AF516119

Sociology and Beyond

Sociology and Beyond

Windows and Horizons

ANANTA KUMAR GIRI

Madras Institute of Development Studies, Chennai

RAWAT PUBLICATIONS

Jaipur • New Delhi • Bangalore • Hyderabad • Guwahati

ISBN 978-81-316-0533-2

Published by
Prem Rawat for **Rawat Publications**
Satyam Apts, Sector 3, Jawahar Nagar, Jaipur 302 004 (India)
Phone: 0141 265 1748/7006 Fax: 0141 265 1748
E-mail: info@rawatbooks.com
Website: www.rawatbooks.com

New Delhi Office
4858/24, Ansari Road, Daryaganj, New Delhi 110 002
Phone: 011 2326 3290

Also at *Bangalore, Hyderabad* and *Guwahati*

Typeset by Rawat Computers, Jaipur
Printed at Chaman Enterprises, New Delhi

For

Arjun Appadurai
John Clammer
Arturo Escobar
Johan Galtung
Hermann Schwengel
Philip Quarles van Ufford and
Surichai Wun'Gaeo

for their inspiring efforts to seek new windows and horizons and cultivate new grounds for mutual fecundation.

Contents

Foreword ix

Preface xv

Acknowledgments xix

Introduction: An Invitation to Sociology and Beyond 1

Part I : Invitation and Cultivation

1 Sociology and Beyond: The Calling of an Ontological Epistemology of Participation 13

2 Sociology and New Paths of Criticism and Creativity 30

3 Beyond Adaptation and Meditative Verbs of Co-Realizations: Towards Creative Nurturance of "I" ,"Me" and "You" and the Transformative Fellowship of Non-Duality 42

4 Rethinking the Human and the Social: Towards a Multiverse of Transformations 52

5 A New Global Humanity: Self-Development, Inclusion of the Other and Planetary Realizations 66

6 Moral Consciousness and Communicative Action: From Discourse Ethics to Spiritual Transformations 75

7 Sociology as a Quest for a Good Society: A Conversation with Robert Bellah 96

8 Understanding 'Social' in Indian Traditions 120

9 Social Science Research in India: Call of Home and the World 136

10 Sociology and the Limits of Loyalty 151

11 The Challenge of Understanding Indian Society: Critique, Generosity and Transformations 163

Part II: Movements and Transformations

12 Social Movements in the Advanced Societies and the Emerging Transnational Spaces 185

13 Building in the Margins of Shacks: Towards a Hermeneutics of Recovery 208

14 Understanding the Chipko Movement 225

Part III: New Horizons of Quality of Life and Societal Co-Realizations

15 Quality of Life and the Method of Science: A Contemporary Critique 239

16 Social Development as a Global Challenge 252

17 The New Built-Environment: New Classes and the New Homelessness in Contemporary United States 267

18 The Aesthetics of Production and Consumption 277

19 Globalizing Economy and the Calling of Dialogues 291

20 Global Justice and the Calling of Peace 296

21 Cultivating Transformative Reconciliation and Striving for Peace: Compassion, Confrontation and a New Art of Integration 307

Part IV : Cultivating Transdiciplinarity and Fields of Mutual Blossoming

22 The Calling of a Creative Transdisciplinarity 317

23 Psychology and the Challenge of the Postmodern Condition 328

24 Conquest of Self? Intimacy and Overcoming of Boundaries 337

25 Anthropological Imagination and Forgetting: A Glimpse into Milan Kundera's *A Book of Laughter and Forgetting* 345

26 Epistemological Crisis in Anthropology: The Case of the Quest for the Real Samoa 353

27 The Power of Word, The Language of Religion 366

28 Sociology, Theology and Spirituality: Nurturing Spaces of Emptiness and Striving from Fullness to a Different Fullness 386

29 Literature, Society and the Calling of Creative Public Spheres: Towards a New Art of Cross-Fertilization 397

30 With and Beyond Plurality of Standpoints: Sociology and the *Sadhana* of Multi Valued Logic and Living 410

Index 433

Foreword

The title of this book, *Sociology and Beyond*, captures the spirit of a serious and timely undertaking to reassess and rethink sociology from a perspective which has recently been opened by a multilevel shift in the constitution of the human form of life and reflection on that process. This shift, sealed by the twenty-first century global crisis, placed us in the challenging contemporary 'post-disciplinary' situation, as it has come to be called. The leading idea for dealing with this situation – an idea which Ananta Kumar Giri previously developed in a penetrating way for instance in an essay entitled 'Transcending Disciplinary Boundaries' – is that of 'transdisciplinarity'. This is obviously a counterfactual normative idea. As such, it allows us not only to imagine and conceive an as yet lacking meaningful interrelatedness of the various disciplines, but also to pursue their transformation and mutual orientation in a committed and active way with a view to realising more closely such relationality. Pointing simultaneously to a desideratum and a structural possibility, the idea both directs us to embark on a certain path and guides our feeling, thinking and action to move towards the destination.

It is this particular structure of thought which allows the sustained critique in this book not only of the current academic disciplinary state of affairs, but more broadly also of those aspects of the contextual status quo which, despite certain promising transformations at a number of levels since the 1960s, continue to exert a debilitating inertia while exacerbating what appears to be the gravest crisis so far in human history. Quite correctly, sociology is taken to task not only for lagging behind in its understanding of the emerging world society and the new subject concurrently in formation, but also for its parochial methodological nationalism, narrow dualistic scientistic epistemology, reified sociologistic ontology and unreflexive utilitarian orientation. These objectionable features, which are more generally reflected in prevailing disciplinary arrangements, correlate moreover with certain negative yet characteristic tendencies of the civilization of modernity which, ultimately, are all conditioned by its instrumentally deformed and hence unsustainable relation to nature – both external and internal nature.

Taking a longer view, the new perspective informing the critical transdisciplinary project pursued in this book owes something to the epoch-making disclosure engendered by the construction and dropping of the atom bomb which, necessitating a deeper level of reflexivity, opened our eyes both to the potentially self-destructive risks generated by our decisions and actions and to the narrow limits of the rather small and exceedingly vulnerable globe forming the shared bio-social system of all life on earth. Global warming and climate change, to which could be added also world poverty and hunger caused by neo-liberal free market globalization, are only the latest indications confirming the relevance of this world disclosure. With the lag induced by the Cold War removed by the European Revolution of 1989 and its reverberations elsewhere, both the risk and global perspectives could start to assume their cognitive framing function and together facilitate the emergence of the cosmopolitan perspective. By the mid-1990s, the role of the leading imaginary was taken by the emotionally gripping image and idea of a locally lived, cosmopolitan world society on an ecologically safeguarded planet Earth – symbolized by the 'Blue Planet', the first photograph of our planetary home from space and the most reproduced picture in human history. The fundamental twentieth-century Gestalt switch at issue here shifted the Copernican-Newtonian heliocentric-mechanistic cosmology and industrial world model underpinning the civilization of modernity to the background in favour of foregrounding the ecological planetary cosmology and cosmopolitan world model of our own time which point towards a new civilizational constellation. By the same token, the interpretative schema of wealth and poverty through which the former was articulated was replaced by the currently ascending cognitive schema of safety and danger. For a growing number of people, consequently, a sense of ontological security could derive no longer from the avoidance of pauperization and sharing in the wealth of the nation, but rather has to be sought in risk aversion and enjoyment of locally rooted living conditions, which are technologically, ecologically and cosmopolitically safeguarded on a global scale – a search, moreover, which requires self-transformation, as Giri has consistently argued in various of his writings, as well as responsible participation in world constitution.

More immediately, of course, the perceived need for transdisciplinarity can be traced back to the drastic intellectual transformation, which has accompanied the shift in epochal self-understanding towards a greater sensitivity for risk, the environment, the global dimension and the demands of cosmopolitan norms. From a certain and, indeed, important point of view, this intellectual transformation is encapsulated by the expression 'post-empiricism' or 'post-positivism' – itself inherently inadequate yet pointing in the right direction. Most of the above-mentioned criticisms of sociology's disciplinary limitations are in fact inspired, even if not explicitly acknowledged, by this new understanding of the philosophy of the social sciences. To begin with, a pluralistic vision is associated with it. Not only must the diverse features and structures of the social world and the different forms and dimensions of rationality inherent in them be acknowledged, but an adequate approach to social reality requires multiple theories to account for the variety of levels, structures and features, while adherence to a single logic or method must be abandoned. An at least weak naturalistic ontology is required to secure appreciation of the continuity between nature and sociocultural reality. Concomitantly, a diverse range of criteria is needed to justify the use of multiple theoretical and methodological concepts. In turn, such criteria must be attuned to the transdisciplinary features of cognition, knowledge and rationality. At a deeper level, epistemology must be historicized and socialized as well as naturalized. On the one hand, the different origins and sources of the diverse theoretical and methodological traditions in the pursuit of knowledge must be identified and kept in mind, while on the other assumptions about cognitive agents or subjects of knowledge and their capacity to generate and maintain social life in its natural environment must be spelled out. This would allow specification both of theoretical goals and of practical purposes. Since transformation, including self-transformation, is centrally implicated here, the accommodation not only of context but also of intentionality and normative intuitions, expectations and structures is vital. Of particular importance is the counterfactual normative moment of idealization, regulative ideas or reflexive rules which, for its part, underlines the need for normative practical criteria of adequacy and the acknowledgement that every cognitive act involves the taking of responsibility for the constitution of the human world and its natural organic substrate.

The disciplines as we have come to know them were institutionalized in the course of the academic revolution which brought the modern university into being. As regards the social sciences, it started in 1810 with the recognition of history at the University of Berlin, was followed by abortive attempts between 1830 and 1850 to secure an institutional foothold for sociology in France, and continued with the establishment of economics in 1870 in Britain, anthropology as well as sociology in 1892 in the United States, psychology in 1910 in the United States, and on the continent sociology again in 1913 and 1918 in France and the German-speaking world respectively. Their institutionalization was the formal recognition of a development which had commenced with the emergence of modern society from the ashes of the medieval feudal order. As the new phenomenon of society, based on the novel principle of association instead of the previously dominant principle of hierarchy, made its appearance between the political domain and the household, a range of new intellectual concerns based on social theory and related to the different dimensions of society displaced practical philosophy together with the ancient-medieval disciplines of politics, ethics and household economics based on the theory of the state. Regarded as being able to take responsibility for studying modern society from different angles and making a contribution to its development, the different disciplines were institutionalized in order to secure the permanent and uninterrupted production of knowledge and thus to free the latter from the vagaries of chance.

This process, however, took place under contradictory and hence distorting conditions. During the eighteenth-century Enlightenment, on the one hand, sociology *avant la lettre* took the form of what contemporaries regarded as a moral science, or what Peter Gay later called the 'science of freedom', which concerned itself in a central respect with both the formation of an appropriate subject for the emerging society based on association and the moral progress of humankind, while simultaneously adopting a global perspective. The context in which sociology took shape at this stage was the early modern rights discourse in which the conditions for a free associational and self-organizing society and civilization based on a new form of subjectivity were publicly argued out, clarified and prepared for establishment in the form of a freedom and equality guaranteeing constitution. As the earlier inquisitorial practices and witch hunts, the victory of the state over the church, the emergence of the mechanistic world view, the state monopolization of the seventeenth-century institution of science and the crystallization of the early form of capitalism foreshadowed, constraints were imposed on the institutionalization of the disciplines, which severely restricted and distorted their focus, scope and depth. With the partial exception of marginalized intellectual orientations, which tried to keep suppressed ideas and normative concerns alive, until the late twentieth century, the mainstream disciplines effectively laboured under the burden of such forces as a mechanistic vision, state cooptation, elite democracy (i.e., oligarchically deformed 'demoarchy'), nationalism, varying forms of liberal economics, possessive individualism and privatism. What was lost sight of in the wake of this contradictory institutionalization is the fact, highlighted for example by the emergence of sociology in its original form as an integral part of a public discourse and a process of problem solving and world creation, that a discipline is not confined to a professional academic context but is at one and the same time a discursive practice which in constant communicative exchange starts from and returns to social life and the practices creating and organizing it.

The aforementioned constricting forces and the concomitant loss of imagination are precisely the aspects of modernity that the criticisms contained in this book rightly target in order to disclose and open up structural possibilities or potentials beyond the long-established disciplinary system and the status quo it serves – possibilities and potentials which sensitise us to the beginnings of a new civilization on the margins and in the interstices of modernity. But there is also a specific aspect which comes in for persistent criticism – the intellectual dimension of modernity, namely, the philosophical orientation, particularly the model of cognition and knowledge based on Cartesian, Baconian and Humean principles.

Intellectually, the disciplines were since their earliest moment of institutionalization dominated by the philosophy of positivism, first in the form of the old positivism of the nineteenth century and then twentieth-century neo-positivism supported by behaviourism and system theory, which all along complemented the mechanistic, experimental, statist, elitist, patriarchal, liberal, capitalist, individualist and privatistic features of modernity. The criticisms levelled against the modernist mode of thinking in this book draw resources from the future, such as the vision of an ecologically safeguarded, planetary, cosmopolitan world society, but at the same time they also feed on achievements of long-standing from the past. The latter become apparent when one turns armed with the new and expanded vision towards the origins and sources of the social sciences and of philosophical reflection upon them. Positivism, of course, is but a more particular manifestation of the scientistic tradition which is rooted in the seventeenth-century institutionalization of science in the Royal Society in 1662 and the *Académie des sciences* in 1666 and propagates the ideal of 'unified science' based on the model of physics. But, the origins and sources of the social sciences are much more diverse and fecund than this. On the one hand, the Reformation concern with the problem of the interpretation of the Holy Scriptures stimulated the rise of hermeneutics and, more broadly, the interpretative tradition to which hermeneutics, phenomenology, pragmatism, linguistics and language philosophy all made contributions. On the other, the Enlightenment most characteristically spawned, far beyond the anaemic and debilitating scientism to which it is nowadays fashionably reduced, the motif of critique which in the hands of, for instance, the left-Hegelian tradition represented by Søren Kierkegaard, the young Karl Marx, Charles S. Peirce and related marginalized twentieth-century developments, opposed the basic features of the emerging modernity – from conventional self-cultivation by means of organized religion, through exploitative and destructive capitalism, to its pernicious dualistic Cartesian assumptions. It found expression in a renewed normative emphasis recognizing the generative and regulative role which ideas of reason play not only in the ethical and moral domains, but also in the intellectual one. In such counterfactual ideas as accountable subject-formation, justice and responsible knowledge production and world creation, needless to say, are to be found potentially fruitful contact points for forging links with other civilizations, intellectual traditions and practices, such as for instance those of India highlighted in this book.

When one considers transdisciplinarity against this background, it becomes apparent sooner or later that it demands much more than going beyond particular disciplinary boundaries. Such border-crossing presupposes and, indeed, is made possible by what could perhaps be called 'transparadigmaticity' – going beyond the philosophical traditions, paradigms or models of cognition and knowledge, i.e., the scientistic as well as the interpretative and critical ones, which underpin the social scientific disciplines. Such a move involves a fundamental philosophical reorientation which is by no means confined to epistemological, ontological and methodological adjustments, but is also guided by a new ethical appropriation of those basic moral principles which guided the original emergence of modernity – for instance, unconstrained association of free and equal people, responsible self-organization, justice, cosmopolitanism and peace – but today appear in a different light and require reinterpretation due to their recontextualization by the recent epochal shift. Moving at one and the same time beyond disciplinary boundaries and the boundaries of philosophical paradigms is essential, but perhaps even this is not yet enough. Strictly speaking, in fact, it is not just a matter of moving beyond, but rather the more demanding one of mediation – mediating among philosophies and disciplines in a way that fulfils the requirements of both immanent and transcendent adequacy. The relative right of each has to be respected, but this has to be achieved in light of the overall purpose or vision they serve. As regards purpose, vision or transcendent adequacy, furthermore, there is the need to renew the sociological imagination by broadening it so as to be co-extensive with the scope of the emerging world society and civilization. In this case, the relevant context of social scientific endeavour requiring mediation includes inter-cultural and inter-civilizational communication and learning, the self-organization of civil society and civilization, and – absolutely vital in the face of the current general crisis of the conditions of life – the impact of all this on the self-regulation of nature.

If it is correct to regard transdisciplinarity comprehensively as a matter of mediation, then a further serious question arises. It concerns the meta-dimension in terms of which it is possible to conceive and clarify the medium of interrelation. Ideally, it should allow for mediation in the full sense of the word – that is, not only the mediation of disciplines, but at one and the same time of the disciplines, their philosophical underpinnings, social life and the natural conditions of the latter. In the post-disciplinary situation, a range of meta-level candidate transdisciplines are currently competing for attention – among them being systems theory, information theory and semiotics. The first is concerned with autopoietic or self-maintaining systems, the second with information flows and selection mechanisms, and the third with semiosis or acts and processes of constitutive meaning production, interpretation, problem solving and world creation. Of these transdisciplines, the third – semiotics – is in my opinion the most appropriate one to cope with the challenge of transdisciplinary mediation. Both systems theory and information theory threaten to continue the pernicious effects of the problematic features of the civilization of modernity, while semiotics bears a different promise. It proceeds from the assumption not only that humans are sign-using beings and that their world as well as their knowledge of that world and of themselves are mediated by signs, but also that they are able to pragmatically participate in an appropriate way in the process of the evolution of both society and nature if they engage in responsible sign interpretation. In its full pragmatically integrated three-dimensional form, in distinction to its popular semiologically reduced two-dimensional version, it therefore precludes an infinite regress of both the real object and the real interpreter by restoring the neglected reality reference of the material sign, on the one hand, and recovering the suppressed subject of knowledge and interpretation through enabling reflexivity, on the other. Creating room for performative self-reflexive or self-referential knowledge linking all the different dimensions, it makes possible an understanding of communicative claims and the contribution they make to the maintenance and expansion of the context of communication as well as of the position of the social scientist as a participant in and contributor to a larger scientific and social communication community which itself, in turn, forms part of an encompassing universe. Ultimately, then, this field of mediation is where we participate in, experience and witness bodily and perspectival engagement with reality, guidance by transcendent counterfactual ideas, social interaction and discourse, cognition and knowledge production, societal learning, the expansion of the human interpretation and communication community, and the assumption of responsibility both for society and the organic foundations of all life on Earth – all of which serve problem solving and, above all, culminate in world creation.

Here global cosmopolitan being in a cared-for planetary bio-social ecosphere, which requires the cultivation of an as yet lacking appropriate subject, is beckoning. Beyond the disjunction of disciplines, their philosophical underpinnings and their social and natural contexts which feeds into the twenty-first century global crisis, it provides the necessary reference points for sociology's new meaning-giving normative vision so urgently required by the emerging society and civilization – what Giri, in a happy turn of phrase, calls sociology's 'normative trigonometry of self-development, inclusion of the other and planetary realizations'.

November 2009
Kinsale

Piet Strydom
Department of Sociology
School of Sociology and Philosophy
University College Cork, Ireland

Preface

Do not give me scissors,
Give me a needle to stitch
Since I do not cut.

— Baba Farid

[...] the more we accumulate new knowledge, the more we deprive ourselves of the means of acquiring the most important of all, and, in a sense, it is by virtue of studying man that *we have become totally unfit to know him.*

— Jean-Jacques Rosseau (1988), *Discourse on the Origin and Foundations of Inequality Among Men*, p. 4, emphasis added

In order to speak of a social pathology [...] we require a conception of normality related to social life as a whole. The immense difficulty involved in this project has been made evident by the failure of social-scientific approaches that have sought to fix the functional requirements of societies solely through external observations. Since what counts as a developmental goal or as normality is always culturally defined, it is only by a hermeneutic reference to a society's self-understanding that social functions of their disorders can be determined. Thus, we may have a defensive possibility of speaking of social pathologies within a culturally contingent notion of normality, since we can limit ourselves to an empirical description of what a given culture regards as a disorder. [...] *A paradigm of social normality must, therefore, consist in culturally independent conditions that allow a society's members to experience undistorted self-realization.* [...] The question then becomes crucial whether it is a communitarian form of ethical life, a distance-creating public sphere, non-alienated labor or a mimetic interaction with nature that *enables individuals to lead a well-lived life.*

— Axel Honneth (2007), *Disrespect: The Normative Foundations of Critical Theory*, p. 34, 35, 37, emphasis added

Since we are a conversation and can hear from one another [..] mankind's conversation with one another and with the divine sound like a single conversation. Because we are a conversation, we are the one story of mankind.

— Hans-Georg Gadamer, (1998), "Culture and the Word," p. 3.

Baba Farid, the inspiring Sufi saint, asks for needles and not scissors; he wants to stich. Social life consists of a lot of works of weaving in the midst of violence and many other processes of pathology. If we do not learn how to do threadwork we feel helpless in the face of threatworks which make us bound to our own closed walls and always ready with scissors to attack the other in oneself, society and the world.

Sociology is a perennial seeking to understand the work of self, culture and society in the midst of the threats of annihilation as well as our many works of weaving, creating threads of beauty, dignity and dialogues in our world. It is a *sadhana,* a quest of active meditation and deep conversation, of understanding how individuals and societies realize their potentials through struggle and creative works of self and co-realizations. This is a fragile journey as our life and societies are in the midst of multi-dimensional challenges of social structures of oppression, unconscious, nature and divine. But there is no way except being with our ways of strivings or *sadhana* of understanding our realities and possibilities, and acting with divine solitude and soulful solidarity to transform our existing realities of domination and exploitation.

For this sociology is our nurturing mother but it is not helpful to bind our mother to a disciplinary prison especially the way this was erected in modern Western world. We should be grateful to our mother for the nourishment she has given us to understand the social world as well as normative struggles emerging out of this very world itself but we are always called upon to go beyond our homes, especially those which are made into prisons by disciplined and disciplinary enthusiasts, and embrace the worlds of many flows, strivings and struggles. This is the *sadhana* of a transdisciplinary and transparadigmatic cultivation of the quest of sociology in which as seekers and communities of seeking we grow together with many other strivings such as literature, philosophy, psychology, anthropology and spirituality as well as reflective mobilization of self and various socio-cultural and socio-spiritual movements.

Sociology and Beyond: Windows and Horizons is a humble effort in this *sadhana* of a transdisciplinary and transformative sociology. I came to the lap of sociology by accident by my meeting with Chitta Ranjan Das, a transformative critic and experimenter from Odisha, who embodies a practice of transformative social criticism. As an undergraduate student at Ravenshaw College, Cuttack in 1982 I used to spend most of my time reading Pitrim Sorokin, Talcott Parsons, Eric Fromm and Carl Gustav Jung, often borrowing these books from Chitta Ranjan Das. I was touched by such works of Sorokin as *Altruistic Love,* Parsons' *The Structure of Social Action,* Jung's *Modern Man in Search for a Soul* and Fromm's *Art of Living, Man for Himself, Escape from Freedom* and *Sane Society*. After my B.A. examination in 1984 I came to my village Jamalpur from Cuttack and wrote three postcards to universities of Madras, Bombay and Delhi. I only heard from University of Delhi stating that I would have to sit in an entrance examination for M.A. in Sociology at the Centre for Advanced studies in Sociology, Delhi School of Economics. I came rushing to Delhi on a train without a proper ticket and after my studies in sociology at Delhi School of Economics the paths of life in an unexpected way brought me to the Department of Anthropology at The Johns Hopkins University, Baltimore, USA. It is at The Johns Hopkins University that my friends and teachers forced me to realize that social theory by itself is not enough unless it is accompanied by grounded fieldwork. I have since then striven to bring sociology, anthropology, philosophy, literature and fieldwork together in a creative trigonometry of philosophy, fieldwork and footwork. I have not only done fieldwork on movements such as Chipko, Habitat for Humanity, Swadhyaya and integral education, I have been on the foot wandering around different themes of life and society such as values, ethics and business, ethics and aesthetics of development and practical discourse and practical spirituality.

I have learnt from all my teachers, friends and colleagues in the last thirty years in this wandering and I am grateful to all of them. I dedicate this book to Arjun Appadurai, John Clammer, Arturo Escobar, Johan Galtung, Hermann Schwengel, Philip Quarles van Ufford and Surichai Wun'Gaeo. Arjun Appadurai is a creative seeker of our times who has brought social science engagement to a new depth and height of grounded normative quest by cultivating such themes as culture and capacity to aspire and anthropology of hope. John Clammer is an inspiring seeker of our contemporary world who has also wandered into many fields and have gifted us many insightful works. I first read an article of John on development anthropology in a library in Amsterdam in 2002 and was quite touched by it. I immediately wrote to him and then we met. It is inspiring for me to walk and dream together with John and nurture many projects such as World Spiritual Transformation Forum and Asian Forum for Social Theory. While the former seeks to bring together scholars and practitioners engaged in practical and transformative spirituality the latter cultivates cross-cultural dialogues on important theoretical and philosophical issues cutting across India, Asia and the world. Arturo Escobar is another inspiring anthropologist of our world who also has a very broad vision of one's life as a scholar and seeker. I recall warmly our meetings, especially a walk we took in Chapel Hill in a winter afternoon in January 2003, where we discussed about many dimensions of human condition – politics and spirituality. Escobar is an embodiment of kindness and beauty. Over the last six years ever since our first meeting at Aalborg University, Denmark, I have also been enriched by my association with Johan Galtung. Galtung himself has started with sociology in a transdiciplinary way, for example, studying mathematics and sociology together and then in his creative *ouvre* over the last half century he has dedicated himself to striving for peace. Galtung himself is a living embodiment of wandering and wonder and his life teaches us how much as students of society we can do to understand the world as well as to transform it.

Hermann Schwengel, who presently teaches at University of Freiburg, Germany, is a thoughtful sociologist who brings sociology and philosophy together in creative ways. He argues that the present phase of globalization must be accompanied by an inner globalization. People across the world should meet with each other in which they should realize the self of other culture as well as their own selves. It has been enriching on my part to have met Hermann in an unexpected way and then have been part of our many conversations.

Philip Quarles van Ufford taught anthropology at Free University, Amsterdam and ever since our first meeting in a conference in London in 1998 we have spent many days and evenings wandering and seeking together in Amsterdam, Chennai and Java. I have learnt a lot with Philip for which I am deeply grateful to him. Surichai Wun'Gaeo is a living embodiment of a creative and critical sociology who has nurtured many students, friends and policy makers in his home country of Thailand and around the world. Being with

Achan Surichai makes one realize how selflessly and effortlessly one can give oneself to the pursuit of sociological understanding, social transformation and friendship. *Kapunkah* (thank you) to Achan Surichai.

This work could not have come out without the kind and enthusiastic support of Pranit Bhai of Rawat Publications and I offer my grateful thanks to him as well as to his team for their kind help.

Finally I hope this reaches all the seeking souls in sociology and other fields of seeking who are striving for more unbound and creative ways of understanding self, culture and society as well as transforming these into ever expanding circles of creative becoming and manifold co-realizations.

Diwali, Festival of Lights
October 20, 2011

Ananta Kumar Giri
Madras Institute of Development Studies, Chennai

Acknowledgments

The chapters in the book draw from my earlier works as presented below and I am grateful to all friends associated with these journeys, especially editors and staff of journals where these were published for their kind interest and help:

Ch 1: It draws on my work on this theme over the last eight years and most recently presented in an essay in *Asian Journal of Social Sciences* 2009.

Ch 2: It draws on my editorial introduction to *Rethinking Social Transformation: Criticism and Creativity at the Turn of the Millennium* (Jaipur: Rawat Pulbications, 2001).

Ch 3: It draws on my key-note presentation at the seminar on "Mead's Theory: Interpretation, Application and Transcendence," Department of Sociology, Fujen University, Taipei, Taiwan, May 23, 2009 and later published in *Journal of Indian Council of Philosophical Research* 2009. I am grateful to Professor Johannes Han-Yin Chang Chai-wang of Fujen University for his kind invitation and to Professor Mrinal Miri for his encouragement.

Ch 4: It is the revised version of a paper first presented in the panel, "The Human and the Social: What Can Human Development and Human Security Discourse(s) and the Social Quality Approach Offer Each Other," 2008 Conference of the Human Development and Capability Association, 11–13 September 2008, New Delhi. It is subsequently published in *International Journal of Social Quality* 2011. I thank Des Gasper for his kind invitation to this session and subsequent comments and Helma and Laurent of European Foundation for Social Quality for their kind help and interest.

Ch 5: Revised version of a paper first presented at the session, "Asian Traditions and a New Humanity," Global Forum on Civilization and Peace, 60th Anniversary of Liberation of Korea, Academy of Korean Studies, Seoul, December 4–7, 2005. My grateful thanks are due to Professor Sang-Jin Han and Dr. Do-Hyun Han for their kind invitation and to President Professor Yoon Deok-hong and staff of Academy of Korean Studies for generous hospitality and participants, especially Professors Willliam Steel and Karl-Heinz Pohl, for their discussions and comments. This also builds on an essay published in *Journal of Human Values* 2009.

Ch 6: *History of the Human Sciences* 1998.

Ch 7: I am grateful to Professors S. N. Eisenstadt and Robert N. Bellah for their kind reading of the draft of this essay. Professor Bellah has very kindly shared with me his recent writings and has commented upon the text for which I am grateful. None of them however are responsible for the views presented here. The essay was presented as a lecture at Institute of Sociology, University of Gottingen, and my grateful thanks are due to Professor Matthias Koening for his kind invitation, hospitality and suggestions and to the members of the audience, especially Professor Ulrich Braukamper, for comments. It is also coming out in *Journal of Human Values*. In the meantime, Professor S.N. Eisesntadt, a doyen of world sociology and a kind pilgrim of seeking and learning, passed away on September 2, 2010. I dedicate this essay to the loving and immortal memory and living legacy of Professor Eisenstadt.

Ch 8: *Journal of Indian Council of Philosophical Research* X1V (3): 169–78, May-August 1997 and the Appendix "Towards a Mutuality of Explorations and the Limits of Assertions: A Dialogue on Self, Society and the Other," *Journal of Indian Council of Philosophical Research* XV1 (3): 123–32, May–August, 1999.

Ch 9: "Social Science Research: Call of Home and the World." *Economic and Political Weekly*, August 2003; "Creating a Community of Discourse in Sociology in India," *Economic and Political Weekly* XXVII (29 & 30): 1538–39, July 17–24, 1993; "Reconstructing Social Sciences," *Review of Development and Change*.

Ch 10: *The Eastern Anthropologist* 2007.

Ch 11: "The Challenge of Understanding Indian Society: Critique, Generosity and Transformations," *Sociological Bulletin* 59(2): 256–277, May-August 2010.

Ch 12: "Social Movements in the Advanced Societies and the Emerging Transnational Spaces," *Guru Nanak Journal of Sociology* 18 (1), 1997: 1–35.

Ch 13: "Building in the Margins of Shacks: Towards a Hermeneutics of Recovery," *Journal of Indian Anthropological Society* 32 (1): 77–85, March 1997.

Ch 14: "Chipko's Understanding of People and People's Understanding of Chipko," *Vision*, 1992.

Ch 15: "Quality of Life and the Method of Science: A Contemporary Critique," *Gandhi Marg*, January 1993.

Ch 16: "Social Development as a Global Challenge," *Social Action*, July-September 1992.

Ch 17: It was first published as a working paper from G.B. Pant Social Science Institute, Allahabad, 1972.

Ch 18: "The Aesthetics of Production and Consumption," *Review of Development and Change* 3 (1): 109–24, 1992.

Ch 19 Revised version of a paper first presented at the International Seminar on "Globalising Economy and Civilisational Agenda," Institute of Asian Studies, Chulalongkorn University, Bangkok, March 21, 2008 and published in the seminar volume. I am grateful to Professor W. Surichai for his kind invitation and friendship.

Ch 20: "Global Justice and the Calling of Peace," *Rajagiri Journal of Social Development* 2 (2): 214–29, 2006. This was first written for the Journal of Attac, Bergen In June 2006. I thank Ase Moller Hansen and friends in Attac, Bergen for their kind invitation.

Ch 21: "Cultivating Transformative Reconciliation and Striving for Peace: The Calling of Compassionate Confrontation and A New Art of Integration," *Current Sociology*, 2011.

Ch 22: "The Calling of a Creative Transdisciplinarity," *Futures* 34: 103–15, 2002.

Ch 23: "Psychology and the Challenge of the Postmodern Condition," *Economic and Political Weekly*, xxviii (40): 2130–33, October 2, 1993.

Ch 24: "The Conquest of Self? Intimacy and the Overcoming of Boundaries," *Economic and Political Weekly*, July 2, 1994.

Ch 25: "Anthropological Imagination and Forgetting," *Man & Development*, June 2010.

Ch 26: "Epistemological Crises in Anthropology: The Case of the Quest for the Real Samoa," *Journal of the Indian Anthropological Society* 30: 115–24, 1995.

Ch 27: "The Power of Word, Language of Religion," *The Eastern Anthropologist*, September-October 2009.

Ch 28: This essay was written in honour of Professor Felix Wilfred and has come out in the book *Negotiating Borders: Theological Reflections in a Global Era* edited by Patrick Gnanapragasam and Elisabeth Schussler Fiorenza (Delhi: ISPCK, 2008). I am grateful to Dr. Patrick Gnanapragasam for his kind invitation and help.

Ch 29: This builds on a presentation at the national seminar on "Literature and Society: Interdisciplinary Transactions", Department of English, North-Eastern Hill University, Shimla, March 2010. I am grateful to Dr Sukalpa Bhattacharjee for her kind invitation and warm hospitality and participants for their comments and reflections. This is also coming out in *IIAS Summerhill Review*, Indian Institute of Advanced Studies, Shimla, and my thanks are due to Professor Satish Aikant, its editor, for his kind interest and encouragement.

Ch 30: I am grateful to Professor Andre Beteille for his kind reading of this essay. I am also grateful to Elaine Desmond of University College Cork, Ireland and Marcus Bussey of University of Sunshine Coast, Australia for their very helpful comments and suggestions.

Introduction

An Invitation to Sociology

ANANTA KUMAR GIRI

Introduction

An Invitation to Sociology and Beyond

ANANTA KUMAR GIRI

> The story of all real sociology is one of breaking open the boundaries. The discipline was originally bound strictly to its specific lines and limitations and it is great that transgressions have been happening all the time. It is becoming increasingly clearer that society and people matter more than the study of society. The older definitions and contours are fast changing and there are more and more people who are less shy and hence willing to transgress the boundaries. More mature days are in the offing and the recluses so far working in the laboratories are becoming more courageous. Yes, courage more than anything else, always helps us ask questions and rewrite our canons of inquiry.
>
> — Chitta Ranjan Das (2009: 580)

> [...] the subject matter of sociology no longer corresponds to its 'classical' definition. [...] it is necessary to substitute a new principle of value orientation to the idea of society [...]
>
> — Alain Touraine (2007: 70)

> [The distinction between instrumental and reflexive knowledge] is a disastrous error [...] the division itself is both a cognitive mistake and a normative delicit, because sociology is simultaneously a cognitive and a moral enterprise. It is precisely by ignoring this fact and letting critical and instrumental production separate themselves in the academy [...] that sociologists have opened themselves to [...] pathologies: self-referentiality and servility on the "instrumental" side and dogmatism and faddishness on the "reflexive" one. These happen not because good "versions" of instrumental and reflexive work have somehow degenerated into something less than themselves but because the two should not be separated in the first place.
>
> — Andrew Abbott (2007: 198)

> The core concern of contemporary social and political theory stems from the problematic nature of modern, particularly late modern society. The latter presents the internally fractured picture of a global, functionally differentiated, ecologically endangered class society that, at least partially, gives rise to normative claims which point far beyond its overwhelmingly functionalist, risk-generating and asymmetrical organization in the tension-laden field between the national and the translational or global constellation. On the one hand, modern society is based on egalitarian presuppositions manifest in expectations about a similar dependence of all on, as well as equal chances of access to, function systems and their products.

> But, on the other, the mode of organization of this society is characterized by a disturbingly unequal distribution of both dependency and access. At a deeper level still, there is the presupposition of a philosophically appropriate, scientifically correct and hence collectively beneficial relationship of society to nature which, likewise, is contradicted by the increasing level of societal self-endangerment, self-injury and potential self-destruction and the highly unequal distribution of manufactured or scientifically and technologically based ecological risk. This fractured and tension-laden nature of society is finally refracted and focalized in the typical yet historically varying ontological insecurity of the modern individual.
>
> Faced with this multi-leveled problematic situation, social and political theory is required today, at least to begin with, to find a theoretical point of articulation of these different apparently disparate dimensions: the gap between function systems and normative claims; the typical modern problems of individualization and social exclusion following this lack of coordination; the globalization of these very problems which are now manifest in the form of global risk society, world poverty and intercultural clashes; and the failure of globalization to mature into adequate worldhood. Such a theoretical means of mediation would entail mitigating long-standing internal divisions – e.g., micro and macro, life world and system or agency and structure, and in particular immanent social obligations and context-transcending normative guidelines – and concurrent tendencies towards one-sidedness. There is no doubt that social and political theory can neglect or ignore any aspect of the diverse range of significant phenomena and developments characteristic of our time only at its peril. The question of how social and political theory could be brought, for instance, to adopt a more consistent global and cosmopolitan perspective or to recognize its own normative poverty, or how one version of political theory could be encouraged to reconsider, for example, its national fixation or ethnocentrism and another opened up so as to acknowledge its ecological blindness, is of central theoretical importance.
>
> — Piet Strydom (2009: 2)

I

Sociology in its disciplinary form emerged in the context of rise of modern society in the West and some of its foundational limitations in terms of disciplinary closure and parochialism are now being realized more and more. As Alain Touraine in an epigraph cited above says, the classical definition of society modeled in terms of bounded nation-state is in foundational crisis and we need a "new principle of value orientation to the idea of society". The present book is a humble endeavour in this quest for a new vision and practice of the idea of society as well as the field of sociology. The first essay in this volume offers a concept of society as ontological society and the third essay, society as a space of meditative verbs of co-realizations – self as well as collective.

The book continues the boundary crossing, transgressing and transformative quest of many of the seekers and savants in our world of knowledge and practice. As Chitta Ranjan Das tells us, sociology is breaking open its known boundaries and seeking new modes of self, social and world realizations as well as new modes of knowing and understanding. This is calling into question earlier dualisms such as between subject and object and instrumental and reflective knowledge. We are also called upon to reflect upon the contemporary challenge before sociological imagination and practice. As Piet Strydom tells in one of opening epigraphs, sociology needs to pursue "far beyond [the] overwhelmingly functionalist, risk-generating and asymmetrical organization in the tension-laden field between the national and the transnational or global constellation" of late modern society, which is also characterized by the "ontological insecurity of the modern individual". Contemporary sociology also needs to acknowledge its "normative poverty" and go beyond its parochial fixation and "ecological blindness". In this spirit, the present book, continuing a journey in my other books – *Global Transformations: Postmodernity and Beyond* (1998), *Conversations and Transformations: Towards a New Ethics of Self and Society* (2002), and *Knowledge and Human Liberation: Towards Planetary Realizations* (forthcoming) – pleads for going beyond parochialism – both metropolitan and native, Western and Indian – and realize sociology as part of multi-dimensional planetary conversations involving both comparative global studies as well as cross-cultural conversations. *Sociology and Beyond* also presents a new vision for sociology as well as sociological practice animated by the passion of self-development, inclusion of the other and planetary realizations.

Sociology and Beyond seeks to cultivate, realize and reconstitute sociology as a field of learning and understanding in a transdisciplinary way. Its approach to the current crisis of disciplinary identity is not one of defense but of renewal and transformation.[1] This *sadhana* of a transdisciplinary sociology is also part of a new *sadhana* of understanding what I have elsewhere called a multi-valued logic of autonomy and interpenetration. This multi-valued logic helps us to go beyond dualism between individual and society, matter and spirit, economic and cultural and helps us realize non-duality. It is part of the transformation from what Gotthard Gunter (1979) calls "the classical period of science" to the "age of trans-classical science" animated by "polycontextuality."[2] We can look at both society and sociology as fields of polycontextuality. Disciplines and distinctions have their contextual necessities but they are not absolute nor monolithic nor destinies. Both individuals as well as institutions are now urgently called upon to experiment with new ways of learning, knowledge gathering and social becoming. It is true that our institutions of knowledge lag behind the need for understanding self, culture and society in a new way but we should not be bound to institutions nor wait infinitely for appropriate institutions to arise before we can practise a transdisciplinary way of pursuing our disciplinary knowledge. We are called upon to be embodiment of creativity in the flow of life in the margins of institutions going beyond what Amartya Sen (2009) has recently called "institutional transcendentalism".

Challenges before contemporary sociology are giving rise to a variety of responses. Some plead for cosmpolitanization of sociology. But such efforts coming from practitioners such as Ulrich Beck (2002) rarely challenge the parochialism of Euro-American sociology and embody comparative global engagement and cross-cultural planetary conversations. Others such as Michael Burawoy (2007) call for a public sociology but this rarely involves the project of self-transformation of the sociologist herself though towards the end of his essay Burawoy could not have but written: "Important though these institutional changes are, the success of public sociology will not come from above but from below. It will come when public sociology captures the imagination of sociologists [...]" (Burawoy 2007: 58). Public sociology is also confronted with the foundational task of reconstituting the public itself as a multi-dimensional field of ontological epistemology of participation (see Chapter 1 in the book). The public is not just public, nor is it only epistemic. If renewal of sociology begins with a foundational acknowledgment of limitations of the modernistic conception of society modeled upon bounded nation-state, then, the project of public sociology also needs an integral transformation of the very idea of the public involving both self and the social in a spirit of co-learning and transformations.

In his response to Burawoy's call for public sociology, Andrew Abbott tells about the limits of separation of instrumental and reflexive knowledge and challenges to realize that sociology needs to cultivate both. But he wants to do it in a successive way: "[...] the cognitive and normative thinking must be perpetually succeeding phases in the research process. [...] We have to alternate between reflection – questioning our assumptions and in particular our value assumptions – and routine cognitive analysis" (2007: 202). But this successive approach may have its limitations and can hide a reality of separation and the challenge here is what can be called a *sadhana* of simultaneity, i.e., to pursue both cognitive and normative thinking simultaneously. This may not be an easy option to begin with but we need to practise this as an ongoing *sadhana*.

Such a *sadhana* of simultaneity accompanied by poly-contextuality (looking at society as well as sociology as fields of poly-contextuality and pluarlizations) and multi-valued logic of autonomy and interpenetration (see Chapter 1) makes sociology a spiritual quest along with it being a cognitive and moral enterprise simultaneously. Going beyond sociology now calls us to be reflective about its primacy of the political and realize sociology as a field of mutual blossoming and social becoming animated by both practical discourse and practical spirituality (see Chapter 6).

II

The essays in this book seek to cultivate sociology as a transdisciplinary and transformative engagement in understanding the dynamics of self, culture and society. It deals with various themes of conceptual, methodological as well as substantive issues. The first chapter, "Sociology and Beyond: The Calling of an Ontological Epistemology of Participation" cultivates such a transdisciplinary and self-critical view of sociology by going beyond the primacy of the social in sociological thinking and cultivating society as a field of ontological sociality. The second chapter, "Sociology and New Paths of Criticism and Creativity" explores different paths of criticism and creativity in contemporary discourses and practice that sociology could embrace, which would help it overcome some of its contemporary limitations, such as isolation from a larger public discourse and lack of will to self-transformation on the part of the practitioners of the discipline. The third chapter discusses the work of George Herbert Mead in going beyond sociological naivety and an acquiescent view of social loyalty. It explores how sociology can help us in going beyond adaptation and cultivate meditative verbs of co-realizations of self and society. It also gives a new interpretation of Mead's perspectives on mind, self and society and shows how creative experiments in these fields can create vibrancy in these fields. The fourth chapter, "Rethinking the Human and the Social: Towards a Multiverse of Transformations" discusses the limits of both humanism and socio-centrism. It argues that thinking about concrete issues, such as human security and social quality in sociological theory and policy discourse, needs to build upon such realization of limits of taken for granted views of the human and the social. The chapter here brings the perspective of *purusartha* of paths of self and social realization from Indian traditions and discusses how human security and social quality approaches in contemporary social discourses can be enriched by such cross-cultural learning and dialogues. The fifth chapter, "A New Global Humanity: Self-Development, Inclusion of the Other and Planetary Realizations" carries such cross-cultural dialogues further and it pleads for striving for a new global humanity on the part of sociology animated by a creative trigonometry of self-development, inclusion of the other and planetary realizations.

These first five chapters describing possibilities in several creative discourses are accompanied by further explorations. Chapter 6 presents the works of Jurgen Habermas and Sri Aurobindo and discusses the challenges for transformation of conventional sociological engagement that they both present, for example, cultivation of post-conventional practical discourse on the part of Habermas and practical spirituality on the part of Sri Aurobindo. The chapter pleads for the need to bring practical discourse and practical spirituality together in a creative sociological engagement. Chapter 7 "Sociology as a Quest for a Good Society" discusses the work of Robert N. Bellah and insights for renewal and transformations that his sociological *oeuvre* presents. Chapter 8, "Understanding 'Social' in Indian Traditions," presents the seminal work of Govind Chandra Pande, a philosopher and historian from India. This chapter read with sections on limits of the socio-centric view discussed in Chapter 4 helps us cultivate sociology as an open field of engagement and realization which is not a prisoner of an *apriori* privileging of the social as it happens in Western academic sociology. Chapter 9 discusses some cross-currents of debates about sociology in contemporary India. It discusses the problem of entrenched parochialism in Indian sociology where practitioners rarely work outside their home universes inside and outside India. This problem of parochialism in Indian sociology mirrors the parochialism of Euro-American sociology where very few practitioners do work outside the charmed circles of the Imperium. Such mirroring parochialisms heighten the need for going beyond sociology as we know and make it part of a new global understanding and planetary conversations. Chapter 10, "Sociology and the Limits of Loyalty," discusses some of theses issues discussing the limits and possibilities in the work of M.N. Srinivas, a doyen of Indian sociology. It discusses the need for sociology to go beyond several lines of its loyalty to modernity, nation-state and the cult of ancestor worship – be it Weber, Durkheim or Srinivas – and make sociology an unbound undertaking of both empirical understanding and creative theorizing. Chapter 11, "The Challenge of Understanding Indian Society: Critique, Generosity and Transformations," discusses further some issues in study of Indian society which has a global relevance.

These eleven chapters in the first section prepare the ground for cultivating sociology in new ways and the following section, "Sociology and Beyond: Movements and Transformations" presents us possibilities of transforming sociology with study of different transformative movements in self, culture and society. The first chapter in this section presents the work of social movements, especially transnational ones, in advanced industrial societies. It discusses resource mobilization and identity formation approaches to the study of movements and pleads for a creative interpenetration of both these perspectives. The following chapter, "Building in the Margins of Shacks: Towards a Hermeneutics of Recovery" presents the work of Habitat for Humanity in the US and its potential for recovery going beyond both the dilapidation of the lived environment and the theoretical landscape of deconstruction. This chapter is followed by Chapter 14 which presents the vision and social dynamics of Chipko, the famous grass-roots environmental movement from Indian Himalayas which had a great influence on the emerging ecological consciousness of the world in the 1970s.

The chapters on movements and transformations are accompanied by seven chapters dealing with several aspects of quality of life, human development and social transformations in the succeeding section, "Sociology and Beyond: New Horizons of Quality of Life and Societal Co-Realizations." Chapter 15 discusses the issues of quality of life and the need to go beyond positivist organization of science and society. Chapter 16 discusses the issue of social development as a global challenge which challenges all societies – so-called developed world and the developing world. It thus seeks to go beyond the hiatus between sociology and development studies (cf. Beteille 2010). If we accept social development as a global challenge, as for example, discussed with regard to the case of homelessness in the United States in the succeeding chapter, it may not be "necessary for us to put the straightjacket of development studies behind us," as Beteille argues, rather sociology can empirically and normatively look into the challenges of global development in all countries around the world going beyond the earlier ideological distinction between the developed and the developing world.[3]

The subsequent five chapters in the book discuss different aspects of contemporary challenges of development such as the new built-environment and homelessness, aestheticization of production and consumption, globalizing economy and the need for cross-cultural dialogues on the vision and practice of economy, global justice and the calling of peace, and the challenge of transformative reconciliation for creative social action, sociology and development studies. Chapter 17 discusses the problem of homelessness in contemporary United States. Chapter 18, "The Aesthetics of Production and Consumption," discusses the aesthetic transformation of both production and consumption. Chapter 19, "Globalizing Economy and the Calling of Dialogues," continues the practice of cross-cultural dialogues in thinking about the very theme of economy itself and seeks to reconstitute economy as a multiverse characterized by strivings to realize happiness, beauty and dignity. Chapter 20 brings our trans-border conversations to the fields of global justice and peace. It also discusses the art of universal self-realization which read together with the earlier trigonometry of self-development, inclusion of the other and planetary realizations can give a new meaning to the practice of sociology. Chapter 21 discusses the challenges of transformative reconciliation, compassion, confrontation and a new art of integration before creative sociological thinking and initiatives in human development and social transformations.

These two sections on movements, social development and new horizons of societal co-realizations help us to come back to bigger, wider and deeper issues. The fourth and final section of the book, "Sociology and Beyond: Cultivating Transdisiplinarity and Fields of Mutual Blossoming" begins with Chapter 22 on cultivating the art of transdisicplinarity involving both authentic embeddedness in our disciplinary homes as well as will to transcend its boundaries. The following chapter discusses the field of psychology especially as it needs to renew itself in the face of questions and challenges from postmodernism. Chapter 24 continues this exploration of transdisciplinarity at the borderland of sociology and psychology by discussing the issue of intimacy, sexuality and spirituality beginning with the work of Anthony Giddens in this field, *Transformation of Intimacy*. Chapter 25 brings such border-crossing conversations to the field of literature discussing the work of novelist Milan Kundera on issues of memory, imagination, resistance and forgetting. Chapter 26 discusses epistemological issues in anthropology, especially crisis of representation and ethnographic authority, with a focus on Derek Freeman's critique of Margaret Mead's classic work, *Growing up in Samoa*.

The last four chapters of this book discuss several issues at the borderlands of sociology, religious studies, theology and spiritual quest. Chapter 27 discusses the relationship between religious language and ordinary language. Chapter 28 discusses the border-crossing between sociology and theology in the direction of spiritual quest. It discusses the seminal work of theologian Felix Wilfred and agues how both sociology and theology need to learn with each other and move towards spiritual quest and realize that self and society are not only characterized by fullness but also emptiness and the need for moving from fullness to a different fullness. Chapter 29 discusses the themes of literature, society and the calling of creative public spheres and cultivates a new art of cross-fertilization. The final chapter of this book carries this exploration further by returning to the issue of plurality of standpoints. It touches themes of beyond sociology developed in the first chapter of the book and pleads for making sociology a *sadhana* of multi-valued logic and living going beyond the absolutism of any one standpoint, be it sociological, political or spiritual.

Notes

1. Anthony Giddens (1996) and Andre Beteille (2002) seem to be offering a defensive response to the crisis of disciplinary identity that sociology is confronted with. But such defensive reactions are not enough though are understandable. In a similar way, Satish Deshpande seems to be reiterating an exclusionary view of sociology as a discipline in India though he himself writes about another meaning of discipline as something "like *riyaaz* required of classical musicians" (Deshpande 2003: 7). The *riyaaz* of sociology is practised in

the institutional context of modern universities and departments who have a vested interest to perpetuate the outmoded notion of disciplines. It might be an accident or a conjunction that so far I have not been required to practise the *riyaaz* of sociology in a university department though I have interacted with students and colleagues in sociology, anthropology and other departments in humanities and social sciences in universities in India and abroad. Probably such a non-university and non-departmental *riyaaz* of sociology and anthropology have enabled me to pursue these disciplines in a transdisciplinary way. I fully realize that friends who work in disciplined departments would have different kinds of existential requirements, anxieties and aspirations and the present book is an offering for sharing our experiences, pursuits and dialogues.

2. As Gunter writes: "What classic science has investigated so far is a subjectless Universe; and a subjectless Universe presents us with a rigorously mono-contextual structure. [...] On the other hand, the turn from classic to trans-classic thinking means that the mono-contextual concept of Reality is abandoned and replaced by a poly-contextual theory of Existence which makes room for the phenomenon of Life within this Universe. In a poly-contextual Universe we do not have to consider Life as an element totally alien to inanimate matter, because matter in itself already contains the seeds of Life in its dialectical contraposition of Being and Nihility" (1979: 304). To appreciate the significance of proceeding with Life as our object of attention we need to remember what Orlando Patterson writes on the subject: "[Sociology adopted] a normal science approach modeled on physics and its experimental methodology rather than on biology" (2007: 182).
3. About this Beteille writes:

> Perhaps the time has come to ask if having a fixed framework of research based on the idea of development may not become an encumbrance in the future, or, even, if it is not already becoming one. It was natural at the time of independence for the advanced industrial countries to think of India as a backward or underdeveloped country. It may have also have been natural for Indian social scientists to regard the problems of growth and development as the ones that needed their most urgent attention at that time [...] But times have begun to change. India is no longer caged in the Hindu rate of growth, and we are ceasing to be regarded as a backward or underdeveloped country. In order to look for new horizons of social science research in India, it may be necessary for us to put the straightjacket of development studies behind us (Beteille 2010: 146).

But Beteille here is himself proceeding with a fixed notion of development studies where practitioners of development studies are themselves interrogating the dichotomous construction of the world and are brining new issues of human development such as ethical, aesthetic and spiritual development which are globally relevant (cf. Quarles van Ufford and Giri 2003). In this context Beteille may have to rethink his own fixed view of development studies and this section in our book helps us come to terms with many intertwined issues of sociology, development studies and qualities of life such as peace, justice and reconciliation together. It is not necessarily true what Beteille writes about development studies and this section in our book thus can help us to go beyond the hiatus between development studies and sociology that Beteille constructs:

> The real problem with the framework of development studies is that it is based on the presumption of a dichotomous division of the world into countries that are

> advanced and those that are backward, or between developed and underdeveloped countries. I do not know any strong advocate of development studies who does not carry somewhere in his mind a dichotomous view of the world as being divided into backward and advanced countries. Such a view is misleading and it is an impediment to the free growth of comparative studies (ibid: 147).

References

Abbott, Andrew. 2007. "For Humanist Sociology." In Dan Clawson et al. (eds.), *Public Sociology: Fifteen Eminent Sociologists Debate Politics and the Profession in the Twenty-First Century*, pp. 195–209. Berkeley & Los Angeles: University of California Press.

Beck, Urlich. 2002. "The Cosmopolitan Society and its Enemies", *Theory, Culture and Society* 19 (1–2): 17–44.

Beteille, Andre. 2002. *Sociology: Essays on Approach and Method*, Delhi: Oxford University Press.

——. 2010. "Social Science Research." In Andre Beteille, *Universities at the Crossroads*, pp. 134–155. Delhi: Oxford University Press.

Burawoy, Michael. 2009. "For Public Sociology." In Dan Clawson et al. (eds.), *Public Sociology: Fifteen Eminent Sociologists Debate Politics and the Profession in the Twenty-First Century*, pp. 23-64. Berkeley & Los Angeles: University of California Press.

Das, Chitta Ranjan. 2009. "Afterword." *The Modern Prince and the Modern Sage: Transforming Power and Freedom* (ed.), Ananta Kumar Giri. Delhi: Sage Publications.

Deshpande, Satish. 2003. *Contemporary India: A Sociological View*. Delhi: Penguin.

Giddens, Anthony (1996). *In Defense of Sociology: Essays, Interpretations and Rejoinders*. Cambridge: Polity Press.

Giri, Ananta Kumar, "Creative Social Research: Rethinking Theories and Methods and the Calling of an Ontological Epistemology of Participation". *Dialectical Anthropology*, 30(No. 3–4).

Gunter, Gotthard. 1979. "Life as Poly-Contextuality." In his *Betrage zur Grundlegung*. Hamburg: Meiner.

Patterson, Orlando. 2007. "About Public Sociology." In Dan Clawson et al. (eds.), *Public Sociology: Fifteen Eminent Sociologists Debate Politics and the Profession in the Twenty-First Century*, pp. 176–194. Berkeley & Los Angeles: University of California Press.

Sen, Amartya. 2009. *The Idea of Justice*. Cambridge, MA: Harvard University Press.

Strydom, Piet. 2009. "Contemporary Social and Political Theory: The Cognitive and Metacognitive Dimension." Manuscript. Included in Gerard Delanty & Stephen Turner (eds.), *Handbook of Social and Political Theory*. London: Routledge.

Touraine, Alain. 2007. "Public Sociology and the End of Society." In Dan Clawson et al. (eds.), *Public Sociology: Fifteen Eminent Sociologists Debate Politics and the Profession in the Twenty-First Century*, pp. 67–78. Berkeley & Los Angeles: University of California Press.

Part I

Invitation and Cultivation

1 Sociology and Beyond

The Calling of an Ontological Epistemology of Participation

Sociology is part of the agenda of modernity which privileges epistemology to the neglect of ontological issues. In the modernist mode, sociology was considered only an epistemic project – a project of knowing about the world with proper procedure and scientific method and neglected issues of consciousness, self, relationship of subject and object and ontological issues of self-nurturance and self-transformation.[1] The neglect of ontology is a crucial gap in modernistic sociology which continues to persist even in contemporary new formulations like cosmopolitan sociology offered by Ulrich Beck (2002). For Beck, sociology now needs to move from methodological nationalism to methodological cosmopolitanism. But this move is primarily methodological and epistemic and does not address ontological preparation needed for transformation of sociology from its contemporary binding in nation-state to a cosmopolitan world. This needs a new self-conception on the part of sociologists not only as citizens of the nation-state and sociological role occupants but also transcendental selves living in varieties of communities but at the same time transcending these.

In this context, the present chapter is an initial striving to transform sociological engagement as simultaneously ontological and epistemological. It seeks not only to go beyond the epistemic privileging and ontological neglect of much of modernist sociology but also to transform sociological engagement as a field of ontological epistemology of participation which embodies transformative interpenetration of ontological and epistemic as processes of walking and co-realizations. It builds upon creative efforts in this field from sociology, anthropology and philosophy. It must be made clear at the outset that while trying to remedy the neglect of ontology in the practice of sociology, the present project is not one of making sociology ontological in a one-dimensional, essentialist and fixed way. On the other hand, those who look at this project with their *apriori* critique of ontology, for example, their being imprisoned within the critique of ontology of Heidegger offered by scholars such as Habermas and Bourdieu, are invited to go beyond their own *apriori* judgment and join in this project of renewal of sociology as a multi-dimensional field of ontological epistemology of participation (see the last section of this chapter).

Beyond Sociology: Rethinking Society and the Calling of an Ontological Sociality

Beyond sociology involves a reconceptualization of society and subjectivity and an important task here is to understand what can be called the work of ontological sociality in self, culture and society. One important challenge here is to go beyond the false dichotomy between individual and society. As Norbert Elias tells us: "We have the familiar concepts of 'individual' and 'society', the first of which refers to a single human being as if he or she were an entity existing in complete isolation [...] Society is understood either as a mere accumulation, an additive and unstructured collection of many individual people, or as an object existing beyond individuals and incapable of further explanation [...] the words available to us, the concepts which decisively influence the thought and action of people growing up within their sphere, make it appear as if the single human being, labeled the individual, and the plurality of people conceived as society, were two ontologically different entities" (Elias 1991: i). For Elias, "[...] the individual person is able to say 'I' because he can at the same time say 'we'. Thus society consists of a simultaneously 'I' and 'we' but the balance between them has changed historically" (ibid.: 61). At the contemporary juncture it is the "I" dimension which seems to be getting more primacy and attention in modern and late modern societies that Zygmunt Bauman calls individualized society (Bauman 2001). In such societies there is a recognition of the limits of the social in many spheres of life such as education, love and ethics (cf. Beck 2000; Beck and Beck-Gernsheim 1995). The ideal of society is now being foundationally rethought as providing a space for self-development of individuals. For example, Andre Gorz (1999) argues that educative relation is not just a social relation.[2] Similarly, ethics is not just acting in accordance with social conventions but with post-conventional awareness and realizations where, as Habermas says, conventional norms of society turn out to be "instances of problematic justice" (Habermas 1990: 108). Morality is not just obeying pre-given command by either society or a benevolent dictator or a wise master but acting according to one's conscience. It is probably for this reason that Alain Touraine writes in his recently provocatively titled essay, "Sociology after Sociology":

> One of the main themes of sociology is therefore the reversal of the conception and role of institutions. These were defined by their function in the integration of a social system. They defined and imposed respect for the norms and instruments for the defense of individuals which enable them to defend themselves against norms. Our society is less and less a society of the subjected and more and more a society of volunteers (Touraine 2007: 191).

The field of society is also a work of ontological sociality, which is not confined only to contemporary, late, modern or individualized societies. It is a reality and possibility in all kinds of societies though degrees may vary (cf. Touraine 2000). In this context, what Michael Frietag writes deserves our careful consideration: "Contrary to a misguided reading of Max Weber's well-known texts, the ontological aspect – the immanent normativity of human/social and historical being is primary, and an understanding of it involves another break with the Weberian heritage: the idea of an ontological reciprocity of individual and society should replace methodological individualism" (Frietag 2001: 2). But acknowledging the ontological aspect of society does not mean only acknowledging its normative dimension but also its "subjective existence" (ibid.). In recent social experience this ontological dimension of society – creativity of self, return of the actor, and self-production of society – comes into play in the work of varieties of social movements. Some scholars suggest that in social movements we get a glimpse of the pathways of an alternative sociality which can be called ontological sociality, the basic ontological relationship characterized by interpretative action. As Martin Fuchs argues: "Humans not only refer to their self and their social environment, the sociality or polity they live in but the world as a [...] latent 'surplus of meaning', as exceeding. The basic (ontological) relationship would be interpretative action. This broadens the reference of human action and interpretation or, rather, transcends the idea of a specific referent [...] Instead of seeing subjectivity as constitutive of the world [... we have to see it] as open to the world" (Fuchs 2004)

There is a recognition of an ontological dimension in varieties of life and disciplines now. For example, in so far as the domain of economy and the field of economics is concerned, Irene van Staveren tells us: "[...] There is a methodological alternative to the utilitarian paradigm of economics to be found in ontology" (van Staveren 2004: 86). Like Frietag's discussion of ontological reciprocity in sociology pointing to the normative and subjective dimensions of self and society, in van Staveren, an ontological approach to economics urges us to understand the value commitments of actors. An ontological approach to economics relies on people's value commitments but these values should not be understood as only utility maximization or profit maximization but reflect values of justice and care, and these values should not be understood through "the dualistic methodology of mainstream economics, separating values from economic behaviour" (ibid.). In her outline of an alternative economic methodology (an ontological methodology for economics grounded on human values) and conceptualization of economics as concerned with provisioning rather than exchange, van Staveren builds on Aristotle but reformulates the essentialist traces of an Aristotelian ontology in the direction of movement and pluralism (also see van Staveren 2001).

For van Staveren, economic actors have plural value commitments of freedom, justice and care. So far, the ontology of economics has been narrowly defined in terms of freedom, market and exchange but for van Staveren we should acknowledge that the domains of justice and care are also integral parts of the reality of economic life. These domains of the economy are autonomous yet interdependent and what is helpful for us to realize is that there is a non-instrumental relationship between them. What van Staveren writes can open new vistas of imagination in our methodological engagement: "[...] in an economic ontology grounded in human values, economic value domains are interdependent but not instrumentally related. Each domain functions on its own terms but at the same time it is a precondition for the functioning of other domains, without being instrumental" (ibid.: 98).

We also get glimpses of an ontological sociality going beyond subject-object dualism in classical formulations of society. For example, building on both Indian and Greek traditions, philosopher Binod Kumar Agarwala (2004) tells us that play was central to Greek and Vedic imagination of society. Central to the practice of play is that the actor or subject loses himself/herself in the play. Furthermore, "The mode of being of *lila* [play] does not permit the *jiva* [person] to behave towards the *lila* as to an object"; "the self-understanding of *jiva* is inevitably involved in understanding of *lila* in such a way that the medium is not differentiated from it" (Agarwala 2004: 263). This suggests an ontology and epistemology of participation which are important components of a creative social research but Agarwala urges us to be open towards the dimension of beyond or transcendence in this ontology and epistemology of participation. Self-consciousness here cannot be completely dissolved into self-knowledge: *"There is always a remainder, an excess of what we are beyond what we know of ourselves"* (ibid.: emphasis added).

Rethinking Society: Some Further Considerations

The perspective of ontological sociality helps us rethink society in a foundational way which can be understood in conjunction with other recent efforts. For example, many contemporary sociologists point to the need for thinking about sociology beyond society. John Urry and Karin Knorr-Cetina point to this which has a much wider currency than acknowledged by anxiety-stricken sociologists of our times.[3] Writes John Urry in his *Sociology Beyond Societies*: "New rules of sociological method are necessitated by the apparently declining power of national societies (whether or not we do in fact live in a global society), since it was these societies that had provided the social context for sociological study until the present" (Urry 2000: 1–2). Urry looks at the emergence of "natural-social" hybrids for contemporary citizenship and explores whether "notions of chaos and complexity" can assist in the "elaboration of a 'sociology beyond societies'" (ibid.: 190).

Social theorist and sociologist of science Karin Knorr-Cetina takes this exploration of a sociology beyond society to inspiring height and depth. Writes Knorr-Cetina in her provocatively titled essay, "Postsocial Relations: Theorizing Society in a Postsocial Environment": "Sociality is very likely a permanent feature of human life. But the focus of sociality are nonetheless changing – in conjunction with concrete historical developments" (Knorr-Cetina 2001: 521). And, one of the most important aspects of the contemporary development is "the loss of social imagination, the slow erosion of the belief in salvation by society" (ibid.: 523). The post-social environment today not only consists of subject-centred imagination but also objects and the non-human world which challenges us to go beyond anthropocentrism. The very beginning lines of Knorr-Cetina (2001: 520) deserve our careful attention from the point of view of overcoming the tight grip of anthropocentrism in our thinking:

> [...] we take it for granted that social reality is the world of human affairs, exclusively [...] Luckman raised the issue from a phenomenological perspective arguing that the boundary we see between the human social and the non-human, non-social was not an essential structure of the life-world. One reason for this was that our sense of humanness itself is not an original or universal projection but arises from revisions and modifications of other distinctions, for example that between living and non-living beings.

For Knorr-Cetina, in contemporary consumer culture and society, we find that social reality consists not only of subjects but also objects. Living in this reality leads to the emergence of a new self: the self as a structure of wanting and the shift from "the inner censor to the mirror image self". Knorr-Cetina writes building on his dialogue with George Herbert Mead and Jacques Lacan: "The lack-wanting system describes contemporary selves better than the I-you-me system" (ibid.: 527). Here, self is characterized by wanting and though in contemporary consumer culture individuals want fulfilment in having more objects, this object-centred consumption may not be our destiny and our structure of wanting has the potential to make us seeker of a more authentic solidarity, an intimate relation with self, other, Nature and God. The task here is to realize the challenge of an emergent subjectivity and what Foucault had written vis-à-vis Nietzsche: "For Nietzsche, the death of God signifies the end of metaphysics, but God is not replaced by man, and the space remains empty" (quoted in Carretto 1999: 85; see also Uberoi 2002; Bhaskar 2002a, 2002b).

In Knorr-Cetina's insightful formulation, solidarity is central to a post-social sociality but solidarity here is not entrapped in a logic of nation-state and society and carries the signature of an ontological sociality. Post-social sociality also calls for a new epistemology of participation. Writes Knorr-Cetina: "[...] we can do less without positioning ourselves on the object's side when the object is non-human than when it is human [...] The process of position-taking involves the subject's 'becoming the object,' a sort of cross-over through which the subject attempts to see the object world from inside, to 'think' as it does, and to feel its reactions. In the words of a biologist, 'if you want to really understand about a tumour, you've got to be a tumour' " (ibid.: 531).

But such an ontology and epistemology of participation calls for overcoming not only anthropocentrism but also egoism. What is interesting is that such a calling seems to be articulated now by scholars with a Marxist background. In his presidential address to World Congress of Sociology, "The Heritage of Sociology, the Promise of Social Science," Immanuel Wallerstein writes: "Human arrogance has been humanity's greatest self-imposed limitation. [...] In all these arrogances we have betrayed first of all ourselves, and closed off our potential" (Wallerstein 1999: 250). Wallerstein transforms the whole logic of familiar sociological discourse when he talks about cosmic creativity which prepares the ground for far deeper radical proposals of thinkers such as Roy Bhaskar to follow who talks about cosmic envelope and transcendental identification: "We live in an uncertain cosmos, whose single greatest merit is the permanence of [...] uncertainty, because it is this uncertainty that makes possible creativity – Cosmic Creativity, and with that of course human creativity" (ibid.).

In the same essay, Wallerstein presents sociology six challenges: (a) rethinking rationality; (b) overcoming its initial Eurocentric bias; (c) rethinking time and temporality; (d) reckoning with complexities and uncertainties; (e) coming to terms with feminist challenges not only in social relations but also in epistemology and questioning objectivity in not only social sciences but also in natural science; and finally (f) rethinking modernity by acknowledging that modernity, the centrepiece of all our work, has never really existed (ibid.: 241). This urges us to realize that the relations between self, other and the world can be more meaningfully imagined and lived than what has been done under the regime of European modernity (Uberoi 2002).

Out of these challenges, we can elaborate the challenge of rethinking rationality and universality as a starting point of a multi-dimensional foundational rethinking of the very category of society itself. Our conception of society in sociology suffers from a "myth of rationality" and "myth of stability" (cf. Toulmin 2001). But society is not only the ground of the rational, it is also the base of much irrational and also the ground for supra-rational aspirations, as Nietzsche and Sri Aurobindo from their very different positions would urge us to understand. And, in so far as universality is concerned, there is a dimension of universality as a reality as well as possibility in particular cultures calling us to transcend the dichotomy between universalism and particularism and understanding the work of a contingent universal. Wallerstein et al. (1996) many years ago had challenged us to understand the work of "particularistic universalism". This is akin to a relational and perspectival universality articulated by literary theorist Radhakrishnan (2003: 34) which is always in process. In their work on cosmopolitanism, Sheldon Pollock et al. (2000) urge us to understand the similar work of what they call "situated universality,"[4] which is different from an opposition between global and local, universal and particular. Ulrich Beck (2002) in this regard also talks about cosmopolitanism with roots and wings. In rethinking universality, along with perspectives such as situated universality and perspectival universality, we are also enriched by a perspective of dialectical universality recently developed by Roy Bhaskar in his project of a deepened critical realism. For Bhaskar, for rethinking universality, we must go beyond abstract universality, understand it dialectically, and relate universality to "irreducible uniqueness" (Bhaskar 2002a: 122). For Bhaskar, dialectical universality of particular beings is sustained by "genuine non-duality and relations of identity" (Bhaskar 2002b: xxv). Bhaskar further writes, "once you describe the world in an abstract universal way as consisting in constant conjunctions of events or actualized empirical uniformities then you put a halt to history" (ibid.: 122). It reflects "ontological monovalence" and a sense of fatalism that the present society is the best of all possible worlds. Instead,

> [...] universality had to be understood dialectically – that is universality together with differentiations and mediations, together with geo-historical trajectories, or what I call *rhythmics,* and together with irreducible uniqueness, all of which defines the concrete singularity of every instance, everything that ever occurs. This would mean in concrete terms that the two members of the working class or two members of human race would always have to be understood in their mediations, that is whether they are women or men, what kind of work they do, and also in terms of their geo-historical trajectories, where they are coming from, their place and past, and where they are going, what their tangential future (ibid.: 122).

Rethinking Subjectivity

In his introduction to an anthology of contemporary European social thought on "Rethinking the Subject," James D. Faubion argues that while Kant's ontology is that of autonomous subject which was followed by Durkheim as he reformulated it in terms of making society "the genuine referent of Kant's transcendental subject," contemporary European thinkers go beyond this in offering an ontology of techno-praxis of the "techno-practitioner". For Faubion, the works of Habermas and Bourdieu reflect this shifting subjectivity: "For

Habermas, the hallmark of the techno-practitioner is his or her capacity – no longer nominal, but instead the product and profit of all in this world that mankind has learned – at once to recognize, accept, and follow the normative principles immanent in communication. For Bourdieu, the hallmark of techno-practitioner is his or her capacity to play a game, to use his or her material and symbolic resources strategically in order to win a context more or less local in its rule but everywhere the same in its covert end: domination" (Faubion 1995: 14–15).

Rethinking the subject as a techno-practitioner, for Faubion, should remind us of Aristotle to realize its promise and limits. For Faubion, "The Ethics [Nichomachean Ethics of Aristotle] sets the technician to one side; it features only the practitioner. But the practitioner it features is, like those of his lineage, a being neither transcendental nor natural but instead a being constructed, trained, and socialized, a being of acquired competence and acquired habit" (ibid.: 15). But Aristotle would also urge us to understand the limit of the contemporary techno-practitioner in terms of "ethical formalism" of Habermas and Bourdieu's "perverse teleology" [This is what Faubion himself writes]. Aristotle's hallmark is *eudaimonia* – happiness – and the techno-practitioner must not only argue and strategize but embody a striving for *eudaimonia* a striving which takes her beyond the contemporary models of the subject as coming from Habermas and Bourdieu. Realization of happiness is not a matter of social practice but also of appropriate subjective cultivation; realization of *eudaimonia* also calls for a spiritualization of practice, as we shall shortly see, and also going beyond Aristotle.

Subject as Not Only a Techno-practitioner but also a Transcendentally Real Self

Thus rethinking the subject urges us to realize the limits of the models of the techno-practitioner which is closer to the earlier sociological model of *homo sociologicus* presented by Ralph Dahrendorf. Neither the techno-practitioner nor *homo sociologicus* as occupants of social roles exhaust the reality and possibility of the subject (see Cohen 1994; Giri 1998) and it is helpful also here to acknowledge that the subject is also a transcendentally real self. Such a deepening and widening of perspective is suggested by Roy Bhaskar. Bhaskar, the pioneer in the movement of critical realism, has now deepened the quest of realism to touch spiritual quest of self-development and social emancipation. Even much before his contemporary spiritual deepening of critical realism Bhaskar had posed some foundational challenges to social sciences. For Bhaskar, in thinking about society we should not commit a collectivist or individualist fallacy as society consists of neither the collective nor the individual but relations. But, what is at the core of relationship? For Bhaskar, it is the ideal and practice of identification what he calls "transcendental identification". Transcendental identification is the work of the transcendentally real self; so in rethinking the subject we have to think of her as also a transcendentally real self and not merely a "techno-practitioner". For Bhaskar, "[...] transcental identification is absolutely basic to life. This means non-duality is absolutely basic to life" (Bhaskar 2002a: 140). And, this "non-duality is not something 'mystical,' not something that depends on any kind of belief or faith, but the necessary condition for our most quotidian states and acts" (ibid.: 261). For Bhaskar (2002a), our ontology has to be "vastly expanded to allow for the possibility for the enfolding layers of being" (ibid.: 16). Parallel to Knorr-Cetina's notion of self as a structure of wanting, Bhaskar refers to absence that affects our ontology and epistemology: "The whole process is really structured by absence: first in the form of incompleteness which initiates it; second it is negativity in the form of contradiction which stimulates the crisis which motivates you to transcend an existing problem field. And, what happens when you are transcending it is that you have a moment of creative discovery which actually cannot be induced or deduced from the existing subject matter; so it comes from the epistemically unknown" (ibid.: 130).

Acknowledging that the subject is also a transcendentally real self urges us to rethink differentiation from a perspective of identification. Bhaskar takes the discourse and practice of identification to a new depth and height by talking of ground state, cosmic envelope and co-presence. Bhaskar writes: "When your action is coming from your ground-state you will see no preference for your own development over the development and freedom of any other being in the universe" (ibid.: 148). Bhaskar urges social scientists to be open to these new pathways of connectivity at work in people's lives rather than just be preoccupied with difference:

> The critique of postmodernism involves accepting the emphasis on uniqueness and differentiation without throwing out our concepts of universality and connection. Indeed the ground-state and cosmic envelope are just precisely the concepts we need to understand differentiation within a unity. But these aspects of being, on which all other aspects ultimately depend, are precisely those which through the generalized theory of co-presence, allows us to see that everything is implicitly enfolded or contained and may be brought to consciousness, implicit or explicit, in everything else, so that anything can be traced or manifest in anything else. The world becomes one in which a quasi-magical or generalized (dialectically universalized) synchronicity is potentially capable of being manifest anywhere (ibid.: 248).

Max Weber spoke about the disenchantment of the world in which modern scientific world view played an important role. Modern social science took part in this disenchantment of the world in the process making us unable to live authentically. Now, there is a need to go beyond the crisis of European sciences and to live a non-dual life and through our ontology and epistemology contribute to the experience and making of a re-enchanted world where "knowledge of" cannot be dissociated from "knowing with" (cf. Sunder Rajan 1998). Bhaskar urges us to attend to this calling of re-enchantment both as subjects and scientists which involves collapse of "subject-object duality" and "fact-value distinction" (Bhaskar 2002b: xxxvii).[5] For Bhaskar we are all enchanted beings, i.e., "bearers of values, meaning and change". Bhaskar writes: "We are involved as totalities in a world which is enchanted in the sense that it is the bearer of values, of meaning and change. This level of critique also enables us to see that the world consists of emergent totalities [...]" (ibid.: 247). Bhaskar elaborates the dynamics of an expanded ontology as a reflection of and striving towards a dynamically moving re-enchanted world:

> [...] we perspectivally re-totalise the field, which we all daily experience, and which is plummeting into global crisis, under the categories of transcendence, duality and non-duality, in the context of an expanded ontology, in which we not only, as in

> hitherto critical realism, think being, thing being processually, and as a totality, and as incorporating transformative agency and reflexivity; but also now think being as multi-planar and n-dimensionally generalised, with mental and emotional *sui generis* realities, bound together within a more basic level which is not only beyond thought but beyond sight, which I have called the cosmic envelope; and within this vastly expanded conception of being, and the very extended ontology it necessitates, we now see being as re-enchanted, that is as valuable, meaningful and containing invisible (more generally unknown and even unmanifest), subtle, mysterious and even magical qualities and connections, which our contemporary sciences know nothing of (ibid.: 257–58).[6]

Beyond Sociology: Sociological Research and the Calling of an Ontological Epistemology of Participation

Rethinking society and subjectivity also calls for rethinking sociological research as a field of ontological epistemology of participation. Research is not just an epistemic activity; it also calls for cultivation of appropriate virtues transgressing the conventional boundaries between epistemology and ontology. As John Greco writes: "Just as virtue theories in ethics try to understand the normative properties of actions in terms of the normative properties of moral agents, virtue theories in epistemology try to understand the normative properties of beliefs in terms of the normative properties of cognitive agents" (Greco 2001: 136). Virtue epistemology makes activities of research "person-based rather than belief-based" (ibid.). While in epistemology there is a move towards "virtue epistemology," in ontology there are moves towards "weak ontology"[7] as pioneered by Vattimo (1999), "practical ontology" and "critical ontology" as striven by Dallmayr (1984, 1987, 1991), and "ontological anthropology" as attempted by Clammer et al. (2004), which interestingly embodies a "relational epistemology" (Clammer et al., 2004: 17). Vattimo's weak ontology embodies vulnerability, self-emptying (*kenosis*), love and non-violence; similar is also Dallmayr's strivings of a practical ontology which touches the height and depth of a practical spirituality. We can bring "virtue epistemology," "weak ontology," "practical ontology," "ontological anthropology" and Bhaskar's expanded ontology or ontology of self-expansion and nurture the ground for an ontological epistemology of participation.

In ontological epistemology of participation, there is attentiveness to and interpenetration of both the subjective and the objective and the whole challenge is to arrive at an objective in spite of our irreducible subjectivity. This calls for a new conception of both the subjective and the objective. As we have suggested, subjective also refers to the dimension of transcendental or non-dual self in the actor/subject/scientist and this would be a companion of an aspired for objectivity. As Eric Fromm tells us: "Objectivity does not mean detachment, *it means respect*; that is, the ability not to distort and to falsify things, persons and oneself" (Fromm 1950: 105). Furthermore, "To be objective is possible only if we respect the things we observe; that is, if we are capable of seeing them in their uniqueness and interconnectedness" (ibid.: 104) (compare this to Bhaskar's perspective of dialectical universality paying attention to uniqueness and singularity).

Ontological epistemology of participation differs from participant observation as it is conventionally understood. Bourdieu asks of participant observation: "How can one be both subject and object, the one who acts and the one who, as it were, watching himself acting? (Bourdieu 2003: 282). As an alternative, Bourdieu proposes *participant objectivation*: "By participant objectivation I mean the objectivation of the subject of objectivation, of the analyzing subject – in short the researcher herself?" (ibid.). But, how can one watch oneself acting and be both subject and object? Does it not involve work on oneself or cultivation of some kind of witnessing self what is called *sakhi pursusha* in Indian spiritual traditions or impartial spectator by Adam Smith (1976)? Can this be only epistemic and does not it also involve some ontological work on oneself? Bourdieu speaks about "epistemic reflexivity" (cf. Bourdieu and Wacquant 1992: 38). His application of statistical analysis to self-understanding is helpful but does it also not involve ontological nurturance?[8]

In this context, Ankersmit's most recent discussion of the methodology of historical representation helps us understand the work of ontological epistemology of participation in a new way. Ankersmit tells us that historical representation of a period may present a "coherent whole of developments on domains that are incommensurable with each other" such as the "cognitive, ethical, aesthetic, religious or technical preoccupations of a period" (Ankersmit 2002: 234). For Ankersmit such a connected picture and free movement "from one domain to another" is possible because of historical representation. He goes on to write: "If we ask ourselves how representation may enable us to do this, the answer is that *the unique contribution of representation […] is that it involves the knowing subject […] The self is activated by representation in a way that would mean the end of objective knowledge*. And from the point of view recommended by representation, suddenly a common ground can be discerned for domains that seemed hitherto completely unrelated and incommensurable" (ibid.; emphasis added).

Here, Ankersmit presents the example of epistemology and politics in 17th century France. For Ankersmit, "at first sight seventeenth-century rationalist philosophy and absolutism will have nothing in common for us. But then the historian may suggest the point of view of the transcendental ego [or it may emerge from any self-initiated historical engagement, not just from historian as a professional expert], of a self that withdraws from the world but in order to get a firmer hold of it" (ibid.). "And this point of view makes us aware of what the Cartesian self, doubting all knowledge in order to gain access to absolute certain knowledge, has in common with Louis XIV withdrawing from the bustle of Paris to Versailles in order to confirm his absolutist mastery of France" (ibid.). Thus, the perspective of transcendental ego born of historical inquiry and representation, an engagement in which all of us seeking souls can participate, not only professional historians, helps us understand the connection between epistemology and politics in seventeenth century France. For Ankersmit, one may not totally identify with such a perspective which emerges from our work of historical representation but nonetheless it shapes our personality and what we are. From the perspective of the calling of an ontological epistemology of participation, what Ankersmit writes, deserves our careful considerations: "Nevertheless, becoming acquainted with the possibility of many such points of view will, add each time, a new, though tiny stone to the mosaic of our personality. And in the end this cannot fail to have its effect on the kind of person that we are" (ibid.: 235).

By the Way of Conclusion

In this essay we have explored the work of ontological sociality in self, culture and society and thus sought to reconstitute society as a field of ontological epistemology of participation. We have also striven to reconstitute sociological research as a practice of ontological epistemology of participation going beyond modernistic privileging of epistemology and neglect of ontology. Such a new view of sociology and sociological research points to the need for cultivation of an appropriate ontology which can help us come to terms with not only some of the theoretical problems such as the postmodern imprisonment within difference but also realize the practical task of establishing solidarity across divides. Ontological cultivation also includes the challenge of cultivating non-dual modes within ourselves as subjects of investigation. Such an ontological cultivation has an epochal significance as our theories and methods have been imprisoned within the modernist privileging of epistemology over ontology. Bringing ontological cultivation back to sociology enables us to go beyond the conventional slogan of renewing sociological research with participation. For the last quarter century participatory research has been much valorized – it has been on everybody's lips starting from anthropologists to development practitioners, and now the agents of World Bank. But our approach to and involvement with participatory research has been mostly procedural and instrumental. In this context, we need to think about and practise research in a new way, in an ontological way, where our whole self – not just the inquiring mind – is involved with research. The valorized discourse of participatory research today needs a radical supplement from Gandhi and Heidegger where research becomes a time and space of laying open oneself and realization of co-being (cf. Dallmayr 1996). The time of research becomes both a time of communication and silence[9] – a time of "lived time" – and the space of research becomes a space of dwelling, in fact a "poetics of dwelling", rather than building. Here, what Pillai writes about Gandhi's modes of participation in social service from a Heideggerian point of view can be helpful in going beyond an instrumentalist approach to participatory research: "Gandhi's participation in the life of his time was always (at the same time) an interior journey, an exploration of his being, and not just working out of a pre-established strategy. It is this insistent questioning of himself which distinguishes his action from all self-sanctifying 'social service' based on representation. Every decision for Gandhi was simultaneously the laying open of himself" (Pillai 1985: 77).

Bringing ontological cultivation to the discourse and practice of sociology is an important calling of our time. But while embodying ontological cultivation we can proceed in the spirit of a journey and evolution rather than with an essentialist, fixed ontology. Much of talk of ontology has in the past suffered from the dangers of essentialism and fixation. But we are not destined to commit the same errors nor should we valorize ontology to the point of excluding the epistemic activity of learning. A way out of the modernist privileging of epistemology and neglect of ontology is not to valorize ontology at the expense of the epistemic practices of learning and inquiry. Here we can supplement Heidegger with Gandhi, not only in politics but also in epistemology, thus rescuing us from complicity with any politics of mastery in the name of the resoluteness of *Dasein* and making *Dasein* and self an involved and emergent participant in learning (cf. Bourdieu 1991b; Dallmayr 2001b; Srinivasan 1998).[10] One arresting aspect of

Gandhi's life and work is his insatiable passion for learning and experiments with truth. At the ripe age of eighty when he was travelling from village to village and trying to calm the fire of communal violence in riot-torn Noakhali, he was devoting an hour everyday to learning the alphabets of the language of the locality, *Bengali*. It is this passion for learning and self-cultivation which can make us humble and rescue us from the danger of using our knowledge, including the knowledge generated out of our research, as an aid to our will to power – an instrument of authority, including ethnographic authority, it can help us realize that what we need is not so much "self-mastery" as an "ethics of servanthood," and a "pathos of shakenness" (cf. Giri 2002: Shanks 2001). As we transform sociology as a field of ontological epistemology of participation, we have to realize that ontology emerges as much from contestation, conversation and learning as it is an initial participant in self and science. We have to open ontology itself to a journey of homelessness (cf. Dallmayr 2001) and an epistemic practice of learning thus crossing the boundaries between ontology and epistemology, a border-crossing which becomes a paradigmatic activity of multiple border-crossing between philosophy and fieldwork, creative research and critical action, self and other, society and cosmos. To sing it with Rabindranath Tagore, the immortal poet of *Gitanjali*:

> Life is perpetually creative because it contains in itself that surplus which ever overflows the boundaries of immediate time and space, restlessly pursuing its adventure of expression in the varied forms of self-realization (Tagore 1961: 45).

Notes

1. As John Clammer writes, "For much conventional sociology, a preoccupation with methodology has driven out any concern with consciousness" (Clammer 2007: 13).
2. Gorz (1999) writes the following about education which embodies a critique of society-centred sociological reasoning and signature of an ontological sociality:

   > This can not be *taught*; it has to be *stimulated*. It can arise only out of the affective attachment of children or adolescents to a reference group who makes them *feel* deserving of *unconditional* love, and *confident* of their capacity to learn, act, undertake projects and measure themselves against others – who gives them, in a word 'self-esteem'. The subject emerges by virtue of the love with which another subject calls it to become a subject and it develops through the desire to be loved by that other subject. This means that the *educative* relation *is not a social relation and is not socializable*.

3. This seems to be the case with Anthony Giddens whose very title, *In Defence of Sociology*, suggests this anxiety. It is no wonder than that Giddens laments the disappearance of the "capacity of sociology to provide a unifying centre for the diverse branches of social research" (Giddens 1996: 2). To be fair to Giddens he is surely not alone, traces of this anxiety are to be found in Andre Beteille (2000) as well. An anxiety to defend one's discipline is not confined to sociology. Habermas (1990) seems to be worried that one day philosophy may be replaced by cultural anthropology and Sidney Mintz (2000) is worried about this being replaced by cultural studies.

4. What Pollock et al., (2000) write below vis-à-vis their elaboration of what they call as cosmofeminism as an example of situated universalism deserves our careful attention:

   Any cosmofeminine would have to create a critically engaged space that is not just a screen for globalization or an antidote to nationalism but is rather a focus on projects of the intimate sphere conceived as a part of the cosmopolitan. Such a critical perspective would also open up a new understanding of the domestic, which would no longer be confined spatially or socially to the private sphere. This perspective would allow us to recognize that domesticity itself is a vital interlocutor and not just an interloper in law, politics and public ethics. From this reconfigured understanding of the public life of domesticity and intimacy it follows that spheres of intimacy generate legitimate pressure on any understanding of cosmopolitan solidarities and networks. The cosmofeminine could thus be seen as subverting those larger networks that refuse to recognize their own nature as specific systems of relations among others. That is, we would no longer have feminism as the voice of the specificity interrogating the claims of other putative universals. Instead we would have the cosmofeminine *as the sign of an argument for a situated universalism that invites broader debate based on a recognition of their own situatedness*. A focus on this extensional understanding of domesticity and intimacy could *generate a different picture of more public univeralisms,* making the domestic sphere subversive of *thin claims to universalism*" (Pollock et al., 2000: 584–85; emphasis added).

5. Reenchantment for Bhaskar also involves a "collapse of the distinction between sacred and profane" (Bhaskar 2002b: xxxviii). For him, "Once this distinction goes we can read the spiritual into the structure of everyday life" (ibid.).

6. Bhaskar's subsequent elaboration deserves our careful attention:

   Our task is to re-become non-dual beings in a world of duality, opposition and strife. Freedom is the elimination of the non-dual components within my embodied personality; that is the elimination of everything inconsistent with my ground-state, the cessation of negative incompleteness. In order to do this, I had to experience duality, heteronomy and change, to grow and fulfill my intentionality. When I have fulfilled my intentionality, when I have no more non-me within me, I am one with my ground state, and one with the ground-states of all other beings in the rest of creation too. I am one with the whole of creation; and as such will reflect back to its creator his work, formation, creation, will or intentionality; and perfectly reflecting his intentionality, I am one with him too. This is self-realisation, the realisation of the divine ingredient within me [...]

   But this is not the end of the odyssey in the world of duality. I am still *positively incomplete,* in so far as other beings are co-present, enfolded within me, are negatively incomplete, that is, unfree. When the whole of creation is self-realized, when it reflects back its own divinity, then and only then will there be *peace*. Even then this peace is only the end of pre-history. I know in the meantime that I will grow and develop while I strive for this goal, a development to which I can see no conceivable end; so if there is an expanded plenitude of possibilities packed into my non-dual being, my agentive self in the world of duality, we cannot even begin to anticipate what possibilities lie within eudemonia. This *eudenomia* is not something removed from ordinary secular speculation [...]; rather, we have found it everywhere as a presupposition of even the most crude and rudimentary forms of ethics (ibid.: 261–62).

7. In the words of Vattimo: "[...] We derive an ethics of non-violence from weak ontology, yet we are led to weak thought, from its origin in Heidegger's concern with the metaphysics of objectivity, by the Christian legacy of the rejection of violence at work within us" (Vattimo 1999: 44).
8. This may still be a helpful step despite Bourdieu's own disdain for "the political ontology of Martin Heidegger" (Bourdieu 1991b). A way out is not to be trapped inside the abominable walls of Heideggerian political ontology and to explore the pathways of spiritual ontologies taking inspiration, for example, from Dallmayr's (1993) exploration of an other Heidegger.
9. Consider here what Niklas Luhman, the sociologist of communication writes:

   [We need] to make a digression at this point and consider whether the participation of consciousness is not perhaps best conceived as a silence (Luhman 2001: 16).
10. It must be noted however that in his later seeking Heidegger himself made a shift from his earlier preoccupation with resoluteness. As Dallmayr helps us understand in an original reinterpretation of the Heideggerian pathway: "[...] Heidegger's middle and later writings came to see the pitfalls and streamlining effects of linear power-seeking and to adumbrate a realm beyond power and impotence, domination and submission under the rubric of a 'power-free' (machtlos) dispensation that allows being (s) 'to be' (Dallmayr 2001b: 190).

References

Agarwala, Binod. 2004. "Humanities and Social Sciences in the New Millennium: Theorizing in/for Society as Play." In Ananta Kumar Giri (ed.), *Creative Social Research: Rethinking Theories and Methods*, Lanham, MD: Lexington Books, pp. 253–272.

Ankersmit, F.R. 2002. *Political Representation*. Stanford: Stanford University Press.

Bauman, Zygmunt. 2001. *The Industrialized Society*. Cambridge: Polity Press.

Beck, Ulrich. 2000. *The Brave New World of Work*, Cambridge: Polity Press.

——. Beck, Urlich. 2002. "The Cosmopolitan Society and its Enemies." *Theory, Culture and Society* 19 (1–2): 17–44.

Beck, Ulrich and Elizabeth Beck-Gernsheim. 1995. *The Normal Chaos of Love*, Cambridge: Polity Press.

Beteille, Andre. 2002 *Sociology: Essays on Approach and Method*, Delhi: Oxford University Press.

Bhaskar, Roy. 2002a. *Reflections on Meta-Reality: Transcendence, Everyday Life and Emancipations*, New Delhi: Sage Publication.

——. 2002b. *Meta-Reality: The Philosophy of Meta-Reality*, Volume I. *A Philosophy for the Present: Creativity, Love and Freedom*, The Bhaskar Series, New Delhi: Thousand Oaks and London: Sage Publications.

Bourdieu, Pierre. 1990. *In Other Words: Towards a Reflexive Sociology*, Cambridge: Polity Press.

——. 1991a. "Epilogue: On the Possibility of a Field of World Sociology", in Pierre Bourdieu and James S. Coleman (eds.), *Social Theory for a Changing Society*, Boulder, CO: Westview, pp. 373–87.

——. 1991b. *The Political Ontology of Martin Heidegger*, (Tr. Peter Collier), Cambridge: Polity Press.

——. 1992. "The Practice of Reflexive Sociology (Paris Workshop)", in Pierre Bourdieu and Loic J.D. Wacquant, *An Invitation to Reflexive Sociology*, Cambridge: Polity Press.

——. 1999. *The Weight of the World: Social Suffering in Contemporary Society*, Cambridge: Polity Press.

——. 2000. *Pascalian Meditations*, Cambridge: Polity Press.

——. 2003. "Participant Objectivation", *Journal of Royal Anthropological Institute* (N.S.) 9: 281–294.

Bourdieu, Pierre and Loic J.D. Wacquant. 1992. *An Invitation to Reflexive Sociology*, Cambridge: Polity Press.

Carretto, Jeremy (ed.). 1999. *Religion and Culture by Michel Foucault*, Manchester: Manchester University Press.

Clammer, John. 2007. "Deep Sociology." Special issue on "Beyond Sociology," *Asian Journal of Social Sciences*.

Clammer, John, Sylvie Piorier and Eric Schwimmer. 2004. "Introduction: The Relevance of Ontologies in Anthropology: Reflections on a New Anthropological Field", in John Clammer et al. (eds.), *Figured Worlds: Ontological Obstacles in Intercultural Relations*, pp. 3–22, Toronto: Toronto University Press.

Cohen, Anthony. 1994. *Self-Consciousness: An Alternative Anthropology of Identity*, London: Routledge.

Dallmayr, Fred. 1984. *Polis and Praxis: Exercises in Contemporary Political Theory*, Cambridge, MA: The MIT Press.

——. 1987. *Critical Encounters: Between Philosophy and Politics*, Notre Dame: University of Notre Dame Press.

——. 1991. *Between Freiburg and Frankfurt: Toward a Critical Ontology*, Amherst: University of Massachusetts Press.

——. 1993. *The Other Heidegger*, Ithaca: Cornell University Press.

——. 1996. *Beyond Orientalism: Essays on Cross-Cultural Encounter*, Albany: SUNY Press.

——. 1998. *Alternative Visions: Pathways in the Global Village*, Lanham, MD: Rowman & Littlefield.

——. 2001a. *Homelessness and Homecoming: Heidegger on the Road*, University of Notre Dame: Manuscript.

——. 2001b. "Resisting Totalizing Uniformity: Marin Heidegger on the *Macht* and *Machenschaft*", in Fred Dallmayr, *Achieving Our World: Toward a Global and Plural Democracy*, Lanham, MD: Rowman & Littlefield.

——. 2002. *Dialouge among Civilizations: Some Exemplary Voices*, New York: Palgrave.

——. 2004. *Peace Talks: Any Body Listening?* Notre Dame: University of Notre Dame Press.

——. (ed.) 1999. *Border Crossings: Toward a Comparative Political Theory*, Lanham, MD: Lexington Books.

Elias, Norbert. 1991. *The Society of Individuals*, Cambridge, MA: Basil Blackwell.

Faubion, James D. (ed.) 1995. *Rethinking the Subject: An Anthology of Contemporary European Social Theory*, Boulder, CO: Westview Press.

Flyvbjerg, Bent. 2001. *Making Social Science Matter: Why Social Inquiry Fails and How It can Succeed Again*, (Tr. Steven Sampson), Cambridge: Cambridge University Press.

Frietag, Michel. 2001. "The Contemporary Social Sciences and the Problem of Normativity", *Theses Eleven*, No. 65: 1–25.

Fromm, Eric. 1950. *Man for Himself*, London: Routledge and Kegan Paul.

Fuchs, Martin. 2004. "Articulating the World: Social Movements, the Self-Transcendence of Society and the Question of Culture", in Ananta K. Giri (ed.), *Creative Social Research: Rethinking Theories and Methods*, Lanham, MD: Lexington Books.

Giddens, Anthony. 1996. *In Defense of Sociology: Essays, Interpretations and Rejoinders*, Cambridge: Polity Press.

Gatens, Moira and Genevieve Lloyd (1999) *Collective Imaginings: Spinoza, Past and Present*, London: Routledge.

Giri, Ananta Kumar. 1998. "Self, Other and the Challenge of Culture", in idem, *Global Transformations: Postmodernity and Beyond*, Jaipur: Rawat Publications.

——. 2002. *Conversations and Transformations: Toward a New Ethics of Self and Society*, Lanham, MD: Lexington Books and Rowman and Littlefield.

Gorz, Andre. 1999. *Reclaiming Work: Beyond the Wage-Based Society*, Cambridge: Polity Press.

Greco, John. 2001. "Virtues and Rules in Epistemology," in Abrol Fairweather and Linda Zagzebski (eds.), *Virtue Epistemology: Essays on Epistemic Virtue and Responsibility*, pp. 117–141, Oxford: Oxford University Press.

Habermas, Jurgen. 1990. *Moral Consciousness and Communicative Action*, Cambridge: Polity Press.

Ingold, Tim. 2004. "A Circumpolar Night's Dream". In Clammer et al., pp. 25–57.

Knorr-Cetina, Karen. 2001. "Postsocial Relations: Theorizing Society in a Postsocial Environment", in George Ritzer and Barry Smart (eds.), *Handbook of Social Theory*, London: Sage.

Luhman, Niklas. 2001. "Notes on the Project of 'Poetry and Social Theory'" *Theory, Culture and Society*, 18 (1): 15–27.

Mintz, Sidney W. 2000. "Sow's Ears and Silver Linings: A Backward Look at Ethnography", *Current Anthropology* 41 (2): 169–189.

Melucci, Alberto. 1996. *The Playing Self: Person and Meaning in the Planetary Society*, Cambridge: Cambridge University Press.

Mohanty, J.N. 2000a. *Self and Other: Philosophical Essays*, Delhi: Oxford University Press.

Pillai, P.V. 1985. "Hind Swaraj in the Light of Heidegger's Critique of Modernity", in *Hind Swaraj: A Fresh Look*, Delhi: Gandhi Peace Foundation.

Pollock, Sheldon et al. 2000. "Cosmopolitanisms". *Public Culture* 12 (3): 577–89.

Radhakrishnan, R. 2003. *Theory in an Uneven World*, Cambridge, MA: Basil Blackwell.

Shanks, Andrew. 2001. "What is Truth?", *Towards a Theological Poetics*, London: Routledge.

Smith, Adam. 1976. *A Theory of Moral Sentiments*, Oxford: Oxford University Press.

Srinivasan, Amrit. 1998. "The Subject of Fieldwork: Malinowski and Gandhi", in Meenakshi Thapan (ed.), *Anthropological Journeys: Reflections on Fieldwork*, Hyderabad: Orient Longman.

Sunder Rajan, R. 1998. *Beyond the Crisis of European Sciences*. Shimla: Indian Institute of Advanced Studies.

Tagore, Rabindranath. 1961. *On Art and Aesthetics*, Calcutta: Orient Longman.

Tuner, Bryan S. (ed.) 1996. *The Blackwell Companion to Social Theory*, Oxford: Blackwell.

Toulmin, Stephen. 2001. *Return to Reason*, Cambridge, MA: Harvard University Press.

Touraine, Alain. 1977. *Self-Production of Society*, Chicago: The University of Chicago Press.

——. 2000. *Can We Live Together? Equality and Difference*, Cambridge: Polity Press.

——. 2007. "Sociology After Sociology". *European Journal of Social Theory* 10 (2): 184–193.

Uberoi, J.P.S. 1978. *Science and Culture*, Delhi: Oxford University Press.

——. 1984. *The Other Mind of Europe: Goethe as a Scientist*, Delhi: Oxford University Press.

——. 2002. *The European Modernity: Truth, Science and Method*, New Delhi: Oxford University Press.

——. 2000. *Sociology Beyond Societies: Mobilities for the Twenty-First Century*, London: Routledge.

Vattimo, Gianni. 1999. *Belief*, Cambridge: Polity Press.

van Staveren, Irene. 2001. *The Values of Economics: An Aristotelian Perspective*, London: Routledge.

——. 2004. "Caring for Economics". In Ananta Kumar Giri (ed.), *Creative Social Research: Rethinking Theories and Methods* Lanham, MD: Lexington Books, pp. 83–111.

Wallerstein, Immanuel et al. 1996. *Open the Social Sciences*, Stanford: Stanford University Press.

Wallerstein, Immanuel. 1999. *The End of the World as We Know It: Social Science for the Twenty-First Century*, Minneapolis: University of Minnesota Press.

2 Sociology and New Paths of Criticism and Creativity

[...] all change or at least all radical change, that is all creative change, begins with self-change, that is with a prior (analytically and/or chronologically) transformation in one's transformative praxis. Moreover, all change also in a certain sense consists in (or involves) self-expansion. [...] man is essentially God (and therefore also essentially one, but also essentially unique); and that, as such, he is essentially free and already en-lightened, a freedom and enlightenment which is overlain by extraneous, heteronomous determinations which both (a) occlude and (b) qualify this essential fact. [...] Since God is also [...] *inter alia* unconditional love (unbounded peace and infinite joy or happiness) and we are essentially Godlike, the most appropriate [...] ethical and political stance is one of unconditional love for our essential selves, and that of each and every being and the environment we inhabit.

— Roy Bhaskar (2000), *From East to West: Odyssey of a Soul*, p. 68, ix

It is society which is called upon to become a means for the free development of the individual, or, more precisely, the space in which each contributes to creating for all, and all for each, the conditions for a free development of their individuality.

— Andre Gorz (1999), *Reclaiming Work: Beyond the Wage-Based Society*, p. 66.

Creative society embodies a methodology of viewing society in terms of liberation from multiple dominations – class, caste, race, ethnicity, gender and many more yet to be discovered sources of domination – and it points at processes already active or yet to be articulated, seeking to reconstitute society. [...] The concept of creative society opposes any formation which suggests a terminal view of the history of society. [...] the advanced industrial society may not be quite the example of a creative society that is fulfilling the people's democratic urges. It may actually be the picture of a system that manages instrumental creativity in a narrow framework. [...] capitalism in modern history represents the taming of creativity and taming of reason. The creative society, therefore, is bound to break out of the capitalist process in pursuit of creativity and liberation.

— Manoranjan Mohanty (1998), "Social Movements in a Creative Society: Of Autonomy and Interconnections," pp. 67–68

We have stepped into a new century and a new millennium and "the expectations of the millennium are of moving towards a better society" (Thapar 2000: xviii). But this movement towards a better society, which is decent (cf. Margalit 1996), is characterized by elimination of humiliation and institution of dignity in the lives of individuals and society, and creative calls for new initiatives in criticism, creativity and transformation. The last century has witnessed the demise of many assured methods of moving towards a better society. Over the last few decades, all societies have been subjected to fundamental processes of transformation, which have challenged the prevalent social and ideological systems. These processes have also challenged the familiar models of social criticism and methods of social transformation. The ideological systems of Marxism and liberal democracy had emphasized the proletarian class and political citizen as the main agents of social criticism. But contemporary changes have pointed to the limits of these categories as bearers of criticism, creativity and transformation. The collapse of state socialism in Soviet Union and Eastern Europe, the contemporary crisis of capitalism and disenchantment with political parties in advanced industrial democracies suggest that now the agenda of criticism and transformation must be broadened.

We thus face the challenge to rethink criticism, creativity and transformation in the context of changes taking place in self, culture and society. In familiar models of emancipation, political movements and political parties were the main agents of social criticism. As a consequence of the postmodern turn in culture and society, we are now recognizing the significance of socio-cultural and socio-spiritual new social movements as agents of social and cultural criticism. But this focus on new social movements now needs to be broadened by acknowledging transformative selves of individuals as agents of criticism and creativity. We get an intimation of such an agenda of criticism and creativity in the vision of many creative interlocutors of our times such as Roy Bhaskar, Alain Touraine, Alberto Melucci, Roberto Unger, Sri Aurobindo, Fred Dallmayr and Chitta Ranjan Das as well as in the work of movements such as Swadhyaya, integral education and the Zapatista movement. To understand self-transformation as an important goal of criticism and creativity and transformative self as the agent of social criticism, we can begin with the recent proposal of Roy Bhaskar. For Bhaskar, all creative change "begins with self-change or transformation of one's transformative praxis" (Bhaskar 2000: 68). The dialectics of self-transformation and social transformation is linked with each other and the task here is to overcome alienation and to practice the art of what Bhaskar calls "de-alienation" or *yoga*. The dialectics of God-realization or self-realization is a mechanics of a "re-enchanted reality". Love plays an important role in this path of criticism, creativity and transformation. As Bhaskar tells us: "The dialectics of de-alienation (of retotalisation) are all essentially dialectics of love of, love of self (Self), of each and all (Totality) and in both inner and outer movements, both as essentially love of God. The essence of liberated man is therefore love of God and God, we could say, is not only essentially love but essentially to be loved" (ibid.: 44).

But to love God is also to love men, women and children and this world and to fight for justice when God is denied in our lives and social systems. In fact, there is a transformation in religion and spirituality now where people are relating to God in a spirit of practical service in the world. As Robert Wuthnow tells us about the emergent contours of practice-oriented spirituality in the contemporary US: "Although it is possible for people's spiritual practices to focus so much attention on themselves or on God that little energy is left for anything else, this possibility does not appear to be the typical result" (Wuthnow 1998: 192). For Wuthnow, "spending time cultivating their relationship with God" frees people from "material concerns and other self-interested process so that they would focus on the needs of the other" (ibid.). Wuthnow further says that in a society like contemporary American society there is a transformation from a spirituality of dwelling to a spirituality of seeking and from a spirituality of seeking to spirituality of practice. "A spirituality of dwelling emphasizes *habitation*: God occupies a definite place in the universe" (ibid.: 10). But a "spirituality of seeking emphasizes *negotiation*: individuals search for sacred moments that reinforce their conviction that the divine exists [...]" (ibid.: 4). In practice-oriented spirituality, such a seeking takes place in varieties of transformative practices which can hold Roy Bhaskar's proposal of universal self-realization as a dialectic of love. Practical spirituality touches all aspects of our life: "[...] the point of spiritual practice is not to elevate an isolated set of activities over the rest of life but to electrify the spiritual impulse that animates all of life" (ibid.: 198).

Practice-oriented spirituality provides us a new relationship with the sacred. The sacred here is not an instrument in fundamentalist mobilization of religion, which is active in all societies now, added as they are by the forces of globalization but points to the realization of limits of instrumental rationality as the foundation of our lives. As Charles Taylor argues: "Acknowledging the transcendent means being called to a change of identity [that is, responding to the call for a] a radical decentering of the self in relation with the divine" (Taylor, quoted in Dallmayr 2001: 20). Transcendental sacred also works as a force of critical interrogation in contemporary societies when the power holders of society present the existing systems as Gods (Unger 1987). As Alberto Melucci argues: "Instrumental rationality has restored the world to mankind's scope of operation, but it also denies humanity all chances to transcend reality, it devalues everything that resists subsumption under the instrumental action. Society thus becomes a system of apparatuses identical with its own actions and intolerant of any diversity. The sacred thus reemerges as an appeal to a possible other, as the voice of what it is not but could be. Divested of the ritual trappings of the churches, the sacred thus becomes a purely cultural form of resistance which counters the presumptions of power by affirming the right to desire [...] to hope that the world is more than what actually is" (Melucci 1996a: 171). And here as Dallmayr would urge us to realize: "There are plenty of signs in our time that a narrowly confined immanence cannot satisfy human longings and aspirations. What needs to be recognised that longings for transcendence, even a transcendental holism, are vibrantly alive today in many societies on the level of the ordinary life-world – far removed from traditional power structures" (Dallmayr 2001: 17).

An openness to beyond in our lives calls for our being attentive to our own "inner planets" (Melucci 1996a: 60). For Melucci, "concerning ourselves with the inner planet of an ecological mentality means that we are called to go beyond an ecology of the system to assume responsibility for our being in the world." In this context, "what we need is *a passionate capacity to change form*, to redefine ourselves" (ibid.: 50; emphasis added). It also calls for an eulogy to wonder in our lives. The work of metamorphosis is facilitated in the work of creative and critical socio-spiritual movements, which provide a laboratory for creative experimentation with self, culture and society. As Melucci writes in his *Challenging Codes*:

"Contemporary movements are prophets of the present. What they possess is not the force of apparatus but the power of the word. They speak a language that seems to be entirely their own, but they say something that transcends their particularity and speaks to us all" (Melucci 1996b: 1). In fact, the ground for moral protest that many contemporary socio-cultural movements provide enables the actors to go beyond their instrumental concerns and engages themselves with something beyond. As James Jasper says: "Protest is like religious ritual: it embodies our moral judgments, so that we can express allegiance to moral visions through our actions. For those who no longer hold to traditional religious practices, protest is one of the few ways to express allegiance to moral visions through our actions" (Jasper 1997: 14). What is to be noted is that movements of protest which take us beyond the realm of instrumental and utilitarian self are not integration-seeking movements – seeking to be included within the existing frames of state and society – but to transform the existing basis of organization and questioning what Homi Bhaba calls the existent "ethics of social affiliation" (Bhaba 2000: 108). Jasper calls some of these movements "post-citizenship" movements: "In the nineteenth century post-citizenship movements often took the form of poor relief and anti-vice crusades; in the last thirty years they have pursued 'post-industrial' or 'post-material' aims like protection of the environments, peace and disarmament, alternative healing, life-style protections, and rights – goals which do not especially interest those seeking jobs, equal pay or the right to vote" (ibid.: 11).

Melucci presents metamorphosis as a path of criticism and transformation and this has close kinship with an appropriate politics and ethics of the subject what Alain Touraine calls developing an appropriate "subjectivation" (Touraine 2000). Touraine tells us in his *What is Democracy?*: "For a long time, modern philosophy regarded the interests of society as the principle of the Good: What was useful to society was good and what was harmful to society was bad. This rationalist, programmist faith in the correspondence between personal interests and collective interests is no longer tenable" (Touraine 1997: 19). For Touraine, "Democracy serves neither society nor individuals. Democracy serves human beings insofar as they are subjects, or in other words their own creators and the creators of their individual and social lives" (ibid.: 19). Touraine further says: "The subject is not merely a form of reason [...] it is also freedom, liberation and rejection" (Touraine 2000: 58); in fact, the "subject is at once reason, liberty and memory" (Touraine 1997: 127). To be a subject now is to recompose the world, especially as it is being torn asunder by the spread of global marketization and communitarian identity mobilization. Market forces recognize no subject nor do collectivist and communal identities. In our contemporary world, both market and collectivist mobilizations of identity are the triumphant forces, which threaten our capacity for realization as subjects. For Touraine, "Our real point of reference is not hope, but the pain of being torn apart. Because the world of objectification and its technologies has been so debased as to be no more than a market, whilst the world of cultural identities is locked into communitarian obsession, the individual who exists inside us all is suffering the agony of being torn apart, of feeling that his or her life world is as decayed as the institutional realm or even the representation of the world itself. [...] We are now experiencing a very different pathology: the pathology of formulating an 'I' because it is either drowning in a mass culture or confined within authoritarian communities"

(Touraine 2000: 55). Touraine urges us to realize that "the reconstruction of the individual can come about only if that individual can recognize and assert himself as a subject, as a creator of meaning and change, as well as of social relations and political institutions" (ibid.: 60).

Touraine's suggestions for developing an appropriate politics and ethics of the subject makes us realize that "the complete fulfillment of each individual now becomes the goal which society must make possible " (Gorz 1999: 61). In this pathway, there is a need to produce alternative socialities which go hand in hand with the creation of alternative subjectivities. But, in contemporary capitalism, production and employment are the dominant modes in which people relate to each other; society today is produced through the media of capitalist work and time. But now we have to think of new modes of creation of self and society other than the media of money and market. This calls for going beyond "work," "employment," "production" as the only foundation of self and society and to have a "multi-active life" (ibid.: 73). As Andre Gorz tells us: "To change society, we have to change 'work' and vice versa. To change it by divesting it of all its reifying constraints [...] which reflect its subordination to capital. To change it by reconciling it with a culture of daily life, an art of living, which would both extend and nourish instead of being cut off from them" (ibid.: 98–99). Gorz further says: "We have to 'widen' as far as possible the gap between society and capitalism, that is to say, to increase as far as possible the space and resources which enable alternative socialities to be produced" (ibid.: 79).

Civil labour as different from capitalist employment can provide such a space for the production of alternative solidarity. In civil labour, people work for each other and for the common good and it is part of a "state-approved exit from the market" (Beck 2000: 126). Today, civil society is in everybody's mouth but what needs to be stressed is that through concrete practices of civil labour where we share time and labour with each other, we can create and recreate civil society in an embodied and meaningful way. For Ulrich Beck who presents us this proposal of civil labour as a way of revitalizing state and society in his *The Brave New World of Work:* "There is no better way of breathing life into civil rights than to convert them, through civil labour, into the self-organised action of the sovereign Many" (ibid.: 134). There is a need now to rethink civil society not only as a space of political empowerment and political argumentation but also as a space of self-realization and creative inter-subjectivity and here practices of concrete labour can give an embodied transformative content to Habermasian disembodied space of moral argumentation (cf. Giri 1999b). Beck makes it clear that civil labour provides opportunity for self-fulfilment also. It is not only a labour for helping the other; it is a labour which helps one to develop oneself. It is a labour which is neither altruistic nor egotistic; in fact, it transcends the conventional boundaries of altruism and egotism. Thus participation in civil labour can create a condition for both the ethical and aesthetic development of self (cf. Giri 1999; Giri and Quarles van Ufford 2000). As Beck urges us to realize the connection between care of the self and attentiveness to the other: "For more and more people, 'social progress' is measured by the extent to which opportunities are created for self-fulfillment in the value dimension of one's own life" (Beck 2000: 152). It is this "often-demonized individualism – and not the traditional duty orientation – which embodies a hitherto untapped source of engagement, a mighty 'social capital' lying dormant" (ibid.).

Beck's discussion of self-fulfilment and civil labour as integrally connected urges us to realize the transformative linkages between self-fulfilment and creation of social capital. As is well known, like civil society, social capital is an all-pervasive discourse of social and economic reconstruction at present (cf. Putnam 1993; Dasgupta and Serageldin 1999). Trust is at the root of the discourse of social capital but the theorists of social capital neither address the issue of how to generate trust nor do they explore ways of developing what Fred Dallmayr has spoken of in another context, the "inner resources that are required to animate public commitment" (Dallmayr 1999: 19). This calls for a deeper foundation for civil labour, for a spiritual regeneration of social capital, a calling which we find animated in the vision and experiment of the socio-spiritual movement of Swadhyaya. Swadhyaya has many *prayogas* or experiments where individuals work together for the generation of impersonal wealth and the creation of common goods. Swadhyayees consider their work in such projects as an instance of *shramabhakti*, devotion of labour. Devotional sharing of time and labour creates trust and social network among the participants and contributes towards a spiritual regeneration of social capital (see Giri 2008).

The vision and experiments of Swadhyaya not only transform the current discourse of social capital in the direction of a deeper spiritual renewal but also urge us to find much more fruitful pathways of connection between self-realization and the building of a just society. Here, we can relate transformations taking place in spiritual horizons to new developments in social theory. The initial proposal of Roy Bhaskar regarding intimate links between self-development and social transformation gets an enriching corroboration in the work of radical sociologist Goran Therborn. For Therborn, it is self-realization, rather than emancipation, which has to be the goal of a movement for a decent society and dignified life. A socialist or radical project can no more be summed up "in terms of emancipation" (Therborn 1991: 300). It is true and cannot be denied that "emancipation remains on the agenda in most parts of the world" and it has a salience in "the form of women's emancipation, but also of ethnicity/nationality and class" (ibid.). "However, the concept of emancipation presupposes that of oppression/exploitation as a clear base line from which to move. In advanced capitalist democracies, it is difficult, and unconvincing, to conceive of women or workers as generally and unqualifiedly oppressed and exploited" (ibid.). In this context, human life-realization as the goal for struggles for liberation and freedom "has the advantage of not being tied to one linear movement, from oppression to freedom, but of connoting, at the same time, an infinite plurality of life-projects and a universal yardstick, the human life-span universally possible at a given level of world resources and medical knowledge" (ibid.). But for this human life-realization to be a reality what is needed is a radical distribution of resources. Realization of universal self-realization calls for a just, humane, decent material and political foundation and in the context of present day systemic inequality it calls for both socio-spiritual and socio-political struggles. While the ruling ideology of neo-liberalism would make us believe that the contemporary moment heralds an end of history as an end of historical struggles for justice, in the contemporary world we continue to witness emergence of radical and anti-systemic people's movements and social struggles (Falk 1999; Wilfred 2000).

Enabling individuals to grow is a goal in both liberalism and democracy. While liberalism has failed in enabling universal self-realization as it is tied to capitalist rationality, the challenge here is to build on the inner resources of democracy and on the way transforming it as well. The task here is to use the emancipatory possibilities of democratic modernity in the fight against capitalist modernity and on the way to spiritualize both democracy and modernity as a project of universal self-realization.[1] As Chantal Mouffe argues: "[...] Once we acknowledge that what constitutes modern democracy is the assertion that all human beings are free and equal, it becomes clear that it is not possible to find a more radical principle for organizing society" (Mouffe 1992: 1). Immanuel Wallerstein, the other radical thinker of our times who has not stopped dreaming even after the collapse of official socialism, makes a similar argument: "to most people democratization translates primarily as the demand for three things as equal rights: a reasonable income (a job and later a pension), access to education for one's children, and adequate medical facilities. To the extent there is democratization, people insist not merely on having these three, but on regularly raising the minimum acceptable threshold for each. But having these at the level that people are demanding each day, is incredibly expensive, even for the wealthy countries, not to speak for Russia, China, India. The only way every one can really have more of these is to have a radically different system of distribution of the world's resources than we have today" (Wallerstein 1999: 18). Thus, along with the contemporary politics of recognition, what needs to be stressed is an ethics and politics of redistribution but the "the left is afraid to speak of distribution, when redistribution is becoming a question of life and death for society. Everything has to be redistributed from the top down – technology, resources, money, knowledge" (Kagarlitsky 2000: 9).

In Therborn, Mouffe, Laclau and Wallerstein striving for universal self-realization is an integral part of realization of radical democracy and in the Indian context this linkage comes most forcefully in the works of Manoranjan Mohanty. Mohanty urges us to pay attention to multiple movements for a creative society in the contemporary world. For him, a creative society is a society where individuals become aware of the multiple sources of oppression and domination and continually seek to overcome these in quest for freedom and solidarity. Mohanty laments that now in the post-colonial societies, "memories of freedom struggle are transcended by new preoccupations" of market-led growth, global accumulation etc. (Mohanty 1994: 105). The task before post-colonial criticism here is to resist this evaporation of memory of struggle and to continue to fight for greater democratic realization. But, such a charting of the path of post-colonial criticism is different from what is globally applauded as post-colonial criticism. Post-colonial criticism has been part of the global cross-current of post-modern and post-structuralist cultural criticism but now it has become domesticated by global capitalism as most of the advocates of post-colonial criticism either work or have migrated to the US academia. Post-colonial criticism now seems to forget the memory and aspirations of freedom struggles. As Arif Dirlik writes: "Post-colonial xx is applicable not to all of the post-colonial period but only to that period after colonialism when, among other things, a forgetting of its essence tends to set in" (Dirlik 2000: 216). For Dirlik, "postcolonial critics have engaged in valid criticism of past forms of ideological hegemony but have had little to say about its contemporary figurations" (ibid.: 231).

This critique of essentialism has a liberatory potential as struggle for liberation calls for "the negation of divinification of every Totality as negation of the negation of human person" (Dussel 1998: 17).[2] But, the problem with post-colonial criticism, as with the broader genre of post-structuralism, is that it makes a fetish of anti-essentialism itself. As David Scott tells us about post-colonial criticism in his *Refashioning Futures: Criticism After Postcoloniality*: "For the antiessentialists criticism is a practice of demonstrating the epistemological naivete of their adversaries" (Scott 1998: 9). "The anti-essentialists are not interested in what constellation of historically constructed demands may have produced the supposedly essentialist formulations" (ibid.: 9). Marxism is often the object of the anti-essentialist wrath of post-colonial critics but here post-colonial critics neither translate Marxism into a national (which is rejected) or local (which is affirmed) vernacular nor replace it with local stories of criticism and creativity but put forward the universalist language of post-structuralism. The entry of an imperialist universalism through the back door should not escape our attention: a "critique that starts off with a repudiation of the universalist pretensions of Marxist language ends up not with its dispersion into local vernaculars but with a return to another First World language with universalistic epistemological pretension" (Dirlik 2000: 218).

Decolonization and establishment of a life of what Gandhi calls *Swaraj* or self-government is the enduring message of anti-colonial struggles for freedom and this has a continued significance in our contemporary world (cf. Terchek 1996). Now, the colonial masters may not be there in their classical forms but we are subjected to ever newer forms of colonialism. As Jurgen Habermas tells us, our life worlds are now increasingly subjected to a colonialism by the system world. The message of anti-colonial struggle needs to be retrieved here in terms of decolonizing our life world from the colonialism of the system and making it a space of *Swaraj* or self-government. The same challenge of criticism and creativity lies in decolonizing our mind, knowledge and future (cf. Nederveen Pieterse and Parekh 1995). As Jan Nederveen Pieterse argues: "The colonialism of the life world' – commodification, bureaucratisation is a familiar metaphor. This includes a routinized process of colonization of futures, because of the concentration of forecasting and planning capabilities in government and computer hands. What is needed is a decolonization of futures or, to use more general language, a democratization of futures" (Nederveen Pieterse 2000: 3).

To decolonize future is to make "futures a matter of public concern" and it calls for decolonization of the public sphere. But, the public sphere is now being colonized by the forces of capitalist marketization and it is the advertisement for money and power which is written in bold letters there. In this context, the task of decolonization of public sphere entails the task of recreating it as a space of inter-subjectivity and freedom where freedom means not only consumer choice but what Zygmunt Bauman calls "communal self-management" (Bauman 1988: 98)). The task of criticism and creativity is to resist the privatization and reprivatization of the public sphere and to rescue it from the clutches of the new colonial masters of both state and market. But, as Bauman again tells us, now there is not only a privatization of public sphere, there is also a privatization of critique. While earlier social criticism was an activity in a "shared household," now it has shrunk into an activity in the camping site (Bauman 2001). In the words of Bauman:

> One can think of the kind of "hospitality to critique" characteristic of present-day modern society as having the pattern of a camping site. The place is open to everyone who has their own caravan and money to pay the rent. Guests come and go, none taking much interest in how the site is run, provided that they have been allocated a plot big enough to park the caravan, that the electric sockets and water taps are in good order and the passengers in nearby caravans do not make too much noise and turn down their portable hi-fi and TV speakers after 10 p.m. If they feel they are being short-changed or find that the managers' promises are not kept, campers may complain and demand their due-but it won't occur to them to challenge and renegotiate the managerial philosophy of the site. They may, at the utmost, make a mental note never to use the facilities again and not to recommend using them to their friends (ibid.: 100).

For Bauman, such a privatization of critique, instead of leading to critique of foundation of social arrangements, leads to a "compulsive *self-critique*" where one blames one for one's own misery, "seeking causes of one's own defeats nowhere except in one's own indolence and sloth" (ibid.: 106). Such a privation of critique at the contemporary juncture makes it urgent the need to retrieve the moral function of criticism as a connected activity in society (Walzer 1988).

Criticism as a connected activity is enriched by heeding to the challenge of "triple transformation" at the contemporary juncture outlined recently by the sympathetic Portuguese sociologist Boaventura dos Santos where "power becomes shared authority, despotic law becomes democratic law; knowledge-as-regulation becomes knowledge as emancipation" (Santos 1995: 482). But realization of this triple transformation calls for creation of new subjectivity and a new mode of knowing. The new subjectivity here is "constituted by the topos of prudent knowledge" (ibid.: 489) and the new mode of knowing overcomes the dichotomy between epistemology and ontology by calling for a new self-understanding of science. This in turn calls for a transformation in modernist positivist science as a secured foundation of knowledge of self and society. The task here is to transform science into a science of hope where it is a "search for new possibilities" (Sunder Rajan 1998: 22). As Sunder Rajan further tells us, science as hope "is a post-critical hope in the transformative resources of the sciences" which strives for "certain intrinsic possibilities of a new self-understanding" (ibid.: 22). This calls for a mutual interpenetration between action, love and knowledge and a new epistemology of participation. In this transformational pathway, there can no longer be a divorce between epistemology and ontology and "knowledge of" is carried out in a caring condition of "knowing with". As Sunder Rajan writes: "Caring gives us a unique mode of access, a kind of knowing which may be called knowing-with" (ibid.: 78).[3]

The preceding pages have presented us multiple visions of a desirable society towards which we need to strive. But this expected movement to a better society and a transformative self is not going to be painless or smooth; it would involve social struggles and we would have to be ready for this. At the same time, we have to be ready for creativity as a foundation and art of life. Creativity is now no longer a choice, it is an obligation: "We feel obliged to create ourselves and choose our values" (Weiner 2000: 268). As Robert Weiner tells us: "Short of divine intervention, it appears that none of our problems can be dealt with unless we think and work creatively" (ibid.). But this task of creativity is not fulfilled by having or promoting extraordinary role models of creativity, rather it is to help all of us and each of us to be creative. Weiner urges us to realize: "It will never suffice to have extraordinary role models of creativity. Our dream is to help everyone gain the insights of being on the margins without anyone being marginalized, to help the average person express him or herself in exceptional ways, and to help all of us progress together" (ibid.: 270).

Hope is an integral aspect of criticism, creativity and transformation. Critical initiatives in criticism, creativity and transformation are founded on hope and it cannot be carried on "without some sense of historical possibility" (Walzer 1988: 17). But, the ideology of neo-liberalism would try to destroy hope for a life beyond the dominance of market. In this context, the fundamental task before us is to preserve, nurture and continually seek to transform what David Harvey calls "spaces of hope" (Harvey 2000). Here, it is a positive sign that despite the picture of no alternative created by state and market, people everywhere are struggling for new hopes, new freedoms. As Felix Wilfred writes in his heart-touching recent meditation, *Asian Dreams and Christian Hopes*: "Fired with hope, ordinary people resist abuses of power, take on the globalizing forces by small initiatives at the local level, affirm their identities against cultural domination and homogenisation, claim their right for land and other natural resources against exploitative forces. Are these not truly the sling of David in the face of the mighty Goliaths? There is only hope and no room for despair" (Wilfred 2000: xvi): What Wilfred writes further provides us further challenges in rethinking criticism, creativity and transformation at the contemporary juncture:

> Hopeless is the situation when one segment of humanity, one culture or civilization pretends to be all. It is a process that weakens humanity. That is why, we look forward to a century of greater human solidarity and togetherness, and not clash of civilization. We cannot forget for a moment that a nuclear conflagration of the world is a real possibility that hangs over the head of humanity like Democles' sword. It provides an added reason to invest our energies in bringing peoples and nations together in mutual understanding and cooperation. The meeting of peoples and races, cultures and regions will be the most hopeful thing that could happen to humanity and signify a fresh epoch of richness. It is the direction in which we need to move and look for ways and means to realize the future of humankind as one family (ibid.: xiv).

Notes

1. Partha Chatterjee (1997) draws our attention to the hiatus between capitalist modernity and democratic modernity. But he does not wish to push democratic modernity in a direction of spiritualization, an agenda which I would like to stress here.
2. What Dussel writes here as the objective of liberation philosophy deserves our careful attention: "It is necessary to negate the moments that negate the person, and to develop the moments that justify liberation. If there is an absolute, it cannot but affirm and develop the person in justice, autonomy, and freedom" (Dussel 1998: 11).

3. Sundar Rajan's call for a new epistemology of participation is partly realized in new computer-mediated communication technologies. Jim Walch (1999) provides us several glimpse of this (also Castells 1997).

References

Bhaba, Homi K. 2000. "Postcolonial Criticism." In Diana Brydon (ed.), *Postcolonialism: Critical Concepts in Literary and Cultural Studies*. London and New York: Routledge, Vol. 1, 105–133.

Bauman, Zygmunt. 1988. *Freedom*. London: Open University Press.

——. 2001. *The Individualized Society*. Cambridge: Polity Press.

Bhaskar, Roy. 2000. *From East to West: Odyssey of a Soul*. London: Routledge.

Beck, Ulrich. 2000. *The Brave New World of Work*. Cambridge: Polity Press.

Butler, Judith, Ernesto Laclau and Slavoj Zizek. 2000. *Contingency, Hegemony, Universality: Contemporary Dialogues on the Left*. London: Verso.

Castells, Manuel. 1997. *The Power of Identity*. Oxford, UK: Basil Blackwell.

Chatterjee, Partha. 1997. "Beyond the Nation or Within." *Economic and Political Weekly*.

Dasgupta, Partha and Ismail Serageldin (eds.), 1999. *Social Capital: A Multifaceted Perspective*. Washington, DC: World Bank.

Dirlik, Arif. 2000. "The Post-Colonial Aura: Third World Criticism in the Age of Global Capitalism." In Diana Brydon (ed.), *Postcolonialism: Critical Concepts in Literary and Cultural Studies*. Vol. 1, London and New York: Routledge.

Dallmayr, Fred. 1999. "Achieving Multiple Countries: Millennial Reflections." *Journal of Contemporary Thought* 10 (Winter): 5–26.

——. 2001. "Global Modernization: Toward Different Modernities." University of Notre Dame: Manuscript.

Dussel, Enrique. 1998. *The Underside of Modernity: Apel, Ricouer, Rorty, Taylor and the Philosophy of Liberation*. New York: Humanity Books.

Falk, Richard. 1999. *Predatory Globalization: A Critique*. Cambridge: Polity Press.

Gorz, Andre. 1999. *Reclaiming Work: Beyond the Wage-Based Society*. Cambridge: Polity Press.

Giri, Ananta K. 1999a. "Self-Development and Voluntary Action." *Gandhi Marg* 21 (2): 195–207, July–September.

——. 2000. "Rethinking Civil Society." *Review of Development and Change* V (1): 99–127.

——. 2008. Self-Development and Social Transformation?: The Vision and Practice of the Self-Study Mobilization of Swadhyaya, Jaipur: Rawat Publications.

Giri, Ananta K. and Quarles van Ufford. 2000. "Reconstituting Development as a Shared Responsibility: Ethics, Aesthetics and a Creative Shaping of Human Possibilities". Madras Institute of Development Studies: Working Paper.

Harvey, David. 2000. *Spaces of Hope*. Edinburgh: Edinburgh University Press.

Jasper, James. 1997. *The Art of Moral Protest*. Chicago: The University of Chicago Press.

Kagarlitsky, Boris. 2000. *The Return of Radicalism: Reshaping the Left Institutions*. London: Pluto Press.

Margalit, Avishai. 1996. *The Decent Society*. Cambridge, MA: Harvard University Press.

Melucci, Alberto. 1996a. *The Playing Self: Person and Meaning in the Planetary Society*. Cambridge: Cambridge University Press.

——. 1996b. *Challenging Codes: Collective Action in the Information Age*. Cambridge: Cambridge University Press.

Mohanty, Manoranjan. 1994. "Swaraj and Jiefang: Freedom Discourse in India and China." In *Understanding the Post-Colonial World: Theory and Method,* Neera Chandhoke (ed.), Delhi: Sterling.

——. 1998. "Towards a Creative Theory of Social Transformation." In *People's Rights: Social Movements and the State in the Third World,* Manoranjan Mohanty and Partha N. Mukherji (eds.), New Delhi: Sage Publications, pp. 9–26.

Mouffe, Chantal. 1992. *Dimensions of Radical Democracy: Pluralism, Citizenship, Community*. London: Verso.

Nederveen Pieterse, Jan and Bhikhu Parekh (eds.), 1995. *The Decolonization of Imagination*. Delhi: Oxford University Press.

Nederveen Pieterse, Jan (ed.), 2000. *Global Futures: Shaping Globalization*. London: Zed Books.

Putnam, Robert D. 1993. *Making Democracy Work: Civic Traditions in Modern Italy*. Princeton: Princeton University Press.

Scott, David. 1998. *Refashioning Futures: Criticism After Postcoloniality*. Princeton: Princeton University Press.

Santos, Boaventura de Sousa. 1995. *Toward a New Common Sense: Law, Science and Politics in the Paradigmatic Transition*. London: Routledge.

Sunder Rajan, R. 1998. *Beyond the Crisis of European Sciences*. Shimla: Indian Institute of Advanced Studies.

Terchek, Ronald J. 1996. *Gandhi: Struggling for Autonomy*. New Delhi: Vistaar Publications.

Thapar, Romila. 2000. *India: Another Millennium?* Delhi: Viking.

Therborn, Goran. 1991. "Virsprung durch Rethink." In Robin Blackburn (ed.), *The Future of Communism and the Future of Socialism*. London: Verso, pp. 298–309.

Touraine, Alain. 1997. *What is Democracy?* Boulder, CO: Westview Press.

——. 2000. *Can We Live Together? Equality and Difference*. Cambridge: Polity Press.

Unger, Roberto M. 1987. *False Necessity: Anti-Necessitarian Social Theory in the Service of Radical Democracy*. Cambridge: Cambridge University Press.

Walch, Jim. 1999. *In the Net: An Internet Guide for the Activists*. London: Zed Publishers.

Wallerstein, Immanuel. 1999. *The End of the World as We Know It*. Minneapolis: University of Minnesota Press.

Walzer, Michael. 1988. *The Company of Critics: Social Criticism and Political Commitment in the Twentieth Century*. New York: Basic Books.

Weiner, Robert P. 2000. *Creativity and Beyond*. Albany: SUNY Press.

Wilfred, Felix. 2000. *Asian Dreams and Christian Hopes*. Delhi: ISPCK.

Wuthnow, Robert. 1998. *After Heaven: Spirituality in America Since the 1950s*. Berkeley: University of California Press.

3 Beyond Adaptation and Meditative Verbs of Co-Realizations

Towards Creative Nurturance of "I", "Me" and "You" and the Transformative Fellowship of Non-Duality

[...] One asks a psychoanalyst to what end he cures his patients. In most cases he has no other answer than the notion of an optimum of adaptation. And to what this optimum is, however, he can say nothing on the basis of his science alone, since every ultimate meaningful end has been eliminated from the very first.

— Karl Mannheim (1936), *Ideology and Utopia*, p. 18

The response of the "I" involves adaptation, but an adaptation which involves not only the self but also social environment which helps to constitute the self; that is, it implies a view of evolution in which the individual affects its own environment as well as being affected by it. [...] *As a man adjusts himself to a certain environment he becomes a different individual; but in becoming a different individual he has affected the community in which he lives. [...] It may seem to be a molding of the individual by forces about him, but the society likewise changes in this process, and becomes to some degree a different society.* The change may be desirable or it may be undesirable, but it inevitably takes place.

— George Herbert Mead (1934),
Mind, Self and Society, p. 214, 215, 226. (emphasis added)

There is no norm but the fullness of the life of the individual, and the attainment of that norm is possible only through the ideas which arise out of past expressions of impulses, this control being the will. Here then arise our subjects which Dewey presents as our interests. The term is favored by him because it expresses both our impulses and desires and that in which they eventuate. It is both subjective and objective, or rather it is a statement of the process of action at the point at which the distinction between subjective and objective disappears. Dewey has four definitions of the moral end, "the realization of the individuality," "the performance of specific functions," "the satisfaction of interests," and "the realization of community of individuals". The first might be called distinctively ethical, the second biological, the third psychological, and last sociological; but they are but different aspects of the same. [...] Dewey's ethics has its home in a social habitat as genuinely as Hegel's, *but the individual is no thrall of society. He constitutes society as genuinely as society constitutes the individual.*

— George Herbert Mead (1935),
"The Philosophy of John Dewey," p. 70 (emphasis added)

George Herbert Mead is an inspiring nurturer of the field of sociological imagination and practice who has cultivated it in a transdisciplinary and transformative way drawing insights from philosophy, psychology, biology and cosmology. Unlike many other founding fathers of sociology, Mead did not suffer from an anxiety to reduce everything to the social nor did he consider society as God. Mead realized the limits of the social as he urged us to realize that an uncritical worship of the social as it happens in mob or patriotic fervour can lead to "self-degradation". This realization of the limits of the social was quite ahead of his time and this finds a resonance in creative and transformative moves in sociology to cultivate sociology beyond the limits of society, or to put in the memorable phrase of Alain Touraine (2007), to practice sociology after sociology. In Mead's sociology individuals just do not passively adapt to the environment rather both the organism and the environment, individual and society co-constitute each other.

Building upon Mead, especially his exploration of dynamics of creative self-expression on the part of "I," the present chapter explores how individual and society, "I" and "Me" can go beyond dualities, take part in multi-dimensional processes of non-dual realizations and meditative verbs of co-realizations. The familiar terms and categories in Mead, such as "I," "mind," "self" and society, are not only nouns but also verbs. But as verbs they are not only activistic but also meditative. While Mead building upon pragmatism can look at these verbs as activistic though touched by reflection in this chapter in a spirit of cross-cultural dialogue, I wish to bring the category of meditation and look at Meadian categories as meditative verbs of co-realizations. For example, "I" and "Me" are either engaged in meditative verbs of co-realizations or they are confronted with such a challenge of co-realization where the "Me' in the name of the generalized other just does not control the "I" but it gives space to it; similarly "I" just neither repeats nor reacts to the "Me" but seeks a higher self-expression and embodies a higher value of integration which seeks to realize a different society.

Mead's pathways of reflections draw upon pragmatism which not only seeks to go beyond dualism, such as body and mind, mind and society, mind and nature, but also emphasizes reflective action and reflective intelligence as characteristics of human being. Mead is quite anthropocentric[1] in his conceptualization of the human vis-à-vis other forms of life and this needs to be transcended. Mead's critique of dualism and his focus on reflective action calls for transformative cross-cultural dialogue such as dialogue between pragmatic efforts to go beyond dualism and efforts in non-dual realizations in other traditions such as Buddhism and Advaita Vedanta. His concept of action also needs to be part of a cross-cultural dialogue, for example, action is not only reflective but also meditative. But pragmatism as an intellectual movement from Pierce to Dewey in Mead's time did not take part in cross-cultural dialogue beyond the Euro-American philosophical universe and this lack of dialogue characterizes pragmatism even now as it is in the works of savants such as Richard Rorty.[2] This parochialism of pragmatism needs to be transcended as Mead's conceptualization of self needs to also invite the integral transcendental dimension of self. Both "I" and "Me" just do not represent the social dimension, they also have a transcendental dimension as evident in our ability to understand and listen to each other which makes communication possible. Mead's influential categories of "I" and "Me" suffer from the entrenched sociological problem of "double contingency" and needs to be understood and realized as a field of triple contingency consisting of "I," "Me," "you," and an observant expanding public (cf. Strydom 2009).

Beyond Adaptation and the Dynamics of Self-Expression

Karl Mannheim (1936), a pioneer in sociology of knowledge, tells us that as individuals we just do not aim at an "optimum of adaptation" but seek to express ourselves and realize meaning. Mead also shares a similar concern of going beyond adaptation or a different view of adaptation itself as creative and just not following blindly the rules of either society or environment. Mead was not just interested in evolution[3] but he had a much more creative and dynamic view of evolution in which organisms and individuals play important roles which resonates with contemporary discourses of evolution as co-evolution and going beyond the dualism of socio-genesis and onto-genesis (cf. Bocchi and Ceruti 2002; Giri 2008; Kropotkin 1902; Rousseau 2006).

Mead looks at mind as part of an evolutionary emergence in which sociality does play an important role. As Morris argues, "In *Mind, Self and Society* Mead develops the theses that mind is essentially social [...]" (1938: xli). But Mead recognizes "the necessity of the conditions for the emergence of mind and society, and in so doing he acknowledges the process of emergence [...]" (ibid.). The category of emergence as Mead draws on Whitehead's philosophy plays an important role in Mead's thinking. "An emergent in its social character belongs to two or more systems at the same time. The two or more systems to which an emergent belongs are interrelated in the sense that systems which arise after others are dependent upon those others for their existence. Thus, a biological organism belongs to at least two systems, the physical and the biological, and the latter is dependent upon the former for its existence. But an emergent is also social in that 'the novel event is both in the older order and the new in which its advent heralds.'" (ibid.). Furthermore, "[...] the future and the past belong to a present characterized by an emergent, thanks to which there is time. There is, consequently, neither an absolute, unchanging past nor future posited as the object of knowledge" (ibid.: lxiii). As Morris helps us to understand: "[Mead's] *The philosophy of the act* [...] explains the interrelationship of the emergent and environment, the causal relationship of mind and events in nature, and the sense in which past and future are merged into a present process which further promotes the creative advance of nature" (ibid.: lxvii).

"I" and "Me" are the influential concepts of Mead: "The "I" is the response of the organism to the attitude of others; the "Me" is the organized set of attitudes of others which one himself assumes. The attitudes of the others constitute the organized "Me," and then one reacts towards that as an "I" (Mead 1934: 175). Mead further writes: "The organized community or the social group which gives rise to the individual this unity of self may be called the 'generalized other'. The attitude of the generalized other is the attitude of the whole community" (ibid.: 154).

But in his reflection on I, me and self Mead also raises some profound questions. "How can an individual get outside of himself (experientially) in such a way as to become an object to himself? This is the essential psychological problem of self-hood or self-consciousness" (ibid.: 138). For Mead, "And it is necessary to rational conduct that the individual thus should take an objective, non-affective attitude toward itself; otherwise we have just consciousness, not self-consciousness" (ibid.). Furthermore, "The importance of what we term 'communication' lies in the fact that it provides a form of behaviour in which the organism or the individual may become an object to himself [...] Communication in the sense of significant symbols, communication which is directed not only to the others but also to the individual himself" (ibid.: 139). In a similar way, Bourdieu also asks how can the subject become an object. But it calls for appropriate self-cultivation which is not addressed by either Mead or Bourdieu (see Giri 2006).

In Mead, the "I" and "Me" are different phases of the self. While "I" is sometimes a response to the dimension of the "Me," in other times it is an agent of creative self-expression. Mead writes: "Over against the 'Me' is the 'I'. The individual not only has rights, but he has duties; he is not only a citizen, a member of the community, but he is one who reacts to this community [...] The 'I' is the response of the individual to the attitude of the community as this appears in his own experience" (Mead 1934: 196). At the same time, Mead draws our attention to the expressive work of I: "But an individual is constantly reacting to such organized community in the way of expressing himself, not necessarily asserting himself in the offensive sense but expressing himself; being himself in such a cooperative process as belongs to any community" (ibid.: 197–98). Also, "The situation in which one can let himself go, in which the very structure of the 'Me' opens the door for the 'I,' is favorable to self-expression. I have referred to the situation in which a person can sit down with a friend and say just what he is thinking about someone else" (ibid.: 213).

For Mead, "[...] every individual self has its own peculiar individuality,[4] its own unique pattern; because each individual self within that process, while it reflects in its organized structure the behaviour pattern of that process as a whole, does so from its own peculiar and unique standpoint within that process, and thus reflects in its organized structure a different aspect or perspective of this whole social behaviour pattern from that which is reflected in the organized structure of any other individual self within that process" (ibid.: 201).

Mead further writes: "This brings out the general question as to whether anything novel can appear. *Practically, of course, the novel is constantly happening and the recognition of this gets its expression in more general terms in the concept of emergence. Emergence involves a reorganization, but the reorganization brings in something that was not there before*" (ibid.: 198; emphasis added). For Mead, "*The possibilities in our nature [...] are possibilities of the self that lie beyond our own immediate presentation.* We do not know just what they are. They are in a certain sense the most fascinating contexts that we can contemplate, so far as we can get hold of them [...]. The possibilities of 'I' belong to that which is actually going on, taking place, and it is in some sense the most fascinating part of our experiences. It is there that novelty arises and it is there that our most important values are located. It is the realization in some sense of this self that we are seeking" (ibid.: 204; emphasis added). Mead tells us: "We seek certainly for that sort of expression which is self-expression. When an individual feels himself hedged in he recognizes the necessity of getting a situation in which there shall be an opportunity for him to make his addition to the understanding, and not simply to the conventionalized 'Me'." (ibid.: 212). What Mead writes below deserves our careful consideration:

> [...] "Me" may be regarded as giving the form of the "I". The novelty comes in the action of the "I," but the structure, the form of the self is one which is conventional.
>
> This conventional form may be reduced to a minimum. In the artist's attitude, where there is artistic creation, the emphasis on the element of novelty is carried to the limit. This demand for the unconventional is especially noticeable in modern art. Here the artist is supposed to break away from convention; a part of his artistic expression is thought to be in the breakdown of convention (ibid.: 209).

Furthermore,

> The value of an ordered society is essential to our existence but there also has to be room for an expression of the individual himself if there has to be a satisfactorily developed society. A means for such an expression must be provided. *Until we have a social structure in which the individual can express himself as the artist and the scientist does, we are thrown back on the sort of the structure found in the mob, in which everybody is free to express against some hated object of the group* (ibid.: 221; emphasis added).

For Mead, "Great figures in history bring about very fundamental changes. *These profound changes which take place though the action of individual minds are only the extreme expression of the sort of changes that take place steadily through the reactions which are not simply those of 'Me' but an 'I'.* These changes are changes that take place gradually and more or less imperceptibly. We know that as we pass from one historical period to another there have been fundamental changes, and we know these changes are due to the reaction of different individuals" (ibid.: 203; emphasis added).

Urging to understand the need to give space to creativity in the midst of routine activities of life Mead says:

> Such men as John Stuart Mill have been able to carry on routine occupations during a certain part of the day, and then give themselves to original work for the rest of the day. *A person who cannot do a certain amount of stereotype work is not a healthy individual [...] Nevertheless, and granting this point, there must be some way in which the individual can express himself.* It is the situations in which it is possible to get this sort of expression that seem to be particularly precious, namely, those situations in which the individual is able to do something on his own, when he can take over responsibility and carry out things in his own way, with an opportunity to think his own thoughts. Those social situations in which the structure of the 'Me' for the time being is one in which the individual gets an opportunity for that sort of

expression of the self bring some of the most exciting and gratifying experiences (ibid.: 213; emphasis added).

But Mead cautions us: "These experiences may take place in a form which involves degradation, or in a form which involves the emergence of higher values. The mob furnishes a situation in which the 'Me' is one which simply supports and emphasizes the more violent sort of impulsive expression. [...] Such expression may involve degradation of self [...]" (ibid.: 213). He goes on: "The response of the "I" may be a process which involves *a degradation of the social state as well as one which involves higher integration*" (ibid.: 218; emphasis added).

The Fields of Mind, Self and Society and Meditative Verbs of Co-Realizations

"I" and "Me" are part of the self. But what is self? Does it consist only of the domain of social role? As we have seen, both "I" and "Me" in Mead are not just extension of the social naively and uncritically conceptualized and represented. Self is a multi-dimensional field of reality, realization and becoming consisting simultaneously of unconscious, social role of techno-practitioner and the transcendental. The relationship among these is one of autonomy and interpenetration (cf. Giri 2006).

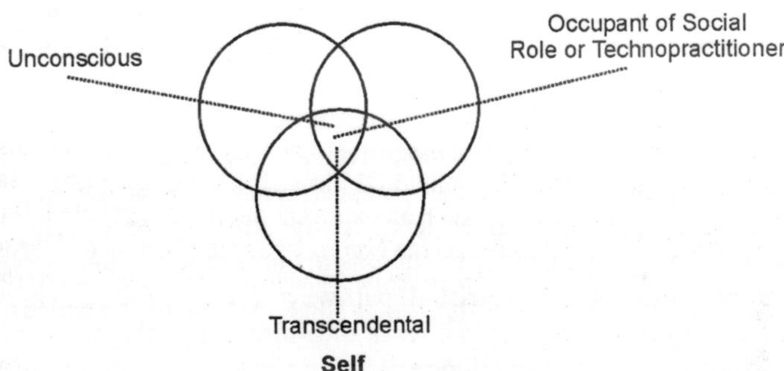

Self

Self is also a field. Some Asian traditions look at self as a field and this is born out in Srimad Bhagvad Gita, a key text in Indian spiritual tradition, which talks about the yoga of the field, *kshetra* (see Clammer 2008). Such a field approach to self has a potential to go beyond a fixed, a point-imprisoned and one-dimensional conception of the human, individual and self and realize their inescapable multi-dimensionality. Self as a field has not only an individualist dimension but also a trans-individual (as it is in certain paths of Buddhism[5] carrying the traces of both Nature and *Anatta* – no Self and also in the philosophy of Spinoza).

Self as a field consists not only of "I" and "Me" but also "you" and the public. The "you" has both vertical as well as horizontal dimension (Buber 1958). While in the ethical philosophy of Levinas and in spiritual traditions the vertical dimension of the self is emphasized (as for example in the famous line of Levinas: your face is not in front of me but above me), in critical theory of Habermas as of much of modern democratic theory the horizontal dimension of the relationship between "I" and "you" is emphasized. But now there is a need for transformative interpenetration of both the horizontal and vertical dimensions in the conceptualization and realization of the self. The field of the self also consists of the triple contingency of the public beyond the double contingency of the "I" and "Me" or self and other.

Self as Field and the Work of Triple Contingency

At this point some discussion on triple contingency is in order. This is a concept recently developed by social theorist Piet Strydom to take us out of the limitations of the double contingency of classical sociology. For Strydom, "[...] the concept of double contingency needs to make way for a more adequate replacement – namely, triple contingency. In the first scenario, two social actors, communicatively acting subjects or black boxes, A and B, face or encounter one another or enter into some relation with each other as 'I' and 'Thou.' In the basic situation of triple contingency, by contrast, there is a third perspective borne by C, who observes what A and B are saying. By so doing C has a constitutive impact on the social situation" (Strydom 1999: 8). Though this third point of view at an earlier stage of Strydom's formulation "represents society" (ibid.), at a later stage it represents discursively engaged and learning public, which is not just a representation of society and is not bound to a society's "internal mode of justification" (personal communication). Strydom also asks a bold question: "the third point of view: within or beyond society?" and suggests that triple contingency is a product of immanent transcendence. For Strydom, immanent transcendence refers to "the relation between immanence and transcendence as defining of the process of the constitution of social reality, and in particular transcendence as it is represented by counterfactuals" (personal communication). But such a work of immanent transcendence can also involve what can be called "transcendental immanence" where transcendence cannot be solely located within society and exists and rises from many other spheres, such as Divine, Nature and in creative engagements such as art and music. The prophetic traditions in many religions and spiritual pathways have embodied a critique of existing society and here critique is a work of transcendental immanence and not solely that of immanent transcendence.

Mind and Society: Creative Mind Works and Experiments with Vibrant Sociality

Continuing our earlier discussion about self as field we can also look at mind and society as fields. For Mead mind is social and this urges us to realize how through creative mind work and by creating alternative vibrant sociality, we can make the mind more creative and porous going beyond, for example, the rigid boundaries between left brain and the right brain. Mead writes: "The medieval saint worked out that method of identifying himself with all beings, as did the religious technique of India" (1934: 219). It is in this context that recent developments in creative mind work and neuro-meditative experiments deserve our attention. Building upon his earlier work on neuro-politics, which also involves an unspoken project on neuro-spirituality, William Connolly tells us: "We should experiment cautiously with body techniques that then find expression in thought and feeling. [...] Such strategies might include visualization, priming dreams by reviewing a perplexing issue before going to sleep, lucid dreaming – meditation, and neurotherapy" (Connolly 2006: 75; also see Connolly 2005). Connolly hopes that "as we move back and forth among experiential awareness, media studies, knowledge of body/brain processes, and subtle technologies of body/brain intervention [in Sri Aurobindo it would be subtle technologies of body/brain transmutation through *Yoga*], we may also gain more insight into how to confront and counteract the politics of cultural revenge that exerts so much of power [...] today" (ibid.). Through such experiments we can "tap a latent reserve of compassion," in ourselves, "a reserve that finds expression in future conduct" (ibid.: 73).[6]

New experiments in sociality also can shape our mind creatively. Loneliness is a key problem in the Euro-American world, which is getting spread globally and people's lack of heart-to-heart communication creates a cold social field, which affects our mind and leads to depression. In this context creation of vibrant spaces of spontaneous and creative sociality nurtured by art and music can create a social context in which vibrant minds would flourish.

"I," "Me," "self," "mind' and "society" can help each other to realize their unrealized possibility and potential as part of fields of actions, reflections and transformations. These processes involve simultaneously action and meditation nurturing what may be called "meditative action". These meditative actions include new experiments in self, society and mind as outlined above.

Fellowship of Transformative Non-Duality

These processes are characterized by an aspiration for overcoming dualism. We began how Mead as well pragmatic tradition seeks to overcome dualism in its own way. Here, building on cross-cultural dialogue, we can cultivate what may be called "transformative non-duality". Transformative non-duality interrogates dualisms of various kinds from within and across the field. It is characterized by a multi-valued logic of autonomy and interpenetration and resonates with Mead's pluralism and overcoming the dualism, as Baldwin (2009) tells us, between skepticism and relativism. Fellowship of transformative duality is always with us as a reality or a potential to be realized depending upon our self-realization and nature of institutional arrangement (see Gandhi 1993; Giri 2009). It calls for not only creative experiments and metamorphoses of action. but also continuous efforts to be aware of the limits of unreflective and naïve dualism and the suffering and illusion it creates. It also demands for social, political and spiritual struggles to transform structures and discourses, which have a vested interest in producing dualism and maintaining it in a military way as a source of oppression and binding of imagination. Transformative non-duality creates fellowship of being and community beginning with a transformative fellowship of "me" and "I" and touching webs of society, Nature and Cosmos.

Notes

1. Out of his many anthropocentric passages note here the following: "Our own fundamental attitude is a social relationship based upon the self; so we treat the acts of domestic animals as if they had selves." But discourse on humanism and talk of animals has moved much further. See, Derrida (2008), Dallmayr (2009) and Nussbaum (2006).
2. Though in his recent insightful reflections Fred Dallmayr (2007b) tells us that Dewey did visit China and studied Confucianism. For Dallmayr, "Despite his deep modesty, Confucius himself can be seen, and was seen, as an 'exemplar' or 'exemplary person' (*chun-tzu*) who taught the 'way' not through abstract doctrines but

through the testimony of daily living. At this point, the affinity with Deweyan philosophy comes clearly into view – a fact which is perhaps not surprising given Dewey's extended visit to China after World War I" (Dallmayr 2007b: 15).

3. As Charles W. Morris writes in his introduction to Mead's *Philosophy of the Act*: "Evolution, emergence, dynamics, process, and sociality characterize Mead's cosmological views" (Morris 1938: xlv).
4. In this context, what John B. O'Malley writes elaborating Gabriel Marcel's concept of personhood deserves our careful consideration: "[...] confusion is often made between the question of individuality and that of personal distinctiveness: the person may be considered in his role of individual member of a class, whether this be humanity or some determinate social group; such individuality however, does not necessarily coincide with his distinctiveness as person" (1996: 2).
5. In his work on new conceptions of identity from Asia, John Clammer finds it creatively elaborated in the vision and work of Buddhist thinker and Thai social critic Sulak Sivaraksa and invites us to be engaged in a transcultural conversation about our presuppositions:

   > In much the same way that Louis Dumont has argued that Western individualism has its roots in Christianity and that the consequences of this individualism are profound for the arrangement of society and assumptions about how relationships within it work, so Sulak is arguing for a 'trans-individualism' that arises from Buddhist roots, and which has profound implications for the ordering of society (2008: 190).

6. Recent collaboration between neuroscientists and spiritual practitioners, such as Dalai Lama and his followers, shows us how creative work with mind makes brain much more porous and open to transformations. See Begley 2007.

References

Baldwin, John. 2009. "Avoiding Extreme Skepticism and Total Relativism-via George Herbert Mead." Paper presented at the seminar on Mead, Fujen University, Taiwan, May 23, 2009.

Bergson, Henri. 1912. *Creative Evolution.* (Tr. Arthur Mitchell). London: Macmillan.

Begley, Sharon. 2007. *Train Your Mind, Change Your Brain: How a New Science Reveals Our Extraordinary Potential to Transform Ourselves.* New York: Balantine.

Bocchi, G. and M. Ceruti. 2002. *The Narrative Universe.* Creskell, NJ: Hampton Press.

Buber, Martin. 1958. *I and Thou.* Edinburgh: T. & T. Clark.

Connolly, William E. 2005. "The Evangelical-Capitalist Resonance Machine." *Political Theory* 33 (6): 869–886.

——. 2006. "Experience and Experiment". Daedalus Summer.

Clammer, John. 2008. *Diaspora and Belief: Identity, Religion and Globalization in Postcolonial Asia.* Delhi: Shipra.

Dallmayr, Fred. 2007a. *In Search of Good Life: A Pedagogy for Our Troubled Times.* Lexington: University of Kentucky Press.

——. 2007b. "Liberal Democracy and its Critics: Some Voices from East and West." *Journal of Indian Council of Philosophical Research* XXIV (4): 1–24, October–December.

——. 2009. "The Return of Philosophical Anthropology." In *Philosophy and Anthropology: Border-Crossing and Transformations*, Ananta Kumar Giri and John Clammer (eds.), Forthcoming.

Derrida, Jacques. 2008. *The Animal That Therefore I Am*. New York: Fordham University Press.

Gandhi, Ramachandra. 1993. *Sita's Kitchen: A Testimony of Faith and Inquiry*. New Delhi: Penguin.

Giri, Ananta Kumar. 2002. *Conversations and Transformations: Towards a New Ethics of Self and Society*. Lanham, MD: Lexington Books.

——. 2006. "Creative Social Research: Rethinking Theories and Methods and the Calling of an Ontological Epistemology of Participation." *Dialectical Anthropology*.

——. 2008. "Beyond West and East: Co-Evolution and the Calling of a New Enlightenment and Non-Duality." *Futures* 40(10): 877–886.

——. 2009. "The Calling of Practical Spirituality; Transformations in Science and Religion and New Dialogues on Self, Transcendence and Society." Madras Institute of Development Studies: Working Paper.

Ingold, Tim. 1986. *Evolution and Social Life*. Cambridge: Cambridge University Press.

Kropotkin, Peter. 1902. *Mutual Aid: A Factor in Evolution*. London: Freedom Press.

Mannheim, Karl. 1979 [1936]. *Ideology and Utopia: An Introduction to the Sociology of Knowledge*. London: Routledge and Kegan Paul.

Mead, G.H. 1934. *Mind, Self and Society*. Chicago: The University of Chicago Press.

——. 1935. "The Philosophy of John Dewey." *International Journal of Ethics 46* (1): 64–81.

——. 1936. *Movements of Thought in the Nineteenth Century*. Chicago: The University of Chicago Press.

——. 1938. *The Philosophy of the Act*. Edited with an introduction by Charles W. Morris. Chicago: The University of Chicago Press.

Morris, Charles W. 1938. Introduction to Mead's *The Philosophy of the Act*. Chicago: The University of Chicago Press.

Nussbaum, Martha. 2006. *Frontiers of Justice*. Cambridge, MA: Harvard University Press.

O'Malley, John B. 1996. *The Fellowship of Being: An Essay on the Concept of Person the Philosophy of Gabriel Marcel*. The Hague: Martinus Nijhoff.

Rousseau, Jerome. 2006. *Rethinking Social Evolution: The Perspective from Middle Range Societies*. Montreal: McGill-Queen's University Press, 2006.

Sri Aurobindo. 1962. *The Human Cycles*. Pondicherry: Sri Aurobindo Ashram.

Strydom, Piet. 1999. "Triple Contingency: The Theoretical Problem of the Public in Communication Societies". *Philosophy and Social Criticism*, 25(2): 1–25.

——. 2009. *New Horizons of Critical Theory: Collective Learning and Triple Contingency*. Delhi: Shipra.

Touraine, Alain. 2007. "Sociology After Sociology", *European Journal of Social Theory* 10(2): 184–193.

4 Rethinking the Human and the Social

Towards a Multiverse of Transformations

My heart leaps up when I behold
A Rainbow in the sky;
So was it when my life began
So is it now I am a man
So be it when I grow old
Or let me die!

The child is the father of Man;
And I could wish my days to be
Bound each to each by natural piety

— William Wordsworth

In Africa recognition of our interdependence is called *Ubuntu* in Nguni languages, or *botho* in Sotho which is difficult to translate into English. It is the essence of being human. It speaks of the fact that my humanity is caught up and inextricably bound up in yours. I am human because I belong. It speaks about wholeness; it speaks about compassion. A person with *ubuntu* is welcoming, hospitable, warm and generous, willing to share.

— Desmond Tutu (2005), *God Has a Dream: A Vision of Hope for Our Time*, p. 26

The whole planet can suffer no greater torment than a single soul.

— Ludwig Wittgenstein

We should not ask: what does a person need to know or be able to do it in order to fit into the existing social order? Instead we should ask: what lives in each human being and what can be developed in him or her? Only then it would be possible to direct the new qualities of each emerging generation into society. Society will then become what young people, as whole human beings, make out of the existing social conditions. The new generation should not just be made to be what present society wants it to become.

— Rudolf Steiner (1985), *The Renewal of Social Organism*, p. 71

In the relations between the individual and the group, this constant tendency of Nature appears as the strife between two equally deep-rooted human tendencies, individualism and collectivism. On one side is the engrossing authority, perfection and development of the State, on the other the distinctive freedom, perfection and development of individual man. The State idea, the small or the vast living machine, and the human idea, the more and more distinct and luminous Person,

> the increasing God, stand in perpetual opposition. The size of the State makes no difference to the essence of the struggle and need make none to its characteristic circumstances. It was the family, the tribe or the city, the *polis*; it became the clan, the caste and the class, the *kula*, the *gens*. It is now the nation. Tomorrow or day after it may be all mankind. But even then the question will remain poised between man and humanity, between self-liberating Person and the engrossing collectivity.
>
> — Sri Aurobindo (1962), *Human Cycles*, pp. 272–73

The human and the social are both adjectival terms and rethinking these invite us to realize both of these as verbs of ongoing and unfolding processes of co-realizations, which strive to transcend many taken-for-granted dichotomies, such as human and animal, human and divine, individual and society, nature and society, and society and transcendence. There are germs of aspiration towards a new way of conceptualizing and realizing the human and the social in both the human security approach and the social quality approach – the former talking about the need for integration and the latter about a holistic approach beyond fragmentations of many kinds, including policy fragmentation and disciplinary fragmentation. This aspiration for integration and holism can be a creative source for foundationally rethinking the human and the social as well reconstituting these conceptually as well as in new practices.

As we move further in this task of rethinking, it is helpful to have a brief glimpse of the concerns of these two approaches – human security approach and social quality approach. Human security approach is part of the broader discourse of human development which emerged in the 1980s but among the family of human discourses such as human development and human rights, it focuses much more on the issues of security and vulnerability not only of groups but also of individuals. As Des Gasper et al. write: human security in its broad 'United Nations' formulation, "means the security of people against important threats to the fulfilment of their basic needs" (Gasper et al., 2008). It treats security "as more than just a problem of the state but also as one of care and psycho-social requirements" (ibid.). "The term 'human security' conveys a message about basic life quality (and quantity) and a claim for its priority in policy." The social quality approach emerged in the late 1990s within the European Union, seeking to find new ways to change the conventional asymmetrical relationship between a dominant (nowadays, neo-liberal) economic policy and all other public policies that distorts the daily life of citizens in the EU and indeed indirectly the lives of people around the world. Initiated with the first book on social quality in 1997 by W. Beck and others and the Amsterdam Declaration on Social Quality, which was signed later by 1,000 European scientists, social quality work became institutionalized with the creation of the European Foundation on Social Quality, located in The Netherlands. By focusing on the concept of the social, "the social quality approach has sought a new meta-theoretical basis to connect different sciences in order to address social and economic changes in Europe in a comprehensive way. Through collaboration with Asian scientists in recent years efforts are being made to develop a common social quality approach between Europe and Asia".

Now, continuing our task of rethinking the concept of the social and the human, Gasper et al's recent essay on the subject does explore some of the pathways of rethinking and reconstitution. They write: "[...] social is realized in the interplay between processes of self-realisation and individual beings and processes leading to formation of collective identities" (Gasper et al., 2008: 15). Social in this latest stage of reflection in the social quality approach is linked to "processes of self-realisation" (ibid.: 18). Gasper and his colleagues recognize that the "social quality approach has developed within fortress Europe" and discuss the need to overcome Eurocentrism in our conceptualization of both the social and the human. Social quality approach is being extended to Asia but at present it seems much more an extension of the taken-for-granted conceptual frame in Europe and exploring and applying in the Asian context rather than a foundational examination of the meaning of the social in Asian traditions, such as China and India. Nevertheless, social quality approach does have this potential to go beyond and be part of cross-cultural, global and planetary conversations and interactions "involving co-learning and co-transformation among persons" (ibid.: 22). They write that Asian scholars may "inherit an ontology or ontologies which accord different meanings to notions of state, human, social and security" which suggest the need for more planetary conversations and cross-cultural and transcultural work on these terms. In this essay, I focus on only two – the human and the social.

Rethinking the Human and the Social: A Prelude to Planetary Conversations

Though there is no unitary Asian conception as there is no unitary Chinese or Indian perspective on these terms, nonetheless, in Asian conceptions, the human is part of nature as at the same time it does contain the divine inviting us to realize human as an evolutionary field holding three autonomous but overlapping and criss-crossing concentric circles of non-human, human and divine. But, the conception of the human in the human development and human security (from now onwards HDS) approach is one-dimensional and it does not explore how insecurities such violence and cruelty may cause partly by the existing continuance of animal in us. The compassion (that is at work even in situations of extreme violence and that we need to cultivate more as suggested in Ogata and Sen's (2003) report on human security) may be partly because of the interpenetrative work of Nature, human and divine in us. The social quality approach criticizes the individualist premise of HDS approach but it does not go far enough, for example, it does not realize that there is a transindividual dimension to the work of the human and the individual just as there is an individual dimension. Vision and practice of the human and individual in Buddhism does suggest this and transindividuality here carries the traces of both Nature and *Anatta* (no Self). John Clammer finds this in the work of Buddhist thinker and Thai social critic Sulak Sivaraksa and invites us to be engaged in a transcultural conversation about our presuppositions:

> In much the same way that Louis Dumont has argued that Western individualism has its roots in Christianity and that the consequences of this individualism are profound for the arrangement of society and assumptions about how relationships within it work, so Sulak is arguing for a 'trans-individualism' that arises from Buddhist roots, and which has profound implications for the ordering of society (Clammer 2008: 31).

Clammer also tells us how Asian conceptions look at self as field and this is born out in Srimad Bhagvad Gita, a key text in Indian spiritual tradition, which talks about the yoga of the field, *kshetra*. Such a field approach to self has a potential to go beyond a fixed, a point-imprisoned and one-dimensional conception of the human, individual and self and realize their inescapable multi-dimensionality. In my recent works I have been exploring a multi-dimensional conception of individual/self as simultaneously consisting of techno-practitioner, unconscious and transcendental (cf. Giri 2006; also see Faubion 1995). Though in modern Western conceptualization of the self the transcendental dimension is missing or it can only be allowed in the form of what Habermas (2002) calls "transcendence from within," creative cross-cultural encounters, conversations and confrontations can lead to memory work where we in the West also can realize that in our traditions of philosophy, literature, spirituality, mysticism and alternative social practice there is also a rich reservoir to realize the transcendental dimension of both the human and the social.

Daya Krishna, the eminent philosopher from India, writes: "Society need not be considered the last term of human thought. The centrality may be restored to the human individual who, then, may be viewed as the nucleus of the social cell from what all creativity emanates or originates. In this perspective, then, society would be conceived as a facilitating mechanism so that the individual may pursue his trans-social ends. Instead of art, or religion, friendship or love being seen as the lubricating oil for the functioning of the social machine, the machine itself would be seen as facilitating the emergence and pursuit of various values [...]" (Krishna 1993: 11).

In many cultures, including the Indian, the social does not have the same ultimate status as it has in modern Western society and socio-religious thought. The social in Indian thought does not have a primal significance: it is considered an intermediate field and an ideal society is seen as one which facilitates our realization of potential as *Atman*, soul. Daya Krishna calls it *atman*-centric approach and contrasts this with the socio-centric approach in not only the modern West but also in religious traditions such as Christianity. But one also finds a socio-centric approach in certain aspects of Confucianism which accords primary significance to social relations and not to the same extent to processes of self-realization. Both the *Atman*-centric and socio-centric approaches have their own limitations, what Daya Krishna calls the "two predicaments" – the *atman*-centric predicament and the socio-centric predicament. The socio-centric predicament does not give enough space to self-realization while "Atman centricity leads a people's attention away from an active concern with society and its betterment" (ibid.: 23). Rethinking the human and the social calls us to overcome the one-sidedness of an *atman*-centric approach and socio-centric approach and Daya Krishna links it to a new realization of freedom. Sri Aurobindo, as suggested in the opening paragraph of this essay, links it to evolutionary transformation, transforming the very constitution of the individual and the social beyond their present-day dualistic constitution.

From the point of view of this aspiration to overcome *Atman*-centredness or self-centrality and socio-centeredness we can look at Asian traditions in new ways. We can here take, for example, the case of Buddhism and Confucianism – two major traditions of discourse and practice from Asia. In its reflections on humanity, Confucianism focuses on webs of relationships while Buddhism emphasizes the need to transcend the limits of social relationships, particularly anthropocentrism. But both the traditions have gone through many inner debates as well as contestations among them giving rise to movements, such as neo-Confucianism, which urges us to pay simultaneous attention to webs of relationships as well as nurturance of self-realization in our quest of human realization (cf. Dallmayr 2004: 152–71). According to Tu Wei-ming, neo-Confucianism involves a "continuous deepening of one´s subjectivity and an uninterrupted broadening of one's sensitivity" (quoted in Dallmayr, ibid.). It also involves a "dynamic interplay between contextualization and decontextualization. Hence, the self as a ´center of relationships´ finds itself simultaneously in the grip of an ongoing decentering or displacement [...] Just as self-cultivation requires self-overcoming, so cultivation of family and other relationships demands a transgression of parochial attachments such as 'nepotism, racism and chauvinism' and ultimately a transgression of narrow 'anthropocentrism' in the direction of the 'mutuality of Heaven and man and the unity of all things'" (ibid.: 164).[1]

Rethinking the Human and the Social: Critiques of Humanism and Socio-Centrism

Broadening and deepening the meaning of the human and the social by being engaged in cross-cultural, transcultural and planetary conversations can also be nourished by critiques of humanism and sociocentrism in Western critical thought. Both HDS and the social quality approaches do not sufficiently base themselves upon critique of humanism and suspicion of both the concepts of the human and the social. In their recent work, Gasper and associates do not take an oversocialized conception of the human but their work can be further fruitfully deepened and enriched by building upon critiques of both humanism and socio-centrism and moving forward.

The critique of humanism in Western thought urges us to be cautious in our valorization of the human and realize the violence that humanism has created. Gasper et al. (2008) talk about the need for a new "political humanism" in the context of Europe but this now needs to be based upon a foundational realization of the critique of humanism and the need for learning to be human in a "post-human" way.[2] Being human in modern West is intimately linked to a power model of the human condition and a new humanism, which is simultaneously social, cultural, political and spiritual, has to overcome this primacy of the political and nurture new modes of conviviality such as *sraddha* or reverence for life.

We are also invited for critical genealogical work, for example, reflecting upon the images of the human in modern Western moral, social and spiritual traditions. As a case in point here we can invite the *weltanaschauung* of Martin Luther and Erasmus. Luther has a much more power-driven view of the human where critique of religious authority surrenders to the authority of the kings to the point of killing those who oppose this new alignment of the church and the state but Erasmus looks at human as embodiment of *sraddha*, or reverence and this has close kinship with the perspective of the human coming from the Bhagvad Gita where humans are looked at not only as characterized by hunger for power but also hunger for *sraddha*, love or reverence (cf. Giri 2009; Wilfred 2009).

The critique of humanism also suggests us to be engaged in a foundational critique of the telos of power as it also invites us for a foundational critique of a nation-state-centred view of the human and the social. Our conception of humanity in modernity was confined to a nation-state bounded conception of self and citizenship and the current processes of manifold globalization and cosmopolitanization challenge us to overcome such a bounded conception of humanity and realize a global humanity facilitated by post-national transformations and the rise of varieties of transnational public spheres and communities of feeling (cf. Ezzat 2005).

Our existent conception of humanity, including much of the anti-humanist declarations in certain postmodern masters, is anthropocentric as well as Eurocentric but the call for new humanism which is "post-human" – both politically and spiritually[3] – challenges us to overcome anthropocentrism, transform the relationship between the human and non-human through acknowledgment of shared suffering[4] and realizing what Martha Nussbaum (2006) calls "cross-species dignity" and Donna Haraway (2006) "companion species". It is also confronted with a foundational rethinking of the human not only as agents of immanence but also as seekers and embodiment of transcendence – in fact of immanent transcendence – but such a realization challenges us to go beyond a Eurocentric Enlightenment*, which arbitrarily cuts off the human and the social world from its integrally linked relationships with transcendence.[5]

Our rethinking of the human and the social can also creatively build upon the critique of socio-centrism in Western sociology. In contemporary societies, especially the Euro-American ones, there is a recognition of the limits of the social in many spheres of life, such as education, love and ethics (cf. Beck 2000; Beck and Beck-Gernsheim 1995). The ideal of society is now being foundationally rethought as providing a space for self-development of individuals (as discussed in Chapter 1). Even in sociological explorations there is now much more a nuanced understanding of the place of the human and the social in the context of non-human and nature which inspires us to look at cultures and societies beyond a conventional understanding of "forms of life". Conventionally building upon Wittgenstein we look at both the human and the social as forms of life but this invites us to reflect further on the meaning of life and not only feel secured with the formality and typology of forms. Veena Das, building upon Stanley Cavell, shares some insightful reflections here which can be helpful in rethinking both the human and the social:

> When anthropologists have evoked the idea of forms of life, it has often been to suggest the importance of thick description, local knowledge or what it is to learn a rule. For Cavell [Stanely Cavell, the noted contemporary philosopher] *such conventional views of the idea of form of life eclipse the spiritual struggle of his investigations*. What Cavell finds wanting in this conventional view of forms of life is that it not only obscures the mutual absorption of the natural and the social but also emphasizes *form* at the expense of *life* [...] the vertical sense of the form of life suggests the limit of what or who is recognized as human within a social form and provides the conditions of the use of criteria as applied to others. Thus the criteria of pain do not apply to that which does not exhibit signs of being a form of *life* – we do not ask whether a tape recorder that can be tuned on to play a shriek is feeling the pain. The distinction between the horizontal and vertical axes of forms of life takes us at least

* Here we must note that such a cutting of, as Des Gasper comments, was true of Descartes and his followers rather than Wordsworth and Goethe (personal communication),

> to the point at which we can appreciate not only the security provided by belonging to a community with shared agreements but also the dangers that human beings pose to each other. These dangers relate to not only disputation over *forms* but also what constitutes *life*. The blurring between what is human and what is not human sheds into blurring over what is life and what is not life (Das 2007: 15–16; emphasis added).

Thus rethinking the human and the social calls for deep reflections and our earlier critique of socio-centrism gets a new height and depth in John Clammer's pathways of a "deep sociology" resonating with pathways of deep ecology (2009). Clammer invites us to explore pathways of a deep sociology going beyond continued "epistemological Eurocentrism" (2009: 333) and taking the philosophical dimensions of globalization seriously. Clammer also urges us to realize that "an oversocialized and overculturalized notion of self cannot provide the foundation for an adequate sociology of the real world, as the sociology of the body demonstrates" (ibid.). Clammer also suggests us to transform the "existential shallowness, culturalism and anthropocentrism of conventional sociology with the possibility of a rich and transforming engagement with the issues and approaches to life that artists, spiritual seekers, poets and deep ecologists have long pioneered and the absence of which is both the source of so much of aridity of sociology and the crises that global society and environment now confront" (ibid.: 344). This resonates with Melucci's inspiring project of playing self and planetary society which helps us in rethinking the human and the social. Writes Alberto Melucci in his *The Playing Self: Person and Meaning in the Planetary Society*: "We live on a planet that has become a global society, a society totally interconnected by its capacity of intervening on its environment and on social life itself, and yet still dependent on its natural home, the planet Earth. This twofold relation to the Earth, as the global field for social action and physical boundary, defines the 'planetary society' in which personal life takes place" (Melucci 1996: 2).

Contemporary rethinking of the human and the social also can creatively build upon savants of an earlier generation such as Sri Aurobindo and Rudolf Steiner who provide a foundational critique of both humanism and sociocentrism in their works such as *Life Divine, Human Cycles* and *Renewal of Social Organism* and urge us to realize that human beings are not only rational and human, they also have a spiritual dimension to their very existence.

Rethinking Human Security and Social Quality: Human Blossoming, Practical Spirituality and the Calling of a New *Purusartha*

The vision of *purusartha* (i.e., of the four main aims of life for humans) in Hinduism urges us to realize how human development calls for realization of *dharma* (right conduct), *artha* (wealth), *kama* (desire) and *moksha* (salvation) in the life of individuals. But this has not been thought of and put into practice at the level of society. Here, both the human security approach and the social quality approach can help widen the traditional conception of *purusartha* to the level of society – local, national, transnational and planetary.[6] Such an extension and deepening calls for new political, economic and spiritual transformations as *purusartha* at the level of society involves creating a space for universal self-realization consisting of elementary blocks of functioning and capacities, human securities, social qualities and spiritual awakening.

But, in order to do this, we would have to overcome an isolated constitution of elements of *purusartha* and look at them instead in a creative spirit of autonomy and interpenetration. Much of illness and ill-being, both in traditional societies as well as in our contemporary ones, emerges from isolation of these elements for example, *artha* (wealth) not being linked simultaneously to *dharma* (righteous conduct) and *mokhsa* (salvation).[7] In this context, Sen's creative connection to the field of human development of the question that Maitreyee had asked to Yajnavalkya is helpful:

> It is not unusual for couples to discuss the possibility of earning more money, but a conversation on this subject from around the eighth century B.C. is of special interest. As that conversation is recounted in the Sanskrit text *Brihadaranyaka Upanishad*, a woman named Maitreyee and her husband, Yajnavalkya, proceed rapidly to a bigger issue than the ways and means of becoming more wealthy: How far would wealth go to help them get what they want? Maitreyee wonders whether it could be the case that if "the whole earth, full of wealth" were to belong just to her, she could achieve immortality through it. "No," responds Yajnavalkya, "like the life of rich people will be your life. But there is no hope of immortality by wealth." Maitreyee remarks, "What should I do with that by which I do not become immortal? (Sen 1999: 1)

Maitreyee's question is a question of *purusartha* urging us to ask the question of relationship between *artha* and *moksha*. It has layers of symbolic and worldly meaning but Sen, worldly bound as he confesses, does not explore the symbolic meaning. He translates its worldly meaning in this way: "If we have reasons to want more wealth, we have to ask: What are precisely these reasons, how do they work, on what are they contingent and what are the things we can 'do' with more wealth" (Sen 1999: 2). Sri Aurobindo (2000), in his *Thoughts and Aphorisms*, has said that there are different kinds of eternities[8] and similarly Maitreyee's concern with immortality refers to different kinds of immortalities, which can be translated into visions and practices of creating a more dignified society that would nurture self and social immortality of a temporal kind, for example, enabling us to overcome our physical and spiritual morbidity, illness and quick breakdown. With the spirit of Maitreyee and in the context of our engagement with creating a more secured humanity and qualitatively rich social life, we can also ask: What do we have to do with that kind of life, society, humanity and pursuit of wealth, which does not ensure human development, human security, human blossoming and social quality? So, we need a new *purusartha* where elements of it such as *kama* (desire) and *artha* (wealth) transcend their boundaries and are creatively interpenetrated by other elements such as *dharma* and *moksha* and vice versa.

Practical spirituality is a multi-dimensional struggle for *anna* and *ananda* – food and bliss – which can help us make creative links between practical issues of human development and spiritual issues of ends for which we live (cf. Giri 2011). Practical spirituality can also help us realize such a new *purusartha* at the level of self and society embodying a spirit of integration and continued quest for realization of connections. It can also help us transform the cult of sovereignty at the levels of both the human and the social and realize both of these as works of shared sovereignties emerging out of their multiplanar existence beyond dualisms, such as human and natural, and social and transcendental. Practical spirituality can transform the discourse of human development to one of blossoming and this transformation resonates with contemporary concerns in development studies with themes such as happiness and well-being. But happiness can be too shallow and practical spirituality here invites us to realize blossoming at the level of self and society as a continued quest for realization of *ananda* (bliss). There is an integral link between *anna* (food) and *ananda* (bliss) as suggested in Taitreya Upanishad and practical spirituality strives to realize *ananda* in ensuring human security and social quality for us, in the process transforming these very terms of discourse and modes of realizations.

Practical spirituality involves new value formations both at the levels of self and society. Along with the values of compassion that Ogata and Sen (2003) talk about in their work on human security, practical spirituality pleads for values of voluntary poverty, voluntary sharing and voluntary insecurity. Today, we are realizing that just structural interventions for the eradication of poverty are not enough unless the middle class and upper class undertake voluntary poverty.[9] Similarly, transformation of the contemporary conditions of risk and insecurity calls us to undertake voluntary insecurity. Some of our fellow beings do it when they go to Iraq, Afghanistan and offer their bodies on the line. An exemplary instance of voluntary insecurity is the life and martyrdom of Rachel Corrie who faced the bulldozers in Gaza in solidarity with people affected by it and gave her life under the wheels.[10] But even though all of us may not go to conflict zones like Rachel and offer our bodies and souls, we can put ourselves imaginatively in the bleeding bodies, souls and hearts of many of our fellow beings and realize what it means to be subjects and objects of many insecurities in the world today. Such voluntary insecurity would create an ontological and social basis for transforming contemporary conditions of insecurity. Voluntary insecurity also helps us realize that some amount of chosen insecurity, which is not imposed upon us by structural conditions, can be a source of creative breakthroughs and new realizations in the lives of self and society.[11] Voluntary insecurity thus puts our concern with security in place, including opening up our craving for security to a fundamental Socratic dissatisfaction and Maitreyee-like *purusartha* question: What do we need security for? What kind of secured life do we wish to lead – secured life of a satisfied pig or that of a dissatisfied Socrates? (Das 1989; Giri 2002).

The new *purusartha* of practical spirituality goes beyond a gendered fixation and helps us realize that our *purusartha* lies in being creative mothers. There is a feminization of spirituality now where spiritual realization lies in our capacity to be mothers to ourselves, each other and society. Human development as human blossoming, collective self-realization and planetary realizations calls us to be mothers including making our society and state a space of mothering where society and state provide a space for self-realization as mothers and do not function only as spaces of control. This involves a reconstitution of both space and time as today much of our insecurity also emerges from an anxiety about time and being helpless victims of spaces of capital. A new *purusartha* of practical spirituality reconstitutes space and time as our mothers but this reconstitution calls for transformation of capitalism and a new spiritual realization of our own capacity to generate time as mother and not only selling our time in the media of money and market. The new *pursuartha* of practical spirituality transforms human security and social quality in the directions of human blossoming, inclusion of the other and planetary realizations.

Notes

1. In his recent insightful reflections on Confucian path, Dallmayr (2007b: 14–15) explores common aspirations in Confucius, Gandhi and John Dewey which deserves our careful consideration:

   > [...] the Confucian "way" or "tao" – akin to Gandhian *swaraj* – involves an "unceasing process of self-transformation as a communal act," and thus a linkage of ethics and social engagement whose seasoning effect "can free us from the constrictions of the privatized ego." [...] Despite his deep modesty, Confucius himself can be seen, and was seen, as an "exemplar" or "exemplary person" (*chun-tzu*) who taught the "way" not through abstract doctrines but through the testimony of daily living. At this point, the affinity with Deweyan philosophy comes clearly into view – a fact which is perhaps not surprising given Dewey's extended visit to China after World War1. As in case of Gandhian *swaraj*, leading a responsible life in society involves self-restraint and the abandonment of domineering impulses. In Confucius's own words, humanness or to be properly human (*jen*) means to "conquer oneself (*ke-chi*) and to return to propriety (*fu-li*).

2. Escobar writes in almost the last sentence of his much discussed book, *Encountering Development*: "For what awaits both the First and the Third World, perhaps finally transcending our difference, is the possibility of learning to be human in post-humanist (post-man and postmodern) landscapes" (Escobar 1995: 226). But what is the meaning of posthuman here? Should Foucault's critique of humanism be taken at face value or should we explore the link between Foucault's critique and the humanistic strivings of savants such as Erasmus especially as Erasmus urges us to move beyond a power-model of the human condition and cultivate *sraddha*, reverence for life. It is Foucault himself who has written: "[...] for Nietzsche, the death of God signifies the end of metaphysics, but God is not replaced by man and the space remains empty" (Foucault, quoted in Carrette 1999: 85).
3. In this context, Dallmayr (2007a) talks about an "Other Humanism" beyond a "high tide of old-style humanism" and embodying a "tentative resurgence of subdued, self-critical and non-Eurocentric (that is, non-hegemonic) view of human".
4. In this context, what Derrida writes referring to Bentham's question vis-à-vis animals "Can they suffer?" deserves our careful consideration: "the question is not to know whether the animal can think, reason or speak, etc., something we still pretend to be asking ourselves (from Aristotle to Descartes, from Descartes, especially, to Heidegger, Levinas and Lacan) [...] but rather to know whether animals *can suffer*" (Derrida 2008: 27).
5. It must be noted here that many contemporary thinkers such as Habermas (2002) and Nussbaum (1990) are comfortable with some conception of internal transcendence but they would like to confine themselves only to the shores of immanence. Consider here what Nussabaum writes in the chapter on "Transcending Humanity" in her *Love's Knowledge: Essays on Philosophy and Literature* Nussbaum: "[...] there is a great deal of room for transcendence of our ordinary humanity [...] transcendence, we might say, of an *internal* and human sort [...] There is so much to do in this area of human transcending (which I also imagine as a transcending by *descent*, delving more deeply into oneself and one's humanity, and becoming deeper and more spacious as a result) that if one really

pursued that aim well and fully I suspect that there would be little time left to look about for any other sort" (Nussbaum 1990: 379).

6. For Daya Krishna: "The development of new *purusarthas* in the history of a culture or civilization would perhaps be one of the more important ways of looking at man's history as it will emphasize ways of making his life significant in the pursuit of new ends of a different kind. [...] The emergence of any new *purusartha* on the horizon of human consciousness should be seen as a breakthrough in human history, providing the possibility of a new kind of pursuit not available earlier" (Krishna 1997: 25).
7. For Daya Krishna, "The oft-repeated traditional theory of the *purusarthas* [...] is of little help in understanding the diversity and complexity of human seeking which makes human life so meaningful and worthwhile in diverse ways. The *kama*-centric and *artha*-centric theories of Freud and Marx are as mistaken as the *dharma*-centric thought of sociologists and anthropologists who try to understand man in terms of the roles that he plays, and society in terms of the norms of those roles and their interactive relationships. For all these theories, the independent seeking of any value which is different from these is an illusion, except in an instrumental sense. [...] Fortunately for the Indian theory of *purusarthas*, it has postulated the ideal of *moksa* which is tangential to all the other *purusarthas*. But it too has no place for the independent life of reason as a separate value, or for that matter for any other life which is not concerned primarily with *artha, dharma, kama* and *moksa*" (Krishna 1991: 204–05).
8. In the words of Sri Aurobindo (2000: 31), "There are lesser and larger eternities, for eternity is a term of the soul and can exist in Time as well as exceeding it."
9. In his recent reflections on religion and democracy, Robert Bellah, the pre-eminent sociologist of our times, has reflected upon the calling of voluntary poverty for our times. For Bellah (2005), earlier voluntary poverty might have been confined to monasteries as exemplified in the vision and life of saints, such as St Francis of Assissi, but now we are all invited to live a life of voluntary poverty. To live a life of voluntary poverty is to live with what is needed and not to run after wealth. It also means to reduce our consumption including that of energy. For Bellah, "[...] a life based economically on a sufficiency rather than the expectation of ever increasing income is, in today's world, a form of voluntary poverty" (ibid.: 31). "Thinking of a life based on sufficiency instead of wealth frees us up to take on all kinds of work that serves others, not just ourselves" (2005: 31). At the same time, a life of sufficiency does not just give us opportunity to serve others, it also gives us time and space to blossom ourselves. Bellah links a life of voluntary poverty to the issue of creativity. For Bellah, "Genuine creativity requires leisure, which, in its original meaning, is not absence of work, but the possibility of a fulfilling form of life [...] a life of sufficiency, of, in modern times, voluntary poverty, might not only have the benefit of allowing one to undertake a life of service to others, it might also allow time for genuine creativity in art or thought or whatever field" (ibid.: 32).
10. Rachel was a young student from the US working with people of Gaza. Her e-mail to her family just days before her supreme offering is heart-touching:

    When that explosive denotated yesterday it broke all the windows in the family's house. I was in the process of being served tea and playing with two small babies. I am having a hard time right now. Just feel sick to my stomach a lot being doted on all the time, very sweetly by people who are facing doom [...]. Honestly a lot of time the sheer kindness of the people here, coupled with the overwhelming evidence of the wilful destruction of their lives, makes it seem unreal to me. I can't really believe that something like it can happen in the world without a bigger outcry about it. It really hurts me, again, like it has hurt me in the past, to witness how awful we can allow the world to be.

11. In his inaugural lecture on human security at Free University, Amsterdam, Thomas Hylland Eriksen builds upon his native Norwegian wisdom, especially the work of Ibsen in his *Peer Gynt*, and asks such a question. He tells us how Peer Gynt is not happy with security of home and accepts the insecurity of the road and the sea. This is also the story of many migrants in modern history. From the other side of the world, Chittaranjan Das (2009) talks about divine discontent and the need to cultivate aspiration which is not bound to the status quo and seeks to transform existing condition of self and society in the direction of mutual dignity, beauty and co-realization.

References

Agarwala, Binod. 2004. "Humanities and Social Sciences in the New Millennium: Theorizing in/for Society as Play." In Ananta Kumar Giri (ed.), *Creative Social Research: Rethinking Theories and Methods* Lanham, MD: Lexington Books, pp. 253–272.

Beck, Ulrich and Elizabeth Beck-Gernsheim. 1995. *The Normal Chaos of Love*. Cambridge: Polity Press.

Beck, Ulrich. 2000. *The Brave New World of Work*. Cambridge: Polity Press.

——. 2002. "The Cosmopolitan Society and its Enemies." *Theory, Culture and Society* 19 (1–2): 17–44.

Beck, W., L.J.G. van der Maesen A.C. Walker et al. (eds.) 1997. *The Social Quality of Europe*. The Hague, London, Boston: Kluwer Law International (Reprinted Bristol: Policy Press, 1998).

Beck, W., L.J.G. van der Maesen, F. Thomese and A.C. Walker (eds.) 2001. *Social Quality: A Vision for Europe*. The Hague, London, Boston: Kluwer Law International.

Bellah, Robert. 2005. The Place of Religion in a Democratic Society. Pamphlet for Fetzer Institute.

Beteille, Andre. 2002. *Sociology: Essays on Approach and Method*. Delhi: Oxford University Press.

Carrette, Jeremy (ed.). 1999. *Religion and Culture by Michel Foucault*. Manchester: Manchester University Press.

Clammer, John. 2008. *Diaspora and Belief: Globalisation, Religion and Identity in Postcolonial Asia*. Delhi: Shipra.

——. 2009. "Deep Sociology." Special issue on "Beyond Sociology," *Asian Journal of Social Sciences* 37 (3): 332–345.

Dallmayr, Fred. 2004. *Peace Talks: Who Will Listen?* Notre Dame, Indiana: University of Notre Dame Press.

——. 2007a. *In Search of Good Life: A New Pedagogy for Our Troubled Times*. Lexington: University of Kentucky Press.

——. 2007b. "Liberal Democracy and its Critics: Some Voices from East and West." *Journal of Indian Council of Philosophical Research* XXIV (4): 1–24, October-December.

Das, Chitta Ranjan. 1989. *Shukara O Socrates [The Pig and Socrates]*. Berhampur (Orissa): Pustaka Bhandar.

——. 2009. *Seprastharu Eprasthaku: Ma Bahira Sannidhyare* [From that Side to this Side: In the Light of Sri Aurobindo's book on The Mother]. Bhubaneswar: Pathika Prakashani.

Das, Veena. 2007. *Life and Words: Violence and the Descent into the Ordinary*. Berkeley: University of California Press.

Derrida, Jacques. 2008. *The Animal That Therefore I Am*. New York: Fordham University Press.

Eriksen, Thomas Hylland. 2005. "Risking Security: Paradoxes of Social Cohesion." Inaugural Lecture, Free University, Amsterdam, 15 March.

Escobar, Arturo. 1995. *Encountering Development*. Princeton: Princeton University Press.

Ezzat, Hebba. 2005. "Beyond Methodological Modernism: Towards a Multicultural Paradigm Shift in the Social Sciences." In Helmut Anhelier et al. (eds.), *Global Civil Society 2004/2005*, London: Sage.

Faubion, James D. (ed.) 1995. *Rethinking the Subject: An Anthology of Contemporary European Social Theory*. Boulder, CO: Westview Press.

Frietag, Michel. 2001. "The Contemporary Social Sciences and the Problem of Normativity", *Theses Eleven*, No. 65: 1–25.

Fuchs, Martin. 2004. "Articulating the World: Social Movements, the Self-Transcendence of Society and the Question of Culture". In Ananta K. Giri (ed.), *Creative Social Research: Rethinking Theories and Methods*, Lanham, MD: Lexington Books.

Gasper, Des et al., 2008. "Human Security and Social Quality: Contrasts and Complementarities." Paper.

Giddens, Anthony (1996) *In Defense of Sociology: Essays, Interpretations and Rejoinders*. Cambridge: Polity Press.

Giri, Ananta Kumar. 1998. "Moral Consciousness and Communicative Action: From Discourse Ethics to Spiritual Transformations." *History of the Human Sciences*.

——. 2002. "Socrates and Pig." In *Conversations and Transformations: Towards a New Ethics of Self and Society*. Lanham, MD: Lexington Books.

——. 2006 "Creative Social Research: Rethinking Theories and Methods and the Calling of an Ontological Epistemology of Participation." *Dialectical Anthropology* 30 (3–4): 227–271.

—— (ed.). 2009. *The Modern Prince and the Modern Sage: Transforming Power and Freedom*. Delhi: Sage.

—— (ed.). 2011. *Practical Spirituality and Human Development*. Special issue of *3D: Journal of Indus Business Academy*, Bangalore.

Gorz, Andre. 1999. *Reclaiming Work: Beyond the Wage-Based Society*. Cambridge: Polity Press.

Habermas, Jurgen. 1990. *Moral Consciousness and Communicative Action*. Cambridge: Polity Press.

——. 2002. *Religion and Rationality*. Cambridge, MIT: Harvard University Press.

Haraway, Donna. 2006. "A Note by a Sportwriter's Daughter". *Concentric Literary Cultural Studies*, 32(2): 239–53.

Knor-Cetina, Karin. 2001. "Postsocial Relations: Theorizing Society in a Postsocial Environment." In George Ritzer and Barry Smart (eds.) *Handbook of Social Theory*, London: Sage.

Krishna, Daya. 1991. "Time, Truth and Transcendence", in *History, Culture and Truth: Essays presented to D.P. Chatopadhyaya*, Daya Krishna and K. Satchidananda Murty (eds), pp. 323–326, Delhi: Kalki Prakashan.

——. 1993. *Social Philosophy: Past and Future*. Shimla: Indian Institute of Advanced Study.

——. 1997. *Prolegomena to Any Future Historiography of Cultures and Civilizations*. New Delhi: Project of History of Indian Science, Philosophy and Culture & Munshiram Manoharlal.

——. 2006. "Rgveda: The Mantra, the Sukta and the Mandala or the Rsi, the Devta, the Chanda: The Structure of the Text and Problems Regarding it." *Journal of Indian Council of Philosophical Research* XX111 (2): 1–13, April-June.

Melucci, Alberto. 1996. *The Playing Sets: Persons and Meaning in the Planetary Society*. Cambridge: Cambridge University Press.

——. 2002. *The Playing Self: Person and Meaning in Planetary Society*. Cambridge: Cambridge University Press.

Mintz, Sidney W. 2000. "Sow's Ears and Silver Linings: A Backward Look at Ethnography", *Current Anthropology* 41 (2): 169–189.

Nussbaum, Martha.1990. *Love's Knowledge: Essays on Philosophy and Literature*. NY: Oxford University Press.

——. 2006. *Frontiers of Justice: Disability, Nationality, Species Membership*. Cambridge, MA: Harvard University Press.

Ogata, Sadako and Amartya Sen. 2003. *The Commission on Human Security Now*. NY: United Nations.

Sen, Amartya. 1999. *Development as Freedom*. NY: Alfred A. Knof.

Sri Aurobindo. 1962. *Human Cycles*. Pondicherry: Sri Aurobindo Ashram.

——. 1970 *Life Divine*. Pondicherry: Sri Aurobindo Ashram.

——. 2000 [1958] *Thoughts and Aphorism*. Pondicherry: Sri Aurobindo Ashram.

Steiner, Rudolf. 1985. *Renewal of Social Organism*. London: Anthropocentric Press.

Touraine, Alain. 2000. *Can We Live Together?* Cambridge: Polity Press.

——. 2007. "Sociology After Sociology." *European Journal of Social Theory* 10 (2): 184–193.

Tutu, Desmond. 2005. *God Has a Dream*. London: Reider.

Urry, John. 2000. *Sociology Beyond Societies: Mobilities for the Twenty-First Century*. London: Routledge.

Wilfred, Felix. 2009. "Play of Power and Struggle for Freedom in Renaissance Humanism: Erasmus between Scylla and Charybdis." In Ananta Kumar Giri (ed.), *The Modern Prince and the Modern Sage: Transforming Power and Freedom*, Delhi: Sage Publications.

5 A New Global Humanity

Self-Development, Inclusion of the Other and Planetary Realizations

The Problem: Introduction and Invitation

The discourse of humanism is at a crossroads now. Many contemporary thinkers, such as Michel Foucault, tell us about the death of the man and dangers of talking in the name of human progress. Such a view of "death of man" is inspired by Nietzsche's conception of "death of God". But when God dies, the place does not remain empty. It is accompanied by, at least, three processes of being and becoming: divinization of the human, humanization of divine and acknowledgment of radical evil lying in between the lines.[1] Understanding such a process is enriched by dialogue with and participations in many traditions of the world, particularly Asian traditions, where being human involves a process of human-divine formation.

Asian traditions, of course, are varied and it is helpful to understand reflections on humanity and humanism not only in different traditions but also the inner conversations and contestations within each of them (cf. Sen 2005). We can here take, for example, the case of Buddhism and Confucianism – two major traditions of discourse and practice from Asia. In its reflections on humanity, while Confucianism focuses on webs of relationships, Buddhism emphasizes the need to transcend the limits of social relationships, particularly anthropocentrism. But, both the traditions have gone through many inner debates as well among them giving rise to movements such as neo-Confucianism which urges us to pay simultaneous attention to webs of relationships as well as nurturance of self-realization in our quest of human realization (cf. Dallmayr 2004: 152–71). We find a similar emphasis on emergent sociality and self-realizations in pathways of neo-Vedanta in India where neo-Vedantins, such as Swami Vivekananda and Sri Aurobindo, urge us to cultivate creative relationships between self and society with additional cultivation of the divine along with and in between. We also find similar strivings for creative social transformations, self-realizations including divinization and cosmic realization in Tagore and Gandhi.

Such a simultaneous attention to webs of relationships and practices of self-realization where self does not mean only the sociological self, the self of the role occupying individuals but also transcendental self[2] is an important help in rethinking humanism now and realizing a global humanity. Our conception of humanity in modernity was confined to nation-state bounded conception of self and citizenship and the current processes of manifold globalization and cosmopolitanization challenge us to overcome such a bounded conception of humanity and realize a global humanity facilitated by post-national transformations and rise of varieties of transnational public spheres and communities of feeling (cf. Ezzat 2005). Our existent conception of humanity including much of the anti-humanist declarations in self-certain postmodern masters is Eurocentric as well as anthropocentric and thus the realization of a global humanity calls for a planetary conversation on the meaning of being human and place of the human in the journey of our cosmos. The calling of a new global humanity is thus confronted with the challenge of overcoming anthropocentrism and realizing what Martha Nussbaum (2006) calls "cross-species dignity". It is also confronted with a foundational rethinking of the human not only as agents of immanence but also as seekers and embodiment of transcendence – in fact of immanent transcendence – but such a realization challenges us to go beyond Eurocentric Enlightenment which arbitrarily cuts off the human and the social world from its integrally linked relationships with transcendence.

Overcoming the Limits of Modernistic Humanism[3] and the Calling of Planetary Conversations

Modernistic humanism privileges individualism. But this is individualism of a particular kind – egotistic and possessive. While this privileging had a contingent historical necessity during the early period of European modernity, now individualism needs to be transformed into a relational individuality animated by a multi-valued logic of autonomy and interpenetration. This is accompanied by transformations in both individualism and communitarian logic. Realization of a dignity of relationship between individual and community can learn from multiple traditions of humanism – the emphasis on individual in Euro-American post-Enlightenment tradition and the emphasis on communities and webs of relationships in many Asian traditions (see Clammer 2008). This in turn challenges us to rethink the dualism between individual and community which becomes a starting point of rethinking and reconstituting varieties of dualisms in our lives and work towards non-dual realization of humanity (cf. Loy 1988).

Modernistic humanism has been animated by a quest of scientific knowledge. Science and rationality have been the guiding inspiration and method in this primacy of knowledge in modernity. Now, this needs to be fundamentally rethought beyond the crises of European sciences where knowledge does not mean only "knowledge of" but also "knowing with" going beyond the dualism of subject and object (cf. Sunder Rajan 1998). We also need to think of the human condition beyond the prism of modernistic rationality. Human beings are not only rational, they are also infrarational as well as suprarational. While Nietzsche and Freud have challenged us to acknowledge the infrarational dimension of modernistic humanism, Sri Aurobindo (1962) urges us to realize that human beings are also supra-rational and supramental. Their supra-rational and supramental modes of existence do not dismiss the significance of rationality in human development and evolution but it seeks to transform the inherent tendency of rationality towards dualistic classifications into a more inclusive understanding and realization.

Modernistic humanism has been primarily anthropocentric. This has influenced our discourse and practice in modernity, for example, our conception of justice. Theories of justice from Marx to Rawls have been primarily anthropocentric and now there is an epochal need to work towards a frame of inclusive justice which also includes the rights and dignity of non-human animals. In recent years, Nussbaum (2006) has probably gone farthest in proposing a political conception of justice for the non-human animals.[4] But her approach to this still remains ethnocentric as she states that she does not want to promote "uncritical nature worship". Her move beyond modernistic anthropocentrism does not sufficiently embody a cross-cultural realization of different relationship between human beings, nature and non-human animals in different traditions, for example, as it is in indigenous traditions all over the world, Indian traditions and Japanese traditions (cf. Clammer 1995).

Thus rethinking humanism now challenges us to ask many foundational questions. One such is the question of what Habermas calls knowledge and human interest. Habermas (1971) has brought the issue of knowledge and human interest – cognitive interest, emancipatory interest and interest of reason to protect itself – to the forefront of modernistic humanism. But, a further critical question before humanism is now a critique of valorization of knowledge itself, especially its one-sided epistemological fixation without accompanying ontological critique and nurturance. Such a foundational critique of knowledge is suggested in the following lines of *Ishopanishada* – one of the foundational texts of spiritual universality coming from India: *Andham Tamah Prabishyanti Jo AVidyam Upasate, Tato Vuya Ibate Tamah Jo Vidyaam Ratah*. It means those who worship ignorance are steeped in darkness but those who are steeped in knowledge are also steeped in darkness. Therefore, to be steeped in the valorization of knowledge and communication to the exclusion of other practices of self-cultivation such as listening, silence and self-emptying vis-à-vis one's will to power and will to arguments, and connectedness with the world – not only the human social world but also with the world of nature and transcendence – is to be steeped in blindness and we now need a new critical theory which helps us to understand the limits of knowledge and human interests.

Habermas talks about knowledge and human interest but does not pay sufficient attention to the calling of human liberation – liberation from social domination as well as one´s own self, especially that part of the self which wants to dominate and annihilate the other. Modernistic humanism suffers from a cult of mastery and now it needs to be transformed into an ethics and aesthetics of servanthood where human beings reconceptualize and realize their calling as that of being servants of each other as well as of non-human animals, nature, god and cosmos rather than as the lord of all that one surveys.[5]

Such a foundational critique of human knowledge involves a radical critique of self along with systems and structures. It also involves a planetary conversation on the meaning of being human which interrogates presuppositions such as those of Habermas that human beings are primarily agents of justification and Weber and Foucault that they are agents of power. Consider, for instance, the following lines from Bhagvad Gita – a text of spiritual seeking from India: *Sradhha Maya Ayam Purusha Jo Jat Sraddha Sa Ebasa.* Here, the *Purusha* [the human person] is characterized by *sraddha* – capacity for love and reverence – one is what one who loves or reveres. These lines also offer some presuppositions about being human which is different from both Habermasian presupposition of justification as well as Weberian and Foucualdian presuppositions of power. These thoughts challenge us to realize that it is not enough just to be able to justify oneself or to acquire power, what characterizes human beings is their capacity for *sraddha* – love as well and reverence. This also urges us to go beyond a one-sided determinism that all knowledge is reducible to dynamics of power.

But reference to relationships in the Confucian traditions, *anatta* (no-self) in the Buddhist traditions or *sraddha* in Indian traditions is not meant to make us blind to the work of power in the dynamics of human life in self, culture and society. In other words, what is called for here is a mutually interrogative dialogue as to the meaning of being human involving a festival of presuppositions in which we do not suffer from enthusiastic totalitarianism of either love or power, tradition or modernity, in our conceptualization of being human. On the other hand, we are confronted with the task of trans-civilizational dialogues and planetary conversations as to our meaning of being human.

A New Global Humanity: Self-Development and Inclusion of the Other

As can be appreciated from the previous discussion, a new humanity involves a new conceptualization of self and path of self-development. But what is self? Does self refer only to the egoistic dimension of individual? Does it mean only *homo sociologicus, homo economicus*, or the *technopractitioner*? Self is all these but at the same time is not exhausted by these and has a transcendental dimension – a dimension of transcendental and transversal connectivity to the other, society, nature, world and cosmos what Roy Bhaskar (2002a) calls "transcendentally really self". In a recent work, I have submitted a plural and multidimensional conceptualization of self as consisting of overlapping and concentric circles of unconscious, technopractitoner and transcendentally real self (Giri 2006). Self-development means development of all these dimensions of self in a spirit of autonomy and intepenetration and non-dual realizations.

Self-development thus includes processes of capacitation in various techno-practical fields of life such as economy, polity, organization, state, civil society and now in the field of interlinked globality and a cosmic humanity. Self-development involves the capacity for freedom as well as responsibility: in the economic field, it means gaining economic independence, market freedom; in the political field it involves development of the capacity for appreciation for as weli as realization of rights, justice and citizenship and deepening and broadening these from their earlier state-centeredness to fulfil the needs of a global humanity.

The project of self-development is linked with a project of inclusion of the other. Cultivation of a new globai humanity involves multidimensional processes of inclusion of the other in economy, polity, culture, society and self. In all these domains there is so much structural as well as contingent exclusions. But, many a time, the discourse and practice of inclusion of the other does not go far enough; it remains paternalistic and does not involve transformation of structures and discourses which produce exclusion in the first place. In this context, we need a vision and practice of transformative inclusion. In the field of economy, an inclusive economy does not just depend upon the trickle-down effect of economic growth to include the poor, landless and marginalized; it involves transformative processes such as land reforms and right to education and jobs. Similarly, inclusive education calls for creating transformation of the existing space and structure of education. In the Indian context, the discourse of inclusive education now refers to the need to include the low-caste, marginalized and the disabled in the classrooms. But without transformation of the very space, structure and discourse of classroom how this inclusion is possible? Of course, transformative inclusion is a long process and many initiatives and struggles do contribute to it. To talk of transformative inclusion is not be imprisoned within a logic of what Amartya Sen calls (2009) "transcendental institutionalism" and to wait till institutions are transformed and do nothing else. But it is important to have the focus on transformation of the very condition which produces exclusion so that our discourse of inclusion contributes to self-development and blossoming of the other.

Jurgen Habermas (1998) too talks about inclusion of the other. For Habermas, the project of inclusion of the other is not just universalistic[6] but sensitive to difference, defending "a morality of equal respect and solidaristic responsibility for everybody" (Habermas 1998: 5). But, in Habermas, inclusion of the other does not go far enough. A case in point is Habermas' approach to other religions. Habermas writes in his *Religion and Rationality*: "We no longer confront other cultures as alien since their structures still remind us of previous phases of our own social development. What we do encounter as alien within other cultures is the stubborn distinctiveness of their religious cores" (Habermas 2002: 156). When pressed to the limits despite his post-metaphysical thinking, Habermas acknowledges the significance of the Judeo-Christian tradition for the project of modernity but he seems not to be offering same acknowledgment to other traditions such as Buddhism. Recently, Habermas (2005) urges us to realize how both modernistic secularism and religion can learn from each other rather than exclude each other but this project now needs to include one's transformative immersion in many religious and secular traditions of the world beyond the Euro-American universe.

Both the projects of self-development and inclusion of the other can be locked in a self-justificatory closure, for example authenticity in the case of the former, and emancipation in case of the later. For example, the movement of self-study in India, Swadhyaya, can do a lot in terms of inclusion of the other, especially the low-caste (cf. Giri 2008a). Similarly, the project of inclusion of the other, as articulated by Habermas, needs a lot more self-development in order that it can realize its own aspiration of respecting the otherness of the other. Similar is also the challenge for a thinker such as Charles Taylor (1991) whose ethics of authenticity needs a project of radical self-criticism so that it also takes part in a trans-civilizational journey of realizing the well-being of all.

An important challenge here is to overcome the binding of concentration of power and to strive towards realization of what Dallmayr (2001), building on Heidegger, calls "power-free existence". This aspect of self-development has a longer lineage in philosophical and spiritual traditions of the West and as well as the rest of the world, for example, in the Christian concept of *kenosis* of self-emptying (cf. Vattimo 1999), Confucian emphasis on self-cultivation (cf. de Barry 1991) and Foucault's (1986) plea for developing self-restraint on the parts of holders of power (also see Toynbee 1956).[7]

Modernistic humanism has been limited by nation-state. Though in the modern world many humanists have tried to overcome the limits of nationalism and strive towards flourishing of the humankind, the predominant identity of being human has been one of being the citizen of a nation-state. This now needs to be transformed into our realization of being the citizen of the world and member of the human family. This is part of an alternative process of cosmopolitan realization what I have elsewhere called "post-colonial cosmopolis" which goes beyond the predominant meaning of cosmopolitanism as citizen of the world and realizes the significance of "Vasudheiva Kutumbakam" (the Vasudha, the mother earth is our family). It also realizes that much of the predominant cosmopolitan discourses such as those of Kant do not realize squarely the challenge of colonial violence and a new global humanity as part of realization of "post-colonial cosmpolis" acknowledges this and strives to go beyond this (see Giri 2006b).

Planetary Realizations

Writes Alberto Melucci in his *The Playing Self: Person and Meaning in the Planetary Society*: "We live on a planet that has become a global society, a society totally interconnected by its capacity of intervening on its environment and on social life itself, and yet still dependent on its natural home, the planet Earth. This twofold relation to the Earth, as the global field for social action and physical boundary, defines the 'planetary society' in which personal life takes place" (Melucci 1996: 2). But, for Melucci, planetary realizations are not unitary and simplistic processes: Melucci speaks of complexity, difference and uncertainty which demand from "individuals the capacity to *change form* (the literal meaning of metamorphosis)" (ibid.: 2–3). This is in tune with de Chardin's stress on "complexification of consciousness" as an important part of the evolutionary unfoldment of "noosphere" a "growing new organ of consciousness" – "an interlinked system of consciousness and information, a global net of self-awareness, instantaneous feedback, and planetary communication" (Judith 1996: 1). Melucci speaks of the inner planet "consisting of the biological, emotional and cognitive structures that underlies the experience and relations of us all" (1996: 56). Melucci also challenges us:

> An ecology of economic, political, and technological choices cannot operate independently of an ecology of the everyday, *of the words and gestures with which we call into being* or annihilate the inner planet. *To pay attention and respect to details*; to be aware that we are part of a whole and we need to connect the different elements into this whole, *to value the path and not only the end* [...] (ibid.: 69; emphases added).

This calling for planetary realizations is in tune with emerging developments in science, philosophy, religion, spirituality and mysticism. As Lynne McTaggart writes presenting us a recent view from the sciences: "At our most elemental, we are not a chemical reaction, but an energetic charge. Human beings and all living things are a coalescence of energy connected to every other thing in the world [...]. There is no 'Me' and 'not-me' duality to our bodies in relation to the universe, but one underlying energy field" (McTaggart 2002: xiii). Planetary realizations thus call for overcoming egoism, dualism and anthropocentrism apart from ethnocentrism. As Roy Bhaskar presents us challenges of planetary realizations from the shores of philosophy, mysticism and spiritual strivings:

> For if mankind is implicit in an amoeba, then self-realization for that amoeba can mean anything from maximum fulfilment for an amoeba (of its particular type, always potentially unique), to attaining the level of self-realization for an explicitly conscious and potentially self-conscious being such as man, into which that amoeba may evolve through various levels and thresholds of realization, some of which may depend upon the wakening of powers and potentials, which are at present only implicit in man and only awakened in species of which we have no knowledge or awareness (Bhaskar 2002b: 26; also see Bocchi and Ceruti 2002).

Planetary realizations then calls for multidimensional transformations in self and society which can build upon struggles for freedom and dignity coming both from traditions of post-colonial struggles and criticism as well as post-modern cosmopolitan reflections. It also challenges us to build upon different traditions of realization of being human and strive for a new global humanity which strives to overcome anthropocentrism and nation-state centred rationality. Thus, the calling of a new global humanity is intimately connected with the project of universal self-realization.

A New Global Humanity as a Calling and an Invitation

A new global humanity is a calling and an invitation, and the adjective 'new' here is not one of a historical arrogance but one of invitation to realize that this has also been a quest with humanity but one that has also been confronted with varieties of violations and violence. A new global humanity challenges us to overcome this violence – violence of not only modernistic historical colonialism but all sorts of violence in the struggle for building a non-violent self and society. This is a very fragile journey, as fragile as the journey of the human in the cosmos itself. As Habermas urges us to realize:

> Only when philosophy discovers in the dialectical course of history the traces of violence that deform repeated attempts at dialogue and recurrently closes off the path to unconstrained communication does it further process whose suppression it otherwise legitimates; mankind's evolution toward autonomy and responsibility (Habermas 1971: 315).

Notes

1. I do not elaborate these three processes in this essay especially the issue of evil but in my work on practical spirituality which is part of the companion volume *Knowledge and Human Liberation* (Giri 2012) I touch upon this.
2. More on this in the later section of the essay on self-development and inclusion of the other.
3. I do not consider modernistic humanism as a monolithic project but it is used here to draw our attention to its dominant constellation in modernity.
4. "The whole idea of justification that looks for a reflective equilibrium and uses the idea of overlapping consensus is an anthropocentric idea. The holism in ethics that Rawls and I share may be contested at this point by a reasonable Benthamite [follower of utilitarian philosopher Bentham] that what justifies changes in our treatment of animals is not the coherence of a family of human theories and judgments, even bolstered by reasonable agreement and overlapping consensus; it is, instead, a fact external to the human point of view, namely animal suffering. This challenge raises profound metaethical issues" (Nussbaum 2006: 390).
5. Consider here what John Ruskin (2004: 17) wrote more than a century ago: "I know not if a day is ever to come when the nature of right freedom will be understood, and when men will see that to obey another man, to labour for him, yield reverence to him or to his place, is not slavery."
6. Consider here also the following comments of Arjun Appadurai (2005: 18) on humanism and universalism: "What is called for is some sort of tactical humanism, a humanism that is prepared to see universals as asymptotically approached goal, subject to endless negotiation, not based upon prior axioms [...] a humanism prepared to negotiate across borders unaccompanied by any non-neogotiable universals."
7. What Toynbee (1956: 74) writes deserves our careful attention:

   > In human life, Suffering is the antitheses of Power, and it is also a more characteristic, and more fundamental element in Life than Power is. [...] Suffering is the essence of Life, because it is the inevitable product of an unresolvable tension between a living creature's essential impulse to try to make itself into the center of the Universe and its essential dependence on the rest of creation and on the Absolute Reality on whic all creatures live and move and have their being. On the other hand, human power, in all its forms is limited and, in the last resort, illusory. Therefore any attitude towards Life that idolizes human power is bound to be a wrong attitude towards Suffering and, in consequence, a wrong attitude towards Life itself.

References

Appadurai, Arjun. 2005. "Tactical Humanism." *In the Future of Values: 21st Century Talks,* (ed.) Jerome Binde. Paris: UNESCO and New York: Oxford University Press.

Bhaskar, Roy. 2002a. *Reflections on Meta-Reality: Transcendence, Everyday Life and Emancipations.* New Delhi: Sage.

——. 2002b. *Meta-Reality: The Philosophy of Meta-Reality.* Vol. 1: *Creativity, Love and Freedom*. New Delhi: Sage.

Carrette, Jeremy R. (ed.). 1999. *Religion and Culture by Michel Foucault.* Manchester: Manchester University Press.

Clammer, John. 1995. *Difference and Modernity: Social Theory and Contemporary Japanese Society*. London: Kegan Paul.

——. 2008. *Diaspora and Belief: Religion, Globalization and Identity in Postcolonial Asia*. Delhi: Shipra.

Dallmayr, Fred. 2004. *Peace Talks: Who Will Listen?* Notre Dame, Indiana: University of Notre Dame Press.

——. 2001. "Resisting Totalizing Uniformity: Martin Heidegger on Macht and Machenschaft." In idem, *Achieving our World: Toward a Global and Plural Democracy*. Lanham, MD: Rowman and Littlefield.

De Barry, Wm. Theodore. 1991. *The Trouble with Confucianism*. Cambridge, MA: Harvard University Press.

Ezzat, Hebba. 2005. "Beyond Methodological Modernism: Towards a Multicultural Paradigm Shift in the Social Sciences." In *Global Civil Society 2004/2005* (eds.) Helmut Anhelier et al., London: Sage.

Foucault, Michel. 1986. *Care of the Self*. New York: Vintage.

Habermas, Jurgen. 1971. *Knowledge and Human Interest*. Boston: Beacon Press.

——. 1998 *Inclusion of the Other: Studies in Political Theory*. Cambridge: Polity Press.

——. 2002 *Religion and Rationality*. Cambridge, MA: The MIT Press

——. 2005. *Between Naturalism and Religion*. Cambridge: Polity Press.

Giri, Ananta Kumar. 2006a "Creative Social Research: Rethinking Theories and Methods and the Calling of an Ontological Epistemology of Participation." *Dialectical Anthropology* 30 (3–4): 227–271.

——. 2006b "Cosmopolitanism and Beyond: Towards a Multiverse of Transformations." *Development and Change* 37 (6): 1277–1292.

——. 2012. *Knowledge and Human Liberation: Towards Planetary Realizations*. London: Anthem Press.

Melucci, Alberto. 1996. *The Playing Self: Person and Meaning in the Planetary Society*. Cambridge: Cambridge University Press.

Nussbaum, Martha. 2006. *Frontiers of Justice: Disability, Nationality, Species Membership*. Cambridge, MA: Harvard University Press.

Pantham, Thomas. 1995. *Political Theories and Social Reconstructions*. Delhi: Sage.

Ruskin, John. 2004 [1853] *On Art and Life*. London: Penguin.

Sen, Amartya. 2005. *The Argumentative Indian*. New Delhi: Penguin.

——. 2009. *The Idea of Justice*. London: Allan Lane.

Sri Aurobindo.1962. *Human Cycles*. Pondicherry: Sri Aurobindo Ashram.

Sunder Rajan, R. 1998. *Beyond the Crises of Eurpean Sciences*. Shimla: Indian Institute of Advanced Studies.

Taylor, Charles. 1991. *The Ethics of Authenticity*. Cambridge, MA: Harvard University Press.

Teilhard de Chardin, Pierre. 1966. *Man's Place in Nature:* The Human Zoological Group. London: Collins.

Toynbee, Arnold J. 1956. *An Historian's Approach to Religion*. New York: Oxford University Press.

Vattimo, Gianni. 1999. *Belief*. Cambridge: Polity Press.

6 Moral Consciousness and Communicative Action

From Discourse Ethics to Spiritual Transformations

In his stress on performative competence Habermas consistently privileges speaking over hearing or listening [...] In *The Theory of Communicative Action,* a categorical distinction is drawn between "cognitive-instrumental" and "communicative rationality" but the distinction is dubious given that both are modes of formal reasoning.

— Fred Dallmayr (1991), *Life-World, Modernity and Critique: Paths Between Heidegger and Frankfurt School,* p. 24, 11

The speculative employment of reason with respect to nature leads to the absolute necessity of some supreme cause of the world: the practical employment of reason with a view to freedom leads also to absolute necessity, but only of the laws of the actions of a rational being as such. Now it is an essential principle of reason, however employed, to push its knowledge to a consciousness of its necessity. It is however an equally essentially restriction of the same reason that it can neither discern the necessity of what is or what happens ... [Reason] cannot enable us to conceive the absolute necessity of our unconditional practical law.

— Immanuel Kant (1987), *Fundamental Principles of the Metaphysics of Ethics,* p. 101

In the wake of metaphysics, philosophy surrenders its extraordinary status. Explosive experiences of the extraordinary have migrated into an art that has become autonomous. Of course, even after this deflation, ordinary life, now fully profane, by no means becomes immune to the shattering and subversive intrusion of extraordinary events. Viewed from without, religion, which has largely been deprived of its worldview functions, is still indispensable in ordinary life for normalizing intercourse with the extraordinary. For this reason, even postmetaphysical thinking continues to coexist with religious practice – and not merely in the sense of the contemporaneity of the noncontemporaneous. This ongoing coexistence even throws light on a curious dependence of a philosophy that has forfeited its contact with the extraordinary. Philosophy, even in its postmetaphysical form, will be able neither to replace nor to repress religion as long as religious language is the bearer of a semantic content that is inspiring and even indispensable, for this content eludes (for the time being?) the explanatory force of philosophical language and continues to resist translation into reasoning discourses.

— Jurgen Habermas (1992), *Postmetaphysical Thinking,* p. 51

The contemporary moment is characterized by unmet challenges both in theory and practice. Processes of change at work in individual social systems as well as interaction among different societies in the global ecumene bring to the fore the unfinished task lying before us with regard to moral consciousness and communicative action. Now, because of globalization, as "moral issues stemming from cultural diversity [...] that used to arise mainly between societies now increasingly arise within them" (Geertz 1986: 115), the nature of interaction between different cultures with widely variant moral standards and the development of a critical reflective consciousness on the part of the actors where moral issues are not easily disposed of either through a convenient relativism or universalism, is an epochal challenge before us. Similar is the task when we come to individual social systems as they are characterized by pervasive structural differentiations and as in these societies "morality gets no clear status in the construction of a structurally differentiated life world" (Habermas 1987a: 92). A related issue here is the unprecedented crisis of institutions that characterizes individual social systems to cope with the contemporary dynamics of change in self, society and culture. For many insightful critics, our contemporary dilemmas are also significantly institutional, in as much as they spring from the irrelevance of existing institutions and lack of availability of new institutions to guide our private lives and the public sphere. These institutional dilemmas are primarily "moral dilemmas" (Bellah et al., 1991: 38) which call for a new moral language to think about our institutions as they are now ridden with "unprecedented problems" (ibid.: 42). For instance, reflecting on contemporary American society, Robert Bellah and his colleagues argue that in the face of the challenge of the present and the dislocations of the post-industrial transition there is an urgency to think of "democracy as an ongoing moral quest," not simply as a political process – "as an end state" (ibid.: 20). They are emphatic in their proposition that we currently need a new "moral ecology" to think creatively about institutions – their predicament and possibility since "the decisions that are made about our economy, our schools, our government, of our national position in the world cannot be separated from the way we live in practical terms, *the moral life we lead as a people*" (ibid.: 42; emphasis added).

The imperative for a moral grounding of institutions in contemporary practice is paralleled by reflective developments in theory as well. This is most evident in the restructuring of theory from structure to reflective self in thinking through moral consciousness and communicative action. The most important sign of this restructuring is the theory of "post-conventional" morality developed by psychologist Lawrence Kohlberg. In Kohlberg's theory of moral development one's moral consciousness is not a mere appendix to social conventions and one is able to differentiate oneself "from the rule and expectation of others" and one's "values in terms of self-chosen ethical principles" (Cortese 1990: 20). The idea of post-conventional morality rescues moral consciousness from unreflective sociologism where morality is looked upon as an extension of social norms and cultural expectations and brings critical reflection to its very core. In this move from unreflective sociologism to critical reflection, the self-justificatory systems of society and culture are critically lived, analysed, and transcended by seeking actors in quest of justice, well-being and freedom.

The current idea of post-conventional morality has a long pedigree in critical and transformation-seeking social theory which can be drawn at least back to John Dewey's insightful distinction between customary and reflective morality at the turn of the century. For Dewey, "the question of what ends a man should live for does not arise as a general problem in customary morality. It is forestalled by the habits and institutions which a person finds existing all around him" (1960: 29). Dewey further writes: "There can, however, be no such thing as reflective morality except where men seriously ask by what purposes they should direct their conduct and why they should do so; what is which make their purposes good" (ibid.: 30). The fact that reflective morality is accompanied by a scheme of critical evaluation is clearly stated by Dewey: "Reflection has its normal function in placing the objects of desire in a perspective of relative values so that when we give up one good we do it because we see another which is of greater worth and which evokes a more inclusive and more enduring desire" (ibid.: 35).

The work of Jurgen Habermas, an important interlocutor of our time, who has engaged seeking souls in reflection on the present challenges of human emancipation, is a significant contribution to both the idea of post-conventional morality and the contemporary discourse of moral transformation of institutions. Habermas' work reflects the challenge of theory and practice outlined above. His *Moral Consciousness and Communicative Action* is an important contribution to the idea of post-conventional morality with his distinction between critical moral reflection and ethical substantialism. He is also a systematic and transformation-seeking critic of institutional life under late capitalism where his political criticism employs not only the familiar variables of class and power but also the less familiar ones of moral consciousness and communicative action. Habermas has written extensively on specific issues in the history and development of Germany, as well as on the wider questions of the history and discourse of modernity. Though Habermas is too easily categorized as the most prominent member of the contemporary European Left, his agenda has always involved a wider critical engagement, critiquing the conventional theories and methods of Marxism as well. In that sense, he has always pursued his task as a critic of the existing methods and systems. In his recent work, Habermas has championed the cause of radical democracy, one important aspect of which is the moral renewal of individuals and the public sphere (Habermas 1990b). Habermas argues that the task of human emancipation today requires a moral approach along with the familiar models of political action. Consider, for instance, the persistent question of poverty and disadvantage in advanced industrial societies. For Habermas, while in the classical phase of capitalism capital and labour could threaten each other for pursuing their interests, today "this is no longer the case" (ibid.: 19). Now, the underprivileged can make their predicament known only through a "protest vote" but "without the electoral support of a majority of citizens [...] problems of this nature do not even have enough driving force to be adopted as a topic of broad and effective public debate" (ibid.: 20). In this situation, for Habermas, a moral consciousness diffusing the entire public sphere is crucial for tackling the problem of poverty and disadvantage. As Habermas argues: "a dynamic self-correction cannot be set in motion without introducing morals into the debate, without universalizing interests from a normative point of view" (ibid.). The same imperative also confronts us in addressing contemporary global problems such as environmental disaster, world poverty and the North-South divide.[1] For Habermas, in addressing these problems we also need a moral perspective, as he (ibid.: 20) writes: "these problems can only be brought to a head by rethinking topics morally, by universalizing interests in a more or less discursive form [...] The moral or ethical point of view makes us quicker to perceive the more far-reaching, and simultaneously less insistent and more fragile, ties that bind the fate of an individual to that of every other, making even the most alien person a member of one's community."

In this chapter, I strive to make a critical assessment of the work of Habermas with regard to his own stated goal of transformation. I begin with Habermas' own assumptions such as "linguistification of sacred" in the field of moral consciousness and strive to look into incoherences in his project considered in accordance with its own norms. In other words, what I am interested in, to begin with, is an internal critique of the Habermasian agenda of transformation. In this way, I share similar goal with the noted Habermas scholar Thomas McCarthy who sums up the objective of his critical engagement: "Rather than confronting Habermas ideas with objections from competing theoretical traditions, I hope to bring out tensions in those ideas themselves" (McCarthy 1992: 52). But while I am interested in bringing out tensions in Habermas' ideas I am also engaged in interrogating Habermas' agenda from outside its own frame of reference precisely because the issues that these tensions raise cannot be resolved within its own frame. Thus, the tradition where I move towards from Habermas' own frame of reference is the tradition of spiritual criticism and spiritual transformation. While Habermas scholar Robert J. Antonio argues that the "secular and intersubjective turn in critical theory begun by Habermas can be completed by encouraging a broader dialogue with pragmatism" (Antonio 1989: 74), I submit that it is the question pertaining to intersubjectivity that requires an opening towards processes of spiritual transformations and criticism. What I argue is that critical theory now must make a dialogue with critical and practical spirituality in order to achieve its own stated objective of transformation.

Moral Consciousness and Communicative Action: Habermas' Agenda

Habermas argues that at the contemporary juncture where the sacred no longer has the unquestioned authority that it once had, morality can no longer be grounded in religion. Rather it has to emerge out of and be anchored in a process of rational argumentation where the actors participate in undistorted communication as members of a community of discourse. For Habermas, the rise of the public sphere of rational argumentation and rationally-motivated communicative action goes hand in hand with the relocation of the sacred from the domain of the "Unspeakable" to our everyday world of language, making it both an object and medium of our ordinary conversation. Habermas' moral theory has to be understood in his evolutionary framework of the "linguistification of the sacred" (Habermas 1987a) and the "structural transformation of the public sphere" (Habermas 1989).[2] Habermas believes that morality, anchored in and emerging out of the rational arguments of participants in discourse, can fill the void created by the demise of the sacred order.

The idea of a rational society and an "ideal communication community" is central to Habermas' agenda of morality. In his emphasis on rationality, Habermas is "closest to the Kantian tradition" (McCarthy in Habermas 1987a: vii).[3] Both for Kant and Habermas, "calculations of rational choice generate recommendations relevant to the pursuit of contingent purposes in the light of given preferences," and "when serious questions of value arise deliberation on who one is, and who one wants to be, yields ethical advice concerning the good life" (ibid.). Like Kant, Habermas understands "practical reason as universal in import: it is geared to what everyone could rationally will to be a norm binding on everyone else" (ibid.). Habermas' discourse ethics, however, "replaces Kant's categorical imperative with a procedure of moral argumentation," shifting "the frame of reference from Kant's solitary, reflecting moral consciousness to the community of moral subjects in dialogue" (McCarthy in Habermas 1990a: vii).

For Habermas, "the projection of an ideal communication community serves as a guiding thread for setting up discourses" (Habermas 1990a). Those who participate in this communication community have an urge to participate in not only communication but also in a discursive transformation, where "in the relationship between the Self and the Other there is a basic moment of insight" (ibid.). Habermas quotes George Herbert Mead, whose work he values a lot and whom he considers as one of the main inspirations behind his theory of communicative action, programmatically: "What is essential to communication is that the symbol should arouse in oneself what it arouses in the other individual" (Habermas 1987a; 15). Habermas tells us: "I think all of us feel that one must be ready to recognize the interests of others even when they run counter to our own, but the person who does that *does not really sacrifice himself, but becomes a larger self*" (ibid.: 94; emphasis added).

For Habermas, an urge for justification of norms that guide individual action is very much part of being human. Though Habermas is dismissive of questions of ontology he proceeds with two basic assumptions about man, viz., that he has a need for communication and an urge for justification.[4] Habermas argues: "From the perspective of first persons, what we consider justified is not a function of custom but a question of justification or grounding" (Habermas 1990a: 20). This universal need for justification has a special manifestation in modern societies where all norms have now "at least in principle lost their customary validity" (Habermas 1988: 227). In this context, the procedure of rational argumentation, which is the other name of "discourse ethics," fulfils this need for justification and provides the "discursive redemption of normative claims of validity" (Habermas 1990a: 103).

Habermas argues that the realization of moral consciousness is based upon our ability to take a hypothetical attitude to the "form of life and personal life history" that has shaped our identities (ibid.: 104). But those who are uncritical about their socialization by and immersion in the society and culture to which they belong are incapable of taking a hypothetical attitude towards these since they fail to realize that though every form of life presents itself as the best possible form of "good life," it is the task of moral consciousness to go beneath such taken-for-granted assumptions and self-proclaimed truths.[5] It is here that participation in the procedure of practical discourse functions as a redeeming process. First of all, it breaks the illusion of the "good life" that has been associated with a particular form of life by the force of custom and habit. While the "formal" ethics of a society binds us to its order and scheme of evaluation, discourse ethics breaks this bondage and enables us to understand our own self as well as the validity of our culture from the point of view of justice. Habermas tells us that "the universalization principle of practical discourse acts like a knife that makes razor-sharp cuts between evaluative statements, and strictly normative ones, between the good and the just" (ibid.).

It is this concern for justice[6] that creates an incessant thrust towards problematization, laying bare the moral problems within our taken-for-granted cultures. For Habermas, a "thrust towards problematization" is essential for moral consciousness to emerge and to be at work in the context of the life world (ibid.: 107). Habermas tells us how in the normal circumstances of what he calls "ethical formalism" this problematization is not possible.[7] But participation in discourse ethics enables the participants to look at one's own culture critically, where criticism means discovering whether the "suggested modes of togetherness genuinely hang together" or not (see Neville 1974: 189). Habermas argues that "for the hypotheses-testing participant in a discourse, the relevance of the experiential context of his life world tends to pale" (ibid.: 107). Habermas believes that "under the unrelenting moralizing gaze of the participants in discourse [...] familiar institutions can be transformed into so many instances of problematic justice" (ibid.: 108).

Critical Discussion of the Idea of Discourse Ethics: Haberma's Self-Criticism

Habermas argues that the abstractive requirements in discourse ethics provide actors a cognitive advantage – a capacity for distantiation. But this is not enough either for the practice of discourse ethics or for the realization of moral consciousness. It calls for parallel emotional maturity, adequate motivational anchoring and growth. He argues that "cognition, empathy and agape" must be integrated in our moral consciousness, especially when we are engaged in the "hermeneutic activity of applying universal norms in a context-sensitive manner" (ibid.: 182). Thus, reminding us of Christian imperatives for love and care, he argues that "concern for the fate of one's neighbour is a necessary emotional prerequisite for the cognitive operations expected of participants in discourse" (ibid.). This integration of cognitive distantiation and emotional care is particularly required when the initial separation between morality and ethical life is to be overcome. He is aware of the difficulties that this separation poses for the practice of morality. Thus, he is not content to leave his agenda only at the "deontological level" like Kant. He is interested to bring back morality as a guide for action and reflection into practice. Habermas himself writes: "Moral issues are never raised for their own sake; people raise them by seeking a guide for action. For this reason the demotivated solutions that post-conventional morality finds for decontextualized issues must be reinserted into practical life. If it is to become effective in practice, morality has to make up for the loss of concrete ethical life that it incurred when it pursued a cognitive advantage" (ibid.: 179). This opening has to be achieved through "an integration of cognitive operations and emotional dispositions and attitude" that characterizes "the mature capacity for moral judgement" (ibid.: 182).

Though a notion of universal human justice is central to Habermas' perspective on moral consciousness, Habermas himself takes great care to emphasize that morality must obey both the principles of justice and solidarity; it must achieve an integration of "the ethics of love and ethics of justice". While the first "postulates equal respect and equal rights for the individual," the second "postulates empathy and concern for the well-being of one's neighbour" (ibid.: 200). For him, "morality cannot protect the rights of the individual without also protecting the well-being of the community to which he belongs" (ibid.). Thus criticism of the taken-for-granted ways of life must be accompanied by a concern for the community. What is important to note is that both these concerns, for him, "should flow from an adequate description of the highest stage of morality itself" (ibid.: 182).

Discourse Ethics and Moral Consciousness: The Limits of the Habermasian Approach

But though Habermas speaks of the need for "adequate description of the highest stage of morality itself," he himself does not inquire into the nature and height of this stage. For him, it is the public sphere which constitutes this highest stage. Habermas speaks of appropriate emotional development and reflective engagement for the project of critical moral reflection to have its desired effect on individuals in society. But he does not look into the issue of how far his own rational approach can facilitate this. Participation in mutually transforming dialogue, which is the key feature of Habermas' discourse ethics, raises the question of intersubjectivity – the mode of relationship between the self and the other. But, the whole question of intersubjectivity – its realization and its needed rich description – for a project of morality to succeed is missing from Habermas.[8]

The question for us here is what kind of relationship between the self and the other is envisaged in discourse ethics – whether the self or the other are just talking to each other in discourse ethics or the non-self is also part of the self. In this context, McCarthy argues that Habermas' agenda only refers to ethical self-clarification and "ethical self-clarification itself cannot get us beyond the value differences that may result from it" (McCarthy 1992: 62). It is perhaps for this reason that Zygmunt Bauman writes: "a post-modern ethics would be one that readmits the other as a neighbour into the hard core of the moral self [...] an ethics that recasts the other as the crucial character in the process through which the moral self comes into its own" (Bauman 1993: 84) But, the process of this dialectic between self and other is not only rational but also spiritual. As Robert Bellah and associates argue, paying attention to the needs of the other is a spiritual process. In their words, "as in the religious examples, we mean to use attention normatively [...] in the sense of "mindfulness as the Buddhists put it, an openness to the leadings of God, as the Quakers say" (Bellah et al., 1991: 256).

The problem with the Habermasian discourse ethics is also its strength, namely, its emphasis on rationality. Rationality is an important starting point but there are problems when it is made the be-all or end-all in life, as it is in the approach of Habermas. Habermas strongly believes that it is a rational philosophy of science that is not scientistic which holds the key to the overcoming of the confusion in which moral consciousness finds itself today (Habermas 1981).[9] But though Habermas distinguishes between instrumental reason and communicative reason and is an ardent critic of modern positivism, his communicative rational agenda still has its limits in coming to terms with the challenge of transforming moral awareness into a basis of transformative communicative action. Bernard Williams' argument in *Ethics and the Limits of Philosophy* is of crucial significance here: "How truthfulness to an existing self or society is to be combined with reflection, self-understanding and criticism is a question that philosophy itself cannot answer. It is the kind of question that has to be answered through reflective living" (Williams 1985: 200). To be fair, Habermas himself is aware of the need for reflective living but not sensitive to its manifold dimensions.

Moral issues raise questions which are not merely rational but also spiritual. This is a point argued by two important interlocutors of our times, namely, Charles Taylor and Govind Chandra Pande, who incidentally come from two different traditions. For Taylor, to speak of moral consciousness is to speak of the qualitative distinction between the higher and the lower desire or scheme of things, a realization which is dependent on spiritual enlightenment.[10]

Moral questions inevitably raise questions of ontology – the nature of the actor and the quality of his/her depth dimension. Though Habermas makes a distinction between ego identity and role identity and speaks of self-reflection in the context of the therapeutic dialogue of the actors (Habermas 1972, 1979), he does not address the question of ontology vis-à-vis moral consciousness. In this he seems to be carried away by the modernist preference for epistemology to ontology. But Taylor here urges us to proceed cautiously. For Taylor, "the whole way in which we think, reason, argue and question ourselves about morality supposes that our moral reactions" are "not only 'gut' feelings but also implicit acknowledgements of claims concerning their objects" (Taylor 1989: 7). "The various ontological accounts try to articulate these claims. The temptations to deny this, which arise from modern epistemology, are strengthened by the widespread accepting of a deeply wrong model of practical reasoning, one based on an illegitimate extrapolation from reasoning in natural science" (ibid.).

Moral ontology is not confined to spiritual ontology alone but is an important part of it. Moral notion requires a reflective self whose source is spiritual. For Taylor, an inquiry into the sources of the self "is not only a phenomenological account but an exploration of the limits of the conceivable in human life, an account of its transcendental conditions" (ibid.: 32). Govind Chandra Pande also makes a similar argument. For him, "it is only a self which is conscious of its ideal universality that can distinguish values from appetites, pleasures and selfish interests and can become the moral subject. It is the question of the ideal self which is the source of the moral law on which social unity and coherence depends. The ideal self is not an abstract transcendental subject in which immediacy and coherence or non-contradiction both coalesce" (Pande 1982: 113). Pande's ideal self is spiritual in its source, actualization and imagination. Pande draws on the concept of man in Indian tradition where it is believed that spirituality is an important dimension of self and identity (see Pande 1985, 1989, 1991, 1992). But this is also true in traditions of spirituality in the West which, as Taylor argues, have encouraged "detachment from identities given by particular historical communities" (Taylor 1989: 37).

Habermas takes for granted that the sacred has become part of modern rational language, which he calls "the linguistification of the sacred". But this view of the modern condition is coloured by Protestant religious experience where religious engagement is not only subservient to the process of rationalization at work in society but also to the power of the word. Habermas' theory of linguistification of sacred is based upon a tradition like Protestantism which privileges words over silence in religious engagement. But this may not be so in the Catholic tradition and certainly not in the Buddhist and Hindu traditions where silence is very much part of reflection; in fact, silence is the source of critical reflection and transforming utterances in acts of discourse. Habermasian discourse ethics is based upon a very naive view of religion and religious evolution in the modern societies. In this context, Robert J. Antonio's critique of Habermas is particularly true of his notion of linguistification of sacred: "the problem of formalism can be overcome, and the true limits of immanent critique clarified, only after all the pseudohistorical baggage is left behind" (Antonio 1989: 741).

Habermas' discourse ethics is procedural[11] but is not serious about the preparation required of participants to take part in the procedure and also does not address the question of normative direction. Habermas does not concentrate on the ontological preparation required of actors to listen and hear in the process of conversation. It is perhaps for this reason that even such a sympathetic critic of Habermas as Thomas McCarthy argues that arguments in which actors are engaged in discourse ethics "themselves remain tied to specific contexts of action and experience and thus are not able wholly to transcend the struggle between Max Weber's warring gods and demons" (McCarthy 1992: 58). This problem can be overcome by opening oneself to spiritual awareness which would enable the actors to "transcend the struggle between warring gods and demons". Participation in spiritual practice or what is called *sadhana* can and does facilitate this.

As a prelude to arguments to follow, at this juncture, it may be helpful to briefly point out the meaning of spiritual engagement referred to here. It refers to a process of multi-dimensional critical movement. First, it is a process of discovering a higher self within oneself – one which is characterized by more intimate subjectivity. If ethics has to do with the challenge of the other, then spirituality as a transformative seeking of values in both inner freedom and in more genuine bonds of intersubjectivity helps us to invite the other into the self. If every dialectic inevitably has a process of self-reflection,[12] this is also true of the dialectic of self and the other and spiritual transformation of the consciousness of actors makes this dialectic more reflective. As Taylor argues of the spiritual point of view vis-à-vis St. Augustine: "[...] radical reflexivity takes on a new status, because it is the space in which we come to encounter God, in which we affect the turning from lower to higher" (Taylor 1989: 140). Spiritual transformation also involves transforming the base of society or the infrastructure of society. It requires transforming the structures of society which subjects human beings into indignity and exploitation. Spirituality has a dimension of institutional criticism as well, which is most evident in traditions of prophetic criticism, martyrdom and the Bhakti movements (Giri 1996; Uberoi 1996; Walzer 1988).

From Discourse to Spiritual Transformation

Though Habermas pleads for post-metaphysical orientations in our moral engagement, a careful reading of him shows that he is deeply aware of the limitations of his agenda. He recognizes that his agenda is anthropocentric[13] but does not explore ways of overcoming the limits of anthropocentrism. Furthermore, while the question of justice is central to his agenda of morality, he does not address whether the pursuit of justice is only a question of socio-political legislation or it involves, as Agnes Heller (1987) argues, a "profound anthropological revolution". For Heller, pursuit of justice almost always involves an engagement with a "Beyond"[14] (also see, Giri 1997; Dallmayr 1993, 1995, 1996; Laclau 1992). By "beyond" Heller refers to something beyond and deeper than mere socio-political legislation. She states quite clearly that "[...] Beyond has the connotation of higher and not only of being different" (Heller 1987: 325–26). But it is this intimation of the "beyond" and a transcendental height that is missing from Habermas which has grave consequences for the realization of some of his own objectives such as the realization of justice and the overcoming of anthropocentrism.

Habermas speaks of "linguistification of sacred" but does not explore the critical potential that a transcendental sacred has in rethinking existing social arrangements and transforming our conventional institutions which chain human dignity in many guises. In this context, the work of Roberto M. Unger (1987) calls for our attention. For Unger, there are two kinds of sacred reality. "The first is a fundamental reality or transcendent personal being; the second, the experiences of personality and personal encounter that, multiplied many times over, make up a social world" (Unger 1987: 576). Though human beings have a tendency to reduce the first sacred reality to the logic of the societal sacred, the transcendental sacred still continues its autonomy and acts as a source of criticism, creativity and transformation.[15] For Unger, when people are only bound to the sacredness of the existing social contexts, "nothing is left to them but to choose one of these worlds and to play by its rules" (ibid.: 577). These rules, though "decisive" in their influence, are ultimately "groundless" (ibid.; also see Laclau 1992). Unger argues that when the decisiveness of the present social world, presenting itself as a sacred order, "arises precisely from its lack of any place within a hierarchy of contexts", then "there is no larger defining reality to which it can seem as the vehicle or from whose standpoint it can be criticized" (Unger 1987: 577).[16] Habermas' agenda of linguistification of sacred suffers from this problem as well.

It is perhaps for these reasons that Fred Dallmayr does not look at Habermas' "discourses ethics" as a categorical shift from the Kantian deontological morality. "Discourse ethics," Habermas writes, "picks up the basic intent of Hegel's thought in order to redeem it with Kantian means" (quoted in Dallmayr 1991: 117). But for Dallmayr there is no scope for genuine redemption in the Habermasian agenda. According to him, Habermas "makes reference to the alleviation of suffering or of 'damaged life' but only as a marginal gloss not fully integrated in his arguments" (Dallmayr 1991: 126). Dallmayr argues that in order to address the questions of justice, suffering, moral responsibility and the self-justification of inhuman social systems as the sacred order, discourse ethics needs a spiritual opening (see Dallmayr 1995, 1996).

Spiritual Foundations of Moral Consciousness: The *Sadhana* of Sri Aurobindo

Habermas uses rational argumentation as the key to the realization of moral consciousness. But, in traditions of spiritual criticisms, there is a much more inclusive approach to rationality and morality which is illustrated in the work of a critic, namely, Sri Aurobindo (1871–1950). Sri Aurobindo is a multi-dimensional critic of the human condition and is noted for his works such as *Human Cycles*, *Life Divine*, *The Synthesis of Yoga*, and *Future Poetry*.[17] Sri Aurobindo does not discount the significance of reason for the origin and growth of morality but wants us to have a proper perspective regarding "the office and limitations of reasons" (ibid.). Much like Habermas, he argues that reason and rational development have played a key role in our being human.[18] Sri Aurobindo himself argues, reminding us of Habermas, that "an attempt to universalize first of all the habit of reason and the application of intelligence and the intelligent will to life" has played a crucial role in the shift from the "infrarational" to the "rational" age (Sri Aurobindo 1962: 179). He also wants us to appreciate the crucial significance of reason in understanding the validity of traditions.[19]

Like Habermas' plea for undistorted communication, Sri Aurobindo also sensitizes us to the distortion that power can introduce in the working of a rational discourse and the realization of even its inherent emancipatory potential.[20] But, for Sri Aurobindo, even though reason is so important for moral development and evolution (both phylogenetic and ontogenetic), it cannot be the sole foundation of morality. Sri Aurobindo accords this role to spirit, not to reason. For him, both order and evolution in life involve "interlocking of an immense number of things that are in conflict with each other" and discovering "some principle of standing-ground of unity" (ibid.: 201). Reason cannot perform this function because "the business of reason is indeterminate [...] in order that it may do its office, it is obliged to adopt temporarily fixed view points" (ibid.). When reason becomes the sole arbiter of life and morality, "every change becomes or at least seems a thing doubtful, difficult and perilous [...] while the conflict of view points, principles, systems leads to strife and revolution and not to basis of harmonious development" (ibid.). For Sri Aurobindo, harmony can be achieved only when the "soul discovers itself in its highest and completest spiritual reality and effects a progressive upward transformation of its life values into those of the Spirit; for they will all find their spiritual truth and in that truth their standing-ground of mutual recognition and reconciliation [...]" (ibid.).

According to Sri Aurobindo, the inadequacy of reason to become the governor of life and morality lies in man's transitional nature – half animal and half divine. He believes that "the root powers of human life, its intimate causes are below, irrational, and they are above, suprarational."

It is for this reason that "a purely rational society could not come into being and, if it could be born, either could not live or sterilize or petrify human existence" (ibid.: 114). He argues, "if reason were the secret, highest law of the universe [...] it might be possible for him by the power of the reason to evolve out of the dominance of the infrarational Nature which he inherits from the animal. But his nature is rather transitional; the rational being is only a middle term of Nature's evolution. A rational satisfaction cannot give him safety from the pull from below nor deliver him from the attraction from above" (ibid.: 206). Sri Aurobindo uses reason but unlike Habermas does not take it as the be all and end all of life. For him, "The solution lies not in reason but in the soul of man, in its spiritual tendencies. It is a spiritual, an inner freedom that alone can create a perfect human order. It is spiritual, *a greater than rational enlightenment*, that can alone illumine the vital nature of man and impose harmony on its self-seeking, antagonisms and discord" (ibid.; emphasis added).

An ideal society, for Sri Aurobindo, is not a mere "rational society" but a "spiritual society". A society founded on spirituality is not governed by religion as a mere social organization where society uses religion "to give an august, awful and [...] eternal sanction to its mass of customs and institutions" (ibid.: 211). A spiritual society is not a theocratic society but a society guided by the quest of the spirit. A spiritual society regards man not only as a "mind, a life and a body, but as a soul incarnated for a divine fulfillment upon earth, not only in heavens beyond, which after all it need not have left if it had no divine business here in the world of physical, vital and mental nature" (ibid.: 213).

Sri Aurobindo's idea of the highest stage of morality is close to the Kohlberg-Habermas idea of the post-conventional stage of moral development. Like the Habermasian idea of post-conventional stage of morality, Sri Aurobindo's idea of morality is not an extension of the collective egoism of a particular society. But what distinguishes his idea of morality is invocation of God not only as a tertiary factor but also as a constituting factor in the dyadic relationship between the self and the other. For him, "the seeking for God is also, subjectively, the seeking for our highest, truest, fullest, largest Self" (ibid.: 136). He further argues that "ethics is not in its essence a calculation of good and evil in action of a laboured effort to be blameless according to the standards of the world – these are only crude appearances – it is an attempt to grow into divine nature" (ibid.: 143). Let us hear him in his own words about the probable more reassuring route towards moral consciousness and communicative action:

> Ethics only begins by the demand upon [man] of something other than his personal preference, vital pleasure or material self-interest; and this demand seems at first to work on him through the necessity of his relations with others. But that this is not the core of the matter is shown by the fact that the ethical demand does not always square with the social demand, nor the ethical standard always coincide with the social standard. His relations with others and his relations with himself are both of them the occasions of his ethical growth, but that which determines his ethical being is his relations with God, the urge of the Divine whether concealed in his nature or conscious in his higher self or inner genius. He obeys an inner deal, not to a social claim or a collective necessity. The ethical imperative comes not from around, but from within him and above him (ibid.: 141).

Beyond the Technology of Power: Spirituality and the Technology of the Self

In his *The Imperative of Responsibility,* Hans Jonas writes: "It must be understood that we are here confronted with a dialectic of power which can only be overcome by a further degree of power itself, not by quietest renunciation of power" (Jonas 1948: 141). This more power, in Jonas' own view, has to emanate from society and supposedly can break the tyrannical automation of power. Jonas is articulating a point of view towards ethical responsibility, which is more widely shared among interpreters and actors today.[21] The crux of this approach lies in the belief that by having more power we can solve the ethical problems confronting us today.[22] But such politicization of morality removes the "inner life from the sphere of the moral," making it impossible to articulate proper moral concepts (Edelman 1990: 53). But, a spiritual approach to ethics and morality, as Sri Aurobindo's work shows, brings the "inner life" of the actors to the heart of their moral consciousness and communicative action. Spirituality not only retrieves the inner life of the actors and juxtaposes it to their outer life but also continuously strives to critically scrutinize the structure of desire of the inner life and subject it to transformative criticism. This transformed inner life becomes a source of transformational criticism of the logic of power in society.

Habermas' discourse ethics shares the above-mentioned problems of an approach to morality where the logic of power reigns supreme over the creative desire and the devotional dynamics of the self. Though Habermas makes a distinction between technology of power and technology of self (see for instance, Habermas 1987b), his critical theory in general and perspective on discourse ethics in particular scarcely scratches the surface of technology of self. To be fair, Habermas is deeply concerned with the need for self-reflection on the part of the actors but he limits this to the context of therapeutic dialogue between the patient and the analyst. Habermas does not explore the possibility of autonomous self-discovery without the mediation of the therapist.

Spirituality here suggests a different route. Spiritual traditions stress that self-knowledge and self-reflection go together. Sri Aurobindo, for instance, proposes yoga as a synthetic mechanism. For him, "Yoga is a methodological effort towards self-perfection by the expression of the potentialities latent in the being and a union of the human individual with the universal and Transcendent Existence" (Sri Aurobindo 1950: 2). Yoga is a practical psychology of self-perfection to help God complete his unfinished task of creation. Its objective is transformation and making possible a higher stage of evolution here on earth, not individual *moksha* (salvation). Yoga also helps us to overcome our "separative ignorance" (ibid.: 618). The practice of yoga helps us to go beyond altruism and egoism, good and evil, where we are able to "take a wider psychological view of the primary forces of our nature" (ibid.). Through the practice of yoga "there grows an immediate and profound sympathy and immixture of mind with mind, life with life, a lessening of the body's insistence on separateness, a power of direct mental and other intercommunication and effective mutual action which helps out now the inadequate indirect communication and action [...]" (ibid.: 615). Yoga enables individuals to have a right relation with the collectivity where the individual does not "pursue egoistically his own material or mental progress or spiritual salvation without regard to his fellows," nor does he "maim his proper development" for the sake of the community but sums up in himself "all its [community's] best and completest possibilities and pour them out by thought, action and all other means on his surroundings so that the whole race may approach nearer to the attainment of its supreme potentialities" (ibid.: 17).

A spiritual approach to self-reflection, for instance as that of yoga, proceeds with a different relationship between knowledge and human interest or knowledge and power. In the spiritual traditions of practice and inquiry, the aim of knowledge – whether of self or other, or of both – is not to have power over the other but to become an instrument of service and creativity in the genuine growth and development of the other. This creative service begins with enhancing the "functioning" and "capability"[23] of the other and aims at the spiritual transformation of their consciousness. The urge of the seekers within traditions of spiritual practice and inquiry, as Rabindra Nath Tagore[24] puts it in one of his poems, is to fulfil one's life through self-sacrifice and presenting oneself as a gift to the other.

The idea of discourse in the traditions of spiritual transformation is different from the over-politically determined view of discourse in modernity. Discourse here is not confined to politically significant utterances nor is it only full of speech acts. In spiritual traditions, silence is also an important part of discourse. It is undoubtedly true that the discourse that the participants in Habermasian discourse ethics are engaged in is not confined to the political; in fact, its critical significance lies in the fact that it is carried out in the life world. But, in order to realize the search for multi-dimensional criticism such as therapeutic criticism and aesthetic criticism that the participants in discourse ethics are engaged in, there is a need for them to participate in the spiritual dialectic of silence and utterances as well.[25]

It is an integral part of spiritual realization that money and power are not the sole measures of a good life; they must be provided normative direction by the quest for meaning in discovering the depth dimension of one's being and creating bonds of intersubjectivity (see Bellah et al., 1991). This realization affects the technology of self that the actors seek to cultivate. Robert Bellah and his colleagues describe some of these ideally imagined modes of practices and criticism (ibid.). The following critique of consumerism that Bellah and his colleagues provide is an instance of spiritual criticism which bears a lot of suggestions for transformation for the participants in discourse ethics: "Consumerism kills the soul as any good Augustinian can see because it places things before the valuing of God and human community" (ibid.: 211). Bellah and his colleagues also suggest pattern of cultivation as an appropriate mode of being in the world today – a pattern characterized by a spiritual attentiveness to the need of the others (please see the following chapter on the work of Robert Bellah).

By the Way of Conclusion: From Practical Discourse to Practical Spirituality

Habermas does not "tie the criterion of rationality to the idea of self-constituting subject of history, he locates it in the basic context of action, in talk between subjects" (Wagner and Zipprian 1989: 103). This is the problem with the Habermasian approach to rationality and morality. The key question is can we have such a view of rationality or what he calls communicative rationality and realize the ends that he sets for himself; adequate motivational development of actors for them to be able to act upon their moral realization as critics and transformers? Can his procedure of rational argumentation actualize his worthy expectation that participants in discourse ethics realize that one who recognizes the interests of others "does not really sacrifice himself, but becomes a larger self" (Habermas 1987a: 94)? Realizing these goals requires a wider view of rationality where it is part of the consciousness of actors – a consciousness which is simultaneously rational and supra-rational, rational and spiritual. Habermas (1979: 93) believes that at the highest stage of moral development internal nature is moved into a "utopian perspective". At this stage, internal nature is not subject to the "demands of ego autonomy; rather through a dependent ego it obtains free access to interpretive possibilities" (ibid.). He also hopes that moral consciousness as a kind of critique would terminate in a "transformation of the affective-motivational basis" of actors (Habermas 1972: 234). But my argument in this chapter has been that his rational approach is incapable of realizing these worthy ideals; it has to be supplemented by spiritual praxis.

Habermas speaks of practical discourse. Communicative interaction is the most important part of this practical discourse. This practical discourse can be part of a practical spirituality (Metz 1970; Vivekananda 1991). Practical spirituality, as Swami Vivekananda[26] argues, urges us to realize that "the highest idea of morality and unselfishness goes hand in hand with the highest idea of metaphysical conception" (Vivekananda 1991: 354). This highest conception pertains to the realization that man himself is God: "You are that Impersonal Being: that God for whom you have been searching all over the time is yourself – yourself not in the personal sense but in the impersonal" (ibid.: 332). The task of practical spirituality begins with this realization but does not end there: its objective is to transform the world. The same Swami Vivekananda thus challenges: "The watchword of all well-being of all moral good is not 'I' but "thou". Who cares whether there is a heaven or a hell, who cares if there is an unchangeable or not? Here is the world and it is full of misery. Go out into it as Buddha did, and struggle to lessen it or die in the attempt" (ibid.: 353). What practical spirituality stresses is that the knowledge that one is Divine, one is part of a Universal Being, facilitates this mode of relating oneself to the world. This knowledge is however not for the acquisition of power over the other; rather it is to worship her as God. In the words of Vivekananda, "Human knowledge is not antagonistic to human well-being. On the contrary, it is knowledge alone that will save us in every department of life, in knowledge as worship" (ibid.: 353).

This plea for practical discourse being part of a practical spirituality has to be understood in the context of emergent contours of religious evolution of our times which point to a new direction. In this direction exists not only religious fundamentalism but also an urge for spiritual realization on the part of the believers, which is not confined to the religions to which they belong (Giri 1994). People of faith also now realize that spiritual realization is possible only through addressing the concrete problems of man and woman who live in their midst. As E.H. Cousins tells us in his *Global Spirituality*: "people of faith now rediscover the material dimensions of existence and their spiritual significance" (Cousins 1985: 7)

The realization of practical spirituality in the dynamics of self, culture and society is as much a normative ideal as the building of a rational society or realization of a state of undistorted communication. The coming of a spiritual society requires both the "reflexive mobilization of self" (Giddens 1991) as well as building up of alternative communities which are founded on the principles of practical spirituality. According to Sri Aurobindo, the coming of a spiritual society begins with the spiritual fulfilment of the urge to individual perfection but ends with the building of a "new world, a change in the life of humanity or, at the least a new perfected collective life in the earth-nature" (Sri Aurobindo 1950: 1031). "This calls for the appearance not only of isolated evolved individuals acting in the uninvolved mass, but of many gnostic individuals forming a new kind of beings and a new common life superior to the present individual and common existence. A collective life of this kind must obviously constitute itself on the same principle as life of the gnostic individual" (ibid.).

These gnostic individuals are seekers and bearers of the multi-dimensional transformation of practical spirituality. But they are not the Nietzschian supermen driven by the will to power; they are animated by a will to serve and desire to transform the contemporary condition and to build a good society. They do not form a type or a caste of chosen people to dominate this world and interpret its urge for meaning. What William Connolly writes below so aptly sums up the spiritual seekers who are going to carry forward the task of moral consciousness and communicative action well into the future:

> But this typological differentiation between man and overman no longer makes much sense, if it ever did. For the overman – constituted as an independent, detached type – refers simultaneously to a spiritual disposition and to the residence of free spirits in a social space relatively insulated from reactive politics. If there is anything in the type to be admired, the ideal must be dismantled as a distinct caste of solitary individuals and folded into the political fabric of late modern society. The 'overman' now falls apart as a set of distinct dispositions concentrated in a particular caste or type, and its spiritual qualities migrate to a set of dispositions that may compete for presence in any self. The type now becomes (as it actually was to a significant degree) a voice in the self contending with other voices including those of resentment (Connolly 1991: 187).

Notes

1. As Hosle argues, it is "clear that the increasing gap between the First and the Third world raises some of the most difficult moral questions of the modern world" (Hosle 1992: 229).
2. Habermas (1987a: 77) describes for us what he means by linguistification of sacred:

   > The disenchantment and disempowering of the domain of the sacred takes place by way of a linguistification of the ritually secured, basic normative agreement; going along with this is a release of the rationality potential in communicative action. The aura of rapture and the tenor that emanates from the sacred, the spellbinding power of the holy, is sublimated into the binding/bonding force of criticizable validity claims and at the same time turned into everyday occurrence.

   Habermas (1987a: 91) further tells us about the implications of such an evolutionary shift:

   > Norm-guided interaction changes in structure to the degree that functions of cultural reproduction, social integration, and socialization pass from the domain of the sacred over to that of everyday communicative practice. In the process, the religious community that made social cooperation possible is transformed into a communicative community striving under the pressure to cooperate.

3. It has to be acknowledged here that there is differing interpretation of the influence of Kant in Habermas. For some, Habermas' categories are less aprioristic than Kant.
4. In this context, we might take note of what William Baldamus, an insightful commentator on Habermas, writes. According to Baldamus, "[...] there can be no doubt that Habermas' graphical diagrams are created intuitively. Ironically, in his

own terminology this means they have no rational foundation, although in logical terms their credibility may be unquestionable" (Baldamus 1992: 102).

5. According to David Bidney, "An individual is said to be morally free insofar as he acts in conformity with the requirements of his 'true good' and his 'true self'. Moral freedom and cultural freedom don't coincide" (Bidney 1967: 453).
6. In this context, Thomas McCarthy tells us:

   If taking modern pluralism seriously means giving up the idea that philosophy can single out a privileged way of life [...], it does not, in Habermas's view, preclude a general theory of a much narrower sort, namely a theory of justice" (quoted in Habermas 1990a: vii).

7. As Habermas writes:

   Within the horizon of the life world, practical judgments derive both their concreteness and their power to motivate action from their inner connection to unquestioningly accepted ideas of the good life, in short, from their connection to ethical life and its institutions. Under these conditions, problematization can never be so profound as to risk all the assets of the existing ethical life, but the abstractive achievements required by the moral point of view do precisely that" (1990a: 109).

8. In so far as the need for describing richly the work of intersubjectivity is concerned, the following lines of Richard Rorty are insightful: "Human solidarity is to be achieved not only by inquiry but by imagination, the imaginative ability to see strange people as fellow sufferers [...] the process of coming to see other human beings as 'one of us' rather than as 'them' is a matter of detailed description of what unfamiliar people are like and redescription of what we ourselves are like" (Rorty 1989: xvi).
9. In stressing such an approach Habermas carries forward the agenda of Kant:

   Thus, when practical reason cultivates itself, their insensibly arises in it a dialectic which forces it to seek aid in philosophy, just as happens to it in its theoretic use; and in this case, therefore as well as in the other, it will find rest nowhere than in a thorough critical examination of our reason (Kant 1987: 26).

10. For Taylor,

    To know who you are is to be oriented in moral space, a space in which questions arise about what is good or bad, what is worth doing and what is not, what has meaning and importance for you and what is trivial and secondary (Taylor 1989: 28).

11. In this regard, what Charles Taylor writes is significant:

    the modern idea of freedom is the strongest motive for the massive shift from substantive to procedural justification in the modern world [...]. And if we leap from the earliest to the most recent such theory, Habermas's conception of discourse ethics is founded in part on the same consideration. The idea that norm is justified only to the extent that all could uncoercedly accept it is a new and interesting variant of procedural idea (Taylor 1989: 86).

12. Here, we can take note of the insightful arguments of philosopher Roop Rekha Verma. Verma writes:

    The dialectic by itself does not explain the possibility of cultural change or critique of culture. What is important to add in this dialectic is that the internalization can be reflective or unreflective (Verma 1991: 534).

13. Habermas himself writes: "compassion for tortured animals and the pain caused by the destruction of the biotopes are surely manifestations of moral intuitions

that cannot be fully satisfied by the collective narcissism of what in the final analysis is an anthropocentric way of looking at things" (Habermas 1990s: 211). But how do we open ourselves for a dialogue with animals and the natural world while Habermas's "communicative action theory clearly privileges interhuman speech or discourse, while adopting an 'objectifying' attitude to nature"? (Dallmayr 1996: 220).

14. In her view, a just procedure is the condition of the good life – of all possible good lives – but is not sufficient for the good life [...] The good life consists of three elements: first, righteousness; secondly the development of endowments into talents, and thirdly emotional depth in personal attachments. Among these three elements, righteousness is the overarching one. All three elements of the good life are beyond justice (Heller 1987: 273).
15. Unger's following argument helps us understand this:

    Whereas the first of these two is illusive and disputable and requires, to be recognized, the power of vision which is the ability to see the invisible, the second seems near and palpable. Whenever they can, men and women try to identify the first of these two sacreds with the second. They want to see the social world graced with the authority of an ultimate reality. But the progress of insight and the disclosures of conflict prevent this bestowal of authority. If there is a common theme in the history of human thought and politics, it consists precisely in failure to sustain claims of unconditional authority on behalf of particular ways of talking, thinking, living and organizing society. As the two sacreds lose their contact with each other, the distant one fades away into an ineffable, longed for reality without any clear message for understanding and conduct. The nearby becomes profane and arbitrary (Unger 1987: 576).

16. Prophetic criticism comes closest to the kind of critical engagement that Unger has in mind here. Not only in the traditional past but also in varieties of contemporary societies criticisms of modern institutions of human indignity such as racism and slavery, etc. have been the work of the prophets – be it Gandhi or Martin Luther King Jr – who, it must not be forgotten, have used the name of God to build their movement against forces of oppression. Even in modern critical social movements we are "back to the beginning," to use the words of Michael Walzer (1988), where social critic is a prophet.
17. Sri Aurobindo was one of pioneers in the freedom struggle of India and left it quite early in his life for the pursuit of his goal of spiritualization of humanity. Based in his Ashram at Pondicherry, India, Sri Aurobindo and his spiritual companion Mira Richards also known as The Mother have contributed a lot to our understanding of the logic of spiritual transformation as an integral process involving both individual and society.
18. In his discussion of "the curve of rational age" in *Human Cycles*, Sri Aurobindo argues that "the present age of mankind" is characterized "from the point of view of a graded psychological evolution by an attempt to discover and work out the right principle and secure foundations of rational systems of society" (Sri Aurobindo 1962: 181).
19. In the words of Sri Aurobindo (1962: 183):

    Reason can accept no tradition merely for the sake of its antiquity or its greatness; it has to ask, first whether it contains the best truth available to man for the government of his life. Reason can accept no convention merely because men are agreed upon it; it has to ask whether they are right in their agreement, whether it is an inert or false acquiescence. Reason cannot accept any institution merely

> because it serves some purpose of life; it has to ask whether there are not greater and better purposes which can be best served by new institutions. There arises the necessity of a universal questioning and from that necessity arises the idea that society can only be perfected by the universal application of rational intelligence to the whole of life [...].

20. In his words,

> The reason which is to be universally applied, cannot be the reason of a ruling class: for in the present imperfection of the human race that always means the fettering and misapplication of reason degraded into servant of power to maintain the privileges of the ruling class. *It must be the reason of each and all seeking for a basis of agreement* (Sri Aurobindo 1962: 184; emphasis added).

21. In the words of Jonas, "From which direction can we expect this third degree power which reinstates man in the context of his power and breaks its tyrannical automatism? It must, in the nature of the problem, emanate from society as no private insight, responsibility or fear can measure upto the tasks" (Jonas 1984: 142).
22. Ulrich Beck (1992), for instance, argues that it is the collective power of society which can address the ecological crises confronting us today.
23. I use "functioning" and "capability" in the same way as Amartya Sen does. See Sen (1987).
24. A great poet and educational experimenter of modern India noted for his Noble Prize-winning collection of poems called *Gitanjali*.
25. Professor Robert Bernasconi (personal communication 1997) argues that there are different kinds of silence and one must not be insensitive to the distinction between self-chosen silence and imposed silence. What spiritual striving seeks is self-chosen silence and aims at breaking all kinds of imposed silences.
26. Another pioneering spiritual seeker of modern India known in the West for his interventions in the World Parliament of Religions at Chicago in 1893.

References

Antonio, Robert J. 1989. "The Normative Foundations of Emancipatory Theory: Evolutionary Versus Pragmatic Perspectives." *American Journal of Sociology* 94 (4): 721–48.

Baldamus, William. 1992. "Understanding Habermas's Method of Reasoning". *History of the Human Sciences* 5 (2): 91–115.

Bauman, Zygmunt. 1993. *Postmodern Ethics*. Oxford: Basil Blackwell.

Beck, Ulrich. 1992. *Risk Society: Towards A New Modernity*. London: Sage Publications.

Bellah, Robert et al., 1991. *The Good Society*. New York: Alfred A. Knopf.

Bidney, David. 1967. *Theoretical Anthropology*. New York: Shocken Books.

Connolly, William E. 1991. *Identity/Difference: Democratic Negotiation of Political Paradox*. Ithaca: Cornell University Press.

Cortese, Anthony. 1990. *Ethnic Ethics: The Restructuring of Moral Theory*. Albany: State University of New York Press.

Cousins, E.H. 1985. *Global Spirituality*. Madras: University of Madras Press.

Dallmayr, Fred. 1991. *Life World, Modernity and Critique: Paths between Heidegger and Frankfurt School*. Cambridge: Polity Press.

——. 1993. *The Other Heidegger*. Ithaca: Cornell University Press.

——. 1995. "Rights" Versus "Rites": Justice and Cultural Transformation. University of Notre Dame: Paper.

——. 1996. *Beyond Orientalism: Essays on Cross-Cultural Encounter*. Albany: State University of New York Press.

Dewey, John. 1960 [1908] *Theory of the Moral Life*. New York: Holt, Rinehart and Winston.

Edelman, John T. 1990. *An Audience for Moral Philosophy?* London: Macmillan.

Geertz, Clifford. 1986. "The Uses of Diversity." *Michigan Quarterly Review*, Winter Issue: 105–23.

Giddens, Anthony. 1991. *Modernity and Self-Identity: Self and Society in the Late Modern Age*. Cambridge: Polity Press.

Giri, Ananta. 1994. "Religious Resurgence in Contemporary United States: A View from India." *Sociological Bulletin* 43 (2): 177–192.

——. 1996. "Social Criticism, Cultural Creativity and the Contemporary Dialectics of Transformations: A Poser." Introductory statement at the workshop on "Social Criticism, Cultural Creativity and the Contemporary Dialectics of Transformations," Madras Institute of Development Studies, Madras, December 4–7, 1996.

——. 1997. "Well-Being of Institutions: Problematic Justice and the Challenge of Transformation". Madras Institute of Development Studies: Working Paper.

Habermas, Jurgen. 1972. *Knowledge and Human Interests*. Cambridge: Polity Press.

——. 1972. *Theory and Practice*. Cambridge: Polity Press.

——. 1979. *Communication and the Evolution of Society*. Cambridge: Polity Press.

——. 1981. *Philosophical-Political Profiles*. London: Hienemann.

——. 1987a. *A Theory of Communicative Action*. Volume 2: *Life World and System: A Critique of Functionalist Reason*. Cambridge: Polity Press.

——. 1987b. *The Philosophical Discourses of Modernity*. Cambridge: Polity Press.

——. 1988. "Law and Morality." In S.M. McCurrin (ed.), *The Tanner Lectures on Human Values*. Volume VII, Cambridge: Cambridge University Press and Salt Lake City: University of Utah Press.

——. 1989. *The Structural Transformation of the Public Sphere*. Cambridge: Polity Press.

——. 1990a. *Moral Consciousness and Communicative Action*. Cambridge: Polity Press.

——. 1990b. "What Does Socialism Mean Today? The Rectifying Revolution and the Need for New Thinking in the Left." *New Left Review*, No. 183–321.

——. 1992. *Postmetaphysical Thinking*. Cambridge: Polity Press.

——. 1994. "Overcoming the Past: Interview with Adam Michnik". *New Left Review*.

Heller, Agnes. 1987. *Beyond Justice*. Oxford: Basil Blackwell.

Hosle, Vittorio. 1992. "The Third World as a Philosophical Problem." *Social Research* 59 (2): 227–262.

Jonas, Hans. 1984. *The Imperative of Responsibility: In Search of an Ethics for the Technological Age*. Chicago: The University of Chicago Press.

Kant, Immanuel. 1987 [1781]. *Fundamental Principles of the Metaphysics of Ethics*. Delhi: Orient Publications.

Laclau, Ernesto. 1992. "Beyond Emancipation." In Jan N. Pieterse (ed.), *Emancipations: Modern and Postmodern*. London: Sage.

McCarthy, Thomas. 1992. "Practical Discourse: On the Relation of Morality to Politics." In Craig Calhoun (ed.), *Habermas and the Public Sphere*. Cambridge, MA: The MIT Press.

Metz, Johannes B. 1970. "Does our Church Need a New Reformation? A Catholic Reply." *Concilium* 4 (6): 81–91.

Neville, Robert C. 1974. *The Cosmology of Freedom*. New Haven and London: Yale University Press.

Pande, Govind Chandra. 1982. "On the Nature of Social Categories." In Ravinder Kumar, (ed.), *Philosophical Categories and Social Reality*, Delhi: Allied Publishers.

——. 1985. *Aspects of Indian Culture and Civilization*. Varanasi: BHU Press.

——. 1989. *The Meaning and Process of Culture as Philosophy of History*. Allahabad: Raka Prakashan.

——. 1991. "Two Dimensions of Religion: Reflections Based on Indian Spiritual Experience and Philosophical Traditions." In Eliot Deutch (ed.), *Culture and Modernity*. Honolulu: University of Hawaii Press.

——. 1992. "Sri Aurobindo: Cultural Perspectives." Paper presented at the National Seminar on Sri Aurobindo at Pondicherry.

Rorty, Richard. 1989. *Contingency, Irony, and Solidarity*. Cambridge: Cambridge University Press.

Sacks, Jonathan. 1991. *The Persistence of Faith*. London: Weidenfeld and Nicholson.

Sen, Amartya. 1987. "The Standard of Living." In Geoffrey Hawthorn (ed.), *The Standard of Living*. Cambridge: Cambridge University Press.

Sri Aurobindo. 1950. *The Synthesis of Yoga*. Pondicherry: Sri Aurobindo Ashram.

——. 1953. *The Future Poetry*. Pondicherry: Sri Aurobindo Ashram.

——. 1962. *The Human Cycles: The Ideal of Human Unity, War and Self-Determination*. Pondicherry: Sri Aurobindo Ahsram.

——. 1970. *The Life Divine*. Pondicherry: Sri Aurobindo Ashram.

Taylor, Charles. 1989. *Sources of the Self*. Cambridge, MA: Harvard University Press.

Uberoi, J.P.S. 1996. *Religion, Civil Society and State: A Study of Sikhism*. Delhi: Oxford University Press.

Unger, Roberto M. 1987. *False Necessity: Anti-Necessitarian Social Theory in the Service of Radical Democracy*. Cambridge: Cambridge University Press.

Vivekananda, Swami. 1991. *The Complete Works of Swami Vivekananda*. Calcutta: Advaita Ashrama.

Verma, Roop Rekha. 1991. "The Concept of Progress and Cultural Identity." In Eliot Deutch (ed.), *Culture and Modernity*. Honolulu: University of Hawaii Press.

Walzer, Michael. 1988. "Interpretation and Social Criticism." In S.M. McCurrin (ed.), *The Tanner Lectures on Human Values*. Cambridge: Cambridge University Press and Salt Lake City: University of Utah Press.

Wagner, G.R. and H. Zipprian. 1989. "Habermas on Power and Rationality." *Sociological Theory* 7 (1): 102–109.

Williams, Bernard. 1985. *Ethics and the Limits of Philosophy*. London: Fontana.

7 Sociology as a Quest for a Good Society

A Conversation with Robert Bellah

Indeed, there are times when the work of contemporary sociologists is characterized by such depth and seriousness that one is inclined to think that they are the true inheritors of the ancient prophetic traditions working in the world today.

— David Smith (2007), *Moving Towards Emmaus: Hope in a Time of Uncertainty*, p. 83

We live in a society obsessed with the self: above all, most of us want to be rich, powerful, beautiful, and admired, or at least one of the above [...] But instead of saying we are so obsessed with the self, perhaps we should say we are not obsessed enough; we have not looked deeply enough into what we really want, which is the just self, capable of treating others justly in the context of a just society.

— Robert N. Bellah (2007), "Ethical Politics: Reality or Illusion?," pp. 67–68

However, the greatest weakness of the book has nothing to do with Japan but with a weakness in the modernization theory I was using: I failed to see that the endless accumulation of wealth and power does not lead to the good society but undermines the condition necessary for any viable society at all. I suffered myself from the displacement of ends by means, or the attempt to make means to ends, which is the very source of the pathology of modernization. [...] What would it mean to reverse the functionalization of religion, the reduction of the realm of ultimate ends to the status of means? What would it look like if religion set the ends, and the means – wealth and power – that have usurped the status of the ends, were reduced to the status of means again?

— Robert N. Bellah (1985), Introduction to the Paperback Edition, *Tokugawa Religion: Cultural Roots of Modern Japan*, pp. xix, xx

[...] in the present situation a politics of the imagination, a politics of religion, may be the only sane politics. There is no hope in any of the competing absolutisms. If the forces at war are locked in their own death like scenarios perhaps the only responsible politics is to unmask the pretensions of all the contending parties and give witness to the enormous possibilities in human experience, in a word, to awaken the actors out of their trance. To this end a human science can perhaps join with a human religion to help create a human politics.

— Robert N. Bellah (1970), *Beyond Belief: Essays on Religion in a Post-Traditional World*, p. xviii

Robert N. Bellah (born 1927) is a creative sociologist of our times who has deepened the craft of sociological practice and imagination as well as made sociology a part of normative public discourse and striving for realizing a good society. Good society for Bellah is a society where both self and society do not suffer from delusions such as considering wealth and power as ultimate ends of life, and strive to realize their potential of blossoming, fulfilment and realization of meaning. The vision and quest for good society is not a prisoner of dualism between good and evil; rather it seeks to realize goodness in both self and society by creating appropriate institutional conditions for self as well as societal blossoming. Realizing good society in Bellah is a multi-dimensional striving and struggle of critique, reconstruction and creativity and sociology fulfils itself by taking part in it. Good society is a space of realization of beauty, dialogue and dignity.

Good Society is the title of a collaborative study that Bellah and his colleagues published in 1991 in which they offer reflections on the visions of and strivings for good society by many men and women in the United States. This follows their earlier collaborative work on normative quest for a good society in *Habits of the Heart* (1985). Apart from these studies, Bellah has written on different aspects of religion, society and modernity in Japan and North America. He has gifted us with such important works as *Tokugawa Religion* (1957), *Beyond Belief* (1970) and *Imagining Japan* (2003) in which we get glimpses of sociological engagement as quest for a good society. Quest for a good society constitutes an abiding concern of Bellah and also one of the co-ordinating themes in his creative *ouvre* spanning last fifty years. The present essay seeks to present glimpses of the sociological works of Bellah beginning with a conversation I had with him in 2003 with quest for good society as a guiding concern in this narrative presentation.

Quest for realizing a good society has a long pedigree in sociological traditions. This is a concern passionately followed in their own ways by pioneers of our field such as Saint Simon and Karl Marx and which reverberates in critical and creative reflections in humanities, social sciences and public pedagogy in the last hundreds of years. A work of significant insight here is a book by Walter Lippmann first published in 1936 entitled *The Good Society*, which presents the centrality of ethical goodness and the cultivation of public virtues as significant parts of realization of good society. Bellah's quest for realizing good society builds upon tradition patiently cultivated by public educators such as Lippmann and it also vibrates with contemporary creative interpretations of Lippman's such as Fred Dallmayr's who is striving towards a global good society (2007) in which global education, multicultural pedagogy and striving for peace are central. Good society also vibrates with the vision of "The Decent Society" offered by Avishai Margalitt (1996) and "Creative Society" offered by Manoranjan Mohanty (1998). For Margalitt, "A decent society is one whose institutions do not humiliate people" (Margalitt 1996: 1) and for Mohanty a creative society is one which is continuously striving to overcome multiple dominations. Realization of good society is a matter of *sadhana*, strivings and struggles to build appropriate institutions in society which would facilitate blossoming of self and society and realize beauty, dignity and dialogue but is not confined within institutionalism what Amartya Sen (2009) calls "entrenched institutionalism" which is imprisoned within the existing logic of state, society and polity. Rather striving for good society has a dimension of creative aspiration and mobilization – political as well as spiritual – to transform the existing structures of closure and bondage and make life better.

Striving for good society has also a long pedigree in critical and creative traditions but it is at the same time contested on the ground that it can offer a singular notion of goodness. In this context, sociology as quest for a good society is confronted with plural visions of the good, a journey of pluralization which Bellah would not hesitate to join given his own sociological quest in another cultural context – Japan. The concept of good society also meets with possible critique from Jurgen Habermas (1990) who talks about the priority of the right over the good and Andre Beteille (2001) who thinks that the concept of civil society is much more deliberative than good society. But without proceeding with a dualism between "right" and "good" and "good society" and "civil society" we can have a multi-dimensional vision of striving for good society in which quest for right and law and realization of ethics and public virtues on the part of both self and social institutions proceed simultaneously and sociology contributes to such a co-realization (cf. Giri 2008c; Uberoi 2003). Bellah's recent work again would be sympathetic to such a multi-dimensional realization of good society.

With this prelude we can proceed with the notion of sociology as quest for a good society to understand the sociological quest of Robert Bellah. But, the chapter does not discuss further this concept nor does it use it as an evaluative variable to judge the works of Bellah. Rather it is presented as an inviting – not enclosing – frame to understand the narrative presentation of the works of Bellah that is offered in this chapter.

A Glimpse into the Sociology of Robert Bellah: Beginning with a Conversation

I first came across Bellah's collaborative study, *Habits of the Heart* in 1986 while doing graduate work in the United States. Since then I have been interested in his works. After years of correspondence occasioned by my review of his *Habits of the Heart* in *Indian Anthropologist* (Giri 1992) it was an enriching experience for me meeting with him and being in conversation with him in is his office at the Department of Sociology, University of California, Berkeley in March 2003 where Bellah is an emeritus professor.

During our conversations Bellah began by pointing out that from the beginning he was interested to study a society other than the mainstream American. As an undergraduate at Harvard he had studied the Navaho religion and wrote his undergraduate thesis on "Apache Kinship Systems". In graduate school he wanted to study something other than American. Alfred Kroeber, the great anthropologist, once said in a lecture at Harvard that "the two cultures that are most different from our own are Japan and India" which helped him to crystallize his interest to do sociological work on a society other than American. But Bellah became drawn to Japan, especially to its aesthetics and traditions of Zen Buddhism. Though himself born into Christianity and raised as a Presbyterian, he soon became deeply interested in Zen Buddhism, as he told me during our conversation, not only academically but also personally. But his participation in paths of spiritual practice such as Zen Buddhism has not made him forget the deep spiritual significance of his nurturing himself in his journey as one who is born into a Christian faith.[1] He could draw spiritual sustenance from his own religious upbringing with notions like sin which made him realize the fragility of human life and our exaggerated claim of authorship of actions. For Bellah: "I saw the worst is only a hair's breadth away from the best in any man and any society. [...] If I am not a murderer it is because of the grace I have received through the love and support of others, not through the lack of murderous impulses within me" (Bellah 1970: xvi).[2]

Bellah carried out his doctoral work on religion of Japan during the Tokugawa period (1600–1868) from the Department of Social Relations of Harvard where Talcott Parsons was one of his main teachers. After his doctorate he joined Institute of Islamic Studies at McGill as a post-doctoral fellow and worked with the eminent scholar of religion and its founder Wilfred C. Smith. He studied Arabic as well as Koran. But he thinks he got a different religious experience in Japan. In his words, "For me, the East Asian perspective was significant for difference. Personally for me the most important part of Muslim tradition is Sufism but most of the modernist movements have been anti-Sufi. The trouble with Islam is that it is all too familiar. Koran is saturated with Moses. Islam is one of the three Abrahamic religions and as such is close to Christianity. 'Orthodox Islam is superheated Calvinism'. At the same time, Islam offers an extraordinary challenge for sociologists; it emphasizes creation of community, *Umma*."

Quest for a Good Society in Bellah's Study of Japan

Bellah's first major work, *Tokugawa Religion* (1957), is a landmark study in sociology of religion applying the insights of Max Weber to the Japanese society and history. Bellah finds the closest equivalent of Protestant ethics in a Buddhist religious movement named Jodo Shinshu. It preached hard work and austerity which contributed to economic rationalization in Japan. But, the book has many other insights about Japanese religion in particular. Bellah shows us how in Japan all religious streams – Shinto, Buddhist and Confucian – interacted with each other and influenced each other. For Bellah, in Japanese religion, "Nature is not alien to the divine or to man but is united with both" (1985: 63). Bellah tells us: "[...] Japanese religion is fundamentally concerned with harmony – harmony among persons and harmony with nature. Each strand of the tradition views harmony somewhat differently and offers its own peculiar approach. And yet each of them eventuates in the idea of life as ceremony, as play, almost as dance, in which what is being expressed is compassion, care for all beings of the universe" (1985: xix). But this harmony is not static but dynamic and what Bellah writes below has a lot of insights for us as we seek ways of harmony in our dynamically changing world:

> What has been said about the unity of man, nature and divinity should not be interpreted as a static identity. Rather it is a harmony in tension. The gratitude one owes to superordinate benevolent entities is not an easy obligation but may involve the instant sacrifice of one's deepest interests or even of one's life. Union with the ground of being is not attained in a state of coma but very often as the result of some sudden shock in daily living. Something unexpected, some seeming disharmony, is more apt to reveal the Truth than any formal orderly teaching. Japanese art and aesthetic attitude toward nature are also concerned with the unexpected [...] (ibid.: 62–63).

Bellah's book discusses several religious movements in the Tokugawa period, which has interesting comparative sociological and historical lessons. He discusses a movement among the peasants named Hotoku, which gave stress on labour. Hoko means labour as a sacred obligation. This resonates with the vision and practice of *shramabhakti* (devotional labour) in Swadhyaya – a socio-spiritual movement where participants farm together and build orchards and other spaces of collective well-being (see Giri 2008a). Bellah also discusses another interesting movement named Shingaku, starting with the merchants but then touching many other social strata in Japanese society. It was founded by Ishida Baigan (1685–1744) who came from humble origins in a village. Being a younger son, and not having right to inheritance, Baigan came to work as an apprentice in a merchant house in Kyoto and with a life of struggle and fortitude to learn the way he had his own house of teaching at the age of 45. Baigan was a teacher in whose meeting "mutual questioning took place" (ibid.: 137). Baigan not only questioned his followers but his followers also questioned him. This spirit of mutual questioning is rare even today in religious and spiritual spaces around the world, most specifically in India, where spiritual gurus hardly want to be questioned, and Bellah's description of this important teacher of humanity has important lessons for all of us concerned.[3]

In his recent book on Japan, Bellah (2003) has an insightful paper, "Japanese Emperor as a Mother Figure: Some Preliminary Notes," in which he shows how the Japanese emperor has been perceived and works as a mother figure and not only as a patriarch. Besides a figure of "austere masculine authoritarianism," the emperor was also a mother figure. For Bellah, "All Japanese authority figures have a maternal succoring aspect to a great extent than would be the case in many other cultures" (ibid.: 183). This maternal aspect is related to the significance of sun goddess Amaterasu o mikami in Japanese mythology, self-perception and social life who exercises her influence in "a very feminine way" (ibid.: 178). For Bellah, "She is no patriarchal despot like Jehovah [...] She is a peacemaker, conciliator, mediator [...]" (ibid.). Bellah's insightful discussion of both Japanese emperor and the Goddess Amatarasu as maternal figures[4] can inspire us to wonder if we cannot only look at but also realize our politics, religion and spirituality as a space of maternal nurturance and not only as a space of authoritarian command and control. Could American Presidents and Indian Prime Ministers also embody maternal nurturance?

Understanding Tribal Religions and Religious Evolution

Bellah is not only interested in different world religions such as Islam and Buddhism but also in tribal religions. During our conversation, Bellah told me: "Tribal religion is important. It is part of our human heritage which we cannot look down upon. In religious evolution nothing is lost." And he writes about this in his self-reflective introduction to a selection of his writings published by Duke University Press entitled *Bellah Reader*: "[...] tribal and then archaic religions and societies needed to be understood in their own terms, especially since, as I came to see, 'nothing is ever lost,' and the whole of human cultural and religious history is still with us. So, while the abiding concern was the understanding of modernity, and most immediately, American modernity, from very early on I knew that modernity was a mere fragment of the whole, that the idea that what went before could be forgotten is a fallacy, and that only coming to terms with the whole would serve us in facing the present and the future. Thus, the lifelong preoccupation with religious evolution" (Bellah 2005b: 5). Tracing his current and long-standing interest in religions of our ancestors to his earlier seeking as a student Bellah told me: "I did my undergraduate work on the Navaho. They have Navaho theologians. We are now seeing tribal people becoming self-conscious about their identity." During our conversation Bellah also drew my attention to the cruelty to which tribal people and their religions have been subjected to. At the same time, he also pointed to the violence practised in some archaic religions such as the Aztec sacrifice.

Bellah told me in 2003 that he was completing a long-nurtured work on religious evolution and in his recent e-mail communication (2008) he wrote me how religious life of ancient India is difficult for him to understand. Bellah wrote his classic paper, "Religious Evolution" more than four decades ago. In this paper, as he does in his book *Tokugawa Religion,* Bellah looks at religion as a "set of symbolic forms and acts that relate man to the ultimate condition of his existence" (Bellah 1970: 21). Nonetheless, without taking a linear evolutionary stance Bellah invites us to understand differentiation that has taken place in the field of religious symbolization in the religious history of mankind. For him, "Neither religious man nor the structure of man's ultimate religious situation evolves [...] but religion as symbol system" (ibid.: 28). Bellah presents five stages in this evolutionary journey of differentiation of symbolic systems of religions: primitive religion, archaic religion, historical religion, early modern religion and modern religion. In primitive religions, there is close identification between the mythical world and the actual world and in rituals "participants become identified with the mythical beings they represent" (ibid.: 28). Here, "The mythical beings are not addressed or propitiated or beseeched. The distance between man and mythical being, which was at best slight, disappears altogether in the moment of ritual when every when becomes now. There are no priests and no congregation, no mediating representative roles and no spectators. present are involved in the ritual action itself and have become one with the myth" (ibid.). In archaic religions, there is move towards differentiation between the mythical and the actual: "Archaic *religious action* takes the form of cult in which the distinction between men as subjects and gods as objects is much more definite than in primitive religion" (ibid.: 30). In historical religions, for the first time, there is discovery and hierarchical articulation of an other world, which is superior to the actual world. All historical religions share elements of world rejecting transcendentalism which are "dualistic" (ibid.: 32). For Bellah, "*Religious action* in the historic religions is [...] above all is action necessary for salvation. The identity diffusion characteristic of both primitive and archaic religions is radically challenged by the historic religious symbolization, which leads for the first time to a clearly structured conception of the self. Devaluation of the empirical world and the empirical self highlights the conception of a responsible self, a core self, of a true self, deeper than the flux of everyday experience, facing a reality over against itself, a reality which has a consistency belied by the fluctuations of mere sensory impressions" (ibid.: 33).

Continuing the journey, Bellah says that in early modern religion, especially in Protestant Reformation, there is collapse of the hierarchical ordering of the other and this world. Even though dualism between the worlds – other and this – remains, there is more confrontation between the two. "Under the new circumstances salvation is not to be found in any kind of withdrawal from the world but in the midst of worldly activities" (ibid.: 36). And, in modern religions, there is the questioning of this dualism between the other and this world: "it is not so much a question of two worlds as it is of as many worlds as there are modes of apprehending them" (ibid.: 40). Besides, there is also questioning of fixed positions but this does not mean abandonment of religious symbolization rather transforming religion as a space for self-exploration and mutual communication without being constrained by rigid structures. In modern religions there is "increasing acceptance of the notion that each individual must work out his own ultimate solutions and that the most the church can do is to provide him a favourable environment for doing so, without imposing on him a prefabricated set of answers" (ibid.: 43–44). Bellah's characterization of modern religion is not to be understood in a linear and literal way as in the contemporary world all stages of religious evolution co-exist in varying degrees. What Bellah provides us is an insightful way of understanding our contemporary religious predicament and possibility: "The historic religions discovered the self, the early modern religion found a doctrinal basis on which to accept the self in all its empirical ambiguity; modern religion is beginning to understand the laws of the self's own existence and so to help man take responsibility for his own fate" (ibid.: 42).

As a student of religion, Bellah laments lack of a deep interest in modern sociology on matters of religion. On being asked about sociology, religion and the calling of spirituality, Bellah said:

> I have not come to terms with the word spirituality. I feel more comfortable with the older word religion. My fundamental understanding of religion is what makes human beings better. It refers to something beyond human beings. Without the transcendental domain the solidarity of the world comes apart. The very root of religion is society. I do not draw a deep divide between theology and sociology.
>
> At the same time, transcendence is a problematic word. There has to be reference something beyond the human, the intrinsically good – Good in itself and not God in a Judeo-Christian way. It is beyond individual and society without which genuine individuality and genuine sociality is not possible.

Bellah finds "comfortable the older word religion". But for many, the word 'religion' is just the beginning of the manifold foundational difficulties of religion, especially the way it has been used by powers to suppress the realization of potential – self as well as societal. Bellah fully agrees with such a critique of religion but still wants to challenge all those who glorify spirituality and do not always realize that the quest in this field – whatever name you may give, religious or spiritual – does not always sufficiently acknowledge that this is not just an individual act, but involves life of a community. The advocates of spirituality can acknowledge this theoretically by referring to the vision and practice of experimenters in human history such as Sri Aurobindo (1970) who talks about the *Life Divine* and building of spiritual communities. But, the actual sociological embodiment of such spiritual communities is not much different from the work of religious communities. For Bellah, spirituality seems too individualizing and for the proponents of spirituality religion is too much bound up with classification, categorization and violence.[5] As the building of spiritual communities with a new practical logic of coordination, community life and power is still an evolutionary task, there is need for transformative dialogue between sociologists like Bellah who are reluctant to abandon religion and other spiritual seekers who want to replace religion with spirituality.

Bellah has been exploring creative pathways of mediations and transformations between religion and modern science, especially social sciences, without falling into the trap of what he calls, "enlightenment fundamentalism and religious fundamentalism" (Bellah 2005: 1). Given the worldwide resurgence of religion now including its violent manifestations Bellah's creative search for moving beyond the battle between science and religion and search for a "new integration" (which is not just superficial but deep)[6] deserves our careful attention. Taking a creative contingent view of history nurtured by cross-cultural realizations, Bellah writes: "The Enlightenment theory of secularization and of the relation of religion and science is understandable as a reaction to a particular religious tradition, one with a strong cognitive bias and a stress on orthodox belief. Had the Enlightenment occurred first in a culture dominated by Zen Buddhism, for example, the outcome would have been very different [...]" (ibid.: 238). But, the split between science and religion need not be our fate as there have been transformations in both, and as both science and religion are continuously invited for further transformations. For Bellah, "[...] there are greater resources now for healing the split between the imaginative and the cognitive, the intellectual and the emotional, and the scientific and religious aspects of our culture and our consciousness than have been for centuries. Social science is now beginning, faintly and crudely, to be able to cope with the richness of reality as religion has seen it" (ibid.: 245). And for Bellah, the view of reality that religion presents is a multi-dimensional one rather than the flat world of secular realism: "For religion is not a kind of pseudogeology or pseudohistory but an imaginative statement about the truth of the totality of human experience. [...] So-called post-religious man, the cool, self-confident secular man [...] is trapped in a literal and circumscribed reality [...] The world of everyday reality is a socially and personally constructed world. If one confuses that world with reality itself one than becomes trapped in one's own delusions, one projects one's wishes and fears onto others and one acts one's madness all the while believing that one is a clearheaded realist" (ibid.: 244).

Quest for Wholeness

For Bellah, sociology must transform itself to understand the quest for the whole, especially "felt whole," of man which "includes subject and object and provides the context in which life and action [...] has meaning" rather than just subject it to scientific study (Bellah 1970: 253). For Bellah, "The canons of empirical science apply primarily to symbols that attempt to express the nature of objects, but there are non-objective symbols that express the feelings, values, and hopes of subjects, or that organize and regulate the flow of interaction between subjects and objects, or that attempt to sum up the whole subject-object complex or even point to the context or ground of that whole. These symbols too express reality and are not reducible to empirical propositions" (ibid.: 252). Bellah calls this approach symbolic realism. For Bellah, sociological study of religion ought to embody symbolic realism rather than a flat empiricist realism. Since Bellah initially wrote about it four decades ago, there have been a lot of new developments in social sciences on the issues of realism, for example, critical realism, constructivism, and a constructivist realism (Bhaskar 2002; Strydom 2008). Bellah's approach of symbolic realism is not an escape for coming to term even epistemologically our empirical reality but it is a plea for understanding our multi-layered reality without falling into a dualism of realism and constructivism. It has to address much more theoretically as well as practically relationship between symbols, social action and social institutions as the symbolic approach to religion both in anthropology and spiritual traditions has sometimes neglected to relate symbols to institutional contexts, for example, as it happens in Clifford Geertz's approach to religion (Giri 2008b).

Bellah offers symbolic realism as "the only approach for the social scientific study of religion" (Bellah 1970: 253). Given the dangers of any assertion, Bellah may consider it as not the only approach but one approach. But, as an approach, it is significant not only in the study of religion but also in science. The objects of understanding in science as well as methods of understanding also have a symbolic dimension. New developments in science tell us that the empirical reality itself is interpenetrated by the supra-empirical and instead of an opposition between the symbolic approach and an empirical approach to reality now there is a need for a new integration. Sociologist and philosopher J.P.S. Uberoi develops such a new symbolic approach to reality – science, religion, self and society-based upon Goethe's method and work on colours and optics (Uberoi 1978, 1984).

But Bellah has not only been trying to heal the split between religion and science, he has also been trying to transcend the wall of separation between religion and public sphere calling for transformation on both sides. For Bellah, secularism is not only the outcome of Enlightenment anti-clericalism[7] nor civil society is only a so-called secular sphere divorced from religious concerns. Bellah does not make an apriori distinction between good society and civil society as does Andre Beteille (cf. Beteille 2001) nor does he exclude religion from the public sphere as did Jurgen Habermas until recently.[8] Bellah acknowledges that there has been violence[9] in the name of religion but religion cannot be expelled from civil society aprioristically; rather all concerned should shun violence which is not only physical but also epistemological (i.e., when one party condemns the knowledge system of another, for example, secularists condemning meditations of religions and vice versa) and take part in arguments as well as sharing of experiences in the public sphere.

Religion and Public Sphere in Quest for a Good Society: Overcoming Normative Poverty and Enriching Public Discourse

Bellah laments that the discourse on civil society and public sphere is not open to voices from religion. But public sphere should move beyond any absolutism, secular as well as religious, and ought to be a space for mutual learning and transformations. For Bellah, public sphere and public discourse become impoverished by excluding religious discourses on themes of contemporary concern. Bellah here draws our attention to important issues such as global poverty and global warming (cf. Bellah 2005a). On both the issues we have a lot to learn from religions. Bellah also draws our attention to both poverty in the US where 13 per cent of adults and 18 per cent of children live below poverty line and world poverty where 40 per cent of world population live below poverty line (ibid.: 24). For Bellah, this is a political, ethical and spiritual issue and discourse on it in the public sphere both locally as well as transnationally can learn a lot from religions especially from anger in religious traditions about production of and indifference to poverty and mindless pursuit of wealth and conspicuous consumption.

Starting with his own tradition, namely, the Biblical tradition, Bellah tells us that in this there is condemnation of and anger about structural poverty or what may be called "involuntary poverty". For Bellah, "The first thing we have to recognize about the biblical teaching about poverty is that there is a lot of anger there. Much poverty comes from the oppression of the poor and weak by rich and strong, and, according to the prophets, God detests that" (ibid.: 13). Secondly, the Bible tells us: "You cannot serve God and mammon" (Luke, 16: 13). The New Revised Standard Edition says, "You cannot serve God and wealth." For Bellah, "The rich are in danger of worshipping their riches, indeed of worshipping themselves" (2005a: 16). Thirdly, for Bellah, the Bible tells us that poverty is a blessing. And Bellah links it to the calling of voluntary poverty which resonates with the vision and practice of Gandhi. For Bellah, earlier voluntary poverty might have been confined to monasteries as exemplified in the vision and life of saints such as St Francis of Assissi but now we are all invited to live a life of voluntary poverty. To live a life of voluntary poverty is to live with what is needed and not to run after wealth. It also means to reduce our consumption including our consumption of energy. For Bellah, "[...] a life based economically on a sufficiency rather than the expectation of ever increasing income is, in today's world, a form of voluntary poverty" (ibid.: 31). "Thinking of a life based on sufficiency instead of wealth frees us up to take on all kinds of work that serves others, not just ourselves" (ibid.: 31). At the same time, a life of sufficiency does not just give us opportunity to serve others, it also gives us time and space to blossom ourselves. Bellah also links a life of voluntary poverty to the issue of creativity. For Bellah, "Genuine creativity requires leisure, which, in its original meaning, is not absence of work, but the possibility of a fulfilling form of life [...] a life of sufficiency, of, in modern times, voluntary poverty, might not only have the benefit of allowing one to undertake a life of service to others, it might also allow time for genuine creativity in art or thought or whatever field" (ibid.: 32).

Realization of Loss, Quest for Meaning and Critique of Society

Bellah has been interested in communities and search for meaning in religion, society and history but from the beginning of his personal and intellectual journey he has been painfully aware of the violence of totalizing communities and the fragility of human life and the existential loss with which we go through. Bellah lost his father at a young age and this personal loss corresponds to the loss of certitude that characterizes human life trajectory in general and loss of traditional certainty in transition of societies from traditional to post-traditional and modern ones. What Bellah (1970: xx–xxi; xix) had written in his moving introduction to *Beyond Belief: Essays on Religion in a Post-Traditional World* can help us in coming to terms with our own sense of loss as we are blown off our feet from many of our taken-for-granted assumptions and as we painfully go through loss as a result of violence committed in the name of religion and totalitarian certitude of many kinds in this troubled worlds of ours:

> It is a story of loss: the lost father, the lost religion, the lost ideology, the lost century. And it is not, finally, a story of existential despair [...] For the deepest truth I have discovered is that if one accepts the loss, if one gives up clinging to what is irreversibly gone, then nothing which is left is barren but enormously fruitful. Everything one has lost comes again out of the darkness, and one's relation to it is new – free and unclinging. But the richness of the nothing contains far more, it is the all possible, it is the spring of freedom [...]
>
> For me the search for wholeness from then on had to be made without totalism. A critical stance towards every society, ideology and religion was henceforth essential.

Bellah´s (1985) collaborative study, *Habits of the Heart: Individualism and Commitment in American Life*, had created a stirring in American sociology as well as public discourse. The subsequent collaborative study, *The Good Society* continued this normative and critical probing. For example, in *The Good Society*, Bellah and his colleagues tell us that contemporary American form of life minimizes seeking of any "larger moral meaning" and Americans have pushed the "logic of exploitation as far as it can go" (Bellah, et al., 1991: 43). Furthermore, "[...] the main line churches have done a lousy job in naming the suffering of middle class existence" – they do not say that it is the competition-driven existence which is a "form of human suffering" (ibid.: 210). In this context, they plead for a new paradigm for the actors and the institutions of the United States what they call the "pattern of cultivation". This paradigm of cultivation refers to the habit of paying attention to the needs of one another and building of communities. Attention is described here normatively which refers to pursuing goals, and relationships which give us meaning, and is different from 'distraction' and 'obsession'" (ibid.). For Bellah and associates, (1991: 273), "Attending means to concern ourselves with the larger meanings of things in the longer run, rather than with short-term pay offs. The pursuit of immediate pleasure, or the immediate pleasure is the essence of dislocation. A good society is one in which attention takes precedence over distraction." Bellah tells us during our conversations: "Both *Habits of the Heart* and *The Good Society* could not have been written without an outsider perspective." He further tells us about these two books during our conversation: "Our perspective is problematic because we are neither right nor left. The Right does not like our critique of the market. And, the Left does not appreciate our emphasis on community and does not realize that individualism is related to market. We get a sympathetic audience among the churches, above all from the politically active religious groups such as liberal Catholics." "On our part, we come from different backgrounds, for example, Ann Swidler [one of the co-authors] is Jewish but all of us are practising members of religious communities."

Both *Habits of the Heart* and *The Good Society* offer critiques of American society and this critique has become far more deepseated in the subsequent works of Bellah. Bellah is a critique of parochialism of American society in general and its recent imperial manifestation in particular. One evidence of this parochialism is that among the rich countries of the world the United States shares the least, only 0.15 per cent of its national income, for reduction of world poverty.[10] Bellah is a critic of recent tendency to an empire in some Americans. Bellah (2002: 6) writes in his essay, "What kind of empire?":

> We remain a profoundly provincial, monolingual nation. [...] when Bush visited Europe after taking office it was said that it was his first trip to that continent. It is not just his ignorance (which has played into the hands of the small cabal of foreign policy advisors that in fact makes the decisions) but his lack of interest in the rest of the world that is typical. Most Americans are not interested in the rest of the world and certainly don't know much about it.

Bellah's critique of American provincialism is linked to his critique of American radical individualism which draws on Protestantism. This weakens provisions for social support in the government as well as impoverishes solidarity in wider society.[11] For Bellah sociology is a critique of society as it is inspired by a passion for reconstruction what Bellah et al. (1991) in their study *The Good Society* had called a "hermeneutics of recovery." But for Bellah this hermeneutics of recovery is not only textual but also practical. In a recent paper, Bellah (2005a) makes a profound critique of tolerated poverty, income inequality and declining standards of quality public education, and lack of access to quality private education on the part of many in contemporary United States. Speaking of condition of life and society in contemporary United States Bellah says: "One segment of our population has the best education, health care and recreation in the world and another segment might as well be in an underdeveloped country. Life expectancy in many of our inner cities is lower than in Bangladesh" (ibid.: 26).[12] And he talks about condition of work in companies like Walmart in the following way:

> If you want to think about what life is like on the bottom look at the employees of Walmart, America's biggest corporation and largest employer. Work discipline at Walmart is almost like life in the gulag. Talking to a fellow employee about anything unrelated to work is called "stealing time" and is punished, only one of many such rules. You can say people couldn't get out of the gulag but they are free to leave Walmart. Yes they are and yes they do. Walmart has a yearly turnover of 50 per cent. For most corporations that would be a catastrophe, but for Walmart it is a price they are willing to pay if it keeps labour costs low. In a society where good jobs grow ever scarcer there will always be those who, in desperation, will work at Walmart – for awhile. Many of Walmart employees work at minimum wages with no health benefits. They overburden the health care system by having to resort to emergency rooms. Since they can't provide for their families on a minimum wage they need food stamps and other public benefits. So when you think you are buying cheap at Walmart, remember you are paying in taxes for those cheap prices. Walmart is a kind of state socialist enterprise that can only exist if there is a state to pick up the pieces it leaves behind (ibid.: 28).

Bellah had begun his sociological journey working on societies and cultures other than American. But he was drawn to American studies inadvertently being invited to write a paper on "Civil Religion in America" for a Daedalus conference on American religion in May 1966. This has been one of the classic papers of Bellah which had a major influence in understanding American religion, culture and politics. In this, Bellah has discussed the role played by the civil religion in

America, which is a "collection of beliefs, symbols, and rituals with respect to sacred things and institutionalized in a collectivity" (1970: 175). There is a belief in God but this is not a Christian God: "Though much is derived from Christianity, this religion is clearly not itself Christianity" (ibid.). For Bellah, American civil religion works autonomously in the interstices of state, civil society and religious communities without being absorbed by any. Besides, "The American civil religion was never anticlerical or militantly secular. Furthermore, it borrowed selectively from the religious tradition in such a way that the average American saw no conflict between the two" (ibid.: 180–181).

Bellah has not used the American civil religion for an idolatrous worship of American nationalism. Bellah shows us, despite attempts to make regressive use of it, that the civil religion in the America has helped Americans to move towards the side of dignified transformations in moments of trial. Bellah discusses two such epochal moments: American independence and civil war for abolition of slavery. In both these times of trial the American civil religion has inspired people to fight for independence and freedom and abolition of slavery. For Bellah, the third time of trial is the "problem of responsible action in a revolutionary world" (ibid.: 184) and in a globally interconnected world. Even forty years ago, Bellah with so much foresight had pleaded passionately for incorporation of responsible internationalism into the American civil religion hoping that the American civil religion will become part of a "new civil religion of the world" (ibid.: 186).[13] Bellah was a passionate critic of American war in Vietnam in the sixties as he is a trenchant critique of American war in Iraq. He used his discourse of civil religion to foster such a critical approach to American penchant for domination and for a responsible and peaceful relationship with the world. Towards the end of his essay on civil religion, Bellah asks some fundamental questions such as: Could there be a civil religion without God? Bellah refers here to the theological crisis of God but it is also an existential crisis and a crisis in existing representation of God as anthropocentric and patriarchal. Could we imagine and realize God not only as father but also as non-human and mother? Furthermore, Bellah himself writes that God in the American civil religion is "also on the austere side, much more related to order, law, and right than to salvation and love" (ibid.: 175). But this austere God is changing not only in shifting theological discourses but also in the work of Christian socio-religious movements, such as Habitat for Humanity which is building houses for the low-income people in the US and around the world inspired by the vision and work of a loving God (Giri 2002). Does the work of loving God in the American civil society transform the image of austere God in the American civil religion? Furthermore, how does the image of God in the American civil religion derived mainly from Protestantism meet the challenge of a multicultural God nourished by different visions and realizations of God in different religious and spiritual communities from within contemporary United States as well as from around the world? Building upon Bellah civil religions have to transform themselves to civil spiritualities where one may not utter the name of God as one is not overtly mentioning the name of Christ in civil religion (cf. Derrida 1998; Giri 2008d). This transformed civil religion as civil spirituality would have multiple relationships with God including agnostic and God as non-human and maternal. But Bellah may choose not to answer some of these questions directly as in our recent communication he wrote to me: "I stopped using the term 'civil religion' in the early 1980s because of too much of the discussion was about definition and too many people, in spite of my repeated argument to the contrary, regarded it as idolatrous worship of the state. In *Habits of the Heart* and *The Good Society* we do not use the term but talk about the same issues in terms of the Biblical tradition and civic republican tradition."

Some Critical Notes on Bellah's Sociology

The above pages in this chapter have presented us a glimpse of creative *oeuvre* of Bellah. This narrative presentation of the works of Bellah has also offered some critiques of his work in the journey of narration itself such as the need for simultaneous cultivation of the religious and the spiritual in Bellah's sociology. But it is helpful here to consolidate some of these critical notes as a prelude to further cooperative search on our part on some of these issues. The first is the issue of the relationship between the religious and the spiritual. As already discussed, there is need for Bellah for further self-critical work on this issue, for example, exploring the mutually transforming relationship between the religious and the spiritual. Bellah considers spiritual individualistic and lacking in community but it need not be the case. Bellah's work on religious evolution is insightful as he does not have a linear approach to evolution. At the same time, Bellah does not confront squarely the problem of violence with rise of what Karl Jaspers calls "Axial Age Religions from 800 BCE to 200 BCE", which includes such religions as Brahminical Hinduism, Buddhism, Judaism and Confucianism. To be fair to Bellah, Bellah does not consider the rise of Axial Age an unmixed bliss as he tells us that though its utopian vision "have motivated some of the noblest achievements of mankinds; they have also motivated some of the worst actions of human beings" (2008: 23). But Bellah does not inquires further how Axial Age Religions is predicated upon the annihilation of the creative spirituality of mother goddesses. Acknowledging this annihilation is crucial for creative evolution of humanity and reconciliation.

Bellah's substantive work on American society, especially his collaborative study, *Habits of the Heart,* has been critiqued as presenting middle class as bearer of genuine American culture (see Giri 1992). But, over the years, Bellah has reflected the pains, sufferings and broken aspirations of vulnerable working Americans as, for example, comparing the condition of workers in Walmart to Gulags. But, at the same time, there is an epochal need to rethink the role of middle class in strivings for a good society. Middle class occupies an important social space now and most of the time they are prisoners of consumerism and now many within this space are also part of fundamentalism mobilizations in religion and polity. But middle classes can also be part of what Korean sociologist Sang-Jin Han (2009) calls "middling grass-roots" embodying spiritual and political mobilization for justice, peace and ecology. In cultivating sociology as quest for a good society there is need to go beyond existing conceptualization of middle class and reconstitute it as part of a normatively animated "middling grass-roots," a project with which Bellah would be sympathetic.

Further critical reflections as part of a cooperative search relates to Bellah's approach of symbolic realism. But is this primarily an epistemological project or does it cultivate an appropriate ontology? Symbolic realism is not simply an epistemological practice; it also calls for appropriate ontological cultivation to understand the meaning of symbols, which is also part of an unfolding self-discovery on the part of self and society. It needs to be part of what I have called in chapter 1 an "ontological epistemology of participation". The approach of symbolic realism also needs to relate symbols to both individual and social action and can be profited by cross-cultural works and meditations on symbols as spaces of self and social realizations. A dialogue between symbolic realism of Bellah and critical realism of Roy Bhaskar could also be helpful, especially as Bhaskar's recent turns in critical realism has taken a spiritual turn seeking to explore non-duality and transcendence in everyday life and society (Bhaskar 2002).

Dynamic harmony is a key insight of Bellah emerging from his study of Japanese aesthetics. It is an integral part of quest for a good society, or in other words, a good society is characterized by a quest for dynamic harmony. If the quality of institutions is quite crucial in the vision and realization of good society (as it is in the just society of Rawls and decent society of Margalitt), then, the way institutions of society create a space for realization of dynamic harmony, rather than static harmony which perpetuates and justifies status quo, especially when it annihilates creativity and dignity in the life of self and society, becomes an important factor.

Dynamic harmony is an animated concern in many cultural and spiritual traditions of the world such as Kashmiri Saivism.[14] It must also be noted that harmony is a key concern in Confucian traditions though in societies and histories an authoritarian structuring of harmony (for example, as it is in patriarchal feudalism in China and other East Asian societies) has made harmony static. So the theme of harmony and dynamic harmony can be the starting point for further work in this field. Taking inspiration from Bellah we can explore dynamic harmony as an important part of quest for a good society in societies, histories and in our pathways to future but this calls for further work on the theme of dynamic harmony cultivating insights from Confucianism, Kashmiri Saivism and Buddhism together as part of a new planetary conversation in which sociology takes part. There is a tradition of quest for dynamic *sunyata* (emptiness) in Buddhism and it is important to understand its significance for realization of dynamic harmony. Dynamic emptiness helps us realize that "things and events are 'empty' in that they do not possess any immutable essence [...]" (Dalai Lama 2005: 49)[15] and an approach of symbolic realism must creatively emerge out of the transformative interpenetration of both dynamic emptiness and dynamic harmony. This quest also can be enriched by making dialogue with the strivings of seekers such as Sri Aurobindo who talks about dynamic unity as contrasted with unity as a fixed thing or a static state (see Das 2009b).

Bellah talks about holism without totalism which can inspire us to cultivate a new art of wholeness or which cultivates many holes in life, society and the world, rather than forcibly erases them. Bellah also talks about the need for integration, for example, between the cognitive and the emotional in our practice of understanding and realization of being. Though Bellah's quest for integration is not totalitarian, it is helpful here to clarify further pathways of integration in our striving for a good society. Is our discourse of integration one of strong integration or weak integration? The discourse of integration in sociology as well as in the wider public discourse in modernity, for example, in the discourse of nationalism and self, has been imprisoned in a logic of strong integration, which has been source of much violence, suffering and annihilation of potentiality. In this place we need to cultivate an art of weak integration where integration begins with realization of weakness and vulnerability and where this acknowledged vulnerability becomes the lubricant and binding thread for integration as an unfolding, evolving and emergent journey of realization of connectedness and wholeness animated by a transformative interepenetration of dynamic emptiness as well as dynamic harmony. The objective is not valorization of strength or mastery, especially over others, but realization of weakness as a companion to realize our common fate and emergent shared potentiality. Sociology as quest for a good society now needs to cultivate an art of weak integration building upon insights from critical theories of post-nationalism and developments, such as weak naturalism, weak nationalism, weak epistemology, weak ontology, weak theology and weak pedagogy.

Weak naturalism,[16] as a companion in quest for weak integration, helps us realize that we are part of nature but we are not determined by it and we should eschew the arrogance of human mastery and social control. This is accompanied by weak nationalism, which interrogates the construction of nation-state as a naturalized entity propagating the cult of unitary strength at the expense of the plurivocity of beings, societies, languages, nations and cultures. Weak epistemology in this journey makes our epistemic certainty humble and urges us to realize the limits of methods in our scientific understanding as well as social life. All these are accompanied by weak ontology, which urges us to realize that ontological cultivation is not only a cultivation of mastery of the self but also cultivation of its humility, fragility, weakness and servanthood facilitating blossoming of non-sovereignty and shared sovereignties (cf. Vattimo 1999). Weak theology as a companion in good society as quest for weak integration makes theology weak rather than strong which then facilitates border-crossing and dialogues between religions and theological systems. Weak theology is also facilitated by the rise of practical spirituality in religions, which relativize pronounced religious beliefs dogmas and lay stress on practice, especially transformative practice, to transform social suffering.[17] Finally, weak pedagogy helps us realize that if the project of realizing good society is a pedagogic one, then as educators we cannot perpetuate the logic of strength imposing our views on others, especially on children, and treating fellow participants and citizens as children, but persuade to take part in collective transformative co-learning where as educators we realize, as Sri Aurobindo challenges us to realize, that "nothing can be taught".

Coming Back to Our Conversations: Further Challenges

During our conversations, Bellah lamented the parochialism and narrowness of present-day sociology, especially American sociology, as it has little interest in other parts of the world. As he said: "It is also positivist and empiricist. The main stream of American sociology is not interested in our work." For Bellah,

American sociologists should have a much broader interest than just with the politically correct emphasis on race and gender. Bellah and his colleagues have drawn much inspiration from philosophically enriched sociologists, such as Jurgen Habermas or sociologically interested philosophers such as Alasdair MacIntyre and Charles Taylor, especially their work on significance of tradition, quest for values and self-realization. But it must be noted that in this company of philosophers and sociologists Bellah is probably the only seeker who knows spiritual quest, social history and cross-currents of transformation outside the Euro-American world personally. One does not find another Bellah with the sole inspiring exception of S.N. Eisenstadt after fifty years in Euro-American sociology who has done fieldwork outside the enchanting imperium and at the same time has raised so many significant contemporary issues about Euro-American modernity and the humanity at large.

On being asked about his current work, Bellah pointed to his long standing work on religious evolution. Bellah is now writing a book on the subject in which he is trying to show "[...] how genealogically the history of religion is singular, that all existing religions have developed out of common roots and have constantly intertwined ever since" (Bellah 2007: 9). Bellah, recognizes that "we are ultimately related, part of a single history, might, just might, if we give it enough effort, move us closer to mutual intelligibility, even toward a recognition that we are ultimately members of one another [...]without abandoning our indelible particularity, the fact that we are our history, we can move to a new history in which we see that those of other faiths are not as Other as the post-modernists like to claim, that we have much in common with them, that, in spite of all the differences, we are part of the same story, the human story" (ibid.: 9, 23).[18]

By the Way of Conclusion

Quest for a good society and realization of it is a multi-dimensional striving involving creative self-transformation, social criticism and institutional transformations. This chapter has presented a narrative presentation of this quest in the creative sociological works of Robert N. Bellah spanning over last half a century. Sociology as quest for a good society, building upon creative experiments in both institutions and mobilizations, right and good, is an epochal challenge before sociological imagination and practice and Bellah's work offers us many helpful insights as pathways as we are also challenged to take these further both theoretically and practically, for example, making these parts of multi-dimensional projects of realization of pluralism and a new art of wholeness and weak integration, which facilitates blossoming of beauty, dignity and dialogue in self and society, rather than annihilate it.

Notes

1. In a recent article though Bellah (2007: 16) tells us that the contingent nature of his own Christian identity:

> Indeed, I almost cringe when I use the term Christian for myself as I know that many, particularly on the Berkeley faculty, will instantly think that I agree with Pat Robertson or Jerry Falwell, whose views, theological as well as political, I in fact almost wholly reject. What I cannot reject is that I share a common history with them, we are variants of the same tradition, but then, I share a common history with all believers of all religions: we are all variants of one religious history of mankind.

2. Bellah sees grace working in society as well especially in the work of social action and social systems. In his own words,

   > Some of the systems theorists such as Parsons and Karl Deutsch have conceived of human action as multi-layered and open. Deutch, for example, has spoken of the propensity for all highly complex systems to break down, and has borrowed the theological term 'grace' to designate the indispensable but unpredictable situational conditions that seem to be necessary in order for any complex system to function at all (1970: 241).

3. On reading the first draft of this essay, Bellah commented on this point: "This is a normal feature of the student/teacher relation in East Asia. The Analects of Confucius contain many questions from students directed to Confucius and this practice continued in the tradition through all of its history." But here the issue is if the students could also challenge the teacher in the spirit of radical questioning of presuppositions of teachers. In Indian tradition and contemporary Indian socio-spiritual field, such radical questioning rarely takes place. This certainly calls for more comparative socio-historical reflection between practices of mutual radical questioning between students and teachers in different traditions of the world including between China and India, East Asia and South Asia.
4. Bellah here may take note that scholars and seekers in the path of Buddha have also realized and presented Buddha as a mother. Nalin Swaris, who shares such a perspective and realization, writes: "The Buddha took the metaphor of Mother Love to epitomize the noblest moral sentiment in his Teaching – *Maitriya* – Universal, Non Discriminating Friendliness towards all:

   > Just as a mother at the risk of her life watches over her own child, her only child, so also let every one cultivate a heart of boundless friendliness towards all beings. Cultivate goodwill towards all the world, a boundless heart of friendliness, above, and below and across, unhindered, without hatred, without enmity. Standing walking or sitting or lying, as long as one is awake, let one *maintain this mindfulness*. This way of living is the best in the world *(Maitriya Sutra)* (Swaris 2008: 1).

5. For Derrida (1998) those who speak of religion speak Latin authorizing themselves in the name of religion.
6. For Bellah (1970: 257), "The radical split between knowledge and commitment that exists in our culture and in our universities is not ultimately tenable. Differentiation has gone about as far as it can go. It is time for a new integration."
7. For Bellah, "To take the American case, freedom of speech and religious freedom were not simply the projects of Eighteenth Century leaders deeply influenced by Enlightenment philosophy, as the American founders certainly were, but by a public made up in significant part of dissenting Protestants, Quakers, but above all Baptists, who had suffered from religious establishments and were committed to ending them. Thus the disestablishment of religion in the early American republic was not the product of intense anti-clericalism (even though some of the founders were privately anti-clerical), but of an alliance of secular and religious

publics with a common end in view. As a result, no significant American religious group rejected the republic on religious grounds" (2005a: 7–8). This resonates with what Uberoi writes about the role of religious movements in the origin of secularism in Europe:

> If we divide the history of mankind into five periods, that is, the prehistoric, ancient, medieval, modern and post-modern, one can say that the history of civil society begins only when the institution of the sacred or the or the divine kingship begins to dissolve into two differentiated institutions at the dawn of the ancient, or at the very latest the medieval, period out of the past. [...] Even if this civil society was indeed the 'child of the modern world,' still it is the Christian society and its early modern reform that we may also have to consider, and not only the bourgeois society of modern capitalism. By this wider definition, the modern civil society was established or revived in Britain at any rate by the struggle of the Nonconformists, the new Christians, who together severed connection with the established Church of England when it accepted royal supremacy at the time of the Reformation [...] The new Christians wanted instead what we may call salvation through religion in society, with pluralist freedom of conscience and worship for all (Uberoi 2003: 115, 120).

8. In his essays, "Faith and Knowledge" (2003) and "Religion in the Public Sphere" (2006) as well as in his celebrated dialogue with Cardinal Joseph Ratzinger in 2004 Habermas argues for the need for complementary learning between insights from religious traditions and secular traditions. See Habermas (2003, 2006), Harrington (2007), Ratzinger and Habermas (2007).
9. Bellah writes:

> As a sociologist of religion I know that religions and spiritual traditions have often served mainly to reinforce commitment to the status quo: to quiet dissent, not to ask difficult questions. But I also know that it is from religious and spiritual communities that, time and again, there have arisen the great questioners, those who look beyond the taken for granted assumptions of their societies and consider them in the light of ultimate reality. Sometimes they have renounced their societies and sometimes they have denounced them. Probably the faithful need continually to move between renunciation and denunciation. But they do so in the full light of day. They demonstrate to the larger society their alternative realities by the way they live. The public sphere would be enormously impoverished without them. None of them have the sole answer, but perhaps together, and learning from each another, they can help move us from the impasse we have reached to a form of life that will be less destructive and more fulfilling for all life on our planet (2005a: 35).

10. Bellah writes about this in a recent paper:

> The UN report thinks that if the developed nations gave even 50 cents of every $100 of revenue, that could create a significant reduction in world poverty. That is 0.5 per cent (half of one per cent) of national revenue. A few rich countries are already giving that much and several more are getting close to it. But how much do you think the United States gives? When a poll asked Americans if we were giving too much, not enough, or just right to aid developing countries, a majority said we are giving too much. Then when asked to tell the pollster how much we do give, the estimate was 10 to 15 per cent of revenue! But in fact until recently it was 0.1 per cent (one-tenth of one per cent), until the Bush administration, under intense international pressure, raised it to 0.15 per cent, that is about a hundredth of what the American public thought we are spending. If nations had to show up at the last judgment as recounted in Matthew 25, would the US be with the sheep or with the goats? Can you imagine our leaders saying "Lord, when was it that we saw you

> hungry or naked or sick or in prison, and did not take care of you?" And not just the leaders. If the poll I quoted is accurate, most Americans don't know or don't care how little we are doing for those in need in the world (2005a: 19).

11. Bellah writes about it:

> [...] the weakness of public provision as an expression of social solidarity in the United States is not the result of a secularizing erosion of notions of common good, but, in part, of a religious tradition that never emphasized, except in moments of emergency, the common good, but which, on the whole, reinforced an individualistic ideology. Dissenting Protestantism was always suspicious of the state and emphasized the self-sufficiency of the saved and the prime necessity of individual salvation. The Christian symbol of the Body of Christ, so central in churches with a strong liturgical tradition, such as Roman Catholicism, was often marginal in Protestant thought. To the degree to which all religious groups in the United States have become Protestantized, the religious resource for solidarity has been weakened (2005a: 11).

12. About condition of public education in contemporary United States, Bellah tells us:

> Let me take an example close to home for any middle class American family: education. I came from a family of very moderate means and went all through primary and secondary education in the Los Angeles public schools, graduating from Los Angeles High School in 1945. I applied to only one college: Harvard, and was accepted with full scholarship or I could never have gone. In the first few months I was at sea compared to the prep school boys (there were only boys at Harvard then), but by the end of that year I was getting better grades than they were. My public high school preparation put me in a position to do very well at one of the best universities in the country in competition with those who had the best secondary education money could buy. In 1945 California was number one among all the states in its public education system. Today it is 46th or 47th, down there with Mississippi and Alabama.
>
> I'm not saying that it is impossible for a bright California high school graduate to go to a good college today, but it is surely much harder than in 1945. Let's think about why. It's not only the decline in the quality of our public education system. College education has become much more expensive than it used to be, partly because the cost of higher education has risen faster than inflation, but in significant part because both federal and state governments have reduced support for higher education dramatically in recent decades. Even good scholarships don't really cover the costs. So, many families of modest means don't even think of sending children to college, or at most to community college. For the past 20 years, college education for the lowest-income quartile has dropped by 12 per cent (2005a: 24–25).

13. With Fred Dallmayr (2001) we could add that such a civil religion strives for achieving our world rather than just achieving our country.
14. In this context, what Harish Deheja writes about the quest for dynamic harmony in Kashmir Saivism deserves our careful attention:

> Kashmir Saivism postulates that Parama Shiva contains the entire universe, pulsating within it, just as the seed of the mighty *nyagrodha* potentially contains the entire tree. At the immanent level, the transcendent *prakashavimarshamaya* splits into *prakasha* and *vimarsha*, Shiva and Shakti, *aham* and *idam*, I and this, subject and object, held together in pulsating, *dynamic harmony* [...] At every level there is differentiation into subject and object, *aham* and *idam*, but the differenti-

ation is based in, and unified by the non-duality of consciousness" (Deheja 2006: 422; emphasis added).

15. Dalai Lama urges us to realize the ethical implications of nurturing emptiness in our thought and practice elaborating Nagarjuna's work in this field:

    Nagarjuna believes that it is belief in intrinsic existence that sustains the basis for a self-perpetuating dysfunction in our engagement with the world and with our fellow sentient beings. By according intrinsic properties of attractiveness, we react to certain objects and events with deluded attachments, while towards others, to which we accord intrinsic properties of unattractiveness, we react with deluded aversion. [...] In the final analysis, for Nagarjuna, the theory of emptiness is not a question of mere conceptual understanding of reality. It has profound psychological and ethical implications (2005: 53).

16. Regarding weak naturalism, what Piet Strydom recently writes is helpful:

    By contrast with strong naturalism and anti-naturalism, weak naturalism allows two things at one and at the same time: ontological continuity between nature and socio-cultural life, within the framework of which an evolutionary explanation of the grounds of human sociality is certainly possible; and epistemological discontinuity according to which the socio-cultural world, without denying the interference of natural or biological factors and the need to take such restraints into account under certain conditions, must be studied in the irreducible pertaining to it as the special world in which social actors become involved (Strydom 2009: 2).

17. Weak theology is at works in movements such as Habitat for Humanity (cf. Giri 2002) and Swadhyaya (cf. Giri 2008a) where participants emphasize not so much belief or doctrinal content but the need for building homes and collective institutions of well-being. We can look at Bellah's project of beyond belief as also contributing to the art of weak theology.

18. Bellah's perspective on religion and our shared human journey finds a sympathetic echo in the following lines of Chitta Ranjan Das (2009), a great experimenter in education, literature and spiritual evolution from India:

    The historian Arnold Toynbee goes to remark that for a true and lasting peace, a religious revolution is an indispensable condition. By religion he means the overcoming of self-centredness, in the life of individuals as well as of communities. Martin Buber has in one of his writings appealed to us to meet the world with the fullness of our being and in this way only will we meet God. The expressions denote that the familiar meanings man has traditionally given to God and religion are fast changing. Religions with the entire world of their paraphernalia are gradually receding giving place to a new spiritual consciousness which we can describe as religious, but which may not be exclusively Hindu, Buddhistic or Christian. Temples, churches, synagogues and mosques are receding making room for a spiritual living as if God were right up here before us. [...] Half-Gods have to recede if God is to be very much visible here. Paul Tillich, the theologian, perhaps suggests something like that when he talks of the God above God.

    As our consciousness grows and expands, our concept of God has also to grow and expand. We are soon approaching an encounter where everybody's heritage will become also everyone else's heritage (ibid.: 16).

References

Bellah, Robert N. 1970. *Beyond Belief: Essays on Religion in a Post-Traditional World*. NY: Harper Row.

——. 1985 [1957]. *Tokugawa Religion*. Glencoe, NY: Free Press.

——. 2007. "Ethical Politics: Reality or Illusion?" *Daedalus*, Fall Issue: 59–69.

——. 2002. "What Kind of Empire." Manuscript.

——. 2003. *Imagining Japan: The Japanese Tradition and Its Modern Interpretation*. Berkeley: University of California Press.

——. 2005a. The Place of Religion in a Democratic Society. Pamphlet for Fetzer Institute

——. 2005b. Introduction to Bellah Reader from Duke University. But the citation is to Bellah's manuscript and not to the printed pages as I do not have access to this book here.

——. 2007. "All Religions are Cousins: Religions in Human Evolution." Text of a Lecture at Pacific School of Religion.

——. 2008. "Challenge of Secularism: Is God Absent?" Text of a lecture at University of Detroit Mercy, April 22.

Bellah, Robert et al., 1985. *Habits of the Heart*. Berkeley: University of California Press.

——. 2001. *The Good Society*. NY: Alfred A. Knof.

Beteille, Andre. 2001. "Civil Society and Good Society." *Sociological Bulletin* 50 (2): 286–307.

Bhaskar, Roy. 2002. *Reflections on Metareality*. Delhi: Sage.

——. 2008b. "The Heritage of Axial Age: Resumes or Burden?", paper presented at the Axial Age Conference, University of Erfurt, Germany.

Bocchi, G. and M. Ceruti. 2002. *The Narrative Universe*. Creskell, NJ: Hampton Press Inc.

Dalai Lama. 2005. *The Universe in a Single Atom: How Science and Spirituality Can Save Our World*. New York: Random House.

Dallmayr, Fred. 2001. *Achieving Our World: Towards a Global and Plural Democracy*. Lanham, MD: Rowman & Littlefield.

——. 2007. *In Search of Good Life: A Pedagogy for Our Troubled Times*. Lexington: University of Kentucky Press.

Deheja, Harsha V. 2006. "Kashmir Saivism: A Note." In Makarand Paranjape (ed.), *Abhinavagupta: Reconsiderations*, pp. 414–428. Delhi: Samvad India.

Das, Chitta Ranjan. 2009a. "Jesus Christ, White, Black or Yellow?." In *On the Side of Life: Perennial Affirmations*. Manuscript.

——. 2009b. *Se Prastharu E Prasthaku [From that Dimension to this]*. Bhubaneswar: Pathika Prakashani.

Derrida, Jacques. 1998. "Faith and Knowledge: Two Sources of 'Religion' at the Limits of Reason Alone." In Jacques Derrida and Giani Vattimo (eds.), *Religion*. Cambridge: Polity Press.

——. 2002. *Building in the Margins of Shacks: The Vision and Projects of Habitat for Humanity*. Delhi: Orient Longman.

——. 2006. "Creative Social Research: Rethinking Theories and Methods and the Calling of an Ontological Epistemology of Participation." *Dialectical Anthropology*.

——. 2008a. *Self-Development and Social Transformations? The Vision and Practice of the Self-Study Mobilization of Swadhyaya*. Jaipur: Rawat & Lanham, USA: Lexington Books.

——. 2008b. "Symbolic Anthropology of Clifford Geertz and Beyond." Ms.

——. 2008c. "Civil Society and the Calling of Self-Development." *Sociological Bulletin*.

——. 2008d. "The Calling of Practical Spirituality: Transformations in Science and Religion and New Dialogues on Self, Transcendence and Society." Madras Institute of Development Studies: Working Paper.

Giri, Ananta Kumar. 1992. "Genuine Culture, Middle Class and the American Project: Towards an Ethnographic Critique of Robert Bellah et al., *Habits of the Heart*." *Indian Anthropologist* 22 (1): 67–73.

Habermas, Jurgen. 1990. *Moral Consciousness and Communicative Action*. Cambridge, MA: The MIT Press.

——. 2003. "Faith and Knowledge." In his *The Future of Human Nature*, pp. 101–115. Cambridge: Polity Press.

——. 2006. "Religion in the Public Sphere." *European Journal of Philosophy* 14 (1).

Han, Sang-Jin. 2009. "Social Transformation in Contemporary Korea: Three Prime Movers in a Contested Civil Society." In *The Modern Prince and the Modern Sage: Transforming Power and Freedom*, Ananta Kumar Giri (ed.), pp. 222–248. Delhi: Sage.

Harrington, Austin. 2007. "Habermas and the 'Post-Secular Society." *European Journal of Social Theory* 10 (4): 543–560.

Lippmann, Walter. 1936. *The Good Society*. New York: Grosset & Dunlap.

Margalitt, Avishai. 1996. *The Decent Society*. Cambridge, MA: Harvard University Press.

Mohanty, Manoranjan. 1998. "Towards a Creative Theory of Social Transformation." In Manoranjan Mohanty and Partha N. Mukherjee (eds.), *People's Rights: Social Movements and the State in the Third World*, New Delhi: Sage Publications, pp. 9–26.

Ratzinger, Joseph and Jurgen Habermas. 2007. *The Dialectic of Secularism: On Reason and Religion*. San Francisco: Igniatius.

Sen, Amartya. 2009. *The Idea of Justice*. London: Allen Lane.

Smith, David. 2007. *Moving Towards Emmaus: Hope in a Time of Uncertainty*. London: SPCK.

Swaris, Nalin. 2008. "A Buddhist Perspective on Human Responsibility." Paper presented at the International Dialogue, "Uniting Responsibilities in a World of Rights," Bangalore, April 4–6.

Sri Aurobindo. 1970. *Life Divine*. Pondicherry: Sri Aurobindo Ashram.

Strydom, Piet. 2008. *New Horizons of Critical Theory: Triple Contingency and Collective Learning*. Delhi: Shipra.

——. 2009. "Contemporary Social and Political Theory: The Cognitive and Metacognitive Dimensions." Manuscript prepared for *Handbook of Social and*

Political Theory, Gerard Delanty and Stephen Turner (eds.), forthcoming from London: Routledge.

Uberoi, J.P.S. 1978. *Science and Culture*. Delhi: Oxford University Press.

——. 1984. *The Other Mind of Europe: Goethe as a Scientist*. Delhi: Oxford University Press.

——. 2003. "Civil Society." In Veena Das (ed.), *The Oxford India Companion to Sociology and Anthropology*, Delhi: Oxford University Press.

Vattimo, Giani. 1999. *Belief*. Cambridge: Polity Press.

8 Understanding 'Social' in Indian Traditions

The order of our social world is that of value-based norms arising ultimately from the idea of the person as the supreme value. The being or reality of person is in self-consciousness which contains within itself a tension between ideality and actuality. Correspondingly, the categories relevant to the comprehension of social reality can only be definitions of norms based upon value which itself truly apprehended in terms of self-enlightenment.

— G.C. Pande (1982), "The Nature of Social Categories"

To confine oneself to the individual alone is to not do justice to the notion of *purusartha*. The idea of *dharma* in traditional thought in India tries to consider the purusartha of society, but the very fact that it does not know how to deal with law and polity on the one hand, and *moksa* on the other, shows that it was not able to deal with the problem effectively. In fact, it did not formulate the idea of a collective *purusartha* without which the real problems of a plurality of *jivas* who are aware of each other for the realization of their own *purusarthas* cannot even be formulated, let alone understood.

— Daya Krishna (1996), *The Problematic and Conceptual Structure of Classical Indian Thought about Man, Society and Polity*, p. 149

An individual's capacity to make sense of the world [...] presupposes the existence of collective traditions; but individuals must be able to experiment with these collective traditions by being allowed to live at their limits.

— Veena Das (1995), *Critical Events: An Anthropological Perspective on Contemporary India*, p. 116

In the previous chapters we had fruitful dialogues with Goerge Herbert Mead, Jurgen Habermas, Sri Aurobindo, Robert Bellah and various other creative practitioners, such as Alain Touraine, Alberto Melucci and Chitta Ranjan Das and saw the way sociology can renew itself by embodying a new moral ecology and simultaneously embodying practical discourse and practical spirituality. In this chapter, we continue this engagement of deepening and broadening sociological imagination by exploring the concept of the social in Indian traditions by undertaking a dialogue with the seminal work of Govind Chandra Pande (1994), a creative interpreter of Indian tradition, *Bharatiya Samaj: Aitihasik aur Tattvik Vivecana* (Indian Society: Historical and Theoretical Reflections).

Pande has written enormously on many aspects of Indian tradition and has enriched our understanding of the wider questions of self, culture and spirituality. His *The Meaning and Process of Culture as Philosophy of History* is a significant contribution to thinking about culture as a spiritual quest (Pande 1989). In the present work, which consists of three lectures delivered at the G.B. Pant Social Science Institute, Allahabad, as part of its annual Govind Ballav Pant Memorial Lecture, Pande discusses the problem of thinking of society from the point of view of classical Indian tradition.

In his first lecture entitled, 'Abadharanatmaka Paripreksya,' Pande offers his critique of sociological reasoning. For him, there are two modes of social inquiry – the classical and the modern. While in all classical traditions, the knowledge of society is linked to philosophical and religious world views, in modernity this is part of science. The foundation of modern sociological knowledge is not 'sastric' text-based and transcendental but scientific. But Pande is quick to point out that modern sociology, claiming scientific status for itself, is not free from philosophical presuppositions. The basic principle of modern science is the presupposition that unconscious matter is the foundation of the world. Such a philosophy is also at the root of modern sociological thinking where the dynamics of consciousness, particularly self-consciousness, has been banished from the sociological conceptualization of society as an objective reality. Pande strives to correct this lopsidedness by bringing the perspective of Indian tradition to bear on our thinking.

For Pande, sociology deals with human beings and the knowledge of human life is linked to their *atmabodha* – self-knowledge – and, in fact, should be based on it. But, self in Pande's thinking is not merely a societal being or even a 'reflective self – a la Giddens (1991) – but a soul – soul which is primarily transcendental and divine. It seems closer to the Heideggerian *Dasein* (cf. Dallmayr 1993) and self in Charles Taylor's (1989) recent formulation. Pande would like sociology to be the study of the work of soul in the field called society. For Pande, soul is not a mere object of knowledge; it is also its subject. He makes clear that in a deeper sense, while being the subject of knowledge, it is also not totally subjective. It occupies an intermediary space between the subjective and objective dimension of the seeking of knowledge.

Pande argues that *'Atmanam Biddhi'* – know thyself – and *'Purusa Ebam Idam Sarvam'* – All this is *Purusha,* All this is God – are the basic principles of the classical approach to sociology. Pande gives primary significance to the knowledge of the soul in the study of society. For him, the awakened conscience is the key to self-knowledge and self-knowledge is the educational foundation of society. Pande argues that in a society it is important for human happiness that the opportunity for self-realization exists for individuals. He finds problems in modern sociology's reduction of self to external and physical determinants without paying attention to its inner dialectics.

Pande urges us to rethink the taken-for-granted belief in the virtue of social inquiry conducted on the model of science. Modern sociology, for him, is closer to science than religion on the ground that the claims of religions are contradictory, while those of science are not. But Pande argues that the existence of non-contradiction cannot be the starting point for any inquiry, if at all, it can be its ideal. "In so far as contradictions between propositions of a philosophical system are concerned, they are characteristics of all philosophies. If for this reason, we keep the spiritual philosophies outside the foundations of our social inquiry then we would also have to leave the scientific ones. But it is not possible for man to leave all philosophical presuppositions and lead one's life only in accordance with the principles of science". To take religious presuppositions seriously in the conduct of our social inquiry may make us feel that it would take us to the Middle Ages but for Pande whether faith is more important than science is not a matter of fact alone, it is also a matter of value. It is a matter of what he calls *drstimulak mulyavibyakti* or perspectival value-expressiveness.

Pande discusses the implication of taking the *atmabodh* or sense of self of human beings seriously in the study of society. Once we turn to the inner world of persons, the evidence of the external world becomes less helpful. Here, Pande builds upon the distinction between *Purusha* and *Prakriti* in the Indian tradition and argues that the Being of the *Purusha* – the soul of the person – is not governed by the objective and norm-governed *Prakriti*. It is governed by the autonomy of consciousness – a consciousness characterized by *swatantrata* (independence) and *atmarthata* (consciousness, conscious of its own significance). Pande admits that the study of society clearly means studying the observable action of individuals in the field of society but the transcendental world views, which inspire human beings are not a matter of direct observation.

For Pande, society is the world of human action; in his words, it is a *karmaloka*. But, the analysis of *karma* takes one on the one hand to study the aspired world of *purusarthas*[1] and on the other the nature of actors, what he calls *kartaka svarupa*. For Pande, understanding the nature of actors is possible only through self-investigation or *atmanusandhana* which can be of two kinds. One is an inquiry into the pure self – a self which is not dependent upon externally attributed identifications. The other is an inquiry into the dialectic between self as pure self and several attributed identities of society which work as a marker of self. Thus, Pande argues that sociology should be concerned with the study of the following four phenomena – self/soul, the attributes of self/soul, the world of action or *karma* and *purusartha*.

In his second chapter entitled, 'Bharatiya Samaj: Sadhana aur Bidhana', Pande argues that society consists of two intertwining streams – one is the stream of *sadhana* – creative quest – and the other is the stream of *bidhana* or regulation. Modern sociology gives primacy to the world of social regulation epitomized by the Durkheimian principle that society consists of coercive social facts of which individuals are bonded/bound bearers. Pande here urges us to realize the significance of *sadhana* in the constitution, functioning and transformation of societies. Recently, social inquiry has reoriented itself from the emphasis on structure to a focus on practice (Ortner 1984; Bourdieu 1977). But *sadhana* refers not merely to the logic of practice – a la Bourdieu; it refers to the world of ideal practice and a continued striving to realize this ideal in relationships. *Sadhana* is the practice of individuals, which is governed by an ideal vision of self and society. While transformation is outside the realm of modern sociological theory of practice, for example, as it is in the case of the work of Bourdieu (see Fox 1984), it is at the heart of *sadhana*. Pande argues that Indian society should not only be studied through the prism of its world of regulations, say the caste system, but also through its *sadhana* such as its spiritual movements. For Pande, the classical Indian culture is the foundation of Indian society and it is characterized by spirituality, tolerance and the influence of Sanskrit language.

For Pande, taking *sadhana* seriously in the study of society means that we would have to attend to the distinction between *sreya* and *preya* in human life. *Sreya* refers to the world of 'ought' while *preya* refers to the world of pleasure. While in modern sociology, *sreya* is the logical culmination of *preya*, in the traditional perspective, *sreya* has an autonomy of its own; it has a locus in the transcendental dimension of self, society and cosmos. Pande seems to suggest that *sreya* has a universal significance. But, how do individuals perceive *sreya* in their lives? Is *sreya* the same for different people? How do people struggle with their *preyas* as they seek for the realization of *sreya* and *preya*? Keeping in view the transformation in the discourse of desire at the contemporary juncture, can we also find *preya* in the *sreya* and *sreya* in the *preya*?[2]

Pande's writing suggests that *dharma* is a source of *sreya* in the life of individuals and society. He argues that *dharma* is not religion as it is conceived in the modern West. An Indian approach to the study of society emphasizes the need to take a *dharmic* view in our understanding of the 'social'. *Dharma* is a creative force in society; in fact, for Pande, it is a primary principle of creativity. *Dharma* is characterized by spiritual *sadhana*, the work of the saints and prophets; it refers to their world and their examples which express highest human possibility. Pande realizes that there is a gap between *dharma* and society in as much as, at a given point in history, the structure and functioning of an existent society does not embody the principle of *dharma*. Therefore, like *sadhana*, *dharma* provides a continuous challenge to a society's existing arrangement and structure. But Pande's uncritical adoration of *dharma* and his failure to realize the distinction between *dharma* and *adhyatma*[3] – religion and spirituality – does not make it clear whether *dharma* is constitutive of society as an ideal or it permeates its real social arrangements. Speaking of Indian society, Pande writes that in this *dharma* is both *niti* and *bidhi*; *svabhava* and *adarsa*; *guna* and *kriya*; system and justice. But, if *dharma* is both the law of the social system and principle of justice, then is there no contradiction between these dual locations and meanings of *dharma*?[4] Pande's explorations do not help us understand the contradiction between these multiple roles of *dharma* in the life of individual and society.

In this context, it must be mentioned that *dharmasankata* (dilemma of *dharma*) is an important aspect of traditional Indian thinking about *dharma*. In other words, what characterizes the calling of *dharma* is not simply a set of clear principles whose significance is unambiguous and universal but *dharmasankata*. As Daya Krishna argues, "[...] the deepest *dharmasankata* is between the conflicting claims of self-consciousness, at every level, to be different from that one is and the claims of others which one's consciousness is aware of all the time" (Daya Krishna 1996: 260). Following *dharma* means confronting a lot of dilemmas.[5] How does a society and an individual deal with such dilemmas? Is the option available at the level of self the same at the level of society? While at the societal level, we require reflexive structures which is the other name of institutions, to deal with the dilemmas arising out of the following of *dharma* at the individual level, we also require a critical reflexivity. But can societies as they exist promote such a critical reflexivity? Can traditional Indian society foster such a critical subjectivity? What kind of institutions can we build upon from the perspectives of classical tradition to cope with the challenge of *dharmasankata*?

Pande himself writes that if the problem with modern sociology is to study self-consciousness in terms of reference of a lower self, then, the problem with the classical/traditional perspective is to look at society through the idiom of rituals and not through the 'eternal sovereignty' of the Vedas.

Both this chapter as well as the succeeding chapter on tradition and change make some remarks about structure of Indian society, which helps us to understand Pande. Pande argues that in classical Indian society caste was conceived not primarily as a division of labour but as an expression of the distinction of *dharma*. Caste was supposedly a system for the exercise of *karmayoga* as it is not important what *karma* has been determined for whom but how one does it. But Pande himself writes that *karma* has been determined in the caste system; it is not an object of self-determination. Then, if the object of one's most important aspect of life, that is, *karma*, is not determined by self-consciousness, then, how does the free and pure self reconcile with such a system of determination? Inviting our attention to the Vedic times, Pande writes that even during that time, the Sudras were debarred only from reading the Vedas but they were free to read other texts. But, the very fact that the Sudras were debarred from reading the Vedas, which for Pande himself are the source of *dharma*, does it not pose any problem of incoherence to the seekers of *dharma*? It also poses the question of assault to the self-realization of the Sudras because of their lack of access to the Vedas? Did the Sudras have no soul in the Vedic times?

These chapters also bring to the fore Pande's dialogue with the ghost of Mandal. Pande resents the fact that castes today are the soldiers of political parties and argues: "the economic condition of the so-called backward castes is not a product of the caste system, rather a product of economic deprivation for which not caste but medieval feudalism and modern colonialism is responsible".

Pande also observes that the Arya in the Indian tradition has not been a category of racial meaning. Such a meaning of Arya is very new while its classical meaning refers to the one who is "sista, sajjana or dharmika", meaning cultivated, gentle and nurtured by *dharma*. Again, for Pande, this certainly was the case in the Vedic Age. Pande sees the ideals of Indian society realized in the Vedic Age. In the Vedic society, the Rishis constituted the frame of reference of society. They were living in the forests and the culture of the forest was considered the highest. Pande writes that in the Vedic society, people had an affirmative attitude to life. They were not characterized by the suffering pathos of the later-day renouncers. The fundamental mantra of their life was: "Isavasayam Sarvam Idam", that is, all this is Brahma, all this is God.

Pande argues that the role of woman in traditional Indian culture was that of a mother while in modern society it is that of worker. For Pande, the contemporary attempts to ameliorate the condition of women are in line with the perspective of tradition while the displacement of *dharmic sraddha* (love or reverence nurtured by *dharma*) from the collective styles of life is a systematic annihilation of it.

Pande's arguments to make self-knowledge the foundation of sociological knowledge is exciting but raises a number of questions. How is self-knowledge going to be the foundation of sociological knowledge? Pande suggests that this should be in both a constitutive and an objective sense. In a constitutive sense, it means that the self-knowledge of the subject of inquiry is an important factor in the study of society. But what are the processes by which self-knowledge of the student of society becomes sociological? Through a deeper knowledge of one's self – its transcendental dimension as well as interactive dimension – one can have illuminative knowledge about society. But knowledge of the transcendental universalism of self is not the same as that of its interactive universalism. Fields of social scientific inquiry such as anthropology and psychology have all along emphasized the significance of self-knowledge of the students of society and culture but have always invited us to understand the complexity of the problem and process of movement from one level to the other. Moreover, even in their critique of positivism, they have pointed to the significance of evidence (see Obeyesekere 1990). True in sociology, validity cannot be scientific and has to be interpretative but how do we establish the interpretative validity of our self-knowledge? How do we distinguish between self-knowledge and self-delusion?

In an objective sense, when sociological inquiry makes self-knowledge of human beings an important object of study, then, it certainly has a much more salutary significance. For instance, it can lead to a welcome emphasis on the narratives of the actors. And here Pande's insights are helpful. The *atmabodha* of persons cannot be understood only through an objective, manifest consciousness. A sociologist has to go down or up to the level of consciousness of the actors.[6] And, in this journey, an inquiry into the rational self-knowledge of actors is not enough.

The sense of self or self-knowledge of the actors is important for the sociological knowledge but what about their sense of the other? Studying the sense of the other or the other-regarding orientation of the actors is important since it is the capacity for otherness which constitutes society as a moral entity. As Swami Vivekananda tells us so forcefully: "The watchword of all well-being, of all moral good is not 'I' but 'thou'. Who cares whether there is a heaven or a hell, who cares if there is an unchangeable or not? Here is the world and it is full of misery. Go out into the world as Buddha did, and struggle to lessen it or die in the attempt" (1991: 353). But Pande's work on religion, spirituality, culture and society privileges self rather than other. Logically as well as contextually, there is no guarantee of one-to-one relationship between the two.

Of course, to be fair to Pande, it has to be noted that he does argue that the task of cultural realization is to overcome the distinction between the self and the non-self, the *atma* and the *anatma*, the self and the other. But, the dissolution of this distinction may not be a fact of life; in other words, we may not encounter our given self this way. Therefore, we need to pay special attention to the reality of the other and attend to its multifarious moral demands on the self. In this context, what Daya Krishna argues is significant. For Daya Krishna, even the Gita, which widens the notion of action and sees it in a 'social and even political context' seems to have completely forgotten that "action is, and ought to be, primarily concerned with others – their happiness, their freedom, their *abhyudaya* and *nisresaya*" (Daya Krishna 1996: 58). Furthermore, once we begin to "see the 'other' as a subject in his or her own right and capable of being affected by one's actions one will begin to see the self as 'responsible' to the 'other' and not just be concerned with the state of one's own being. Yajnavalkya's *atman*-centric analysis of the human situation and his contention that everything is dear for the sake of the self would, then, seem to result from a one-sided analysis" (ibid.: 58).

Working on the question and practice of inter-subjectivity can certainly help us mediate the relationship between the self and the other. But if the problem with modern sociology and even the critical theory of interlocutors such as Habermas is that it does not have a rich notion of inter-subjectivity (cf. Giri 1995), similar is also the case with scholars such as Pande. Pande argues that the soul is neither objective nor subjective but does not describe its nature in this space of mediation. Nor does he discuss the sociological implication of such a perspective on soul.

In his critique of sociological knowledge, Pande builds upon the distinction between *purusha* and *prakriti* in the Indian tradition. *Purusha* is self-conscious while *prakriti* is not. But this is an outmoded view of reality as the narrative of quantum physics now attests. In quantum physics, an all-pervading consciousness permeates reality, physical and social, and this can have radical implications for our conceptions of society (cf. Zohar and Marshall 1994). A quantum view of reality can help us break the hierarchic conception of society existing in the Indian tradition where the Brahmins are all *purushas* and Sudras are all *Prakriti*. Even contemporary social scientists seem to have gone a step ahead of the Advaita Vedantins as they urge us to overcome the distinction between the human and the natural in our conceptualization of relationships (see, Gulbenkian Commission 1995; Haraway 1990; Habermas 1990).

Coming to the existing social relationship in the Indian tradition as presented by Pande, one fails to see how one can defend the caste system in consideration of some esoteric notion of *dharma* or in the light of what supposedly existed in the Vedic times. Pande does not find it problematic that even in the Vedic times the Sudras were debarred from the reading of the Vedas. *Varnashrama Dharma*, for Pande, is the foundation of Indian society but as Daya Krishna argues: "The so-called *varnashrama dharma* is a misnomer as every *varna* is not entitled to all the *ashramas*" (Daya Krishna 1996: 60). "As is well known, the Sudras are not entitled to sannyasa and vanaprastha and presumably not to brahmacarya if it is interpreted in the technical sense of going to the guru and living in the gurukula after the upanayana of the yangyopavita ceremony" (ibid.: 61).

Purusartha is another important concept in Indian tradition with which Pande works and it has a wider significance. But, the four conventional *purusarthas* are drawn by the ideal of *moksa* – salvation. Usually, salvation has meant the salvation of the self and this does not necessarily mean the salvation of the world. The predominant significance of *moksa* as a *purusartha* has tended to obliterate the need for developing the capacity for otherness in other *purusarthas*. Daya Krishna (1996: 28) again helps us understand this: "from the perspective of *moksa, dharma* is seen not as an other-oriented consciousness or even as the fulfillment of categorical imperatives, but rather in terms of the effects it has on one's consciousness. The consciousness-centric perspective of *moksa* thus turns the 'other-centric' perspective of *dharma* completely around the discussion of one's consciousness. Thus, instead of being concerned with the consciousness and self-consciousness of others. [...] One begins to be concerned with the effects that actions have on one's own consciousnesses."

Finally, Pande argues that tolerance has been an essential ingredient of Indian culture and Islam has been an integral part of it. But Pande has maintained total silence over the demolition of the Babri Masjid, which took place one year after the delivery of these lectures and two years before their publication. What would be the response of traditional faith to such fundamentalist onslaught on society which paradoxically uses some of the elements of the same vocabulary, for instance as that of *sanatana dharma*, as Pande does?

Notes

1. The vision of *purusartha* in India tells us four goals of life: *dharma* (right conduct), *artha* (wealth), *kama* (desire) and *moksa* (salvation).
2. The pursuit of pleasure and the seeking of *sreya* or a noble desire may not be altogether different processes. In fact, in the journey of our self-development, the seeking of *sreya* can be pleasure-giving.
3. In this context, it is important to recall the arguments of Sri Aurobindo (1962) that because of their proximity to the structure of power, history is replete with examples where systems of religions have annihilated spirituality.
4. For understanding the disjunction between systemic law and principles of justice which uphold human dignity, see Unger (1987), Das (1995) and Giri (1996).
5. The same is true about the predicament of ethics today which is characterized by the persistence of ethical dilemmas. See, Giri (1994).
6. Such an approach is different from the interpretative approaches in contemporary anthropology, for instance, as in the work of Clifford Geertz. Geertz argues that understanding the form [...] of native's inner lives is more like grasping a proverb, catching an allusion, seeing a joke [...] than it is like achieving a communion" (quoted in Buraway 1991: 4). But Pande would like to emphasis the communion that takes place between two souls in conversations and anthropological interactions.

References

Bourdieu, Pierre. 1977. *The Outline of a Theory of Practice*, Cambridge: Cambridge University Press.

Buraway, Michael. 1991. *Ethnography Unbound: Power and Resistance in the Modern Metropolis*, Berkeley: University of California Press.

Dallmayr, Fred R. 1993. *The Other Heidegger*, Ithaca: Cornell University Press.

Das, Veena. 1995. *Critical Events: Anthropological Perspectives on Contemporary India*, Delhi: Oxford University Press.

Fox, Richard G. 1984. *The Lions of Punjab: The Making and Unmaking of Culture*, Berkeley: University of California Press.

Giddens, Anthony. 1991. *Modernity and Self-Identity: Self and Society in the Late Modern Age,* Cambridge: Polity Press.

Giri, Ananta Kumar. 1994. "Values, Ethics and Business: Challenges for Education and Management", Monograph prepared for Ravi Matthai Centre for Educational Innovations, Ahmedabad: Indian Institute of Management.

——. 1995. "Moral Consciousness and Communicative Action: From Discourse Ethics to Spiritual Transformation", Working Paper, Madras: Madras Institute of Development Studies.

——. 2002. "Well-Being of Institutions: Problematic Justice and the Challenge of Transformation", paper presented at the Silver Jubilee Seminar of Madras Institute of Development Studies, April 1996. This has been later published in *Sociological Bulletin* (1998) and also forms part of author's *Conversations and Transformations: Towards a New Ethics of Self and Society*, Lanham, MD: Lexington Books.

Gulbenkian Commission. 1995. Open the Social Sciences: Report of the Gulbenkian Commission on the Restructuring of Social Sciences, Lisbon.

Habermas, Jurgen. 1990. *Moral Consciousness and Communicative Action,* Cambridge: Polity Press.

Haraway, D. 1990. "A Manifesto for Cyborgs: Science, Technology and Socialist Feminism in the 1980s", in Linda J. Nicholson (ed.), *Feminism Postmodernism,* London: Routledge.

Krishna, Daya. 1996. *The Problematic and Conceptual Structure of Classical Indian Thought about Man, Society and Polity,* Delhi: Oxford University Press.

Obeyesekere, Gananath. 1990. *The Work of Culture: Symbolic Transformations in Psychoanaylist and Anthropology,* Chicago: The University of Chicago Press.

Ortner, Sherry. 1984. "Theory in Anthropology Since the Sixties", *Comparative Studies in Society and History.*

Pande, G.C. 1982. "On the Nature of Social Categories", in Ravinder Kumar (ed.), *Philosphical Categories and Social Reality,* Delhi: Allied Publishers.

——. 1989. *The meaning and Process of Culture as Philosophy of History,* Allahabad: Raka Prakashan.

——. 1994. *Bharatiya Samaj: Eitihashik Aur Tattwik Vivechan.* Delhi: National.

Sri Aurobindo. 1962. *The Human Cycles, The Ideal of Human Unity, War and Self-Determination,* Pondicherry: Sri Aurobindo Ashram.

Taylor, Charles. 1989. *Sources of the Self,* Cambridge, Mass: Harvard University Press.

Unger, Roberto M. 1987. *False Necessity: Anti-Necessitarian Social Theory in the Service of Radical Democracy,* Cambridge: Cambridge University Press.

Vivekananda, Swami. 1991. *The Complete Works of Swami Vivekananda,* Calcutta: Advaita Ashrama.

Zohar, Danah and Ian Marshall. 1994. *The Quantum Society: Mind, Physics and a New Social Vision,* London: Flamingo.

Appendix

Towards a Mutuality of Explorations and the Limits of Assertions: A Dialogue on Self, Society and the Other

> Ontology as a state of affairs can afford sleep. But love cannot sleep [...] Love is the incessant watching over of the other [...]
>
> — Emmanuel Levinas (1995), *Ethics of the Infinite,* p. 195

> Once the participants in dialogue have let go of clinging to their own points of view. the second stage begins – the resynthesis. People discover they can I listen to each other in a new way, that there is some common ground to be I discovered.
>
> — Donah Zohar and Ian Marshall (1994), *Quantum Society: Mind, Physics and the New Social Vision,* p. 237.

Review of any work is a work of dialogue. This dialogue begins with a description of the *weltanschauung* and the arguments of the author but in the process seeks to widen the universe of discourse. The act of criticism here has no axe to grind but seeks to explore the truths about the human condition in a spirit of mutuality where both the critic and the author are co-travellers. If the critic were to total subscribe to the foundational assumptions of the author then can an act of criticism lead to a widening of the universe of discourse and enable us to raise new questions and understand the multi-dimensional constitution of the object of discourse and the subject of meditation? At the same time, if in the name of critical encounter a critic superimposes his own beliefs on the text and the author then is an understanding possible in the first place? I believe that the task of criticism is to overcome the temptations of both and to pursue one's journey in a spirit of what Jurgen Habermas (1996) calls 'cooperative search for truth' in which both the critic and the author are fellow travellers. I have followed such an approach to criticism in my dialogue with Professor Govind Chandra Pande in his book, *Bharatiya Samaj: Eitihashik Aur Tattwik Vivechan.* Therefore, I am at pains to read Dr Badri Narayan Tewari's allegation about the massacre of meaning of the text that supposedly takes place in my review. It is certainly true that a text has multiple meanings and a reviewer focuses on some (because this is what is humanly possible) but that does not mean that this leads to a hierarchy of meanings nor their massacre.

To begin one's response with such charges unfortunately does not help in the further continuance of a dialogue. I am grateful to Tewari for writing a rejoinder to my essay but it would have been helpful if he had spent a little time in exploring the 'remaining and untouched aspects of the book' that he refers to and I have supposedly left out. It would also have been helpful if Tewari had tried to make a dialogue with my whole argument rather than the ones with which he disagrees. For example, Tewari differs with me on the issue of self-knowledge. I raise the question of self-delusion towards the end of a long paragraph in which I seek to understand a number of issues for making self-knowledge the foundation of sociological knowledge. as Professor Pande envisions. For facilitating the present conversation, I repeat these concerns:

> Pande's arguments to make self-knowledge the foundation of sociological knowledge is exciting but raises a number of questions. How self-knowledge is going to be the foundation of sociological knowledge? Pande suggests that this

> should be in both a constitutive and an objective sense. In a constitutive sense, it means that the self-knowledge of the subject of inquiry is an important factor in the study of society. But what are the processes by which self-knowledge of the student of society becomes sociological? Through a deeper knowledge of one's self – its transcendental dimension as well as interactive dimension – one can have illuminative knowledge about society. But knowledge of the transcendental universalism of self is not the same as that of its interactive universalism. Fields of social scientific inquiry such as anthropology and psychology have all along emphasized the significance of self-knowledge of the students of society and culture but have always invited us to understand the complexity of the problem and process of movement from one level to the other. Moreover, even in their critique of positivism, they have pointed to us the significance of evidence. True in sociology, validity cannot be scientific and has to be interpretative but how do we establish the interpretative validity of our self-knowledge? How do we distinguish between self-knowledge and self-delusion? (Giri 1997: 174–5).

It would have been helpful if Tewari had thought through all these issues. At the same time, his admittance that 'if self-knowledge is inconstant or fails to deliver one from suffering, it is reasonably suspect' can enable us to see beneath all the claims of self-knowledge.

But when we come to the next two paragraphs we are in the company of a lot of puzzles and unfortunately of assertions, too. Consider here the following lines of Tewari: "It must, however, be remembered that self-knowledge in its transcendental aspect differs from empirical and logical constructs". This itself suggests that the transcendental aspect of self-knowledge is only one aspect of it. What are its other aspects? It has been my argument that self has both a transcendental dimension as well as an interactive dimension. But how does the transcendental knowledge of the self relate to its interactive universe? This question remains unanswered and the following line again makes assertions but does not help us come to terms with this central question: "In so far as self-knowledge is transcendental, it is self-authenticating". This again makes clear that all self-knowledge is not transcendental. By Tewari's arguments, self-knowledge becomes self-authenticating when it is transcendental. But what happens to the problem of authenticity when self-knowledge is not transcendental? But even when transcendental, and granted that this self-knowledge is self-authenticating, how is this shared with others and perceived by others? One may consider one's knowledge self-authenticating but others may not consider it so. In such a situation, how do we go beyond the binding of ontology and meet the world on its own terms? The challenge of communication, sharing and mutual validation is integral to any knowledge and that is why I believe that an agenda of self-knowledge cannot be nonchalant about the question of validity. Of course, this validity, as I have argued in my essay, is not merely scientific but interpretative where the self and the other arrive at points of mutual validation through dialogue and deliberations.

Immediately after this line about 'self-authenticating knowledge', Tewari writes: "The interactive knowledge of self and other or knowledge of person as social objects is different from the transcendental knowledge ultimately presupposed in societal knowledge which directly is based on empirical self-consciousness". This sentence is based on a lot of unsubstantiated presuppositions and makes assertions which ought to be argued out and looked into closely. This suggests that the empirical knowledge of self and the other is different from the transcendental knowledge. It may be so but that does not free itself from the responsibility of relationship, i.e., the relationship between transcendental knowledge and empirical knowledge. Moreover, even for Tewari, 'empirical self-consciousness' is not insignificant since by his own admission societal knowledge is directly based on it. Moreover, the above line of Tewari suggests that in social knowledge, transcendental knowledge and empirical self-consciousness meet. But how do they meet? In what way they talk to each other and mutually transform? I was eagerly looking for help in coming to terms with this challenge while going through Pande's book. Instead of thinking through some of these issues which confront a reader, Tewari defends the positions with which he feels at home and further asserts that transcendental knowledge is presupposed in societal knowledge? How?

Frankly speaking, I am unable to understand what Tewari means by the 'magic circle of transcendental illusion'. Tewari writes with enviable certainty that "sociology as an empirical discipline cannot escape the magic circle of transcendental illusion" which should make any of us applaud him in these days of deconstruction. He looks at sociology in a formulated eye. Sociology and its kin anthropology are empirical disciplines and modern thought has to be grateful to these fields of inquiry for urging us to realize the significance of paying attention to the facts, empirical details and the configuration of human relationships as they exist and unfold in this world. Speculative philosophy certainly has its use but it is always enriching if it is combined with a dialogue with people's experience. Certainly the knowledge that is produced from such a dialogue with people and the facts of their living is not absolute and may not have the status of what Tewari calls but rarely defines 'transcendental knowledge' but for that matter such a knowledge does not become an illusion. Moreover, while sociology and anthropology are empirical pursuits they are not bereft of post-empirical philosophical and theoretical reflections. Both sociology and anthropology today consider it their vocation to be attentive to both facts and interpretations. In this context, what noted theoretical anthropologist Tim Ingold writes helps us to clarify the vocation of sociology and philosophy:

> If we study ourselves it is because we (men and women, adults and children) are all fellow travellers on this earth, and because we care about where we have come from and where we are going. In fieldwork we go to study with, or under, other people who become our guides and tutors. And we do so because the knowledge that these people can impart to us, sharpened as it is by their practical experience of everyday involvement in the world, can help us to reach a deeper and richer understanding of the human predicament. Philosophers, of course, have speculated on this predicament for centuries, and might even claim such activity as their special preserve. Rarely if ever, however, do they enlist the help of ordinary people in their enterprise, or test their insights against the wisdom of common sense. Anthropology is a kind of philosophy too, but it is not so exclusive. [...] *Anthropology is a Philosophy with the people in.*

And it is needless here to add that sociology is also philosophy with "people in." But for Tewari, it seems, 'the knowledge of the people is a matter of common sense and one does not need sociology in order to have a knowledge of "oneself" in relation to one's own tradition'. But is the knowledge of the continued relationship between the self and the other that self-evident? Moreover, the relationship between the self and the other does not include the face-to face interactions but many webs of relationships which bind one with the farthest on the globe and cosmos. Is all this knowledge evident? Even in the face-to-face interactions among people psychoanalysts tell us how enriched our relationship can be if we relate to each other with a measure of therapeutic touch and subtlety. This, of course, does not mean that we deride our common sense and make it subservient to the claimed professional expertise of sociology or psychology. What is certainly true is that at present the relationship between self and the other is full of much antagonism and hostility at all levels – from the personal to the impersonal. Students of sociology and anthropology believe that the pursuits of knowledge through their description of the dynamics of human relationships at work at different levels can enable participants to transcend their egos and see the world through a third eye, through the eye of the mid-point of relationships. It is to be noted that such a belief in the work of description to engender a critical reflective consciousness in us is emphatically stressed in our recent times by none other than a philosopher. Richard Rory tells in the very beginning of his *Contingency, Irony and Solidarity:* "Human Hearty is to be achieved not by enquiry but by imagination, the imaginative ability to describe our strangers, those who are different to me ourselves and to redescribe ourselves. This is task not for theory Jut for genres such as ethnography" (Rorty 1989: xvi).

Thus sociology is an invitation to understand the dynamics of life as it unfolds in the field of self, culture and society. It is not primarily concerned with prediction and we should only remember Max Weber who nearly a century ago had taught us that the primary vocation of sociology is understanding. The significance of sociological understanding lies in the fact that our everyday life may be full of conventions and may be islands of what Jurgen Habermas (1990) calls 'problematic justice'. Tewari believes that "the self and the other is given to everyman in his moral consciousness". Such a view takes for granted that the everyday consciousness of a person can be moral as well. When Guru Dronacarya sent the seeking Eklavya back to the jungle refusing him to teach, he might be operating within the realm of existing conventions but was his consciousness moral? It is a deeper reflection on what we take for granted as facts of everyday life that enables us to make a distinction between the conventional and the moral (Giri 1998a, 1998b). The significance of sociological seeking to understand life lies in its humble aspiration to contribute to the cultivation and growth of a post-conventional moral development in society where society is not sufficiently aware and wakeful towards its divine potentiality and possibilities. Such a sociological seeking contributes to an enriched self-understanding as well. As Anthony Giddens, a doyen of contemporary sociology, tells us, "As individuals all of us know a great deal about ourselves and about societies in which we live yet there are definite boundaries to such self-knowledge. People make many common sense judgments about themselves and others which turn out to be wrong, partial or ill-informed. Sociological research both helps us to identify the limitations of our social judgments and at the same time 'feed back' this context. [...] Sociology can provide self-enlightenment, increased self-understanding" (Giddens 1993: 17–18, 23). And closer to home, as Professor Andre Beteille, who has devoted a life-long career to the task of sociological understanding, tells us: "We must surely deplore the mystification of the simple through the display of technical virtuosity; but we must also recognize that common sense is not always successful, by its own unaided effort, in making complex things simple" (Beteille 1996: 2361).

It should be clear to the readers by now how unfortunate it is that Tewari should look at sociology as a child of imperialism. Apart from its lack of veracity at the contemporary juncture such an indictment raises wider questions about the way we carry our cross-disciplinary conversations. If two disciplines start throwing stones at each other from their walls of home-grown truths, then what is the possibility for creating a mid-point where both can stand and continue to learn from each other? In India, cross-disciplinary conversation.

From these wider issues of cross-disciplinary conversation, now let us come to Tewari's points about the self and the other. For Tewari, self-knowledge is not individual's knowledge of oneself. Then, what it is? I agree with Tewari that "the whole quest of self-knowledge is to move beyond the separateness of selves". But this quest did not make it redundant and irrelevant the continued fact of separation of selves at a given point of time. Tewari is certainly right that I begin with a plurality of selves but these selves, I also believe, are not egotistic monads (cf. Harvey 1996) but share a dimension of universality in their constitution of both particularity and plurality. In fact, this constitutive universality – as an ideal, value and a fact of life – makes connections possible. But I do not therefore subscribe to the 'ultimacy of their empirical particularity'. What I am interested to explore is the shared space that this plurality of selves inhabits and seeks to create. For me the empirical self is not ultimate, what is my ultimate concern is the ethics and aesthetics of relationships which touch both the ground of immanence and the sky of transcendence.

I also believe that by privileging either the self or the other we cannot adequately prepare ourselves for the calling of the ethics and aesthetics of relationships. In a recent essay "The Galling of an Ethics of Servanthood", I have discussed the problems that afflict us when we privilege the self as the Vedantins do and the other as the contemporary deconstructionists such as Jacques Derrida (see Giri 1998c). What I argue is that relationship requires dialogue between the self and the other and this I do not because as Tewari alludes "the goal of overcoming the distinction of self and other may not actually realizable". I turn to the other because in the name of overcoming the distinction between the self and be other, the self sought to swallow the other. As I have argued in my review essay on Professor Pande, I find it problematic that 'the only way to know other is through self-knowledge and empathy', as Tewari argues. In order to know the other one has to come out of oneself and touch the face of the other on her own terms. This, of course, does not mean absolutizing or reifying the other but to bend one's knee before the face of the other and to share her pain and be responsible for her growth (1995). This is crucial to a friendship and love between the self and the other and in leading an ethical life of what Emmanuel Levinas (1995: 195) calls 'permanent wakefulness'. I also turn to the other because the other does not vanish just because the Vedantins assume, believe and assert that the self is universal and all pervasive. It is true that the Vedantins speak of 'unitive self-consciousness' (cf. Chakraborty 1995), but this self-consciousness now has to probe the nature of this unity in the light of the movement of differentiation and the celebration of difference that has taken place in the course of evolution and history. The contemporary discursive movement of deconstruction as well as the socio-political movement of ongoing democratization have reiterated the significance of difference and now the Vedantic self has to come to terms with it instead of asserting its universality and transcendental knowledge. If the self is universal, then let its universality be demonstrated and embodied in webs of care and love rather than asserted.

The concluding comments of Tewari relate to my argument about Advaita Vedanta and Quantum Physics. He is right that I do not explore the pathways between Sankhya and Quantum Physics and this is an important criticism. Regarding my point out the equivalence about the distinction between Brahmana and Sudra and *Purusa* and *Prairiti*, I had made a metaphorical point but this is a metaphor which is so close to experience despite the recent movement of emancipation of the depressed castes. In my review essay I did not argue that Professor Pande defends current caste system. Nobody can defend it really! But the very fact that Sudras were debarred from reading the Vedas in the Vedic time is written by Professor Pande himself in the book under discussion. Professor Pande (p. 70) writes: 'Adhyana nishedhvi sudras ke like sirf Veda adhyan tha, na ki adhyana matraki [Insofar as exclusion from reading was concerned; the Sudras were only debarred from reading the Vedas, not from other kinds of Reading]. As I have already argued in my review essay, Professor Pande does not find it problematic that the Sudras were debarred from reading the Vedas even though they supposedly did not have any such restriction in reading other materials.[1]

Finally, about the demand of my description! As readers and Participants of a conversation, all of us have so much to learn from an engaging master interlocutor of our times such as Professor Pande. I do not have the audacity to take Professor Pande to task for his silence on the demolition of the Babri Masjid. But when the past[2] 'and the present so viciously flow into each other as it happens in contemporary India, Tewari's defensive reactions to my eagerness to learn about Professor Pande's public stance on this issue smacks of evasion of responsibility. When the fundamentalists are using the same language of Sanatana Dharma to kill human beings, destroy our places of worship and grab power for the sake of ego-aggrandizement then we can certainly expect our historians and philosophers to help us meet with these forces of destruction with the resources of a caring and responsible spirituality – a spirituality that is prepared to die for the sake of Truth and for the celebration of Life.

Notes

1. In this context, what Amartya Sen (1997: 33) writes deserves our careful attention:

    > When in the 11th century, the Arab-Iranian mathematician Alberuni came to India, and studied extensively Indian mathematics, astronomy, general sciences, linguistics and history, he already spoke of the real deprivation of "those castes who are not allowed to occupy themselves with science". That substantive deprivation remains largely untouched even today (after nearly a millennium), with half of the adult population of India (and nearly two-thirds of the adult women) still illiterate,

and there is very little evidence except in some specific regions, of a serious effort to bring education and science to the large mass of the citizens of India.

2. Here again, Amartya Sen's arguments are helpful:

> The interpretation of India's past cannot but be sensitive to the concerns of today. Our identities cannot be defined independently of our traditions and past, but this does not indicate a linear sequence whereby we interpret our past first, and then arrive at our identity, equipped to face contemporary issues. On the contrary, our reading of the past and understanding of the present are interdependent. [...] (Sen 1997: 35).

References

Beteille, Andre. 1996. 'Sociology and Common Sense', *Economic and Political Weekly*, 2361–2365.

Chakraborty, S.K. 1995. *Ethics in Management: Vedantic Perspectives*, Delhi: Oxford University Press.

Giddens, Anthony. 1993. *Sociology*, Cambridge: Polity Press.

Giri, Ananta Kumar. 1997. 'Understanding the "Social" through the "Indian" Tradition: The Ideal and the Real', *journal of Indian Council of Philosophical Research*, xiv (3): 169–78.

——. 1998a. *Global Transformations: Post modernity and Beyond*, Jaipur: Rawat Publications.

——. 1998b. 'Moral Consciousness and Communicative Action: From Discourse Ethics to Spiritual Transformations', *History of the Human Sciences*, 11 (3): 1–27.

——. 1998c. 'The Calling of an Ethics of Servanthood', *journal of Indian Council of Philosophy Research*, xvi.

——. 1998d. 'Transcending Disciplinary Boundaries: Creative Experiments and the Critique of Modernity', *Critique of Anthropology*, 18(4).

Habermas, Jurgen. 1990. *Moral Consciousness and Communicative Action*, Polity Press, Cambridge.

——. 1996. *Between Facts and Norms: Contributions towards a Discourse Theory of Law and Democracy*, Polity Press, Cambridge.

Harvey, David. 1996. *Justice, Nature and the Therapy of Difference*, Cambridge: Basil Blackwell.

Levinas, Emmanuel. 1995. "Ethics of the definite".

Rorty, Richard. 1989. *Contingency, Irony and Solidarity*, Cambridge: Cambridge University Press.

Sen, Amartya. 1997. 'On Interpreting India's Past', in Sugata Bose and Ayesha Jalal (eds.), *Nationalism, Democracy and Development: State and Politics in India*, Delhi: Oxford University Press, 10–35.

Simon, Herbert. 1992. 'Living in Interdisciplinary Space', in Michael Szenberg (ed.), *Eminent Economists: Their Life Philosophies*, New York: Cambridge University Press.

Zohar, Donah and Ian Marshall. 1994. *Quantum Society: Mind, Physics and the New Social Vision*, Londan: Flemingo.

9 Social Science Research in India

Call of Home and the World

[...] under a regime of pluralist non-dualism, all human differences and partitions are negotiable in civil society as a 'community of sovereignties' because no one reality or truth falsifies another. [...] In effect our common humanity thereby returns to the perennial fashion of the Hermetic tradition of Europe, and produces neither simple homogeneity (equality) nor heterogeneity (inequality) but a new non-dualist axis of correlation and mediation, correspondence and complementarity.

— J.P.S. Uberoi (2002), *The European Modernity: Truth, Science and Method*, p. 130

History may at best be a critical teacher who tells us how we ought *not* to do things. Of course, it can advise in this way only if we admit to ourselves that we have failed. In order to learn from history, we must not allow ourselves to push unsolved problems aside or repress them; we must remain open to critical experiences – otherwise we will not even perceive historical events as counter-evidence, *as proof of shattered expectations*

— Jurgen Habermas (1998), "Can We Learn from History?", p. 13

Ramachandra Guha's (2003) recent reflections on social science research in India raises a number of issues which call for further critical explorations. One of these is the issue of self and other and the conjoint calling of trying to understand and contribute towards transformation of both the home and the world. Guha writes at one place in his magisterial reflection: "My own hope is that in time the diaspora shall turn from its current absorption with the self towards the serious study of history and politics of the West. Or of other countries around the world" (ibid.: 1124). But should it be expected only of diasporic scholars? What about social scientists who are in India or even those who stayed behind? Are they destined only to collect data and study issues and problems confined within India? Don't they have a primary responsibility to understand and study issues and problems both in India and the world?

There is no disagreement with Guha's argument that the current hype about diasporic scholars from India are misplaced and should be put in proper perspective. Guha celebrates the tradition of social science research and publications that were built by the 1960s in India much before the global sweep of contemporary postcolonial intellectuals from India. But as much as we should celebrate this tradition is there any scope for critical self-reflection here? The social science research that was patiently cultivated in this period for which all of us concerned can only be profoundly grateful to the pioneers was preoccupied mostly with self, i.e., India and it had no interest even in its immediate environment in South and South-East Asia what to speak of carrying out fieldwork in Europe and the Americas. Thus, the other aspect of the story that Guha tells about is that this social science tradition that got built after independence was too parochial. Hardly any scholar worked on culture and society outside India. Guha writes about scholars from the US who have done outstanding empirical and theoretical work on India in history and anthropology. But how many social scientists from India have cared to work on cultures and societies outside India? Is this lack of engagement in the world not a gap in our scholarship and does it not affect our confident engagement with socially relevant problems at home?

It may be argued that fifty years ago we were busy building our home and it is too much to expect us to be engaged with the world. But in what way can we explain our lack of desire to study any other part of the world even now when we have such a huge social science infrastructure in this country? Many of us from India now go to all parts of the world as students and teachers but how many of us are interested in carrying out study of other cultures and societies? We have access to many networks and resources but are they ever used to fulfil the responsibility that Indian scholarship owes to the world? In India we accuse other scholars, especially from the West, of ethnocentrism but what needs critical self-reflection here is an entrenched parochial fixation in Indian scholarship. In India, many of us are proud of our long intellectual tradition. But what has been its contribution to the creation of basic and critical knowledge about – the other, the world? Huen-Tsang came on foot to India from China and wrote about it but how many "Brahmins" from India undertook a parallel walk and wrote about China? Now, many of our best students go to do their doctoral research in universities abroad but they invariably come back to India to do their field research. The hold of our parochial fixation dies hard even when we are studying abroad with possibilities to do fieldwork in Brazil, Africa, Thailand or Japan. We do not feel excited about the world. Here apart from the structure of parochial fixation in Indian intellectual tradition has the valorized yardstick of research relevant to India something to do with it?

There of course have been some outstanding exceptions who have carried out study on culture and societies in other parts of the world even though in some cases dealing with Indic issues there. We can remember here the pioneering work of J.P.S. Uberoi both in theoretical reflection and empirical work in Melanesia, Afghanistan and Europe, Satish Saberwal's work in Africa, Manoranjan Mohanty's work on China, Triloki Nath Pandey's work among the American Zuni's, Ravinder Jain's work in Malay plantations, Ratna Naidu's work in Malyasia, and most recently Mukulika Banerjee's work on the north-west frontier (Banerjee 2000; Mohanty 1978, 1992; Naidu 1980; Saberwal 1972, 1995; Uberoi 1959, 1978, 1984, 2002). Banerjee writes in her book, *The Pathan Unarmed: Opposition and Memory in the North West Frontier*: "The Delhi School of Economics turned down my research proposal on the grounds that it was unfeasible for an Indian to do prolonged fieldwork within such a strategically sensitive part of Pakistan and I therefore relocated to Oxford to begin my doctorate" (Banerjee 2000: 4). But, the same Indian from Oxford could carry out fieldwork there and write an outstanding book in history and ethnography. But, why could not Delhi School of Economics nurture such a work? It must be noted here that even after all the water that has flown in the Ganges and Thames, Guha considers Delhi School of Economics and Jawaharlal Nehru University as outstanding centres of social science research in India. But, are they also not islands of "shattered expectations" considered from the point of view of our responsibility to the world? How many students and scholars from these institutions have studied problems other than Indian? Banerjee could continue her project in Oxford but how many projects like her to study other societies and cultures have been nipped in the buds in these centres?

Both Delhi School of Economics and Jawaharlal Nehru University bring students and teachers from many parts of India but do they ever become interested to study a culture and society other their own not only outside India but also within it? Do their mentors ever challenge them to go beyond their parochial fixations? Do students in Delhi from Odisha become interested to study a problem in neighbouring Bengal or Andhra Pradesh? The same problem of parochial fixation which is camouflaged as loyalty to roots is compounded when we come to social science research in rest of India. Now scholars from some parts of India such as Bengal and Kerala have achieved remarkable prominence in both India and the world but how many of them are interested in language, culture and problems even in their neighbouring states? How many people from universities in Odisha work on Bengal what to speak of working in far off areas such as Kashmir and Meghalaya? Is it that difficult to send our students to do fieldwork to other parts of the country far from the place where our home is? The problem here is not at all one of resource but a lack of vision and total insensitivity to our responsibility of understanding the other and the world. We have an indispensable responsibility to understand our self and therefore all of us have a responsibility to work on our local issues and problems but does not this also call for an integrally linked engagement with the other and the world both empirically as well as theoretically?

One outstanding contribution of M.N. Srinivas in this regard is that he encouraged some of his best students to go to a region other than the ones from where they came. Thus, Andre Beteille, originally from Bengal came to Tamil Nadu to do his fieldwork, Anand Chakraborty from Andhra Pradesh came to Rajasthan, and Veena Das from Punjab ending herself studying the caste *puranas* of Gujarat. Though Srinivas did not send his students to Thailand or Burma, he did send them out of their native universes. But to what extent this outstanding legacy of Srinivas is being followed now? Do those of us who celebrate his legacy encourage our students to be at least sensitive to the need for doing fieldwork in another part of India? But, while Srinivas sent his students to other parts of the country, he himself worked only in his native Karnataka. As Srinivas himself writes: "As an anthropologist, I am somewhat of a maverick in that I study my own culture and not any distant Other" (Srinivas 1997: 1). Would it be too much a hubris here to ask to what extent Srinivas' confinement within his native culture and society impoverished the possibility of emergence of a truly pan-Indian vision of Indian sociology and anthropology which is open to the world? How Indian sociology and anthropology would have looked like if one of its founding fathers had also done fieldwork in a culture and society other than one's own?

To avoid misunderstanding, let me make clear that we have as much responsibility to do fieldwork at home as about other cultures and societies in the world. Anthropology is neither exclusively about the other nor solely about the self; it involves a dialectical engagement with both and a mutual reflection. But, the problem in Indian social science research has been that we suffer from a reverse Orientalism: We are too preoccupied with ourselves and have little opening and engagement with the world. And, the issue here, as Guha himself writes, is not one who stay behind versus those who go out in search of greener pastures. Guha writes that diasporic intellectuals do not represent India but those who are at home do they represent it? In Guha's words, "They have gone from being elites in their own society to being elites in North America" (Guha 2003: 1123). But what about those social scientists who stayed behind or are at home? Are they not elites in their own society? One critical consideration here is the language in which we write and the kind of universes we belong to. A majority of acclaimed social scientists in India write only in English but does it enrich or impoverish the nature of public discourse in India? There are some social science books written in regional languages but how many of them even find a mention what to speak of being reviewed in journals such as *Contributions to Indian Sociology* or even *Economic and Political Weekly*?

Guha writes: "a list of key texts and authors in India might begin with "Ambedkar, Beteille, (the) Constitution, Dharampal [...]" whereas the diasporic list may begin with 'Althusser, Bourdieu, Certeau, Derrida.' The point cannot be over-stressed: that one discourse is located firmly in the cultural and political milieu of the sub-continent, whereas the other discourse is deliberately distancing itself from that milieu" (ibid.: 1122). But can we too sure of our locations? Our locations and relationships even with people of our society suffer from what Habermas calls "islands of problematic justice" when we open our self-assured homes into processes of critical moral argumentations (Habermas 1990). The issue of language is one but pertinent here is also the question of lifestyle. How many social scientists in India would feel comfortable to sleep in the *verandahs* of *Adivasis* and Dalits on whom they write? On the other hand, though diasporic intellectuals may be using thinkers such as Derrida in a "distantiating way" (this needs more evidence) we in India are not bound by such a reading and we can make a creative dialogue between insights of thinkers such as Derrida, Habermas and Levinas with issues and themes in culture, society and history in the sub-continent. Guha presents these two lists as one of either or which precludes any possibility of learning.

Let us take the example of Derrida. Derrida has sensitized us to the work of difference what he calls "differance" which resists both spatial and temporal integration in self, culture and society and this has enormous potential to understand movements for self-assertion and dignity and also autonomy movements in many parts of India (see Khare 1984). In a recent essay of him on religion, Derrida writes: "[...] the world today speaks Latin (most often via Anglo-American) when it authorizes itself in the name of religion" (Derrida 1998: 27). This Derridean engagement with religion and at the same time a critique of authority claimed in the name of religion can provide significant insights in understanding spiritual movements in India history and critical dialogues on religion and secularism at present (Giri 2002b). The same could be said of many other thinkers whom Guha puts in two different tables. But the scholars from these two different tables are interacting among themselves. Consider here the interaction between Beteille's work and that of Bourdieu. Beteille himself writes that in his work on reproduction of inequality he found Bourdieu's pioneering prior work on social and cultural reproduction useful (Beteille 1991). Thus, the calling here is one of learning and this is not possible when we proceed with an aprioristic and self-confident judgment that "poststructuralism and cultural studies are trends of dubious intellectual worth" (Guha 2003: 1123). How can we be so sure about ourselves?

Creative social research everywhere, not only in India, needs an interpenetration between empirical research and theoretical reflection, fieldwork and philosophical engagement. But what has been our record here? Guha refers to elegant match between sophisticated theoretical inquiry and field materials in some of our social scientists. But what has been the nature of this theoretical enterprise? Has theoretical engagement in the work of these scholars been accompanied by a critical interrogation of presuppositions of modernist social theorists such as Weber and Durkheim? (I am not suggesting here that this should be the only criterion of judgment but it may be one of the ways of critically looking at our past and the present.) Has there been any dialogue between Weberian and Durkheimian presuppositions about power and solidarity with presuppositions about man, culture and society coming from India? For example, in *Bhagvad Gita*, it is written: "*Sradhha Maya Ayam Purusha Jo Jat Sraddha Sa Ebasa:* This Purusha [the human person] is characterized by sraddha – capacity for love and reverence – one is what one who loves or reveres." These lines also offer some presuppositions about self, culture and society. For a broadened understanding of culture and society should not there be a dialogue among such presuppositions? If we consider social theory as an engagement in such trans-cultural and trans-civilizational dialogue on self, culture and society, then what has been our record in India? Here, it may be helpful to invite a perspective of bracketing that phenomenologically-oriented philosophers talk about. While modernist social scientists in India have bracketed the presuppositions of Indian traditions, have they bracketed the presuppositions of theorists of Western modernity whose presuppositions many of them uncritically adore? To what extent their presuppositions can be considered universal even sociologically?

It is sad to note that there is an undercurrent of disdain for theory in Guha's reflections which reflects the nature of social science tradition that he celebrates. There is an unspoken assumption here that our main task is to do so-called socially relevant research and we should not busy ourselves with "abstract, theoretical issues". But theoretical issues do not vanish, they come back with a vengeance even if we wish them to evaporate. We may castigate Derrida and Foucault as just fashion but could the same critical observers castigate Weber, Durkheim and Parsons also as suffering from serious lack considered from the need for a dialogue between Indian and Western presuppositions about self and society? The task here is not of *a priori* rejection but creative, critical engagement.

But, because of a disdain for theoretical work in social science in India, there is no space for carrying out serious work in critical social theory even with an objective of a trans-civilizational dialogue or a trans-cultural exploration. If one is working on Habermas, or Foucault, or for that matter Derrida, then, which among the journals that Guha celebrates in his essay would accept even such a submission let alone publish it? Would *Contributions to Indian Sociology* publish a paper on critical social theory such as a trans-civilizational dialogue with Kant or Habermas? *Economic and Political Weekly* may consider this but it is a question of many ifs and buts and also a matter of luck. The fact of the matter is that there is no space for serious theoretical engagement in social science journals in India and here one is compelled to submit one's papers to the gate-keepers of social theory in the Euro-American world who are only too happy to throw you to the dustbin if you challenge their presuppositions. But, the key question is why a journal like *Contributions to Indian Sociology* be confined only to field-based research on India and why cannot it also be a vibrant space for theoretical issues? Is *American Journal of Sociology* or *European Journal of Sociology* confined only to empirical work on Europe and America? Moreover, does this almost near total lack of space for autonomous theoretical reflection in pages of a journal such as *Contributions* not reflect the colonial and neo-colonial mentality that in the West they would produce theory and here in India we shall do only fieldwork and produce data?

This disdain for theory seems to influence the way Guha refers to without naming the theoretical work in historiography done by scholars such as Dipesh Chakraborty (2000). To provincialize Europe Chakraborty makes a critical dialogue with Marx and Heidegger. The fact that Chakraborty could provincialize Europe only with dialogue with European thinkers and not even refer to seminal work of scholars such as J.P.S. Uberoi's work on Goethe and the hermetic tradition of Europe needs further critical scrutiny. But Guha's problem with Chakraborty is not this. His problem, it seems, is with Chakraborty's theoretical engagement itself. Guha probably would have been happy if Chakraborty had confined himself only to the problems of labourers in the jute mills of Calcutta and not be engaged with Heidegger. But, despite Heidegger's problem of brief Nazi association, the question about home and the world that Heidegger had raised is receiving a lot of critical attentions even from social scientists around the world. Consider here what David Harvey wrote nearly a decade ago in his book, *Justice, Nature and the Geography of Difference*: "Marx regards experience *within* the fetishism as authentic enough but superficial and misleading, while Heidegger views that the same world of commodity exchange and technological rationality is at the root of an inauthenticity in daily life which has to be repudiated. This common definition of the root of the problem (though specified as particularly capitalist by Marx and modernist – i.e., both capitalist and socialist – by Heidegger provides a common base from which to reconstruct a better understanding of place" (Harvey 1996: 315). In this context, the dialogue with Marx and Heidegger that Chakraborty initiates is a welcome move and can provide us new insights in our study of society and history in Europe and India. Social science research in India can profit from a dialogue with Heidegger, especially Heidegger's call to abandon our homes and be in a journey of homelessness around the world (Dallmayr 1993; Giri 2002a). It can urge us to leave our familiar homes in Coorg and Orissa and come back to our roots with a spirit of commitment and distantiation.

The need for overcoming our parochial fixations and combining theoretical reflection with empirical research is not just a pious hope; it is a functional necessity for revitalizing social science research in India in creative and critical ways. My point is that our lack of autonomous work on other cultures and theoretical reflections has impoverished the kind of social sciences we do in India even in the name of urgent social relevance. Think of how much different our understanding of Indian society would be if some of us had come to it with personal field experience in other cultures and societies such as the US, Brazil, South Africa, Thailand, Korea and Japan?

Thus, in coming to terms with the calling of creative social research, the issue is not only one of those who stay here and those who fly there. This is undoubtedly an important factor and we are grateful to Guha for raising this in such a provocative manner. But it is also true that all locations are problematic and those of us who are in India cannot be too confident that we relate to and represent people of India in a better way compared to those who stay abroad. In this context, what philosopher J.N. Mohanty writes in his autobiography *Between Two Worlds: East and West* may help us to understand the situation of diasporic scholars. At least it has helped me to come to terms with my personal sense of grief in seeing some of our most inspiring critical social scientists leaving the country in recent years. Mohanty is a distinguished philosopher of India and the world who after teaching for nearly two decades in West Bengal moved to the US in the early 70s. Writes Mohanty: "What was the reason for my immigration? Did I immigrate without reason? Any reason that I may give are likely to be afterthoughts. It was another of those historical accidents which have given shape to my life. [...] So I began a new phase of my life, a life cut off from my roots. But is not the very idea of 'root' questionable?" (Mohanty 2002: 79). The point here is not that we should read such an argument as a justification for abandoning our roots; it is rather where ever we belong our relationship with our roots have a problematic moral dimension about which we need to be aware of.

Mohanty did his doctorate in philosophy from Gottingen in Germany and after that spent a year in walking with Binoba Bhave. Mohanty quotes one of the sayings of Binoba from his padayatra: "In ancient India, the philosophers (who were also saints) traveled on foot all over the country, thereby educating not merely the elite but also the common folk. I look upon my *padayatra* or 'journey by foot, a modern way of following in their footsteps. I want to educate the common people in matters of ideas [...]" (ibid.: 59). Mohanty tells us how his participation in Binoba's *padayatra* gave him a new sense of philosophical vocation. This can also give us a new sense of sociological vocation. These days, many of our critical social scientists in India including Guha are telling us that social sciences ought to take part in public discourse and contribute to public enlightenment (see Chatterjee 2002). But if this is our normative ideal, then, all of us can only work more to realize this. Here, an understanding of the integral insufficiency of our rootedness and irrelevance is a prerequisite for a more responsible relationship with the people of our locales.

Mohanty has worked not only on Gandhi and Sri Aurobindo but also on Kant and Husserl. He is engaged with both home and the world and surely there are many social scientists in India who also embody a simultaneous sensitivity. The self-identity that Mohanty provides as a philosopher can also help us to broaden our self-identity as social scientists. As he tells us in his *Reason and Tradition in Indian Thought*.

> My tradition is constituted not by *sruti* alone but by all those texts with which I think: Plato, Kant, Hegel, to name a few. My tradition as an Indian philosopher needs then to represented as a series of concentric circles opening out to many other traditions, to the large conversation of mankind at the outermost fringes. This picture rehabilitates my self-understanding as being both an Indian philosopher and an universal thinker (Mohanty 1992).

Similarly, the challenge before us is to be a student of both India and the world in a spirit of concentric interpenetration, mutual interrogation and learning. Many of the pioneering social scientists in India have also embodied in their own way an aspiration to be an Indian scholar and universal thinker. Guha (2000) himself has done this in his engagements with environmental movements with both North and South. We can build on this fertile tradition and continue, broaden and deepen this simultaneous engagement with home and the world. But this calls for a radical interrogation of our presuppositions and transformation of our modes of being in the world.

References

Banerjee, Mukulika. 2000. *The Pathan Unarmed: Opposition and Memory in the North-West Frontier.* Oxford: Jame Curry.

Beteille, Andre. 1991. "The Reproduction of Inequality: Occupation, Caste and Family." *Contributions to Indian Sociology* (ns) 25 (1): 3–28.

Chatterjee, Partha. 2002. "Institutional Context of Social Science Research in South Asia." *Economic and Political Weekly,* August 31.

Chakraborty, Dipesh. 2000. *Provincializing Europe: Postcolonial Thought and Historical Difference.* Princeton: Princeton University Press.

Dallmayr, Fred. 1993. *The Other Heidegger.* Ithaca: Cornell University Press.

Das, Veena. 1993. "Sociological Research in India: The State of the Crisis." *Economic and Political Weekly,* June 5.

Derrida, Jacques. 1998. "Faith and Knowledge: Two Sources of 'Religion' at the Limits of Reason Alone." In *Religion,* (eds.) Jacques Derrida and Giani Vattimo, Cambridge: Polity Press.

Giri, Ananta Kumar. 2002a. "Transcending Disciplinary Boundaries: Creative Experiments and Critiques of Modernity." In *Conversations and Transformations: Towards a New Ethics of Self and Society.* Lanham, MD: Lexington Books.

——. 2002b. "Spiritual Cultivation for a Secular Society." Madras Institute of Development Studies: Working Paper.

Guha, Ramachanda. 2000. *Environmentalism: A Global History.* New York: Longman.

——. 2003. "The Ones Who Stayed Behind." *Economic and Political Weekly,* March 22.

Habermas, Jurgen. 1990. *Moral Consciousness and Communicative Action.* Cambridge: Polity Press.

——. 1998. "Can We Learn from History?" In *The Berlin Republic.* Cambridge: Polity Press.

Harvey, David. 1996. *Justice, Nature and the Geography of Difference.* Cambridge, MA: Basil Blackwell.

Khare, Ravinder. 1984. *The Untouchable as Himself.* Cambridge: Cambridge University Press.

Mohanty, J.N. 1992. *Reason and Tradition in Indian Thought.* Delhi: Oxford University Press.

——. 2002. *Between Two Worlds: East and West.* Delhi: Oxford University Press.

Mohanty, Manoranjan. 1978. *The Political Philosophy of Mao Tse-Tung.* Delhi: Macmillan.

——. 1992. (ed.) *Chinese Revolution: Comparative Perspectives on Transformation of Non-Western Societies.* Delhi: Ajanta.

Naidu, Ratna. 1980. *The Communal Edge to Plural Societies: India and Malaysia.* Delhi: Vikash.

Saberwal, Satish. 1972. *Embu of Kenya.* New Haven: Human Relations Area File.

——. 1995. *Wages of Segmentation: Comparative Historical Studies on Europe and India.* New Delhi: Orient Longman.

Srinivas, M.N. 1997. "Practicing Social Anthropology in India." *Annual Review of Anthropology* 26: 1–24.

Uberoi, J.P.S. 1959. *Politics of the Kula Ring.* Manchester: Manchester University Press.

——. 1978. *Science and Culture.* Delhi: Oxford University Press.

——. 1984. *The Other Mind of Europe: Goethe as a Scientist.* Delhi: Oxford University Press.

——. 2002. *The European Modernity: Truth, Science and Method.* Delhi: Oxford University Press.

Appendix One

Building a Community of Discourse in Sociology in India

In her provocative article "Sociological Research in India: The State of Crisis" Veena Das (2003) has raised some important questions regarding the practice of sociological research in India. One cannot disagree with Das' description of the lack of competence in sociological research in India today. Her plea for restoring "a dignity to dull, honest, plodding research" calls for critical reflection and creative response from all of us who are concerned with the problem.

Das is keen to pursue such research and "build up a critical mass of empirical data" within "the accepted paradigms of a discipline" (Das 1993: 1161). But what are the accepted paradigms of the sociological discipline in India? Over the last 70 years of practice of sociology in India have we really cared to create a curriculum of sociology and anthropology in India which takes seriously our own cultural predicament and the Indian point of view? Das finds it alarming that many students whom she has interviewed have forgotten where Malinowski did his fieldwork. But, is it not equally alarming that some of the thoughtful interpreters of the human condition from within the Indian tradition, such as Gandhi, Sri Aurobindo and Tagore, do not find a place in the sociological curriculum of even the centres of advanced study in our country? Das takes for granted the discursive field of sociology in India. But, apart from the lack of competence in the average research scholar that she points to, the real crisis of Indian sociology continues to lie in the fact that it is a colonial and metropolitan implant. Our curriculum is flooded with material coming from the West. If one is teaching religion in a department of sociology, then, why should one teach only Emile Durkheim's *Elementary Forms of Religious Life*? Why, for instance, is a student not also taught Sri Aurobindo's *Life Divine?* If one is teaching theories of culture and society, then, why should only Giddens and Geertz steal the show? In our curriculum, does a scholar such as Govind Chandra Pande find a place?

In fact, when one reads carefully Das' text, he/she is pained to discover that an uncritical metropolitanism permeates her thinking and vision. There is no denying that an efficient knowledge of English is a must for the practice of sociological research in India. But, is it also not true that competence in one's own mother tongue and several Indian languages is a must for carrying out research in India and understanding our culture? Actually, our problem is that we are more interested in reading and writing in English than in the Indian languages. Writing in English provides us a quick access to a global audience and brings laurels for us. It also provides us access to national and international publishers. We hardly write in our mother languages. But, if we do not publish in our own mother languages, then, how are we going to communicate the perspective gathered from empirical research to the people of our land? In any critical reflection on research the question 'knowledge for what?' cannot be altogether avoided in the name of competence or keeping off populism. As practitioners of sociology, we must widen our audience by writing in one or several Indian languages. We must not forget the fact that we are teaching and carrying out research in India, not in the US or England. It is very much possible to write efficiently in both one's mother language and in English and this I consider to be a national task. But Das seems to be prejudiced against writing dissertations in the Indian languages. One agrees with her that "sociological works in the regional languages nor regional contributions add up to a sufficient body of literature" (ibid.: 1160). But, instead of trying to remedy this situation by encouraging us to read and write in one or several Indian languages, Das ends up only with a plea for English.

This metropolitanism gets in the way of our being enriched by the work that is produced in India. The problem with the practice of sociology in India is that we have hardly cared to build up a community of discourse. A community of discourse requires egoless interaction and communication among those who think they belong to it by either professional role playing or choice. But our egoism whipped up by our metropolitanism does not make us interested in the work of fellow research scholars of our land. We hardly care to know about the work that is produced in the social science departments across the country. Das remarks that only five or six departments are competent to guide research scholars, but what kind of a community of discourse are we to create with such a bent of mind? If a majority of departments lack in competence, then, the challenge is to better the situation rather than withdraw support from these. Instead, if only five or six departments thrive it would further accentuate the alienation of Indian sociology by confining it to the language and reality of the metropolis.

Das also draws our attention to the problems of sub-standard publications and plagiarism in India. This is a problem and we must face it squarely. But here we must also realize that the problem is not merely that of sub-standard publications but lack of publications. As members of the academic community in India, a majority of us do not have the urge to publish. Therefore, even when scholars publish in their university or departmental journals they should be read with care rather than ignored because of our a priori biases. Utkal University's department of anthropology produces an annual journal, *Man in Society.* But how many in India know about it? On the other hand, we are mostly acquainted with such departmental journals as *Cambridge Anthropology.* Even ill-papers published in journals such as *Mm in Society* do not compare favourably with those published in *Cambridge Anthropology,* we have a duty to read the former because they are written by scholars in our country. Without such care and humility born out of one's commitment in building a community of discourse in India, the prospects for sociology in India are going to be gloomy. Das gives more importance to publication in rèferred journals than elsewhere. There is no denying that refereed journals demand more professional competence from the authors. But we cannot decide a priori about the quality and competence of articles published in either referred or non-referred journals. As there are very few professional journals of sociology in India, we must welcome young scholars publishing in any forum they get and look for the best in them in unknown places.

Das is worried that "there may not be a next generation" for sociology in India which has been nourished by "such eminent scholars as Radhakamal Mukherjee, G.S. Ghurye, N.K. Bose, D.N. Mazumdar and M.N. Srinivas" (ibid.: 1161). But the next generation has to be prepared, it will not fall from the air. The problem in contemporary India is that institutions are so little concerned about their own survival and reproduction by being open to and welcoming of the young who are going to join them. In fact, the youth in India face a problem of institutional closure. Positions lie vacant in universities and institutions of research for ages without being filled up. When there is call for interview, in 99 per cent of the cases, especially the first timers, candidates are not provided any support for travel and stay. Both the experts and the interviewees are called for the same purpose, but while the experts are taken care of by the universities, the poor students are left to the streets. The experts are men and women of means, while the students might have borrowed their bare travel money by mortgaging their mother's bangle. Is such a treatment fair? With such a framework for the meeting of generations, what kind of inter-generational solidarity can we expect?

Das describes her disappointing experience in interviews. But she does not subject the existing framework of recruitment to critical scrutiny. First of all, is the prevalent mode of recruitment through a haphazard interview the best way of getting the most efficient scholars into our academic institutions? What can the experts find out in a mere 15–20 minutes? As an alternative, we could have a two-tiered process of selection. An interview with experts can lead to a short-listing of candidates, who then should make presentations to an audience of students, teachers and concerned citizens. This is a better mechanism of recruiting the best than the prevalent method of interviewing where an expert sometimes does not care to read the whole of a paper written by a student and presented before the board but asks about some author cited in the text. A commutative interaction requires fairness from all sides and an interviewee should not be given the impression that he or she is being asked questions out of context.

Das refers to the Indian Sociological Society in her essay. She wants this body to prepare a report on the state of the crisis that she highlights. It has not had its annual convention for years.[1] It also seems that it has not been able to involve the majority of practising sociologists in India its work. We, interested sociologists in India who want to interact with our colleagues, do not have any platform for interaction and exchange of ideas. This is tragic and unfortunate. Without regular annual meetings of our supposedly provisional bodies, such as the Indian Sociological Society, we continue to live within our own particular oases and have opportunity for interacting with fellow scholars which could transform our taken-for-granted assumptions about the self and the other. The plight of Indian Sociological Society heightens the urgency to build functioning professional bodies, which would have an all-India character and not simply be metropolitan in their composition and ethos. It also underscores the importance of building a community of discourse in India where we give as much importance to good work coming from Coimbatore as we give to that coming from Cambridge. But, in building such a community of discourse, the problem of egoism, though less visible, is far more threatening than the problem of invidious politics.

Appendix Two

Reconstructing Social Sciences: Burdens of the Past, the Stagnation of the Present and the Challenges of the Future*

The 1996 Annual Meeting of the Heads of Departments of Universities in South India was held at the Madras Institute of Development Studies (MIDS) on January 31, 1997. The theme of the meeting was "Reconstructing Social Sciences". The theme paper was presented by Professor Narasimha Reddy of University of Hyderabad. In his paper, Reddy presented a critical account of the report *Open the Social Sciences*, commissioned by the Gulbenkian Foundation of Spain and authored by the distinguished American sociologist Immanuel Wallerstein and nine other eminent scholars from different disciplines. Reddy presented the main arguments of the report and pleaded that these arguments have a lot of relevance for the predicament in which social science and social scientists are in India (for a detailed description of the report, please see Reddy's review of it in *Review of Development and Change* 1 (2): 277–85, July-December 1996). Some of the insights from the report that Reddy specially focused on are:

(a) Modern social science disciplines have emerged in the context of the Newtonian revolution in science and formation of nation-states in politics.

---

*This is the excerpt from a report of a workshop prepared by the author and published in *Review of Development and Change* 3 (1), Jan-June, 1998. It is presented here with a hope that the readers would find deliberations presented here of interest.

Now social scientists have to go beyond both these legacies in order to make themselves relevant to the needs of the present and prepare for the future;

(b) Social sciences have to be much more historical; and

(c) There should be new structures in the institutions of knowledge for the pursuit of interdisciplinary and cross-disciplinary research. Members of the faculty should have joint appointments in two departments and graduate students should have compulsory training in two disciplines.

While supporting the overall arguments of the report, Reddy nonetheless raised some critical questions. Reddy considered it a crucial gap in the report that it does not demystify the ideological biases, fixations and preoccupations of modern social sciences – their class and other interest biases. Reddy further argued that there is an "overwhelming impression that emerges out of the Report that all is well with social sciences and that disciplines are capable of evolving into creative endeavors responding to the emerging challenges". Reddy pleaded that social sciences are in a deep crises heightened by the present processes of globalization and structural adjustment; in this context, it is not enough just to open the social sciences but to ask what are the social and ideological foundations of the social sciences which are opened and in which direction they are to be opened.

Reddy's presentations and posers led to an enriching discussion on these issues. Warming up the ground, Professor C.T. Kurien (MIDS), who chaired the morning session, asked whether the basic problem with social sciences lie in their imitation of natural sciences. Kurien, in this context, reiterated the centrality of Newtonian mechanics to modern consciousness and ways of understanding reality. Professor Paul Appaswamy (MIDS) joined the debate by arguing that though the Newtonian model is faced with problems, what is still relevant in it is the search for and promise of order. Newtonian logic has enabled social sciences to order the realities studied and this, for Appaswamy, has a continued relevance even in the contemporary context. Other participants urged us to understand and interrogate this quest for order as well as ordering. Here, both Drs. Manikumar (M.S. University, Tirunelveli) and M.S.S. Pandian (MIDS) pointed to the problem in social sciences proceeding with natural sciences as their role models. Pandian particularly took issue with the reluctance in the community of scholars as well as citizens to interrogate the ideological foundations and biases of natural as well as social sciences. Giving the examples of what he thought three important critiques of modern enlightenment – Marxian critique of fetishism of commodities, Freudian critique of unconscious and the post-structuralist critique of society and history – Pandian argued that what we find in these instances is that freeing oneself from the claims to science has opened up new possibilities.

These arguments about criticism of science in the modern discourse led to further explorations and contestations. Professor A. Vaidyanathan (MIDS) argued that while being enthusiastic about these critiques of science, the question still remains how and why these critiques continue to remain marginal. For Vaidyanathan, it is because the marginal movements do not open up a space for a common platform for the "mainstream" and the "marginal". Vaidyanathan argued that it should be an integral part of any criticism to formulate a common rule for discourse. Vaidyanathan also argued that though social sciences have dealt with a world of complexity, which is not amenable to a law-governed understanding, still they have been able to pursue their inquiries with rigour and in the name of criticism of the mainstream, this rigour should neither be scoffed at nor sacrificed. Responding to these posers, Pandian argued that the criticisms of the "mainstream" have remained marginal not for their faults; rather, they have been marginalized. At this point, Kurien joined the deliberations and discussed the role of institutions of knowledge in maintaining the status quo of the mainstream. Kurien also argued that while finding problems with social science disciplines, we should not think that we can do away with the frames of disciplines. Disciplines provide very important vantage points for looking at reality and in the name of criticisms of science these vantage points should not be sacrificed.

Towards the end, Ananta Kumar Giri (MIDS) took issue with Reddy's prescription about historicizing social science disciplines. Giri argued that to think that social science disciplines can redeem themselves by being solely historical is a reflection of the uncritical bondage of some radically inclined social scientists to the ideology of history. Radical thought from Marx to the most recent had posited a faith in history to redeem human beings from their miseries. Giri argued that the authors of the report such as Wallerstein and Trouillot are bound to such modernist faiths in the redemptive power of history without interrogating the ideology of history in the way, for instance, as an interlocutor such as Ashis Nandy does. For Giri, social sciences can be made relevant and energetic by not only being historical but also by making them partners in struggles for a life of dignity at present and fighting for a more dignified future. At this point, Kurien clarified that there are two meanings of history – genealogical and contextual. To historicize a discipline is to contextualize it and in this sense there may be a common ground between the contemporaneous thrust of Giri and the thrust towards history of Wallerstein et al. and Reddy.

The afternoon session continued the deliberations with a focus on the problems with social science research in India. Dr Masood Ali Khan of ICSSR Southern Regional Office, Hyderabad argued that one great problem here is that there is no vibrant link between teaching and research. In India, there is a breakdown of communication between institutions and universities of teaching. Moreover, those who are in institutions are not interested in research itself but in their personal gains. Dr Manikumar continued the critical discussion by drawing our attention to the pathologies of funding institutions in India. According to him, the first pathology revolves around the step-motherly attitude to social science research on the part of state funding. For Manikumar, "While for a shoddy proposal you can easily get Rs 10 lakh from Department of Science and Technology, it is difficult to get Rs l lakh from ICSSR for a comparatively better proposal. That too, if you are lucky, you get it after 3–4 years." Such structural constraints, accompanied by the bureaucratic administration of universities which has absolutely no concern for research pursuits, throttle creativity.

On the issue of institutional obsolescence, Professor D. Sundaram of University of Madras argued that existing institutions such as the Academic Staff Colleges are in a dormant state and they should be revitalized. Further, both UGC and ICSSR should pull their resources and energies together and should provide helping hands to all – both to people in universities as well as research institutes. It may be noted here that at present the persistent feeling is that UGC is for universities and ICSSR is for institutions of research.

Apart from the problem of institutional malaise, there is also the problem of motivation on the part of researchers. Professor S. Ambirajan asked how much money Kamban got for writing Ramayan and even for that matter how much money P.V. Kane, the noted historian of the *Dharmasastras*, had got from the government for his monumental work, *The History of the Dharmasastras*. Ambirajan argued that lack of state funding should not be used as an excuse for our lack of motivation and perseverance and social scientists must pursue their inquiries against all odds. The real challenge lies in keeping pace with fast developments in one's own discipline. So researchers must continuously learn. But that there is tremendous reluctance and laziness on this front was pointed out by Dr D.S. Tewari, Professor of Geography, University of Madras. He argued that social scientists fail to learn from the changes taking place in the world.

Dr J. Josephine of University of Madras argued that apart from reluctance to learn, our scholars and institutions also suffer from reluctance to talk to each other and be engaged in a dialogue. Ajit Menon of MIDS discussed the problem of lack of interaction between faculty and students. He argued that in order to revitalize social science disciplines, institutions of research and teaching should also be strengthened, which are in a state of stagnation and dormancy now. Menon argued that the Wallerstein report is much more relevant in the US than in India since the institutional infrastructure for the pursuit of socially relevant and multidisciplinary research is at a dismal state here. Professor J.K. Pillai, former Vice-Chancellor, Mother Teresa University, who chaired the session, argued that social research in India is in such a pathetic state now because it is imitative of western concepts on the one hand and alienated from social problems and social reality on the other. Social science research uses people as tools for their study. It is no wonder then that people now talk back to the researchers: "You are wanting us to talk but what we are going to get from this study?" Pillai also pointed to the intractable problem of egoism in the academy where people are confined to their narrow egoistic and disciplinary walls and do not want to come out at all. For Pillai, this is a pity since many of the emerging urgent areas of research such as gender studies and Dalit studies require a multidisciplinary approach.

Note

1. Since this article was written in 1993 this situation has changed. Now, Indian Sociological Society does hold its annual convention every year and publishes its journals, *Sociological Bulletin*, thrice a year, regularly.

10 Sociology and the Limits of Loyalty

> Intellectual life is first of all conflict and disagreement, teaching may give the opposite impression when initiates relate to novices what we claim to know; but the forefront where ideas are created has always been a discussion among oppositions. This heartland of disagreement is difficult to avoid; to deny it is to exemplify it. This is not say that no agreement ever happens [...]
>
> — Randall Collins (1998),
> *The Sociology of Philosophies: A Global Theory of Intellectual Change*, p. 1

> Sociology confers on you an autonomy, especially when you don't use it as a weapon against others, or as an instrument of defence, but rather as a weapon against yourself, an instrument of vigilance.
>
> — Pierre Bourdieu (1990), *In Other Words: Essays Towards a Reflexive Sociology*, p. 27

> [...] To follow in the most demanding and authentic way, it implies 'anacol,' the not following [...] in order to follow in a consistent way, to be true to what you follow, you have to interrupt the following.
>
> — Jacques Derrida (2003), "Following Theory", p. 7

I

Debates and discussions in an intellectual field help us to come to terms with our existing condition and work towards its needed transformation. Debates and discussions have been very much part of traditions of sociological reflections in India. In the 1950s there was a debate about the "book view" and "field view" of studying Indian society in which the works of M.N. Srinivas and Louis Dumont were discussed (cf. Das 1995). A recent debate has arisen on the need for Indian social sciences to overcome their entrenched parochial fixations and be simultaneously interested in fieldwork at home and the world. The present writer had initiated such a dialogue as a response to an earlier essay on the subject by Ramachandra Guha (see the previous chapter). On the issue of our parochial fixation I had written: "Many of us from India now go to all parts of the world as students and teachers but how many of us are interested in carrying out study of other cultures and societies? [...] In India we accuse other scholars, especially from the west of ethnocentrism but what needs critical self-reflection here is an entrenched parochial fixation in Indian scholarship"

(Giri 2003: 3605). I had also written: "The same problem of parochial fixation which is camouflaged as loyalty to roots is compounded when we come to social science research in rest of India. [...] How many people from universities in Orissa work on Bengal what to speak of working in far off areas such as Kashmir and Meghalaya? Is it that difficult to send our students to do fieldwork in other parts of the country far from the place where our home is? The problem here is not at all one of resource but a lack of vision and total insensitivity to our responsibility of understanding the other and the world. We have an indispensable responsibility to understand our self and therefore all of us have a responsibility to work on local issues and problems but does not this also call fro an integrally linked engagement with the other and the world both empirically and theoretically?" (ibid.).

A.M. Shah (2003) and Yasmeen Arif (2004) have made valuable rejoinders to this argument. On the issue of parochial fixation of Indian sociologists not doing enough fieldwork outside India, Shah argues that this has not been the case, i.e., sociologists from India, particularly Delhi School of Economics, have always been engaged with societies and cultures other than one's own.[1] In this context, what Yasmeen Arif writes in her article, "Passages Out of India," deserves our careful consideration: "Notwithstanding A.M. Shah's statements on this, particularly in the way they interlocute M.N. Srinivas' thematic concern with the study of 'other' societies, I will still have to say that out of the 97 PhDs awarded by the Department since its inception in 1959, not more than a couple are based on direct field work in locations outside India. A very few others, in ratio, would have been on and about locations within India which are removed from the students Personal Universe" (Arif 2004: 301). What Andre Beteille, himself a student of Srinivas and presently a doyen of world sociology, writes also helps us to put in perspective our parochial fixations and predicament: "Sociologists in India have been much more confined in their interests, and in the early decades of independence their work ran the risk of being absorbed into Indian studies. *It is true that India offers enormous scope for comparative studies within its own boundaries but the development of the subject has undoubtedly suffered from the absence of sound empirical work by Indian sociologists on societies other than their own.* New entrants into the profession feel discouraged when they find that western sociologists write freely about all societies whereas the leaders of the profession in their own country have very little to say about societies outside India" (Beteille 2002: 4; emphasis added). Beteille also tells us how very few Indian scholars work on societies and cultures other than their own: "[...] Indian research scholars [...] rarely choose to do fieldwork in a region other than the one to which they belong; this enables them to dispense with the trouble of learning a new language, and it allows them to take other shortcuts that in the end detract from the quality of their fieldwork" (Beteille 1996: 234).

On this issue of parochial fixation of Indian scholars, Shah writes: "Giri makes a grand statement, 'The problem here is not at all one of resources but a lack of vision and total insensitivity to our responsibility of understanding the other and the world' (Shah 2003: 4491). Shah considers this statement grand but by characterizing this adjectivally does it help us to address the issues and challenges at hand? The key question here is what is our approach to criticism, self as well as social? Such an adjectival mode of quick judgement and *a priori* fixation is akin to what Bourdieu talks about the violence of classification: "The logic of the classificatory label [in this context labels such as 'grand' and 'careless'] is very exactly that of racism, which stigmatizes its victims by imprisoning them in a negative essence" (Bourdieu 1990: 28). The key question once again is: can we and should we be critical of ourselves and the traditions with which we work?

Shah concludes his article with a suggestion that one's own backyard is as good as 'Trobriand islands'. Shah quotes Srinivas: "As an over protected Brahmin [...] boy growing up on college road, I experienced my first culture shocks not more than fifty yards from the back wall of our house [...] The entire culture of Bhandikeri (the area behind our house where lived a colony of shepherds, immigrants from their village, located a few miles from Mysore) was visibly and olfactorily different from that of college road. Bhandikeri was my Trobriand Islands, my Nuerland, my Navaho Country and what have you" (Shah 2003: 4492). But, in the very next pages, Srinivas also writes: "There are also important differences among 'the others.' A Sholiga tribesman in the elephant-infested jungles of the Biligiri mountains, about 60 miles from my house, would be very different from my neighbour while a Naga or a Mizo in the North-Eastern Hill areas would be even further removed. There are then varying degrees of the 'other,' and in the extreme case 'the other' can be totally different culturally from the self" (Srinivas 1992: 142). Therefore, how to read Srinivas' statement – "Bhandikeri was my Trobriand islands, my Nuer land, my Navaho country and what have you"? Should we read it literally? As Shah himself acknowledges, despite Srinivas himself having done fieldwork only in his native Karnataka, Srinivas' commitment was to a broad-based comparative sociology and anthropology. As Srinivas urges us to realize in his co-authored article with M.N. Panini, "The Development of Sociology and Social Anthropology in India": "Paradoxical as it may seem the very need to understand Indian society requires from Indian sociologists a commitment to a comparative approach in which the problems, processes and institutions of their society are systematically compared with those of neighbouring countries in the first instance, and later with other developing countries [...] There are also areas and problems which should be studied on a global basis, for instance, backwardness and poverty, ethnicity, urbanization, generation gap and student unrest" (Srinivas and Panini 1992: 181–82).

But in what way did Srinivas realize this project of a global comparative sociology and anthropology from India? In this regard, Shah writes: "Aware of the constraints of circumstances in India, Srinivas followed two main strategies to put his vision into practice. First, he devised for BA and MA students of sociology syllabi that were comparative. He introduced a number of books on Africa, America, Australia, Europe and parts of Asia other than India along with India in the syllabi both at Baroda and Delhi. [...] If such students went on to do research in his own society, his knowledge and understanding of other societies would help him to understand his own society better" (Shah 2003: 4491). But, the whole question is whether the project of a global comparative sociology and anthropology be realized only by having courses on other cultures or does it also call for fieldwork in other cultures and societies?[2] Is there any contradiction between an aspiration for a global comparative sociology and anthropology and the literal belief, not necessarily of Srinivas himself as Srinivas had a much more subtler sense of self and other, that one's backyard is one's Trobriand islands? It is Srinivas himself who also tells us: "The phrase 'studying one's own society' needs some clarification: very few are ill-advised enough to take up their natal village or town or quarter for study" (Srinivas 1989b: 177–178).

A great contribution of Srinivas to post-independent Indian intellectual landscape is his emphasis on fieldwork (Beteille 1996). Srinivas, Beteille and many of the founders of the Department of Sociology in University of Delhi plead for fieldwork as an integral part of sociological and anthropological engagement. In the words of Beteille, "Sociology and social anthropology are empirical disciplines which will languish in the absence of a deep respect for facts and close attention to their observation and description; in other words, a disciplined as against a self-indulgent attitude towards facts" (ibid.: 247). But what is our preparation for nurturing respectful observation of and relationship with facts? In many of our centres of sociological learning, there is not much training worth the name either in statistical method or fieldwork?[3] In Department of Sociology at Delhi School of Economics and at the Centre for the Study of Social Systems, Jawaharlal Nehru University – two of our premier centres of sociological teaching and research – now students begin their empirical research and ethnographic fieldwork only when they reach the doctoral level. Students here even in their post-MA/M. Phil research do not do fieldwork. With such a "solid preparation in and for fieldwork" then it should not be a surprise that tradition of empirical research is weak in India (cf. Beteille 1996). But, the reason for this weakness is not the invasion of the barbarians or the proponents of cultural studies and deconstruction as some scholars (cf. Guha 2003) might suggest but our own lack of training in and commitment to fieldwork and nurturance of habits of empirical research.

For Beteille, sociology and anthropology are empirical disciplines but this begs the question of the meaning of the empirical? Is empirical reality only what we observe and is it so unproblematically amenable to observation in the way we know it in traditions of empiricism and anthropological traditions of participant observation? Does not the domain of the empirical consist of multiple layers of reality, as Roy Bhaskar (2002), the philosopher of critical realism, would challenge us, and in understanding this stratified reality in which the empirical and supra-empirical interpenetrate to what extent empiricism is adequate? In putting forward the view of sociology and anthropology as empirical disciplines, are we uncritically following empiricism as an epistemology as well as ontology? Moreover, for being empirical does a person or a discipline have to be empiricist? A collapse of the empirical and empiricist epistemology and ontology impoverishes the nature of sociological engagement as sociologists proceed with a naïve sense of reality without letting themselves being challenged by both the empirical and supra-empirical dimensions of reality. This self-confident sociological empiricism is also based upon little foundational reflections on the nature of our assumptions, assumptions of reality thus based upon a divorce between philosophy and sociology, rather than a mutually enriching and transforming dialogue between the two.

We are grateful to Srinivas and Beteille for emphasizing fieldwork in Indian intellectual engagement. But is it a question of either theoretical engagement or fieldwork? In case of Srinivas himself, as he writes in his autobiographical reflections, "Itineraries of an Indian Social Anthropologist," while proceeding to do fieldwork among the Coorgs in South India, he himself wanted to write on theories of society taking some Indian traditions of thought as his point of departure. But he could not proceed on this because of threat of lack of fellowship for such a work from his mentor G.S. Ghurye:

> While the field study of Coorgs in their forested mountains had its appeal for me, I was troubled by the fact that I was becoming a chronicler of customs and not the theoretician of society which I wanted to be [...] I thought I should take up a 'theoretical subject' for my PhD. I went to the late Professor M. Hiriyana in Mysore whose understanding of Indian philosophy was profound and asked him whether a person who did not have a knowledge of Sanskrit could make a study of how the relation between individual and society was formulated in Indian thought. Hiriyana said I could undertake such a study. But the project was nipped in the bud by Ghurye who told me that no fellowship would be forthcoming if I chose a theme which did not involve fieldwork. Ghurye took a dim view of my hankering after 'theory.'
>
> I was bitter with Ghurye at that time but in retrospect I cannot help being thankful to him for being firm about fellowship being available for fieldwork only (Srinivas 1989a: 190–91).

But what happened to this desire for theory in Srinivas in his subsequent years? If there is a disdain for theoretical engagement in Indian sociology and anthropology could it be linked to such foundational experiences?[4] Indian sociology and anthropology began with a dualism between book view and field view but as Srinivas himself tells us there was a part in him which wanted to be a theoretician of society. And, as Beteille writes nearly sixty years after this foundational experience of Srinivas in his own autobiographical epilogue: "Perhaps it was a mistake to have presented the book-view and field-view as if they stood in complete mutual opposition. A comprehensive scheme for the understanding of Indian society and culture must find a place for the book-view as well as the field-view [...]" (Beteille 1996: 247).

II

In her article, "Passages Out of India," Yasmeen Arif (2004) raises a number of important questions on the issue of parochial fixation of Indian social scientists. For her, the issue here is not only one's desire to work on other cultures and the availability of mentors but also of availability of funding. From her own experience of carrying out fieldwork in Beirut, she shows how in India there are virtually no institutions which support fieldwork in other cultures and societies. Arif quite rightly writes: "Apart from combating possible intellectual insularity towards a research agenda that falls outside the 'local,' a sustainable interest in 'other cultures' in India has to be nurtured through various interconnected institutional and practical measures" (ibid.: 302). Thus, for overcoming our parochial fixation, we need transformation of our ethos, existing institutions such as universities, University Grants Commission and Indian Council of Social Science Research, as well as creation of new institutions.

Arif welcomes the plea for more nuanced theoretical engagement on the part of Indian social scientists but wonders whether in this context dialogue with Indian traditions is a must: "If my specific research agenda is best informed by theoretical reflections that have not emerged from the category of the indigenous, should that be a predicament about my 'responsibility' as a student of social science in India?" She suggests the difficulty of taking part in such a dialogue as we do not have adequate preparation in languages such as Sanskrit, Persian and Pali for this. But this itself calls for appropriate pedagogical transformations. Her question also raises important issues about the nature of theories that we deal with in social sciences as well as to the nature of dialogue itself. The theoretical frames that we deal with reflect specific socio-cultural presuppositions, for example, the social theory we deal with being primarily Euro-American reflects particular socio-cultural presuppositions. As India is not just an empty slate for application of sociological theory originating from elsewhere, there is a need to engage ourselves with a dialogue on the presuppositions of theories that we are dealing with. The emergent theoretical reflection is not an extension of the indigenous but emerges from open-ended and mutually interrogating dialogue between reflections on self, culture and society in a specific locale such as India, Europe and Japan and more universalizing theoretical models. But this dialogue is a dialogue of exploration not of *a priori* assertion about the timeless virtue of "Indic wisdom". For example, if one is engaged in a dialogue between contemporary critical theory and insights of texts such as Bhagavad Gita and Upanishads, then, he or does not treat the later as store houses of wisdom. The objective is not to make a war between "native view" and the established "metropolitan hegemony" but a "better understanding of human society," as Arif so inspiringly aspires for and through this to transform sociology into varieties of planetary conversations.

Arif also raises questions about the nature of relationship between self and other in extending one's anthropological engagement to other societies. For Arif, an important question is whether in doing fieldwork in other countries as Indian anthropologists we are also constituting these 'places' as "field sites for empirical research" within a "gaze". But doing fieldwork in other countries is not destined to be done in an "otherizing gaze" and despite our inherent finitude in any self-other relationship, an effort to understand other culture and society can be carried out in a spirit of mutual learning and transformation – transformation of our initial starting points. This calls for, as Arif herself writes, "new epistemologies of understanding": "The impasse has to be dislodged, in terms of both empiricism and theory, preferably in the same breath, to create new epistemologies of understanding rather than create innumerable contrasts of interpretation" (ibid.: 303). Arif also challenges us: "[...] a critical reflection on some new modalities of interaction between parochial selves and hegemonic others, on the outside and inside must be worth the effort" (ibid.). This indeed is a key challenge but addressing this is not only an epistemological task but it also calls for work on ontology exploring what may be called an "ontological epistemology of participation" (Giri 2005b). In the spirit of the very important question that Arif has raised, it may be helpful to explore this pathway further.

To begin with, the very categories of "parochial self" and "hegemonic self" can be further opened up both epistemologically and ontologically. Self is not only parochial, it has also a connected and relational dimension which is an aspect of its transcendental dimension. Similarly, the other is not just hegemonic, it also has a potential and desire to love and understand despite all problems of violence and history.[5] Therefore, a new modality of interaction between self and other calls for multi-dimensional realizations in case of both self and other, i.e., there is a universal dimension in the so-called parochial self and a non-hegemonic dimension in the hegemonic other. But cultivation of this new modality of interaction is not possible only epistemologically or sociologically, it also involves work on self and ontology. As discussed in Chapter 1, it is a part of ontological epistemology of participation involving border-crossing between transformational epistemology and transformational ontology.

III

Ontological epistemology of participation as it crosses the boundaries of self-certain epistemology and fixed ontology seeks to bring both virtue epistemology and virtue ethics together (cf. MacIntyre 1999). What are some of the virtues in an ontological epistemology of participation? To begin with, it is gratitude. Life begins and is nourished further by gratitude, so does science and scholarship. Shah wonders whether I have forgotten my MA studies at Delhi School of Economics. No. I am ever grateful to my teachers at the School as well as to our earlier pioneers such as M.N. Srinivas but this gratitude itself urges us to ask questions, explore further. This is different from loyalty. The calling of creative social research, for that matter science or philosophy, cannot proceed by loyalty but by gratitude. However, sociological reasoning itself may have its limitation in understanding the limits of loyalty. Sociology not only in India but also in its Euro-American home suffers from an intractable problem of loyalty. The primary loyalty of sociology has been to modernity[6] but is it not committing both epistemic and ontological violence in its modernist epistemology of understanding where not only subjects of sociology but also sociologists themselves live a variety of forms of life simultaneously – traditional, non-modern, modern as well as postmodern? In this context, sociology's loyalty to modernity needs to be transcended by a mode of gratitude which while making us grateful to modernity does not make us its prisoners. It is an important challenge of a sociology of Indian sociology to understand to what extent its practitioners suffer from an *a priori* post-traditional and modernistic telos or are they open simultaneously to tradition, modern and postmodern as co-constitutive dimensions of reality that we are seeking to understand.

Sociology also has been a loyal subject of nation-state but in this loyalty has forgotten its duty to both critical aspirations of people in such contested spaces as Kashmir as well as post-national and cosmopolitan formations which challenges the easy equations between society and nation-state (cf. Mathur 2005; Oommen 2004; Beck 2002). It is encouraging that there is some acknowledgment of the limits of nation-state in sociological engagement. Ulrich Beck (2002), in this context, argues that understanding many of the sociological themes such as inequality challenges us to go beyond the nation-state but the present-day conventional sociology reflects the biases of a methodological nationalism. Beck challenges sociology to overcome its loyalty to methodological nationalism and embrace a new one of methodological cosmopolitanism. Even though Beck's cosmopolitan sociology is primarily Euro-American[7] and has very little planetary conversations as to the very conceptions of self, culture, society, sociology and social theory, it is an important move in going beyond the complicity of sociology in the project of the nation-state. Similarly, in Indian sociology, there is a move now to go beyond the confinement of the Indian nation-state and to look at our engagement from a broader South Asian and comparative global vantage point.[8]

Sociology has also been loyal to varieties of ideologies. In each of these axes – modernity, nation-state justification, and ideology – our challenge is to understand the limits of loyalty and the significance of gratitude. Shah's rejoinder challenges us also to understand the problem of loyalty to our pioneers. Sociology like any tradition of learning is enriched by the ongoing creative work of pioneers who are alive even in their physical absence but this calls for a relationship of gratitude, which in turn is nurtured by systematic learning and training about their works and methods,[9] and continued critical and creative explorations rather than only ritual ancestor worship.

Notes

1. We are grateful to Shah (2003) for telling us that R. Jayaraman, one of the early students of Srinivas, had completed his doctoral work on Sri Lanka, and Anand Chakrabarty who had done fieldwork in another society other than the one in which he was born was not originally from Bengal but from Andhra Pradesh. Though it would have been helpful instead of advising us to look at the annual reports of the Department of Sociology, University of Delhi, Shah had helped us with some detailed facts and figures including the nature of the project about the Pakistan Area Study Program and the North Eastern Hill Areas Program in which the department took part.
2. Because of many constraints, fifty years ago, Srinivas might have had to take recourse to course work on other cultures as an important companion to comparative orientation of Indian scholars but do we do justice to the outstanding legacy of Srinivas by repeating the same strategy now? Is there not an indispensable need to combine coursework on other cultures with fieldwork in some of these?
3. In this context, Sujata Patel tell us that "[...] to this day Delhi University's Department of Sociology does not teach quantitative methodologies" (Patel 2002: 277). Patel furthermore writes: "Unlike the sociologists from Lucknow, Srinivas did not place his sociology in context with a debate and discussion with Marx and Weber or other thinkers. He was also against the survey method being popularized by American sociology, and disapproved of its teaching in Indian universities because, in his opinion, it diluted the qualitative understanding of the structure [...]" (ibid.).
4. Exploring this is not a matter of "Oedipal struggle" about which Patricia Uberoi (2000) writes in her reflections on sociologists reflecting on their own profession in India.
5. Here Said's (1978) reflections on the self-other relationship in *Orientalism* can be supplemented by a new hermeneutics and spirituality of this as suggested in pathways of *Beyond Orientalism* charted by Fred Dallmayr (1996).

6. For Anthony Giddens (1994), sociology is essentially characterized by "a post-traditional telos" and for Beteille (2002: 6)), "sociology is a modern and not a postmodern [...] discipline."
7. Another limitation here is that Beck's methodological cosmopolitanism seems to be primarily epistemic and does not involve work on ontological nurturance and transformation as suggested in the pathway of ontological epistemology of participation (cf. Giri 2004, 2005b).
8. In a seminar on this theme convened by Professor M.N. Panini at Jawaharlal Nehru University (January 27–28, 2006) several participants challenged Indian sociology to go beyond the nation-state perspective and adopt a broader civilizational and regional perspective. In his concept note, Panini writes: "The need for such a seminar arises from the fact that social scientists working in the region tend to be confined to their own niches and do not look out across national boundaries to make comparisons and evolve perspectives that may generate new insights in the understanding of South Asian cultures and communities" (Panini 2006: 1). In this seminar Professors J.P.S. Uberoi and T.K. Oommen, among others, led this move to go beyond the limitations of Indian and South Asian sociology by adopting a civilizational and frontier perspective. But, in his keynote address, Professor Andre Beteille quite rightly challenged us to go beyond programmatic statements and be engaged in serious comparative studies across the borders. He also challenged us to acknowledge that just as there are limits in reifying the nation-state there are also limits in reifying the region. For example, for him, sociologists in Pakistan would find enriching not only sociological work from other South Asian countries but also from Iran.
9. Beteille (1997: 98) challenges us to understand the problem of amnesia in Indian sociology: "In India, each generation of sociologists seems eager to start its work on a clean slate with little or no attention to the work done before." Cultivating a relationship of gratitude to our pioneers challenges to overcome this amnesia and be engaged in creative memory works. But this itself is nurtured by systematic training in history of sociological, anthropological, and social thought in India and South Asia in Indian universities which, in most cases, does not exist. Our amnesia of our pioneers may be related to this lack of training in traditions of social thinking in India. In this context, the proposed work of gratitude and memory work has significant pedagogical implications: in schools of sociology and anthropology in India there is a need for teaching the work of our pioneers as well as many other related thinkers. Apart from this, there is also a need for a critical discussion of our contemporary fellow sociologists and anthropologists. Post-independent India has produced some seminal sociologists and anthropologists of world significance but except pioneering figures of an earlier generation such as G.S. Ghurye and M.N. Srinivas it seems there is not even a single M.Phil work critically discussing works of scholars such as J.P.S. Uberoi, Andre Beteille, T.K. Oommen and Veena Das what to speak of full-length doctoral work on their works. This is also a part of our amnesia but here again much of this may be related to the character of our pedagogy and training.

References

Ankersmit, F.R. 2002. *Political Representation*. Stanford: Stanford University Press.

Arif, Yasmeen. 2004. "Passages out of India." *Economic and Political Weekly*, January 17: 301–303.

Beck, Ulrich. 2002. "The Cosmopolitan Society and its Enemies." *Theory, Culture and Society* 19 (1–2): 17–44.

Beteille, Andre. 1996. "Epilogue: Village Studies in Retrospect." In *Caste, Class and Power*. 2nd Edition, New Delhi: Oxford.

——. 1997. "Newness in Sociological Inquiry." *Sociological Bulletin* 46 (1): 97–110.

——. 2002. *Sociology: Essays on Approach and Method*. Delhi: Oxford University Press.

Bhaskar, Roy. 2002. *Reflections on Meta-Reality: Transcendence, Everyday Life and Emancipations*. New Delhi: Sage.

Bourdieu, Pierre. 1990. *In Other Words: Essays Towards a Reflexive Sociology*. Cambridge: Polity Press.

——. 1991. *The Political Ontology of Martin Heidegger*. Cambridge: Polity Press.

——. 2003. "Participant Objectivation." *Journal of Royal Anthropological Institute* (N.S.) 9: 281–294.

Bourdieu, Pierre and Loic J.D. Wacquant. 1992. *An Invitation to Reflexive Sociology*. Cambridge: Polity Press.

Clammer, John, Sylvie Piorie and Eric Schwimmer. 2004. "Introduction: The Relevance of Ontologies in Anthropology: Reflections on a New Anthropological Field." In *Figured Worlds: Ontological Obstacles in Intercultural Relations*, (eds.) John Clammer et al., pp. 3–22. Toronto: Toronto University Press.

Collins, Randall. 1998. *The Sociology of Philosophies: A Global Theory of Intellectual Change*. Cambridge, MA: Harvard University Press.

Connolly, William E. 1995. *The Ethos of Pluralization*. Minneapolis: University of Minnesota Press.

Das, Veena. 1995. *Critical Events: Anthropological Perspectives on Contemporary India*. Delhi: Oxford University Press.

Dallmayr, Fred. 1987. *Critical Encounters: Between Philosophy and Politics*. Notre Dame: University of Notre Dame Press.

——. 1991. *Between Freiburg and Frankfurt: Toward a Critical Ontology*. Cambridge: Polity Press.

——. 1993. *The Other Heidegger*. Ithaca, NY: Cornell University Press.

——. 1996. *Beyond Orientalism*. Albany: SUNY Press.

——. 2001. "Resisting Totalizing Uniformity: Martin Heidegger on the *Macht* and *Machenschaft*." In *Achieving Our World: Toward a Global and Plural Democracy*. Lanham, MD: Rowman & Littlefield.

Derrida, Jacques. 2003. "Following Theory." In *Life After Theory*, Michael Payne and John Schad (eds.), London: Continuum.

Fromm, Eric. 1950. *Man for Himself*. London: Routledge and Kegan Paul.

Giddens, Anthony. 1994. "Living in a Post-Traditional Society." In *Reflexive Modernization: Politics, Tradition and Aesthetics in Modern Social Order*, (eds.) Ulrich Beck, Anthony Giddens and Scot Lash, Cambridge: Polity Press.

Giri, Ananta. 2002. *Conversations and Transformations: Towards a New Ethics of Self and Society*. Lanham, MD: Lexington Books.

——. 2003. "Social Science Research: Call of Home and the World." *Economic and Political Weekly*, August 23, 3605–08.

——. 2004. "Self-Development, Inclusion of the Other and Planetary Realizations." In *The Religion of Development/Development of Religion*, (eds.) Ananta Kumar Giri et al., Delft, Netherlands: Euborn.

——. 2005a. *Reflections and Mobilizations: Dialogues with Movements and Voluntary Organizations*. New Delhi: Sage.

——. 2005b. Creative Social Research: Rethinking Theories and Methods and the Calling of an Ontological Epistemology of Participation. Madras Institute of Development Studies: Working Paper.

Giri, Ananta Kumar (ed.) 2004. *Creative Social Research: Rethinking Theories and Methods*. Lanham, MD: Lexington Books and New Delhi: Sage.

Greco, John. 2001. "Virtues and Rules in Epistemology." In *Virtue Epistemology: Essays on Epistemic Virtue and Responsibility*, (eds.) Abrol Fairweather and Linda Zagzebski, Oxford: Oxford University Press, pp. 117–141.

Guha, Ramachandra. 2003. "The Ones Who Stayed Behind." *Economic and Political Weekly*, March 22.

Hardt, Michael and Antonio Negri. 2004. *Multitude: War and Democracy in the Age of Empire*. London: Penguin.

Ingold, Tim. 2004. "A Circumpolar Night's Dream." In Clammer et al., 2004: 25–57.

Lunman, Niklas. 2001. "Notes on the Project 'Poetry and Social Theory.'" *Theory, Culture and Society* 18 (1): 15–27.

MacIntyre, Alasdair. 1999. *Dependent Rational Animals*. London: Duckworth.

Mathur, Shubh. 2005. "Torture, Empire and Nation." *Economic and Political Weekly*, March 5–11: 993–995.

Oommen, T.K. 2004. *Nation, Civil Society and Social Movements: Essays in Political Sociology*. Delhi: Sage Publications.

Panini, M.N. 2006. Concept Note to the Seminar on Sociology of South Asia, New Delhi: Jawaharlal Nehru University.

Patel, Sujata. 2002. "The Profession and its Association: Five Decades of the Indian Sociological Society." *International Sociology* 17 (2): 269–284.

Pillai, P.V. 1985. "*Hind Swaraj* in the Light of Heidegger's Critique of Modernity." In *Hind Swaraj: A Fresh Look*, (ed.) Nageswar Prasad, New Delhi: Gandhi Peace Foundation.

Said, Edward. 1978. *Orientalism*. New York: Random House.

Sen, Amartya. 2002. "Justice Across Borders." In *Global Justice and Transnational Politics: Essays on the Moral and Political Challenges of Globalization*, (eds.) Pablo De Greiff and Ciaran Cronin, Cambridge, MA: The MIT Press, pp. 37–51.

Shah, A.M. 2003. "The Matter of Facts." *Economic and Political Weekly*, October 18, 4491–92.

Shanks, Andrew. 2001. *What is Truth? Towards Theological Poetics*. London: Routledge.

Smith, Adam. 1976. *A Theory of Moral Sentiments*. Oxford: Oxford University Press.

Srinivas, M.N. 1989a. "Itineraries of an Indian Social Anthropologist." In *Cohesive Role of Sanskritization and Other Essays*. New Delhi: Oxford University Press.

——. 1989b. "The Insider versus Outsider in the Study of Cultures." In *Cohesive Role of Sanskritization and Other Essays*. New Delhi: Oxford University Press.

——. 1992. *On Living in a Revolution and Other Essays*. Delhi: Oxford.

Srinivas, M.N. and M.N. Panini. 1992. "The Development of Sociology and Social Anthropology in India." In Srinivas, 1992: 151–188.

Srinivasan, Amrit. 1998. "The Subject of Fieldwork: Malinowski and Gandhi." In *Anthropological Journeys: Reflections on Fieldwork*, (ed.) Menakshi Thapan, Hyderabad: Orient Longman.

Uberoi, J.P.S. 2002. *The European Modernity: Truth, Science and Method*. Delhi: Oxford University Press.

Uberoi, Patricia. 2000. "Déjà vu?" Seminar. Retrieved from http://www.india-seminar.com/2000 on November 11, 2004.

Vattimo, Giani. 1999. *Belief*. Cambridge: Polity Press.

The Challenge of Understanding Indian Society

Critique, Generosity and Transformations

Work for your contemporaries; but create what they need, not what they praise.

— Freidrich Schiller (1982),
On the Aesthetic Education of Man, p. 61

Understanding a society is a journey and in this as we build upon the work of pioneers we are continuously challenged to go beyond settled foundations, explore further and cultivate new modes of understanding and create new communities of inquiry and intimacy. This challenge is also equally true of understanding Indian society. T.K. Oommen's 2007 M.N. Srinivas Memorial Lecture, "The Disjunction between Field, Method and Concept: An Appraisal of M.N. Srinivas" (Oommen's 2008) and subsequent responses of A.M. Shah (2008) and M.V. Nadkarni (2008) have raised a number of important issues, which call for further explorations, cultivation and probing. In this chapter I focus mainly on the following issues in Oommen's essay – his reflections on methodological pluralism; application of the label of "methodological Hinduism" to characterize the work of Srinivas; and the conflation of language and social reality in Srinivas' use of the word "Sanskritization" which Oommen misses in his critique. I do not analyse in details all the arguments of Oommen and responses of Shah and Nadkarni to these and only focus on the above issues as they relate to the wider challenge of understanding Indian society.

On Fields, Methods and Methodological Pluralism

Oommen talks about the disjunction between field and method and the need for methodological pluralism. He argues that one particular method, for example, participant observation is not suitable to all situations of fields. Instead of methodological monism we need to practise methodological pluralism. Oommen attributes methodological monism to parts of Srinivas' works but he himself presents Srinivas' argument for the need for "methodological catholicity and resilience, and an ability to choose the appropriate method for tackling a particular problem" (Oommen 2008: 68). Cultivating methodological plurality is an indispensable challenge before us but this urges us to have a multi-dimensional and plural realization of method itself. It seems by method

Oommen mainly refers to techniques of data collection. Such a view is part of modernistic view of looking at method only as a tool, as an aspect of epistemology. But method is not only a tool of understanding outside reality, objective world, it is also part of the constitution of self, an aspect of ontology. Thus, method is not only epistemic, it is also ontological. Method is part of what I have elsewhere called "ontological epistemology of participation" (Giri 2006) involving both epistemology and ontology in interpenetrative and transformative ways.

With a broadened and deepened realization of method involving both epistemology and ontology and more than just techniques of data collection, we can overcome some of the difficulties that Oommen finds in the method of participant observation. Oommen writes: "[...] If one is studying one's society defined in the narrowest possible terms (for example, Sri Vaishnava Brahmins, in the case of Srinivas), is not participant observation a contradiction in terms because the observer and the participant are rolled into one?" (ibid.: 62). But is it not the fact that in all situations of participatory learning (I am deliberately not using the word "participant observation" because of the limitation of the primacy of the observing – more on it later) one is simultaneously an observer and participant? In fact, modern science has long ago questioned absolute separation between observer and observed. Not only in the study of one's own community but even in the study of distant other is it possible to separate the participant dimension from the observing dimension? Oommen finds this contradictory possibly because he is still working within a dualism between participation and observation. It is probably because of this binding that Oommen finds Srinivas' call for making oneself an object of anthropological study problematic. Oommen writes: "Including the study of self and not only the other within the ken of social anthropology has a logical consequence, namely, the study of individual self, not just the societal self, can also become the unit of research! And Srinivas did reach this logical destination when he proposed the following 'field' for anthropological investigations. He asks: 'Why can't an anthropologist treat his life as an ethnographic field and study it? [...] The life of every individual can be regarded as a 'case study' ad who is better qualified than the individual himself to study it" (ibid.: 62). Oommen reads the implication of this in this way: "If these proposals are accepted, not only the 'field' of social anthropology expands exponentially but its methods too have to multiply because it has to study the distant other, the immediate other, one's own society and even the individual self" (ibid.: 62–63). But Oommen associates social anthropology with one method only – participant observation. Anthropology itself has a plurality of methods, which includes life history. Some classic works in anthropology, such as Sidney Mintz's (1960) *Worker in the Cane: A Puerto Rican Life History*, has involved life study method where case study of a single individual tells us a lot about society in which one lives and histories within histories that flow through individuals and societies. Anthropologist Robert Murphy (1987) has gifted us an excellent autobiography-cum-ethnography of his predicament as not being able to move in his *The Body Silent*. Thus, in putting forward self as a field of investigation, which is not meant to be confined only to the discipline of anthropology and which ought to overflow also into fields like sociology, Srinivas is indeed articulating many creative streams in social sciences and, at the same time, challenging us to go beyond the dualism of subject and object. Why should we study only objects and others, why our own life and self not be a subject of study?

Thus reflections on methods now and call for methodological pluralism invite us to take part in fundamental methodological transformations in this field where there is a move towards going beyond dualism of participation and observation and realization non-duality as a journey. Tim Ingold probably has this in mind when he writes:

> Yet all science depends on observation, and all observation depends upon participation – that is, on a close coupling, in perception and action, between the observer and those aspects of the world that are the focus of attention. If science is to be a coherent knowledge practice, it must be built on the foundation of openness rather than closure, engagement rather than detachment. And, this means regaining the sense of astonishment that is so conspicuous by its absence from contemporary scientific work. Knowing must be connected with being, epistemology with ontology, thought with life (Ingold 2006: 19).

Understanding the relationship between field and method also invites us to explore if we can look at method itself as a field. For example, participant observation as a method can itself be looked and realized as a field. Such a field view of method would help us to realize and embody pluralities in each of these methods. Each of the methods that Oommen talks about, for example, the qualitative and the quantitative have inbuilt pluralities within it. For development ethicist Des Gasper (2003), what is often labelled as case approach includes a varieties of cases or different kinds of cases, for example – "thick case studies; thin case studies; real life choice situations; real life anecdotes and other illustrations; conceivably true fictions; and impossible fictions" (Gasper 2003: 196). Thus, Oommen's call for methodological pluralism invites us to pluralize each of the methods which are conceived in a unitary and monolithic way.

One important challenge of methodological pluralism is to combine description of the field and the voices of actors who constitute such a field. The voice of individual actors and communities is missing from Srinivas' account of Sanskritization, which is presented mainly in macro terms.[1]

For Oommen, social anthropology began as study of non-western society while sociology study of West. But both sociology and social anthropology involve study of both western and non-western society, self and other. This is not only true of the present but also of what happened in the past as Shah also makes this point in his response. Oommen writes: "Participant observation was an appropriate method to study the other, but to study one's own society one can resort to a plurality of methods" (Oommen 2008: 70). But participant observation is helpful not only in the study of the other but also in the study of the self. At the same time, there is a foundational limitation of participant observation which we need to explore. Participant observation gives primacy to observation in the practice of participation and this is limiting. It subjects the object of study to the gaze of observation. Participation involves many processes of interaction and communications – verbal, non-verbal and visual. In order to realize methodological pluralism as an ongoing process of pluralization, we need to pluralize the monolithic conceptions of available elements of methods, such as quantitative and qualitative and strive to overcome the dualism between participation and observation.

On Methodological Hinduism

Oommen writes: "Social scientists differ in their methodological orientations. For example, Durkheim gave primacy to society and hence his methodological orientation may be designated as societal determinism. Similarly, Marx's methodology is often labeled as economic determinism. In contrast Weber's obsession with individual action prompted analysts to designate him as a methodological individualist. The tendency to conflate state and nation and treating nation-state as a self-contained unit of analysis is referred to as 'methodological nationalism [...] Following the same trail, the methodology pursued by Srinivas to understand Indian society may be designated as methodological Sanskritic Hinduism. This qualifier to Hinduism is crucial because he did not take into account Dravidian Hinduism [...] But for purposes of brevity and elegance I will refer to this orientation as Methodological Hinduism" (ibid.: 76).

Methodological Hinduism is the label Oommen uses to describe the methodology used by Srinivas to understand Indian society. Srinivas (1952) used the methodology of participant observation from social anthropology and sociology to understand Indian society and his first major work *Religion and Society Among the Coorgs of South India* sought to understand Indian society through the understanding of religion and society among the Coorgs. It is mainly through study of Hindu religion and society by applying the methods of participant observation that Srinivas not only made Hinduism an object of study but also Indian society. As Andre Beteille argues:

> [...] Srinivas's representation of Hinduism in *Religion and Society* is that of the social anthropologist and not of the philosopher or the moralist. [...] his task was to present an account of its actual beliefs and practices as seen from the vantage point of a particular Hindu community. [...] As a social anthropologist, he valued observation and description above introspection and speculation. He knew that introspection had been valued far above observation in the Indian intellectual tradition, and in his early and most productive years as a sociologist, he felt that he had to swim against the current. Those productive years began with the writing of *Religion and Society among the Coorgs* (Beteille 2003: xxiii–xxiv).

So, we can understand Oommen's application of label of methodological Hinduism in this way that with Srinivas Hinduism became an object of study and also methodological as opposed to merely textual or self-valorizing.

In modernity method has been looked at as an epistemological process; it has been looked at only as a tool. But method is not only a tool of understanding social reality; it also plays a role in constitution of self and society (Ankersmit 2002; Giri 2004). This is the ontological dimension of method. In modernity only the epistemological dimension of method was emphasized. But, once we look at method as having both the epistemological and ontological dimensions, then, it opens up new vistas, horizons, realities and possibilities. Look at for example the term "methodological individualism". Methodological individualism treats individuals as a unit of study. Its problem, like methodological nationalism, is that it treats both of them as self-contained units. But methodological individualism is also an individualism that emerges out of methodological meditations and engagements which is different from egoistic individualism. For example, methodological individualism as an ontology has the potential to make individualism more self-reflexive and different from either possessive individualism or egoistic individualism. Similarly, once we realize that method constitutes self and society, as also our reality, then methodological Hinduism also becomes methodological, as different from what is just uttered by people or written in the texts. Methodological Hinduism thus has a potential to make it much more self-critical and open-ended. Similarly, methodological religion and theology is also much more self-critical and open-ended (see Beteille 2009; Wilfred 2004).[2] Thus, one implication of applying the label of methodological Hinduism to Srinivas' construction of Hinduism is that he understood Hinduism through the methodology of participant observation, which presented a different portrait of Hinduism than what appears in the texts or in the valorized speeches and articulations of its practitioners. Thus, Hinduism that emerges from such engagement is methodological, it is not just what is written in the texts and what is spoken by the people.

Methodology has another implication – an act of valorization. Methodological individualism sometimes valorizes individualism as does methodological nationalism valorize nationalism. Applying the label of methodological Hinduism thus urges us to ask the question: Did Srinivas valorize Hinduism? Here Srinivas' approach is much more complex and multi-dimensional. In some passages we can find an element of valorization of Hinduism but in others it is an engagement of non-valorization and critique.[3] Srinivas has not only used the language of cohesion, he has also used the language of revolution. In his 1986 essay "On Living in a Revolution" Srinivas writes: "A most depressing scenario for the future is that concerning the relations between dominant, landowning castes and the scheduled castes. The conflict between the two is likely to become more and more bitter, and violent. It will be a primary arena for the struggle for equality in India" (2009: 381). If Srinivas had written in 1956[4] that if caste dies then also Hinduism his last major essay before his death which was posthumously published is entitled "An Obituary on Caste as a System" (2003). In this essay, while writing an obituary on caste as a system facilitated by transformations in production relations, Srinivas does not write any obituary about Hinduism nor does he show any anxiety about this.

Oommen writes that Srinivas used methodological Hinduism to understand Indian society. India is a plural society but Srinivas did not study any other religion except Hinduism. Even Srinivas' 1987–88 essay, "Social Significance of Religion in India," does not discuss much the work and dynamics of non-Hindu religions in India. Oommen applies the label of methodological Hinduism to Srinivas to suggest that he used Hinduism in an exclusive way to understand Indian society. Such an exclusionary emphasis is also noticeable in Srinivas' first work, *Marriage and Family in Mysore* (1942). As Charsley argues about this study:

> The framework of "after castes" i.e. "discrete, classifiable castes" already promoted by the succeeding Censuses of India [...] provided the frame for the project which Srinivas was given by his teacher Ghurye. [...] This framework already served to focus discussion and make important sections of the Mysore population peripheral to the argument. In fact, religious orientation – being Hindu – is introduced as the initial qualification for relevance. The chief result was to rule out and make invisible major sections of the population which did not relate positively to the Brahmans. These were first the Muslims, making up 6 per cent of the total in 1931 but more important than this proportion implies. [...] To his exclusion of Muslims, Srinivas adds 'Christians,

Jains and even Lingayats,' though 'the last mentioned are no doubt Hindus' (Charsley, 1998: 533).[5]

But, the use of the label "methodological Hinduism" also urges us to probe this: What are the methods of Hinduism? Different ways of logic, argumentations and philosophical systems within Hinduism have a rich repertoire of methodology and ways of argumentations. This is a vast topic but let us explore what are some of the methodological reflections and practices in these ways of argumentations and philosophical systems. And then we can critically probe whether Srinivas built upon these methodological insights to deepen the vision and method of participant observation or he just applied the method of participant observation and the theory of social structure from British social anthropology to the study of Indian society. The methods of argumentation and conversation in the Upanishads[6] have a potential for participatory discussion and learning, which is also aimed at in the methods of participant observation in sociology and anthropology. As Godavarish Mishra argues: "The most important method is the method of inquiry where certain simple but critical questions are raised and answered. [...] In the Upanishads we repeatedly find that the questions are asked in different ways and answers are given till the students are [...] satisfied. [...] The underlying intention is to provide clarity of the concepts and create a corresponding experiential base in the interlocutor [...] This method of questioning is adopted in many systems of Indian philosophy to ensure that no view was accepted without being examined for its experiential validity" (Mishra 2004: 278–79).

Sruti or listening is an important method in ways of thinking in Vedas but it is also accompanied by *pramanas*, or evidences, which give us "objective knowledge" (ibid.: 275). These *pramanas* make methods empirical thus having a possibility for building bridges with methods in social sciences such as participant observation and survey research. "Sankara does not dogmatically follow *Sruti*. He says that there should be experiential domain for *Sruti*, as 'even a hundred scriptural texts declaring fire to be cold or non-luminous, will not be authoritative'" (ibid.: 287). To this method of *pramanas* the Mimanshakas developed hermeneutical methods "for the understanding and the interpretation of the Vedas" while at the same time acknowledging the limitations of hermeneutical method and the need for it to be open to revelation (ibid.: 279–80). "In order to resolve the seeming contradictions of the text, Mimamsaka proposes that the subject matter (*visaya*) has to be identified first. This has to be followed by statement of possible doubts (*samsaya*). Then comes the prima facie view (*purvapaksha*) which postulates a set of meanings [...] based on which the doubt is answered. This is followed by the suggested view (*uttara-paksha*), which refutes the meaning proffered by the prima facie view, through rational arguments and offers an alternative set of meanings. Then comes *nirnaya*, the definitive judgment on the meaning of the text. The chief aim of this hermeneutic method is to identify the proper context in which the Vedic passages could be related to human needs in a more meaningful way and to show its all time applicability beyond the temporal justification" (ibid.: 280).

Advaita Vedanta has a method of what is called as *adhyaropa-apapada* (superimposition and de-superimposition). While *adhyaropa* points to the fact that many of our concepts and languages are superimposition upon reality, *apapada* reiterates the need for de-superimposition. Languages and concepts we use are many a time a superimposition upon reality which need to be accompanied by a process of de-superimposition. Language does not only help us communicate, it also creates illusion and distortion of reality. In this context, it is worth asking whether the language and concept of Sanskritization is a superimposition upon reality? As we shall shortly see, the word "Sanskritization" conflates language and society which is a superimposition upon reality which not only constructs reality in a particular way but also distorts it. In this context, Shankara emphasizes de-superimposition as an inevitable part of understanding reality. As Ramakrishna Puligandla helps us understand: "advancing an argument and rescinding it at the end; one advances an argument in order to inspire and orient the listener; and one finally rescinds the argument" in order to enable one understand reality in an open-ended way (Puligandla 1996, quoted in Giri, 2004: 354).

Thus methodological practices from these broadly conceived Hindu modes of thinking have important implications for methods in social sciences. Methods like de-superimposition help us overcome illusions and not to be bound to the prisons that we ourselves create through the use of language and concepts. "It is part of movement from *adhyàsa* – illusion (which is a very important concept in the Indic epistemology) to ever greater approximation to truth" (Wilfred 2004: 167). It also urges for purification of methods and consciousness in its stages of sense perception, rational and theoretical understanding, and at the stage of wisdom. Methodology in these systems of thinking is not only confined to sense perception and rationalization but also includes movement towards the "third stage of *prajna* or wisdom" (ibid.: 168). Thus, if we talk of methodological Hinduism, then the methodological implication of working with some of these ways of thinking and being is to realize the limits of both sense perception as well as rationalization and impregnate these practices with perspective and practice of wisdom. Here, a facile distinction between Indic speculation and modern-day social science methods of either empiricism or rationalism does not help us realize that not only speculation creates illusion, empirical work, concept formation as well as theoretical construction, application and analysis can and do create illusion. There is a need to purify our sense perception and rational mode of thinking and embody an art of *prajna* or wisdom. As Felix Wilfred helps us understand this: "At this level there takes place a purification of the rationalizing process. For the latter process could be seriously conditioned by interests, passions and desire. [...] Wisdom is a stage in which intellect and will, reason and passion, desire and restraint are reconciled and not polarized. The stage of *prajna* is able to do that precisely because it is a stage of wholeness in which various layers and dimensions of the real are held together" (ibid.: 169).

In his methodology did Srinivas build upon such methodological insights from broadly conceived Hindu intellectual traditions? In his unease with the Indological approach and cultivation of an anthropological approach, Srinivas did not build upon such methodological insights from Hindu traditions. Srinivas did not carry out a dialogue between methods of social sciences and such insights from Hindu traditions. Such a dialogue is by and large absent in Indian social sciences including most of the followers of Srinivas and his critics.[7] Oommen, for example, has not carried out such a dialogue. Oommen is critical of the project of indigenization which for him promotes "pathological nationalism" (2007a: 12) but the dialogical project presented here is different from the project of indigenization. The task here is one of learning, going deeper and across, and be engaged with dialogues across traditions of thinking – modern social sciences and traditions of argumentations in India. This is a major poverty of Indian sociology and the need for such a dialogue can be easily put under carpet by constructing the challenge of understanding Indian society in terms of a facile dualism between book view and field view.[8] Oommen (2007a) himself urges us to go beyond the dualism of universalization and indigenization and focusing on contextualization (see Welz 2009). But contextualization also calls for dialogues. Undertaking dialogues across boundaries, for example, between modern social sciences and traditions of thinking such as Shankar's *adhyaropa-apavada* is also an important challenge here. Contextualization also calls for going beyond surface view of context.

Sanskritization: The Foundational Problem of Conflation of Language, Religion and Dynamics of Self and Social Transformations

The primary problem with the word "Sanskritization", which is offered as a concept, is that it uses the category of a language to connote religion and dynamics of self and social transformations. Srinivas uses this word keeping in mind Sanskrit as a language but such an innocent phrase hides many deeper processes such as Brahminization or difficulty of expressing the dynamics of change that Srinivas wants to present through the category of Brahminization. As A.M. Shah himself writes: "A question is often asked, particularly in discussions of the concept in regional languages: is this word based on *Sanskrit* (name of the language) or *sanskriti* (meaning culture, civilization)? Both Srinivas and Chatterjee [Chatterjee who had independently used this word to describe cultural change in Indian history] based it on the former rather than the latter. For both of them, the concept was inextricably linked to the religious and cultural complex found in classical Sanskrit literature" (Shah 2005: 239).

The word for culture in Sanskrit as well as in several Indian languages is *sanskriti*. *Sanskrit* comes as a shorthand for the description of the work in the field of culture, *sanskriti*, a process which is also primarily looked at in cultural terms rather than structural terms. As Srinivas himself writes, he looks at Sanskritization primarily in cultural terms rather than in structural terms.[9] The use of the linguistic category of Sanskrit to describe the dynamics of change in the field of *sanskriti* (culture) contributes to the conflation of language and social reality. This has been a foundational problem with Srinivas right from the days of his MA thesis on "Marriage and Family in Mysore." As Simon Charsely helps us understand this: "This term 'Sanskritic', of such significance for the future, slips into discussion without introduction or definition" (Charsley 1998: 531). It is probably for this reason that Sanskritists objected to use of the word "Sanskritization". As Srinivas himself writes: "[...] The Sanskritists condemned my use of the word Sanskritization [...] The term has been uniformly condemned by Sanskritists everywhere, but in spite – or because – of that, Sanskritization has been used extensively by those writing on social and cultural change in South Asia" (2009: 680–81). It seems Srinivas did not pay any heed to the objection of Sanskritists possibly because as a non-living language lacking in political power Sanskrit had its own limitation in modern India to force Srinivas to realize that he was using the category of language to bail him out of his conceptual and methodological difficulty of describing and representing social and cultural change in India. As Srinivas himself writes:

> *Sanskritization is no doubt an awkward term, but it was preferred to Brahminisation for several reasons: Brahminisation is subsumed in the wider process of Sanskritization though at some points Brahminization and Sanskritization are at variance with each other*. For instance, the Brahmins of the Vedic period drank *soma*, an alcoholic drink, ate beef, and offered blood sacrifices. Both were given up in the post-Vedic times. It has been suggested that this was the result of Jain and Buddhist influence. Today, Brahmins are, by and large, vegetarians: only the Saraswat, Kashmiri, and Bengali Brahmins eat non-vegetarian food. All these Brahmins are, however, traditionally teetotallers. *Had the term Brahminization been used, it would have been necessary to specify which particular Brahmin group was meant, and at which period of its recorded history* (2009: 201; emphasis added).

But in so far as the word "Sanskritization" is concerned, A.M. Shah reiterates: "In any case, however, in scientific discourse the substantive content of a term is far more important than its etymology" (Shah 2005: 239). But, what is the substantive content of the term? As Srinivas writes in one of his early formulations of Sanskritization in the chapter on social structure in his Coorg book:

> Every caste tended to imitate the customs and ritual of topmost caste, and this was responsible for the spread of Sanskritization. When this process is viewed in a continental scale and over a period of at least 2, 500 years, it is easy to see how Sanskritic ideas and beliefs penetrated the remotest hill tribes in a such a manner as not to do violence to their traditional beliefs (Srinivas 1952: 30).

But the key question is why call it Sanskritization? Etymology, as Shah seems to suggest, is not innocent here. It is deliberately used to conflate language with religion and dynamics of self and social change and as Srinivas himself acknowledge in such construction "facts have been oversimplified in order to make some general statements" (ibid.: 27–28). Such oversimplification facilitated by the conflation of language, religion and social dynamics constitutes the foundational problem of the discourse of Sanskritization, which is rarely realized by its supporters or problematized by its critics.

But, let us hear Srinivas in his words about different aspects of Sanskritization. Srinivas offers Sanskritization to present a dynamic view of caste mobility. In the same book, Srinivas writes:

> It is not always the Brahmin priest who is the agent of Sanskritic Hinduism. In every part of the Kannada country, and in Coorg, the Lingayat sect, consisting exclusively of non-Brahmins, have exercised in the past a Sanskritizing influence. Lingayat ritual is Sanskritic (though not Vedic), and the Lingayat Rajas of Coorg have been responsible for the Sanskritization of the customs, manners, and rites of Coorgs. Customs like marking the forehead every morning with three stripes of sacred ashes (*vibhuti*), celebrating the festival of Sivaratri, and erecting tombstones, surmounted by the figure of the Nandi Bull, over the graves of important persons reveal Lingayat influence (ibid.: 226).

Srinivas further writes:

> The Brahmin too has been influenced by non-Sanskritic modes of worship, and impressed with the power of village deities and, very rarely, through a non-Brahminical friend, of an animal to the village deities like Mari during an epidemic of small pox or plague or cholera (ibid.: 226–27).

In his 1956 essay, "A Note on Sanskritization and Westernization," Srinivas himself writes: "However thoroughgoing the Sanskritization of an Untouchable group may be, it is unable to cross the barrier of untouchability" (Srinivas 2009: 215).

For Srinivas,

> It is necessary to undermine the fact that Sanskritization is an extremely complex and heterogeneous concept. It is even possible that it would be more preferable to treat it as a bundle of concepts than as a single concept. *The important thing to remember is that it is only a name for widespread social and cultural process, and our main task is to understand the nature of these processes. The moment is discovered that the term is more a hindrance than a help in analysis, it should be discarded quickly and without regret* (ibid.: 218; emphasis added).

Srinivas himself outlined the need for more research which is yet an unmet challenge in Indian sociology after more that fifty years:

> One way of breaking down Sanskritization into simpler and more homogeneous concepts would be to write a history of Sanskritic culture taking care to point the value systems subsumed in it and to delineate the regional variations. The task would be a stupendous one even if the period beginning with British rule were excluded. Such a study is not likely to be forthcoming in the near future and anthropologists would be well advised to continue studying Sanskritization as they are doing at present: study each field instance of Sanskritization in relation to the locally dominant caste and other factors. The next task would be to compare different instances of Sanskritization in the same culture-area, and the third task would be to extend the scope of comparative studies to include the whole of India. Such an approach might also enable us to translate historical problems into social problems (ibid.: 219; also see Shah 2005).

Sanskritic Hinduism is fundamental to the concept of Sanskritization.[10] The term "Sanskritic Hinduism" is used by both Srinivas as well as his supporters such as Shah and critics such as Oommen. But, what does Sanskritic Hinduism mean? Is it Hinduism where its practitioners – priests, for example – speak Sanskrit as a language or some of its important sacred books are written in Sanskrit? If Sanskritization conflates language, social reality and social dynamics to overcome the difficult social and ritual issue of the role of Brahmins in Hindu social structure and dynamics, then, the word "Sanskritic Hinduism" continues the same conflation of language, social reality and religion. Let us read what Srinivas writes about Sanskritic Hinduism: "Sanskritic Hinduism is Hinduism which transcends provincial barriers and is common to the whole of India" (Srinivas 1952: 74). But, why it should be called Sanskritic Hinduism? Is it because priests use Sanskrit language in some ritual occasions or is it that some important texts of Hinduism are written in Sanskrit? Srinivas writes: "The sacred literature of the Hindus in Sanskrit (or inspired by Sanskrit but in regional or other languages) has played a vital part in enabling Sanskritic Hinduism to absorb local cults" (Srinivas 2009: 223) But, the sacred literature in their original text and translation do not just propagate one monolithic version of Hinduism. Moreover, when translated in mother languages of India, these texts have also interrogated existing hierarchy as for example one finds in Sarala Das' translation of Mahabharata into Oriya in 15th century. Srinivas writes: "Paradoxical as it may seem, the use of the ordinary languages of the people for religious purposes, the advocacy of a single-minded love of God as the simplest means of achieving salvation, and the general anti-elitism of Bhakti cults, greatly enhanced the spread of the ideas associated with Sanskritic or higher Hinduism" (ibid.: 365). But Bhakti movements are complex formations of contestations in language, religion and society. For example, Bhakti poets in medieval Odisha have interrogated both the dominance of Sanskrit language and caste hierarchy. The literature of Bhakti movement simply did not reproduce the so-called values of higher Hinduism. In this context, what M.V. Nadkarni writes in his rejoinder to Oommen deserves our careful consideration: "But there is also a vast body of non-Sanskritic literature, composed by *bhakti* sants, which is considered equally sacred by its followers as the *shruti*, which is strongly opposed to the caste system. This dates from about 6th century AD itself from Tamil Nadu, spreading all over India" (Nadkarni 2008: 404). It is Srinivas himself who has also written about the significance of Bhakti movements in cultivating non-Sanskritic language but it seems this has not affected his model of Sanskritization.[11]

In his 1956 essay on Sanskritization, Srinivas himself wrote: "The spread of Sanskrit theological ideas increased under British rule" (Srinivas 2009: 206).[12] Furthermore, "The discovery of Sanskrit by Western scholars, and the systematic piercing of India's past by Western or Western-inspired scholarship, gave Indians a much needed confidence in their relationship with the West" (ibid.: 207). Sanskritic Hinduism as a discourse as well as practice is produced by the process of Westernization and is inconceivable without Orientalism. We have to take into account the wider historical and discursive field in which not only Sanskritic Hinduism is produced but Orientalism has also played a significant role. The colonial government with the aid of Orientalists formalized Hindu customs and gave primacy to what is written in Sanskrit texts. Such codification had profound implication for what constitutes authentic Hinduism and the constitution of a new legal order. It also gave a primacy to Sanskrit language, which was not there in the life of the people thus undoing the creative work of Bhakti movements in questioning the primacy of Sanskrit language[13] as well as Brahminical hegemony.

But the discourse of Sanskritic Hinduism was limited as it did not embody pluralities within Hinduism. The concept of Sanskritic Hinduism, as used uncritically by Srinivas and his followers such as Shah and critics such as Oommen, does not adequately reflect plural streams of living, contestation and creativity in Hinduism not only in the present times but also in the past.

Pluralism is an important challenge in understanding not only Indian society but also Hinduism and Srinivas' stance on it is quite complex. In his vast *ouvre*, there are some passages which are more plural than the others. But one issue needs to be noted. Even in his 1987–88 essay on "The Social Significance of Religion in India," there is not much substantial discussion of the work of non-Hindu religions and their social significance. Srinivas also did not work on any other non-Hindu religions to understand their dynamics in India society and their significance for understanding Indian society.

In his critique of Sanskritization, Oommen does not address the foundational problem of conflating language, religion and society in it, rather he himself continues this conflation by offering phrases such as Tamilisation.[14] Like Sanskritization, these are words which are supposed to be concepts and have a self-generating conceptual effect holding us in awe and amazement. Oommen also does not interrogate the construction of Sanskritic Hinduism itself as monolithic produced under the joint regime of Orientalism and colonialism. Instead, in an exercise of critique which at this foundational level does not go beyond an act of mirroring and reproducing the very terms of discourse, Oommen proposes Dravidian Hinduism as an alternative to Sanskritic Hinduism.[15] But both of these are complex mirrors of each other. As M.S.S. Pandian (2007) helps us understand this in his significant work, *Brahmin and Non-Brahmin: Genealogies of the Tamil Political Present*, it is Orientalism which produced Hinduism as Brahminical and the non-Brahmin movements in Tamil Nadu, instead of interrogating this construction, accepted such a construction of Hinduism uncritically. Hinduism of non-Brahmin movement became a mirror opposite of the Sanskritic Hinduism constructed by the Orientalists. For Pandian, Orientalist notions of Hinduism "celebrated Sanskrit texts and Brahmins as true bearers of Hindu authenticity" (ibid.: 51). Pandian further says: "The anti-Brahminism of Iyothee Thoss and Maraimalai Adigal was no different, for the metaphysics of caste as an enforced hierarchy remained in their discourses, largely in tact. [...] Negating Brahmanism, they respectively valorized Buddhist Parayar and Saivite Vellalar. Regrettably, this substitution only recast their ideal in more or less in the image of the Brahmin [...]" (ibid.: 143, 142). For Pandian, "The Brahmin as a Trope" continued unquestioned in the much valorized self-respect movement of Periyar EV Ramasamy: "[...] Ramasamy's idea of an essentialized Hinduism was premised on Brahmin self-representation based on Orientalist knowledge. [...] the Orientalist conception of Hinduism became the basis of advancing a new critique of Brahmin power " (ibid.: 204, 187).[16]

It was not only Brahminical Hinduism which was not only exclusionary, the Hinduism of the non-Brahmin movement including what Oommen seems to be celebrating as Dravidian Hinduism opposing Sanskritic Hinduism was and continues to be exclusionary. It excluded the low castes and the Dalits. Such exclusion continues in the present strengthened by the reign of Dravidian politics in the last eight decades which has created a politics and language of closure on the path of self-realization and emancipation of Dalits.

In his mirroring critique of Srinivas, as different from a foundational one, Oommen writes: "Srinivas did not pay attention to the challenge of Tamilisation. This is the reason behind designating his orientation as methodological Hinduism [...] (Oommen 2008: 77)." Here, Oommen invokes the notion of Tamilakkam presented by Burton Stein: "Tamilakkam connotes the home of Tamil language, culture and/or people and symbolizes the distinction between Tamils who are internal to Tamil Nadu and contrasts them with the 'external other,' the Aryan Hindus, who follow Sanskritic Hinduism" (ibid.: 74). But those who spoke Tamil in the past practised different religions such as Hinduism, animism, Buddhism, Jainism, Islam and Christianity. Oommen constructs the oppositional categories of Dravidian Hinduism and Sanskritic Hinduism but Tamilakkam was and is not a space for Dravidian Hinduism only. It was and is a space of pluralities including plural religions but homogenous construction of Tamilakkam makes many people who live inside it feel alienated. Roy Gowthamam, a contemporary Dalit cultural critic from Tamil Nadu writes: "Tamil culture, though being talked of as if a homogeneous one, contains several contradictory elements" (quoted in Pandian 2007: 341). Giving expression to the pain of the marginalized such as Dalits in what Oommen celebrates as Tamilakkam, Gowthamam writes: "All are hunters. We can call our Tamil culture as the culture of the hunters" (ibid.: 241).[17]

In order to appreciate the significance of Oommen's critique of Sanskritization via Tamilisation, let us read what Srinivas writes about it: "In the Tamil country, however, there has been an attempt to reject the older epic Ramayana on the ground that it is Northern, Aryan and anti-Dravidian. The organized hatred for the Ramayana is part of the Tamil non-Brahmin movement, a cultural and political movement, which began towards the end of World War I" (Srinivas 2009: 226). In his essay, "A Brief Note on the Ayappa: The South Indian Deity", Srinivas writes:

> A student of South Indian ethnography cannot help becoming deeply interested in Ayyappa. To call him South Indian is not to deny him all-India and Sanskritic affiliations, but only to stress the fact that the form he assumes in South India is different from the form he assumes in the North. Quite frequently, a deity's character changes from one region of South India to another. The Sanskritic and popular names are often different, and occasionally, there is no relation between the deity as he is represented in Sanskrit literature and the deity and his devotees in any small local area conceive him to be. These differences are important to the ethnographer, and a fieldworker has to be specially careful to see that he does not allow the Sanskrit name of a deity into attributing to him all the characteristics which are found in *Vedas* and *Puranas*, and other works (ibid.: 347).

Thus, it is clear that Srinivas was aware of differential work of Hinduism in different parts of India, especially in South India, and in the Tamil country.

In his essay, Oommen refers to Islamization in talking about Sanskritization. He does not explore this further. But there is a need to explore the link between Islamization and Sanskritization. Hindus, especially low-caste, down the centuries have found a way of escaping caste hierarchy by embracing or converting to other religions such as Islam, Christianity and Buddhism. Thus understanding the dynamics of change in Indian society requires looking at Sanskritization and these forces of conversion together.

Labour and Love of Mutual Understanding: Critique, Generosity and the Challenge of Learning

In their responses to Oommen, Shah (2008) and Nadkarni (2008) have raised many important issues. Nadkarni urges us to go back to the texts and argues that the hierarchy of caste is not legitimized in Purusasukta. Nadkarni also refers to *guna* and *karma* in Gita as important markers of caste but these have not been able to transform the caste system. The only thing that has given a jolt to the caste system is the transformation of *jati*-based division of labour and caste-based production system. As Srinivas writes: "[...] the localized system of food grain and other necessities [...] based on a caste-wise division of labour is fast breaking down all over rural India, and is likely to disappear in near future. This event is of momentous importance for it augurs the end of a social order which has continued for 2,000 years or more" (Srinivas 2003: 455). Srinivas goes on to argue that just an ideological attack on the caste system as it happened in Buddhism, Jainism and Bhakti movement which is "not backed up or underpinned by a mode of social production ignoring or violating caste-based division of labour [...] is totally inadequate" (ibid.: 459).

In his rejoinder Shah has made important contributions about the method of anthropology and history of the discipline in India and Britain. But his critique of Oommen is not accompanied by generosity as Oommen's application of the label of methodological Hinduism to Srinivas without elaboration of its many implications also seems to lack in generosity. Shah writes: "Oommen should read all of Srinivas's writings, and in full, rather than pick on a couple of convenient sentences as he has done repeatedly" (Shah 2008: 397–98). But how does Shah know and can be so sure that Oommen has not read Srinivas in full. Shah accuses Oommen of "violation of norms of academic discourse". But what is the norm that Shah has followed in offering such an accusation? What example is Shah setting? Shah writes towards the end of his rejoinder: "Srinivas wrote a great deal on secularism, pluralism, and other values enshrined in the constitution of India, but Oommen has not read them, and if he has, he has either not understood them or ignored them deliberately" (ibid.: 399). Critique needs to be accompanied by generosity, which is not simply a matter of charity or academic courtesy, but is also a fundamental aspect of integrity and responsibility. It is not only Srinivas who has written a great "deal on secularism, pluralism, and other values enshrined in the constitution of India" but also Oommen (2002). Oommen has not only written about these issues extensively in his creative *ouvre* of the last fifty years but embodies an inspiring passion for nurturing plural spaces of conversations, realizations and transformations in India and the world. Has Shah read or felt the obligation to read any of Oommen's writings including the one most relevant to his discussion, *Knowledge and Society* (Oommen 2007)?

The anger and accusation manifest in Shah's critique of Oommen is not only personal; it is a reflection of the nature or Indian sociology as a discursive and interactive field. In Indian sociology very rarely there is dialogue among its practitioners.[18] There is studied and deliberate ignorance of each other's work in Indian sociology. We, practitioners, very rarely feel that we all belong to an intertwined field of strivings in which we have a moral responsibility, ethical and professional obligation to read each other's work. Most of the time we relate to each other with profound mutual disrespect. Here, we hardly read each other's work and here a study of referencing could be a very creative project of sociology of knowledge of Indian sociology. As practitioners of this field, we embody not only profound mutual disrespect but also disrespectful indifference. Most of the time, in our normal interactions, we do not even care to respond. But apathy is more dangerous than unfair criticism. Given the lack of normal critical dialogue in Indian sociology among fellow practitioners the only way it can express is through angry explosions.

Mutual understanding is a matter of love and labour. It does not put under the carpet existing envy, hatred, jealousy, apathy and unfair criticism but through love and labour of learning it seeks to transform such conditions. Post-independence Indian sociology has produced some seminal sociologists and anthropologists whose works need careful consideration. Here barring work on Srinivas there is not a single M.Phil work on any of these scholars what to speak of a full-length doctoral dissertation or book. This is also an indicator of the state of apathy in Indian sociology and lack of mutual engagement of love and labour of learning and deepening and broadening our discourse.

The challenge of understanding Indian society needs to be met by transforming such conditions of apathy and creating conditions of mutual learning, dialogue and respect. Here interrogating some of our foundational assumptions such as the conflation of language and social reality as it happens in the word "Sanskritization" is important. There is also a need for dialogue between methods of modern social sciences and traditions of argumentations in India. Indian sociology as a field need to nurture generous critique as a mode of being, inter-subjectivity and mutual engagement, where critique is accompanied by generosity, which is a matter of not only charity but also integrity and responsibility.

Critique and generosity can also be accompanied by work of humour. Satish Deshpande (2003) tells us that sociologists as a tribe have very few jokes in their field. But probably in Indian sociology we have some jokes about each other which are spoken in the backyard rather than in the frontyard. Such jokes if spoken to each other in front can help us have a sense of humour and thus contribute to creation of ripples of mutual reading, learning and conversation in the pool of sociology, which bereft of such interactions, unfortunately faces the danger of stagnation.

Jokes could be disrespectful and we need to have a sense of respectful humour. Here Srinivas with his inspiring ease and humility can be our teacher and fellow-traveller. I was once speaking with an anthropologist from abroad and he told me of the following conversation. Srinivas has told this in a conversation with fellow-scholars: "He [referring to a student of Srinivas] complains that I am not a theorist but I do not complain that he is not a Buddhist."

Notes

1. As Charsley argues, towards the end of his life, Srinivas realized that in his account of Sanskritization he has not addressed "personal Sanskritization": "the deliberate adoption of a Sanskritized life-style by individuals, which he had not previously sufficiently noticed" (1998: 544).
2. Probably with this spirit Andre Beteille (2009) makes a distinction between sociology of religion and theology of religion.
3. We can read here passages such as the following originally written in his 1967 essay, "The Cohesive Role of Sanskritization":

> One of the most important tasks confronts independent India is to draw all sections of India's heterogeneous population into the mainstream of national life while at the same time retaining what is valuable in Sanskrit thought and culture. To do this it is necessary for Hindus to accept the entire tradition to which all sections of the population have contributed, and for the latter to regard the Sanskrit heritage as their own. This can only be the result of slow process of cultural osmosis [...] (Srinivas 2009: 235).

In the following passage in his essay, "The Social Significance of Religion in India," we find that Srinivas (2009: 363) did not valorize Hinduism as a tolerant religion:

> Hinduism is regarded as a tolerant religion both by its votaries and others [...] However monotheism occurs in Hinduism at the sectarian level, and it is usually accompanied by intolerance towards other sects.

Srinivas has been a critique of Hinduism from his first encounter with it in his MA theses. As Charsley writes about it:

> Indeed a recurring theme in the book, the work of a modern and progressive young Brahman is to challenge the patriarchal nature of Sanskritic culture and in particular its disadvantages for women (Charsley 1998: 535).

4. In the words of Srinivas (2009: 217):

   > To the question whether the threat to religion from westernization is common to all countries in the world and not something peculiar to Hinduism, the answer is that Christianity and Islam are probably better equipped to withstand westernization because they have a strong organization whereas Hinduism lacks all organization excluding the caste system. If and when caste disappears, Hinduism may also disappear [...]

5. Charsely however urges us to realize that despite such emphasis, Srinivas' sociology is not a Hindu sociology (personal communication).
6. Upanishad means to seat nearby and discuss.
7. It is worth noting here the work of M.V. Nadkarni who carries out dialogue between methods of modern social sciences and insights from Bhagavad Gita in his essay, "Limits of Analytical Method: A Perspective from Bhagavad Gita for Holistic Social Science Research" (Nadkarni forthcoming).
8. It is worth noting what Beteille (1996: 247) has written about this: "Perhaps it was a mistake to have presented the book-view and field-view as if they stood in complete mutual opposition. A comprehensive scheme for the understanding of Indian society and culture must find a place for the book-view as well as the field-view [...]." This also resonates with Oommen's plea for studying both the fields and the texts.
9. Srinivas admits that he looks at Sanskritization primarily in cultural terms though it can also be looked at structurally: "To describe social changes occurring in modern India in terms of Sanskritization and Westernization is to describe it primarily in cultural and not structural terms. An analysis in terms of structure is much more difficult than an analysis in terms of culture" (2009: 212).
10. Note here what A.M. Shah (2008: 398) writes: "The concept of Sanskritic Hinduism, the foundation of the concept of Sanskritization, is essentially a culture concept."
11. But here we need to keep in mind that those who wish to creatively cultivate their mother languages need not be necessarily at logger heads with Sanskrit. For

example, Gandhi wrote in Gujarati but he read Sanskrit. In his essay "Gandhi and Gita" Bakker helps us understand this:

> [...] We need to be aware of the extent to which the articulation of Gandhian social philosophy is 'Sanskrit-based.' [...] In addition to his native Gujarati it was the study of Hindu (and Hindu-Buddhist) scriptures, often in the 'original' Sanskrit, that influenced him most deeply (Bakker 1998: 225).

12. In his essay, "The Social Significance of Religion in India," Srinivas writes: "As a result of two centuries of contact with the West, the activist streak in Hinduism is receiving greater emphasis, the Bhagvad Gita is becoming the single most important book of the Hindus" (2009: 369).
13. It must be noted that when Britishers came, the official language of Mughal courts was Persian. We need to understand the dialectic of valorization of Sanskrit in Orientalism as well as in colonial government with Persian as well as mother language spaces of India.
14. Here we can compare Oommen's present critique of Sanskritization with his earlier critique of Srinivas' concept of dominant caste (Oommen 1970) It seems that the later critique is more foundational than the former. While his critique of dominant caste raises foundational questions to the very concept of dominant caste, in his critique of Sanskritization we do not find a parallel critique, for example, of the conflation of language and social reality in this.
15. Oommen considers Saivism as the core of Dravidian Hinduism but was there no relationship between Saivism in Tamil Nadu and Saivism in Kashmir?
16. From a comparative historical perspective, we can note similar processes of Orientalist influence in the construction of Buddhism in Thailand. This has been commented upon in discussing the work of Buddhist reformer Budhadasa Bikhu in Thailand (see Jackson 1987).
17. It is this pain that we must understand in the dynamics of social and cultural change. Srinivas' account of Sanskritization misses the pain of people who do not make it in their striving for emulation. As Oommen rightly argues, imitation also can be protest. See Rao 1979.
18. Oommen here argues that a dialogue between Y.B. Damle and M.N. Srinivas on Sanskritization and reference group behaviour could have enriched discussion and understanding of such issues in Indian sociology. For Oommen,

> Damle applied "reference group theory to analyse mobility within caste. [...] Merton's unit of analysis in reference group behaviour is the individual who functions in American society characterized by acute individualism. The mechanism adopted is anticipatory socialization, that is, gradually internalizing the norms and values of the group in which s/he aspires membership. It is an individual-group dynamic [...]
>
> In contrast, given the fact that the Indian individual has little autonomy [...] and it is the lower castes which aspire to move upward, by adopting the norms and values of the upper castes, the dynamic involved is an inter-group one. Admittedly, M.N. Srinivas' formulation of sanskritization can be justifiably described as the Indian variant of anticipatory socialization. [...]. By so doing the power of reference group theory could have been considerably enhanced. Unfortunately Damle has not attempted this and Srinivas has ignored reference group theory. To my mind this was a missed opportunity for Indian sociologists/social anthropologists for extending the frontiers of social theory (Oommen 2007b: 10–11).

References

Ankersmit, F.R. 2002. *Political Representation.* Stanford: Stanford University Press.

Bakker, J.I. (Hans). 1998. "Gandhi and the Gita: Sanskrit and Satyagraha." In *Ethics, Religion and Culture: Facets of Mahatma Gandhi.* Vol. 4, (eds.) Subrata Mukherjee and Sushila Ramaswamy. New Delhi: Deep & Deep Publications, pp. 203–233.

Beteille, Andre. 1996. *Caste, Class and Power.* 2nd Edition. Delhi: Oxford University Press.

——. 2003. "Introduction to the New Impression." *Religion and Society among the Coorgs of South India,* Delhi: Oxford University Press, pp. xvii-xxix.

——. 2009. "Sociology and Ideology." *Sociological Bulletin* 58 (2): 196–211.

Charsley, Simon. 1998. "Sanskritization: The Career of an Anthropological Theory." *Contributions to Indian Sociology* (ns) 32 (2): 527–549.

Deshpande, Satish. 2003. *Contemporary India: A Sociological View.* New Delhi: Viking Penguin.

Gasper, Des. 2003. "Anecdotes, Situations, Histories: Varieties and Uses of Cases in Thinking about Ethics and Development Practice." In Philip Quarles van Ufford and Ananta Kumar Giri (eds.), *A Moral Critique of Development: In Search of Global Responsibilities*, London: Routledge, pp. 194–220.

Giri, Ananta Kumar. 2006. "Creative Social Research: Rethinking Theories and Methods and the Calling of an Ontological Epistemology of Participation." *Dialectical Anthropology* 30 (3 and 4): 227–271.

——. 2004. "The Calling of Creative Transdisciplinarity." In *Creative Social Research: Rethinking Theories and Methods,* (ed.) Ananta Kumar Giri, New Delhi: Vistaar, pp. 345–358

Ingold, Tim. 2006. "Rethinking the Animate, Re-animating Thought", *Ethnos* 71(1): 9–20.

Jackson, Peter A. 1987. *Buddhadasa: Theravada Buddhism and Modernist Reform in Thailand.* Chiangmai, Thailand: Silkworm Books.

Mishra, Godavarish. 2004. "Transdisciplinary Methods and Tools of Experiment: Insights from the Philosophical Traditions of Buddhism and Vedanta." In *Creative Social Research: Rethinking Theories and Methods,* (ed.) Ananta Kumar Giri, New Delhi: Vistaar, pp. 273–296.

Mintz, Sideny W. 1960. *A Worker in the Cane: A Puerto Rican Life History.* Yale: Yale University Press.

——. 1979. "The Anthropological Interview and Life History." *The Oral History Review* 7: 18–26.

Murphy, Robert F. 1987. *The Body Silent.* New York: W.W. Norton.

Oommen, T.K. 1970. "The Concept of Dominant Caste: Some Queries." *Contributions to Indian Sociology* (NS) IV: 73–83.

——. 2002. *Pluralism, Equality and Identity: Comparative Studies.* Delhi: Oxford University Press.

——. 2007a. *Knowledge and Society: Situating Sociology and Social Anthropology.* Delhi: Oxford University Press.

——. 2007b. 'Y.B. Damle: The Teacher, the Researcher and the Scholar'. Department of Sociology, University of Pune: Occasional Paper.

——. 2008. "Disjunction between Field, Method and Concept: An Appraisal of M.N. Srinivas." *Sociological Bulletin* 57 (1): 60–81.

Nadkarni, M.V. 2008. "Hinduism and Caste." *Sociological Bulletin* 57 (3): 402–404.

——. Forthcoming. "Limits of the Analytical Method: A Perspective from Bhagvadgita for Holistic Social Science Research." In *Pathways of Creative Research,* (ed.) Ananta Kumar Giri.

Pandian, M.S.S. 2007. *Brahmin and Non-Brahmin: Genealogies of the Tamil Political Present.* Delhi: Permanent Black.

Puligandla, Ramakrishna. 1996. "The Central Upanishadic Insights and their Significance to Deconstruction and Theory of Everything." Department of Philosophy, University of Madras: Memorial Lecture.

Rao, M.S.A. 1979. *Social Movements and Social Transformations: A Study of Two Backward Class Movements in India.* Delhi: Macmillan.

Shah, A.M. 2005. "Sanskritization Revisited." *Sociological Bulletin* 54 (2): 238–249.

——. 2008. "On M.N. Srinivas and Indian Society: Violation of the Norms of Academic Discourse." *Sociological Bulletin* 57 (3): 388–404.

Srinivas, M.N. 1942. *Marriage and Family in Mysore.* Bombay: New Book Company.

——. 2003 [1952]. *Religion and Society among the Coorgs of South India.* Delhi: Oxford University Press.

——. 2003. "An Obituary On Caste as A System." *Economic and Political Weekly* 38 (5): 455–459.

——. 2009. *The Oxford India Srinivas.* Delhi: Oxford University Press.

Welz, Frank. 2009. "100 Years of Indian Sociology: From Social Anthropology to Decentering Global Sociology." *International Sociology* 24 (5): 635–655.

Wilfred, Felix. 2004. "Indian Theologies: Retrospect and Prospects: A Socio-Cultural Perspective." In *Encounters with the World: Essays to Honour Aloysius Pieris, S.J.,* Edited by Aloysius Pieris, Marshal Fernando and Asanga Tilakaratne. Colombo: Ecumenical Institute for Study and Dialogue, pp. 145–176.

Part II

Movements and Transformations

12 Social Movements in the Advanced Societies and the Emerging Transnational Spaces

The menaces of the programmed society are global and strongly related to symbolic and cultural processes.

— Peter Gundelach (1990)
"Hopes and Menaces of the Programmed Society", p. 6

No period in post-war era has witnessed such a massive and unexpected emergence of new movements on a global scale as has the eighties. *And rarely has the discrepancy between the practices and analyses of new movements been so acute.* [...] The movements of the seventies were characterised by their basically cultural dimension. Beyond their different and multiple significance, they were the agents of a major cultural change: the shift from industrial to post-industrial values. Theoretically, this led to an essentially and often cultural definition. In contrast, without having lost this cultural dimension, the movements of the eighties are characterised by their basically ethical dimension. They do not appeal to alternative sensibility, and even less to collective interest, but to personal responsibility for a collective future at a local, national, and planetary level.

— Zsuzsa Hegedus (1990)
"Social Movements and Social Change in Self-Creative Society: New Civil Initiatives in the International Arena", p. 263, 266

Contemporary India, by virtue of its bicultural experience, manages to epitomize the global problem of knowledge and power in our times. There is a continuity between the Indian experience of an increasingly violent modern science, encroaching upon other traditions of knowledge and social life [like the rising debate over large-scale dams that displace thousands, can erode the landscape and cause long-term ecological damage, and transform the nature of agrarian relations], and the Western experience with modern science as the dominant cultural experience resisting the emergence of new cultures of knowledge [like the resistance to investigating in exploration and production of alternative forms of energy].

— Ashis Nandy cited in Michael M.J. Fischer (1995),
"Eye(I)ing the Sciences and their Signifiers (Language, Tropes, Autobiographies): InterViewing for a Cultural Study of Science and Technology", p. 55

Until recently, theories in the social sciences have paid little attention to grass roots movements, especially those of a transnational character. Whether it is the Durkheimian and Parsonian sociological theory of "the social system" or the Boasian concept of culture, theories have tended to focus instead on the nation-state or its various microcosms: formal organizations, rational bureaucracies, political parties and cultural systems. Thus little attention has been given to the social movements as part of the *weltanschauung* of the social scientists. Since the 1960s, however, following the post-war boom, there have been several crises in socialist and capitalists nation-states, as well as a "crisis of representation" in the social sciences. As a result of these changes, the last two decades witnessed the emergence of new movements in the realms of social organization, and in various domains of social scientific inquiry. The growth of grass roots "critical social movements" in "world regional locales as diverse as North America, Japan, Europe, China & Mexico" (Wallerstein et al., 1986) have parallelled the growth of new frames of reference in the social sciences, including postmodernism, "practice," "body," "language game," "structuration," and the renewed significance of "everyday life" (Geertz 1983; Ortner 1984; Turner 1984; Vincent 1984). To make sense of the contemporary human condition, it is useful to note these parallel crises in the "nation-state" and in social science "representation," and the critical responses of various emerging social and theoretical movements to these crises.

In this chapter, I discuss the emergence of different social movements in the contemporary advanced industrial societies. These societies have witnessed the rise of new kinds of social movements in the last quarter century – movements which articulate their agenda as different from the old party-based socio-political movements. I discuss the work of such movements in the advanced societies and the response they embody to the challenge of post-industrial transformation at work in these societies. I also discuss how these movements are looked upon as bearers of new frames of interpretation for the actors and institutions of these societies. Besides, I discuss too some theoretical issues in the study of social movements in general and the new social movements in particular.

As we shall see below, social movements in the advanced societies are emerging in the context of the "legitimation crisis" (cf. Habermas 1973) of nation-states and I discuss this as well as the related issue of globalization by describing the emerging transnational spaces as a result of the interface between globalization and new social movements. Though the chapter discusses the question of social movements and transnationalism mainly from the vantage point of actors and institutions in advanced industrial societies, it briefly discusses the rise of new movements in the developing societies in the context of their crisis of the discourse of development (see Wignaraja 1993). It argues that the challenges to the discourse of development and the developmental logic of state in the developing societies parallels the challenges to structure and state that new social movements pose in advanced industrial societies and taken together they help us make sense of the transnational world in the making – a world which just does not mirror the logic of modernity but in many ways go beyond it.

Social Movements in the Advanced Societies

Over the last decades, critical social movements of various kinds have proliferated in advanced industrial societies of Europe and North America. For instance, ecological movements in these societies have challenged the modernist discourse of development and organizational logic of political parties. In West Germany, the Green movement had introduced a "new style of politics" into the electoral system, according to which it is a committee rather than an individual which provides leadership to grass roots groups (Capra and Spretnak 1984). The peace movement in advanced industrial societies represents, on a normative level, "the penetration of a communicatively based democratic process of will formation into the private preserves of technocratic rationality" (Hegedus 1987). The social bases of the peace movement have combined secular and religious currents with flexible left-of-centre politics (Berman 1982; Hirsch 1982). Anti-nuclear protest in Europe has fought against miliary expansion by proposing an alternative model of development and industrial reconversion. In this movement's trajectory, "the militants passed from a cultural critique of the state" (Touraine 1983: 60). Thus, their main objective is – as one of Touraine's informants puts it – "to testify, to alert others" and "not to win something" (Touraine 1983a: 45). Finally, women's movements in these societies have challenged phallocentric discourses and patriarchal social institutions. Feminist movements have used the non-conventional political methods of consciousness raising, collectives and caucuses (Hellman 1987).[1]

The Challenge of Post-industrial Transition

Advanced industrial societies are now confronted with the challenge of a post-industrial transformation. Post-industrial transformation is accompanied by both the pangs of de-industrialization and dislocation as well as by what Fred Block (1990) has called "post-industrial opportunities". But, the realization of post-industrial opportunities depends not only on the social operation of critical movements but also on cultivating what could be called a movemental ethos in the actors and the systems. Indeed, the proliferation and dynamics of critical grass roots social movements can challenge simplistic definitions of post-industrialism and its consequences (Burns and Uberhost 1989). Post-industrial societies are increasingly dependent on new technologies and electronic communications which have, in turn, created a tightly integrated "system world" at the local, national and global levels. But a variety of communitarian and other populist political movements have brought a significant measure of participatory democracy to these societies, bringing the perspective of the dialogic "life world," as formulated by Habermas (Calhoun 1986, 1988).

The new technologies of computers and micro-electronics are rapidly transforming the nature of work in advanced industrial societies. New technologies facilitate the growth of corporate mega-structures (Derber 1982; Touraine 1988). But, the crucial challenge in making sense of contemporary social reality is to understand how new technologies interact in the contemporary stratified social reality and how grass roots social movements can point to the alternative application of these technologies. Advanced technologies in post-industrial societies are being used as an instrument to control workers and ordinary people. But they also have a more non-hierarchical and democratizing potential: according to Zuboff, they simultaneously "automate" and "informate" (Zuboff 1988; Rapp 1988; Shaiken 1984). Shaiken's study of the Numerical Control Machine shows how, in some cases, technology is viewed as a tool for the enhancement of the power of the machinist (who often does a considerable amount of programming), rather than as a vehicle to control the worker. In the operation of new technologies, "the questions that we face today are finally about leadership. Will they be able to create the organizational conditions in which new visions, new concepts, and a new language of work place relations can emerge?" (Zuboff 1988: 64). Grass roots social movements, for observers such as Zuboff and Shaiken, are the instruments for democratizing the social base of the new technology.

In similar ways, Manuel Castells' (1985) study of high technology and space in contemporary global capitalism shows how the "political dynamics of the decision-making process partially restores the space of historical meaning" in the context of the internationalization of capital and information flows made possible by advanced technology (also, see Gale 1984). In high-tech areas such as Silicon Valley, California, and Route 128, Boston, powerful grass roots social movements resist limitless growth (Saxenian 1985). High technologies are restructuring the spatial configuration in the cities, and understanding this high-tech induced spatial and social transformation requires an ethnographic understanding of the "social-political processes such as the new neighborhood movement" (Castells 1985: 33). Furthermore, in the case of new reproductive technologies, grass roots political activism has become a clear option. Rapp (1988: 155) argues that new reproductive technologies create wider choices about disability and reproductive rights, but they also create silences which "[have] to be lifted out of the medical context and negotiated as part of popular culture".

The Discourse of Social Needs

In the case of the "new service sector" where information technology plays a major role, we must understand the tensions between the social movements that define new "collective identities" and the more intensified and localized business planning system (Hirschorn 1985: 185). In the case of the post-industrial service sector and the accompanying discourse on "social needs," it is the grass roots social movement that makes public the so-called private needs and "contest the administrative logic of the social state as they struggle for the power to interpret their members' needs and to institute democratic, dialogic and empowering communicative relations" (Fraser 1987: 31). For Nancy Fraser, in order to comprehend contemporary late-capitalistic societies, we must contextualize the changes in social structure with respect to the "change in the characteristics of social discourse". "Needs-talk" is the centre of the late capitalist social discourse, which has given rise to a contested terrain of interpretation and representation, between the states on one hand, and various collective agents or social movements on the other (Gans 1988; Kothari 1986, 1987, 1988; Preteceille and Terrail 1985). If postmodern society is characterized by the centrality of interpretation (cf. Bauman 1987), then social movements are significant interpretive agents in the ongoing discourse on social needs. Their need interpretation is dialogical, while that of the social state is monological (Fraser 1987). While the economy, the state and other large-scale institutions in this contested terrain appear to most citizens as alien forces of the "system world," the rights advocacy of "social movements is an extension of people's "life world". These social movements not only resist the encroachment of the system world, they "also try to understand the system world through the extension of life-world categories" (ibid.). Fraser shows how by initiating a social movement social welfare clients can create a "life world" among themselves and can transform their position from a "stigma connoting dependence, atomization and disempowerment into a political identity, the identity of a constituted collectivity" (ibid.: 28).

Urban Social Movements

In the advanced societies, we also see the emergence of urban social movements which strive to redefine the meaning of the city, emphasizing its use value over exchange value, which is historically connected, among other things, to "the feminist theme of identity and communication" (Lowe 1986: 53). Cities in advanced industrial societies have become major locations for a variety of social movements and political struggles. Urban social movements are distinct from conventional political parties, pressure groups and voluntary associations (Castells 1983). Urban issues cut across basic class divisions as a result of exposure to common consumption problems and link different social classes, especially the middle class and the working class (Harvey 1973; 1985). In this context, the significance of urban social movements has to be understood through such vantage points: these movements remove the social care system from the market place and "decommodify" them (Scarpaci 1991). However, urban social movements "are not agents of structural social change, but symptoms of resistance to the social domination even if, in their effort to resist, they do have major effects on cities and societies" (Castells 1983: 329).

The Coming of New Social Movements

While studies of contemporary post-industrial societies point to the contextual operation, inevitability and necessity for grass roots social movements, the literature on contemporary political practice (cf. Castells 1983; Walker 1988) and the consciousness of the subject (cf. Harvey 1987; Martin 1987) point to "critical social movements" as the emerging type of political activism. In this context, many observers have proclaimed the coming of "the new social movements" (cf. Cohen 1985) in the advanced societies which "fight for symbolic and cultural stakes, for the achievement of new meaning in social action" (Walker 1988: 96). These movements are considered socio-cultural, rather than socio-political, insofar as they strive to create a new collective cultural identity for people instead of fighting for resource mobilization, as did earlier social and political movements (Frank and Fuentes 1987; Touraine, 1981).

Advocates of new social movements theory tells us that these new movements are not only cultural; they also derive their inspiration and strength from traditional culture (Cox 1984; Touraine 1983a 1983b). At present, science is a part of the established discourse. Hence, it is people's traditions, or what Nandy calls "critical traditionalism," which are the source of anti-systemic thinking and practice (Nandy 1987a, 1987b, 1988; Touraine 1988). There is a divorce between social structure and culture in post-industrial societies because social structures become cogs in the huge corporations, while culture becomes the local practice (Bell 1973; Touraine 1988). What becomes very clear, especially in the works of Castells (1983), Touraine (1988) and Martin (1986) is that the subject's ability to resist the system comes from the realm of culture. In this context, it seems that the distinction between "civilization" and "culture" that Robert MacIver had made is helpful in understanding the cultural basis of grass roots social movements in responding to the crisis in the contemporary global system. For MacIver, civilization is what we have and culture is what we are. It is interesting to note from a comparative perspective that Sunderlal Bahuguna, leader of the famous socio-ecological movement in the central Himalayas called Chipko, defines it as a "response of culture" to the "crisis in civilization" (Bahuguna 1987).

The new social movements not only derive their inspiration from local tradition, they also emphasize local action and are firmly rooted in a specific topography. They are also local to the extent that they struggle to revitalize civil society and to emphasize individual action (Walker 1988). These critical social movements are often modest in their struggle and outcome (Touraine 1981). In some cases, they may be "less concerned with challenging the structures of exclusion than with resisting their worst effect in particular ways" (Walker 1988: 107). Their mode of resisting may be very subtle, where "everyday life" itself becomes a site of struggle and resistance (Falk 1987). Their practices draw on "the clear understanding that people are always engaged in politics" (Walker 1988: 107). As Joe Bailey (1988: 279) writes: "The idea that politics is lived is not new [...]. But the idea of politics as primarily expressed through a way of life is a popular phenomenon mainly of the last twenty years." The practices of the grass roots social movements embody a new micro-macro dialectic, where the imperative is to "think locally and transform globally" (Kothari 1987: 285). This politicization of everyday life is essential for "the take-off point of humane governance" (ibid.: 279).

For many observers, the new social movements are not only cross-class alliances, but they also provide a unique context for intellectuals to participate actively in addressing vital social issues (see Burdick 1995). Because of the increasing role of "knowledge" and "information' in the definition of many issues that the new social movements confront, solidarity between concerned actors and activists becomes inevitable (Downey 1988).

The new social movements must be appropriately situated in the ongoing structural and discursive transformation taking place in the advanced societies; understanding their genealogy requires placing them in the context of the coming of the post-industrial society and the "culture shift" (Inglehart 1990) that it is facilitating. Alain Touraine (1981) helps us in situating these new social movements in the transformed organization of social life, in the transformed organization of what he calls as the "programmed societies" (ibid.). For Touraine, class domination in programmed societies "consists less in organizing work than managing the production and data-processing apparatus, i.e., ensuring the often monopolistic control of the supply and processing of a certain type of data, and hence of a way of organizing social life" (ibid.: 6). According to Touraine, "What is crucial now is no longer the struggle between capital and labour in the factory but that between different kinds of apparatus and user-consumers" (ibid.). For Touraine, "The institutionalization of labor conflicts which transform the worker's movements into a truly political force has made it lose its role as a central social movement while at the same time increasing its role in national life. In post-industrial society, social movements formed around what is called consumption in the name of personal or collective identity, yet at the heart of the greater apparatus of production and management – not in relation to the system of ownership" (1977: 323). Social movements are agents of historicity and "self-production" in programmed societies where "society's work upon itself is no longer carried out only in the economic order but almost always in the domains of culture" (Touraine 1981: 73).

It is here that attention to the culture shift in advanced societies becomes crucial in understanding new social movements as they are emerging in the discursive field of this culture shift and as a very significant bearer of this culture shift itself. For Ronald Inglehart (1990), the most crucial dimension in this culture shift is the shift from materialist to post-materialist values. For Inglehart, because of unprecedented prosperity and the absence of war in western countries since 1945, younger birth cohorts place less emphasis on economic and physical security than do older groups. On the other hand, they tend to give a high priority to non-material needs, "such as a sense of community and the quality of life" (ibid.: 56). The rise of post-materialism, as a widespread social value, has led to the blurring of the familiar political boundaries between the Left and the Right and has created the genealogical context for the rise of the new social movements as a novel mode of relating to oneself and as a new political practice. Inglehart has noted: "[...] the Materialist/Postmaterialist dimension has played a crucial role in the rise of the wave of the new social movements" (ibid.: 372). Inglehart further shows us how "the rise of postmaterialism has placed existing party systems under chronic stress" and post-materialists of the middle class origin articulate the "non-economic" issues as "the most heated" ones in political discourse (ibid.: 278).

This account of the shifting trajectory of the political orientations, the "recomposition and 'fragmentation' of the historical relations of representation between classes and parties [...] the emergence of new arenas of contestation, new sites of social antagonism, new social movements, and new social subjects and political identities in contemporary society'" (Hall 1988: 2) seems to be corroborated by commentaries coming even from the scholars with committed Left leanings. David Harvey's outstanding inquiry (1989) into the origin of contemporary cultural change is a case in point. If Inglehart places the contemporary culture shift in the habitus of the post-materialists, Harvey situates it in the material and ideological practice of what he calls the "cultural mass" (Harvey 1991). For Harvey, the cultural mass – large number of people who work in the academia, the media, journalism and cultural production – constitutes the core of the new social movements and they raise many significant questions which are often labelled as postmodern. For Harvey, "In recent years, the cultural mass has pursued a whole host of political and ideological struggles that have generated significance: anti-racism, feminism, the struggles concerning ethnic identity, religious tolerance, cultural decolonization and the like. Because postmodernism is associated with a democratization of voice within the cultural mass, many of the struggles against a central source of authority and power [...] have enlisted under the postmodern banner" (ibid.: 75). But, unlike other enthusiastic commentators discussed so far, Harvey adds a note of caution and sarcasm in his assessment of the new social movements. For Harvey, "the problem is that these fights are being waged in a homogeneous class context" (ibid.). Harvey puts the new social movements in a critical perspective: "New social movements gained a stronger purchase on political consciousness [...] seeming to represent alternatives to the working class as agents of human emancipation. But these movements were frequently victims of capitalist co-optation [...]" (ibid.: 69). The segment of the left in the cultural mass lost its tenuous link with the weakened working class movement and spent their energy in "deconstructing discourses and engaging in all manner of language games" (ibid.). Harvey's sarcasm requires special attention: "Radicals within the cultural mass became charmed by fields like semiotics, as if the really interesting thing about the homeless were the variety of coded messages of protest that cardboard boxes could convey" (ibid.).

But Harvey's critical reflection does not end with this sarcasm only and he appreciates the significance of the postmodern turn for the rise of the new social movements: "The postmodern turn within the cultural mass has placed the treatment of difference and 'otherness' firmly on the political agenda" (ibid.: 75). Indeed, in advanced societies, there is the politicization of all sorts of differences and a struggle over their definition and rights vis-à-vis the state – be it the welfare mothers or the homosexuals or the alien undocumented workers or the Latin American refugees in the American heartland. The social movements are the key articulator of this differential politics.

The Idea of New Social Movements: Some Critical Notes

Much of the discussion on the new social movements in advanced industrial countries has come from one particular theoretical camp, namely, the New Social Movement (NSM) theory, and it is important to understand that it is a particular point of view and it does not exhaust the varieties of perspectives on contemporary movements. What we should call a new social movement is a question of ethnography and description, and has less to do with our enthusiasm. In this context, it is also important to realize that much of our enthusiastic interpreters of the new social movements – be it R.B.J. Walker or Jurgen Habermas or even Alain Touraine – have provided little actual ethnographic description of how social movements work on the ground. At the same time, the NSM theory and its stress on identity formation has to be understood in the context of the claims of the Resource Mobilization (RM) theory. In the RM theory, the contemporary resurgence of movement activity is explained not by the system's "legitimation crisis," but by the increase in the resources needed to express dissent. As Zald and McCarthy (1987: 328), two influential proponents of the RM theory, write: "The existence of marginal resources, gathered from many middle class suppliers, or large amounts of resources, gathered through churches, philanthropic organizations, and labor unions, permits movement entrepreneurs to find an organizational niche even when a mass base of activists [...] are difficult to find." In the resource repertoire of movements, technological developments like computer-personalized letters play a crucial role. The success of these movements depends upon their organizational infrastructure. For instance, Zald (in Zald and McCarthy 1987) argues that the pro-life movement in the US has had an edge over the pro-choice movement because of its ability to use the infrastructure of existing organizations such as the church (also see Ginsburg 1989). Fund-raising is a very important preoccupation of many movements which could be called "new social movements" and they spend a lot of energy in manufacturing a particular image that could be sold to the public at large for raising funds, which is crucial to carrying out the social objectives of these movements. Thus, in the work of contemporary movements, "identity formation" and "resource mobilization" interact with each other in manifold ways – a reality which is lost sight of by the stark opposition that has been made in contemporary theories between new social movements as seekers of identity formation and old social movements as striving for resource mobilization.

Indeed, it is true that the recent paradigm shift in the field of social movements has been the "reassertion of the political" (McAdam et al., 1988: 699), focusing on "the politics of collective action: its relation to the state, to conventional forms of political exchange and to political and to policy change" (Tarrow 1988: 422). But, the politics that the NSM theorists focus is the politics of the life world. But such an argument of the NSM theory is contested by other students of collective action even in advanced industrialized countries. For Tarrow, "although there is a continuing reason to distinguish between the internal logic of social movements and that of conventional groups, the dynamics of collective action – even in its most expressive and anti-political forms – are best understood in relation to the political process" (ibid.). For Charles Tilly, the NSM theorists such as Melucci still operate with the image of the special sort of group as the basic units of social movements. But, the "proper analogy of social movement is neither a party nor a union but political campaign. What we call social movement actually consists in a series of demands of challenges to power holders in the name of a social category that lacks an established political position" (Tilly 1985: 736). Tilly and his associates show that local, regional and national struggles for power account for a high proportion of collective action in Europe. They stress a "co-occurrence between social movement activity and increases in conventional political participation," pointing to the students of the new social movements that "the stark division often drawn between new and old might be overdrawn" (cf. Tarrow 1988: 424).

In talking about the RM theory, it must be stressed that the RM theory has moved away from its initial Olsonian (Olson 1965) moorings in the work of Tilly (1978) and Hirschman (1982) and stresses the linkage between movement and other institutions in the polity. Rather than seeing organization and movement as contrasting phenomena, this theory has begun to see them as embedded (Oommen 1990). In the context of the new social movement theory's distinction between the organized movements and the spontaneous movements, the RM theory allows the possibility of a variety of organizational forms of movements. For instance, Hertz (1982) found a segmentary organizational form in case of the welfare mothers' movement (also see Schester 1982). But what is more significant is that the RM theorists have also begun to be sensitive to the question of identity formation and "frame alignment processes" (Snow et al., 1986) in collective action. This prepares the context for developing an analytical framework that goes beyond the limitations of both the NSM theory and the RM theory. In his study of European anti-nuclear movements, Thomas Rochon finds both these theories inadequate: an RM theorist "would have trouble understanding the local activities of the Peace Movements, many of which do not have a political target at all" (Rochan 1988: 22) and an NSM theorist would have difficulty in interpreting the fact that the "political strategy of Peace Movement has not been determined by the new social movement ideologues" (ibid.: 210). What Ronald Inglehart writes from the other camp is also significant:

> Clearly, the emergence of new values has not been the sole factor involved. Objective problems, organizations, and ideologies have all been at work. And the emergence of the new social movements owes much to the gradually rising level of political skills among mass publics, as education has become more widespread and political information more pervasive. But the emergence of new value priorities has also been an important factor (Inglehart 1990: 372).

In this context, in order to make sense of the dynamics of contemporary social movements, there is the urgent necessity for a dynamic and creative fusion of perspectives. This lies in being sensitive to the "dialectics of resource mobilization and identity formation in the constitution of social movements" (Giri 1989: 336). This also calls for taking note of the variety of collective movements and what configuration the three important elements of collective action – mobilization, institutionalization and consciousness formation – have in a particular movement. There are two broad kinds of movements in our times: organizational movements and discursive movements. These two kinds of movements require different emphases from a student vis-à-vis the question of discourse and power. While in case of the organizational movements, one can identify a solid organization which can be subjected to sociological research, discursive movements are those which are primarily discursive in nature where movemental activism does not manifest itself in a well-defined organizational form and where activism starts with a discourse and strives to create a new language of self, society and cosmos (Giri 1992). In studying a discursive movement, besides mobilization and institutionalization, what needs careful attention from a sociologist who, in fact, has very few tools to make sense of it, is the process of consciousness formation – the process by which members of a movement become part of an "imagined community," the way participants of a community become a community of discourse. This requires careful attention to texts that inspire rather than simply the context of operation, to the issue of persuasion and the articulation of a new language rather than the sole sociological question of protest and power. But this idea of a discursive movement is proposed not in diametrical opposition to the idea of organizational movements, but with a degree of differential emphases. The fundamental challenge to the sociological imagination is to understand the dialectic between values and power; hence one has to be always on the guard so that these differential emphases do not degenerate into a kind of symbolic involution re-enacting the familiar cockfight between symbolism and the analysis of power.

Another problem in the theory of new social movements is its distinct Eurocentrism. This comes out clearly in the distinction between the social movement and the political party that the NSM theorists make. Such a distinction reflects the particular cultural experience and the social history of Western Europe. The non-party and non-institutional nature of collective mobilization revealed in the practice of the new social movements in the post-war period seems to have struck European social scientists as a uniquely new experience. Yet, in the case of the United States, non-party, grass roots associations and movements have spearheaded the cause of social justice more frequently than the organized labour (Tocqueville 1966; Sorokin 1950).

Another crucial point in the discussion of new social movements is to what extent one can globalize the NSM perspective in understanding contemporary collective actions. New social movements in the Third World would have a different relationship between meaning and production, than it would have in the First World. For instance, Pramod Parajuli (1991: 181) argues that new social movements in the Third World are not simply about the crisis in quality of life, but about production as well.

The broadly middle class origin of the new social movements in advanced societies is agreed invariably by all. But what happens to the issue of poverty and unemployment in these societies? Is there any taker for these causes? However, one agrees with Stuart Hall (1988) that even in case of poverty referring to the real experience would not do, i.e., this has to be ideologically constructed, but who is going to be engaged in a discursive construction of poverty? As one of Touraine's informants puts it: "The ecology movement has been totally incapable of explaining to workers and discussing with them importance of those themes for their day-to-day problems" (Touraine 1983a: 71).

These cautions can certainly help us in our understanding of both contemporary social movements and the emerging transformational challenges confronting us. But we cannot underestimate the theoretical and practical significance of the study of contemporary movements. For instance, the problem of the dualism of the structure and agency is one of the most fundamental theoretical challenges of our times a resolution of which has also significant practical correlation. It seems the study of creative grass roots movements can suggest how structures and agencies together create a communitarian space through a process of "structuration," a process of mutual transformation. As Anthony Giddens argues:

> The challenges facing sociology at the end of the twentieth century reflect the issues the new social movements have brought to the fore. On the extensional level, accelerating processes of globalization demand direct analysis and threaten to sweep away sociologists' traditional preoccupation with the study of 'societies' [...]. A global perspective must increasingly become central to sociological work,

> with all the complexities and difficulties that this entails. On the intensional level, transmutations are occurring in gender relations, personal life and conditions of day-to-day activity. How should we seek to interpret these changes in a world in which distance and proximity combine in ever tangled a fashion (Giddens, 1991: 221)?

But how do we come face to face with this challenge of interpreting "changes in a world in which distance and proximity combine in ever tangled a fashion?" Is world survey the answer to this epochal challenge? Giddens, the sociologist, writes: "All social research [...] presumes ethnography" (1991: 219). Here is the crucial role for cultural anthropology to play. The epochal challenge of our time is how to create solidarity at different levels – local, regional and the global – with its particular mix of familiarity and strangeness, identity and difference (Connolly 1991). At the contemporary moment, writes philosopher Richard Rorty, "[...] human solidarity is to be achieved not by inquiry but by imagination, the imaginative ability to see strange people as fellow sufferers [...] this process of coming to see other human beings as 'one of us' rather than as 'them' is a matter of detailed description of what we ourselves are like. This is a task not for theory but for genres such as ethnography" (Rorty 1989: xvi). Indeed, ethnographies of critical movements, which are also transnational in their articulation and operation, can help us in widening our horizons, rethink more concretely our identities and differences and be awakened by the portrayal of an alternative form of live. This description might help us discovering our "variant subjectivity" (Giri 1991a) and discover alternative spaces both within ourselves and in the contemporary globalizing world.

The Emerging Transnational Spaces

Current global reality, both in advanced industrial centres and in the developing peripheries, is characterized by the proliferation and dominance of critical social movements (Eide 1986; Esteva 1987; Falk 1987; Kothari 1986; Ruiz 1988). The world in which we live today has a different image (cf. Appadurai 1991) of itself, succinctly put in the following words: "Historians no longer need to invent the world in order to study world history. The world exists as a material fact. It lies before us demanding explanation, not as some distant chimeras, but as everyday experience" (Bright and Geyer 1987: 1). Social movements, which cut across the boundaries of nation-states and can be called transnational movements, are an important feature of our contemporary world and the emerging transnational spaces in it. These movements are not simply the extension of the networks of the nation-state; instead they embody a solidarity between people as citizens of the world and not solely as members of nation-states. An example of contemporary transnational initiative is the "sister-city movement" launched in the advanced societies. This initiative establishes partnership between a city in the developed world and one in the developing world. Wilbur Zelinsky, who has studied the contemporary process of "The Twinning of the World," writes: "Something new and remarkable, if not revolutionary, has been going on in the social geography of our late-twentieth-century world: the sister-city phenomenon. Over the past forty years, more than 11,000 twinning have been formalized among a wide variety of communities in at least 159 countries – people-to-people relationships, one is inclined to believe, are generally inspired by quite laudable ideals" (Zelinsky 1991: 2) These laudable ideals refer to a transnational and a global consciousness. The sister-city movement leads to a lot of traffic in personal contacts across the borders. The human and socio-cultural significance of such large-scale people-to-people contact must be understood. For instance, in Europe, with a total of 5,600 twinned towns, over a million people are involved in contacts every year. Most of the work in this sister-city twinning or even "trinning" is carried out by unpaid volunteers. According to Zelinsky, "With or without the encouragement of national agencies, the decision as to whether to enter into a particular arrangement is initiated at the local level by the townspeople, not by any central leadership" (ibid.: 3).

Apart from the socio-cultural significance of the meeting of cultures and peoples that takes place in the sister-city movements, there is also a political dimension which is reflected in the opportunity for "citizen diplomacy" that the sister-city phenomenon creates. This citizen diplomacy has sometimes been instrumental in effecting a turn in the foreign policy of the powerful countries. Here, one remembers the impact of the sister-city movement in turning public opinion in the US in favour of Nicaragua and against the US policy of launching a contra-led war in that country. According to Zelinsky, "More than any other single development, it is the Nicaraguan situation that illustrates the potentialities of an autonomous sister city movement and related transnational forms of citizen activism" (ibid.: 27). Moreover, for Zelinsky, citizen diplomacy in the sister-city movement undermines the integrity of the nation-state system. It is against this background of the twilight of sovereignty of the nation-state and the emergence of various non-state actors in the global domain that we must undertake our efforts of making sense of the contemporary world.

Twilight of Sovereignty: Transnational Movements as the Third System of Power

The contemporary global reality presents us three different configurations of power. The first refers to the power of the nation-states and inter-state organizations, which still exhausts the conventional analysis of the world system. The second refers to the power of the multinational and transnational corporations, which as global economic power could be, at least analytically, distinguished from the first configuration of the global political power. The third configuration refers to the power of the people's movements connected globally and operating across nation-states. This configuration of power, which development theorist Bjorn Hettne (1990) has aptly called "The Third System Politics," refers to the power of the transnational people's movements. They demonstrate that formal statist organizations and transnational corporations do not exhaust the scenario of non-state actors in the contemporary world. Different private citizens, transnational networks and global movements have "increasingly intruded in world politics without reference to governments or interstate organizations" (Mansbach et al., 1976: 26).

These transnational initiatives reflect Brandt's (1980) perspective that "the shaping of our common future is much too important to be left to governments and experts alone" (see also, Galtung 1980). The third system politics symbolizes a system of power "represented by people acting individually or collectively through voluntary institutions and associations" (Hettne 1990: 165). For Hettne, this third system politics, be it in the First World or in the Third World, is more issue-oriented, rather than functional – fulfilling the functional need of either the nation-state or the statist design of development. Hence, it is rooted more firmly and meaningfully in problematic locales and specific topographies, although the issues it deals with are translocal.

Instances of these transnational initiatives abound in our times. To start with, Habitat for Humanity, an ecumenical housing movement in the United States, which is building "homes" for the low-income families in thirteen hundred American communities and in nearly forty-five overseas countries (Fuller 1986; Giri 1994). Dan Chekki tells us about different "people-centred" transnational initiatives in Canada such as "Project Ploughshares," and the Canadian Catholic Organization for Peace and Development which, creates grass roots awareness for diverting "precious resources from military to socially useful purposes" (Chekki 1988: 392). Similarly, Kovack's study (1988) of local towns in Hungary shows the significance of local influences on its international relations. Ecological movements in the contemporary world have also generated a transnational network of concerned activists such as Petra Kelly, E.P. Eckholm and Sunderlal Bahuguna who provide inspiration for alternative striving across the globe. The Peace Movement and the Human Rights Movements are other instances of transnational initiatives where the concerned citizens of the world participate "to act locally, but to transform globally" (Kothari 1987: 285). These transnational initiatives get their pedigree from the student uprisings in the 1960s in Europe and North America (Habermas 1971; Touraine 1971) to "the Jacobite movement which played a pivotal role in the international politics of Europe at various times between 1688 and 1746" (Mansbach et al., 1976: 46).

The transnational movements have emerged in the context of what Jurgen Habermas calls the "legitimation crisis" of advanced societies. This refers to two different processes: on the one hand, the colonization of the life world by the system world makes the legitimacy of the states problematic in the consciousness of the actors; and on the other hand the "unintended consequences of the successful nation-building project" is the emergence of various meaningful transnational identities and identifications. The latter process takes place "where high level of education and welfare – the results of a successful nation-building project – are transformed into transnational identifications and concerns embraced by a reasonably large segment of the population" (Hettne 1990: 31). For Hettne, "The latter types of identifications are expressed for instance through the new social movements which due to their global concerns also challenge the legitimacy of the state" (ibid.).

If transnational movements in advanced societies are emerging in the context of the "legitimation crisis" of the nation-state, in the developing world they are coming into being in the context of the legitimation crisis of the discourse of development (cf. Apter 1987). Indeed, in the developing societies, development policy has formed an "integral part of the nation-building project" (Hettne 1990: 30). But, in the developing societies, the process of development as a logic the state has led to the annihilation of tribes, cultures and peoples. Thus, people's movements of various kinds question the developmental logic of the state; they fight against the displacement of people, culture, symbols and habitats that takes place in the name of modernization and development. It is significant to attend to the discourse of the people's movements as they are engaged in reconstructing the process of modernization and development from the vantage point of the victims and the displaced.[2] The people's science movement in contemporary India is an example of this critical reflection on modernity and development. Modern science and technology as the "Reason of the State" is the subject of attack here (Nandy 1988). Different science and technology groups in contemporary India are engaged in a serious evaluation of the relevance of modern science and technology for the predicaments of a developing society like India (Giri 1992). These movements are not simply romantic critics of science and technology; they also offer fundamental critiques of modern science and show how these assumptions, when carried out in public policies, bring havoc to the people (see Laughlin 1995). Here, Professor C.V. Seshadri's critique of the Second Law of Thermodynamics and implications for energy policy is remarkable. For Seshadri (who directed a technology group working on rural transformation named Murugappa Chettiar Research Centre, based in Chennai), because of the law of entropy, there is an inherent bias towards high-temperature energy sources and when this becomes the fulcrum of the energy policy in a developing society like India, we have neither the wisdom nor the resource to attend to the low-temperature energy sources like bio-mass which constitutes 53 per cent of the source of total energy consumed in India. Vinod Raina (1991), another key figure in the All India People's Science Movement, also offers a radical critique of the project of development which, for him, has led to one of the greatest man-made disasters in history. Varieties of critical movements, be it the Chipko or Swadhyaya[3] or the All India People's Science Movements, reflect this sensibility and their emergence coincides with the "declining hegemony of the development discourse [...]" (Parajuli 1991: 173).

The decline of the hegemony of development discourse has been caused by the contradiction inherent in the state-building project in the post-colonial world, especially due to the problem of the forcible collapse of the genuine distinction between state and society. Hence, it is not a coincidence that all these questions – the decline of the hegemony of state and development, the nature of the relationship between state and society and the rise of the transnational movements – are emerging simultaneously in the same space of critical movement and critical reflection. In this context, Hettne speaks of "the social project" whose significance for creating a genuine transnational space requires a closer look: "The concept of 'social project' transcends conventional social science analysis, whether it takes 'social class' or 'nation-state' as point of departure, and tries to make justice to both territorially orientated local action and transnational actors which are responding to world system politics" (Hettne 1990: 205; also see, Avadhuta 1985; Towsey 1990; Uberoi 1996).

The declining hegemony of the development discourse and the rise of alternative movements in the developing world, such as Chipko, Liberation Theology, and Swadhyaya have a global significance. These movements bring concerned actors from different countries together and have a potential for creating transnational solidarity. Different social movements in the developing world which fight against the developmental logic of the state become rallying points for transnational activism for the actors of new social movements in the advanced societies. If the building of Sardar Sarovar Dam over Narmada represents one kind of transnational integration, one made possible by the instrumentalities of powerful global actors such as the World Bank, then the movement against the dam (cf. Baviskar 1995) also becomes the rallying point for a different kind of transnational solidarity. Movements, such as Chipko and Narmada Bachao Andolana, have found additional support and strength from sympathetic and concerned citizens in Japan, Europe and North America.

But alternative movements in the Third World have another, far important, global significance too. These movements pursue many critical questions that are of concern to the actors of new social movements in the advanced societies such as the crisis of science, rationality, and state and the accompanying quest for establishing a "good society" (cf. Bellah et al., 1991). But, the prospects for real recovery and transforming the existing systems seem so much a distant dream in advanced industrial countries.[4] However, in the societies of the Third World, alternative visions of life and modes of livelihood exist not only in imagination but also in practice. Elements of the non-modern and pre-modern that exist in science, society and economy in these societies can provide a real basis for launching alternative efforts to go beyond the predicament of modernity (Nandy 1982; Giri 1995a, 1995b). These efforts can generate hopes for a different form of life – a life founded on values of reciprocity, sharing, productivity, dignity of labour, and recognition of irreducible human dignity – especially for the people of advanced industrial countries who are otherwise so wedded to the formal systems of money and power in the organization of their life and in the vision of it. As Giddens argues:

> An agenda of more thoroughgoing reform, starting from the Third World end rather than the First World, is needed to break this deadlock. Such a programme must place in question the very notion of development as economic growth, while still recognizing the enormous problems that global poverty presents. It has to be a challenge to modernity rather than an attempt to generalize it successfully everywhere (1994: 158).

Some Concluding Reflections

The worldwide rise of social movements in general and of "new social movements" in the advanced societies in particular is receiving increasing attention in social theory today. But students of social movements have not paid sufficient attention to the transnational dimension of their vision, consciousness formation and mobilization. This is clearly the case with the New Social Movement Theory which, in the recent years, has become such a globally significant mode of interpreting collective actions. In this chapter, apart from describing the specific experience of advanced industrial societies and the new social movements, a preliminary attempt has been made to understand the making of a transnational world from the vantage point of vision and practice of social movements.

But barring a brief discussion about social movements in the developing world, the transnational movements discussed here are primarily from the advanced societies. At this point, it is probably essential to spell out some of the reasons behind this. The first is, even though transnational movements originate from all sorts of locales[5] and the advanced societies are, certainly, not their sole incubators and exporters, they proliferate more in the advanced societies rather than in other locales in our contemporary world. Hence, understanding these movements from the vantage point of the experience of self and cultural transformation taking place in advanced societies helps us to understand the contours of these emergent formations from the "native point of view" (see Giri, 1995c). The second reason behind an extended discussion of the particular experience of the advanced societies is that this experience itself is becoming globalized. The condition of postmodernity, which is probably the most important genealogical context for the origin of social movements in the advanced societies, is now in a process of global diffusion. Even in a society such as India, one would ignore this postmodern dimension of contemporary development only at one's own perils. Many critical movements in contemporary India have a predominantly middle-class repertoire of actors and they are being subject to a similar global process of doubt, disintegration and reconstruction, as their counterparts in the advanced societies.

Notes

1. Hellman's study, for example, shows the feminist challenge to the model of militancy in the Italian Communist Party.
2. In this context, what Paul Ekins (cited in Giddens 1994: 158–159) writes deserves our careful attention:

   > On the one side are scientism, developmentalism and statism, backed by the big battalions of the establishment: modern technology, and the institutions of world capitalism and state power. On the other are the people, principally the 30 per cent of humanity that is disposable as far as the modern project is concerned, but aided and abetted by many from the other 70 per cent who regard this project as ethically, socially and environmentally intolerable.

3. Swadhyaya is an exciting initiative in multi-dimensional transformation of self and society in contemporary India (see, Giri 2008; Roy 1993; Seth 1994).
4. In this context, we can take into account the argument of Claus Offe and Rolph G. Heinze about building alternative socio-economic institutions, which are not founded on the hegemonic and exclusionary logic of money and market but on the socialization of time and labour. Offe and Heinze argue that exchange networks, what they call "co-operation circles," perform an important role in mitigating the burden of the poor in the advanced industrial countries. However, for them, these networks cannot supplant the system; instead, they have to work as supplements. In their view, by "their very nature cooperation circles can only be marginal gap-fillers. For that reason they should not encourage hopes of far-reaching social reform [...]" The advocates of such initiatives also should not abstain from broader political intervention since the facilitating support from other institutions in society are crucial to their functioning.

   Offe and Heinze are cautious in their evaluation of the promise of the "co-operation circles" to create value because the society in which they live has destroyed this as a viable one. But in many societies in the world even today such as in contemporary India, there is a greater possibility for the success of moneyless exchange system where "time" and "labour" are the main currencies of exchange, not money.

5. Until recently, the construction of globalism used to be the sole prerogative of the modern West. But, at present, global movements emanate not only from the developed post-industrial world where there is the obvious advantage of resource and communication for carrying out a global movement, but also from the developing societies which then diffuses to the whole world.

   Anand Marg and International Krishna Consciousness are instances of transnational initiatives from India which work in many countries.

References

Adorno, Theodore et al. 1972. *Aspects of Sociology*. Boston: Beacon Press.

Appadurai, Arjun. 1991. "The Global Ethnoscape: Notes and Queries for a Transnational Anthropology." In Richard G. Fox (ed.), *Recapturing Anthropology: Working in the Present*. Santa Fe, New Mexico: School of American Research Press.

Apter, David. 1987. *Rethinking Development: Modernization, Dependency and Postmodern Politics*. Beverly Hills, CA: Sage.

Avadhuta, Acharya Tadbhavananda. 1985. *Samaj: A New Dimension in Politics*. Calcutta: Proutist Universal Publications.

Bahuguna, Sunderlal. 1987. *The Crisis of Civilization and the Message of Culture*. Lucknow: Rajendra Prasad Memorial Lecture.

Bailey, Joe. 1988. "New Movements?" In *Pessimism*. London: Routledge.

Bauman, Zygmunt. 1987. *Legislators and Interpreters: On Modernity, Postmodernity and the Intellectuals*. Oxford: Polity Press.

Baviskar, Amita. 1995. *In the Belly of River: Tribal Conflict Over Development in the Narmada Valley*. Delhi: Oxford University Press.

Bell, Daniel. 1973. *The Coming of the Post-Industrial Society: A Venture in Social Forecasting*. New York: Basic Books.

Bellah, Robert et al. 1991. *The Good Society*. New York: Alfred A. Knof.

Berman, Russell. 1982. "Opposition to Rearmament and West German Culture." *Telos* 51: 141–148.

Block, Fred. 1987. *Revising State Theory: Essays in Politics and Postindustrialism*. Philadelphia: Temple University Press.

——. 1990. *Postindustrial Possibilities*. Berkeley: University of California Press.

Bluestone, Barry and Bennett Harrison. 1982. *The Deindustrialization of America*. New York: Basic Books.

Brandt, Willy. 1980. *North-South, A Programme for Survival: Report of the Independent Commission on International Development Issues*. Cambridge, Massachusetts: MIT Press.

Bright, Charles and M. Geyer. 1987. "For a Unified History in the 20th Century." Unpublished Manuscript.

Burns, T. and R. Uberhst. 1989. *Creative Democracy: Systematic Conflict Resolution and Policy Making in a World of High Science and Technology*. New York: Praeger.

Burdick, John. 1995. "Uniting Theory and Practice in the Ethnography of Social Movements: Notes Towards a Hopeful Realism." *Dialectical Anthropology* 20: 361–385.

Calhoun, Craig. 1986. "Computer Technology, Large-Scale Social Integration, and the Local Community." *Urban Affairs Quarterly* 22 (2): 329–349.

——. 1988. "Populist Politics, Communication Media and the Large Social Scale Integration." Unpublished Manuscript.

Capra, F. and C. Spretnak. 1984. *Green Politics*. New York: E.P. Dalton Books.

Castells, Manuel, 1983. *The City and the Grassroots: Towards a Cross-Cultural Theory of Urban Social Movements*. Berkeley: University of California Press.

——. (ed.) 1985. *High Technology, Space and Society*. London: Sage.

Chekki, Dan. 1988. "Transnational Networks in Global Development: Canada and the Third World." *International Social Science Journal.*

Cohen, Jean. 1985. "Strategy or Identity: New Theoretical Paradigms and Contemporary Social Movements." *Social Research* 52 (4).

Cox, Harvey. 1984. *Religion in a Secular City: Towards a Post-Modern Theology*. New York: Simon and Schuster.

Connolly, William. 1991. *Identity/Difference: Democratic Negotiations of Political Paradox*. Ithaca, NY: Cornell: University Press.

Derber, Charles. 1982. *Professionals as Workers: Mental Labor in Advanced Capitalism*. Boston: G.K. Hall and Co.

Davidson, Miriam. 1988. *Convictions of the Heart: Jim Corbett and the Sanctuary Movement*. Tucson, Arizona: University of Arizona Press.

Downey, Garry L. 1988. "Structure and Practice in the Cultural Identities of Scientists: Negotiating Nuclear Wastes in New Mexico." *Anthropological Quarterly* 61 (1): 26–38.

Eide, Asbjorn. 1986. "The Human Rights Movement and the Transformation of the International Order." *Alternatives* 11 (3): 367–402.

Elias, Norbert. 1982. *The Civilizing Process*. New York: Pantheon Books.

Esteva, Gustavo. 1987. "Regenerating People's Space." *Alternatives* 13 (1): 125–152.

Falk, Richard. 1987. "The Global Promise of Social Movements: Explorations at the Edge of Time." *Alternatives* 12 (2): 173–196.

Fischer, Michael M.J. 1995. "Eye(I)ing the Sciences and their Signifiers (Language, Tropes, Autobiographies): InterViewing for a Cultural Study of Science and Technology." In George Marcus (ed.), *Technoscientific Imaginaries: Conversations, Profiles, and Memoirs*. Chicago: University Press, pp. 43–84.

Frank, Andre G. and Marta Fuentes. 1987. "Nine Theses on Social Movements." *Economic and Political Weekly* 22 (35): 1503–1510.

Fraser, Nancy. 1987. *Social Movements vs Disciplinary Bureaucracies: The Discourse of Social Needs*. Minneapolis: University of Minnesota Press.

Friberg, Mat and Bjorn Hettne. 1984. "The Greening of the World: Towards a Non-Deterministic Model of Global Processes." In H. Addo et al. (eds.), *Development as Social Transformation*. Tokyo: United Nations University Press.

——. 1988. "Local Mobilization and World System Politics." *International Social Science Journal.*

Fuller, Millard. 1986. *No More Shacks: The Daring Vision of Habitat for Humanity*. Waco, Texas: Word Books Publisher.

Gale, D. 1984. *Neighborhood Revolution and the Postindustrial Cities*. Lanham, MD: Lexington.

Gans, Herbert. 1988. *Middle American Individualism: The Future of Liberal Democracy.* London: Macmillan Books.

Galtung, Johan. 1980. *The True Worlds: A Transnational Perspective.* NY: Free Press.

Geertz, Clifford. 1983. *Local Knowledge: Further Essays in Interpretive Anthropology.* NY: Basic Books.

Giddens, Anthony. 1975. *The Class Structure of Advanced Societies.* NY: Harper and Row.

——. 1981. *The Nation-State and Violence.* Berkeley: University of California Press.

——. 1991. "Structuration Theory: Past, Present and Future." In C.G.A. Bryant and D. Jarry (eds.), *Giddens' Theory of Structuration: A Critical Appreciation.* London: Routledge.

——. 1994. *Beyond Left and Right: The Future of Radical Politics.* Cambridge: Polity Press.

Ginsburg, Faye. 1989. *Contested Lives: Abortion Debate in an American Community.* Berkeley and Los Angeles: University of California Press.

Giri, Ananta. 1989. "Narratives of Creative Transformation: Constituting Critical Movements in Contemporary American Culture." *Dialectical Anthropology* 14(3)

——. 1991a. "Notes of a Traveller from an Andhra Village." *Mainstream,* February 9, 1991.

——. 1991b. "Contemporary Crisis of the Idea of the System." *Man and Development,* December, 1991.

——. 1992. "The Portrait of a Discursive Formation: Science as Social Activism in Contemporary India." National Institute of Science, Technology and Development Studies, New Delhi: Working Paper.

——. 1994. In the Margins of Shacks: The Vision and Practice of Habitat for Humanity. Johns Hopkins University, Baltimore, PhD Thesis.

——. 1995a. "Exclusion and Integration: The Moral Struggles." *Gandhi Marg.*

——. 1995b. "The Dialectic Between Globalization and Localization: Economic Restructuring, Women and Strategies of Cultural Reproduction." *Dialectical Anthropology* 20 (2).

——. 1995c. "Building a Global Covenant? The Overseas Work and the International Partners of Habitat for Humanity." Madras Institute of Development Studies: Working Paper.

——. 2008. *Self-Development and Social Transformations? The Vision and Practice of the Self-Study Mobilization of Swadhyaya.* Jaipur: Rawat Publications.

Goldthorpe, J.H. (ed.) 1984. *Order and Conflict in Contemporary Capitalism.* New York: Oxford University Press.

Gundelach, Peter. 1990. "Hopes and Menaces of the Programmed Society." Department of Political Science, University of Aarhus, Denmark.

Habermas, Jurgen. 1971. *Towards a Rational Society.* Boston: Beacon Press.

——. 1973. *Legitimation Crisis.* Boston: Beacon Press.

——. 1990. "What Does Socialism Mean Today? The Rectifying Revolution and the Need for a New Thinking on the Left Today." *The New Left Review,* No. 183: 3–21.

Habermas, Jurgen (ed.) 1984. *Observations on "The Spiritual Situation of the Age: Contemporary German Perspectives".* Cambridge, MA: MIT Press.

Hall, Stuart. 1988. *The Hard Road to Renewal: Thacherism and the Crisis of the Left.* London: Verso.

Harvey, David. 1973. *Social Justice and the City.* Baltimore: Johns Hopkins University Press.

——. 1987. *Consciousness and the Urban Experience.* Baltimore: Johns Hopkins University Press.

——. 1989. *The Condition of Postmodernity.* Oxford and Cambridge, MA: Basil Blackwell.

——. 1991. "Flexibility: Threat or Opportunity?" *Socialist Review* 21 (1): 65–77.

Hegedus, Zsuzsa. 1987. "The Challenge of the Peace Movement: Civilian Security and Civilian Emancipation." *Alternatives* 12 (2): 197–216.

——. 1990. "Social Movements and Social Change in Self-Creative Society: New Civil Initiatives in the International Arena." In Martin Albrow and Elizabeth King (eds.), *Globalization, Knowledge, and Society,* London: Sage, pp. 263–183.

Hellman, Stephen. 1987. "Feminism and the Model of Militancy in an Italian Communist Federation: Challenges to the Old Style of Politics." In M.F. Katzenstein and C.M. Fuller (eds.), *The Women's Movement of the U.S. and Western Europe.* Philadelphia: Temple University Press.

Hertz, S. 1982. *The Welfare Mothers' Movement.* Washington, DC: University Press of America.

Hirsch, Joachim. 1982. "The West German Peace Movement." *Telos* 51: 135–141.

Hirschmann, A. 1982. *Shifting Involvements.* Princeton: Princeton University Press.

Hirschorn, Larry. 1985. "Information Technology and the New Services Game." In Castells, 1985: 172–190.

Hettne, Bjorn. 1990. *Development Theory and Three Worlds.* Essex: Longman.

Horowitz, I. 1970. *The Struggle is the Message: The Organization and Ideology of the Anti-War Movement.* Berkeley: Glendessary Press.

Inglehart, Ronald. 1990. *The Culture Shift in Advanced Societies.* Princeton: Princeton University Press.

Kothari, Rajni. 1986. "On the Non-Party Political Process: The NGOs, the State and World Capitalism." *Lokayan Bulletin.*

——. 1987. "On Humane Governance." *Alternatives* X11: 277–290.

——. 1988. *Transformation and Survival: In Search of the Humane World Order.* New Delhi: Ajanta.

Kovack, Ilona. 1988. "Local Influences on International Relations in Hungary." *International Social Science Journal.*

Laughlin, Kim. 1995. "Rehabilitating Science, Imagining Bhopal." In George E. Marcus (ed.), *Technoscientific Imaginaries: Conversations, Profiles and Memoirs.* Chicago: University Press.

Lowe, Stuart. 1986. *Urban Social Movements: City After Castells.* New York: St. Martin's Press.

McAdam, Doug et al. 1988. "Social Movements." In Neil Smelser (ed.), *Handbook of Sociology.* Newbury Park, CA: Sage.

Marcus, George and Michael Fischer. 1986. *Anthropology as Cultural Critique: An Experimental Moment in the Human Sciences.* Chicago: Chicago University Press.

Mansbach, Richard et al., 1976. *The Web of World Politics: Non-state Actors in the Global System.* Englewood, NJ: Prentice-Hall.

Martin, Emily. 1986. *The Meaning of Money in China and United States.* Lewis Henry Morgan Lectures.

——. 1987. *Woman in the Body: A Cultural Analysis of Reproduction.* Boston: Beacon Press.

Nandy, Ashis. 1982. "Science for the Unafraid." *Mainstream,* June 26.

——. 1987a. "Cultural Frames for Social Transformation: A Credo." *Alternatives* 13 (1): 113–123

——. 1987b. *Traditions, Tyranny, and Utopia.* Delhi: Oxford University Press.

——. (ed.) 1988. *Science, Hegemony and Violence: A Requiem for Modernity.* New Delhi: Oxford University Press.

Offe, Claus. 1985. "New Social Movements: Challenging the Boundaries of Institutional Politics." *Social Research* 52 (4).

Offe, Claus and Rolph G. Heinze. 1992. *Beyond Employment.* Cambridge: Polity Press.

Olson, Mancur. 1965. *The Logic of Collective Action.* Cambridge: Harvard University Press.

Oommen, T.K. 1990. *Protest and Change: Studies in Social Movements.* New Delhi: Sage Publications.

Ortner, Sherry. 1984. "Theory in Anthropology Since the Sixties." *Comparative Studies in Society and History* 26 (1): 126–166.

Parajuli, Pramod. 1991. "Power and Knowledge in Development Discourse: New Social Movements and the State in India." *International Social Science Journal* 127: 173–190.

Preteceille, Edmond and Jean-Pierre Terrail. 1985. "Social Needs and State Monopoly Capitalism." In Sarah Matthew (tr.), *Capitalism, Consumption, and Needs.* Oxford: Basil Blackwell.

Raina, Vinod. 1991. "Formal and Informal Communication Channels for Disaster Preparedness." Lecture delivered at the 1991 Meetings of the Indian Science Congress.

Rapp, Rayna. 1988. "Chromosomes and Communications: The Discourse of Genetic Counselling." *Medical Anthropology Quarterly* 2 (2).

Rochon, Thomas. 1988. *Mobilizing for Peace.* Princeton: Princeton University Press.

Rorty, Richard. 1989. *Irony, Contingency and Solidarity.* Cambridge: Cambridge University Press.

Roy, Ramashray. 1993. "Swadhyaya: Values and Message." In Wignaraja, 1993.

Ruiz, Lester Edwin J. 1988. "Theology, Politics, and the Discourse of Transformation." *Alternatives* 13 (2): 155–176.

Sassen, Saskia. 1988. *The Mobility of Capital and Labor.* Cambridge: Cambridge University Press.

Saxenian, A. 1985. "Silicon Valley and Rt. 128: Regional Prototypes and Historic Exceptions." In Castells, 1985.

Scarpaci, Joseph L. 1991. "Primary Care Decentralization in the Southern Cone." *Annals of the American Association of American Geographers* 81 (2): 181–209.

Schester, Susan. 1982. *Woman and Male Violence: The Vision and Struggle of the Battered Women's Movements.* London: Pluto Press.

Seth, N.R. 1994. Children of the Same God. Gujarat Institute of Development Research, Ahmedabad: Working Paper.

Shaiken, Harry. 1984. *Work Transformed: Automation and Labor in the Computer Age.* Cambridge: Cambridge University Press.

Sheshadri, C.V. 1982. "Development and Thermodynamics." Murugappa Chettiar Research Centre, Madras: Occasional Paper.

Snow, David et al., 1986. "Frame Alignment Process, Micromobilization, and Movement Participation." *American Sociological Review* 51: 461–481.

Sorokin, Pitrim. 1950. *Altruistic Love: A Study of "American Good Neighbors" and Christian Saints.* Boston: Beacon Press.

Tarrow, Sidney. 1988. "National Politics and Collective Action: Recent Theory and Research in Western Europe and United States". *Annual Review of Sociology* 14: 421–40.

Tilly, Charles. 1978. *From Mobilization to Revolution.* Reading, MA: Addison-Wesley.

Tocqueville, Alexis de. 1966. *Democracy in America.* Tr. G. Lawrence. New York: Harper & Row.

Tomsho, Robert. 1987. *The American Sanctuary Movement.* Austin: Texas Monthly Press.

Touraine, Alain. 1971. *Post-Industrial Society.* New York: Random House.

——. 1977. *The Self-Production of Society.* Chicago: University of Chicago Press.

——. 1981. *The Voice and the Eye: An Analysis of the Social Movements.* Cambridge: Cambridge University Press.

——. 1983a. *Anti-Nuclear Protest.* Cambridge: Cambridge University Press.

——. 1983b. *Solidarity.* Cambridge: Cambridge University Press.

——. 1988. *Return of the Actor: Social Theory in Postindustrial Society.* Minnesota: University of Minnesota Press.

Towsey, Michael Vaktavirya. 1990. *A Sociology for the New Age: An Introduction to the Social Science of P.R. Sarkar.* Maleny, Australia: Prout Research Institute.

Turner, Bryan S. 1984. *The Body and Society: Exploration in Social Theory.* Oxford: Basil Blackwell.

Uberoi, J.P.S. 1996. *Religion, Civil Society and the State: A Study of Sikhism.* Delhi: Oxford University Press.

Vincent, Joan. 1984. "System and Process, 1974–1985." *Annual Review of Anthropology* 15: 99–119.

Walker, R.B.J. 1988. *One World, Many Worlds: Struggles for a Just World Peace.* London: Zed Books.

Wallerstein, Immanuel et al. 1986. "Dilemmas of Anti-Systemic Movements." *Social Research* 53: 185–206.

Wignaraja, P. 1983. *New Social Movements in the South.* New Delhi: Vistaar Publications.

Young, Neil. 1986. "The Peace Movement: A Comparative and Analytical Survey." *Alternatives* 11 (2): 185–218.

Zald, M.N. and J.D. McCarthy. 1987. *Social Movements in an Organizational Society.* New Brunswick, New Jersey: Transaction Books.

Zuboff, Soshana. 1988. *In the Age of Smart Machine: The Future of Work and Power.* New York: Basic Books.

Zelinsky, Wilbur. 1991. "The Twinning of the World: Sister Cities in Geographical and Historical Perspective." *Annals* 81 (1): 103–126.

13 Building in the Margins of Shacks

Towards a Hermeneutics of Recovery

I came in search of not social or cultural America, but the America of the empty, absolute freedom of freeways, not deep America of mores and mentalities, but America of desert, speed, of motels and mineral surfaces. I looked for it in the speed of the screenplay, in the different reflex of television, in the film of days and nights projected across an empty space, in the marvelously affect less succession of signs, images, faces, and ritual acts on the road. [...] I sought the finished form of the future catastrophe on the road.

— Jean Baudrillard (1989), *America*, p. 5

Deconstruction alone is not enough. [...] It must be accompanied by an at least tentative reconstruction grounded in the political and theoretical demands of contemporary world.

— Edward Soja (1989)
Postmodern Geographies: The Reassertion of Space in Critical Social Theory, p. 74

Without the energizing effect of spiritual commitments, American values would be little more than hollow ideals.

— Robert Wuthnow (1988)
The Restructuring of American Religion: Society and Faith since World War II, p. 60

The Problem: Deconstruction, Recovery and Freedom

In this chapter, I discuss some of the problems in the contemporary world of action and interpretation, revolving around the theme of deconstruction and reconstruction, recovery and freedom. My primary concern here has to do with the pervasive influence of philosophies of deconstruction in the sub-culture of intellectuals of our times which harp on the simultaneous death of the subject and the social dissolution of the author and the text. The philosophers of deconstruction deride any notion of foundation and prefer to look at the human condition as a surrealistic web of contingencies and a frivolous play of signifiers. In this chapter, I intend to interrogate this dominant frame of interpretation of our times by presenting the case of an initiative in collective action and critical reflection, which is building houses in many communities in the US and around the world. This is a movement which originated in the United States of America in 1976 and now works worldwide. Habitat for Humanity – this movement – builds houses because its volunteers share the faith that to build a house for the one who cannot afford to buy or find it difficult to rent is to build an altar for God. In this chapter, I intend to present briefly the "reflexive mobilization of self" (cf. Giddens 1991) and the "connected criticism" (cf. Walzer 1988) of culture that is at work in Habitat for Humanity and analyse its implications for a hermeneutics of recovery for the actors and institutions of our times. But before I present the narrative of the actors and the movement, I would like to make the following remarks about the wider issue of reconstruction and recovery, emancipation and freedom in our world today.

Let us begin this reflection with Edward Soja who argues that deconstruction alone is not enough; it must be accompanied by the practical and theoretical demands of the contemporary world. When we take this task seriously – the task of confronting the practical and theoretical demands of the contemporary world – we realize that we have enormous tasks of reconciliation and reconstruction at hand before us. We realize that philosophy and textual analysis cannot sit idle when our communities and forms of livelihood are being systematically destroyed by the globalization of the threatening logic of speculative capital. We are bound to ask to our interpreters and philosophers as G.B. Madison does in his provocative *The Hermeneutics of Postmodernity:* "Is there nothing for the philosopher to do after the demise of the metaphysical seriousness but to be an intellectual *kibitzer, a* concern-free creator of abnormal discourse, an insouciant player of deconstructive and fanciful word games, an agile figure shaken on the thin ice of a bottomless chessboard?" (Madison 1988: 107). When we confront the challenges in the real world, we find that in our recent past, to quote David Harvey, "Radicals within the cultural mass became charged by fields like semiotics, as if the really interesting thing about the homeless were the variety of coded messages that card board boxes could convey" (Harvey 1991: 69). An urge to meet with the demands of theory and practice in the contemporary world immediately makes us realize that the striving for a "good society" and meaningful life is not over and in order to participate in this striving of reconciliation, reconstruction, and new creation deconstruction alone is not enough. As Robert Bellah and his colleagues tell us: "[...] We are not likely to give up what some philosophers call the hermeneutics of suspicion – the tendency in the West since Enlightenment to call all received traditions into question. But without hermeneutics of recovery, through which we can understand what a living tradition is in the first place hermeneutics of suspicion is apt to be an exercise in nihilism" (Bellah et al., 1991: 174).

A reflexive engagement with the challenges of the contemporary world in the context of structural processes and discursive transformation at work also urges us to realize the close link between the theme of building and the theme of freedom. Parallel to the hegemony of deconstruction in our modes of theorizing today is the euphoria about global democratization. But democratization as a formal process evidences such attributes as the collapse of the dictatorial system and the conduct of elections for political office not the same thing as realization of freedom. What is worse, in this moment of euphoria, we confuse emancipation with freedom. But, while emancipation is concerned with, as David Apter argues, "reducing the negativity of otherness, as embodied in the colonial, the subaltern, and the prisoner, vis-à-vis mainstream," freedom is concerned with the liberation of "the mainstream from itself" (Apter 1992: 162). Perhaps, for this reason, Anthony Giddens makes a distinction between "emancipatory politics" and "life politics". According to him, life politics is concerned not with hierarchical but generative power, and is a politics of reflexively mobilized order and a politics of self-actualization "where reflexivity links and body to systems of global scope" (Giddens 1991: 9). In the same vein, Ernesto Laclau concludes his provocative plea for beyond emancipation with the following lines:

> We are today coming to terms with our own finitude and the political possibility that it opens. This is the point from which the potential liberatory discourses of our postmodern age have to start. We can perhaps say that we are at the end emancipation and at the beginning of freedom (Laclau 1992: 137).

But, as we are at the beginning of freedom, how does our discourse of freedom prepare us for intended transformative leap into the future? We are familiar with the modern experience of the degeneration of freedom into narcissistic individualism and the current fight against equality in the name of freedom. To take us out of the current impasse of freedom against equality, Amartya Sen (1989), building upon Isaiah Berlin, proposes a distinction between positive and negative freedom. Sen hopes that by portraying positive freedom as the freedom to enhance the "functioning" and "capability" of individuals and negative freedom as preoccupation with one's individual rights and security, one can make a tight link between food and freedom – a link which is deliberately obscured by the reigning ideologies of our times. But even such a reconstruction the agenda of freedom in the work of Amartya Sen does not take us very far since it is still haunted by the problem of dualism, namely, dualism between positive and negative freedom. But there is a need to transcend this dualism and Sen is not of much help to us here because he cannot tell us how same individual can integrate his concern for negative freedom with positive freedom. This integration is as much a task of self as it is of the social order. But Sen's agenda does not have a project of self-nurturance and overcoming and is not aware of its transformative capacity to overcome the distinction between positive and negative freedom. Overcoming the distinction between positive and negative freedom – both in biography and history – is an important part of self-cultivation, political transformation and spiritual enlightenment. It calls for a view of freedom as spiritual transformation where spirituality means an integral change covering the whole space from food to freedom and the agent of freedom is a transformative self (see Pande 1989, 1991; Giri 1995). Such a view of freedom is available in the thought of Sri Aurobindo who presents freedom as a *synthesis of yoga*. For instance, Sri Aurobindo argues that spirituality "transforms the needs desires onto a divine work and *Ananda* [joy or bliss]". "It transforms the mental and moral aspiration into the power, truth and perfection that are beyond them. It substitutes for the divided training of the individual nature the passion and strike of the separate ego, the calm profound, harmonious and happy law of universalized person within us" (Sri Aurobindo 1950: 193). For Sri Aurobindo, the discovery of the secret Godhead within us helps us create a universal ground within us where the social distinction between the individual and the collective, the negative and the positive freedom, gets a new frame of reference for criticism and transcendence.

Is it a hubris to utter the name of God while speaking of politics and freedom? Probably not. May be, it is a sign of recovery of our times that even contemporary political theory is coming back in search of a ground and a God.[1]

Even political scientists have begun lamenting the missing God in contemporary discourse of transformation. At the same time, some of them also talk of the need for transformation of our desire in order that individual freedom can be an object of social commitments. For example, Claus Offe and Ulrich K. Preuss tell us that we face conflict not only between different social groups but also between different kinds of desires – the "inner conflict between what the individuals themselves experience as their more desirable and their less desirable desires" (Offe and Preuss 1991: 166). Insofar as the connection between freedom and spirituality is concerned in no place in contemporary political theory it is better articulated than in the following lines of Laclau:

> If, on the one hand, modernity started by seriously typing representability to knowledge, the constitutive opaqueness resulting from the dialectic of emancipation involves not only that society is no longer transparent to knowledge, but also since God is no longer there to substitute knowledge by revelation that all representation will be necessarily partial and will take place against the background of an essential unrepresentability. On the other hand, this constitutive opaqueness withdraws the ground which made it possible to go beyond the dialectic of incarnation, given that there is no longer a transparent society in which the universal can show itself in a direct unmediated way. But again, as God is no longer there, ensuring through his word the knowledge of a universal destiny which escapes human reason, opaqueness cannot lead to a restoration of the dialectic of incarnation either. The death of the ground seems to lead to the death of the universal and to the dissolution of social struggle into mere particularism (Laclau 1992: 131–32).

But, the problem in such a promising agenda of Laclau is that it lacks a project of self-transformation. Though Laclau speaks of the "dialectic of incarnation," there is no reference to self-reflection in his outline. But, according to Indian philosopher Roop Rekha Verma, "the dialectic by itself does not explain the possibility of cultural change or a critique of culture. [...] What is important to add in this dialectic is that internalization can be reflective or unreflective" (Verma 1991: 533). Thus having a notion of transformative self as a seeker of freedom is essential to go out of the current impasse of deconstruction and destruction in our search for recovery and reconstruction.

Habitat for Humanity

The above provides us an appropriate background to discuss Habitat for Humanity. Habitat identifies itself as a God's movement and is based upon what it calls "partnership between God and Man". It operates with the Biblical principles of "Economics of Jesus" and "Theology of the Hammer" – the former believing that it is immoral to charge interest from the poor and the latter believing that one has to express one's love for God through the instrument of hammer. Habitat believes that it is interest which locks the poor in a condition of perpetual renting and determines the critical distinction between living in a shack and owning one's own home. Habitat's mission is "No More Shacks" (Fuller 1986) and it strives towards this realization by creating what it calls a "revolving fund for humanity". Habitat builds homes and communities through the donated money and labours of the volunteers but does not give houses to the homeowners for free. Homeowners are required to pay back their mortgage payments to the local Habitat project, which is utilized for building more houses and widening the circle of gift and reciprocity.

Habitat has many programmes and activities. One of them is called covenant church programme, and other corporate partnership. The former builds partnership with interested churches while the latter with corporations in order to mobilize resource and support for its building programme. Former President Jimmy Carter leads a Habitat work camp every year building "homes" in a community for a week. For instance in 1988, the Carter work camp raised 20 houses – an entire neighbourhood – in Atlanta. Its leader says about the significance of this work camp for the homeowners: "People whose lives were debased by the violence of poverty now pay taxes and become contributors themselves; suburban volunteers far removed from the pain of material deprivation gain more substance and sensitivity from a hard day's work for the benefit of another" (quoted in Fuller and Fuller 1990: 25).

Habitat for Humanity builds houses in different communities around United States in partnership with the local affiliates. These affiliates are autonomous and mobilize their own resources to build houses in their respective areas. Habitat affiliates vary in size, resource base and texture. Some operate in more favourable environments with little resource problems while others strive with little internal resource of the community. Here, we take the work of two Habitat affiliates as illustrations: the Habitat affiliate in Fort Meyer, Florida and the affiliate in Pembroke, Illinois. The former works in an environment of wealth while the latter struggles with little community resource. Lee County Habitat for Humanity, the Habitat Project in Fort Meyers, Florida, builds in the Gulf Shore town of Fort Meyers. With a large population of retirees and a constant stream of tourists, "it has an air of comfortable affluence" (McDonald 1992: 5). "But for many working people in this town the reality is different. The economy of Fort Meyers and the surrounding Lee County depends almost entirely on tourism. The industry requires a lot of labour, but the jobs creates are mostly unskilled – hotel and restaurant jobs – that pay only the minimum wage. Thus, while Lee County has a healthy median family income of $36,500 it has a large population of working poor. Affordable housing is a particular problem" (ibid.). Demand from wealthier retirees and vacationers has raised real estate prices and has, at, the same time, lured developers to build expensive homes. As a result, there is a shortage of decent housing for the less affluent.

In response to this need, Lee County Habitat has built three new communities in the past twelve years. Lee County Habitat began in 1979 with the acquisition of twenty acres of vacant county-owned in an area called Harlem Heights. Since then, it has worked steadily to develop the Habitat North and Habitat South neighbourhoods on that site. More recently, it has begun to build in Dunbar a new neighbourhood about five miles away. Today, 35 Habitat houses stand in Harlem Heights, and site development is underway that would add another thirty-five homes. The Dunbar neighbourhood now has twenty-three Habitat houses with three more currently under construction.

McDonald, writing in *Habitat World,* the bi-monthly publication of the Habitat for Humanity, tells about this affiliate: "The Heights neighborhood today has a real estate value of $2 million. But for homeowner Dolan Rosado, the word 'value' means something completely different. 'Now', she says 'my children have safe place to play and grow up'" (ibid.).

But all Habitat affiliates in the United States do not share such an advantage. Affiliates in small towns and poor communities strive with little. One such affiliate is the Habitat project in Pembroke, Illinois. In this not-so-wealthy neighbourhood "the work of the affiliate is maintained by people who are struggling to improve their own lives" (ibid.). The affiliate's bookkeeper is Pam Ward, single mother of six, who owns the fourth home that was renovated by the Pembroke affiliate. The work of Pembroke Habitat is done mostly by volunteers. This is also the case with most of the affiliates where there is either no or very few salaried staff. The former President and the continuing volunteer of a Habitat affiliate in New York's McGrath Country Habitat for Humanity helps us understand this:

> Most of the work which is done by groups in US affiliates is by people who volunteer their time, talent and money. It is a very generous-minded atmosphere [...] Habitat appeals to many vigorous retired people, middle-aged to elderly, who want to go on work at something which has meaning and connection with society. Sometimes the skills of older America are not well-utilized in our society. I believe that in Habitat projects many of these people are willing to show their abilities in work that they feel has real value.

Connected Criticism and the Interrogation of Self

Students of reconstructive movements tell us that the discourse of a movement ought not be a mere projection of existing reality, "it must be sufficiently far-reaching to exercise a visionary pull" (Unger 1987). Habitat founder Millard Fuller uses such a language and a style to infuse people with the spirit of Habitat. Fuller begins with his own story. He had become a millionaire at an early age. But, as wealth and reputation were expanding, his wife Linda left him because she felt he loved more his business than her and their children. Fuller reconciled with his wife and they distinctly felt the calling of God for a full-time Christian service. They decided to leave all their wealth and to start their life anew. They joined Koinonia Farms, an intentional, self-sufficient Christian community in south-eastern Georgia, and started a partnership housing programme for the poor workers and sharecroppers of Sumter County, Georgia in 1968. They were influenced by the life and thought of Clarence Jordan, the founder of Koinonia and a proponent of radical discipleship of Christ (Jordan 1964; Lee 1971). This effort grew into Habitat for Humanity in 1976 (Fuller 1977).

Fuller tells the story of Habitat through numerous personal tales which touch the heart of the listeners. When we read Fuller's books on Habitat and listen to his cassettes, we find that this language is not simply elocutionary and imperative in the instrumental sense but also in a constitutive sense. His books and lectures tell us how he solves human problems employing the perspective of God.

It is not only that the language of a transformative movement has to use personalized parables, any current effort at transformation must also involve a "personalist program" (Unger 1987: 175). According to Roberto Unger, the "personalist program" of transformation gets manifested in participating in the "exemplary conflicts" of our times. In case of Habitat, housing is an "exemplary conflict" of our times and Habitat presents its solution of Christian love and sharing as a radical one. The following narration of Milliard Fuller shows what it means to solve "exemplary conflicts" by involving a "personalist program": Once a pastor of a church came to Clarence Jordan and asked for his advice in resolving a dilemma. The pastor was concerned about the low wage of the janitor who had a big family of nine to take care of and had a long way to drive to work. Despite his passionate plea to the deacons for raising the janitor's salary they were not forthcoming since they were not able to raise the budget of the church. Jordan asked the pastor whether he made more money than the janitor and whether his family was smaller compared to his. When the pastor replied him in the affirmative, then Jordan told him: "Well, why not just swap salaries with him? That wouldn't require any extra money in your budget. You live right here by the church, so you don't have any commuting expenses, and you have only two children while he has eight. Surely you 'Could live more easily on his salary than he can" (quoted in Fuller 1980: 66). Fuller tells us about this story:

> John, a white man, turned whiter: He hadn't expected that kind of solution. Clarence was aware of his discomfort. "What's wrong, John? What's wrong with that solution? Is it contrary to Christian doctrine? There's nothing at all wrong with it, Clarence, from a Christian point of view. That's why it, upsets me! (ibid.).

The above is an example of the resolution of a conflict where an actor considers himself as a part of the problem. Fuller tells such stories all across the United States and creates a constituency for his moral criticism. For both Clarence Jordan and Millard Fuller, to see social problems from a God's perspective means that one cannot abdicate one's responsibility. Such an engagement involves a total criticism of one's self, culture and society where the familiar institutions of society appear as "instances of problematic justice" (Habermas 1990: 108). Fuller draws upon both Bible and his knowledge of other societies to criticize the contemporary American lifestyle of affluence and greed – one which is, for him, also devoid of compassion. He tells his wealthy Christian partners in North America: "Many of our African Christian friends lack the material things of this world, but they have much to teach our affluent Christian world about true values in Christian life" (Fuller 1977: 113). He argues with his fellow Americans that homelessness is a violation of the lofty meaning of the "American dream". The following is an illustration of his argument with his fellow Americans:

> God does not mean, for his people to, go hungry or to do without adequate clothes and shelter. [...] "Whoever has two shirts must give, one to the man he has none, and whoever has food must share it." A few years ago I spoke at a meeting at a large church in Florida, using this text from Luke for my talk. I knew that many people in that church had a house in Florida and another one (or two) up North. So I decided to make the scripture as relevant as possible.
>
> I wonder if this teaching of John about shirts could also be applied to houses?' I asked but I really didn't expect an answer. [...] But one men did respond. 'Mr Fuller, excuse me. I think your analogy between shirts and houses is unfair. After all, a person can't really wear more than one shirt at a time, but he-uh-he (Fuller 1980: 94–95).

Fuller told his interlocutor that the teaching of Jesus is as much applicable to the example of houses as it is to that of shirts. Fuller employs the idiom of the "Kingdom of God" to pursue his critical strategy of what he himself calls "educating the conscience of the world" about the stupendous problem of global poverty housing (Fuller 1986). Fuller's criticism of the existing arrangement and his vision of transformation makes him a "connected critic," to borrow the words of Michael Walzer (1988). Walzer makes a distinction between the "connected critics" who make their point or fail to earn their authority "by arguing with [their] fellows" and the marginal critics who are never meaningfully related to their own culture and suffer from the problem of "ambiguous connection" (Walzer 1988: 32). When we read closely the texts of Fuller, which are sources of evocative or sentimental mobilization for sympathetic citizens of the United States as well as for many around the world, we see such a "connected criticism" at work.

Motivation and the Contours of Meaning: Some Habitat Narratives of Participation

In the United States the work of Habitat is carried out mainly by the volunteers. There are, of course, some paid staff in Habitat affiliates as well as in the Habitat headquarters at Americus, Georgia, but the employees of Habitat identify themselves primarily as volunteers rather than as mere paid workers. Therefore, their tie with Habitat is much more than the tie of "work" and "exchange" one notices in modern organizational life. It is their dedication to the cause of "No More Shacks" and their faith in God which brings them to work with Habitat at a substantially low salary, and many times even without any remuneration.

The volunteers of Habitat come from different backgrounds. Young, old, middle-aged and retired people – all are found in Habitat. The young and middle-aged, who are in search of a different lifestyle or more meaningful work engagement, by which they can contribute to their spiritual growth and social development find an attractive space in the mobilization of Habitat. For the retired people, Habitat provides a scope for meaningful spending of time rather than just "playing golf".

Volunteers of Habitat invariably feel that opportunities for job, education, and housing are decreasing in contemporary American society. They particularly feel appalled by the deplorable housing condition in contemporary US and have been attracted to Habitat because it strives to solve this problem, and encourages "the needy to improve their situation". They attribute various causes to this problem. For some, it is caused by high interest rates, increased cost of building and widespread unemployment and while for others "Reaganomics" is the main cause behind this.

The volunteers of Habitat deplore the fact that "hard working men and women cannot afford to have a place of their own" because of the housing crisis and the "pessimistic attitude" that it gives rise to among America's working poor. Some of them say in unambiguous terms that "it is a scandal to have homeless amid such affluence" and wonder if "the country has lost its connection with God even though there are many who claim to know". They believe that this nearly intractable problem can be solved by raising the consciousness of all concerned – government and people. Some of' believe that the affluent should "lead a simple lifestyle so that others can simply live". For the volunteers of Habitat, "the problem of housing cannot be solved by governments alone but by the grass roots participation of all our citizens".

It is also interesting that some of the volunteers were in real estate business before joining Habitat while some others had difficulty in finding a house to stay – one of them saying that she "grew up in a run-down home and was ashamed to bring friends home". Another volunteer, a former Methodist minister, tells us that during his young days he had a Habitat-type assistance in owing a home which is an "unforgettable experience" in his life. Those who "left their real estate business to join Habitat say that do not operate well in the profit motive" and find their work as realtors "frustrating and stressful". They work with Habitat for no salary and in some cases with considerable less pay but find in their work a "tremendous source of satisfaction".

Over the last years of its existence Habitat has drawn many seeking souls to its paths from many different backgrounds and with different aspirations and motivations. They tell us different stories which cannot be easily put into either an aggregate picture or fit into neat ideological/sociological categories. I present below the stories of some of them which hopefully can provide sense of the innumerable volunteers who now make, up the striving called Habitat for Humanity.

Let us begin with Jane (a pseudonym; in fact all the names in this essay are present pseudonyms), an engaging female volunteer from Burke, New York. Jane tells us that though her community has a staggering housing problem, there are no homeless even though there are people who live in homes that have been condemned. About her own situation vis-à-vis housing, she tells us: "It has sometimes been difficult to find a good apartment or house to rent, but generally we have been to succeed by virtue of considerable effort." It is in this context that Habitat plays for her a significant role. She agrees with the Habitat philosophy of building for people in need, and not asking them to change their faith. It was the opportunity to get involved in actually trying to do something for the poor housing – "the opportunity to implement my beliefs in action" – that attracted over to Habitat. She says that she works with Habitat for nothing because in it she realizes both her "self-aspiration and social goals". Jane says that while "much Christian work seems detached from the needy" Habitat is truly a "hands-on-involvement". Habitat has not only made her aware of the housing problem but also influenced her relationships with other workers. She has found more friends while working at Habitat. Habitat has broadened her outlook on life. She thinks that it enables her to use her skills and reveal the best of herself, in spite of the frustration that comes from the knowledge that not all of her actions are successful.

Forty-three-year-old Julia is another volunteer, who left her real estate business to work with Habitat. She came to know about Habitat ten years ago during the time of Jimmy and Roselyn Carter's Habitat work camp in Bronx, New York. She says that she does not "operate well on the 'profit motive' and found her work as a realtor "sometimes financially rewarding and sometimes not, but almost always frustrating and stressful". She quit her "high-paying job" (this is how she describes her previous work in the questionnaire) to work part-time at a low salary with Habitat. Her husband's good income and the "tremendous satisfaction" she derives from her work with Habitat facilitated this turn in her life.

Julia is not alone in having left a profitable career in real estate to volunteer for Habitat. Many volunteers came from high-paying jobs, an experience which provides them sometimes a negative frame of reference to positively relate to Habitat's goal of making a difference in the housing situation.

Hillary is a 51-year-old retired realtor. She first heard about Habitat four years ago from her son, who had been drawing house plans for the local Habitat. She has been associated with the local Habitat for the last one-and-one-half years as a committee member, a board member, and as an executive director. She appreciates Habitat's vision and practice of "uplifting families". In her words, "A person cannot think about their spiritual life if their physical life is 'roach infested'. What better way to demonstrate our Christianity than through a building programme for all people and all faiths?" She is specifically attracted to "Habitat's concept of building volunteers" and to the fact that the "building programme is being funded by contributions from churches and individuals".

Before working with Habitat, Hillary was volunteering for the Salvation Army through which she could meet many homeless. Though she says that her life has not been adversely affected because of her service for Habitat, she has at the same time reached a point, as she tells us, where she needed to make a decision as to the amount of time she could spend as a volunteer. Her current reflection has been partly triggered off by the loss of earning she has incurred after leaving her previous job.

Hillary is an Episcopalian. About the nature of Habitat as a Christian initiative, she comments: "Habitat's mission is visible for all to see. We do what many others only talk about. Quoting a Bible verse will not keep a family warm in the snow or dry in a rainstorm. The need to help others is very strong in many people and there will always be those who need our help. Habitat's evangelism reaches all people connected with the programme, not just the families being helped."

Thirty-three-year-old Mark, the executive director of the Habitat project in his area, is another engaging interlocutor whose views we should hear. He had worked as a programme director of the Minneapolis Red Cross for four years. He thinks that there have always been two types of evangelism: "evangelism that 'talks' and evangelism that 'does' " For him, "Habitat is a 'doing' evangelism, which is the best way [...] and its work is greatly needed in our contemporary world." It is because of this that he "gladly" left his other jobs to become the executive director of the local project. Now that he is with Habitat he realizes that his work "integrates his faith into his daily life". In his words, "My experience with Habitat has certainly been intense: I would say it is one of those rare 'peak experiences in my life." For him, "The source of this lies in the fact Habitat helps poor families stabilize their lives and climb out of poverty."

Grace is another Habitat volunteer. She lives in the inner city in a "room" provided by the local affiliate as part of her "voluntary stipend" and her income is below the taxable range. At the same time, she does not think that she has made any sacrifice in working with Habitat. Rather her experience has been just the opposite – a wonderful experience of working with "an organization which enables one to try to live out one's conscience, where there's virtually no sacrifice of values". She says, "Being from the white, privileged, educated minority, I will always be middle to upper-middle class. My choosing to be below taxable income is yet another 'privilege,' i.e., *voluntary poverty*" (emphasis added).

Grace feels that we are all interconnected by a God of Love who has set forth various ways and means to manifest her/himself. She has the following graphic metaphors to share about Habitat: "I knew how the housing crisis can best be solved. Habitat has a very effective philosophy – kind of like the Amish barn-raising parties where everyone from the community comes together to help their neighbor their own barn".

Understanding the Significance of Habitat: Dilemma, Movement and Transformations

The actors of Habitat embody an urge to do something to make a difference in their own lives and in the lives of those for whom they build. But even joining Habitat out of a deeper conviction to find meaning in one's life is not without doubt and dilemma on the part of the actors. This is even true of those who consider their participation with Habitat to have been definitely a turning point in their lives. Rick Hathaway, a former General Electric (GE) engineer from Massachusetts and now the director of Habitat Affiliates, is one such. His participation with Habitat, he says, has been a turning point in his life. He worked with GE for five years. Then he took a year off and built houses for Habitat in Lynn, Massachusetts. It was then that he decided to leave his job and work full time on the staff at the Habitat headquarters. It was a challenging decision for him since it meant "leaving a lot of security". He remains fully aware that he has left a well-trodden and secure path, and I think he experiences some ambivalence. Rick's story sensitizes us to the dilemmas and doubts that accompany the process of self-transformation as initiated by one's participation in social movements so persuasively captured in McAdam's study (1988) of the Freedom Summer.

Nevertheless, social movements are processes of ongoing self-transformations, which can change movement actors into critics of culture (Bright and Harding 1984). One gets an intimation of a critical consciousness among the Habitat folks at Americus, Georgia – the headquarters of Habitat. In commenting contemporary American society, Sky – a Habitat volunteer – declares that it is becoming a credit card society which for him is also the "sign of the beast" (his words). As he envisions it, this might become a society where currency would become superfluous while the access to exchange would be more and more restricted. Sky thinks that eventually power and control could be concentrated in the hands of a few. Another volunteer, who identifies himself as a "hippie", says that the United States is heading for a civil war. In his words, "If this happens, then people will realize the practical significance of liberation theology." Many volunteers, not all of whom are necessarily wealthy and able to afford a "voluntary poverty," feel that their participation in Habitat has given them a less "materialistic perspective" on life. They articulate what Inglehart (1990) calls a "post-materialist" perspective on life which does not consider money and power as the sole measures of life. This is put into practice by what Unger (1987) calls the "personalist programme". With hammers in their hands Habitat actors bring their "personalist programmes" to bear upon the unfoldment of self, culture, society. Habitat actors do not just wait for the government or a more significant other to arrive and solve problems of shelter; they pick up their hammer and go to build. They also share their resource with the projects and enjoy leaving their well-paying jobs to either volunteer with

Habitat or work at substantially salary. Their "voluntary poverty" helps us appreciate what Unger says, "The citizen renounces [...] because *his concessions are transfigured by the affirmative inclinations and attachments*" (Unger 1987: 379; emphasis added).

Giddens provides us a perspective to make sense of the aspirations of Habitat actors vis-à-vis their search for a more meaningful "career". Giddens argues that to understand not only individual but also society in our "late modern age" we will have to take seriously the "reflexive project of the self" which "consists in sustaining a coherent, yet continuously revived biographical narrative" in face of "multiple choices filtered through abstract systems" (Giddens 1991: 5). Such a project involves the choice of a particular lifestyle "among a diversity of options" (ibid.). A reflexive mobilization of self is also at work in the life of the actors of Habitat for whom their house-building engagement is a significant marker of their "lifestyle". When actors under late capitalism are by and large robbed of their power to synthesize and conceive of their life as a meaningful whole, this lifestyle gives Habitat volunteers an opportunity solidarity and "de-differentiation" (Habermas 1984: 25), an alternative to the "internal colonization of life world" (Habermas 1987). As Dorris Poole (1993), a volunteer at Habitat International headquarters, who left her job in an insurance company after nineteen years of service to work full time with Habitat, tells us: "I really feel that Americans today live a compartmentalized lifestyle. We don't want our jobs, our religion, our friends, our social lives to mix together. Coming to Habitat has given me a more integrated lifestyle."

Reflexive mobilization of the self involves both conflicts with the existing system – new conflicts now emerge along the seams "between system and life world" that target at roles created by "the media of money and power" (Habermas 1987: 395) – as well as movements for reconstruction and affirmation. In Habitat we see such moves at work which in their own ways try to deconstruct the monolithic language of money and power, "work and exchange" (Unger 1987: 431). What we also see in Habitat is how new forms of religion and spirituality help in this deconstruction and reconstruction by trying to "directly address issues of the moral meaning of existence which modern institutions so thoroughly tend to dissolve" (Giddens 1991: 207).

Involvement with Habitat provides its volunteers an opportunity to come to terms with their life crises and actualize their life aspirations. In other words, their Habitat engagement helps them in their "identity formation". But, the process of this "identity formation" is complex. The identity of Habitat volunteers is crucially dependent upon the performance of the homeowners. Homeowners must repay regularly, which help Habitat volunteers to feel secured in their identity of belonging to a movement where their money and labour is not given either as a dole or a charity but becomes a link in an ever-widening circle of "Revolving Fund for Humanity". They feel threatened when the homeowners default. In order to secure this identity from all probable threats the actors of Habitat would not hesitate to impose their own middle-class identity upon the homeowners by insisting on the destruction of the dilapidated trailer of a selected homeowner. This, in fact, is a rule in Immokalee, Florida where I carried out my fieldwork. Some of them also would not feel the prick of conscience in throwing out a defaulting homeowner to the streets of Chicago in a cold winter night (that this actually happened in the Chicago Habitat affiliate was once reported widely in the newspapers in the United States about which Habitat World had also written a commentary) or suggesting to take out the roof of a poor farmer's Habitat house (this was suggested by an international volunteer of Habitat in a project in India during the drive for the collection of mortgage payment from the defaulting homeowners), thus blurring the thin separating line between vicarious and creative identity formation.

It is perhaps for this reason that there are some volunteers in Habitat who articulate disenchantment with it. A Habitat couple who had served for three years as international partners in two different Habitat projects in East Africa tells us: "Participation in Habitat has made us cynical about developmental efforts in general. The arrogance of the First World people overrides many of the benefits. This experience has confirmed our belief in the need for true grass roots development, which Habitat is not." They further add: "[...] Habitat is a good model if it can be freed from the control of the middle class, both in the United States and in the Third World." Another volunteer of Habitat who works in a project in Peru also tells us: "The organization is a paternalistic disgrace in Peru where a bunch of rich snorts feel very good about themselves for helping those 'poor people' get a material good, while the poor themselves are allowed no meaningful participation in the program and, far from being taught that they can improve themselves, are led to believe that they can only get ahead through the beneficence of rich Peruvians and North Americans. My impression is that the projects in United States vary, but that in general they aren't much better than Peru." The following statement of Habitat homeowner Margaret Dellucenay of Eckhart, Indiana, helps us understand this: "After a while, reality struck and I found that these Habitat 'angels' were really just ordinary people. They didn't always understand me and I just could not figure out what they didn't like about me. They would ask me my opinion and would get very upset when I give it to them" (quoted in Fuller and Fuller 1990: 57). It is perhaps for this reason that a recent commentator of Habitat has written:

> [...] apart from the bickering over whether to pay bigots to change, their habitats or to hope that the zealots will live like missionaries out of the goodness of their hearts, the marginality of the poor remain in the margins and spaces of the text. Those inhabiting the world of greed invite the marginal people 'in'; those inhabiting world of love go out to meet the marginal people, to minister to their needs. In both cases, the marginal people are out there, ripe for domination because their needs must be met from without by the resources of the greedy middle class folks or loving middle-class folks (Corlett 1989: 9).

Towards a Hermeneutics of Recovery

We began this reflection with an interrogation of the discourse of deconstruction and with a plea for understanding the urge for recovery and building in the life of actors and institutions in contemporary societies. Habitat articulates a different agenda of self-criticism and rebuilding of the built-environment than that provided by the discourse of deconstruction. But, its complex embodiment, especially the continued urge of some volunteers to control the life-space of the homeowners, suggests that Habitat is not a pure counter-example of the narrative of self and society deployed by deconstruction. Probably, in interrogation of any theoretical metanarrative, examples do not work as pure evidences to support or refute a theory; a creative engagement with them help us to be critical of our taken-for-granted assumptions and the reigning ideologies of the time, and widen and deepen our universe of discourse (see Giri 1994; Lieberson 1992). As complex as the process of "identity formation" at work and the embodiment of the vision of "No More Shacks" in Habitat is, the significance of Habitat for what its actors perceive as the destruction of the US moral economy and the redemption seen in building houses cannot be discounted. The actors of Habitat are appalled by the processes of economic, political and social change; they seek to arrest this disintegration process and create new sites of integration by building houses. By building houses for the less privileged, they not only build communities but rebuild themselves – rejoin several disjointed fragments in their lives and arrive at a new synthesis.

In their recent moral critique of institutional arrangement in the contemporary United States, Robert Bellah and his colleagues tell us that contemporary American form of life minimizes seeking of any "larger moral meaning" and Americans have pushed the "logic of exploitation as far it can go" (Bellah et al., 1991: 43). In this context, they plead for a new paradigm for the actors and the institutions of the United States what they call the "pattern of cultivation". This paradigm of cultivation refers to the habit of paying attention to the needs of one another and building of communities. Attention is described here normatively which refers to pursuing goals, and relationships which give us meaning, and is different from "distraction" and "obsession" (ibid.). For Bellah et al., "Attending means to concern ourselves with the larger meanings of life in the longer run, rather than with short-term pay offs. The pursuit of immediate pleasure or the promise of immediate pleasure is the essence of distraction. A good society is one in which attended takes precedence over distraction" (ibid.: 273).

In Habitat we see a mode of attention at work. If the actors in Bellah's conversation on good society express their attentiveness through the idiom of cultivation, the actors of Habitat express it through the idiom of "love in the mortar joints". The paradigm is a paradigm of building – building homes and building communities. Fuller talks about pursuit and building as appropriate models of the care of the self – as appropriate modes of being in the world and self-engagement. Like Bellah's actors Fuller also presents his idea of pursuit normatively and argues that "a spiritual dimension to our various pursuits is essential to make sense of what life is all about" (Fuller 1992c: 4–5). Fuller speaks simultaneously of "pursuing peace and building up one another" (Fuller 1992a) and challenges for "building a better world" (Fuller 1992b). Many commentators of the emergent American consciousness also point to a pervasive spiritual urge within a section of population so that critical exhortations from interlocutors such as Millard Fuller do not fall only on deaf ears. For instance, one observer tells us that a strong social ethic, which is "an activist form of mystic endeavor, for it supports transformative work in society as an outgrowth and manifestation of transformation of the self", is emerging as a major component of the new spirituality (Albanese 1993: 138). Another observer of contemporary American religiosity argues that the religious scene is characterized not only by "pastiche styles of belief and practice," but by a "profound searching" (Roof 1993: 165) which is "not so much that of navel gazing, but a quest for balance – between self and others, between self-fulfillment and social responsibilities" (ibid.). It is noteworthy that in his remark on this emergent social ethic and spirituality, Roof mentions Habitat for Humanity.

The paradigm of building, which animates movements like Habitat for Humanity, has a potential for recovery – recovery of meaning in individual lives as well as recovery of communities from the threatening logic of speculation where speculation on profit takes an upper hand over the human need for decent shelter. This paradigm of building also embodies a hermeneutics of recovery for our ways of world-making and frames of interpretation. The disintegration of built-environments in advanced industrial societies has gone hand in hand with the rise of deconstruction in social theory and anti-foundationalism in American philosophy. But "[...] in challenging all consensual standards of truth and justice, of ethics, and meaning [...] deconstructionism ended up, inspire of the best intentions of its more radical practitioners, reducing knowledge and meaning to a rubble of signifiers" (Harvey 1989: 350). "It thereby produced a condition of nihilism" (ibid.) which in turn has made the need for a "hermeneutics of recovery" urgent in the theory and partial of the actors.

In Habitat we see such a hermeneutics at work. A hermeneutics of recovery requires trust in one another and communities which sustain us and give our interdependence a moral meaning (Bellah 1989; Bellah et al., 1991). If as a result of economic decline and post-industrial transition contemporary United States is now "falling from grace", then Habitat's vision of "No More Shacks" and its paradigm of building is a sign of recovery. It is undoubtedly true that it is just a sign and has not yet become a symbol. Still its potential for engaging Americans in a hermeneutics of recovery cannot be missed.

Note

1. But it must be noted that this ground is not necessarily a solid, self-assured and arrogant ground but a nurturing ground realizing its inherent fragility. God discovered is not just the Sovereign, all Powerful, but a small God, God with small g. See Dallmayr 2005.

References

Albanese, Catherine. 1993. "Fisher Kings and Public Places: The Old New Age in the 1990s". *Annals of the American Academy of Political Science* 527: 131–143, May1993.

Apter, David. 1992. "Democracy and Emancipatory Movements: Notes for a Theory of Inversionary Discourse". In Jan N. Pieterse (ed.), *Emancipations, Modern and Postmodern*. London: Sage Publications.

Baudrillard, Jean. 1989. *America*. London: Verso.

Bellah, Robert. 1989. "Interview with Robert Bellah." In Bill Moyers, *A World of Ideas*. New York: Doubleday.

Bellah, Robert et al. 1991. *The Good Society*. NY: Alfred A. Knof.

Benjamin, Roger. 1981. *The Limits of Politics: Collective Goods and Social Change in Post-industrial Societies*. Chicago: The University of Chicago Press.

Boyte, Harry. 1980. *The Backyard Revolution*. Philadelphia: Temple University Press.

Corlett, William. 1989. *Community with Unity: A Politics of Derridian Difference.* Durham: Duke University Press.

Dallmayr, Fred. 2005. *Small Wonder: Global Power and its Discontents.* Lanham, MD: Rowman & Littlefield.

Ewen, Stuart. 1988. *All Consuming Images: The Politics of Style in Contemporary Culture.* New York: Basic Books.

Fuller, Millard. 1977. *Bokotola.* Chicago: API Fullet.

——. 1980. *Love in the Mortar Joints.* Clinton, NJ: New Win Publishing, inc.

——. 1986. *No More Shacks: The Daring Vision of Habitat for Humanity.* Waco, Texas: Word Books Publisher.

——. 1992a. "Pursuing Peace and Building up One Anther". Bacealaureate Sermon, Lynchburg College, Lynchburg, VA, May 1.

——. 1992c. "Building a Better World". Commencement Address at Technical University of Novascotia, May 9.

——. "Housing Things Which Make for Peace". Baccalaureate Sermon, North Park College, Chicago, May 22.

Fuller, Millard and Linda Fuller. 1990. *The Excitement is Building: How Habitat for Humanity is Building Roofs Over Heads and Hopes in Hearts.* Dallas: Word Publishers.

Gaylin, Willard. Interview with Bill Moyers. In Bill Moyers, *A World of Ideas: Conversation with Thoughtful Men and Women about American Life Today and the Ideas Shaping Our Future.* New York: Doubleday.

Giddens, Anthony. 1991. *Modernity and Self-identify: Self and Society in the Late Modern Age.* Cambridge: Polity Press.

Giri, Ananta. 1994. "Some Contemporary Notes on Method." *Man and Development,* June 1994.

——. 1995. "Self, Other, and The Challenge of Culture". Manuscript. This is later part of my *Global Transformations: Postmodernity and Beyond.* Jaipur: Rawat Publications.

Habermas, Jurgen. 1987. *The Theory of Communicative Action.* Cambridge, MA: The MIT Press.

——. 1990. *Moral Consciousness and Communicative Action.* Cambridge: Polity Press.

Habermas, Jurgen (ed.). 1984. Observations on *"The Spiritual Situation of the Age:" Contemporary German Perspectives.* Cambridge, MA: The MIT Press.

Harvey, David. 1989. *The Condition of Postmodernity: An Inquiry into the Origins of Cultural Change.* Cambridge, MA: Basil Blackwell.

——. 1991. "Flexibility: Threat or Opportunity." *Socialist Review* 21 (1) 69–77.

Inglehart, Ronald. 1990. *The Culture Shift in Advanced Societies.* Princeton: Princeton University Press.

Jordan, Clarence. 1964. *Practical Religion or the Sermon on the Mount and the Epistle of James in the Koinonia "cotton patch" Version.* Americus, Georgia: Koinonia Farms.

Laclau, Ernesto. 1992. "Beyond Emancipation". In Jan N. Pieterse (ed.), *Emancipations Modern and Postmodern.* London: Sage Publishers.

Lee, Dallas. 1971. *The Cotton Patch Evidence: The Story of Clarence Jordan and the Koinonia Farm Experiment*. Americus, GA: Koinonia Partners.

Lieberson, Stanley. 1992. "Einstein, Renoir, and Greeley: Some Thoughts on Evidence in Sociology."*American Sociological Review* 57 (1) 1–15.

Madison, G.B. 1988. *The Hermeneutics of Postmodernity.* Bloomington: Indiana University Press.

McAdam, Doug. 1988. *Freedom Summer.* NY: Oxford University Press.

McDonald, Malarie. 1992. "Low Wages, High Prices Make Resort Area a Tough Place to Live." *Habitat Word* 9 (5) 5.

Offe, Claus and Ulrich K. Preuss. 1991. "Democratic Institutions and Moral Resources." In David Held (ed.), *Political Theory Today.* Cambridge: Polity Press.

Pande, G.C. 1989. *The Meaning and Process of Culture as Philosophy of History.* Allahabad: Raka Prakashan.

—. 1991. "Two Dimensions of Religion: Reflections based on Indian Spiritual Experience and Philosophical Traditions." In Eliot, Deutch (ed.), *Culture and Modernity.* Honolulu: University of Hawaii Press.

Poole, Dorris. 1993. "Dorris Poole, Americus, GA." *Habitat World* 10 (3): 9.

Roof, Wade Clark. 1993. "Toward the Year 2000: Reconstructions of Religious Space." *The Annals of American Association of Political and Social Science.*

Sen, Amartya. 1989. "Food and Freedom." *World Development* 17(6): 769–781.

Soja, Edward. 1989. *Postmodern Geographies: The Reassertion of Space in Critical Social Theory*. London: Verso.

Sri Aurobindo. 1950. *The Synthesis of Yoga.* Pondicherry: Sri Aurobindo Ashram.

Taylor, Charles. 1989. *The Sources of Self.* Cambridge, MA: Harvard University Press.

Unger, Roberto M. 1987. *False Necessity: Anti-Necessitarian Social Theory in the Service of Radical Democracy*. Cambridge: Cambridge University Press.

Verma, Roop Rekha. 1991. "The Concept of Progress and Cultural Identify." In Eliot Deutch (ed.), *Culture and Modernity*. Honolulu: University of Hawaii Press.

Walzer, Michael. 1988. "Interpretation and Social Criticism". In S.M. McCurrin (ed.), *Tanner Lecture on Human Values*. Cambridge: Cambridge University Press. and Salt Lake City: Utah Press.

Warren, Mark. 1992. "Democracy and Self-Transformation." *American Political Science Review* 86 (1): 8–23.

Wuthnow, Robert. 1988. *The Restructuring of American Religion: Society and Faith since World War II.* Princeton: Princeton University Press.

14 Understanding the Chipko Movement

Chipko was a socio-cultural movement in the Central Himalayas of India focusing on the protection of forest resources, and fighting for regional economic development, ecological conservation and social justice. The movement originated in the Uttarakhand region (now a separate state) of the state of Uttar Pradesh around 1972 or 1973. It was not a centralized and homogeneous movement, either ideology or in terms of organization. People with different ideological commitments, the communists and Gandhians, participated in this movement and contributed to its operation and success. Villagers spontaneously participated in this movement because they wanted the outside contractors to leave so that they might utilize the forest resources themselves. The Chipko activists fought the contractors by hugging the trees that were threatened by logging operations. The word for "hugging" in the native language is "Chipko". Therefore, the movement came to be known as the "Chipko Andolan" or the "Chipko Movement".

I did my fieldwork with Chipko during June-August, 1987. The movement was spread all over the Uttarakhand region, but the fight against the contractors and government forest policy had become a thing of the past. After its success with the forest problem, the Chipko movement turned to issues such as mining enterprise abuse. But, the original forest problem has meanwhile become a historical narrative for the people of Uttarakhand. Villagers in many districts participated in it, without always being linked organizationally and ideologically. In the district of Gopeswar Chandi Prasad Bhatt, a Gandhian leader was influential, while in the two adjacent districts of Tehri and Pouri, Sunderlal Bahuguna, the noted Gandhian leader, inspired people's protest. In the district of Uttarakashi, the communists led the forest agitation. These particular features of the movement required a fieldwork plan, and I had to do considerable oral history. It was necessary to do fieldwork in all the representative command areas of the movement and places where decisive Chipko fights took place. I did fieldwork in Khirakot (Almora district), Gopeswar (Chamoli district), Reni (Chamoli district), Silyara and Bariyargarh (Tehri district), and in Naikala (Dehradun district) in the summer of 1987. Since I was interested in how people perceive and feel about the consequences of the movement, the popular understanding of Chipko was my prime object of investigation. Linked with it was the question of the operation and embodiment of this movement in an actual context of inequality and stratified social reality. I wanted to investigate how two major facts of social inequality – caste and gender – affected and were in turn affected by the Chipko movement.

Chipko started as a socio-economic movement. Its primary objective was the economic development of the hills through modernization and industrialization. Chipko wanted the abolition of the contractor system and the establishment of forest-based industries for generating local employment (see Pant 2011) . This would have the effect of stopping the migration of manpower from the hills to the plains. After 1977, however, Chipko took a predominantly ecological view of the problem in the hills. A group of Chipko activists, under the leadership of Sunderlal Bahuguna, proposed an alternative model of hill development. Instead of pleading for scientific cutting of the trees for the establishment of forest-based industries, they demanded a total ban on green felling in Central Himalayas. In place of a western model of economic development, the group pleaded for the principle of "ecology as permanent economy".[1] The struggle of this ecological group led to a cleavage in Chipko – between those who supported the scientific cutting of trees and those who demanded a total ban on tree-cutting in Himalayas. In 1983, the ecological group won out. The Government of India announced a temporary ban on green felling in Central Himalayas for an interim period of 15 years.

My objective here is to discuss what common people thought about the shift in Chipko priorities and its ideological struggle. I discuss how people felt about the Chipko leaders and their popular basis. I also discuss the gap between Chipko's understanding of people and people's understanding of Chipko. I discuss the initial socio-economic objectives of Chipko, as they have been determined by the socio-economic system of Uttarakhand and the history of a continuous diminution of local forest rights. I relate the key features of Chipko's initial socio-economic concern to certain salient features of Uttarakhand's culture and history. Then I shall discuss how, why and when Chipko took an ecological turn. In the discussion of people's understanding of Chipko, I relate this to the issue of social inequality in Chipko.

Society and Culture in Central Himalayas

The six hill districts of the state of Uttar Pradesh, the then biggest state in India, constitute the region of Uttarakhand. This region is the most sacred of the Himalayas and has a unique place in Indian culture[1]. The two most significant rivers, the Ganga and Jamuna, flow from this region. The people of Uttarakhand include two indigenous ethnic groups: (a) the Hindu and Muslim subsistence farmers and castes, living in the lower heights of the Himalayas (up to 7,000 ft. above the sea level); and (b) the Tibetan-speaking Buddhist Bhotiyas, living at the higher altitudes, who are nomadic herders and traders. The region constitutes a distinct culture area within the framework of North Indian Aryan culture (Berreman 1962), which can be contrasted with culture and society on the plains. One of the crucial distinctions in culture and in people's consciousness is the "Pahari" (mountains)/"Deshi" (plains) people contrast. Compared to the plants, the amount of land available for cultivation and habitation in this highland region is limited. Relative landlessness is common to people living in mountain regions all over the world (Eckholm 1976). Yet landlordism has not existed in this area, because land distribution has not involved much inequality. Traditionally, the untouchables have had less land, but the differences in landholding are not substantial. Unlike other parts of India, in this region, not much social unrest has been based on land disputes. This helps to explain why social unrest here revolved around forest resources instead.

The scarcity of surface is reflected in the architectural pattern. People live in an upper story and keep cattle on a lower story. Women in this village say, "We are all animals, but we are tied up in the upper story". Like the Munduruou village in Murphy and Murphy (1974), the physical layout and architecture of this society tell us something about its socio-cultural system. Because of land scarcity, the economy has always been based on subsistence. At the same time, forest and animal husbandry have been very important, the forest has been a fundamental source of sustenance. For centuries, its vegetation has fertilized the topsoil. The forest provides fodder for animal husbandry. People also get vegetables, tea leaves, medicinal plants and wood for making their ploughs and houses from the forest.

For centuries, this area has been relatively isolated from the outside world though there have always been pilgrims and other traditional messengers. After the 1962 Indo-China war, when this region opened up, people from this region have migrated to work on the plains and people from the plains have intruded upon this space to exploit the indigenous forest resources. Migration of the males from highland villages to the plains creates a peculiar situation for the socio-economic system of the hills. This is basic to our understanding of the unique position of women in the hills. Since men mostly stay on the plains, women now do most of the work on the land and also all the work in the domestic domain. In the sexual division of labour, most of the difficult tasks are assigned to women. They go to the forest to collect fodder and firewood and also work in the field, planting the saplings and harvesting the paddy. Since almost all the women in the village go together to the forest, they share a sense of collectivity and solidarity. They have to take decision in many concrete situations when males have been away in the plains for years. Therefore, women have a greater sense of independence compared to women in many other parts of India. Raju, a boy in Kheti village, told me that when a young girl is required to do all the household work the boy is not usually pressured because it is he who will migrate and bring money for the family. Because it is the women who go to the forest, the forest stands in a special relationship of "affection and sentiment" to women. To quote one male in Kheti village, "The relation of woman to the forest is one of Dil (heart)." Radha Behn, my distinguished informant, who herself has led many women's movements in the region argued, "Here women do not conceptualize forest and field as source of money. When we have any problem, we go to the forest and cry there." The forest is as much an intimate space for women as is the village. Eliade (1959) tells us about construction of sacred and profane space, and argues that it is from the boundary of the village that the realm of the profane starts. Similarly, Beidelman (1986) reports the same contrast between village and bush in his study of Kaguru. But for people in this region, especially women, forest space is not differently conceived, as compared to the village. The forest is conceived as a mother. Radha Behn went on, "If the forest is cut down, then where shall we go for our physical and emotional existence since part of our soul and substance lies in the forest?" This is basic to understanding women's role in the Chipko movement.

For Berreman, in this region, "Rajputs and Brahmins are allied castes possessing decisive dominance" (Berreman 1979). But, compared to the plains, there is much more informal encounter between people of different castes, even though the notion of purity and pollution is more rigidly applied here. The untouchables, as in almost all Indian villages, live in a segregated settlement and they are mostly landless. Harijans usually plough the land for the high-caste landowners. In Pakhi, Harijans once refused to plough. Then, the high-caste youths in the village, who serve in the military, coerced them to do it. But, in Garhwal, Brahmins do plough. This distinctive caste structure is basic to understanding the issue of social inequality in Chipko.

Certain Decisive Moments in the History of Uttarakhand

The two decisive moments in the history of Uttarakhand are: (a) British annexation; and (b) the opening up of the region to the outside world mainly after independence and the Indo-Chinese war in 1962. The history of the region has been the history of the diminution of the rights of the local people over the forest resources. Before the advent of British rule in India, there was only customary regulation of people's rights over forest lands and products. But, the British realized the commercial value of forests and began to regulate the people's rights over them. After independence, there was a basic continuity between the colonial forest policy and post-colonial forest policy. On October 25, 1980, the Government of India issued the Forest Conservation Ordinance prohibiting the state government from allowing any forest land to be used for any non-forest purpose without prior approval. This situation of "stolen rights" has been very similar to the situation described by E.P. Thompson (1975). In Thompson's analysis, the struggle between the Whigs and Hunters has basically involved "the alternative definition of property rights". Similarly, writes Ramachandra Guha, "The history of conflict and struggle can be seen essentially as emanting from alternative conceptions of property rights and obligations" (Guha 1983: 1886).

In the post-1947 situation, there has been enormous growth of forest industries which have made high demands upon the forests in Uttarakhand. The opening up of this region in terms of road transportation, especially after the 1962 Indo-Chinese war, has brought the commercial, imperial and capitalistic interests more fully into forests. Now, the contractors from the plains with their networks in the forest department and government could cut down the forests. This has led to what Berreman (1979) aptly calls "Fourth World Colonialism". This explains the ambivalent attitude of the people and social activists of the region towards the road. For Dr Samser Singh Bist, an economist and the leader of the influential Uttarakhand Sangharsh Vahini, "The role of the road has been similar to the role of the East India Co. in India" (Bist 1979: 208).

The continuous diminution of people's rights over the forests has set the context for the agitational movement in Uttarakhand. The peak of this popular protest was the Tilhari agitation on May 30, 1930 where there was a firing on peaceful protesters in Tilhari, a village in Garhwal. The Tilhari firing has an important place in the "Collective Unconscious" of the people even today. It is perhaps for this reason that the Uttarakhand Sarvodaya Mandal on May 30, 1968, the anniversary of the Tilhari firing, declared May 30 as Martyr's Day and Forest Day. On this Forest Day, the Mandal took the pledge to generate local employment by establishing forest-based industries. Chipko's socio-economic goals were being formulated long before the beginning of the actual Chipko fight in 1972.

The penetration of commercial forces not only led to the destruction of the forests, but also to their transformation from "a community of living beings" to a "mine of mono-cultural species".[2] The forest department planted the commercial species which earned revenue, but were ecologically unsuitable for holding air and water and also for enriching the soil. This affects the eco-system of the region. Mira Behn, another disciple of Gandhi, while working in the hills, had long before warned about this ensuing ecological disaster in an article entitled "Something wrong in the Himalayas" published in the late 1940s (quoted in Dogra 1983). In this article, Mira Behn pointed out how penetration of commercial and imperialistic interest in the region has led to vital changes in the species of trees being encouraged to grow. The species of trees that are being nurtured by the forest department are more useful commercially. The species, such as the Banjo, which are an ideal absorber of the monsoon, are being replaced by commercial species such as Chirpine, which produces just the opposite effect. R. Tucker makes this point very clear: "One of the most dramatic changes has been the transfer of large areas of Third World's forests into crop-lands or monoculture tree plantation, to meet the metropolitan countries' demands for industrial raw material and consumer goods" (Tucker 1985). The writings of Serla Behn and Mira Behn created an ecological awareness in the region. This is important to understand why some Chipko activists felt the need for emphasizing economic development through ecological conservation rather than short-run economic gain through commercial forestry and tree felling.

The Origin of Chipko and its Socio-Economic Demands

Chipko movement, in its present form, started simultaneously in many parts of Uttarakhand sometimes around 1972–73. By this time the exploitation and denudation of the forest by the contractors had reached its peak in this region. Sarvodaya workers since the early 60s had established a number of labour co-operatives and village-based industries known as Gram Swaraj Sanghas. These were actually Gandhian institutions and with the help of the Khadi and Village Industries Commission were trying to check the flow of manpower from the hills by offering employment in the local forest-based industries. The Swaraj Sanghas were run by local contractors and when their demand for raw materials from the forest increased, their interest inevitably came into conflict with the interest of the big contractors from the plains (Singh 1987). With the climate of isolation and seclusion that has been a significant aspect of the "Collective Unconscious" in Uttarakhand, this confrontation could also very easily be given a regional interpretation. The contractors and capitalists were not simply contractors, they were also outsiders, who were stealing their life-sustaining substances from their "Mother Forest". In 1972, there was a public meeting in the village, Purola, in which Sunderlal and his influential colleague Surrendra Dutt Bhatt led the public agitation against the contractors. This was followed by public meetings in Uttarakashi on December 12. All these meetings were organized by Gandhians. For example, in Uttarakashi, it was Sunderlal who was leading the agitation while in Gopeswar another Gandhian Chandi Prasad was leading the people's protest. Hence, we should remember that to reach Uttarakashi from Gopeswar it takes at least one day by bus, and the only connecting link might be the Uttarakhand Sarvodaya Mandal – the organization of Gandhian workers in Uttarakhand.

This conflict between contractors and the government on the one hand, and the local people and local mini-contractors on the other, reached its peak in March 1973 when the Uttar Pradesh government gave a permit to a sporting goods company called Simon & Co. in Allahabad to cut the valuable ash trees in Mandal Valley near Gopeswar. Earlier, Chandi Prasad had requested the forest department. to give a few ash trees to his organization for making ploughs but his request was refused. As a result, a public meeting was organized in Mandal village on April 24, 1973 to discuss their future plan in which Alam Singh Bist, the Mandal village council chairman, presided and Bachanlal, an influential Harijan leader from the village, participated. By talking to villagers of Bairangana and Khalla in Mandal Valley, it becomes clear that in this meeting the decision to do "Chipko" that is, to hug the threatened trees to stop the contractors from cutting them down was a collective decision. Hence, it was not the sole idea of Chandi Prasad, as has been suggested in certain studies, notably Mishra and Tripathy (1978) and Berreman (1987). As a result of public pressure, Simon & Co. were allotted trees in Rampur Phata by the forest department and the trees in the Mandal Valley were saved. Then, the venue of the fight shifted to Rampur Phata, where Chipko also won. By this time, the main demands of the Chipko were consolidated into five major points:

(a) The abolition of the contractor system; local labour co-operatives should be entrusted with the responsibility for utilizing the forest resources.
(b) Raw materials from the forest should not be drained from the hills; small-scale industries based upon forest resources should be started, and the villagers should be given governmental assistance.
(c) Based upon the needs of an increasing population, there should be a new forest policy.
(d) There should be a new plantation scheme for soil erosion.
(e) In forest administration and in the governmental measures to protect the forest, village people should be involved.

When we talked to the villagers of the Mandal Valley, it became very clear that their sole aim was the abolition of contractor system and the establishment of forest-based industries. This also became clear when we discussed the Bayali forest agitation led by the communists. But, before this, we need to discuss the best-known Chipko fight in Reni.

Chipko's third and the most famous fight was in Reni, a village in the Joshimath block of district Chamoli, which is situated very close to the Indo-Tibetan boarder. In this village, on March 27, 1974 village women under the leadership of the head of village women's association, Goura Devi, successfully resisted the contractors when their menfolk had been called to Gopeswar under the pretext of certain administrative problems. The local women's association was a tiny organization through which housewives helped each other in times of distress. For the last four months before the date of actual confrontation, Govind Singh Rawat, C.P. Bhatt and other activists had been organizing public meetings in Reni and advising people that they should never allow the trees to be cut down by the contractors. While resisting the contractors and their axemen, the women of village Reni said, "Bhula (Brothers), do not cut the forest. It provides us with cheap herbs. If this forest goes, this mountain will fall on our village. Floods will come and our 'bagads' will be swept away. We will be ruined. Please do not cut these trees. When our menfolk will come back, then you can settle this with them." But, the axemen did not listen. At one point they were out to shoot Goura Devi, the leader. But, when the women fearlessly faced the axemen, the axemen were forced to come back from the forest. After this successful confrontation, there was a public meeting under the leadership of Goura Devi in which approximately 6,000 people participated. After this, the UP government set up the Reni Investigation Committee to investigate the ecological danger that deforestation brings under the chairmanship of noted botanist Dr Virendra Kumar of Delhi University. Based upon the committee's recommendations, tree felling was banned in the vast catchment areas of Alakananda and its tributaries for 10 years.

While the people of Reni were fighting against the contractors at one extreme of Uttarakhand, at another distant forest, called Bayali, in the district of Uttarakashi, the communists were fighting against the contractors and government; this later came to be known as the famous Bayali forest agitation. In almost all the studies of the Chipko movement, there is almost no mention of the work of the communists in the Bayali forest. The deliberate exclusion of the communists may be ideological, since any reference to it explodes the usual picture that the forest movement was all Gandhian and completely non-violent. The studies by H.K. Singh (1987) show that it was the communists who, since the mid-1950s, have been organizing forest labourers. Since land is not a significant factor of inequality, the attention of the communists shifted to the forest. So, they started the "Save the Forest, Save Forest Labourer Movement". The Boyali forest agitation in July 1974 was a concrete manifestation of this ongoing movement. The labourers working in the Bayali jungle, in a letter written to the District Magistrate of Uttarakashi, had complained that they had to work from 14 to 16 hours a day.[3] Like slaves, they were sold from one contractor to another and the intermediary seller earned commission from them. The letters that they got from home were not delivered to them. They demanded a wage of Rs 15 for making each sleeper, i.e., a log of wood. They reached Bayali forest on 25th July and stayed there until August 15. On August 15, this movement achieved final victory when the agitators and the government reached an accord in which most of the demands of the communists were accepted.

As a result of Chipko's socio-economic fight, the Uttar Pradesh government was forced to settle their socio-economic demands with the Chipko activists. On April 24, 1974 the Chief Minister of Uttar Pradesh reached an agreement with Sunderlal Bahuguna and Chandi Prasad, the two most influential Chipko leaders. It was decided that the contractor system would be abolished; forest-based industries would be established with the help of local

Gandhian co-operatives; and forest contracts would be small scale, so that local people could participate in the auction and scientific cutting of the trees, to be carried out by forest department in place of the contractors. As a result, raw mills and turpentine factories were established all over the region with the help of local Gandhian institutions.

The Ecological Shift in Chipko

The ecological shift in Chipko was led by Sunderlal Bahuguna and a group of his committed colleagues. Before his participation in Chipko, Sunderlal had participated in many social movements in the region, including the freedom movement. Right from the 1960s until 1977, Sunderlal was thinking in the language of western development. But from 1977 he began to see that even after the local contractor system, nothing much really comes to the forest labourer. While in the forest with the labourers, he also noticed that the forest department is converting the forest from a community of living species to a mine of commercial trees, which is very dangerous to the eco-system of the Himalayas. Deforestation and the change of forest into a mine of monoculture timber-giving species are causing soil erosion, floods and landslides. As far back as 1974 he had argued, "The two main problems in the hills are (a) landslides and (b) migration of males" (Bahuguna 1974). In the forest, he studied "Losing Ground" by the famous ecologist E.P. Echolm with the forest labourers. He also studied Gandhi's "Hind Swaraj" and discussed Jagdish Bose's book *The Sacred Life of Plants*. By this time, Sunderlal himself had been influenced by the Stockholm Conference on Environment. Instrumental in his shift to an ecological approach was his association with Swami Chidananda, a great Hindu monk and the head of the Life Divine Society, which has its headquarters at Rishikesh. After the eventful Stockholm conference in 1972, it was Swami Chidananda who toured the hill villages with Sunderlal and spread the message of the conference on the issue of ecology and environment. It was Swami Chidananda's propagation of Upanishadic philosophy that "God exists in everything," which had inspired Sunderlal and his followers to treat trees as another living entity in the universe.

People's Understanding of Chipko and Political Action

People's dissatisfaction with excessive environmentalism of Chipko and the forest laws got expressed in the works of two political groups, viz., Uttarakhand Fighting Force and Jhapat Chino Andolan or "Snatch back your rights" movement.

Uttarakhand Sangharsa Vahini (Uttarakhand Fighting Force)

The Vahini operated mainly in the district of Almora under the commandership of Dr Samser Singh Bist, who ran a printing press and published a journal called "The Voice of the Forest" or "Jungle ki Dabedar". It was predominantly a radical Marxist organization and treated Gandhian work on forest conservation and hill development as status-quoist. Dr Bist opposed the formation of a separate hill state like Sunderlal and stressed the need to strike at both the internal stratification system and the overall capitalistic system, which creates misery in the hills. After the ban on green felling in the Himalayas, the Vahini held Sunderlal responsible for the problems people faced in getting trees from the forest for house construction and for fuel. In 1983, the Vahini had spearheaded the anti-wine movement called "Not Wine, But Bread" in the district of Almora (Pathak 1985).

From Chipko to "Jhapat Chino": The Programme Govind S. Rawat's Group

As pointed out before, Govind had played a crucial role in the Chipko fight at Reni. But like many villagers, he was dissatisfied with the ecological turn of the Chipko movement. He thought that it was a conspiracy of the Gandhians to halt development in the hills. Moreover, when village people could not cut trees, the forest department cut down these illegally and took truckloads of woods to the plains. Hence, Govind started "Jhapto Chino" movement. "Jhapto Chino" means "jump over and snatch back your rights," the rights appropriated by the government. As a modus-operandi, Govind and the agitators started obstructing the trucks of the forest department. Bachanlal in Mandal village and Bali Devi in Reni village showed me Govind's pamphlets and were telling how this movement embodied people's discontent against the ecological emphasis of the Chipko movement.

By the Way of Conclusion

I started with the question how ordinary people were affected by the shift in Chipko ideology and the consequent government legislation. It seems that there was a gap between Chipko's understanding of people and people's understanding of Chipko. This gap was due to the lack of communication between Chipko leaders and the common people. No Chipko leader had a widespread mass basis. After the initial success with the forest issue, a sustained popular movement widening its scope did not develop. The ecological group in Chipko, under the tireless efforts of Sunderlal Bahuguna, was successful in creating a country-wide awareness regarding the ensuing ecological disaster in the Himalayas. This perhaps influenced the late Prime Minister of India, Mrs Indira Gandhi, to order an interim ban on green felling in the Himalayas. As we saw, despite its good intentions, it has added to people's miseries.

At the heart of the problem was the question of two alternative models of hill development. One group in Chipko followed the model of rural industrialization. This group was mainly led by Chandi Prasad. But even translation of this objective required a sustained political and social fight. It required a fight against the existing political structure and the internal stratification system of caste, class and power. But as has been pointed out, Chandi did not have contact even among the people of his own village, Gopeswar. His sole programme had been conducting tree-planting camps with the help of village women's associations. For this, he was funded by department of environment of Government of India. So, one who is funded by the government for his work on environment is simply incapable of making Chipko into a fight against it. Though what Bhatt himself writes about this deserves our careful consideration: "We reliased that there is nothing wrong in cooperating with the government when it is responsive to people's demand" (Bhatt in Pant 2011: 118).

The case with Sunderlal was different. Sunderlal had always been a relentless critic of the government. He had a devoted band of supporters such as

Dhum Singh Negi. He never took any government grant. He lives by free-lance journalism. His institution Parvatiya Navajivan Ashram has stubbornly refused any government grant since its inception in 1957.[2] Wherever he conducted his Chipko fight, he was able to arouse people's participation for the cause. If people in a particular village face any problem and they seek his assistance in fighting against the forest department or the mine-owners, Sunderlal rushes to the area with his supporters immediately. He himself has dedicated his life to the cause of the highlanders. His ecological approach to hill development seems particularly suitable and appropriate for the problems of the hill people. But translation of this vision into reality requires a sustained political movement. Till now, Sunderlal has not thought in terms of cadre-based movement. He has spent his energy in creating an ecological awareness in the country and abroad for the cause of the Himalayas. Being a Gandhian, he does not operate in terms of organized political party and group. He works through concerned individuals and in terms of emerging issues. In my discussion with him, he himself acknowledged the need for creating a wider and a more sustained social movement. But, at the moment, he does not have sustained cadres in the region. This explains the gap between his vision of hill development and people's understanding of it.

So, in order to narrow the gap between Chipko's understanding of people and people's understanding of Chipko, the committed groups in it like Sunderlal's have to make Chipko a wider and a more sustained socio-political movement. In the end, the destiny of the people of Uttarakhand depends upon the extent to which Chipko succeeds in this transition and translation.

[This was written in October 1987 based upon my fieldwork on Chipko in June–July 1987. In the mean time, the situation in Uttarakhand has changed and Chipko is no longer a vibrant people's movement it was once].

Notes

1. This account of the socio-cultural system of Uttarakhand is based on my fieldwork and also on works by Bahuguna (1974, 1980, 1984); Berreman (1963, 1979, 1983, 1987): Bhatt (1987a); Bist, A. (1987); Bist, S. (1979); Dogra (1983) and Mishra and Tripathy (1978).
2. Though tragically this is now submerged because of the construction of the Tehri dam.

References

Bahuguna, S. 1974. "Uttarakhand main ekshobish din", Terhi.

——. 1980. Chipko: A Novel Movement for Establishment of Cordial Relationship between Man and Nature, Silyara.

——. 1984. Chipko Message, Silyara.

——. 1985. Interview with Sunderlal, *Illustrated Weekly of India*, June 23–29, Bombay.

——. 1986. *Three Weeks in Himalaya,* New Delhi: Gandhi Book House.

——. 1987. Letters and Documents of Sunderlal, unpublished.

Bandopadhyaya, J. and V. Shiva. 1987. "Chipko Rethinking India's Forest Culture," *The Ecologist* 17(1).

Beidelman, T.O. 1986. *Moral Imagination in Kaguru Modes of Thought.* Bloomington: Indiana University Press.

Berreman, G.D. 1962. *Hindus of the Himalayas.* Berkeley: University of California Press.

——. 1979. Himachal: Science, People and "Progress" IWGIA Document 36. Copenhagen: International Work Group on Indigenous Affairs.

——. 1983. "Identity Definition, Assertion, and Politicisation in the Central Himalayas". In A. Jacobson-Widding (ed.), *Identity: Personal and Socio-cultural.* Atlantic Highlands, New Jersey: Humanities Press, 289–319.

——. 1987. *Chipko: A Movement to Save the Himalayas and the Chipko Movement.* Gopeswar: DGSS.

Bhatt, R. 1987 (a). "Mining: Development or Destruction to the Hills", *Himalaya,* April.

——. 1987 (b). "Laxmi Ashram: A Gandhian Perspective in the Himalayan

Foothills", in Eck and Jain (eds.), *Speaking of Faith,* Philadelphia: New Society Publishers.

——. (ed.), *Saarla Smruti Granta,* Kaushani.

Bist, A. 1987. "The Actual Meaning of Chipko Movement" (in Hindi), unpublished manuscript.

——. 1979. "An analysis of the Economic Development of Kumayoun and the principle of its Regional Development", unpublished Ph.D. dissertation in Hindi, Kumayoun University, Nainital.

Bishnoi, R.S. *Where Conservation is Creed: Teaching of Jamleswar in Action.* Unpublished manuscript.

Chatterjee, P. 1984. "Gandhi and the Critique of Civil Society", in Guha, 1984.

Chidananda, S. 1973. *Uttarake Shaila Sikharase* (in Hindi). Rishikesh: Life Divine Society.

Dogra, B. 1983. *Forests and People,* New Delhi: Dagra.

Eckholm, E.P. 1976. *Losing Ground.* Washington, DC: World Watch Institute.

Eliade, M. 1959. *The Sacred and the Profans,* New York: Harcourt.

Fitzwilliams, J. 1987. "A Leaf out of St. Barbe's Book," *The Ecologist,* 17 (1).

Guha, Ramachandra. 1983. "Forestry in British and Post-British India: A Historical Analysis." *Economic and Political Weekly* 18 (44 and 45–46): 1882–1896 and 1940–1947.

Guha, Ranjit (ed.) 1982–1985. *Subaltern Studies: Writings in South Asian History and Society* (4 vols.), Delhi: Oxford University Press.

Hardiman, D. 1992 "Indian Faction: A Political Theory Examined," in Guha, 1982.

Joshi, G. 1980. "Bare Himalayas", *Gandhi Marg.*

Kanyal, K. 1987. "Chipko' Garb to Exploit Himalayan SC/STs". *Dalit Voice,* July 1–15.

Mangalagiri, A. 1983 "Chipko: A Wider Perspective." *Himalaya.*

Mishra, A. and S. Tripathy. 1978. *Chipko Movement: Uttarakhand Women's Bid to Save Forest Wealth.* New Delhi: People's Action for Peace and Justice.

Murphy, Y. and R. Murphy. 1974. *Women of the Forest.* New York and London: Columbia University Press.

Nandy, A. 1983. *The Intimate Enemy: Loss and Recovery of Self Under Colonialism.* Delhi: Oxford University Press.

Pant, Pushpesh. 2011. "A Conversation with Chandi Prasad Bhatt". *India International Center Quarterly*. 38(2): 108–120.

Passmore, J. 1974. *Man's Responsibility for Nature: Ecological Problems and Western Traditions.* New York: Charles Scribner's Sons.

Pathak, S. 1985. *Wine is a Conspiracy for the Hills* (in Hindi), Nainital.

Rabin, Ran. 1987. Personal Letter to Sunderlal.

Rao, M.S.A. 1979. (ed.), *Social Movements in India.* Vols.1 and 2, Delhi: Manohar Publications.

Schumacher, S. 1973. *Small is Beautiful.* London: Blend & Briggs.

Singh, H.K. 1987. Politics of Environmentalism: A Study of the Environmental Groups in Garhwal Himalayas. Unpublished manuscript.

Thomas, K. 1983. *Man and the Natural World.* New York: Pantheon Books.

Thompson, E.P. 1975. *Whigs and Hunters: The Origin of the Black Act.* London: Allen Lane.

Tiwari, K.M. 1982. *Role of Social Forestry in Village Economy.* Dehradun.

Tucker, R. 1985. "Pastoralism and British Colonial Management in the Western Himalayas". Manuscript.

Turner, V. 1969. *The Ritual Process: Structure and Anti-Structure.* Ithaca: Cornell University Press.

Uberoi, J.P.S. 1984. *Other Mind of Europe: Goethe as a Scientist.* Delhi: Oxford University Press.

Vaihinger, H. 1924. *The Philosophy of "As If".* New York: Barnes & Noble.

Part III

New Horizons of Quality of Life and Societal Co-Realizations

15 Quality of Life and the Method of Science

A Contemporary Critique

What is the impact of science and technology on quality of life? How do we come to terms with this question? Science and technology have enhanced the productive capacity of societies and, for their votaries, have led to an improvement in quality of life. But such a claim has not gone without contestation even from the early days of modern scientific revolution.[1] Science and technology, though have contributed immensely towards creating a more efficient productive base, have not necessarily led to a better standard of living for the majority of the people. For some of our contemporary critics of science, modern science as a "reason of the state"[2] has led to violence, death, and poverty. Instead of widening our choice and enhancing our quality of life, modern science and technology have created an illusion of prosperity.

How do we then assess the impact of science and technology on quality of life? At one level, the answer lies in the point of view that we have or where our interests lie. But is there any "legitimate standing ground outside the contexts of point of view?"[3] In other words, is there any way to overcome this problem of complete relativism. Information about familiar indices of quality of life, such as mortality rate and life expectance over a longitudinal historical period, might seem as a secured independent ground outside the "contexts of point of view" for carrying out such a task. But while these data certainly help us to examine our own biases, they themselves are furnished by the agents of the state who have used science and technology as instruments of economic development. The unreliability of the official data[4] and the derivation of varied, often contradictory, interpretations[5] from the same "information space" suggest that an uncritical return to the facts cannot very much help us in coming to terms with our problem, though such a recourse is not without advantage.

It seems that there are two ways in which we can appraise our problem when it is subject to two or more incommensurable perspectival interpretations. One way is to record shift and transformation within a perspective and to discover the pluralities and dispersions within it. As philosopher Alasdaire MacIntyre would say, such an approach is interested in knowing how "each has been confronted by successive sets of problems and difficulties, identified by the standards internal to each of these."[6] This requires a historical description of points of view which might help us in discovering the commonality or lack of it between the votaries and critics of modern science vis-à-vis the challenge of enhancing our quality of life. Though I follow such an approach and have applied it elsewhere,[7] carrying out a historical sociology of our ways of world vis-à-vis science and quality of life is not my objective here. My objective is rather derived from the second way of coming to terms with such problems and draws its inspiration from sociologist Andre Beteille's discussion of Marxism and anthropology.[8]

In order to understand the relationship between Marxism and anthropology, Beteille proceeds with one particular interpretation of Marxism (in this case Gramsci) which best articulates the spirit of Marxism and one interpretation of anthropology which is closer to its ethos (in this case, Levi Strauss). Then, he explores the relationship between the two and discusses their inherent tension. Similarly, I aim at a sharper delineation of the problem at hand by critically examining a particular influential interpretation of the issues involved. Quality of life has many indices and interpretations and so is the case with the method of science. By quality of life I mean, following Amartya Sen, the "functioning and capability" of the individuals.[9] By method of modern science, I mean the dominant method of positivism.[10]

This chapter seeks to highlight the tension between the positive method of modern science and its proclaimed goal of enhancing the quality of life. We also try to show how science and technology can be transformed so that they can genuinely help us in enhancing our quality of life.

Quality of Life: Towards a Critical Understanding

Of late, social scientists have been more and more interested in the problem of quality of life. But even in our current enthusiasm, quality of life is either another variable of social research or at best a technique of appraisal of social reality. While economists, after their disillusionment with statistical profiles of human reality, tend to treat quality of life as a fertile ground for gathering more qualitative information about the human condition, sociologists do not have much to add at all. For instance, here, we can take the work of Ramakrishna Mukherjee as a case in point. For Mukherjee, quality of life is nothing more than a new technique of social research. In this mode of appraisal of social reality, as Mukherjee tells us, "social research implies progression of objectivity from subjectivity in reference to quality and quantity."[11] Mukherjee prescribes an "inductive-inferential method of empirical research" for recording the "information space" constitutive of quality of life. In the words of Mukherjee, "the adoption of inductive-inferential method of empirical research will bring the enquirers and the enquired together because both will be concerned with, theoretically, an infinite but enumerable space of information of social reality with a view to appraising the quality of life."[12] This, for Mukherjee, an "inductive-inferential method"[13] will bring about a fusion between the object and subject of social research and open both of them to the qualitative dimension of the human condition. While this is a first-order evaluation in the "quality of life research," there is also a second-order evaluation which seeks to evaluate whether the "data items are desirable undesirable, or of no consequence to improving the quality of life."[14] Mukherjee further tells us: "Moreover, both the primary and secondary valuations of a phenomenon are ordinal valuations made by the enquirers and the enquired in the course of identifying distinguishing, and interrelating the commonalities with respect to the phenomenon."[15] But Mukherjee warns us that "polemics on the ordinal valuations of enquirers for forming commonalities of the enquired ones would generate more heat than shed light unless there is a common yardstick for the evaluation of all ordinal valuations made by the enquirers and the enquired."[16]

But how can the enquirer and the enquired come together for evolving a common yardstick for the evaluation of quality of life? How can the subject and object of social research come together in appreciating the worth of life and making a criticism of it? How can social research contribute towards making a "good life" and creating a decent society? In Mukherjee, we do not get much help in tackling these perennial questions. In Mukherjee's framework of quality of life, culture is just an epiphenomenon of social process and cannot "assume a processual role as a self-productive phenomenon."[17] But without a cultural sensibility and the accompanying urge for creativity, how can the enquirer and enquired come together and enhance the common good? Treating social research as a technology for the appraisal of social reality would not help us very much. Without a perspective of culture as a quest for progressive self-realization and without a notion of persons as seekers of freedom and critics of cultural practices as dead habits, any reflection on and even intervention for enhancing the quality of life is beset with problems, even to start with.[18]

Thus quality of life is not simply a technique of social research nor can it be understood narrowly as an "appraisal of social reality". It is a perspective on life and an integral critique of it when criticism means, as philosopher Robert C. Neville tells us, exploring whether "the suggested modes of togetherness genuinely hang together."[19]

We get such a treatment of the question of quality of life in the seminal work of Amartya Sen. For Sen, the perspective of quality of life or standard of living refers primarily to the quality of life one leads "rather than of the resources and means with which one has to lead one's life."[20] Surely enhancing the quality of life of all of us and primarily of the truly disadvantaged who constitute the "wretched of the earth" requires an increase in resources and the productive capacity of individuals and societies. But resources cannot be an end in themselves since increase in resources does not automatically guarantee a more meaningful life for the individuals nor does it guarantee a more meaningful sharing among the members of a community. There is a crucial distinction between availability of a resource and entitlement to it, and even formal entitlements without a social commitment and sustained collective action does not guarantee a better standard of living.[21]

For Sen, happiness, pleasure, utility, resource and opulence are not adequate indices of quality of life. He opines: "The standard of life cannot be so detached from the nature of the life the person leads. As an object of value, happiness and pleasure (even with a bread coverage) cannot possibly make a serious claim to exclusive relevance."[22] Be it happiness, pleasure, or even utility, it is not delinked from a process of valuation which is a "reflective exercise with a complete and unstraightforward linkage with pleasure."[23] Sen makes a trenchant criticism of the "utility-based approach to well-being" showing us its inadequacy in understanding the perspective of quality of life. He writes:

> Sometimes it might make sense to use utility-type information about strength of desire as reflecting valuation, even though the two are neither identical, nor invariably closely related to each other. Sometimes even market choice information can be used to arrive at weights to be attached to commodities and from them to guess the valuation of the corresponding functionings. But the derived and contingent informational role of these observations must be distinguished clearly from the claimed fundamental role of those variables under some impact of the utility-based approach to well-being.[24]

In Sen's framework, neither utility nor opulence is an adequate measure of quality of life. For Sen, the crux of the matter lies in "functionings and capabilities".[25] As he writes: "The main point here is that standard of living is really a matter of functionings and capabilities, and not a matter directly of opulence, commodities, or utilities."[26] What he means by "functionings and capabilities" is "a functioning is an achievement, whereas capability is the ability to achieve."[27] For Sen, "functionings are, in a sense, more directly related to living conditions, capabilities have a direct role too, since the idea of the living standard has an aspect that is not quite independent of the perspective of freedom."[28]

Understanding standard of living through the vantage point of functioning and capability helps us to go beyond the dualism of absolute and relative poverty. For Sen, "there is no great difficulty in sorting out the different elements in the relativity of poverty line in the space of incomes (and that of commodities) since the conception of the standard of living is given an adequate formulation in terms of capabilites."[29] This also helps us in going beyond absolute cultural relativism, while not disregarding the cultural construction of human need and the very meaning of standard of living. The index of standard of living or, for that matter, of poverty is not the same in the United States as it is in India, but the perspective of "functionings and capabilities" enables us to evaluate the quality of life of individuals in societies without falling prey to either absolute relativism or absolute universalism. The question is whether human beings, even in terms of their own social standards and cultural constructions, have the capacity to function meaningfully and effectively in society and have an ability to live, be educated, and send their children to school.

If such is the perspective of quality of life, then what role do commodities play in enhancing it? Or, what is the relationship between commodities and capabilities? Sen tells us that commodities have an instrumental role to play in our lives.[30] For some time, increasing the amount of flow of commodities and consumer goods has been the stated objective of economic policies worldwide. This has created an illusory atmosphere to essentialize commodities, forgetting their instrumental role. Sen argues: "If the objects of value are 'functioning and capabilities,' then the so-called basic needs in the form of commodity requirements are instrumentally (rather than intrinsically) important. The main issue is the goodness of life that one can lead."[31] Thus, Sen discounts a commodity-based approach to well-being as he discounts a utility-based approach. But critics of Sen argue that "commoditization" is still crucial for improving the standard of living and there is the need for a sharper delineation of the notion of capability. For instance, Keith Hart argues that Sen's formulation of the problem of quality of life in terms of capability is vague.[32] Hart suggests that a focus on labour productivity, that is, how much time people spend in earning their livelihood (which includes both acts of self-provisioning as well as industrial work) can provide us with an adequate measure of quality of life. Hart argues: "In particular I hold that underlying trends in labour productivity are the key to improvements in the standard of living; and these have historically depended on advances in commercial division of labour (while being in no way guaranteed by market expansion as such)."[33] Hart further tell us that freedom from drudgery may ultimately be more crucial to living standards than commodity-based indices of material consumption and adds that "perhaps a focus on labour productivity offers a compromise between the usability of commodities and the relevance of capabilities."[34] Sen responds to this criticism by arguing that his is not a total disregard of commodities in the making of human well-being and that Hart does not understand his distinction between the intrinsic and the instrumental.

Bernard Williams raises a more pertinent question regarding the relationship between rights and capabilities. Sen discounts an approach to standard of living solely on the basis of individual rights. It is here that Sen makes the crucial distinction between "negative freedom" and "positive freedom".[35] For Sen, "the negative view sees freedom exclusively in terms of the independence of the individual from interference by others, including governments, institutions, and other persons. The positive view sees freedom not in terms of the presence or absence of interference by others, but in terms of what a person is actually able to do or to be."[36] To understand Sen's framework, it is not only important to understand the distinction between the capacity for primary good and capacity for freedom, it is also important to realize that a discourse on individual rights cannot help us in understanding "individual freedom as a social commitment".[37] Unlike some of our contemporary theorists of justice such as John Rawls, Nozick and Dwarkin, Sen's reflection on the human condition is not simply a move away from utility to "rights".[38] His focus is rather on capability. Nonetheless, the notion of capability cannot be separated from the notion of rights, though it is easy to hide this under the carpet. William's formulation of the problem deserves a full quotation:

> The apparently innocent and descriptive-looking notion of the standard of living or well-being may turn out to contain considerations about the goods to which we believe people have a basic right. Thus, we actually believe that people have a basic right to breathe clean air without having to go somewhere else to do it, but we do not believe that they have a similar right to go to expensive winter holiday resorts. The notion of basic human rights seems to me obscure enough, and I would rather come at it from the perspective of basic human capabilities. I would prefer capabilities to do the work, and if we are going to have a language or rhetoric of rights, to have it delivered from them, rather than the other way round. But I think that there

> remains an unresolved problem: how we should see the relation between these two concepts.[39]

These comments help us in understanding Sen's framework of quality of life better. Central to it is a perspective of freedom – freedom to choose not only the commodities available in the market but also the kind of life one wants to lead. Modern societies create an illusion of free choice. But, the question is whether we have the real option to choose from various institutional alternatives or life trajectories and whether we can criticize institutions and pursue a life which we consider meaningful in a real sense. Sen makes it clear for us:

> To consider acts of substantial choosing as being among the relevant "functioning" is supportable from the point of view that the quality of life a person enjoys is not merely a matter of what he or she achieves, but also of what options the person has the opportunity to choose from. In this view, the "good life" is partly a life of genuine choice, and not one in which the person is forced into a particular life, however rich it might be in other respects.[40]

Sen reiterates that economic development must be assessed in terms of "the enhancement of basic positive freedoms to avoid premature mortality, to escape morbidity, to eliminate undernutrition, and so on."[41] "Freedom is not a remote consideration in policy-making" and has both an instrumental and intrinsic significance. Sen discusses this with reference to food policy. Raising food productivity requires "economic incentives in the expansion of natural output in general and food production in particular."[42] But using this to tackle poverty and famine requires the work of intrinsic freedom in the social and political systems. Here, Sen cites the example of India and China both of which have witnessed many a famine in the last decades. For Sen, India's more successful handling of the situation, as compared to China, is not merely due to the raising of food output per head but because of its democratic system. The lack of a democratic system, Sen argues, is responsible for the inability of the Chinese government to respond efficiently to the crisis of famine even though the governmental policy there has led to an increase in gross availability of food. Thus, Sen argues:

> In assessing the relevance of freedom in the making of food policy, both the intrinsic and instrumental perspectives have to be kept very firmly in view [...]. At the same time, the instrumental perspective has to be extended from the freedom to earn profits to freedoms of broader kinds, including political freedom in the form of freedom of opposition, freedom of information, and journalistic autonomy [...] these freedoms can be quite crucial in delivery and use of food.[43]

But here we must remember that by intrinsic freedom Sen means both the "freedoms of broader kinds" such as political freedom as well as the basic capabilities to function what he calls "elementary freedoms".[44] And once we assess economic development "in terms of the important indications of elementary freedoms," we get a different picture of the recent economic reforms. For instance, discussing in great detail the recent economic reform in China, Sen shows that economic reform there has not been accompanied by a better "food and health services required for the positive freedoms to survive."[45] Sen argues that the post-reform period shows not only "some decline from the previously achieved peak of high life expectancy" but also "an increase rather than a reduction in death rates."[46]

Peter Nolan and John Sender contest this argument of Sen and, using the same official data, contend that "the shift from Maoist policies towards an embryonic social market economy brought substantial gains in welfare for most Chinese citizens."[47] Nolan and Sender use the same official statistics to argue that "post-Mao China saw a geographically widespread decline in death rates."[48] Thus, for Nolan and Sender, economic reform in China has led to an improved standard of living for a majority of the Chinese. They further contended that Amartya Sen in his preoccupation with distribution and well-being has "consistently downplayed the contribution which can be made by rapid output growth."[49]

In his response to Nolan and Sender, Sen argues that the same official figures show an increase in death rates and accuses them of distortion. He also makes it clear that he does not discount the significance of economic growth in enhancing quality of life but the real challenge lies in showing how it works. Sen tells us: "The issue is not whether economic growth is quite unimportant or a complete solution. It is neither. We have to understand how it works, what it does achieve, and what problems it cannot handle well on its own."[50]

Thus, we learn from Sen that in order to enhance the quality of life, we must focus on our "functionings and capabilities" and have a proper perspective on life. We must use commodities and resources for the satisfaction of our need but not for the aggrandizement of our greed. But our current economic restructuring seeks to maximize profit through the stimulation of our desires. In our contemporary phase of "late capitalism, valorization of capital is predicated upon the valorization of our desire."[51] But we do not have adequate resources to sustain such a model of development which thrives on a culture of consumption. Desires have no end and restraint is the key to a happy and a good life. Moreover, the relationship between persons and commodities has to be rethought for enhancing our quality of life. In this process of rethinking and recreating the relationship between ourselves and commodities, we have to realize that even Adam Smith, the author of *The Wealth of Nations*, had felt the need to write a book called *The Theory of Moral Sentiments* in which he admonishes us thus: "It is an invisible hand that drives men to work and to the earning of money and which in a way deceives them since the 'trinkets and baubles' which are brought with those earnings are nothing but 'trifling conveniences'."[52] Economic growth, while important, cannot lead to well-being unless we realize that the resources it puts at our disposal are "only trifling conveniences" and, as they enhance our capability and make our life comfortable, we must learn how to live without them.

It is in this context that Gandhi had spoken of the need for "voluntary poverty" and this is a lesson which can be ultimately traced back to Buddha. E.F. Schumacher has taught us the significance of the lessons of Buddha for coming out of our present ailments and in our effort to create a good society.[53] But this is a lesson which we also learn from Aristotle. What a recent interpreter of the Western political tradition has written about Aristotle's reflection on the subject is important. Interpreting Aristotle's reflection on the need for the limitation of desire, Jerry Weinberger says:

> Yet given the paucity of the very simplest needs, scarcity exists only concurrently with the desire for luxury and the capacity to produce it. Strictly speaking, scarcity could be overcome (and freedom could be possible) not when some level of productive capacity has been reached but only with a limit on the desire for luxurious acquisition. For Aristotle, this limit requires drawing a clear distinction between needlike luxuries and goods that are genuinely noble and beautiful. Therefore, Aristotle follows his account of the origins of the p[illegible]s with a discussion of the natural limits to acquisition. For Aristotle, there is such a limit, situated between penury and unlimited acquisitiveness. But this limit is neither easy to see nor realizable by all because it is in conflict with material production itself.[54]

For the practice of restraint and a life of "voluntary poverty", which is just part of a quest for a more meaningful life, culture and transformative education have to be taken seriously. Transformative education would help us learn and live by a new "technology of self".[55] Thus enhancing the quality of life is a multi-dimensional task which requires simultaneous increase in production as well as a transformative education which can help us not only in restraining desire for more and more consumption but also in realizing that meaning and happiness of life lie primarily in creation.

Quality of Life and the Method of Science

If such is the challenge of "quality of life" as a perspective and a meditation on life, then how does the method of science prepare us for such a call of life? Science is one of our ancient and eternal pursuits and it is certainly a cultural fact, even though it has a universal language. By method of science here is meant the method of modern science which is broadly a method of positivism.[56] This positivistic method of modern science constructs the predicament of human condition in the image of the technique where life as such does not have a sacred meaning. For instance, utilitarianism in economics as an example of such a positivistic science is interested neither in quality nor in life but simply in utility. As two recent commentators tell us: "Utilitarianism imposes, by implication, severe informational constraints. These constraints rule out great deal of information from taking into consideration in arriving at moral judgements. This amounts to taking in the context of moral situation, a remarkably narrow view of being a person."[57]

This narrow conceptualization of being a person in the positivistic method of modern sciences leads to a systematic denigration of human practice. As Jurgen Habermas tells us, it leads to a technological interpretation of the human condition where technique is thought of as a guide to both "theory and practice".[58] In ancient science and philosophy, *praxis* and *poiesis* were parts of the same meditation of life, but the method of modern science is built upon their artificial divorce. This divorce has been made possible by the one-sided accentuation of technical rationality and a complete disregard for the question of ethics and morality. This positive method and *weltanschauung* of modern science has permeated the whole ethos of modernity – from natural law to the art of governance. Habermas tells us:

> While in classical natural law the norms of moral and just action are equally oriented in their content towards the good – and that means the virtuous life of the citizens – the formal law of the modern age is divested of the catalogues of duties in the material order of life, whether of a city or of a social class. Instead, it allows a neutral sphere of personal choice in which every citizen, as a private person, can egoistically follow goals of maximizing his own ends."[59]

It is the technology of power, not the interpretative quest to make life more meaningful, that has also characterized the modern art of governance. Modern welfare state executes policies and programmes to improve people's standard of living on the "basis of scientific analysis of factual social conditions."[60] The consequence of this has been "a scientification of government praxis."[61] Sciences – including social science and social philosophy – no longer visualize their role as critiques and interpreters of life. They are only busy in providing us and our masters of power technical recommendations. In the words of Habermas, "Modern science no longer proceeds hermeneutically, but analytically. They can furnish technical recommendations for effective instrumentalities, but can no longer normatively give any orientation to the goals themselves."[62] As Habermas says, modern science is characterized by the change in methodological approach "from practical knowledge to the pragmatic art of techniques of power and social organization."[63] Thus, social sciences, as enthusiastic collaborators of modern positivism, have been more concerned with social engineering and its accompanying "technology of power" rather than with the more fundamental question of the "technology of the self".

Such a method of science cannot help us in enhancing quality of life as analysts, what to speak of enhancing that of those with whom we are supposed to work. In our age of science and technology, "the social potential of science is reduced to powers of technical control" and votaries of science and technology are no longer bothered about its "potential for enlightened action".[64] The positive method of modern science, for Habermas, threatens our civilization by "splitting of human beings into two classes – the social engineers and the inmates of closed institutions."[65] The danger of an exclusive technical construction of the contemporary condition is that it not only perpetrates a hiatus between the technical experts and the lay public but also splits our consciousness including that of the scientists.

But now that a hiatus between meaning and self-interest and between self-realization and technical organization has been created, how do we overcome it? While it is easy for Habermas to speak of degeneration from classical integrity to the dismemberment of consciousness and communicative action, brought about by modern positivism, it is not that easy for him to tell us who is the culprit in this drama. Here, we must not lose sight of the fact that even modern positive sciences arose in Western history as contentious movements. Of course, their heterodoxies soon turned into new orthodoxies. Nonetheless modern positivism was part of a broader social and cultural movement. Such an understanding helps us in putting the problem in a proper perspective, especially in the context of social evolution. But in no way can it make us complacent about the need for overcoming the hiatus between meaning and technical interest that modern positivism has perpetuated.

The answer lies not in a total abandonment of modern science and technology but in transforming its entrenched positivism and all-pervasive technical rationality. The task is to make science work not only as a "productive force" but also as an "emancipatory force". For Habermas, this, to begin with, requires us to understand that "to set free the technical forces of production is not identical with the development of norms which could fulfil the dialectic of moral relationships in an interaction free from domination."[66] But, the same Habermas who argues that social philosophy has taken on a "monologic form" in the regime of positivism also tells us that it can redeem itself by becoming a philosophy science which strives to make science self-reflective. The need is for more self-reflection, measures of self-correction, and a transformation of its positivist bias, not a total eclipse into unreason. Thus, Habermas says:

> If there exists a philosophy in the face of which the question "does philosophy still have a purpose?" need no longer be raised, then today, according to our reflections, it would have to be a philosophy of science that is not scientific. It would incur a politically effective task, inasmuch as it went against the twofold irrationality of a positivistically restricted self-understanding of the sciences and technocratic administration isolated from publicly discussive formation of will. [67]

Considering the increasing decisiveness of science and technology in modern life, how can science be subjected to a discursive critique? As one recent commentator tells us, this "requires different organizational forms of science and business, science and the public sphere, science and politics, technology and law."[68] There is need for the creation of a public sphere which, "armed with scientific arguments, is capable of separating the scientific wheat from the chaff and allowing the institutions for directing technology politics and law – to reconquer the power of their own judgement."[69] For Ulrich Beck, "the public sphere in cooperation with a 'wind of public science' would be charged as a second centre of the 'discursive checking' of scientific laboratory results on the crossfire of opinions."[70]

This making of science as a public "discursive formation of will" and a process of critical self-reflection is possible only when science addresses itself to the question of human praxis – not simply understood as the horizontal issue of day-to-day survival but as the question of spiritual praxis as well.[71] In order that science as a method can perform its classical function of both knowing and achieving a good life, science has to transform itself from its modernist positivism to a contemporary critique of life. But for this it has to widen its basis through varieties of social and cultural movements so that it can be part of a broader "discursive formation of will".[72] It has also to take spirituality seriously which can provide a "cosmology of freedom"[73] to both the actors and the analysts.

Thus, in order to address meaningfully the question of quality of life, we need a new method of science which can enable us to realize the meaning of life – a realization which also seeks to transcend the contrived opposition between food and freedom and between meaning and materiality. We also have to realize that we cannot understand, much less solve, the global problem of survival unless we prepare ourselves for a radical "defamiliarization" vis-à-vis conventional categories of economics and technology and unless we also realize that such an experience is closely related to a major epistemological or paradigmatic shift.

Notes

1. For instance, Albert O. Hirschman tells us how "the discontents of industrialization led in England to a lament over irreparable damage to the quality of life." See Albert O. Hirschman, "Industrialization and its Manifold Discontents: West, East, and South," *World Development*, Vol. 29(9), p. 1228.
2. See Ashis Nandy, ed., *Science, Hegemony, and Violence: A Requiem for Modernity* (Delhi: Oxford University Press, 1988).
3. I am adapting this phrase from Alasdair MacIntyre. See Alasdair MacIntyre, "Incommensurability, Truth, and the Conversation between Confucians and Aristotelians About the Virtues," in Eliot Deutch, ed., *Culture and Modernity* (Honolulu, Hawaii, 1991).
4. For instance, commenting upon the very data base that they have used for their interpretation of the effect of current economic reforms on quality of life in China, two economists write: "There is much room for doubt the correctness of the official Chinese mortality rate." See Jean Dreze and Amartya Sen, *Hunger and Public Action* (New York: Oxford University Press, 1989), p. 216.
5. Here we can take the recent debate about life and death in China between Amartya Sen on the one hand and Peter Nolan and John Sender on the other as a case in point. They use the same data base but provide two different pictures about the impact of economic reform on quality of life. See Peter Nolan and John Sender, "Death Rates, Life Expectancy, and China's Economic Reforms: A Critique of A.K. Sen," *World Development*, Vol. 20(9), pp. 1279–1303, 1992; and Amartya Sen, "Life and Death in China: A Reply," *World Development*, Vol. 20(9), pp. 1305–12, 1992.
6. Alasdaire MacIntyre, "Incommensurability, Truth, and the Conversation between Confucians and Aristotelians about the Virtues," op. cit., p. 117.
7. See Ananta Giri, *Critique of the Comparative Method and the Challenges of a Transnational World* (Allahabad: G.B. Pant Social Science Institute, 1992), Occasional Paper.
8. See Andre Beteille, "Marxism and Anthropology," In Andre Beteille, ed., *Essays in Comparative Sociology* (Delhi: Oxford University Press, 1987).
9. Amartya Sen, "The Standard of Living," in S.M. McCurrin, *The Tanner Lecture on Human Values* (Cambridge: Cambridge University Press, 1986), Vol. 7.
10. See J.P.S. Uberoi, *Science and Culture* (Delhi: Oxford University Press, 1978).
11. Ramakrishna Mukherjee, *Quality of Life: Valuation in Social Research* (New Delhi: Sage Publications, 1989), p. 21.
12. Ibid., pp. 16–17.
13. Ibid.
14. Ibid., p. 20.
15. Ibid., p. 21.
16. Ibid.

17. Ramakrishna Mukherjee, *Culture, Society, Development* (New Delhi: Sage Publications, 1991), p. 67.
18. Here we can take the pioneering work of G.C. Pande as a case in point. For him, "culture items" are "items in an evolving context of meaning, that is to say, items in the quest of self-realization". See. G.C. Pande, *The Meaning and Process of Culture as Philosophy of History* (Allahabad: Raka Prakashan, 1989), p. 20.
19. Robert C. Nevlille, *The Cosmology of Freedom* (New Haven: Yale University Press, 1974), p. 189.
20. Amartya Sen, "The Standard of Living", op. cit., p. 22.
21. See Amartya Sen, *Poverty and Famines: An Essay on Entitlement and Deprivation* (Delhi: Oxford University Press, 1981); Amartya Sen, "Individual Freedom as Social Commitment," *India International Center Quarterly*, Spring 1992, pp. 101–115; and Ananta Giri, "Tackling Hunger: Reflections on Collective Action," unpublished manuscript.
22. Amartya Sen, "The Standard of Living," op. cit., p. 12.
23. Ibid., p. 11.
24. Amartya Sen, *Commodities and Capabilities* (Delhi: Oxford University Press, 1987), p. 32.
25. Amartya Sen, "The Standard of Living," op. cit., p. 12.
26. Ibid.
27. Ibid., p. 48.
28. Ibid., p. 26.
29. Ibid., p. 49.
30. See Amartya Sen, *Commodities and Capabilities*, op. cit.
31. Amartya Sen, "The Standard of Living," op. cit., p. 34.
32. Keith Hart, "Commoditisation and Standard of Living," in Goeffrey Hawthorn, ed., *The Standard of Living* (Cambridge: Cambridge University Press, 1987), pp. 70–93.
33. Ibid., p. 93.
34. Ibid., p. 89.
35. Amartya Sen, "Food and Freedom," *World Development*, Vol. 17(6), pp. 769–81.
36. Ibid., p. 770.
37. See Amartya Sen, "The Standard of Living", op. cit.
38. For understanding the discursive shift from utility to rights, see Simon Caney, "Liberalism and Communitarianism: A Misconceived Debate," *Political Studies*, Vol. 90, pp. 273–89.
39. Bernard Williams, "The Standard of Living: Interests and Capabilities," in Geoffrey Hawthorn, ed., *The Standard of Living*, op. cit., pp. 94–102, 100.
40. Amartya Sen, *Commodities and Capabilities*, op. cit., p. 415.
41. Jean Dreze and Amartya Sen, *Hunger and Public Action*, op. cit., p. 778.
42. Ibid., p. 779.
43. Ibid.
44. Ibid.

45. Peter Nolan and John Sender, "Death Rates, Life Expectancy, and Chinese Economic Reforms: A Critique of A.K. Sen," op. cit., p. 1279.
46. Jean Dreze and Amartya Sen, *Hunger and Public Action*, op. cit., p. 779.
47. Peter Nolan and John Sender, "Death Rates, Life Expectancy, and Chinese Economic Reforms: A Critique of A.K. Sen," op. cit., p. 1298.
48. Ibid., p. 1300.
49. Ibid.
50. Amartya Sen, "Individual Freedom as Social Commitment," op. cit., p. 1310.
51. See Ernest Mandel, *Late Capitalism* (London: New Left Books, 1975).
52. Adam Smith as quoted in Albert O. Hirschman, "Industrialization and its Manifold Discontent: West, East, and South," p. 1220.
53. E.F. Schumacher, *Small is Beautiful* (London: Blond and Briggs, 1973).
54. Jerry Weinberger, "Political and the Problems of Technology: An Essay on Heidegger and the Tradition of Political Philosophy," *American Political Science Review*, Vol. 86(1), pp. 112–28.
55. I owe this phrase to Jurgen Habermas. See his *Philosophical Discourses of Modernity* (Cambridge, MA: The MIT Press, 1987).
56. Jurgen Habermas, *Theory and Practice* (Cambridge: Polity Press, 1987).
57. Amartya Sen and Bernard Williams, *Utilitarianism and Beyond* (Cambridge: Cambridge University Press, 1982), p. 4.
58. See Jurgen Habermas, *Theory and Practice*, op. cit.
59. Ibid., p. 84.
60. Ibid., p. 14.
61. Ibid.
62. Ibid.
63. Ibid., p. 56.
64. Ibid., p. 281.
65. Ibid., p. 282.
66. Ibid., p. 169.
67. Jurgen Habermas, *Philosophical-Political Profiles* (Cambridge, MA: MIT Press, 1981), p. 17.
68. Ulrich Beck, "From Industrial Society: Questions of Survival, Social Structure, and Ecological Enlightenment," in *Theory, Culture, and Society*, Vol. 9 (1), pp. 97–123, 1992, p. 119.
69. Ibid.
70. Ibid.
71. Concerning the idea of spiritual praxis, see G.C. Pande, *Foundations of Indian Culture* (New Delhi: Books and Books, 1984).
72. See Jurgen Habermas, *Philosophical-Political Profiles; and Ananta Giri, The Portrait of a Discursive Formation: Science and Social Activism and Cultural Criticism in Contemporary India* (New Delhi: NISTADS, 1992).
73. See Robert C. Neville, *The Cosmology of Freedom*, op. cit.

16 Social Development as a Global Challenge

Social development is an all-pervasive global challenge now, a challenge which confronts all societies head on – be they developed countries or less developed ones. In fact, the contemporary global challenge of development arising in the context of a structural transformation from an industrial to a post-industrial society and the discursive shift from modernity to post-modernity obliterates the familiar distinction between the developed and the developing societies. Development is a challenge as much in contemporary "post-modern" USA as it is in contemporary "traditional" India. In the face of contemporary structural transformations in economy and politics and the imperative for social development and institutional transformation that these raise, all societies are confronted with this challenge squarely. Moreover, the dynamics of contemporary change questions the familiar indices of development and urges us to widen our universe of discourse.

Development dialogue once used to be exhausted with the index of economic development. Engineers and economists were the high priests of modernity, state formation and the statist agenda of development. But, over the decades, the discourse on development has widened itself to include a vision of a "good society" and a perspective of freedom (Sen 1987, 1989) in the index and agenda of development. The dynamics and moral vision of critical social movements and social scientists have brought the question of social development to the centre of the agenda of development, thus broadening the vision and pursuit of development which once used to solely mean "economic development" (see Tambiah 1985). Planners and economists who were once only preoccupied with the gross national product of a nation in their agenda of development now show their concern for the question of "the quality of life" (Mukherjee 1989) and "standard of living". Standard of living, as a measure of social and economic development, challenges us to go beyond an economistic and utilitarian view of development and raises the basic questions of "functioning and capabilities" (Sen 1986: 34). As Amartya Sen so insightfully tells us:

> The standard of living is not a standard of opulence, even though it is inter alia influenced by opulence. It must be directly a matter of life one leads rather than of the resources and means one has to lead a life. [...] The main point here is that

standard of living is really a matter of functioning and capabilities, and not a matter directly of opulence, commodities, or utilities (ibid.: 22–23).

Developing the Developed Countries

In the advanced societies, the contemporary global challenge of development has presented itself in the context of the overwhelming restructuring of these societies in the wake of a post-industrial transformation. Revolutionary changes in technologies have been the key factor in the restructuring of the advanced capitalist societies. The innovation, dynamics and diffusion of high technologies has been instrumental in restructuring the economy, politics, culture and even the "script of life" in these societies (Buchman 1989; also Bluestone and Harrison 1982; Harrison and Bluestone 1988). The dynamics of high technology has enabled the restructuring of industrial location from the "Snowbelt" to the "Sunbelt" in a country like the U.S.; and has restructured the very composition and organization of industries leading to an eventual "deindustrialization" (Bluestone and Harrison 1982) and the growth of a "global assembly line". The restructuring of industries and the accompanying spatial restructuring has broken down the historic relations of representation between classes and political parties (Hall 1988: 2). Deindustrialization has led to the "destructuration" (Offe 1988) of solidarities of classes and parties. That is how economic and industrial restructuring, facilitated by the dynamics and diffusion of high technologies, eventually has led to a political restructuring in advanced capitalist societies. This political restructuring has manifested itself in the attack on the welfare state and the rise of the "New Right" as a determinant discourse as well as a ruling ideology.

Restructuring in economy and politics has brought back development as a vital challenge to these societies. Post-industrial transformation has given rise to a "Great U-Turn" (Harrison and Bluestone 1988) in American society creating new dislocations and new disparities, what radical American commentator Michael Harrington had called as "The New American Poverty" (Harrington 1984) The new American poverty is manifested in the phenomenon of high-tech, low pay; the declining standard of living of the majority of the population; and rise of homelessness as an archetype of structural disadvantage in the midst of unprecedented prosperity. All this had led to what anthropologist Katherine Newman (1988) so aptly calls "Falling from Grace" on the part of not only the low class but also of the middle class. Moreover, contemporary restructuring has made the once developed locales and regions backward and underdeveloped. Capital and industries have flown from the locales and regions which were once the industrial heartland of America. Detroit is no more the symbol of the American dream. Now, it is California's Silicon Valley. This simultaneous creation of the post-industrial frontier and the erasure of the industrial ones makes regions backward and underdeveloped within the developed countries calling for special programmes of economic revitalization and economic development. This is a point which has been brilliantly discussed by Harvard Professor David Osborne in his *Laboratories of Democracy* (Osborne 1988). Osborne shows the making of regional backwardness in the contemporary post-industrial America and efforts by the state governments to develop these areas and to create well-being and prosperity in the space of the post-industrial despair. Here it must be noted that deindustrialization has been a fight between what could be called the space of capital and the space of communities. This fight between the "life world" and the "system world", to use the words of Jurgen Habermas, has however raised the question of economic revitalization and social development. There have been different political initiatives of late which are trying a variety of public-private partnerships as a strategy of development. Partnership is now a key word in the development discourse of the advanced capitalist societies.

The Challenge of New Technologies

The innovation and diffusion of new technologies have been important in deciding the contours of social development. Without taking an extreme line of technological determinism, it is still possible to discern that contemporary economic and political restructuring of the advanced societies have taken place in the context of the revolutionary manifestation of new technologies (Giri 1991), which create a new context for realizing the meaning of work which is not just lost in between the contradiction of capital and labour. For many commentators, those who are engaged in data processing are not solely concerned with physical execution, but deeply interested in meaning and interpretation. Thus, one engaging student of meaning of work in the context of new technologies writes:

> As the new technologies integrate information across time and space, managers and workers each overcome their narrow functional perspectives and create new roles that are better suited to enhancing value-adding activities in a data-riching environment (Zuboff 1988: 6).

Furthermore, new technologies have had a dual identity and a dual role: they have simultaneously created a post-industrial despair as well as post-industrial opportunities. However, while new technologies call for a new workforce and a new work culture, the same new technologies have been used for the control of the workers and ordinary people and the powerless subjects like women. According to anthropologist Ryana Rapp, reproductive technologies have been used to enhance the power of the professionals rather than widen the range of choice of women (Rapp 1988).

This brings us face-to-face with the crucial question of the complex relationship between technology and politics. Many commentators of the post-industrial scene believe that the dynamics of high technology has resolved the contradiction between capital and labour that is characteristic of an industrial society. But though new technologies have restructured the relationship between capital and labour, they have not resolved the contradiction between them nor does it mean that capital as a factor does not enter the intervening variable of politics. Indeed, dynamics of politics in the operational and genealogical context of new technologies determines the end for which high technologies are being used in contemporary societies. It is the configuration of politics that determines to what extent emancipatory potentials embedded in new technologies can be realized in the actual context of an egalitarian society. Thus, Soshana Zuboff (1988) argues that new technologies simultaneously automate and informate. But what use new technologies will be put to – whether they would be the new "panopticon" of surveillance and control or a new "laboratory of democracy" (Burns and Uberhst, 1989).

But what is the nature of politics that can help one realize "creative democracy" and create "collective goods" (Benjamin 1980) in society? It is a politics of transformation, not the conventional politics of opposition. Our conventional rhetoric and habits of politics are posited in an either/or mode of conflict of interests and conflict of interpretations. But, the political practice that we urgently need to cultivate today has to create new meanings and solidarity for all of us. In another context, Johann Galtung had once observed that transnational politics is the politics of the individual human being (Galtung 1980). The transformative politics proposed here is similarly the politics of conscience, not simply the politics of the party. However, this does not discount the significance of solidarities in the realization of meaning and capabilities. Thus, while the question of politics cannot be lost sight of in the name of high technology and its imperatives, simultaneously the idea of politics cannot be applied mechanically and as a blank concept in our contemporary reflection on technology and society, and the striving for a more meaningful alternative.

As we would see, new social movements have been the key articulators of this transformed politics which are playing out not simply a politics of opposition, but primarily one of transformation. Grass-roots movements are the instruments for democratizing the social base of new technologies and their power equations. Moreover, the realization of prosperity and the creation of a decent standard of living that new technologies are capable of, depends not only on the social operation of new social movements but also by creating what could be called a movemental ethos.

High Technology and Human Freedom

Ultimately, the dynamics and operation of high technology raises the question of freedom. High technology has enabled some to choose freely out of a range of options, but that does not mean that one can really choose out of a range of structures. The structure is not an object of choice, rather it creates an illusion of infinite choices in every field – from fashion to the fast food. New technologies have also made possible a wide range of choices in the field of consumption. But, in reality, it has led to a vicarious consumption of the few. Coming through the operation of "possessive individualism" and the post-modern narcissism of self-realization through the very act of consumption, new technologies have meant only "negative freedom". The freedom that new technologies have brought have been the freedom to choose out of a range of options and in many cases it has meant to protect oneself from the encroachment of others. But, the dynamics of new technologies and the culture of consumption that it has created have not been accompanied by the practice and pursuit of positive freedom where freedom means not only widening the range of choices for oneself but also enhancing the capacities and capabilities of all (see Giri 1992; Sen 1989). Positive freedom means a vision of freedom where "free development of each is a condition for the free development of all". The perspective of freedom, namely, the discourse of positive freedom, asks basic questions of elementary freedom – whether women have access to the institutions of society, whether a child can go to school and whether all have food to eat. Thus, the perspective of freedom is ultimately one of combining food and freedom in a grand saga of human liberation and the realization of a "good life" in society. It is perhaps for this reason that Amartya Sen writes:

> Food and freedom are both central concerns in human life, and they have links that are both crucial and diverse. These links demand our attention. The elementary freedom to live long and live well for a great many million people is at stake (Sen 1989: 779).

Sen argues that considered from the point of view of elementary freedoms, our exercises in development planning call for critical self-reflection and positive social intervention. Thus, Amartya Sen challenges us to reassess economic development "in terms of important indicators of elementary freedoms" (ibid.: 779). In the words of Sen:

> In assessing economic development and social progress, it is natural to think of the enhancement of basic positive freedom to avoid premature mortality, the escape morbidity, to eliminate undernutrition and so on (ibid.: 788).

Paraphrasing Sen, we can say that links between food and freedom demand attention from the proponets and votaries of new technologies. It is particularly because new technologies have now power and potentiality to make an intervention in production, increase productivity and enhance the standard of living. But, unfortunately, new technologies are now operating in a discursive climate of conservatism and "The New Right Libertarianism". New technologies are now operating in a climate where the determinant discourse is not equality nor even human dignity but efficiency and individual rights (see Beteille 1986). In fact, new technologies are operating in a discursive climate of "negative freedom". It is perhaps for this reason that Manoranjan Mohanty sensitizes us to the decline of the freedom discourse in the contemporary development dialogue (Mohanty 1992). But what Mohanty argues is not only true of India and China but also of America and Japan. In advanced capitalist societies, the discussion of freedom in the wake of recent technological transformation has been mainly couched in the language of negative freedom. The only concern is the encroachment upon individual space that new technologies give rise to. But there has been very little discussion on how to use high technology to expand the radii of "positive freedom" – enhancing the capabilities of millions of people whose life is now at stake because of hunger and homelessness – to live with dignity and to search for meaning. And here it must be stressed that hunger and deprivation are as much a fact of life in Kalahandi as they are in the streets of New York City.

Moral Consciousness and Communicative Action

Linked with this question of freedom is equally important question of what Habermas calls "Moral Consciousness and Communicative Action" (Habermas 1990). This question is linked with the fact that the dynamics of new technologies has given us "technology of power" but not any "technology of self". We are not even sensitive to developing an appropriate technique of the self that would use the techniques of new technology. Thus, no wonder that new technologies have been used as "panopticon" in the path of social development rather than as a source of creative energy.

The unattended question of moral consciousness is most prominent in the field of contemporary professional practice. New technologies have created a new body of professional knowledge. While in the structural realm, societies have become more complex because of the diffusion of new technologies into the societal process, in the realm of the operation of society it has created a new significance for professional knowledge and expertise. Professional knowledge is now being considered important not only to accelerate the momentum of development but also to resolve the dilemma emerging out of it. It is in this context that intellectuals are now the new interpreters of our times supplanting the legislators who were once at the commanding heights of modern society (Bauman 1987).

But if the professionals are the new priests of our times, they can also be our greatest enemies. This happens when they do not use their special knowledge to expand the radii of positive freedom in society, rather they use it to enhance their power not only as individuals but also as members of a secret society. Thus special knowledge is now in the hands of members of a secret society, not in the hands of members of a community of discourse which looks at discourse as a condition for the possibility of new knowledge. Or, in other words, professional knowledge, which is the fruit of new technology and science, is now in the hands of those who do not want to share it with people. As Robert Dahl tells us, such professional apathy and unwillingness to communicate is the greatest danger to democracy in our times (Dahl 1991). If democracy means genuine sharing in the infinite and ever widening webs of intimacies in societies, then the greatest danger to democracy comes from those professionals who do not have the moral consciousness to participate in communicative action – communicating their specialized knowledge with all of us in society. Dahl argues that "complexity threatens to cut the policy elite loose from effective control by the demos" (ibid.: 335). "Moreover, intellectuals seem loath to give to their own influence the same severe and critical scrutiny they so readily give to that of others." So, Dahl argues:

> [...] I am inclined to think that the long-run prospects for democracy are more seriously endangered by inequalities in resources, strategic positions, and bargaining strength that are derived not from wealth or economic position but from special knowledge (Dahl 1991: 333).

The Dialectic of Complexification and De-Differentiation: New Social Movements and the Return of the Actor

New technologies have led to the increasing complexification of our societies: they have made social systems more complex. But, the challenges that new technologies pose cannot be met only at the level of structural complexities. Response to the challenge of the new technologies requires the quest for new meanings and the creation of new solidarities. In other words, the move towards infinite differentiation and fragmentation of society at the structural level has to be met by the vision and practice of "de-differentiation" in the human practice. The contours of contemporary development pose this vital question of the dialectic between complexification and de-differentiation in the structuration of consciousness and society.

New social movements embody this quest for a new cultural identity that is an enbodiment of solidarity and "de-differentiation" in human practice (Habermas 1984). For Habermas, they are the "exploratory movements" whom we can find "beneath the threshold of the well-institutionalized orders of science and technology, law and morality," and "beneath a politics reduced to administration, and on the periphery of a highly moblised economic system" (Habermas 1984: 25). These movements are not socio-political but primarily cultural. They take seriously the challenge of culture (see Giri 1992). According to Govind Chandra Pande, cultural consciousness in primarily a consciousness of closing the gap between Self and the Other (Pande 1989). Overcoming the distinction between the Self and the Other in the practice and meditation of one's Being enables the creation of solidarity and de-differentiation in society. Thus, two things are simultaneously important – de-differentiation in Being and de-differentiation in society.

According to many commentators, new social movements embody de-differentiation in both Being and Society (Giri 1989). They create new solidarities and new "imagined communities" both in the realm of society and in the lives of individuals. It is perhaps for this reason that Alaine Touraine presents us his observation on the prospect of the new social movements under the title "Return of the Actor" (Touraine 1988).

But, for Touraine, new social movements not only contain responses to the challenge of new technologies and the accompanying development dilemma, they have also come into being in a social field diffused and dominated by technologies. New technologies have created a social context which has facilitated the origin and proliferation of the new social movements. This has been because of direct as well as not so direct influences and effects. The restructuring of industry and occupation that new technologies have made possible has created a "new class" which form the main constituency of the new social movements. For Touraine, if the working class used to be the main constituency of the old political movements (namely, the labour movement), then the new class is the key "need interpreter" (Fraser 1987) in the new social movements (see also Kriesi 1989). Thus, the links between new technologies and the new social movements are complex. Touraine helps us to understand this: "Class domination in (programmed societies) consists less in organizing work than managing the production and data-procession apparatus. What is crucial now is no longer the struggle between capital and labour in the factory but that between different user-consumers" (Touraine 1981: 36). New social movements embody the struggle of this new class.

But there is another symbiotic relationship between new technologies and the new social movements in the dynamics of social development in post-war Europe and North America. This is due to the prosperity that science and technology have been able to create even for the middle class or the upper-middle class in the Western societies. Because of unprecedented prosperity, some people in Western Europe have developed what political scientist Ronald Inglehart calls "post-materialist" values (Inglehart 1990). The new classes are more concerned about post-materialist values like ecology and the "quality of life" than about enhancing production and earning more money. These post-materialists form the main constituency of the new social movements in Europe who make culture and other "post-materialist" values central in the agenda of politics and society. In the words of Inglehart, "as a result of the historically unprecedented prosperity and the absence of war that has prevailed in Western countries since 1945, younger birth cohorts place less emphasis on economic and physical security than do older groups...(they) tend to give a high priority on non-material needs, such as a sense of community and the quality of life" (ibid.: 56). Thus, Inglehart arues: "the Materialist/Postmaterialist dimension has played a crucial role in the rise of the wave of the new social movements"(ibid.: 372).

If Inglehart places the contemporary culture shift in the habitus of the post-materialists, Harvey situates it in the material and ideological practice of what he calls the "cultural mass" (Harvey 1991). For Harvey, the cultural mass – large number of people who work in the academia, the media, journalism and cultural production – constitutes the core of the new social movements and they raise some significant questions which are often labelled as "post-modern". For Harvey, "In recent years, the cultural mass has pursued a whole host of political and ideological struggles that have generated significance: anti-racism, feminism, the struggles concerning ethnic identity, religious tolerance, cultural decolonization, and the like. Because post-modernism is associated with a democratization of voice within the cultural mass, many of the struggles against a central source of authority and power [...] have enlisted under the postmodern banner"(Harvey 1991: 75). But, unlike the enthusiastic commentators discussed so far, Harvey adds a note of caution and sarcasm in his assessment of the new social movements. For Harvey, "the problem is that these fights are being waged in a homogeneous class context [...]." (ibid.). Harvey puts the new social movements in a critical perspective: "New social movements gained a stronger purchase on political consciousness [...] seeming to represent alternatives to the working class as agents of human emancipation. But these movements were frequently victims of capitalist co-optation [...]." (Harvey 1991: 69). The Left within the cultural mass lost its tenuous link with the weakened working class movement; its supporters spent their energy in "deconstructing discourses and engaging in all manner of language games" (ibid.). Harvey's sarcasm deserves notice: "Radicals within the cultural mass became charmed by fields like semiotics, as if the really interesting thing about the homeless were the variety of coded messages of protest that cardboard boxes could convey" (ibid.).

The broadly middle-class origin of new social movements in advanced societies is agreed to by all. But what happens to the issues of poverty and unemployment in advanced societies? Are there takers for these causes? One may agree at the outset with Stuart Hall (1988) – even in the case of poverty, referring to the real experience is not enough. A movement must be ideologically constructed. But who will engage in a discursive construction of poverty? Are the new social movements concerned about the question of poverty? As one of Touraine's informants puts it: "The ecology movement has been totally incapable of explaining to workers and discussing with them the importance of those themes for their day-to-day problems" (Touraine 1983: 71). However, it must be noted that even new social movements have become sensitive in their own ways to these structural problems of disadvantage in advanced societies. For instance, Habitat for Humanity (a global Christian housing movement, originating in the US and building houses in poor American communities), which has a predominantly middle class origin (an instance of "yuppie radicalism"), is striving to achieve God's realization through building homes for those who do not have anything to claim as an altar of God. Another crucial point in the discussion of new social movements is to what extent one can globalize the new social movement perspective in understanding contemporary collective actions. New social movements in the Third World would result in a different relationship between meaning and production, than would be the case in the First World. Thus, Pramod Parajuli argues that new social movements in the Third World are not simply about the crisis in quality of life, but about production as well (Parajuli 1991: 181).

But these critical remarks should not distract ourselves from understanding the significance of the new social movements. Even Harvey's critical reflection does not end with mere sarcasm. Harvey appreciates the significance of the postmodern turn for the rise of the new social movements. For Harvey, "The post-modern turn within the cultural mass has placed the treatment of difference and 'otherness' firmly on the political agenda" (Harvey 1991: 75) Thus, it must be stressed that new social movements are not simply passive reflections of the structural context created by new technologies. Rather, they are primarily to create a new cultural and symbolic meaning in a space of technocratic logocentrism and rationality. Besides creating new cultural values which erase the distinction between the Self and the Other, they also help overcome the contemporary dilemma of development in the advanced capitalist societies.

Science, Technology and Development in the Developing Societies

Development has been at the centre of politics and planning in the developing societies at least since the beginning of their independence from the former empires. From the beginning, science and technology have played an important role in setting the content and the direction of the developmental agenda in the developing societies. But, the experience of development in developing societies has not been an unmixed blessing. Three points need to be made clear here: (a) both the discourse and the practice of development have been confined to the machinations of the state with very little involvement of the people (in a participatory and a dialogical sense); (b) science and technology have played a key role in this developmental logic of the state; and (c) this kind of state-centric development though meant for the well-being of the people has, in fact, led to their widespread displacement.

It is in this context of the predicament of development that many people's movements have come up questioning the statist models of development and regenerating people's spaces within the developmental dynamics. These movements not only criticize prevalent models of development, but also reconstruct the available theories of modernization and development and strive towards a genuine alternative. In the Indian context, examples of these movements abound: from *Chipko* to the All India People's Science Movement. People's movements in the developing societies not only question the developmental mobilization of the state, they also question modern science and technology which is the "reason of the State" (Nandy 1988). Thus science movements in contemporary India question the models of science and technology which have led to development as displacement. Here, we can look at the work of both alternative science movement and the people's science movement. Alternative science movement seeks to "build upon the ongoing intellectual and political battles in societies where alternatives, at least baseline alternatives, exist in the present, in the form of traditional systems of knowledge that have survived and are struggling against the hegemony of modern science" (ibid.: 12). As Ashis Nandy further makes it clear:

> [...] many representatives of dissenting movements don't have in mind only the environment of science but also its text [...]. They try to relate to other science movements...(and) build upon not only the experiences of suffering but also the cognitive orders of the victims of modern science (ibid.: 21).

Critique of Science and the Striving for Alternatives

One critical interlocutor of science movements in contemporary India who deconstructs not only the environment of modern science but also its text is Professor C.V. Seshadri, who shows us the connection between a faulty science and a faulty model of development (Seshadri 1982). For Seshadri, the law of entropy is culturally biased, as it is biased in favour of the rich, the affluent and the industrialists. Regarding the cultural bias in the idea of entropy, Seshadri tell us:

> Entropy has a profound history and is such a foundational concept of modern science that it would have been invented at any event. To me, it represents a compromise between the post-Galilean science and the Church. The entropy concept has much to do with messianic Christianity which affirms that there is no cycle of birth and death – these events take place once, and you go to heaven or hell thereafter; things happen once and for all [...]. These beliefs give rise to a notion of unidirectional time, and entropy is the modern concept which fixes that direction. I would point out the kind of hold that such a concept has on thinking at various levels: for example, political leaders in the Christian West often behave the way they do because in their vision, the destruction of the world is certain and they want to control the process. The entropy concepts and such beliefs, I believe, are mutually reinforcing (Seshadri 1990: 93).

Furthermore, for Seshadri,

> The law of entropy, backed by authority, provides a criterion for utilisation of energy available from various sources. This criterion, known as the concept of efficiency, is corollary to the law of entropy and came into existence along with the law. The efficiency criterion stipulates that the loss of available energy in a conversion becomes smaller as the temperature at which the conversion is effected is higher above the ambient. Therefore, high temperatures are of high value and so are resources such as petroleum, coal etc. [...] (Seshadri quoted in Alvares 1988: 89).

Thus, Seshadri shows how the second law of thermodynamics gives preference to high temperature energy sources and values these sources more in the development process. In turn, energy as a value in the developmental process leads to "a sweeping transfer of resources from the *bahiskrit* (excluded) to *paschimkrit* (westernised) *samaj*" (Sahashrabudhey 1988: 26).

It is in this context of the dissatisfaction with the prevalent formulations in modern science that Seshadri develops two important concepts: *Shakti* as a new energy-quality marker and DNA model of development. Seshadri develops his concept of *Shakti* with the postulate of mass energy:

> All forms of energy have mass equivalents (with suitable dimensionalising factors). Thus, the internal energy or energy of combustion of a material can be considered to have equivalents in terms of mass. This enables us to redefine a new class of property functions, *Shakti*, that combines mass and energy in such a way that quality markers can be assigned to various materials for comparison on a common basis [...] *Shakti* is a property that combines the energy of combustion and, say, the food value of the material. It should be noted that combustion is a highly irreversible reaction that oxidises the material rapidly and edibility is akin to combustion (especially of carbohydrates) but goes through a series of slower step with conditions closer to reversibility, and leading to the same end products. Hence, in defining one kind of *Shakti*, we have really used the same oxidising property of the material. It should also be noticed that *Shakti* is defined as a class of property functions that can combine various kinds of energy and their mass equivalents (Seshadri 1990: 22–23).

Seshadri's second concept of a DNA model of development is a plea for social transformation which is generically multidimensional. Seshadri begins with two structural forms: the "helix" and the "spiral". While spiral as a form is two-dimensional, "helix is a form that is purely three-dimensional and neverless"(Seshadri 1980: 31).

> The most fundamental components of living systems are helical...the double helix of DNA, the triple helix of collagen and so on. In fact, the double helix of DNA is mechanically and structurally a strong form [...]. It is this mechanical property of DNA that has been made use of in a wind motor at MCRC [...]. When compared to a Darreus Triposkein wind device, the DNA device has a higher packing fraction and offers a greater surface to the wind. It can be conjectured that the most fundamental unit of self-organisation, self-replication and repair must have evolved to be very sound mechanically, structurally and otherwise. Thus, one asks the next question: if DNA is helical, larger living forms are helical or use the helix widely, can systems of organism be 'helical, ' can society be DNA-like (ibid.: 34).

From Power to *Shakti*: Towards Transformative Realizations

In the same paper, Seshadri develops his concepts of *Shakti* and the DNA model of development. Is there a link between the two? Perhaps, Seshadri seems to be suggesting that a *Shakti* approach to energy is the basis for the multidimensional social development that would be DNA-like. Energy as value has led to highly unequal pattern of development in Indian society. Moreover, energy conversion, according to the law of entropy, always leads to degradation and degeneration. Ultimately, it leads to a degrading view of the cosmic situation and the human condition. In this context, the idea of *Shakti* proposes a transformative view of the human condition with a notion of time which is not only unidirectional and irreversible, but also reversible and cyclical. This transformative model of *Shakti* can enable us to even transform the "waste" produced from energy generation to something useful. According to Seshadri,

> [...] it is possible to conceive of interconnections or processes which would convert what is 'rejected' to environment, the 'waste' from energy use, into food. For example, the off-gas, the waste from combustion of fossil fuels (to generate useful energy) may be used in food production. Thus, we arrive at an important concept, namely, that in a country like ours, 'waste' is a free good, a resource. The whole science, or the knowledge system, will have to be modified to suit this view which enables use of waste as a resource (Seshadri 1990: 92).

If modern western physics has given us a view of energy which is intimately tied to degradation, modern western social theory has given us a concept of power which is inherently tied to displacement and domination. For instance, Max Weber defines power as the ability to carry out one's will against the resistance of others. In this view, to have power means to engage oneself in a battle of displacement. In this context, some anthropologists have recently formulated a different concept of power based on Indian cosmology where power does not simply mean displacement but also nurturance and transformation. It is really striking that one anthropologist has used the very word *Shakti* to speak of an alternative idea of power (Marglin 1985). Unlike power, *Shakti* is primarily concerned with the "capacity to bring forth life" (Cox 1988: 57). Hence, the broader implication of Seshadri's distinction between *Shakti* and energy in modern physics must be understood in the context of the distinction between *Shakti* and power in anthropology and how the idea of *Shakti* leads to a transformative view of the human condition and a DNA model of social development.

People's science movement in contemporary India are also playing their critical role in widening the discourse of development. In this context, it must be noted that people's science movements in India are not simply uncritical appendages to the state nor are they to unpack the package of development. They also question the contemporary practice of development as displacement. They are now operating in varieties of critical areas: literacy, science education, pedagogy, science policy, resource mapping, and crucial policy issues such as the intellectual property rights. It is perhaps for this reason that Vinod Raina, one of the key leaders in the All India People's Science Movement, writes:

> The role of a people's science movement...is defined as not merely that of communicating and simplifying science (though that is essential) but also questioning each aspect of such (alienating) progress and development, in particular, the S&T (Science and Technology) issues involved, and intervening wherever necessary with the active participation of the so-called ordinary men and women (Raina 1989: 2).

Confronting the Challenge of Social Development

Thus development is an all-pervasive global challenge now. Contemporary forces of change as they have come to us in the context of the revolutionary manifestation of new technologies make development a challenge everywhere. All societies are now trying in their own ways to come face to face with this challenge. They are trying to enhance production by taking the help of modern science and high technology. All societies are now restructuring their economies and polities. But such restructuring is not being accompanied by a restructuring of values. Thus societies in the so-called Third World are caught in a paradoxical situation of doubt and conflict. At a deeper level, this conflict is one of interpretation. While high technologies originating from the advanced societies are proliferating globally, there is very little effort to domesticate these technologies in the light and the image of civilizational values. But without addressing the broader question of human values and freedom, high technologies will not be a boon. Instead of being catalytic forces of development, they will be forces of destruction and division. It is here that there is a crucial need for a genuine and authentic retrieval of traditions which will provide resources to thing about and practice human values as we are using new technologies as instruments of social development. Thus restructuring of societies must go hand in hand with a genuine retrieval of tradition in order that pursuits of social development can create a "good life" and "good society" for all of us globally. New social movements embody such quests for an authentic retrieval of traditions. Thus, it is no wonder that in the last All India People's Science Congress, one of the favourite songs of the delegates was: "For a cultural revolution for the whole of humanity, for a cultural revolution for India, let men not be a slave of the machines."

References

Alvares, Claude. 1988. "Science, Colonialism and Violence: A Luddite View, " in Ashis Nandy (ed.). *Science, Hegemomy and Violence: A Requiem for Modernity.* New Delhi: Oxford University Press.

Bauman, Zygmunt. 1987. *Legislators and Interpreters: On Modernity, Postmodernity and the Intellectuals.* Cambridge, MA: Basil Blackwell.

Benjamin, Roger. 1980. *The Limit of Politics: Collective Goods and Political Change in Postindustrial Societies:* Chicago: University of Chicago Press.

Beteille, Andre. 1986. "Individualism and Equality." *Current Anthropology,* 27(2): 121–134.

Bluestone, Barry and Bennett Harrison. 1982. *The Deindustrialization of America.* New York: Basic Books.

Buchman, Marlis. 1989. *The Script of Life in Modern Society: Entry into Adulthood in a Changing World.* Chicago: University of Chicago Press.

Burns, T. and R. Ueberhost. 1989. *Creative Democracy: Systematic Conflict Resolution and Policy Making in a World of High Science and Technology.* New York: Praeger.

Cox, Harvey, 1988. *Many Mansions: A Christian's Encounter with Other Faiths.* New York: Simon & Schuster.

Dahl, Robert. 1991. *Democracy and its Critics.* New Delhi: Orient Longman.

Fraser, Nancy. 1987. *Social Movements vs Disciplinary Bureaucracies: The Discourse of Social Needs.* Minneapolis: University of Minnesota Press.

Fuller, Millard. 1986. *No More Shacks.* Americus: Habitat for Humanity.

Galtung, Johan. 1980. *The True Worlds: A Transnational Perspective.* New York: Free Press.

Giri, Ananta. 1989. "Narratives of Creative Transformation: Constituting Critical Movements in Contemporary American Culture," *Dialectical Anthropology,* 18 (n.2).

——, 1991. *The Portrait of a Discursive Formation: Science as Social Activism and Cultural Criticism in Contemporary India.* Unpublished Monograph.

——, 1992. "Understanding Contemporary Social Movements," *Dialectical Anthropology,* 17 (n.1).

Habermas, Jurgen (ed.) 1984. *Observations on the Spiritual Situation of the Age: Contemporary German Perspectives.* Cambridge: The MIT Press.

——, 1987. *The Philosophical Discourses of Modernity.* Cambridge, MA: The MIT Press.

——, 1990. *Moral Consciousness and Communicative Action.* Cambridge: Polity Press.

Hall, Stuart. 1988. *The Hard Road to Renewal: Thatcherism and the Crisis of the Left.* London: Verso.

Harrington, Michael. 1984. *The New American Poverty.* New York: Holt, Reinhart & Winston.

Harrison, Bennett and Barry Bluestone. 1988. *The Great U-Turn: Capitalist Restructuring and the Polarising of America.* New York: Basic Books.

Harvey, David. 1991. "Flexibility: Threat or Opportunity," *Socialist Review,* 21 (n.1), pp.65–77.

Inglehart, Ronald. 1990. *The Culture Shift in Advanced Societies.* Princeton. Princeton University Press.

Kriesi, Hans. 1989 "New Social Movements and the New Class in Netherlands," *American Journal of Sociology,* 94(n.5).

Marglin, F. 1985. *The Wife of God-Kings.* Oxford: Oxford University Press.

Mukherjee, Ramakrishna. 1989. *The Quality of Life: Valuation in Social Research.* New Delhi: Sage.

Nandy, Ashis (ed.). 1988. *Science, Hegemony and Violence: A Requiem for Modernity.* New Delhi: Oxford University Press.

Offe, Clause. 1988. "Democracy Against the Welfare State: Structural Foundations of Neoconservative Political Thought, " in J.D. Moon, (ed.), *Responsibility, Rights and Welfare: The Theory of the Welfare State.* Boulder, CO: Westview Press.

Osborne, David. 1988. *Laboratories of Democracy.* Harvard: Harvard University Press.

Pande, Govind Chandra. 1989. *The Meaning and Process of Culture as Philosophy of History.* Allahabad: Raka Prakashan.

Parajuli, Pramod. 1991. "Power and Knowledge in Development Discourse: New Social Movements and the State in India," *International Social Science Journal,* 127, pp. 173–190.

Raina, Vinod. 1989. "Education within the Framework of People's Science Movement," Paper presented at the Third People's Science Congress at Calcutta.

Rapp, Ryana. 1988. "Chromosomes and Communications: The Discourse of Genetic Counselling," *Medical Anthropology Quarterly,* 2 (n.2).

Sahashrabudhey, Sunil. 1988. *Freedom from the Degrading Laws of a Degrading Order.* Varanasi: Gnadhian Institute of Studies.

Seshadri, C.V. 1980 "Energy in the Indian Context," invited lectures at Madurai Kamraj University, September 8–9, 1980.

——, 1982. *Development and Thermodynamics*. Madras: Murugappa Chettiar Research Centre.

——, 1990. "Interview with C.V. Seshadri," *PPST Bulletin*.

Sen, Amartya. 1986. "The Standard of Living, " in S. McCurrin, (ed.), *The Tanner Lectures on Human Values*. Vol.7. Universities of Cambridge and Utah Press.

——, 1987. *On Ethics and Economics*. Delhi: Oxford University Press.

——, 1989. "Food and Freedom," *World Development*, 17(n6), pp. 769–781.

Tambiah, Stanley. 1985. *Culture, Thought and Action: An Anthropological Perspective*. Harvard: Harvard University Press.

Touraine, Alain. 1981. *The Voice and the Eye: An Analysis of the Social Movements*. Cambridge: Cambridge University Press.

——, 1983. *The Anti-Nuclear Protest*. Cambridge: Cambridge University Press.

——, 1988. *Return of the Actor: Social Theory in Post-industrial Society*. Minneapolis: University of Minnesota Press.

Zuboff, Soshana. 1988. *In the Age of Smart Machine: The Future of Work and Power*. New York: Basic Books.

17 The New Built-Environment

New Classes and the New Homelessness in Contemporary United States

> A whole history remains to be written of spaces – which would at the same time be history of power [...] from the great strategies of geopolitics to the little tactics of the habitat.
>
> — Michel Foucault

> Yet a global strategy of resistance and transformation has to begin with the realities of place and community. The problem is to discover a centralized politics that matches the increasingly centralized power of flexible accumulation while remaining faithful to the grass roots of local resistance.
>
> — David Harvey

The Problem

Shacks seem to be the new global signs: they are everywhere. They were once a "sign" of the so-called Third World; but now they are to be seen even in the most advanced societies. In fact, as one thoughtful commentator on the global problem of shacks writes: "So far as housing is concerned, the whole world remains underdeveloped because the problem is all-pervasive" (Poulose 1988: 42). The challenge of shelter is posed everywhere. This challenge is integrally linked to transformations in the economy, culture and politics of advanced societies, as well as to the dynamics of contemporary global restructuring. Residence and shelter pose a fundamental crisis for late capitalistic societies. One can take the new American homelessness as a sign of the times, as a sign of advanced, not solely "underdeveloped", societies. Owning one's home has been an important element in the American dream. In American cultural discourse and representation, homeownership is not simply a matter of "economic externality and possession": it is a precondition of the very constitution of the American self, linked almost ritually with adulthood, independence and coming of age. In American culture, homeownership also provides the key elements of the language of ideal citizenship and personhood (Perin 1977, 1988). But, during recent decades, the dream of owning one's home has frequently not come true in America. Many people there now are virtually on the streets, with no place to stay except a street corner or a city shelter. More and more people are not able to afford a place to rent, let alone to own. Crisis in homeownership is a critical problem in the contemporary United States, brining to risk assumptions of the "associations between housing, independence and adulthood" (Williams 1988: 72).

The New Homelessness: The American Case

Homelessness is now an all-pervasive sign or – following Jean Baudrillard – a "simulacrum". But, as a postmodern "simulacrum", homelessness requires understanding both in and of itself, as well as in relation to the broader universe of economy and power. Contemporary American society is in the midst of a whirlwind of restructuring, what two recent commentators have so aptly called the "The Great U-Turn" (Harrison and Bluestone 1988). The all-encompassing restructuring in American society is affecting people from all social strata, especially the lower and the middle classes, some of whom, as Katherine Newman shows us, are now "falling from grace" (Newman 1988).

How does this falling from grace actually manifest itself in individual lives? American social critic Jonathan Kozol presents us a moving portrayal of the work of disintegrating communities and homes in his evocative ethnography, *Rachel and Her Children* (Kozol 1988). Kozol looks at what homelessness represents: "systematic inequities are the real issue" here (ibid.: 97). He describes the life and world of homelessness women in New York City who, along with homeless children, constitute an important element in the phenomenon of the new homelessness. Kozol describes in detail the struggle for survival of a homeless woman, named Rachel. In the "landscape of despair," her children constitute her source of strength, stability and identity. They provide some home-like stability, even though she does not have a roof over her head. She rejects the provision of foster care for homeless children because, as she tells Kozol, "My children is what is holding me together" (ibid.: 78).

Children staying in the shelters have to travel far to attend school; they are often late for school, and they are treated contemptuously by teachers and fellow students. Shelter children are not provided with admission to schools in the surrounding neighbourhoods and communities, but must sometimes attend at schools far away. Kozol notes the case of one four-year-old child travelling over thirty miles a day to school. Systematic social inequities, in Kozol's view, are behind the structuration of such arrangements for residence and education.

Another very moving life in Rachel's world is Richard Lazarus, an educated thirty-six-year-old Vietnam veteran whom Kozol met in the subway underneath Grand Central Station. Three months before, Lazarus had undergone the loss of job, children and wife – all in a single stroke. As in almost all of these situations, it was such a near-simultaneous event that drove him out of his home. Lazarus tells us his story: "Always, up until last summer, I (have) found a job that paid at least $ 300. Now I could not find a job that paid $ 200. When I found an opening at a departmental store they said that I was overqualified. If someone has asked me a year ago who are the homeless, I would not have known what to reply. Now I know the answer. They are people like myself" (ibid.: 170). Lazarus had a job in data processing for seven years until last summer when the company shut down without a warning and moved out of state. Then Lazarus looked for a job everywhere and got one for two months in the summer – a part-time job as a security guard in one of the hotels for homeless families. But he himself did not have a home. "I slept in Washington Square and Central Park" (ibid.). During this time, he wanted to be reunited with his wife. Lazarus continues his narrative:

> For me, the loss of work and loss of wife had left me rocking. Then the welfare regulations hit me. I began to feel that I would be reduced to trash. You're never prepared for this. It's like there isn't any bottom. It's not like cracks in a safety net. It's like a black hole sucking you inside. Half the people I know are suffering from chest infections and sleep deprivation. The lack of sleep leaves you debilitated, shaky. You exaggerate your fears. If a psychiatrist comes along he would say that I was crazy. But I was an ordinary man. There was nothing wrong with me. I lost my kids. I lost my home [...] I was a pretty stable man. Now I tremble when I meet somebody in the ordinary world.
>
> I'm trembling right now. One reason that I didn't want to leave the subway was that I feel safer underground. When you (Kozol) asked if I would come outside and get something to eat, my first thought was that you would see me shaking if we sat down for a meal and you'd think I was an alcoholic" (Kozol 1988: 172).

From a close look at the life history of Lazarus as he narrates it to Kozol, many aspects of the dispossession of the homeless become salient. Lazarus says that the people, staying in the shelter, are given two subway tokens. Lazarus goes on:

> When you are sick, there is no way to get better. You cannot sleep in at the shelter. You have got to go outside and show you are looking for a job. I had asthma as a kid. It was gone for twenty years. Now it's back [...] Asthma is common at the shelter. There's a lot of dust. That may be why. Edema (swollen feet) – you get it from sitting up so much and walking all day long. If you are very hungry and you want a meal you can get it at St. Francis. You can get a sandwich at Grand Central every night at ten o'clock. So if you want to keep from starving you are always on the move. If you have no subway tokens then you jump the stile (ibid.: 172).

Lazarus narrates how he is constantly harassed by the welfare workers. He explains to Kozol how he can work inside the shelter for a token salary. For twenty hours' work, he gets only $ 12.50. "Even sixty cents an hour makes you feel that you are not completely dead. It may be slave labour but it gets certain privileges like being first in line for meals" (ibid.: 173).

After listening to Lazarus, let us enter briefly into the life of another homeless person whom I met during my fieldwork in a shelter in Baltimore in the summer of 1988. James is one of the many persons I had talked with during my study of a shelter named Baltimore Rescue Mission.

James is a white middle-aged man, forty-two years of age. For the last one year, he has been in the street. He is single. He is now working in a labour co-operative as a temporary worker. He earns some three dollars and fifty cents per hour. James leaves the shelter at 6 A.M. every week morning. He reaches his place of work at 8 A.M. He finishes for the day at 3.10 P.M. every afternoon. When he leaves the mission early in the morning, he goes without breakfast from the mission. James thinks that living in the shelter is not particularly suitable for those working in a regular job. In his words, "to be able to work in all the weeks a year, one is required to have an apartment oneself". Hence, he is saving his money to have an apartment and to be able to see television for which there is no provision in the mission.

That living in the shelter is not suitable for working in a regular job is a view shared by one Mr. Sam whom I met only once in the mission. He told me that the time schedule of the mission has no consideration for employed homeless people. As he puts it, "to compel an adult to go to bed at 9 in the night and rise up at 7 A.M. in the morning is dictatorial and disgusting. When the homeless are required to report at the mission by 8 P.M. at the latest, it does not leave scope for the varieties of jobs that they could have done if they were allowed in till 10 or 11 in the night."

To come back to James again, during the last ten years that he has been in the street, he has had a variety of experiences. In this period, at some point, he was a drunkard, even thrown in prison once for heavy drinking. He was also imprisoned for indecent exposure. The term was for three years. Initially, it has to be noted that he wanted to become a street person not because he was unable to pay the rent, but because of the constant change of jobs. It seems that it was not possible on his part to find residence near his place of work each time his job changed. This was why he ended up on the street. In spite of a myth of opportunities for limitless geographical mobility, the distance between the place of work and place of residence remains a constraining factor in case of the working people in the U.S.

While carrying out this study, when I met James two weeks after our first conversation, he greeted me: "Hi, Anna. Nothing new with me besides what I have already told you. Only change is that I have grown two weeks older and my company has fired two people from the job."

Other ethnographies of the shelter situation in contemporary American society give a similar picture. For instance, the work of Kim Hopper and his associates in the Community Services Society of New York shows us the making of America's homelessness from the Skid Row to the new poor (Hopper and Hamberg 1984). Hopper argues that the homeless in the contemporary U.S. are not simply the people staying in the skid rows, but the new poor from all parts of America's stratum of dispossessed.

Contrary to "the skid row approach", psychological disability seems to have replaced alcoholism as a major cause of homelessness since the 1970s. Hopper et al. provide data from the survey they conducted in 1985. The survey involved a two-hour interview with 223 respondents by skilled interviewers. It shows that the majority of men entering the New York City shelters are now black (compared with 24% in the city's population as a whole). In fact, since whites leave the shelters more rapidly, a sample of men staying at any time shows an even higher proportion of blacks. Close to half of the new entrants are under the age of thirty. The educational status of men and their parents suggests that their families of origin were poor, but not part of an extremely deprived "underclass". The vast majority of entrants to the shelters have been in unskilled and low-skilled positions offering neither decent pay nor security. Only a small fraction of the new shelter entrants – between 10 and 25 per cent of the total newcomers – appear to have been in positions with any possibility of stability or advancement. The best jobs they have had seem to be the jobs at the periphery of the service sector. These jobs are low-waged, non-unionized, and highly sensitive to fluctuations in demand, owing to even slight shifts in the competitive positions of their employers.

From the above data, as well as from their previous extensive ethnographic research, Hopper et al. conclude that men from working class families, many of them young members of minority groups, constitute the majority of the new shelter entrants in New York City. Their occupational histories reflect the inter-generational horizontal nobility of the prevailing of deindustrialization in many communities. These people have had peripheral jobs which suggest that, even by the standards of their home communities, their labour market participation has been marginal. Hopper and his colleagues also argue that these homeless do not represent a cross-section of the displaced communities, such as those hard hit by the process of deindustrialization. They are not typical of the communities from which they originate. There is a higher level of disability among homeless persons, and they represent the most marginalized persons from a community that is growing poorer.

Yet the new poor do not exhaust the scenario of homelessness in contemporary America. Mental problems constitute an independent but related variable. In the sample of the above 42 per cent of the homeless show a history of overnight treatment for psychiatric problems, a drug problem or a drinking problem. Psychic disability among the homeless is far higher than typically found in community studies. Of course, the rise of mental illness among the homeless has to be understood in the light of deinstitutionalization. In his later work, Hooper (1988) argues that disability has replaced alcoholism as a predominant cause of homelessness. But Hopper does not want to treat psychic disability as an independent causative factor. It is not psychiatric disability and deinstitutionalization that is responsible for the explosive rise of the homeless in American streets, this work argues. The psychiatric model, for Hopper

> ignores the telling fact of a time lag between the major waves of deinstitutionalization in this country (early and later 1960s) and the appearance in large numbers of psychiatrically disabled on the streets (late 1970s) [...] what this lag points to is the necessity of considering a host of changes in the economy and the ecology of the city, the net effect of which has been to lower the threshold at which personal impairment translates into social handicap (Hopper 1988: 160).

For Hopper, so long as resources in the community – especially affordable dwellings – were plentiful enough, severely disabled individuals, including many with disturbing behavioural traits, could be accommodated. Whatever their hardships, they suffered for the most part silently. Even when forced to move from hospitals and mental institutions, vacancies in inferior but cheap housing meant that most of them could find replacement accommodations. But, as Hopper argues:

> Under the combined forces of gentrification and abandonment, decent affordable housing grew scarce and competition intensified for what remained. 'Undesirable' tenants become expendable 'nuisances,' dilapidated housing became a commodity to be 'warehoused' against its future exchange value, rather than one prized for itsimmediate utility; and the displaced poor were left in the cold (Hopper 1988: 160).

What these materials reveal are the changing structural forces at work in the political economy of the advanced societies. Contemporary homelessness is "not the result of general poverty. Rather, it is occurring in one of the most advanced industrial economies of the world, in the midst of unprecedented wealth" (Harrington 1984); both of which are integrally linked with "deindustrialization of America" (Bluestone and Harrison 1982). Bluestone and Harrison help us to look at the process of deindustrialization as a fight between "life space" and "capital space." But this fight is written not simply in individual lives nor even in the life of the communities, but in the built-environment itself. Deindustrialization has its spatial implication as well, leading to fundamental spatial restructuring of the American cities. Deindustrialization leads to a very different spatial formation in the city, where investment in the urban centres becomes a matter of strategic significance for the "valorization of capital" (Mandel 1973) in the new competitive global reality of late capitalism. While other sources of "valorization of capital" seem to have exhausted their profitability in a post-industrial world, "there are abundant opportunities for the productive employment of capital through the creation of the built-environment for production and consumption" (Harvey 1985: 15).

The New Built-Environment

The cities in advanced capitalist societies are witnessing a "restless formation and reformation of geographical landscapes" (Harvey 1985: 150). The new built-environment and the new homelessness are linked by intermediary processes of spatial restructuring, such as gentrification and abandonment.

As a consequence of occupational restructuring and deindustrialization, cities are transformed from industrial to commercial centres, i.e., centres of financial and real estate transactions, information trading, and the allied professional and technical services. In this context, Hopper et al. write: "Gentrification describes the process whereby rundown, but often occupied, neighborhoods are 'reclaimed' for residential use by high income owners/tenants. In the process, low income residents are displaced, land values in the surrounding areas rise, and old staples of neighborhood service give way to a more affluent clientele" (Hopper, Susser and Conover 1985: 184). Peter Marcuse links this process of spatial restructuring with another related process of restructuring known as abandonment. Both gentrification and abandonment, even though seemingly independent of each other, occur together. "Abandonment of a unit occurs when all those having a private profit-oriented economic interest in a unit lose any incentive for continued ownership beyond the immediate future, and are willing to surrender title to it without compensation, because of the absence of effective demand for its continued use or reuse" (Marcuse 1985: 200). Abandonment of an entire neighbourhood occurs when public or private parties do feel no incentive to engage in long-term neighbourhood investment.

For Marcuse, abandonment and gentrification are reflections of a single long-term process, resulting from the economic restructuring of the cities. The city tries its best to protect property values in the downtown from discordant land use and discordant population. The pull of the professional and gentrifying forces to the downtown occurs simultaneously with the push of the poor from the residential areas. The net effect of all these is the displacement of the poor.

But these processes do not work in some simple mechanical manner. Conscious decisions by landlords, lenders and financial institutions play a crucial in the abandonment process (Meyerson 1986). For Meyerson, the lending institutions withdraw credit based upon racial considerations and consideration of locations thus acting as an "independent causative factor in the neighborhood decline process" (Meyerson 1986: 194).

In the new built-environment, housing is no more a habitat, a marker of one's own identity. Rather, it is a very important speculative element in the accumulation of capital. In this new built-environment, "the housing sector in particular has become a major tool in macroeconomic policy for a stabilizing economic growth, particularly in the United States, where it has openly been used as a Keynesian regulator [...]" (Harvey 1985: 48). As housing becomes a commodity for capital, the prospect for producing affordable housing for low-income people worsens. This is accentuated by the policy of the state, where the state withdrew from this vital domain not only as a producer but also as a facilitator. This withdrawal of the government "decreases the available supply of housing, reduces the ability of the poor to provide additional housing or even maintain existing ones" (Marcuse 1988: 77).

The new built-environment not only embodies the contemporary transformation of capitalism from a Fordist to a regime of post-Fordism and flexible accumulation, it also carries practice and values of a new social formation. The new built-environment is now being occupied by new classes which Bourdieu calls the "new bourgoisie" – with a marked interest in commodity aesthetics and refined consumption, which are also significant factors in contemporary class differentiation (Bourdieu 1984). While from the point of view of the users and the consumers, there is an increased demand for culture as an item of consumption, in the realm of production itself, production of culture becomes a very significant part of the total field. Thus, from the sides of both consumption and production, culture is making new grounds for itself, blurring established genres and crossing familiar boundaries of self and society. The new class in its new built-environment wants "more culture", more sophistication, more meaning through the process of consumption itself. This is at the root of the demand for postmodern architecture and postmodern space in the new built-environment. Scott Lash writes of these peoples: "Their identity and habituses can be fixed, rigid, status-conscious on the caricatured model of the yuppie, that is, on the model of distinction" (Lash 1990: 23).

This new class is moving from the "vulgar functionalism" of modernist mass consumption to the "aestheticized commodity" of postmodernity, where secondary connotations, such as status, chic, humor, etc., rather than the function of the object itself, are important. They opt for new (postmodern) cultural goods and residential settings. "Gentrification, loft living, and the appropriation of historic preservation" is the spatial practice of this new class in the new built-environment (Knox 1991: 186). In the spatial practice of the new class, there is an increasing demand for a postmodern spatial configuration and a postmodern architecture. A very important element in the craving for a postmodern space is the craving for traditions and historical preservation. For David Harvey, in the urban context, postmodernism signifies a break with the idea that planning and development should focus on the large scale and that vernacular tradition and local history [...] should be appreciated with a much greater eclecticism of style (Harvey 1987). Paul Knox writes: "Historic buildings and districts lend both distinctiveness and identity; they also form an obvious linkage with that aspect of postmodern culture that emphasizes the past, the vernacular and the decorative" (Knox 1991: 193).

What does postmodernism in the new built-environment really mean? For Knox, postmodern design is by definition wide-ranging and eclectic, anarchical and combinatorial. It is preoccupied with richness, decoration, context and history. The postmodern new built-environment is peppered with columns and arches. For Lash, the postmodern approach sees the new built-environment as a cultural object, simultaneously material and cultural. He argues that there are two important aspects of postmodern architecture: (a) its sense of play, and (b) its sense of community. "Architectural modernism broke with historical styles, for principles of function and a sense of geometric rationality in building" using the latest building materials "steel, concrete, glass." But, the postmodern urban vision is based on the "Gothic labyrinth of the medieval city" (Lash 1990: 35, 33); it "foregrounds a strong sense of locality (invoking) the metaphysics of the 'street'" (ibid.: 3).

But, the new built-environment is also a contested terrain. To start with, there is a struggle over the meaning of the city between different categories of residents, mainly the low-income and the affluent. Both the low-income and the affluent have different emphases in their spatial practices. In case of low-income, as Harvey shows, "exchange values are scarce, and so the pursuit of use values for daily survival is central to social action [...] Within the community of space, use value gets shared through some mix of mutual aid and predation, creating tight but often highly conflictual interpersonal social bonding in both private and public spaces" (Harvey 1987: 20). It is this community of space that is also a space for carnival – a space for coming together for the residents to celebrate this mutuality (Harvey 1989). The space of use value is also a space of "stalled gentrification" where neighbours grow many kinds of vegetables (Williams 1988). As Williams, who has studied the process of upscaling the downtown in Washington, D.C., tells us: "When the plants thrive, they reflect one's skill as a gardener and may ratify the desire to participate in the alley community. The thick roots and green wide leaves of these healthy blooming plants are approximate methaphors for being settled and committed to the alley world" (Williams 1988: 37). In such a neighbourhood, gardening is a crucial way to socialize and incorporate the new residents to the neighbourhood. Gardening also shows a concern with cycles and repetitions and through this, the residents root themselves into the alley world.

In the some ethnography, Williams remarks: "Collard greens stand for a process that offers opportunities for many variations on a theme" (Williams 1988: 41). In varying ways, they symbolize the concern for use, rather than for exchange. The immigrants who stay in this neighbourhood use their home as a sanctuary for the Central American refugees. The main street of Elm Valley (the neighbourhood that Williams studied) is a space for coming together, where shopping is "so involved with memories" (ibid.: 86). It is in the street itself that residents sometimes use a special dish called souse "which is an appropriate symbol for the personal, dense, textured small town world of the street" (ibid.: 83). Collard greens in Elm Valley also symbolize the fact that the street in Elm Valley is not yet completely incorporated, here the "incorporation of America" is not yet complete (Rose 1987; Trachtenberg 1982).

But what is important to realize is that the open-endedness of the street has not yet completely lost its voice in the heartland of the new built-environment. The new sites for consumption, such as the Baltimore Inner Harbor or the Harbor Front in Boston, are also sites of carnival; and even though the creation of these sites is a reflection of "ruling class alliance", they are also necessary manifestations of the way "class relations and accumulation unfold in space" (Harvey 1985: 150). In this context, the new class in the new built-environment is not simply a bearer of "invidious distinction"; it is also the articulator of a politics of critical difference. Moreover, this new class in this new built-environment is also the key factor in varieties of new social movements. As Scott Lash writes:

> On the other hand, these same social groupings form in large part a constituency for the new social movements. Their habituses or identities can thus be constructed importantly along lines of gender, minority ethnicities, minority sexual practices and environmentalism in opposition to nuclear war. That is, along lines of difference rather than of invidious distinction (Lash 1990: 23).

This new class is also articulating a new language of place and self, which is manifested in varieties of urban religious movements as they "abound to define an alternative sense of community" (Harvey 1985). Even for Harvey, "the construction of community within the frame of capitalist urbanization contains a tension" (ibid.). Paul Knox also argues that the postmodern value or the new class in the new built-environment creates tension within the new urban landscape. Here, postmodern architecture, also, has a critical effect in creating community and "de-differentiation" (Lash 1990). Postmodern architecture is characterized by a sense of play where there is a community regulation and a striving towards achieving a non-separation between work and leisure. For Scott Lash, postmodern architecture exemplifies a set of de-differentiations in introducing a populist and playful style and where there is a constant experimentation of building materials and where "a principle is abandoned in favor of pastiche" (Lash 1990: 36). Thus, the new built-environment, which simultaneously houses the new homeless and the new social classes, is not without contention over meaning and struggles to build humane habitats and an urge to create a humane city.

References

Bratt, R.G., C. Hartman and A. Meyerson (eds.), 1986, *Critical Perspectives on Housing*. Philadelphia: Temple University Press.

Bluestone, Barry and Bennett Harrison, 1982, *The Deindustrialization of America*. New York: Basic Books.

Harrington, Michel, 1984, *The New American Poverty.* New York: Holt Reinhert & Winston.

Harrison, Bennet and Barry Bluestone, 1988, *The Great U-Turn: Capitalist Restructuring and the Polorizing of America.* New York: Basic Books.

Harvey, Davis, 1985, *Consciousness and the Urban Experience.* Baltimore: The Johns Hopkins University Press.

——. 1987, "Flexible Accummulation Through Urbanization: Refections on Postmodernism in American City". *Antipode* 19(3): 260–86.

——. 1989, "Between Space and Time: Reflection on Geographic Imagination". Keynote address delivered at the annual meetings of the American Geographical Association.

Hopper, Kim, E. Baxter, S. Cox and L. Kloin, 1982, *One Year Later: The Homeless Poor in New York City.* New York: Community Service Society.

Hopper, Kim and Jill Hamberg, 1985, "Economies of Makeshift: Deindustrialization and Homelessness in the New York City". *Urban Anthropology* 14(1–3): 183–236.

Kozol, Janathan, 1988, *Rachel and Her Children.* New York: Crown.

Knox, Paul, 1991, "The Restless Urban Landscape: Economic and Socio-Cultural Change and the Transformation of Metropolitan Washington, D.C.". *Annals of the Association of American Geographers,* 81(2): 181–209.

Lash, Scott, 1990, *Sociology of Postmodernism.* London: Routledge.

Mandel, Ernest, 1975, *Late Capitalism.* London: New Left Books.

Marcuse, Peter, 1985, "Gentrification, Abandoment and Displacement: Connections, Causes and Policy Responses in New York City". *Washington University Journal of Urban and Contemporary Law.*

Meyerson, Ann, 1986, "Housing Abandonment: The Role of Institutional Mortgage Lenders". In Bratt et al. (eds.), 1986.

Newman, Katherine, 1988, *Falling from Grace: The Experience of Downward Mobility in the American Middle Class.* New York: The Free Press.

Perin, Constance, 1977, *Everything in its Place: Social Order and Land Use in America* Princeton: Princeton University Press.

——. 1988, *Belonging in America: Reading Between the Lines.* Madison: University of Press Wisconsin.

Poulosp, Thomas, 1988, *Innovative Approaches to Housing the Poor: Role of Voluntary Agencies.* Trivandrum.

Rose, Dan, 1987, *Black American Street Life,* South Philadelphia, 1969, 1971. Philadelphia, University of Pennsylvania Press.

Salerno, D. et al., 1984, *Hardship in the Heartland: Homelessness in Eight U.S. Cities.* New York: Community Services Society.

Savitch, H.V., 1988, *Postindustrial Cities.* Princeton: Princeton U. Press

Trachtenberg, Alan, 1982, *The Incorporation of America.* New York: Hill and Wang.

Williams, Brett, 1988, *Upscaling the Downtown: Stalled Gentrification in Washington D.C.* Ithaca: Cornell University Press.

18 The Aesthetics of Production and Consumption

> Man has become the object of science for man only since automobiles have become harder to sell than to manufacture.
>
> — John Kenneth Galbraith

> We don't realize how much the current indoctrination into systematic and organized consumption is the *equivalent and the extension, in the twentieth century, of the great indoctrination of rural populations into industrial labor*. [...] Having socialized the masses into a labor force, the industrial labor force, the industrial system had to go further in order to fulfill itself in consumption. The ideology of consumption would have us believe that we have entered a new era, and that a decisive "human revolution" separates the grievous and heroic Age of Production from the euphoric Age of Consumption, where justice has finally been restored to Man and to his desires. But there is no truth in this. Production and Consumption are, *one and the same grand logical process in the expanded reproduction of productive forces and of their control.*
>
> — Jean Baudrillard (1988)
> "Consumer Society," p. 51 (emphaśes in the original)

> An aesthetic sociology [...] would entail an attentiveness to the different kinds of shape and significance that humans give to their creativity; it must involve historically specific investigation into that aspects of humans that problematizes them as free beings, that is, as capable of a creative and autonomous elaboration of life. An aesthetic sociology would not, then, be in any sense an *aestheicist* sociology, but would be a sociology concerned with the aesthetic problematization of life as a work of freedom. And the very existence of such a sociology might itself be indicative of the state of society's involvement in the question of freedom.
>
> — Thomas Osborne (1997), "The Aesthetic Problematic", p. 130

The last quarter of 20th century has witnessed profound changes in self, culture and societies in advanced industrial countries – changes which are now becoming globalized. One significant aspect of this change involves an aestheticization of life, which deconstructs the space of the social as a space of structure and control and makes it a flexible space of mediation, mutuality and sociality, inhabited by the reflexive individuals. This general aesthetic turn is however full of contradictory implications and the task before us is to understand these and critically interrogate its root assumptions in order to create a dignified society which nurtures dignified relationships among individuals (cf. Dave and Roberts 1996). As we shall see in the course of this dialogue, on the one hand, aestheticization of contemporary life promises the potential for generation of aesthetic reflexivity and creativity in us. Such a turn can create a generalized context for the cultivation of the subtler dimension of our life and help us make a move from the raw, gross and the grotesque.[1] It can enable us to attain the sublime in the very ordinary facts, figures, routines and objects of our life. At the same time, aesthetic turn also carries the dangers of a narrow conceptualization of beauty and aesthetic pleasure where one's sense of beauty is confined to attractive signs and charismatic leaders and is not related to expanding webs of relationships in society. Thus, the task before us at the contemporary juncture of the so-called aesthetic turn in human history is not to be swayed by its alluring temptations and cultivate a relational meaning of aesthetics where beauty of signs and objects is integrally related to the quest for a beautiful society and qualitatively rich relationships. As the contemporary aesthetic turn is integrally linked with the aestheticized consumption of a few, a mode of consumption which is dependent on the blood, sweat and tears of many who constitute the wretched of the earth, the challenge before us is to carry out a critique of elitism of the contemporary aesthetic turn and its integral hedonism. As American social critic Christopher Lasch (1995) reminds us, we are now confronted with a new revolt, the revolt of the elites,[2] who betray the spirit of democracy of our times, and this revolt calls for a critique of their hedonistic consumption and domination. When the elitist bearers of aesthetic turn reduce the meaning of aesthetics to vicarious consumption of culture, the task before us is to realize that aesthetics also means asceticism. To cultivate an aesthetic approach to life and existence and to consider life as a work of art requires of us to cultivate a reverential attitude to it in contrast to the hegemony of the utilitarian motive in the contemporary aesthetic turn. As one recent insightful commentator urges us to realize: to treat life as a work of art means to cultivate a sense of "disinterestedness" which means to have "comportment towards the beautiful that is devoid of all ulterior references to use" (Osborne 1997: 107). And, this requires an "ascetic commitment" which is facilitated by the "elaboration of ourselves for the release of what has proper worth only in itself" (ibid).

Production and Consumption

With this as a prelude to our conversation, let us understand the manifestation of the contemporary aesthetic turn in different domains of our lives. Let us start with the domain of production. The production process in advanced industrial societies, which is now spreading out to the selected areas of production in other parts of the globe, is going through an aesthetic transmutation. The aesthetic turn in the process of production in contemporary industrial capitalism refers to the increasing production of aesthetic objects as well as the aestheticization of the very process of production itself. Contemporary students of such processes tell us that the objects of production here are not material objects but "reflexive objects, produced through an aesthetic operation" (ibid.: 113). The objects of production are cultural objects, which are characterized by their aesthetic appeal. Describing the aesthetic character of and turn in contemporary production, sociologists Scott Lash and John Urry write in their exciting

Economies of Signs and Space: "What is increasingly produced are not objects but signs. These signs are of two types. Either they have a primarily cognitive content and are post-industrial or informational goods. Or they have primarily an aesthetic content and are what can be termed postmodern goods. The development of the latter can be seen not only in the proliferation of objects which possess a substantial aesthetic component (such as pop music, cinema, leisure, magazines, video and so on), but also in the increasing component of sign-value or image embodied in material objects. This aestheticization of material objects takes place in the production, circulation or the consumption of such goods" (Lash and Urry 1996).

Here, it must be noted that research and design (the R&D side) play a greater role in the production process now. This is as much true of the manufacturing industries as the culture industries. For Lash and Urry, "More work is proportionately going on in developing models, and less work in producing them" (ibid.: 122). Here, what goes on in culture industries provides the paradigm for industrial production. In culture industries "greater proportion of work goes on in 'developing' the model – by the pop band and book author. And much less goes on in the 'production' of the model once it is developed [...]. That is, in the culture industries R&D is the main activity, while production is secondary" (ibid).

The significance of research and reflection in production has been accompanied by rise of what Lash and Urry call "reflexive production". It is reflexive production in the sense that much work must go into the design of new products; these are typically long-cycle, job-tasks entailing a whole series of judgments and decisions between alternatives in regard to product quality and process optimality" (ibid). Here, employees "must make decisions more often on the best process suited for new products". Those engaged in production now must be reflexive and creative and this must be registered in their 'shop floor' habitus. As Lash and Urry help us understand this: "This sort of reflexive economic actor is no longer to such a great extent circumscribed by the constraints of 'structure,' subject to the rules and resources of the shop floor. Instead he/she operates at some distance from these rules and resources; he/she makes decisions as to alternative rules and resources; and he/she is finally responsible for the continuous transformation of both shop floor rules and (in process and product) resources" (ibid).

The aesthetic turn in the production process transgresses the familiar, conventional and still-prevalent dichotomies between infrastructure and superstructure, economy and culture. For example, the conventional idea in culture industries is that what the author does is production, while the process of duplication is 'reproduction'. But, in real economy, "what is commonly called reproduction is in reality production. And what is called production is in fact design, product development or R&D" (ibid.: 123). In the aestheticized production, production of culture does not follow the logic of commodity production in the manufacturing industry. While the aestheticization of production in the manufacturing sector is something recent, this has been the case with the culture industries for a long time, even in the heydays of Fordism and industrial mass production. "Whereas the sign value has only challenged the use and exchange value of manufactured goods more recently in culture industries, both use-value and exchange value have always been sign values" (ibid.). But now this fact of culture industry is being globalized: production in general is becoming "not just more knowledge infused, not just a question of raw primacy of information processing, but of more generic symbolic-processing capacities" (ibid). In this context, *"the economy is increasingly culturally inflected and culture is more and more economically inflected.* Thus, the boundaries between the two become more and more blurred and the economy and culture no longer function in regard to one another as system and environments" (ibid.: 64; emphasis added).

The aestheticization of production takes place in the context of a post-industrial transition. As is well-known, post-industrial transition is characterized by the ascendancy of the service sector and the relative decline of the manufacturing sector. Post-industrial transition is also characterized by the rise of knowledge-based production, the rise of high-tech industries and the de-industrialization of the manufacturing sector.

The aesthetics of production in contemporary capitalism goes hand in hand with the aestheticization of consumption. It refers to the fact that the valued objects of consumption today are increasingly not the conventional material goods but the aestheticized symbolic goods. But aestheticized consumption also refers to the aesthetics and telos of the very process of consumption itself. It refers to the familiar phenomenon of Veblen's conspicuous consumption, which however is no longer an idiosyncratic attribute. Consumption has now become a new religion inasmuch as it provides meaning to individual lives and defines our sense of purpose and *purusartha.* It is in the sphere of consumption that people now "seek to express their sense of freedom, their personal power, status aspirations" (Tomlinson 1990).

In order to understand the aestheticization of consumption, it is essential to understand the new symbology of consumption. Earlier commodities were thought of primarily in terms of their functional utility and integrity but now the "commodity has acquired, in late consumer capitalism, an aura beyond just its function" (ibid.: 9). It now performs the function of distinction; it distinguishes one individual from another and a group from the other. As French sociologist Jean Baudrillard, who has continuously striven to help us understand the socially structured and compulsive character of contemporary consumption, tells us, "In the field of connotations the object takes on the value of a sign. In this way a washing machine serves as an equipment and plays as an element of comfort, or, of prestige, etc. It is the field of play that is specifically the field of consumption" (Baudrillard quoted in Lee 1993: 23).

The rise of aestheticized consumption challenges us to understand the complexity of consumption as an attribute of fantasy rather than as a function of human need and use value. In certain reflections on the human condition, such as the Marxian and the Gandhian, the realization of use value is accorded much significance. But, both Marx[3] and Gandhi have a simplistic notion of use value inasmuch as they fail to understand the creation of needs and their presentation as indispensable use values. But, in the contemporary aestheticized consumption, "the organic relation between needs and material use is shattered as consumption becomes increasingly determined by desire and fantasy" (Haug 1994: 20). But desire and fantasy do not work in the vacuum; they are as much a part of the generalized climate of consumption – a climate where the titillation of individual desire is the primary object of production – as it is a part of individual psychology. Such desire and fantasy is also "founded on the aestheticized appearance of the modern commodity form" (Lee 1993: 20). The real ideal of commodity aesthetics is "to deliver the absolute minimum of use-value, disguised and staged by a maximum of seductive illusion ..." (ibid).

In the aestheticized consumption, objects of consumption turn into subjects – subjects of seduction. Commodities now seduce us through their sexual appeal As W.F. Haug tells us in his provocative work, *Critique of Commodity Aesthetics:* "All manners of goods are enveloped by [the surface of sexuality], and this background of sexual enjoyment becomes the commodity's most popular attire, or the gilded backdrop against which the commodity appears" (Haug 1994: 72).

The aestheticized consumption via the appropriation and consumption of symbolic goods works as a marker of distinction in case of both individuals and groups. For instance, the new classes in contemporary capitalism strive to distinguish themselves as a group through their mode of consumption. For these classes, the object of consumption is nothing other than pure symbolic utility. "It is this mode of consumption, in its signifying capacity of a superior difference, which is exchanged with other (inferior) modes of consumption and which valorizes the capital of the group and may elicit for them cultural profits" (Lee 1993: 172).

Towards a Critique

The rule of commodities as sign values "represents the final triumph, of capitalism in its attempt to impose a cultural order compatible with the demands of large-scale commodity production" (ibid.: 23–24). "Individuals have here been reduced to the status of mere consumers, and consumers have become nothing but the vehicles for the transmission of controlled and predetermined differences [...]" (ibid). The valorization of consumption has made human beings passive and also devoid of seeking of any larger meaning of life. This is depicted provocatively in the novel *American Psycho* where the protagonist is a perfect embodiment of aestheticized consumption. The hero Bateman is a young wall street financier and is an archetypal yuppie. But, he is also a violent, psychopathic killer. As Lee interprets his case for us: "Bateman personifies the dark reality of modem consumer culture when it is taken to its logical ends. [...] Bateman's consciousness itself is assembled from nothing other than fragments of the commodity form; it is a consciousness from which all social meaning has been evacuated save that evoked by the endless succession of commodity-signs through which Bateman's experiences are channeled" (ibid.: 176).

But even in case of the elites of society who are the bearers of aestheticized consumption, consumption does not and cannot provide them self-actualization and fulfilment in stark contrast to what they are made to believe by the ideologues of consumption. What to speak of self-actualization, it also does not fulfil the need for pleasure on our part since in our act of aestheticized consumption which we mistake as a source of pleasure and happiness, we are not satisfying ourselves – our needs and urges for happiness – but are letting ourselves inside the traps set for us by the champions of aestheticized consumption and production. And, here again, Baudrillard provides us much invaluable insights. In his words, "As a social logic, the system of consumption is established on the basis of the denial of pleasure. Pleasure no longer appears as an objective, as a rational end, but as the individual rationalization of a process whose objectives are elsewhere. Pleasure would define consumption *for itself*, as autonomous and final. But consumption is never thus. Although we experience pleasure for ourselves we never do it on our own (the isolated consumer is the carefully maintained illusion of the *ideological* discourse on consumption)" (Baudrillard 1988: 46). And, from Baudrillard, it is not difficult to carry out a dialogue with the distinguished normative sociologist of our times Robert Bellah who tells us along with his equally engaging co-authors in the book *Good Society:* "Consumerism denies the needs of the poor in the name of our own anxious desire. But, most of all, consumerism kills the soul, as any good Augustinian can see, because it places things before the valuing of God and human community" (Bellah et al., 1991).

From a critique of consumption, now let us come towards a critique of production. The post-industrial transition in advanced industrial societies, which has created the condition for the rise of aestheticized production, has not transcended its dependence on the industrial mode. As it happens, many of the industries, which risk the ecology of advanced industrial societies, are being relocated to the poor countries of the world. The de-industrialization of the advanced societies has gone hand in hand with the most brutal industrialization of the peripheries with scant regards to the requirements of environment and those of human capital. The material infrastructure of the aestheticized production is provided by the resources extracted from the cheap labour and other advantages of the developing countries. The aestheticized production crucially depends upon the industrial mode of production for its basic sustenance and survival. But, the industrial mode of production is dependent upon the non-industrial mode of production and forms of life for its basic survival – not simply for profit-making. As economist N. Georgescou-Roegen had told more than a quarter century ago, the industrial mode of production operates through severe thermodynamic constraints; its superior terms of trade with forms such as agriculture is parallelled by its negative thermodynamic equations. The industrial mode is incapable of autonomous reproduction and cannot survive unless 'low entropy is pumped from the environment into the economic process" (Georgescou-Roegen 1971). Anthropologist Alf Hornborg also helps us understand this: "Whereas hunter gatherers, even in areas such as the Kalahari desert, may retrieve 9.6 times the energy they spend on hunting and gathering, industrial agriculture often yields only a fraction of the total, human-orchestrated energy input. Such a wasteful mode of production can only continue as long as it is 'subsidized' by an asymmetric world trade in energy" (1992: 10). In this context, the "technomass of industrial society must be fed specific kind of substances in order to grow" (ibid.).

But, the real problem with the industrial mode, which is now repeated in its post-industrial guise, is the problem of imperialism. Hornborg calls it "thermodynamics of imperialism". The thermodynamic need of the industrial mode compels it to subjugate other modes of livelihood – which are based upon relatively more favourable entropic configuration and which do not suffer from the same thermodynamic constraint – to its own logic of production and reproduction. This leads to the destruction of the self-subsistent modes of production in the world – a destruction which is in full swing now in the current phase of globalization and marketization of human provisions. What people could produce on their own now must be purchased from the market and their bases of self-sustenance and nurturance are being systematically destroyed by the regnant system of production, which is engulfing the world today.

At the same time, the second law of thermodynamics works as an energy-quality marker and provides a guide to the utilization of resources to the grave detriment of the poor and all those who are outside the structure of modern industrial sector, its safe "system world". Philosopher and technologist C.V. Seshadri helps us understand this. For him, "the law of entropy, backed by authority, provides a criterion for the utilization of energy available from various sources. This criterion, known as the concept of efficiency, is corollary to the law of entropy and came to existence along with the law. The efficiency criterion stipulates that this loss of available energy in a conversion becomes smaller as the temperature at which the conversion is effected is higher above the ambient. Therefore, high temperatures are of high value and so are resources such as petroleum, coal etc. [...]" (Seshadri quoted in Alvares 1988: 89). It is no wonder then that "modern energetic is only a tool to allocate resources so as to promote modern industry and modem lifestyle at enormous costs to those outside the modern structures" (Sahashrabudhey 1988: 40).

But those who are outside the system world today are not only the non-industrial forms of life in the periphery but also people at the core. Poverty and unemployment are chronic problems in post-industrial societies, which valorize aestheticized production and consumption. Lash and Urry look at this problem as a problem of lack of participation on the part of the poor in the communication flows of society. For them, the underclass is outside the communication structures of the contemporary economy of signs. But they do not realize that such exclusion is generated by the structure of industrialism and post-industrialism itself. Let us consider here the problem of poverty in advanced industrial societies. The poor have free time and free labour but they cannot sell these in the market. Without the mediation of money, market and capital, time and labour have no autonomous significance and capacity for production of goods and well-being. The present socio-economic institutions, as the noted political sociologists Claus Offe and Rolph Heinze (1992) write in their provocative *Beyond Employment,* cannot exploit the activity potential of the poor at present lying unused. The poor today do not have any institutional access for the utilization of their free time and free labour without the mediation of the market and the logic of market works through the principle that full employment is an impossibility. This constitutes what Offe and Heinze call a "modernization trap". Because the alternative traditions of production, uses of time, sharing of labour, creation of well-being through co-operative labour[4] have been destroyed by industrial modernization, the excluded, unemployed and the poor in the core as well as periphery have no resource to fall back upon (Giri 1996). A critique of industrial production must lead us to a critique of the institution of wage labour itself.

The aestheticization of production and consumption is part of the broader aestheticization of life which has brought about the decline of the social in society inasmuch as social structures are now being replaced by communicative structures (Lash and Urry 1994). But, the decline of the social is fraught with dangerous consequences if its celebration is not accompanied by efforts to create new relationships between the self and the other. The celebration of the aesthetic turn for its engendering of a reflexive subjectivity must not make us blind to the fact that these reflexive individuals are narcissistic and their world view is governed by the philosophy of negative freedom and withdrawal from a larger public discourse.

It is true that interlocutors such as Theodore Adorno have celebrated the aesthetic turn as containing the germs of an emancipatory critique at the contemporary juncture. Adorno claimed that "with the marginalization of class struggle critique today has passed from working class to the aesthetic realm" (Lash and Urry 1994: 142). Lash and Urry interpret the significance of Adorno's agenda for us: "Adorno's agenda was crucially a very 'hands-on' aesthetic, featuring not abstract reason, but the concrete working through of the possibilities in the aesthetic material" (ibid.: 143). For Lash and Urry, "these aesthetic materials are to be largely found among circulating signs of the information and communication structures. Thus, the flows of signs of the various culture industries also provide the materials for aesthetic critique. On the reception-side this is conducive not just to niche-marketed individuation, but simultaneously to authentic aesthetic-reflexive individualization" (ibid.).

But how is such a reflexive individualization at work? The referred to critical and reflexive individualization is at best a sign today which has some social referents in the work of the new social movements in advanced industrial societies (Giri 1997a). But, by and large, it is narcissism and lack of political-moral judgment which rules the roost today. The aestheticization of everyday life works through the ubiquity and deification of popular culture objects and culture figures. The aestheticization of social life today goes hand in hand with the aestheticization of politics and new racism which seeks to annihilate the other for the sake of preservation of one's authentic identity and one's aesthetic pleasure (see Giri 1998; Stolcke 1995).

The aestheticization of politics works through hero worship. David Harvey (1989) calls it "aesthetics of empowerment" which is an illusion of empowerment since it does not lead to the empowerment of individuals but to their vicarious dependence on charismatic leaders. It is charismatic leaders – whether it is a Reagan or a Thatcher or a Yeltsin – who guide our imagination now. These leaders have done everything for the destruction of the social space through their image-based politics. Historically, aestheticized politics has gone hand in hand with the rule of fascism whose ontological ground is the lack of critical judgements in the life of individuals. It is no wonder then that Lash and Urry themselves write: "The negative consequences of this are that the ubiquity and centrality of such popular culture objects [...] *can swamp the moral-practical categories available to young people*" (Lash and Urry 1996: 133; emphasis added).

In the regime of aestheticized production and consumption, culture is an important factor. But, the meaning of culture here is a narrow one; as an object of production and consumption it does not have any link to a larger meaning of life – a meaning which can provide us a framework to evaluate the significance and worth of our lives. The dissolution of the distinction between "high culture" and "low culture" today has made culture devoid of any transcendental and ontological significance. But every lived culture contains within it a dimension of ideal seeking vis-à-vis self-realization, modes of inter-subjectivity and the constitution of a good society. For a philosopher, such as G.C. Pande (1989), cultural realization is not confined only to self-satiating activities but is inevitably linked with efforts to reach out to the other. Culture refers to a dialectical process of value seeking in the life of individuals where to seek a value means to "seek progress in infinite direction" (Pande 1982: 25). At the societal level, such a transcendental vision and reality of culture refers to a moral order which seeks to inspire all members of a society to be concerned with each other's well-being and to create the collective foundations for a good society. The moral order of culture inspires individuals of a social group for "the formulation of the vision of the good into a path of praxis" (ibid.: 29) – a praxis whose motto is the realization of happiness for all. The aspirations such as *"Sarve Bhabantu Sukhino, Sarve Santhu Niramaya, Sarve Bhadrani Pashyantu, Ma Kaschid Dukhabag Bhabct* [Let everybody be happy, let everybody be free from disease, let all see good things and let nobody be unhappy]" are the essence of culture. Thus, a radical universality and urge to reach out to the other characterizes cultural seeking and cultural realization.

Once we understand the meaning of the vision and practice of culture in this sense of radical universality, how do we understand/make sense of the work of culture in the contemporary regime of aestheticized production and consumption? The process of production and consumption is now not driven by the goal of providing well-being to everybody in society. If this were the case, we would not have to live with such debilitating misery and poverty despite the existence of so much wealth and progress in science and technology. Moreover, cultural realization in the life of individuals is not being accompanied by an integral desire to reach out to the fellow beings. If one loves eating ice cream, then any genuine cultural realization also creates an urge within oneself to bring it to as many people as possible. It is akin to Gurudev Tagore's experiential statement on love where love cannot hide itself in a dark corner but inevitably radiates like a light into the whole world. But now our modes of lives are tying us to our own caves where we are satisfied with our own consumption alone. Consumption of culture has become so privatized that it is divorced from any larger public sphere and a concern about the well-being of other human beings.

Anthropologist Edward Sapir had made a distinction between "genuine culture" and "spurious culture" more than half a century ago. For Sapir, a genuine culture is characterized by the quality of human heart and human relationships what Sapir called *"herzenbildung"* (Sapir 1966). From this point of view what we see today in the regime of aestheticized production and consumption is not the work of genuine culture but the dance of spurious culture. It is a culture which has no concern for the collective foundations of well-being and is not animated by a desire to guarantee minimum happiness to all. Thus, contrary to the celebration of the cultural turn in production and consumption *a la* Lash and Urry, what we urgently need is a cultural criticism of contemporary capitalism as an institutional regime. For this, the meaning of culture itself has to be radically expanded and deepened. This expansion and deepening have to be made a matter of quantum leap in the life and relationships of individuals. As Alf Hornborg (1993: 317) argues, "The counterdrive to total commoditization is the cognitive discrimination we know as culture."

And, as the transformative Indian critic Chitta Ranjan Das argues, culture is not a *sampatti* – a property to be possessed but a *prerana* – an inspiration to live for and live by (Das 1992; also Giri 1997b). Realizing the inspirational and depth dimension of culture will make us realize that aestheticized production, such as the production of aesthetically beautiful and lofty apartments, is a vital part of the speculative regime of late capitalism which makes many people homeless. In fact, aestheticized production is a sign of the shift from production to speculation where speculation on basic human needs becomes the primary source behind the "valorization of capital".

One important aspect of the aesthetic orientation is the significance it attaches to the worth of the particular. Many theoreticians of aesthetics – from Kant to Adorno – have drawn our attention to it. But how does the contemporary regime of aestheticized production and consumption relate to particular forms of life? It seeks to conquer the whole world for the sake of the market. It also seeks to make the whole world a graveyard where the flag of McDonald and Coca Cola fly high killing everybody who sells tender coconut on the streets. Those commentators who see only the expression of consumer subjectivity in the current phase of globalization of aestheticized consumption and the "McDonaldization of the World" (cf. Ritzer 1996) speak from the shores of global affluence and their livelihood itself is not at stake when the coconut vendors lose their markets to the multinationals. For instance, it was reported sometime ago in *Pragativadi*, an Oriya daily, that the vendors who were selling coconut drink in the streets were subjected to harassment by the police in the town of Satyavadi in the district of Puri in Orissa. The coconut vendors were harassed because now they must give up their occupation for the triumphant march of the Coca Colas. This instantaneously reminds one of the cutting of the fingers of the weavers of India during the British Raj. Commentators such as Carol A. Breckenridge and Arjun Appadurai would contest such reading of the contemporary scene by arguing that Americanization or commodification is not seducing the world into sameness and "creating a world of little Americas", but they look at it from the vantage point of the globalizing middle class and not from those who do not have means for food and safe drinking water and whose livelihoods are systematically being destroyed by the forces of globalization (cf. Appadurai and Breckenridge 1996).

In Quest for Alternatives: Stepping Stones for a Creative Society

Despite the thermodynamic constraint of the industrial mode, it is this which has triumphed over other modes of livelihood but since the industrial mode owes its existence to the non-industrial it has a moral responsibility to contribute to enhancing the well-being and standard of living of those who are its victims. The industrial mode must compensate for what it takes from the non-industrial mode and for the destruction of its bases of self-subsistence. This compensation must not be thought of primarily in terms of monetary subsidy and non-participatory paternalistic welfare but in terms of sustaining institutions of self-production of provisioning within them (see Joshi 1992; Unger 1987). There must exist and flourish multiple forms of production and consumption; the industrial mode now must have the moral consciousness to recognize this and contribute to its flourishing. It has a moral responsibility to enhance the functioning and capability of people living inside other modes and must exercise self-restraint and self-criticism vis-à-vis its motive of profit maximization and the propensity towards the marketization of the human condition.[5] It must also create institutions within its homeland which embody the principle of labour sharing and creation of value through exchange of labour and not money. The proponents and beneficiaries of the industrial mode must be guided by a sense of trusteeship in their relationship with people subsisting in other modes of livelihood.

It is important, as Offe (1992) again reminds us, that such a moral consciousness must have an institutional manifestation as without institutional correspondence gestures of morality face the danger of melting into thin air. A society which inhabits multiple forms of livelihood (such as Indian society which simultaneously has the industrial, agricultural and the tribal mode) must protect all and especially the vulnerable ones and in this pursuit of universal well-being it must be guided by a sense of justice. The democratic deliberations and institutions of society must ensure this. In fact, the democratic institutions of society must provide the moral resources and moral imagination to the industrial mode to fulfil its responsibility to the agricultural and the tribal mode.

There is a similar challenge vis-à-vis consumption. Today, when a majority of people do not have the ability to satisfy their basic consumption needs, fulfilment of these needs is a matter of moral responsibility on the part of the state, economy and society. But consumption today has become a religion for a few – for an exploitative and uncreative minority – but unlike other religions it lacks a connectedness to a much wider cosmos and an ultimate concern. A creative society has to think of ways to confront this challenge. While realizing the instrumental[6] significance of consumption for the generation of well-being, it must strike a middle ground. It must enable us to make 'consumption choices' (cf. Croker 1995) and help us live a balanced life – balanced between individual well-being, environmental preservation and the well-being of the humanity.

A creative society must have institutions which provide alternative values to individuals such as love, sharing, commitment to relationships, and striving for a just and good society which provides basic minimum to all. Such institutions must enable individuals to make a distinction between their "more desirable" and "less desirable" desire (cf. Offe and Preuss 1991) and to realize that consumption for the sake of consumption constitutes a "less desirable desire" which they must be able to transcend or at least put it in its place for the sake of more worthwhile realities of life such as a productive life and the building of a caring society.

But today it is the value of money and power which gets the unquestioned significance in the public spheres of contemporary societies. The stepping stones for a creative society which sings the glory of man must begin with a conquest of the public sphere for the "son of man". But considering the state in which both religion and politics are today the realization of such a goal seems an impossible task. But humankind cannot ignore this challenge forever and this challenge of basic human dignity of all must engender radical mutations in our vision and praxis now.

Notes

1. We can note here the critique of capitalism offered by Deleuze and Guattari which is an "artistic critique" for "in this critique the artist emerges as a prime example of one who affirms multiplicity" (Bell 2011: 12).
2. In the words of Lasch (1995: 25):

   > Once it was the 'revolt of the masses' that was held to threaten social order and the civilizing traditions of Western culture. In our time, however, the chief threat comes from those at the top of the social hierarchy, not the masses. Today, it is the elites – those who control the international flow of money and information, preside over philanthropic foundations and institutions of higher learning, manage the instruments of cultural production and thus set the terms of public debate – that have lost faith in the values, or what remains of them, of the West.

3. In this context, what Martyn Lee argues deserves our attention. Lee argues that for "orthodox Marxism, use value is established as the material basis for humanity's potential for self-development". But Marxian use value is "immune from processes of social determination" and 'goes "unrecognized as a repressive aspect of the commodity form' " (Lee 1993: 21).
4. As it happens in case of the tribal forms of livelihood. The late anthropologist Bikram N. Nanda (1994) has drawn our attention to this.
5. Claude Meillassoux (1981: 144) helps us understand the dangers of such marketization:

   > [...] the family is coming to be regarded, by reason of the few affectionate relationships it preserves, as one of the last bastions of individual liberty. *It is, however, a very fragile bastion, for nothing any longer predestines it to withstand the corrosive influence of money-relations; and in this we have the measure of the totalitarian menace with which capitalism is heavy.* Totalitarianism, which the bourgeoisie holds up as a bogey before the masses [...] is flourishing [...] in the foreseeable changes in capitalism, in the necessary destruction of all ties of affection. All it can put in the place of these ties is the barbarism of absolute profitability – the last stage of the metamorphosis of human beings into capital, – their strength and intelligence into commodities, and "the wild fruit of women" into investments (emphasis added).

6. What Fine and Leopold (1993: 303) write below deserves our careful consideration:

   > The rise of home entertainment/video/microwave culture is another trend that is thought to lend weight to the increasing privatization of consumption. But the efforts are no more clear-cut or unilateral in this arena. First, the rise of domestic consumption implies restructuring of the systems of provision which supply the necessary goods and services. Second, innovations designed for private consumption have sometimes enhanced collective consumption as well; the availability of the microwave and other innovations in convenience foods have bolstered the rise of eating out [...]. Third, the nature, causes and implications of the microwave culture are also intimately bound up with the increased participation of women in the work force, in a variety of ways, so that they become more socialised as consumption becomes apparently more privatized.

References

Alvares, Claud. 1988. 'Science, Colonialism and Violence: A Luddite View,' in Ashis Nandy (ed.), *Science, Hegemony and Violence: A Requiem for Modernity*. Delhi: Oxford University Press.

Appadurai, Arjun and Carol A. Breckenridge. 1996. 'Public Modernity in India', in Carol A. Breckenridge (ed.), *Consuming Modernity: Public Culture in Contemporary India*. Delhi: Oxford University Press.

Baudrillard, Jean. 1988. *Selected Writings*. Edited and Introduced by Mark Poster. Cambridge: Polity Press.

Bell, Jeffrey. 2011. "Whistle While You Work: Deleuze and the Spirit of Capitalism," *Deleuze and Ethics*, Nathan Jun and Daniel W. Smith, pp. 5-20. Edinburgh: Edinburgh University Press.

Bellah, Robert N. et al., 1991. *The Good Society*. New York: Alfred A. Knof.

Croker, David A. 1995. 'Consumption and Weil-Being.' *Report from the Institute for Philosophy and Public Policy* 15 (4): 12–17, University of Maryland, College Park: School of Public Affairs.

Dahrendorf, Ralph. 1995. *Economic Opportunity, Civil Society and Political Liberty*. Geneva: United Nations Research Institute for Social Development.

Das, Chitta Ranjan. 1992 *Sukara O Socrates* [The Pig and the Socrates]. Berhampur: Pustaka Bhandara.

Dave, Beech and John Roberts. 1996. 'Spectres of the Aesthetic,' *New Left Review* 218.

Fine, Ben and Ellen Leopold. 1993. *The World of Consumption*. London: Routledge.

Giri, Ananta K. 1996. 'Exclusion and Integration: The Moral Struggles,' *Gandhi Marg*, April-June.

——. 1997a. 'Social Movements in the Advanced Societies and the Emerging Transnational Spaces', *Guru Nanak Dev Journal of Sociology*, XVIEI (1): 1–35.

——. 1997b. 'Literature and the Tapashya of Transformation: A Glimpse into the Creative Worlds of Chitta Ranjan Das', paper presented at the National Seminar on 'Recent Trends in Literary and Cultural Criticism in Contemporary India,' Indian Institute of Advanced Studies, Shimla, November 4–7.

——. 1998. *Global Transformations: Postmodernity and Beyond*. Jaipur: Rawat Publications.

Georgescou-Roegen, N. 1971. *Entropy Law and the Economic Process*. Cambridge, MA: Harvard University Press.

Haug, W.R. 1994. 'Critique of Commodity Aesthetics', in *Polity Reader in Cultural Studies*, Cambridge: Polity Press.

Harvey, David W. 1989. *The Condition of Postmodernity: An Inquiry into the Origins of Cultural Change*. Cambridge, MA: Basil Blackwell.

1996. *Justice, Nature and the Geography of Difference*. Cambridge, MA: Basil Blackwell.

Hornborg, Alf. 1992. 'Machine Fetishism, Value and the Theory of the Unlimited Good: Towards a Thermodynamics of Imperialism,' *Man* (n.s.).

——. 1993. 'Money and Meaning: Towards a Multi-Centric Economy', in *Entropy and Bioeconomics*, Milano: European Association for Bioeconomic Studies.

Joshi, Nandini. 1992. *Development without Destruction*. Ahmedabad: Navjivan Press.

Lasch, Christopher. 1995. *The Revolt of the Elites and the Betrayal of Democracy*. New York: W.W. Norton & Co.

Lash, Scott and John Urry. 1994. *Economics of Sign and Space*. London: Sage.

Lee, Martyn J. 1993. *Consumer Culture Reborn: The Cultural Politics of Consumption*. London: Routledge.

Meilliassoux, Claude. 1981. *Maidens, Meal and Money: Capitalism and the Domestic Community*. Cambridge: Cambridge University Press.

Nanda, Bikram N. 1994. *Contours of Continuity and Change: The Story of the Bonda Highlanders*. New Delhi: Sage.

Offe, Claus and Ulirch K. Preuss. 1991. 'Democratic Institutions and Moral Resources', in David Held (ed.), *Political Theory Today*. Cambridge: Polity Press.

Offe, Claus. 1992. 'Bindings, Shackles, Brakes: On Self-Limitation Strategies', in Alex Honneth (ed.), *Cultural-Political Intervention in the Unfinished Project of Enlightenment*. Cambridge, MA: The MIT Press.

Offe, Claus and Rolph G. Heinze. 1992. *Beyond Employment*. Cambridge: Polity Press.

Osborne, Thomas. 1997. 'The Aesthetic Problematic', *Economy and Society*, 26(1): 126–147.

Pande, G.C. 1982. 'The Nature of Social Categories', in Ravinder Kumar (ed.), *Philosophical Categories and Social Reality*. Delhi: Allied Publishers.

——. 1989. *The Meaning and Process of Culture: As Philosophy of History*. Allahabad: Raka Prakashan.

Ritzer, George. 1996. 'McDonaldization Theses: Is Expansion Inevitable?' *International Sociology*, 11 (3): 291–308.

Sahashrabudhey, Sunil. 1988. 'Freedom from the Degrading Laws of a Degrading Order', Working Paper, Gandhian Institute of Studies, Varanasi.

Sapir, Edward. 1966. 'Culture, Genuine and Spurious,' in David Mandelbaum (ed.), *Culture, Language and Personality*. Berkeley: University of California Press.

Seshadri, C.V. 1982 *Development and Thermodynamics*. Madras: Murugappa Chettiar Research Centre.

Stolcke, Verena. 1995. 'Talking Culture: New Boundaries, New Rhetorics of Exclusion." *Current Anthropology*, 36 (1): 1–24.

Tomlinson, Alan. 1990. 'Introduction: Consumer Culture and the Aura of Commodity,' in Alan Tomlinson. (ed.), *Consumption, Identity and Style: Marketing, Meanings, and the Packaging of Leisure*. London: Routledge.

Unger, Robert M. 1987. *False Necessity: Anti-Necessitarian Social Theory in the Service of Radical Democracy*. Cambridge: Cambridge University Press.

19 Globalizing Economy and the Calling of Dialogues

Carrying out this dialogue on globalizing economy and the civilizational agenda in Bangkok,[1] it is helpful to begin our conversation with Sulak Sivaraksha (2006), the noted critic from Thailand:

> Tolerance for socio-economic diversity and alternative models of development is terribly low to the point of being non-existent. The global economy is the only future. Refusing to accept this rationale is a sign of weakness, immaturity and inferiority [...] The global economy does not really cherish a diversity of ideas, cultures, aspirations and views. The diverse ways of life worldwide are increasingly dancing to the same tune of culture/ideology of consumerism which insists that ultimate happiness can be achieved by the never-ending consumption of goods and services.

Sivaraksha's above critique of the contemporary globalizing economy suggests the need for a dialogue in thinking about not only the global economy but economy itself. Sarvaksha begins from his Buddhist starting point, a Buddhism "with a small b"[2] and here we can begin from each of our perspectival, cultural, religious and civilizational starting print in a non-valorizing and dialogical way and think of economies as different forms of life rather than just a machine for the production of profit. Such an engagement in dialogue is facilitated by a parallel thought offered by Johan Galtung who tells us in his dialogue with Daisaku Ikeda: "Development must concentrate on decreasing *dukha* or suffering. This is certainly not synonymous with economic growth as it is understood today. The dimension that really matters is the *dukha-sukha* (suffering-happiness) ratio" (Galtung and Ikeda 1994).

This calls for rethinking not only the contemporary globalizing economy but economy itself. For C.T. Kurien (2000), an inspiring economist from India, no matter what has happened in the name of different alternative experiments from socialism to capitalism and now to neo-liberal economic globalization, the relationship between economy and human beings is still the unresolved question. This question continues to be the subject of transformative strivings in both theory and practice. In his *Rethinking Economics: Reflections based on the Study of Indian Economy* (1996), Kurien makes a distinction between economics and economy. Economy is a field of relationship while economics is a disciplinary reflection on it. In the contemporary moment of neo-liberal economic globalization the disciplinary reflection has become narrower and narrower even forgetting the much broader concerns of its founders such as Adam Smith who was concerned with moral sentiments not to speak of the critical tradition of political economy of Karl Marx and varieties of experiments on alternative economies in the human history.

We need to think about economy as a multi-dimensional field consisting of overlapping circles of markets, state and family.

Economies as Forms of Life and Ontology of Economics: A Multi-Valued Logic of Autonomy and Interpenetration

Irene van Staveren (2001) talks about the ontology of economic life and value of economics from an Aristotelian perspective. An Aristotelian perspective also influences the work of Amartya Sen (1999) who critiques contemporary preoccupation with economic growth. Sen is a critique of utilitarianism and neo-classical economics. His capability approach offers some critique of contemporary neo-liberal economic globalization but the Aristotelian roots of both Sen and van Staveren needs to be opened to further cultural and trans-civilizational dialogues. From the Aristotelian perspective self is a techno-practitioner and in the field of economics it gets manifested itself as homo economicus. But homo economicus as techno-practitioner also co-exists with self as transcendental or self as *anatta* (non-self) as it is in Buddhist tradition. Contemporary rethinking of economics from an Aristotelian perspective needs to acknowledge the transcendental dimension of self. This can provide new imaginations and practical possibilities to contemporary transformative concerns such as a deeper view of human well-being, and economics and happiness. This raises question not only about what is economy – the ontology of economic life – but also what it means to be human. Contemporary globalizing economy proceeds with a narrow Euro-American view of being human with primacy on profit maximization and this needs to be opened up for trans-cultural and trans-civilisational dialogues from varieties of our locations and traditions of our world.

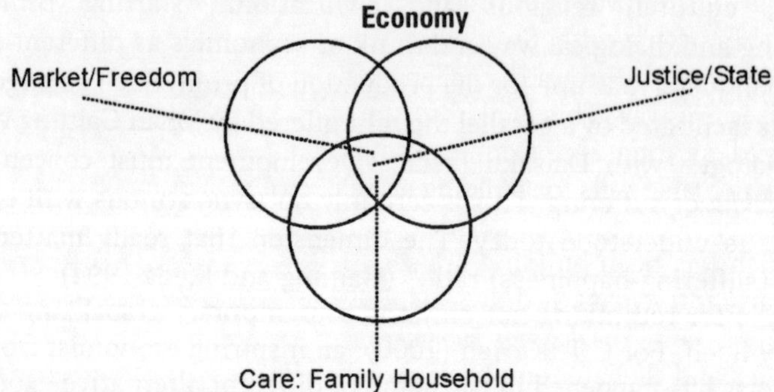

Economics as Forms of Life and the Quest for a Good Society: Glimpses from Different Traditions and the Calling of Dialogues

I would like to clarify that I am not using culture, religion and civilization as synonym with each other nor each of them as unitary. Each of them are complex articulations for human flourishing with traditions of heterodoxies not only orthodoxies. With this, let us consider the way different religious traditions think of economy and challenge practitioners to strive for good society.

In the Islamic tradition, interest on loan is banned and a premium is placed on welfare of the community – the *umma*. Though this has been the normative articulation, its practical realization has varied in society and history. In Hindu perspective wealth is treated as *Laxmi*, which means not only prosperity but also beauty. This beauty has a much broader connotation of beauty radiating in dignified relationships in a prosperous and creative society. This challenges us to understand the relationship between economics and aesthetics. Where only a few people in a society lead a life of over-possession and over-consumption while many lead a life of misery and destitution it is ugly. On the other hand, where all members of society can fulfil themselves materially as well spiritually and there is a smile in everybody's face it is a condition of contagious social beauty. It is this sense of social aesthetics which can now challenge contemporary preoccupations in welfare economics by taking it to deeper and higher levels of quality of life, quality of social relationships and nature of dignity. This way *artha* (economy) is not divorced from *dharma* (path of righteous conduct) and *moksha* (salvation).[3]

Swadhyaya is a socio-religious movement from contemporary Hindu space which seeks to generate what it calls *Apouresheya Laxmi* (impersonal wealth) from different projects of co-operative devotional labour. The idea of devotional labour is different from the familiar conceptions of voluntary labour. In devotional labour one realizes that one is not the sole actor. God is a co-labouring actor in all one's acts of labour and thus one cannot lay exclusive proprietary claim to the fruits of this labour. In the villages of Gujarat and Maharashtra where Swadhyaya is active its practitioners take a piece of land on lease and cultivate it on the basis of devotional labour, i.e., for this labour no one is paid. But, the harvest does not belong either to the individual or community but to God. This has a much wider global significance. After collapse of state socialism we have come to realize that neither socialization nor etatization (state take over) of property is not enough for coming out of the ravages of private capital. What needs to be practised is a new relationship with wealth. Swadhyaya's vision of impersonal wealth, in spite of its own failings on the ground[4], challenges us to relate to wealth in a new way – in a non-possessive way. This is akin to the spirit of trusteeship as Gandhi had also challenged us long ago. Gandhi also challenges us to build an inclusive economics, which also calls for building an inclusive self and inclusive polity.

Habitat for Humanity is a socio-religious movement from Christian tradition which has been building houses for low-income families around the world for nearly forty years. It draws inspiration from the Christian tradition of *Economics of Jesus* and *Theology of Hammer*, the former pleading for sharing of one's resources and the later emphasizing labour for solving concrete problems of the world such as the problem of housing for poor. Theology of Hammer urges practitioners to hold hammer and build houses for and with the poor. There are many contemporary critical engagements with Christian economic thought. Some of it offer a radical critique of contemporary marketization of man and the globe. For example, taking inspiration from his Christian heritage, Desmond Tutu (2005) argues that it is a sacrilege to treat one as worthless because one is not successful. For him, every being is inherently imbued with worth. Similarly, Irene van Staveren (2006) presents some glimpses from Dutch Christian economic thought. Some strands of it emphasize that using one's talent in an appropriate way is a Christian moral obligation.

We can invite here glimpses from our tribal heritage of humanity as well. In tribal modes of production co-operative labour and sharing are primary modes of production and distribution. This co-operative mode is also at work in varieties of co-operative movements in our modern world, some of which have been described for us by Dada Mahesvarananda (2002) in his *After Capitalism*.

Beyond the Globalizing Economy

Thus globalizing economy is not destined to be imprisoned in the logic of neo-liberal global capitalism which is the dominant economic model now. It also calls for understanding the multiverse of economy as a field of relationship, of happiness, beauty and quest for human and social excellence. But this calls for a new ontology of economy where it is a relational field and a new view of self and society. A new economics calls for an appropriate self-development, a new model of self-realization going beyond the contemporary model of self-realization through money and profit maximization. It also calls for new models of societal and collective realizations. Thus globalizing economy calls for self-development, inclusion of the other and planetary realizations. Economics as planetary realization takes into consideration our fragile ecology and also the issue of global justice not only for the vulnerable human beings but also non-human beings (Giri 2006; Nussbaum 2006, also see the following chapter). Contemporary ecological economics and movement such as fair trade provide intimations to us of a different economics of self-development and planetary realizations.

Notes

1. This was first presented in a seminar at Chulalongkorn University, Bangkok in March 2006.
2. By Buddhism with a small b, Sivaraksha urges us to understand the significance of humility in talking about our religions and traditions. This can challenge all of us to bring perspectives from our religions, cultures and traditions in a spirit of small r, c, and t. In thinking about self, culture, society and economy we can draw upon multiple traditions of humanity but with an attitude of tradition with a small t. In tune with pathways of Buddhism with a small b, we need to embody Hinduism with many small h, Christianity with a many small c, and Islam with many small i. Giani Vattimo's (2002) *After Christianity*, and Fred Dallmayr's (2005) *Small Wonder* can facilitate such an humble participation in our multiverse of conversations on cultures and economies.
3. Hindu paths of life emphasize four-fold goals – *dharma, artha, kama,* and *mokhsa*. In a spirit of multi-valued logic of autonomy and interpenetration it is helpful to realize *artha* as a circle of life is interpenetrated by not only *kama* (desire) but also by *dharma* (righteous conduct) and *moksha* (salvation).
4. My fieldwork suggests that many a time this generated impersonal wealth is not used for the upliftment of villages (cf. Giri 2008).

References

Dallmayr, Fred. 2005. *Small Wonder: Global Power and its Discontents.* Oxford: Rowman & Littlefield.

Galtung, Johan and Daisaku Ikeda. 1994. *Choose Peace.* London: Verso.

Giri, Ananta Kumar. 2006. "Cosmopolitanism and Beyond, Towards a Multiverse of Transformations.", *Development and Change* 37(6): 1277–1292.

——. 2008. *Self-Development and Social Transformations? The Vision and Practice of the Self-Study Mobilization of Swadhyaya.* Lanham, MD: Lexington Books.

Kurien, C.T. 1996. *Rethinking Economics: Reflections Based upon the Study of Indian Economy.* Delhi: Sage Publications.

——. 2000. "Globalisation: An Economist's Perspective." Manuscript.

Nussbaum, Martha. 2006. *Frontiers of Justice: Disability, Nationality, Species Membership.* Cambridge, MA: Harvard University Press.

Maheshvarananda, Dada. 2002. *After Capitalism*, Washington, D.C. Prout Publications.

Sen, Amartya. 1999. *Development as Freedom.* New York: Alfred A. Knof.

Sivaraksha, Sulak. 2006. "Buddhism and the Challenge of Modernity in the 21st Century." Paper downloaded from the internet.

Tutu, Desmond. 2005. *God Has a Dream: A New Vision of Hope for Our Times.* London: Rider.

Van Staveren, Irene. 2001. *The Values of Economics: An Aristotelian Perspective.* London: Routledge.

——. 2006. "Dutch Christian Economic Thought." Manuscript.

Vattimo, Giani. 2002. *After Christianity.* New Your: Columbia University Press.

20 Global Justice and the Calling of Peace

Peace and justice are eternal as well as epochal challenges and it is helpful to reflect further on these issues. Justice is weeping in our world today as her sisters dignity, peace and responsibility. Our everyday life and institutions that govern us from our local communities to the global structures contain many "islands of problematic justice" (cf. Habermas 1990; Giri 2002a), which block fuller realization of our potential. Institutions of problematic justice around the world block paths of universal self-realization (cf. Bhaskar 2002). Universal self-realization means that each of us have opportunity to realize our potential through a creative life of labour, love, health and learning. Many of our fellow beings around the world – and not only in the so-called developing world – are prevented from adequate opportunities for fuller self-realization, societal realization and world realization by not having opportunity to participate in creative education, love and labour. Not only millions in the world die of starvation but many, especially in the so-called affluent global North, are slowly killing themselves in their routine lives of work. They do so as servants of profit-making and life-commoditizing capital and an aggrandizing will to power. They do not have time to express themselves, be with oneself as well as each other, and be together in art, dance and music of life. This is also a condition of slavery and social death as the many millions whose lives are statistically portrayed in such figures as: one billion people live on the equivalent of less than one dollar a day,[1] and are targets of global will-formation such as Millennium Development Goals.

The project of universal self-realization that everybody should have the opportunity for their creative self-realization through unfoldment of their various capabilities and functioning – through access to education, health and creative engagement with labour, love and learning – is linked with projects of global justice. While universal justice is a part of global justice, it also involves a profound rethinking and reconstitution of justice. Today, the issue of justice is no longer the issue of mathematical equality between haves and haves not but the challenge of creating condition of fuller human realization – universal self-realization – everywhere. It is this spirit of universal self-realization that animates the moving spirit in us who weep at the fact that so many die because of hunger and so many kill themselves – albeit slowly – in the name of money and power. When individuals and institutions as slavish instruments of power and capital block our self-realization it is a question of problematic justice that urgently calls for transformative strivings. In our multi-linked globality now we find many such instances of problematic justice in the continued existence and production of poverty, disease and anxiety. Transforming these conditions of destruction of potential for fuller self-realization, co-realization and societal realization in the multiple locales of our world is a subject of global justice, and is facilitated by dialogues, including dialogues on the theme of justice and modes of its realization.

The project of global justice is multi-dimensional both in its constitutive conceptualization as well as in modes of realization. In terms of conceptualization we have to rethink global justice by rethinking the project of justice itself. In contemporary theories of justice, for example in the seminal works of John Rawls (1971), justice is primarily thought of as political and is divorced from considerations of morality. But, is justice mainly a project of politics? Does it not touch our moral concerns? Jurgen Habermas extends a primarily political conception of justice to our contemporary global predicament and writes: "The burning issue of a just global economic order poses itself primarily as a political problem [...] The unjust distribution of good fortune in the world was certainly a central concern of the great world religion. But in a secularized society, this problem primarily belongs on the political and economic table, not in the cupboard of morality" (Habermas 2002). Here, Habermas is within our habitual traditions of opposition between political and moral in thinking about and realizing justice. But overcoming this dualistic opposition is an important theoretical and practical task in our projects of justice. This also calls for overcoming another opposition in modernistic projects of justice, namely, the opposition between knowledge and sympathetic personal participation in transformation, between epistemology and ontology. Global justice involves not only knowledge of suffering in the world but also our own personal involvement in transforming the conditions of such suffering which, again, is multi-dimensional – suffering of malnutrition as well as suffering of alienation, including alienation from one's higher self, a self which strives for friendship and solidarity across the borders. As Amartya Sen would challenge us: "[...] justice across borders must not be seen merely as 'international justice' [...] A feminist activist in America who wants to help, say remedy some features of female disadvantage in Africa or Asia, draws on a sense of identity that goes well beyond the sympathies of one nation for the predicament of another" (Sen 2002: 48; also see Sen 2009).

Thus, the project of justice is a personal project, and not only a project of state and society. It is not only a matter of epistemology, a matter of instituting rights procedures and interventions but also an ontological project where ontology means practical action of labour, love and learning (cf. Giri 2004, 2006a). As Gerrry Cohen challenges us in his *If You're an Egalitarian, How Come You are so Rich?*: "[...] egalitarian justice is not only, as Rawlsian liberalism teaches, a matter of the rules that define the structure of society but also a matter of personal attitude and choice [...] a change in social ethos, a change in the attitude people sustain towards each other in the thick of daily life is necessary for producing equality" (Cohen 2000: 3). Thus global justice calls for ontological involvement not only epistemic procedures and interventions. Here such knowledge of numbers as one billion people live with less than one dollar a day is not enough. Global justice, as with justice, involves both knowledge and transformative action, epistemology and ontology going beyond the dualism between the two. It is a project of an ontological epistemology of participation where "knowledge of" is integrally linked with our manifold practices of "knowing with"(cf. Giri 2004, 2006a; Sunder Rajan 1998). In ontological epistemology of participation we learn from and with each other and in the process also transform ourselves.

There is an epochal challenge to create spaces of mutual learning and self-transformation – an ontological epistemology of participation – for nurturance and realization of global justice. The emergent global civil society through the work of varieties of movements across borders, transnational movements and NGOs, as well as the work of such forums as World Social Forums, European Social Forums, Bergen Social Forum and Brazilian Social Forum – creates spaces for an ontological epistemology of participation where all concerned can share their knowledge of suffering around the world as well as renew their commitment to transforming these conditions. This also finds a resonance in varieties of political, religious and spiritual movements around the world. Much of alternative globalization movement involves travel to varieties of alternative political experiments in the world – Brazil, Chiapas, Bangladesh, and India, for example. The socio-religious movement of Habitat for Humanity originating in the US nearly forty years ago and now working world wide has a project of global village where people from the materially affluent countries come to build houses with low-income families in low-income countries (cf. Giri 2002b). The socio-spiritual movement of Swadhyaya originating from India but also now working among diasporic Indians in England and the US, among others, has a project of *bhaktipheri* or devotional travel where people move from village to village, from one country to other, and share time and space with fellow beings (cf. Giri 2004). Global justice calls for varieties of global *bhaktipheris* – political and spiritual – and creation of global public spheres in our multiple locales of our world, in fact wherever we are and where we belong. In these global public spheres emerging locally we can discuss about issues of justice and dignity as well as take concrete steps to realize these in our lives and institutions.

John Rawls (2001), the principal philosopher of justice in 20th century, speaks about the necessity for "overlapping consensus" in realizing the project of justice. In overlapping consensus all parties may not agree about everything but they agree on some. But is overlapping consensus a matter of fixed point or fixed star? What is the process of generation of this overlapping consensus? Does not overlapping consensus involve the overlapping circles of our existence – rich and poor, happy and anxious, knowledgeable and those of us who need a hand? Overlapping consensus, which is crucial to project of justice, is facilitated by the work of overlapping circles at many levels of our interlinked globality today – self, family, community, nation, region and our worlds. Our emergent global public spheres, which emerge locally but reach out to the world in a series of concentric circles, provide a space where these different overlapping circles for example can meet and interpenetrate. The work of overlapping circles and concentric circles is a work of autonomy and interpenetration where involved actors and institutions are related with each other and continuously challenged to overcome their self-interest and domain interest and acknowledge the interpenetrative presence of the other. We can, for example, look at the issue of rich and poor. If the poor people in the world continue to live a life of degradation, then, it is not good for the rich even from the point of view of their own interest. Similarly, if the poor wish to kill all the rich, it also does not contribute to their own self-interest. At the same time, the logic of self-interest alone is not enough for such a realization; we need to overcome our self-interest as the sole criterion and acknowledge the other. But overcoming one's interest calls for transcendence of interest, at least, in some ways. Thus, overlapping consensus and overlapping circles crucial for realization of justice, including global justice, call for work of transcendence. This work of transcendence has various manifestations – spiritual and artistic as well – but our habitual traditions of justice do not speak much about it, and here again is an important conceptual and practical task for all of us concerned.

Rawls' "overlapping consensus" was primarily confined to nation-state but his conception of international justice in his later works, for example, in his *Laws of Peoples* (1999), does not overcome this binding. In her recent work, *Frontiers of Justice,* which has important implications for projects of global justice, Martha Nussbaum (2006) challenges us that we must rethink the Rawlsian analogy between person and state. But here we have to think much deeper as well. Not only the analogy between person and state is inadequate, our conception of person and self in modernity as only the citizens of nation-states are inadequate as well. We need a richer and multi-dimensional conception of self, which can facilitate the work of overlapping circles of interpenetration and transcendence of exclusivistic interest required for realization of justice. But, in our conventional conceptions of justice, the subject of justice is primarily a political self, a right-seeking agent. But this self is also a sharing self, willing to transcend one's self-interest to realize an overlapping circle of consensus. We need to realize that the subject of justice is not only political but also aesthetic and spiritual.

Global justice is related to enchancing functioning and capabilities of each of us. It is the aesthetic and spiritual dimension of our self, which can help us understand our own limitations and facilitate connections and solidarity across borders. This is a project of education – *Bildung* – and here art, including public art, can play a greater role. In the history of struggle for justice, we have to remember the significance of novels, art and music in arousing our sensibility in anti-slavery, anti-colonial, post-colonial, racial justice and gender justice movements. For realizing global justice we need a new art, a new public art, literature and music to arouse our sensibility to the predicament of global justice. We see it in varieties of arts and images emerging in our emergent global public sphere, for example, in the evocative images of suffering, joy and shared humanity that I saw last year in a public exhibition in a park in Paris organized by *Reporter Sans Frontier.*[2] We see such globally sensitive art and music in various emerging global foras today such as World Social Forum.

Enhancing the functioning and capability of individuals is an important goal of social development in our present-day world (cf. Sen 1999). Nussbaum (2006) urges us to globalize our capabilities and presents us the following, among others:

1. Overdetermination of responsibility that domestic never escapes it.
2. Prosperous nations have a responsibility to give a substantial portion of their GDP to poorer nations.
3. Multinational corporations have responsibilities for promoting human capabilities in the regions in which they operate.
4. The main stream structures of the global economic order must be designed to be fair to poor and developing countries.
5. We should cultivate a thin, decentralized, and yet forceful global public sphere.
6. All institutions and (most) individuals should focus on the problems of the disadvantaged in each nation and region.
7. Care for the ill, the elderly, children, and the disabled should be a prominent focus of the world community.
8. The family should be treated as a sphere that is a precious but not "private".
9. All nations and individuals have a responsibility to support education, as a key to the empowerment of currently disadvantaged people.

But realizing the above as well as related proposals of global justice has economic implications. For example, it touches upon the issue of global redistribution of resources. As Naila Kabeer tells us: "It requires measures of the kind proposed by the Brandt Commission at the end of the 1970s, and more recently by a number of countries that countries be taxed on a sliding scale related to national income in order to generate revenue for a global social fund" (Kabeer 2005: 25). We need adequate resources for transforming our condition of misery into one of shared joy and happiness around our planet. Here projects for a global fund for universal self-realization are important, and Attac's struggle for Tobin Tax is an important part of creative global will formation here. But, the founders of Attac themselves realize that Tobin Tax is not a panacea. As Bernard Cassen (2003) writes: "We treated the Tobin Tax as a symbolic terrain [...] We never for a second thought that the Tobin Tax was the only solution to the dictatorship of financial markets". But does the per cent flag of Attac predominantly give the message of money and number? During a conversation last year in his office in Paris I asked this and Cassen did not give a direct reply but only an advice: "Do not read much into the symbol."

The Calling of Sharing

I was in an Easter lunch with a friend's family in Northern Jutland, Denmark, in April 2004. After our moments of togetherness, our host, a senior person who works as an electrician in the locality, shared his pain: "Oh, all the jobs from Denmark are now going to China and India." I said, "There is possibility to use this in a creative manner. If jobs are going to other countries then people of Denmark can have more free time but they should not leave on unemployment benefits. Given the centrality of employment in people's self-perception, everybody in society, especially those needing it, should have some hours of jobs. Retrenchment on the wake of job flight should not be born by only the poor and the low in companies and the wider society. If our labour and free time are shared equally, then, it would create a condition for a more creative and happy life. At the same time, people in India and China who are getting some of these jobs should have a salary and life of dignity. They should not be subjected to brutal conditions of work as it is happening in such places of work as call centres."

I also said, "But we also have to ask why jobs are flying from one country to the other now? This has to do with the high cost of production and management in the so-called affluent countries. The salary difference between the highest and lowest paid in many companies now is more than 500 times. Why has it to be like this? Here, we need a much shared conception of time and labour, happiness and joy so that only high economic differential does not become a sole measure of our self-worth."

Global justice calls for new initiatives in sharing, sharing of resources, knowledge, pain, joy and suffering. Shared joy and shared suffering are keys to global justice in our contemporary moment. Here, we can learn from our many different traditions of practices of sharing from around our world. Various experiments in creative socialism and cooperative production abound in societies and histories some of which are presented to us by Dada Mahesvarananda in his *After Capitalism* (2002). While doing fieldwork with the environmental movement of Chipko in the Himalayas way back in 1987, I was staying in Laxmi Asrham, Kaushani, India, for a few days. Every morning before breakfast we used to pray and then save a handful of grain saying: *ek muthi anname biswasanti he* (in this handful of grain lies world peace) (also see Bajaj and Srinivas 1996; Tutu 2005).

The Calling of Peace

There is an integral link between food and peace, material fulfilment and peaceful co-existence. Peaceful co-existence contributes to better human development, while an inclusive infrastructure for development including realization of autonomy and dignity contributes to the realization of peace. Both Kim Dae Jong and Richard von Weizsacker point to this. As Dae Jong tells us, "In Europe, the United States and other Asian countries, we see the widening gap between the rich and the poor emerging as a main cause for social conflict. On the basis of terrorism, the biggest threat to world peace in the 21st century, always lies this issue, directly or indirectly. Left unresolved, such conflicts would lead to catastrophes in the future" (Dae Jong 2005: 2). This is in tune with the perspectives of some of the leading scholars in the field such as John Clammer and Johan Galtung. For Clammer, "[...] Peace, conflict and social development are intimately linked and that the achievement of peace and resolution of conflict are to a very great extent the product of equitable and just social development, both at the global and local levels [...] the conditions for peace are created by equitable development – development that respects the social, cultural and psychological dimensions of human needs and attempts to integrate them with the economic" (Clammer 2006: 6). Similarly, Johan Galtung, the inspiring scholar of peace studies, challenges us to take an interconnected perspective on peace by linking peace to health.[3] Inspired by Gandhi, especially his view that "there is no way to peace, peace is the way" Galtung challenges us to pursue peace by peaceful means which is an alternative to the contemporary dominant ideology of peace by war. For Galtung, "[...] there is cognitive, intellectual road to peace" (in Galtung and Ikeda 1996: 19).[4] This means that mutual dialogue and learning can contribute to peace while lack of knowledge of each other can perpetuate mutual suspicion and hatred. Thus peace is a project of knowledge of the self and other including working on self-cultivation for a better mutual understanding. This way peace is a project of both epistemology and ontology; like our discussion of justice before, peace is also a project of an ontological epistemology of participation.

Dialogue is a multi-dimensional process of mutual knowledge and self-transformation and it is an integral part of peace. Like peace, dialogue itself is a way pregnant with new possibilities and beginnings. Today, the pursuit of peace calls for dialogue. Dialogue is not only a road to peace, it is also a way to justice.

Such a practice of peace calls for a new vocation of peace in our everyday life and commitment to it. Our religious traditions have also glorified martyrs who can die for the cause of their faith. Modern nationalism has also glorified martyrs for the cause of nationalism. Today, the calling of world peace calls for a new vocation of martyrdom in our lives. It calls for us to sacrifice our small egos and if necessary our lives for the sake of peace, and not for war. As Felix Wilfred challenges us:

> Religious traditions need to counterbalance the classical ideal of martyrdom with education for tolerance and peace. [...] Today, the world needs *witnesses* (original meaning of "martyr") of love, justice, peace and tolerance who will be ready to sacrifice their very selves for greater understanding among peoples, nations and religions. [...] They will belong to the whole of humankind since, through their sacrifice, steadfastness, fidelity and fortitude, they bear witness to the universal values of truth, love, justice and peace. Could the various religious traditions jointly create the climate for the emergence of such *universal martyrs*? (Wilfred 2005: 181).

But this task of preparing for universal martyrs for the sake of peace is not a challenge for different religious traditions but also other traditions of thought such as nationalism. All these traditions of discourse and practice, which had valorized martyrdom for mutual annihilation, can contribute to generate universal martyrs for the sake of peace and realization of human unity.

Ideals of Human Unity

Today, the nation-state model is not sustainable and is a source of much violence and agony. In this context, quest for peace has to be part of post-national transformations within and across national borders. Realizing unity across fractured borders is a perennial human challenge but unity itself is not a monolithic Absolute, unity itself has to be a multiverse of diversity. Both Richard von Weizsacker and Kim Dae Jong discuss the challenge of unification in the context of Germany as well as Korean peninsula.[5] But German unification has been a process of one-sided absorption where East Germany lost some of its finest traditions of social security and co-operative education. Weizsacker seems not to acknowledge the pains that East Europeans have gone through as a result of German unification in which West Germany absorbed East Germany. There was also a promise of a new constitution for the new united Germany after the 1990 unification. Since it happened during Weizsacker's presidency, Weizsacker can help us understand why there has not been a new constitution for united Germany. Weizsacker also refers to a United European Union but here again the challenge is a multiversal Europe, which strives for a better life for everybody and not just for a more profitable Europe. European Union needs a new social pact. The debates over European Constitution are important here. At the moment, major proponents want to make European identity Judeo-Christian but why not also acknowledge religious and cultural pluralism in the very European Constitution itself? Europe is not just Judeo-Christian in its identity; Islam has been a part of Europe for a long time so has other religions influenced modern European consciousness and imagination.

Reflecting on the challenge of unification in the Korean context, Kim Dae Jong writes: "Unification through absorption will only cause catastrophe [...] Unification should be achieved when both feel reassured that right conditions are set. Whether it may take ten years or twenty, a stable process of unification must be pursued based on the principles of Sunshine Policy[6] of peaceful coexistence, peaceful exchange and peaceful unification" (Dae Jong 2005: 4). Dae Jong's cautious approach to the challenge of Korean unification is helpful to think of challenge of unification at the world level. Today, pursuit of human unity has to have a cautious approach realizing dangers of monolithic and gigantic structures of human unity. It has to be part of post-national transformations and dialogues across borders working towards a coordinated framework of shared sovereignties.

But this is a challenge for us to overcome. In modernity, our self, society and nation-state valorize sovereignty. Today different movements of fundamentalism and terrorism also celebrate the cult of sovereignty. Not only nation-states unleash violence in the name of sovereignty, anti-state actors – whether it is LTTE in Sri Lanka or global terror groups – valorize the cult of sovereignty. Our habitual selves, societies, states and anti-state actors celebrate the logic of the sovereign – the One. This valorized One has to learn to share space with the Many (cf. Hardt and Negri 2004). This is the calling of shared sovereignty or the calling of a new logic of multiversality and multitude.

In this context, some of the reflections on ideals of human unity offered by Sri Aurobindo – a seeker and visionary from India – are worth living with. In his *Ideals of Human Unity* written in 1919, Sri Aurobindo tells: "A free world-union must in its very nature a complex unity based on free self-determination" (Sri Aurobindo 1962: 517). Hinting at the challenge of post-national transformations, Sri Aurobindo writes: "[...] in a free world-union though originally steering from the national basis, the national idea might be expected to undergo a radical transformation; it might even disappear into a new and less strenuously compact form and idea of group-aggregation which would not be separative in spirit, yet would preserve the necessary element of independence and variation needed by both individual and grouping for their full satisfaction and their healthy existence" (ibid.: 524). Sri Aurobindo challenges us with a question: why do we need unity, a unity which is not a uniformity?[7] For Sri Aurobindo, "It must be remembered that a greater social or political unity is not necessarily a boon itself; it is only worth pursuing insofar as it provides a means and a framework for a better, richer, more happy and puissant individual and collective life" (ibid.: 263).

Like this foundational question of unity, Sri Aurobindo also raises basic questions about the relationship between the individual and the collective. So far this relationship has suffered from much opposition and violence and the task is how do we work out a transformative relationship between the individual and the collective, the state idea and the person idea. These questions are as much a challenge in a primary group such as family as in an expected condition of world unity.[8] Sri Aurobindo hints that the future task is to realize a unity "based upon the completest individual freedom and freedom also of natural unforced grouping" (ibid.: 391). Our proposed paths of shared sovereignty resonates Sri Aurobindo's plea for meeting of self-determination with mutual determination: "There remains the problem of relations, of the individual and collective self-determination and of the interaction of the self-determination of one on the self-determination of another. That cannot be finally settled by any mechanical solution, but only by the discovery of some meeting-place of the law of our self-determination with the common law of mutuality, where they begin to become one. It signifies the fact of discovery of an inner and larger self other than the mere ego, in which our individual self-fulfilment no longer separates us from others but at each step of our growth calls for an increasing unity" (ibid.: 604).

The pursuit of ideals of unity is a multi-dimensional one – political, psychic and spiritual. Sri Aurobindo challenges us to understand the significance of the psychic unity of humankind. For realization of global justice and peace, Sri Aurobindo challenges us to move in the direction of a spiritual evolution of humanity: "A spiritual oneness which would create a psychological oneness not dependent upon any intellectual or outward uniformity and compel a oneness of life not bound up with its mechanical means of unification, but ready always to enrich its secure unity by a free inner variation and a freely varied outer self-expression, this would be the basis for a higher type of human existence" (ibid.: 555).

Notes

1. We have to ask ourselves what do such figures mean. Living with less than dollar a day: does it mean living miserably? In many places around the world I know one can live creatively with a dollar a day if he or she cooks oneself and if he or she does not have to purchase bottles of water for drinking. Such figures do not also raise the issue of quality of life and the joy of life. We need a much more nuanced global sensitivity which can understand varieties of creative and joyous lives that people live with less and while not romanticizing poverty seeks to transform it in the direction of dignity.
2. Reporter Sans Frontier (RSF), based in Paris, is an international voluntary organization working for the freedom of the press.
3. For Galtung, "Exploitation and cancer resemble each other in that a part of the social or human organism lives at the expense of the rest. Peace research and health research are metaphors for each other; each can learn from the other. Similarly, both peace theory and medicinal science emphasize the role of consciousness and mobilization in healing" (in Galtung and Ikeda 1995: 39).
4. Galtung here draws our attention to the life and works of Spinoza: "[Spinoza] bridges the moral and the cognitive. For instance, he says that lack of understanding produces evil whereas understanding brings good" (ibid.: 7).
5. This sharing took place at the 60th anniversary of Korean liberation in 2005 at the Academy of Korean Studies, Seoul in which the author had taken part and the

present section is in dialogue with some of the thoughts of Kim Dae Jong and Richard von Weizsacker.

6. Sunshine policy is the policy of peace and dialogue initiated by President Kim Dae Jong during his tenure in relationship with North Korea.
7. Sri Aurobindo tells us: "Unity we must create but not necessarily uniformity" (ibid.: 401).
8. For Sri Aurobindo,

> In the relations between the individual and the group, this constant tendency of Nature appears as the strife between two equally deep-rooted human tendencies, individualism and collectivism. On one side is the engrossing authority, perfection and development of the state, on the other the distinctive freedom, perfection and development of individual man. The State idea, the small or the vast living machine, and the human idea, the more and more distinct and luminous Person, the increasing God, stand in perpetual opposition. The size of the State makes no difference to the essence of the struggle and need make none to its characteristic circumstances. It was the family, the tribe or the city, the *polis*; it became the clan, the caste and the class, the *kula*, the *gens*. It is now the nation. Tomorrow or day after it may be all mankind. But even then the question will remain poised between man and humanity, between self-liberating Person and the engrossing collectivity (1962: 272–73).

References

Bajaj, J.K. and M.D. Srinivas. 1996. *Annam Bahu Kurivita*. Chennai, Centre for Policy Studies.

Bhaskar, Roy. 2002. *Reflections on Meta-Reality*. Delhi: Sage.

Cassen, Bernard. 2003. Article on Attac in *New Left Review*, downloadable from internet.

Clammer, John. 2006. "Social Development and Peace." Paper presented at the Workshop on "New Horizons of Human Development," Chennai, February.

Cohen, Gerry. 2000. *If You're an Egalitarian How Come You are So Rich?* Cambridge, MA: Harvard University Press.

Dae Jong, Kim. 2005. "A New Beginning for Peace and Coexistence." Text of the video-taped message for the "Global Forum on Civilization and Peace," Seoul, December 5.

Galtung, Johann. 1996. *Peace by Peaceful Means*. London: Sage Publications.

Galtung, Johann and Daisaku Ikeda. 1996. *Choose Peace*. London: Zed Books.

Giri, Ananta K. 2002a. *Conversations and Transformations: Towards a New Ethics of Self and Society*. Lanham, MD: Lexington Books.

——. 2002b. *Building in the Margins of Shacks: The Vision and Projects of Habitat for Humanity*. Delhi: Orient Longman.

——. 2004. *Reflections and Mobilizations: Dialogues with Movements and Voluntary Organizations*. Delhi: Sage.

——. 2006a. Creative Social Research: Rethinking Theories and Methods and the Calling of an Ontological Epistemology of Participation. Aalborg U, DIR: Working Paper.

——. 2006b. "Cosmopolitanism and Beyond, Beyond Cosmopolitanism: Towards a Multiverse of Transformations." *Development and Change*, 37(6): 1277–1292.

Gorringe, Timothy. 1999. *Fair Shares: Ethics and the Global Economy*. London: Thames and Hudson.

Habermas, Jurgen. 1990. *Moral Consciousness and Communicative Action*. Cambridge: Polity Press.

——. 2002. *Religion and Rationality*. Cambridge, MA: The MIT Press.

Hardt, Michael and Antonio Negri. 2004. *Multitude: War and Democracy in the Age of Empire*. London: Penguin.

Kabeer, Naila. 2005. (ed.), *Inclusive Citizenship: Meanings and Expressions*. London: Zed.

Mahesvarananda, Dada. 2002. *After Capitalism*. Washington, DC: Prout Publications.

Nussbaum, Martha. 2006. *Frontiers of Justice: Disability, Nationality, Species Membership*. Cambridge, MA: Harvard University Press.

Rawls, John. 1971. *A Theory of Justice*. Cambridge, MA: Harvard University Press.

——. 2001. *Justice as Fairness: A Restatement*. Cambridge, MA: Harvard University Press.

——. 1999. *Laws of Peoples*. Cambridge, MA: Harvard University Press.

Sen, Amartya. 1999. *Development as Freedom*. New York: Alfred A. Knof.

——. 2002. "Justice Across Borders." In *Global Justice and Transnational Politics: Essays on the Moral and Political Challenges of Globalization*. (eds.), Pablo De Greiff and Ciaran Cronin, Cambridge, MA: The MIT Press.

Sri Aurobindo. 1962. *The Human Cycle, The Ideal of Human Unity, War and Self-Determination*. Pondicherry: Sri Aurobindo Ashram.

Sunder Rajan, R. 1998. *Beyond the Crises of European Sciences: New Beginnings*. Shimla: Indian Institute of Advanced Studies.

Tutu, Desmond. 2005. *God Has a Dream: A New Vision of Hope for Our Times*. London: D. Reidel.

Wilfred, Felix. 2005. *The Sling of Utopia: Struggle for a Different Society*. Delhi: ISPCK.

21 Cultivating Transformative Reconciliation and Striving for Peace

Compassion, Confrontation and a New Art of Integration

Pity the land that needs heroes.

— Bertolt Brecht

[...] Communication is always ambiguous and always an expression of latent violence. But when this description of violence is ontologized, when one sees "nothing but" violence in it, one misses the essential point, namely, that the critical power to put a stop to violence without reproducing it in new forms can only dwell in the telos of mutual understanding and our orientation to this goal.

— Jurgen Habermas (2006)
The Divided West, p. 18

Compassion brings inner strength, and compassion also brings truth. [...] Compassion involves a feeling of closeness to others, a respect and affection that is not based on others' attitudes towards us. We tend to feel affection for people who are important to us. That kind of close feeling does not extend to our enemies – those who think ill of us. Genuine compassion, on the other hand, sees that others, just like us, want a happy and successful life and do not want to suffer. That kind of feeling and concern can be extended to friend and enemy like, regardless of their feelings towards us. That's genuine compassion.

— The Dalai Lama (2009)
The Middle Way: Faith Grounded in Reason, pp. 2–3

In the experience of reconciliation, some of the true inner historicality of man presents itself as does something of his inner possibility of development; so it is one of the deepest experiences that people can have. For wherever there has been disunity, discord and disintegration, wherever we have fallen out with one another, wherever our sociability has collapsed [...] we always experience how the reconciliation brings an increase into the world. That is the mystery of reconciliation.

— Hans-Georg Gadamer (1998)
"Culture and the Word," p. 14

Introduction and Invitation

"The emergence of an 'ethics of reconciliation' is a significant phenomenon of our recent history." Thus begins Ari Sitas' creatively crafted and deeply moving essay, "Beyond the Mandela Decade: The Ethic of Reconciliation" (Sitas 2011). In his essay, Sitas presents us contours of this emergent ethics of reconciliation which calls for careful and attentive participation of each one of us interested in realizing a different world which is more beautiful, dignified and animated by dialogues in place of violence and monological assertions. For Sitas, an emergent ethics of reconciliation of our times emerges from painful and annihilating violence in the midst of which we learn failingly from our failures and despite setbacks do not quickly give up hope. It is a fragile emergence but it is here to stay as some of us concerned, especially victims of violence, realize that there is no other way except to strive for reconciliation and peace.[1] But this reconciliation is not just repetition of the existing status quo and peace here is not an apology for continuing the existing logic of violation and humiliation. For Sitas, ethics of reconciliation "socializes people into specific dispositions towards others" where the other is not "eliminable surplus" and "non-enslaveable and non-exploitable" (Sitas 2011: 572). It navigates "both individual behaviour and broader forms of group and collective action" (ibid.: 2). An important aspect of the emerging ethics of reconciliation which sociology ought to take note of is that "there are an increasing number of people whose 'dispositions' display in a 'Bourdieuan' sense openness to reconciliation," a disposition which emerges out of interaction, exposure and participation.[2]

For Sitas, the emergent ethics of reconciliation "points to a remarkable negotiated revolution. Nelson Mandela's gesture of reconciliation resonates everywhere, moving people from Mexico to China. It was disarming and however difficult, it allowed for transcendence and co-existence in South Africa" (ibid.). Along with this, Sitas presents us four more sources for the emerging ethics of reconciliation: "the predominance of neo-Gandhian ideas and practices in the so-called third world and the global south; the self-reflexivity of modernity of modernity in the West; the increasing convergence between socialist (read: anti-Stalinist) and human rights discourses and, finally the subterranean and usually underrated work of the 'arts' and 'literature'" (ibid.: 573).

In my walking with Sitas in this important, exciting and arduous journey I wish to present pathways of transformative reconciliation as multidimensional fields and flows animated by creativity, compassion, confrontation, dynamic harmonization and striving for peace which is simultaneously structural as well as soulful. Transformative reconciliation and striving for peace are ever called upon to realize compassionate confrontation and a new art of integration.

The Calling of Transformative Reconciliation

In order to appreciate the significance of Sitas' arguments in his essay, it is helpful to begin with his co-authored insightful study of prospects for reconciliation in Cyprus (Sitas et al., 2007). In this, Sitas et al. are explored the prospects for reconciliation in Cyprus between the Turkish Cypriots of the North and the Greek Cypriots of the South after decades of ethnic conflicts, invasion of Turkey and subsequent de facto partition and efforts towards reconciliation. For Sitas et al., "the Cyprus case did not end up in murderous ethnic cleansing because of self-restraint which speaks to a humanism that precedes the conflict" (Sitas et al., 2007: 3). In their study, they find that those affected by violence have a disposition towards reconciliation: "First in the midst of the narratives collected there is a thick description of very violent and traumatic experiences. Yet in approximately a third of the narratives there appears to be remarkable acts of kindness and humanism even in extreme situations of combat and fight" (ibid.: 37). Similarly, in her work on peace and reconciliation in South Africa, anthropologist Fiona Ross (2004) tells us about individuals and groups who are creatively engaged in reconciliation and peace as an ongoing work of "remaking the everyday". But she also tells us about the limits of the existing discourse of reconciliation especially in South Africa. As Sitas seems to be proceeding with a rather celebratory approach to the Mandela model and the South African model of reconciliation, it is important to note that in the Mandela-Tutu-South African model, as Ross tells us, "responsibility for breaking with the unjust past" "rests precisely on those whose futures have been curtailed by the damages to them" (ibid.: 15). Such a model of reconciliation places a heavy onus on the victims and is not accompanied by material reparation of inequality such as inequality in landownership as a result of colonialism and apartheid. In this context, we need to transform the emerging ethics of reconciliation into a much broader and deeper process and cultivate transformative reconciliation which involves structural transformation addressing some of the limitations of a celebratory approach to South African model of reconciliation and its uncritical global claims.

Transformative reconciliation is a dynamic process animated by both compassion and confrontation. While compassion enables the participants to share in their suffering as well as joys of coming out of closures of violence and counter-violence confrontation enables them confront each other as well as structures of domination which still determine the existing condition of lack of peace (cf. Giri 2010b). This confrontation is face to face as well as takes place at the wider institutional level. This is not necessarily violent. In fact, the work of Randall Collins (2008) shows that in the face to face confrontation people understand their limitation to inflict harm on the other. Confrontation also takes place in non-violent ways and it does and can involve compassion giving rise to reality and further emergent and evolutionary possibility of compassionate confrontation. Ross' study of reconciliation process in South Africa shows how varieties of confrontations took place in the court room itself between perpetrators and victims. We can also read the significance of the Cyprus study by Sitas et al. in terms of opportunities for compassion and confrontation that it presents to interested actors. Those who meet with each other from across the border can understand each other compassionately and they can also confront each other especially the more fundamentalist, ethno-nationalist and heroic construction of identities from each other's sides.

Sitas argues that ethics of reconciliation is not a philosophy of being but a philosophy of praxis and he also creatively interprets pathways of Gandhi and neo-Gandhian moves beyond the person of Gandhi. Though Sitas may not necessarily have in mind a dualism between being and praxis, it is important to cultivate ethics of reconciliation as a multidimensional field of non-duality consisting simultaneously of being and praxis, ontology and epistemology. Transformative reconciliation involves the dynamic creative interpenetration of both ontological nurturance, especially adequate self-preparation and self-transformation, and epistemic learning involving the work of what I have elsewhere called "ontological epistemology of participation" (Giri 2006). In their study of prospects of reconciliation in Cyprus, Sitas et al. talk about hard variables such as class and soft variables such as participation in peace organizations and other border-crossing and boundary crossing meetings. For them, "[...] the more our hard variables influence swings in dispositions, the less space exists for individual and collective action. The more soft variables swing dispositions, the more space exists for individual and group action. [...] The remarkable finding is that the soft variables swing disposition towards reconciliation, co-existence and forgiveness in a more vigorous way that the hard ones" (Sitas et al., 2007: 53). We can look at the significance of these soft variables as creating condition for creative collaborative learning and necessary work on self, for example, nurturing the self as part of a vibrant sociality towards reconciliation.

Transformative reconciliation is an aesthetic project as it is an ethical one. Sitas urges us to realize the significance of art for the practice of reconciliation: "What artists bring to consciousness is a unique attention to the 'particular', to life forms, to *living rights* [...] Unlike sociological theorization that needs to move to determinate and systematic abstractions to illuminate the field, the artist is haunted by it – she lives the field, invents another with its subconscious, pregnant from all other fields she has known or imagined" (Sitas 2010: 10; emphasis added). Thus, we need to realize reconciliation as simultaneously ethical and aesthetic and in this context we need a new language and practice of aesthetic ethics of reconciliation. This in turn builds upon border-crossing between the aesthetic and the ethical. The language of ethics has some inherent limitations, for example, ethical suffers from a preoccupation with the other while not cultivating self appropriately as the aesthetic suffers from some aspect of self-closure and not opening oneself to the face of the other, as Levinas would urge us to realize (cf. Quarles van Ufford and Giri 2003). Aesthetic ethics helps us overcome the limits of both the ethical and aesthetic and it also involves a project of social aesthetics and art of building bridges across borders while one oneself becomes a bridge.[3]

Transformative reconciliation grapples with suffering – self as well as social – and is a manifold process of healing. In this there is a spiritual dimension at work. Though there is an implicit spiritual dimension in Sitas' pathways, it is helpful to creatively express and explore it with its integral open-endedness and connectedness. Trasnformative reconciliation is linked to spiritual as an ongoing and emergent process of critique, creativity and transformation and is part of what can be called practical spirituality (cf. Giri 2009). Practical spirituality is animated by quest for beauty, dignity and dialogue in our world still burdened with much ugliness, violence and monological assertion of oneself and one's singular and imperial truth. Transformative reconciliation also involves mediation, meditation and transformation. We can further creatively look at the spaces created by the work of Sitas' soft variables as spaces where not only mediation and mutual learning in compassion and confrontation takes place but also meditation. We can look at meditation in an open-ended way. Sitas looks at the emergent ethics of reflection through what he calls "self-reflexivity of modernity". But, the discourse and practice of reflexivity may not necessarily involve meditation especially what I have elsewhere called meditative verbs of co-realizations (see chapter 3).[4] Understanding the significance of meditation poses foundational challenge for both the existent practice of reconciliation as well as to sociological discourse of reflexivity which is the reflexivity of a self-reflexive subject where both self and reflexivity are predominantly defined in rationalist ways. The practice of reconciliation in South Africa was deeply influenced by a mode of Christian practice; it was an act of forgiveness also in the public. It probably lacked spaces of self and co-meditations. Imagine what would have happened if along with followed practices of reconciliation the participating agents would have also meditated together in Cyprus, South Africa and beyond. Thus, we can cultivate fields of transformative reconciliation as fields of meditations – sitting, walking as well as dancing.[5] For this existing models of reflexivity, mediation and reconciliation have to go out of their initial locations and learn together with humility and festivity with and around the world what can be called the dance of a new planetary co-learning. In this process, "the anxiety of incompleteness" (cf. Appadurai 2006) is transformed into what can be called "festivity of incompleteness" where with mediation and meditation we help each other to realize our fuller potential which has bee so far stunted by ongoing violence and intractable conflicts. We thus complete each other and create what Vygotsky would call "zones of proximal development" (cf. Holzman 2009).

Transformative Reconciliation and Striving for Peace

Transformative reconciliation is related to the ongoing striving for peace where peace is also a creative mediation of and meditation on tensions. It involves, at the same time, necessary and courageous steps towards transformations. Like reconciliation, peace is not a noun but a verb and as a verb both of them are not only activistic but also meditative.[6] Peace is an ongoing arduous journey in Cyprus, South Arica, Kashmir, Tibet, Palestine and around the world and in the recesses of our hearts; it is an ever present challenge calling for fuller realizations. Peace embodies here what Galtung calls structural peace and what I would like to call soulful peace which embodies both inner peace as well as peace and striving for soulful togetherness in our world of fragmentation, isolation, violence, violation and annihilation.

Striving for peace works in the existing condition of conflict and violence, "negative peace" (which is characterized by the absence of violence – as in a ceasefire) and "positive peace" characterized by presence of harmony (cg. Galtung and MacQueen 2010). This harmony is not static but dynamic; striving for peace is animated by processes of dynamic harmonization which unsettles many accepted foundations of statis and domination. For Galtung and MacQueen, striving for peace is a *"joint project,* building on and building positive cognitions and emotions. A project is something spiritual, imbuing the parties with meaningful lives together" (ibid.: 17). Along with structural peace which involves equity and reciprocity, striving for peace also "implies *integration* in the sense of all relating to all, as all parties, as opposed to segmentation" (ibid.: 18).

Towards a New Art of Integration

But this integration is a weak and gentle one and different from the telos and ideology of strong integration characterizing models of both social system and self-integration in modernity. An evolutionary challenge before both transformative reconciliation and realization of peace is the challenge of cultivating a new art of integration what I have elsewhere called weak and gentle integration (Giri 2010c). In Galtung and Macqueen this can be related to the battle between hard and soft sides of each of us and our traditions including traditions of science, secularism and religion and the epochal need to cultivate soft dimensions of each of us as self and creative practitioners of traditions. This can be also creatively related to the significant discussion of Sitas about the work of soft variables in practices of reconciliation. Bringing Galtung and Sitas together a challenge before creative sociology, peace studies and contemporary practice is to cultivate creative softness and weakness in us building upon manifold weakness of our contemporary field of discourse and practice such as weak nationalism, weak ontology and weak religion (cf. Giri 2010d). Cultivating softness is an evolutionary challenge now but an important practical and theoretical challenge before is how do we cultivate weakness, softness and gentleness in a world full of violence and without our softness being wiped out. Here we need to develop what can be called weak strength and energetic softness which is not cowardly, fearful and afraid but has the courage to practise compassionate confrontation and weave a new art of integration from our wounds and fragments. But cultivating this is a multidimensional task involving manifold transformative struggles and transformations including profound transformation of the sociological project itself. Apart from being an artist as suggested by Sitas, a sociologist herself has to be an embodiment of compassionate confrontation and a new art of integration through her scholarship, activism and soul-filled and heart-touching communication. Working together with fellow seeking souls, she strives to transform sociology into a multidimensional field of mediation and meditation and realization of transformative reconciliation and structural and soulful peace.

Notes

1. This is also born out in my study of communal violence in Kandhamal, Orissa, India. See Giri 2010a.
2. Here Sitas quotes Bourdieu: "One might say that we are disposed because we are exposed" (Sitas 2011: 572).
3. Here we can consider the work of Joseph Beuys and his work in social aesthetics. Chitta Ranjan Das (2008) also talks about two wings of aesthetic consciousness touching both *Anna* and *Ananda* – food and bliss.

4. Meditation as meditative verbs of co-realizations refers to practices of self and relationship where through meditation we co-realize each other and help each other to breathe together, feel our pulses and establish a rhythm of harmony. I am now trying to re-realize the project of self-other relations including sociality as meditative verbs of co-realizations.
5. In this context, what Galtung and MacQueen (2010: 184)) write deserves our careful consideration:

   > In Cambodia the Center for Peace and Reconciliation, established chiefly by Buddhists, has attempted, through nonviolence training, peace walks and other programs, to begin the process of healing and restoration in Cambodia of a peace culture, while in Sri Lanka, a healing garden for children traumatized by the conflict has been established in the Batticaloa region. Although it has been designed to be non-denominational so as to transcend the religious and ethnic divisions, the garden has drawn upon earth-centered symbols of peace and wholeness.
6. Note here what Ross writes: "In English, 'peace' is not a verb. This observation appears commonplace, but it signals the necessity of action, a force or energy that is brought to bear to produce a result. In turn, this implies human action and a temporal dimension. The verbs that precede 'peace' require that we think about its and its lack in everyday life and about the diverse ways in which 'peacefulness' might be generated, encouraged, coaxed or allowed to emerge from prevailing conditions of possibility" (2004: 1). But here the verb that that Ross talks about is mainly activistic and is not meditative. Gandhi looks at peace as a verb when he says: "There is no way to peace, peace is the way" (quoted in Galtung 1996) but the verb here is both activistic and meditative.

References

Appadurai. Arjun. 2006. *Fear of Small Numbers: An Essay on the Geography of Evil*. Durham: Duke University Press.

Collins. Randall. 2008. *Violence: A Micro-Sociological Theory*. Princeton: Princeton University Press.

Dalai Lama. 2009. *The Middle Way: Faith Grounded in Reason*. Boston: Wisdom.

Das, Chitta Ranjan. 2008. "Soundarya Bodhara Duiti Akhi [Two Eyes of Aesthetic Consciousness]." *Eshana* June: 117–131.

Galtung, Johan and Graeme MacQueen. 2010. *Globbalizing God: Religion, Spirituality and Peace*. Transcend University Press.

Galtung, Johan and Daisaku Ikeda. 1996. *Choose Peace*. London: Pluto Press.

Giri, Ananta Kumar. 2006 "Creative Social Research: Rethinking Theories and Methods and the Calling of an Ontological Epistemology of Participation." *Dialectical Anthropology*.

——. 2008 "The Calling of Practical Spirituality." In *Science, Spirituality and the Modernization of India*, pp. 238–254, Makarand Paranjape (ed.). Delhi: Anthem South Asian Studies.

——. 2010a "Peace in Kandhamal." *Mainstream*. April.

——. 2010b "Knowing Together in Compassion and Confrontation: The Calling of Transformative Knowledge." Madras Institute of Development Studies: Working Paper.

——. 2010c "Towards a New Art of Integration." Paper presented at the international symposium on "Learning Across Boundaries." Luxemborg.

Habermas, Jurgen. 2006. *The Divided West*. Cambridge: Polity Press.

Holzman, Lois. 2009. *Vygotsky at Work and Play*. London: Routledge.

Quarles van Ufford, Philip and Ananta Kumar Giri (eds.). 2003. *A Moral Critique of Development: In Search of Global Responsibilities*. London: Routledge.

Ross, Fiona. 2004. "Peace, Reconciliation and the Accomplishment of Everyday Life: Interpersonal Relations in South Africa." Paper presented at the EASA meet in Vienna.

Sitas, Ari et al., 2007. *Prospects of Reconciliation, Co-Existence and Forgiveness in Cyprus in the Post-Referendum Period*. Oslo: PRIO.

Sitas, Ari. 2011. "Beyond the Mandela Decade: The Ethic of Reconciliation." *Current Socology*.

Part IV

Cultivating Transdiciplinarity and Fields of Mutual Blossoming

Part IV

22 The Calling of a Creative Transdisciplinarity

> There is today among the human sciences a sense of confusion about the identity of the social disciplines which expresses itself in a lack of clarity about the limits of their own validity – hence also a failure to understand their own interrelations; in a situation of blurred identity, relationships appear threatening – that is as true of persons as of intellectual disciplines. [...] To overcome the feeling of threat by means of an inwardly felt need for the other point of view is the ultimate goal of interdisciplinary studies. The basic task before such a programme is not merely the learning of new concepts and methods, nor merely new ideas and thoughts, but what we have to learn is a new way of thinking. But how do we think ourselves into a new way of thinking?
>
> — R. Sunder Rajan (1998), *Beyond the Crisis of European Sciences*, p. 1

> What we are proposing is 'border crossing with a difference' – as an act of creation rather than one of violation. In methodological terms, remapping the border between disciplines contributes to the larger intellectual project of rethinking culture, canon, and disciplinarity. [...] Border crossing yields what W.E.B. Du Bois calls 'double vision' – it expands our field of vision without being expansionist; it includes without consuming; it appreciates without appropriating and it seeks to temper politics with ethics.
>
> — Mae G. Henderson (1995)
> "Introduction: Borders, Boundaries, and Frame(works)", p. 27

Academic disciplines have exercised a dominant influence in the way we think, perceive and seek to understand reality and the universe in the modern world. Modern modes of inquiry into the human condition have been characterized by a disciplinary mode – we make sense of the world through particular, specialized and bounded disciplines. We look at the world through the eyes of the discipline to which we belong and tend to think that the whole world is characterized by a disciplinary significance. If one is a sociologist, he or she tends to firmly believe that the world is sociological and sociology holds the ultimate key to the understanding of reality, while if one is a psychologist then the world presents itself to him/her only through psychological themes and figures – through the eyes of Sigmund Freud, as it were. To put it in the evocative words of Clifford Geertz (1983: 155): "In the same way that Papuans or Amazonians inhabit the world they imagine, so do high energy physicists or historians of the Mediterranean in the age of Philip II [...] to set out to deconstruct Yeat's imagery, absorb oneself in black holes, or measure the effect of schooling on economic achievement is not just to take up a technical task but to take on a cultural frame that defines a great part of one's life [...]". Academic disciplines provide not only cultural frames to us but also social identity and locations in the institutions of knowledge. Also, academic disciplines not only help us classify the world but also classify ourselves. And, both of these functions and objectives are fulfilled by the erection of rigid boundaries between them.

But, if the rigid boundaries between disciplines have been characterized by the triumphant moment of the modern world (1850–1950) (cf. Trouillot 1991 1996; Wagner 1989; Wallerstein et al., 1995; Uberoi 1978, 1996), the recent moment has shown us a different picture. It is a picture of "blurred genres" (cf. Geertz 1980) where the rigid boundaries between the disciplines are slowly breaking down and we find more fluidity and permeability. This blurring of disciplinary boundaries is easily noticeable in the way new disciplines and sub-disciplines are emerging that embody the limits of conventional disciplinary boundaries and the quest for a new mode of engagement, which cuts across various disciplines (Katz 1995). The blurring of disciplinary boundaries in the frontier areas of several disciplines and in the works of master interlocutors of our times, such as Michel Foucault, Jurgen Habermas, Amartya Sen and Andre Beteille, has been accompanied by a call for interdisciplinary approach in our studies. But, as Clifford Geertz tells us, "most of the discussion which arise around it seem to be condemned to a certain sterility [...]" (Geertz 1983: 16). This sterility arises partly from the fact that we talk about interdisciplinarity in the same language of bounded disciplines and our conversation lacks a perspective of transcendence. Our rhetorics and practice of interdisciplinary studies is still within the predominant model of a bounded ontology and epistemology which, while open for occasional negotiation of one's boundaries, is reluctant and even resistant for a transmutation of one's initial disciplinary identity and for participation in a relational field of transdisciplinarity. Another major source of sterility seems to be the confinement of the entire effort of creating transdisciplinary knowledge at the level of institutional procedures without focusing on self-preparation that is required on the part of the researchers and community of researchers. So, the discourse and practice of interdisciplinary studies requires a transcendental interrogation, opening and trasmutation which transforms the pious hopes and waiting for interdisciplinarity into a calling of transdisciplinary striving.

In this striving, we are enriched by the work of philosopher R. Sunder Rajan who tells us in his important work, *Beyond the Crisis of European Sciences: Towards New Beginnings*: "The principle of transcendence is the clue to our understanding of the world and the principle of interdisciplinarity is the clue to our understanding knowledge and experience" (Sunder Rajan 1998: 3). Transcendence is central to a perspectival view of life and disciplines. In the evocative words of Sunder Rajan, "Every act discloses the object but discloses it as transcending the act itself" (ibid.). For Sunder Rajan, "Each perspective or point of view is such only as a member of a community of points of view; this is a community and not a collection, for each perspective, from within its own resources, refers to the possibility of others" (ibid.: 4). The problem with modern disciplinary thinking is that it fails to realize that its claim to universality needs to be relativized by recognizing the significance of other disciplines in gaining multiple perspectives about the world to which both one's as well as another's discipline contribute. In this context, for Sunder Rajan, "Each discipline must shed an illusory universality to gain a perspectival universality" (ibid.: 3). The task here is to realize that "the possibility of other perspectives is not merely a contingent or incidental feature but is essential to the very form of a perspective; a perspective is because it is one among others" (ibid.). Sunder Rajan calls this "interperspectivity" which resonates with what Foucault calls "interpositivity". The calling for transdisciplinarity requires a practice of interperspectivity and interpositivity.[1]

Looking at a discipline in terms of perspectives helps us to transcend disciplinary boundaries. Here, a discipline is not defined in terms of subject matter and even less by method of study but by its perspectival emphasis on the human condition (see Sivakumar 1986). Here, let us take the example of anthropology. What characterizes anthropology as a discipline at the present juncture is not so much it being a guardian of study of primitive society nor its method of participant observation but its emphasis on human voice and description of this voice (see Das 1995). This perspective can be internalized by a philosopher such as Jurgen Habermas (1990) or Richard Rorty (1989) or an economist such as Amartya Sen (1981) or a sociologist who considers his/her task to look at large-scale processes and be engaged in big comparisons.

In interdisciplinary striving, the other perspective, the other discipline needs recognition and invitation into the hard core of the disciplinary self (cf. Bauman 1993). Such a recognition and invitation makes our efforts transdisciplinary rather than interdisciplinary. The calling of creative transdisciplinarity urges us to realize the limitation of the language of interdisciplinarity as "inherent in the interdisciplinary format is a mechanistic and aggregative, at best integrative, process rather than transformative process which is what really takes place" (Kothari 1988: 34). In transdisciplinary striving, relationship rather than our separate disciplinary being is the ground of our identity. This calls for looking at disciplines in relational terms rather than in isolationist or oppositional terms. But, the relational approach to disciplines has to face the primary task that in many a case this relationship has to be created. In interdisciplinary striving relationships may not be there to start with. The practice of interdisciplinarity then calls for reconstituting interaction between different disciplines as a field of relationship.

But if transdisciplinarity is a field of relationship, then what kind of preparation is required on the part of self, discipline and department in order to partake in such a relationship? To begin with, it requires an ability to recognize the significance of one's disciplinary perspective without essentializing and absolutizing it and recognizing the significance of other perspectives for oneself as well as for the world. In the words of Sunder Rajan, "Each discipline sees itself as a perspective on the whole; in these terms it maintains a certain autonomy and is irreplaceable [...] but each discipline is enabled to give us this access to the world precisely because it is a member of a community of representations. It is this republic of perspectives which underwrites each one, such that each perspective has to enter into the dialectic of recognizing and being recognized by others" (Sunder Rajan 1998: 5). In the practice of creative transdisciplinarity neither the self nor the other is valorized and absolutized. In a relationship of giving and receiving, disciplines discover their true perspectival significance but the de-absolutization and relativization at work in such an endeavour does not make one less focussed and less committed in so far as bringing certain aspects of one's disciplinary perspective to the field of conversations is concerned. Here again, we can come to the example of anthropology. There is now a need to speak with commitment the perspectival emphasis on human voice and description in anthropology. Another aspect of the anthropological perspective, which needs to be universalized and pursued further with commitment, is the practice of and attentiveness to description. In fact, the perspectival uniqueness of anthropology in emphasizing the need for description and the need for other disciplines to cultivate this is attested to by thinkers as varied as Amartya Sen, Paulo Friere, Richard Rorty and Jurgen Habermas who may not have been anthropologists in a disciplinary sense (Giri 1998). The practice of a creative transdisciplinarity does not dispense with the notion of commitment but it is a perspectival commitment; it is not the disciplinary commitment of a missionary zealot who seeks to convert the entire world into one's dogma. We get a glimpse of such a perspectival commitment in what Eric Wolf writes about his own home field of anthropology: "Working with small populations in exotic settings, we discovered that the different aspects of social and cultural life intertwine – that social relations are simultaneously psychological, economic, political, ideational; and we are thus given to combine what others would cut asunder. We are hence able to entertain the possibility of multiple causation. This has made anthropology an integrative science – a rarity today – one that crosses the boundaries of different domains and resists the dismemberment of relations and contexts" (Wolf 1999: 13). And, Sunder Rajan helps us further in understanding the significance of perspectival commitment and universality:

> In terms of disciplines, when, for example, anthropology becomes truly interdisciplinary, it does not become false; on the contrary, it is now that we can understand what the anthropological perspective really means. By relating itself to other disciplines, in one sense, it loses the pretensions of being the whole, but in another sense, it achieves a form of totality possible within human thought. Anthropology is not one part of human reality but a perspective on the whole of reality – so also sociology, politics, economics – each discipline must shed an illusory universality to gain a perspectival universality (1998: 3).

The practice of creative transdisciplinarity is enriched not only by the work of such a perspectival commitment and universality but also by the cultivation of appropriate virtues. A transcendental perspective makes us aware of the contingent nature of our locations but in order that these contingent locations are not left unattended to degenerate into closed ponds where the water is stagnant and stinky, it requires the art of establishing connection among different contingent locations. This is an aspect of cultivation of virtues. What are then some of the virtues that are important for cultivation in the field of transdisciplinarity?

The first virtue is probably the virtue of dialogue. The field of interdisciplinarity involves interaction between different disciplinary perspectives which can be mutually competitive and sometimes at loggerheads with each other. But it is the virtue of dialogue which transforms this field of interaction into a relation of transdisciplinarity. It is the virtue of dialogue which enables us to let go or suspend our own point of view "as the only point of view" (Zohar and Marshall 1994: 235). But, the suspension of one's point of view does not put a full stop to the quest for understanding; rather it prepares the ground for an emergent synthesis. As Zohar and Marshall tell us, "Once the participants in dialogue have let go of clinging to their own points of view, the second stage begins – the resynthesis. People discover they can listen to each other in a new way, that there is a common ground to be discovered: 'When the rigid, tacit infrastructure is loosened, the mind begins to move in a new order. This new order is a whole new, emergent level of consciousness [...]'" (ibid.: 237).

The virtue of dialogue requires the cultivation of authentic embeddedness within one's discipline. Dialogue is not just an other-oriented activity; in fact, the willingness to listen to the other is facilitated by the discovery of a true self within. Similarly, interdisciplinarity is not just a gesture of benevolence towards other disciplines; it also requires nurturance in the perspectival universality of one's own discipline. Transdisciplinarity calls for an art of authentic embeddedness in one's discipline and transcendence does not mean cutting off from the ground where one stands but widening one's horizons. In the practice of creative transdisciplinarity, transcending our disciplinary point of view provides us a new experience of immanence, of our immanent existence within our disciplinary homes – homes whose doors and windows are ever open to the world. A transdisciplinary dialogue and practice enables us to realize that our own discipline has within it multiple perspectives, multiple perspectival universality. Our own discipline is not an integrated whole, nor is it a seamless field of homogeneity. In our discipline itself there are diversities and differences. There is a transdisciplinary undercurrent within each of our disciplines. As Stanley Katz tells us in his provocative essay, "Do Disciplines Matter?": "Today's political scientist, for instance, probably belongs not only to the American Political Science Association, but also a subdivision there of such as an association of legal theorists. [...] Most of these new affiliations are reductionist in these sense that they are merely subgroupings of traditional fields, but many are cross-disciplinary. Thus traditional academic taxonomies built solely upon the traditional disciplinary categories do not reflect the profusion, confusion and richness the working scholars use to think of themselves (Katz 1995: 871).

The art of authentic embeddedness requires an art of distantiation and the courage to abandon one's home discipline in the pilgrimage of one's quest and research. Sometimes the hold of our own discipline is so much upon ourselves that it requires a conscious abandonment of the secured ground of our home discipline and movement in uncharted lands. We find the glimpses of such a creative transdisciplinarity in the work of Herbert Simon. Though awarded the Noble Prize for the Economic Science in 1978, Simon had abandoned the field of economics since 1955. His interest in economics began in 1935 as an interest in human decision-making. Pursuing this interest has led him to what he calls a "long, but pleasurable, search through a tortuous maze of possibilities" (Simon 1992: 265). Simon describes his journey in the following way:

> To understand budget decisions, one has to understand decision-making in general. And to understand decision-making, even in its material aspects, it is necessary to

> study processes of decision making, and more generally, the process of human thinking. To study thinking, I had to abandon my home disciplines of political science and economics [...] for the alien shores of psychology and, a little later, of computer science and artificial intelligence. There I have remained since, except for occasional brief visits to the home islands. My emigration took place about 1955, with some interdisciplinary commuting for a few years thereafter (ibid.).

Simon's commitment to travel and live in the twilight zone of "interdisciplinary space" suggests us a way out. He argues that as a sociologist if one wants to travel inside economics, then he/she must speak the language of economics and not stick to one's previous vantage point and look at the newly arrived land through it. In his words, "When in economics, there is no substitute for talking the language of marginal analysis and regression analysis – even (or especially) when your purpose is to demonstrate their limitations" (ibid.: 269). Simon goes on to say: "It is fatal to be regarded as a good economist by psychologists; and a good psychologist by political scientists. Immediately upon landing on alien shores, you must begin to acquire the local culture, not with the aim of denying your origins, but so that you can gain the full respect of the natives" (ibid.). He offers the ideals of a pilgrim or a journeyman in place of the tight-necked professional and urges us to realize: "Disciplines, like nations, are a necessary evil that enable human beings of bounded rationality to simplify the structure of their goals. But parochialism is everywhere, and the world sorely needs international and interdisciplinary travellers who will carry new knowledge from one cave to another" (ibid.).

But abandonment in Simon has not precluded the possibility of a homecoming. But that without this art of abandonment, our conversation across disciplines cannot go very far from our initial starting point becomes clear when we discuss the work of two other important interlocutors in the field: Amartya Sen and Andre Beteille. To begin with Amartya Sen, though trained as an economist, Sen's work represents a creative transgression of many disciplinary boundaries – economics, sociology and philosophy, to name just a few. What is quite inspiring is that Sen brings a perspective of what he himself calls "ultimate concern" to his practice of cross-disciplinary efforts. For Sen, "Economics is ultimately not about commodities; its ultimate concern has to do with the lives we can or cannot lead. That is of course a complex concern and the working of these lives cannot be really understood without bringing in society in which all this takes place" (Sen 1990: 206). Creatively moving from the existing problems of identification and classification to the aspired world of integration, Sen further tells us: " I believe the task of integration of economics and sociology would be much easier if we recognize clearly how large an area of congruence we have. The immediate objects of attention are much more disparate than our respective ultimate concerns" (ibid.). But, in his autobiographical reflection, Sen tells that he read economics quite early in his life and took an interest in other subjects such as sociology and philosophy at a relatively late stage. He then read some of the works of Weber and Durkheim and some other sociologist who influenced his thinking. Still, they never stuck to his mind "as firmly as those works" with which he "grew up" (ibid.: 253). In the words of Sen, "When I am thinking, for example of a particular point and I find it similar to a point by somebody else but not quite the same, then my natural preference is to those things over which I have better command. And that command was acquired at a time when my receptivity was greater, namely when I read Marx or Mill, rather than later on when as it were the foundations of my own mental make up had already been largely made up" (ibid.).

Like Sen, social scientist Andre Beteille has creatively combined multiple perspectives in his work. He has combined the perspectives of sociology and anthropology which has enabled him to make some original contributions in thinking about modern themes and ideals like equality (Beteille 1974). For instance, his essay "Individualism and Equality" (Beteille 1986) is a unique contribution to thinking about the tensions in these two ideals of modernity – a contribution which would not have been possible if he were sticking to either the disciplinary regime of sociology or anthropology (also see Beteille 1996). But despite exchanges with anthropology and economics, Beteille would like to stick to his identity and vocation "as a sociologist" (Beteille 1993: 299). Self-identifying phrases like "as a sociologist" and objectifying phrases like "as a subject of sociology" (consider here some of the titles of Beteille's papers – "Religion as a Subject for Sociology", "Individual, Self and Person as Subjects of Sociology") proliferate in Beteille's writings which make one wonder whether there is an urge to transcend disciplinary boundaries in Beteille (1990, 1992, 1997). There is a clinging to disciplinary identity here which reiterates the need for cultivating the art of abandonment in our transdisciplinary strivings.

In cultivating this art of abandonment we can gain insights from both philosopher Martin Heidegger and the Indian perspective of *vanaprastha*. Heidegger says that it is important for human beings to abandon their homes and be strangers to themselves (see Dallmayr 1993). For discovering the meaning of life, Heidegger states, it is important for us to move in strange lands. The Indian perspective of *vanaprastha* also says that after the completion of prior stages of life – *brahmacharya, grahasthya* – one has to abandon his/her home and the world and be a *vanaprasthee*, a wanderer in the woods. The perspective of *vanaprastha* states that after one has accumulated his/her wealth and power he/she should abandon all these and search for truth. This seems to have immense enriching suggestion for our task of abandonment at hand. Academic disciplines provide wealth, prestige, power and acclaim to the practising professionals. But having gained all these through our respective disciplines, at a certain stage, we have to abandon our assuring grounds in order that we are able to discover the unexpected truths of reality in the borderland and wilderness, as it were. This should not be a difficult task for people at the midpoint or end of their professional careers since they have already achieved to a great extent all the material and professional accomplishments that they needed. At the same time, in a Heideggerian sense, abandonment as a goal can be always with us no matter at what stage of our life-cycle and professional life we are. In fact, this is how we can reinterpret the agenda of *vanaprastha* for our contemporary times (cf. Das 1993).

The Heideggerian goal of moving in strange land is part of his wider commitment not to grant any essential boundary to Being and reality. Such a view of reality is now buttressed by developments in quantum physics and contemporary interpretations of Upanishadic agenda of transcendence and the Buddhist notion of sunyata (Zohar and Marshall 1994; Puligandla 1996; Dallmayr 1993, 1996). Since the idea of determinate reality has contributed much to our notions of academic disciplines as essential boundaries, it is important for us to gain insights from all these experiments in order to be free from our conceptual models of essential and bounded reality. Let us begin with the Upanishadic insights where it is believed that reality is beyond our categorical formulation and comprehension. Whatever categories and concepts we use to make sense of reality, they are not adequate to provide us a total picture. The Upanishadic insights refer to the simultaneous need for concept formation as well as their abandonment. The first exercise is an exercise of "superimposition" of concepts and forms upon reality and according to Upanishads and Shankara, this superimposition is a manifestation of avidya (ignorance of concrete reality, true self) (Puligandla 1996). It is only when one fully and thoroughly disengages oneself from superimposition, does he/she open himself/herself to an experience of reality. Shankara emphasizes de-superimposition as an inevitable part of understanding reality and calls it *Adhyaropa-apavada*. As Puligandla (1996) helps us understand: "advancing an argument and rescinding it at the end; one advances an argument in order to inspire and orient the listener, and one finally rescinds the argument" in order to enable one to launch upon the quest for reality which defies determinate structuration and is essentially open-ended (also see Witz 1995).

In developing this alternative notion of reality and alternative methods of studying it, we can also draw inspiration from the Buddhist notion of *sunyata*. In this view, what characterizes reality is not an essential and determinate structure but a "dynamic *sunyata*," a vacuum to put it in the language of quantum physics (cf. Dallmayr 1996; Zohar and Marshall 1994). The significance of dynamic *sunyata* or the vacuum is not merely genealogical, i.e., reality has emerged out of the vacuum but its role as a permanent destabilizer of any stabilized form. As Dallmayr interprets, *sunyata* or emptiness "denotes not simply a vacuum or empty space; nor does it coincide with logical negation. Far from serving as a vacuum preamble to conceptual determination, the term signals an absent-present matrix allowing conceptual distinctions to arise in the first place (while simultaneously placing them in jeopardy)" (Dallmayr 1996: 177). Reality has a *sunyata* aspect or a vacuum aspect as an integral part of it and our methods of study must be sensitive to this aspect of reality. As a mode of engagement, taking emptiness or *sunyata* seriously means that we are not totally and arrogantly certain about our methods, objects and subjects of study and we have the courage to take part in "self-emptying process" – to be free from the privileges, securities, and the power of essential categories (cf. Wilfred 1996). The significance of the above mode of being for transcending disciplinary boundaries should not be difficult to discern. When we endow our disciplines with essential truths and rigidify the boundaries between them, dynamic *sunyata* as a mode of engagement has the courage and capacity to rupture these boundaries and make us seekers in a wonderland.

The process of abandonment in the practice of transdisciplinarity is not devoid of difficulties, pangs and suffering involved in the process of transdisciplinary conversations and journeys. This journey involves moments of despair – the pangs of leaving one's familiar ground and entering inside uncharted lands. What happens then is not a smooth negotiation but painful transition and transmutation. Thus, the calling of a creative transdisciplinarity also calls for a preparation for pain and suffering. Acknowledgement of pain and suffering probably helps us to accept it with equanimity, or at least with less disturbance and inner turmoil.

But the acknowledgement and acceptance of pain and suffering becomes easier when we look at and participate in the field of transdisciplinarity as a field of relationship. Recently, Alasdair MacIntyre (1999) has argued that participation in a field of relationship of what he calls "acknowledged dependence" is facilitated by the cultivation of the virtues of justice and generosity. Cultivating the virtue of justice in a field of relationship enables the actors to realize what she owes to the other. At the same time, cultivation of the virtue of generosity in the field of relationship can enable us to realize that what the self owes to the other is an "uncalculated giving" or an "unconditional obligation" and to fail in this is to "fail in respect of generosity" (MacIntyre 1999: 121). MacIntyre's insights can help us to reconstitute interdisciplinary striving as a field of acknowledged dependence. In the relational field of transdisciplinarity disciplines are dependent on each other for their identity. But participation in such a field of mutual dependence – a field which may not exist *a priori* to start with especially in a climate of disciplinary hostility and which emerges out of a process of conscious striving and evolutionary aspirations – is facilitated by the cultivation of the virtues of justice and generosity. It is the virtue of justice which enables us to realize that in interdisciplinary striving and transdisciplinary engagement, we have a calling of justice in a more fundamental sense. Without being transdisciplinary we may not be able to do justice to the scope of the subject we are studying. And, the virtue of generosity makes us caring both with regard to our own disciplines and others. As Sunder Rajan tells us:

> In the labor of caring there is first of all a skilled activity, often time consuming and involving great bodily exertion. But there is skill and adaptability here such that one has an experience of growth in the art of nurturance. [...] Caring is a manifestation of love and concern; one feels deeply for what one cares about. [...] The object of our care is, at the moment of our care a source of value and very often of intrinsic value. In caring therefore there is a commitment to the well-being and flourishing, a joy in its perfection and sorrow in its stresses and strains. And lastly, caring gives us a unique mode of access, a kind of knowing which may be called knowing – with (Sunder Rajan 1998: 78)

Note

1. For Foucault, "A configuration of interpositivity is not a group of neighbouring disciplines; it is not only an observable phenomenon of resemblance; it is not only the overall relation of several discourses to this or that discourse; it is the law of their communications" (1972: 161–62).

References

Bauman, Zygmunt. 1993. *Postmodern Ethics*. Oxford: Basil Blackwell.

Beteille, Andre. 1974. "Sociology and Anthropology". In Andre Beteille, *Six Essays in Comparative Sociology*. Delhi: Oxford University Press.

——. 1986. "Individualism and Equality." *Current Anthropology* 27 (2): 121–134.

——. 1990. "Individual, Person and Self as Subjects for Sociology." In Andre Beteille, *Society and Politics in India: Essays in a Comparative Perspective.* Delhi: Oxford University Press.

——. 1992. "Religion as a Subject for Sociology." Delhi School of Economics: Working Paper.

——. 1993. "Sociology and Anthropology: Their Relationship in One Person's Career." *Contributions to Indian Sociology* (n.s.) 27 (2): 291–304.

——. 1996. "The Mismatch Between Class and Status." *British Journal of Sociology* 47 (3): 513–525.

——. 1997. "Newness in Sociological Enquiry." *Sociological Bulletin* 46 (1): 97–100.

Dallmayr, Fred. 1993. *The Other Heidegger.* Ithaca: Cornell University Press.

——. 1996. "Sunyata East and West: Emptiness and Global Democracy." In F. Dallmayr, *Beyond Orientalism: Essays on Cross-Cultural Encounter.* Albany: SUNY Press.

Das, Chitta Ranjan. 1993. *Sukara O Socrates* [The Pig and the Socrates]. Berhampur, Orissa: Pustak Bhandar.

Das, Veena. 1995. "Voice and the Birth of Culture." *Ethnos.*

Foucault, Michel. 1972. *The Archaeology of Knowledge and the Discourse on Language.* London: Tavistock.

Geertz, Clifford. 1983. "Towards an Ethnography of Modern Thought.," In C. Geertz, *Local Knowledge.* New York: Basic Books.

——. 1980. "Blurred Genre: Refiguration of Social Thought." *American Scholar* 49: 165–179.

Giri, Ananta K. 1998. *Global Transformations: Postmodernity and Beyond.* Jaipur: Rawat Publications.

Habermas, Jurgen. 1990. *Moral Consciousness and Communicative Action.* Cambridge: Polity Press.

Henderson, M.G. 1995. "Introduction: Borders, Boundaries and Frame (works)." In Henderson (ed.), *Borders, Boundaries and Frames: Cultural Criticism and Cultural Studies.* New York: Routledge, pp. 1–27.

Katz, Stanley N. 1995. "Do Disciplines Matter? History and the Social Sciences." *Social Science Quarterly* 76 (4): 863–877.

Kothari, Rajni. 1988. *Rethinking Development: In Search of Humane Alternatives.* Delhi: Ajanta.

MacIntyre, Alasdair. 1999. "The Virtues of Acknowledged Dependence." In *Dependent Rational Animals.* London: Duckworth.

Puligandla, Ramakrishna. 1996. "The Central Upanishadic Insights and their Significance to Deconstruction and Theory of Everything." A Memorial Lecture Delivered at University of Madras.

Rorty, Richard. 1989. *Irony, Contingency and Solidarity.* Cambridge: Cambridge University Press.

Sen, Amartya. 1981. *Poverty and Famines: An Essay on Entitlement and Deprivation.* Oxford: Clarendon Press.

——. 1990. Interview in Swedberg, 1990.

Simon, Herbert. 1992. "Living in Interdisciplinary Space." In Michael Szenberg (ed.), *Eminent Economists: Their Life Philosophies*. Cambridge: Cambridge University Press.

Sivakumar, S.S. 1986. "Is Method All Madness? Comments from a Participant-Observer Economist." *Social Research* 53 (4): 615–646.

Sunder Rajan, R. 1998. *Beyond the Crisis of European Sciences*. Shimla: Indian Institute of Advanced Studies.

Swedberg, Richard. 1990. *Economics and Sociology, Redefining the Boundaries: Conversations with Economists and Sociologists*. Princeton: University Press.

Trouillot, Michel-Rolph. 1991. "Anthropology and the Savage Slot: The Poetics and Politics of Otherness." In R.G. Fox (ed.), *Recapturing Anthropology: Working in the Present*. Santa Fe, New Mexico: School of American Research Press.

——. 1996. "Open the Social Sciences." *Cross Currents in Culture, Power and History* 3(2), The Johns Hopkins University.

Uberoi, J.P.S. 1978. *Science and Culture*. Delhi: Oxford University Press.

——. 1996. *Religion, Civil Society and the State: A Study of Sikhism*. Delhi: Oxford University Press.

Wilfred, Felix. 1996. *Leave the Temple: Indian Paths to Liberation*. Trichy: Carmell Publications.

Wagner, Peter. 1989. "Social Science and the State in Contemporary Europe: The Political Structuration of Disciplinary Discourse." *International Social Science Journal* 122: 509–528.

Wallerstein, Immanuel et al., 1995. *Open the Social Sciences*. Lisbon: Report of the Gulbenkian Commission.

Wolf, Eric. 1996. "Pathways to a Global Anthropology." In Sing C. Chew and Robert A. Denemark (eds.), *The Underdevelopment of Development: Essays in Honor of Andre Gunder Frank*. London: Sage Publications.

——. 1999. "Anthropology among the Powers." *Social Anthropology* 7 (2): 121–134.

Witz, Klaus. 1995. "Science and the Object of Study in Vedanta." Paper presented at the International Congress on Vedanta, University of Madras, January.

Zohar, Donah and Ian Marshall. 1994. *Quantum Society: Mind, Physics and the New Social Vision*. London: Flemingo.

23 Psychology and the Challenge of the Postmodern Condition

We are living in the midst of fundamental processes of transformations, which are global in nature and which touch almost all the domains of our lives impacting both the contours of our social structure and the contours of our cultures. Postmodernism is a descriptive label for some of these processes of restructuring in contemporary societies. Even though as a framework for understanding contemporary structural as well as discursive transformation, postmodernism has originated in Western Europe and North America, as a perspective it has a global relevance partly because of the globalization of the cultural and structural change that started decades ago in advanced societies. Contemporary Indian society is as much a part of the postmodern condition as North America is even though the degree of belongingness might vary. In this context, what is the challenge of the postmodern condition – the crisis of representation and the crisis of social organization it entails – for the way we think about issues and imagine our universe? Indeed, we are now living in a time of structural and discursive liminality where our familiar categories are collapsing and our ways of world-making are disintegrating beyond recognition. The collapse of our familiar boundaries calls for a readjustment in our rhetorical habits which would enable us not only to study the world of "difference" that postmodernism creates, but also to live more meaningfully in this changing world. Contemporary transformations in culture and consciousness, politics and social structure pose the greatest challenge to social science as a community of imagination. This calls for an alternative process of knowledge formation where we celebrate interdisciplinarity at the very level of our being, realizing that the constitution of reality – the constitution of both society and subjectivity in contemporary period – defies any bounded disciplinary signification. If postmodernism, as the sociologist Scott Lash would argue, refers primarily to anew "mode of signification,"[1] then its significance for social science lies in challenging us to transcend our disciplinary boundaries and to cultivate what the noted anthropologist Clifford Geertz calls "imaginative entry into an alien turn to mind."[2]

What does postmodernism mean? Philosophers and literary critics would like to treat it as simply a philosophical movement built around the deconstructionist enterprise of people like Jacques Derrida. But, as a cultural anthropologist, I do not treat postmodernism as an isolated movement of doubt and reinterpretation in metaphysics. I treat postmodernism as a part of the field of contemporary transformation; hence I prefer the word "the condition of postmodernity" to postmodernism. The method of looking at postmodernism as a field has drawn inspiration from some of the most insightful commentaries on the postmodern condition, such as geographer David Harvey's, *The Condition of Postmodernity*, sociologist Scott Lash's *The Sociology of Postmodernism*, and historian Mark Poster's *The Mode of Information: Post-Structuralism and the Social Context*.[3]

But even after all these prefatory remarks, the fundamental question still remains: What does exactly postmodernism mean? My intention here is not to provide a definition of postmodernism but to attempt a description of it. In describing postmodernism, I would use two differentiating (not diametrically opposed) notions: flexibility and differentiation. Postmodernism is a movement both in the field of culture as well as in social structure, which strives towards flexibility from a centralized and standardizing regime and to recreate de-differentiation in a world already differentiated by the modernizing process. As a movement towards flexibility, postmodernism in economic activity breaks away from a regime of standardized mass production to a flexible regime of production, distribution and exchange. This movement towards flexibility is being accompanied by the rise of the "informal economy,"[4] by the reorganization of "the internal labour market" of the industries and by the deregulation and transformation of bureaucracy. In the realm of politics, postmodernism strives to create a flexible relationship between state and civil society through the transformative politics of grass roots movements. These movements are different from conventional political parties insofar as they are motivated less by "questions of distribution than by the concern for the grammar of forms of life".[5]

But this incessant striving towards flexibility is not simply confined to economy and politics, it has also not left untouched the script of life in modern society. Postmodern restructuring not only creates a flexible specialization on the shop floor, it also necessitates a flexible life course. As Buchman, in his study *The Script of Life in Modern Society: Entry into Adulthood in a Changing World* writes: "Unemployment due to structural (technological) change or economic factors undermine the life long integration in the occupational system that has characterized male occupational careers since World War II. Thus, the individual's movement through the occupational system is gradually losing its highly standardized form."[6] This loss of a standardized and predictable life course on the part of the blue-collar workers is accompanied by the rise of a "postmodern self" in case of the professional and the new middle class in advanced societies. Wood and Zurcher, in their study, *The Postmodern Self*, write that this embodies a "post-individualist" "charismatic reaction to the contradiction between formal and substantive authority embodied in the modern self."[7]

There are, however, two broad approaches to the nature of self and subjectivity in the postmodern condition. One approach celebrates the coming of a new form of subjectivity which is, to adapt the word of philosopher Fred Dallmayr, "post-individualist"[8] and is able to transcend the dualism between structure and agency, collective and the individual. Social movement theorist Alain Touraine discovers in this new subjectivity "The Return of the Actor,"[9] an actor who is not simply an egoistic monad, but who also realizes his or her own individuality through community and transformation. The other view looks at the postmodern self as a sign and a simulacrum without having any foundation whose solidarity is only a product of the frivolous play of irony and contingency.[10] Mark Poster writes: "In electronically mediated communications, subjects now float, suspended between points of objectivity, being constituted and reconstituted in relation of the discursive arrangement of the occasion."[11] In the electronic stage, "the self is decentered, dispersed, and multiplied in continuous instability."[12] In this context, sociologist Scott Lash speaks about the double identity of the new middle class in advanced societies: one built on the model of distinction and the other built on the model of difference. In Lash's insightful words, "Their identities and habituses can be fixed, rigid, status conscious on the caricatured model of the *yuppie* that is on the model of 'distinction'. On the other hand, these same social groupings also form in large part of constituency of the new social movements. Their habitusés and identities can thus be constructed importantly along lines of gender, minority ethnicities, minority sexual politics, environmentalism. [...] This is, along lines of difference rather than of invidious distinction."[13]

Indeed difference is the new language of self and society in the postmodern condition, a new mode of talking and thinking about the human condition made sacred by the deconstructionist enterprise of philosopher Jacques Derrida. Derrida challenges "hierarchy" and "opposition" as fundamental categories of human existence – the categories which provided focal metaphors during the modernist regime. Derrida argues that "such philosophical opposition as nature/culture, theory/practice, mental/manual and life/death are differentially constituted."[14] These differences are not simply passive signs or lifeless categories in a system of classification. Derrida makes us to understand the critical power of differences in resisting incorporation into a totalizing system of inequality through both "spatial and temporal deferral".[15] If human reality is differentially constituted rather than hierarchically constituted, then what about human needs? Are these still hierarchically constituted? How to think about Abraham Maslow's hierarchy of needs in the face of Derrida's postmodern differential onslaught? Its implication for psychology is, perhaps, to supplant the hierarchy of needs with a vision of simultaneity and difference, which would have more a spatial configuration rather than a simple linear ordering. I think postmodernism does pose a question to Abraham Maslow when Scott Lash writes: "[...] postmodernism can promise a subjectivity whose classificatory schemata have more in common with difference than they with the hierarchy or 'distinction'."[16] Ronald Inglehart has studied at great length the question of value and valuational ordering in case of the post-industrial societies. Inglehart writes: "[...] People tend to give priority to the safety and sustenance needs on the one hand, or to higher order needs, on other hand without assuming that there is any specific ordering within the latter group."[17] For Inglehart, who has studied at depth the contemporary culture shift in advanced industrial societies: "There does not seem to be clear hierarchy within the last set of needs, which Maslow called 'self-actualization needs'."[18]

Ashis Nandy also provides us a contemporary critique of Maslow's hierarchy of needs.[19] For Nandy, a hierarchical construction of human needs and the separation of the higher from the lower needs can obscure the fact that the pursuit of higher form of needs by those who have already fulfilled their basic needs can be carried out in a social and cultural context of narcissism and deprivation. Nandy sensitizes us to the sociological structuration of hierarchy of needs. "The privileged, having had fulfilled their basic needs, can pursue their 'Being Love' with a total unconcern for the deficiency needs of the majority."[20] Moreover, for Nandy, such asceticism of the rich "can become in the psychological sense, a defensive denial of real life suffering."[21] Nandy makes his argument clear: "But the spirit denying consumerism of the rich and the obsessive compulsive concept of monetized work of the powerful too, can be neurotic defenses against recognizing the decadence and degradation of the privileged. Concretization of happiness, success, morality, creativity and work can be pathological too. As this century has shown, there is not only Maslow's theory of hierarchy of needs but also a half articulated anti-Maslowian logic which says that if freedom can be an ego-defense and not a real substitute for bread, bread too can be an ego-defense and not a real substitute for freedom."[22] Thus, for Nandy, "[...] the so-called deficiency needs and growth needs can be, indeed must be, pursued synchronically because the two kinds of needs are vital to each other."[23]

But even though postmodernism questions Maslow's hierarchy of needs, some trends in postmodernism can corroborate Maslow's psychology of Being.[24] Maslow's Being is not simply a Fruedian Id full of instincts to start with and then socialized into a new cultured Being through familiar processes of psychological internalization and cultural socialization. It is a Being which is full of possibility to start with and socialization process is a process of mutual unfolding of this potentially Divine Being, and the patterns of culture. Sociologist Anthony Giddens' new vision about socialization which he calls "structuration" is very much along similar lines.[25] For Giddens, the process of growing up individual is not simply a product of either society or culture. This way of conceptualizing the individual and the socialization process helps us to understand the process of moral development in a new way where morality refers not simply to an obedience to a collective norms, but to have the critical faculty of one's being regarding a proper and a good life, a faculty which might question one's own cultural construction of such a good life. In a hierarchical society, patterns of culture might and, in fact, support structures of in-human inequalities, but it is the Being which has the critical faculties to transcend the givens of one's own exploitative culture and celebrate Eros rather than Thanatos.

Two contemporary philosophers help us to put in perspective this treatment of culture and Being vis-à-vis the striving for a good and meaningful life understood intersubjectively rather than simply through the prism of "possessive individualism". Agnes Heller argues in her *Beyond Justice*: "[...] a just procedure is the condition of the good life, of all possible good lives [...] but it is not sufficient for the good life. [...] All the elements of the good life are beyond justice."[26] Heller stresses that the pursuit of a good life cannot simply be a matter of particular cultural convention; it requires that vision of the Being which has the capacity of going beyond a particular cultural construction of justice which to an outsider might seem very unjust. Heller further writes; "[...]

Beyond has the connotation of 'higher', and not only being different."[27] Jurgen Habermas further illumines this process of critical consciousness of the Being which has the critical power to question cultural convention. Habermas develops his notion of "discourse ethics" where individuals are participating in a transformational process of moral argumentation not simply with the model of the socialized cultural convention but with a "moralizing gaze" which is, to some extent, beyond culture. To quote Habermas, "Under the unrelenting moralizing gaze of the participant in discourse [...] familiar institutions can be transformed into many instances of problematic justice."[28] Habermas makes this clear in his *Moral Consciousness and Communicative Action*: "Within the horizon of the life-world, practical judgments derive both their concreteness and their power to motivate action from their inner connection to unquestioningly accepted ideas of the good life, in short, from their connection to ethical life and its institutions. Under these conditions, problematization can never be so profound as to risk all the assets of the existing ethical substance. But the abstractive achievements required by the moral point of view do precisely that. This is why Kohlberg speaks of a transition to a post-conventional stage of moral consciousness. At this stage, moral judgment becomes dissociated from local conventions and historical coloration of a particular form of life."

Postmodern challenge to psychology is not confined solely to the reconceptualization of the human need and rethinking the process of moral development. It is a challenge to the very authority of psychology itself – particularly to the authority of psychoanalysis. In this way, it is a part of the global decentering of authority – be it the authority of the state or the authority of the anthropologist or authority of the psychoanalyst.[29] Postmodernism argues that our clinical ground is not as absolute as we once thought. In his essay, "The Unconscious in a Postmodern Depth Psychology," Paul Kugler argues that modernism refers to a central focus on "authorial intention" while postmodernism refers to "an epistemological crisis" emerging out of the crisis of this modernist authority and textuality. Kugler writes:

> The modernist hermeneutic was guided by the implicit assumption that the real meaning was to be found in authorial intention. What the creature intended in the process of the text is the 'real' meaning. In depth psychology, during the same period, a similar interpretive attitude was cultivated in the case of the interpretation of dreams. The analyst, as detached observer, "objectively" viewed and interpreted the patient's dream text through a knowledge of the person's psychiatric history, psychodynamics, and free associations. Through an "objective" analysis of the clinical material, it was thought to be possible to discover the patient's unconscious intentions and therefore, the 'true' meaning of the dream text.[30]

Kugler further tells us:

> The tendency to ground the set of interpretation in a transcendental signified is characteristic not only of Western metaphysics but of depth psychology as well. Psychoanalysis has traditionally grounded clinical diagnosis and therapeutic understanding on just such absolutes. To understand a symptom, we look to one of these ultimate to give authority to our diagnosis and interpretation. We look for the 'origin' of the symptom, or we attempt to discover what 'really' happened in the patient's 'history', or we view the symptom from the point of view of the 'self' and its innate tendency to 'centre' or bring 'unity' to personal life. For these 'absolutes'

to perform their interpretative function, they must themselves transcend the very clinical phenomena they seek to explain.[31]

But these absolutes are not only temporally located in the past, "the authorities for clinical interpretation might also be grounded in a posited absolute located in the future."[32] This kind of psychoanalytic explanation in terms of the transcendental absolute and "first principles" works teleologically and like Western linear historiography does violence to the case in hand. "For example, the clinical material might be interpreted as moving toward and referring to a posteriori ultimates such as the self, archetypes, wholeness, unity, spirit, soul, death and so forth. For these first principles to perform their explanatory function, they cannot be implicated in the very system of thought and language they are being used to explain; nor can their meaning have the same semantic status as other meanings within the system".[33] In this context, "postmodernism, with its intense focus on the problematic of self-reflection, textuality and the process of psychic representation, has revealed that these unquestionable 'absolutes' are not eternal, archetypal structures we once thought them to be, but are rather temporal and linguistic by-products resulting from a representational theory of language. Any such transcendental term is a fiction heuristically and clinically valuable perhaps, but nonetheless fictional."[34]

In situating postmodernism in psychology in the linguistic turn in psychoanalysis, Kugler is building upon the seminal work of Jacques Lacan. Speaking about "Depth Psychology's Turn Toward Language" Kugler writes:

> The importance of Lacan's contribution of theories of textual interpretation lies in his emphasis on the process through which personality development is dependent on and invented in a matrix of culturally determined 'symbols' (signifiers) making up our textural environment. For without the capacity of the self to represent itself, either as an image or as a word, and thereby look back at itself from another vantage point, the construction of personality and its characteristic capacity for consciousness and self-reflexibility would be impossible.[35]

In the text cited above, Kugler is referring to the representational theory of language. But postmodernism, in a way, questions this representational theory of language – the view that language represents reality. In a way, the whole postmodern movement questions the very distinction between representation and reality not only in contemporary communicative practices but also in contemporary cultural practices. In the context of the contemporary electronic "mode of information," "the representational character of language is especially fragile and problematic."[36] As Mark Poster writes: "The function of representation comes to grief when words lose their connection with things and come to stand in place of things, in short, when language represents itself. The complex linguistic worlds of the media [...] are each realms in which the representational function of language has been placed in question by different communicational patterns each of which shift to the fore point the self-referential aspect of language."[37] But to be fair to Kugler, even though Kugler is using the word "the representational theory of language," he is going beyond the divorce of reality and representation associated with it. In the same text, Kugler writes: "There is no linguistic concept that is exempt from the metaphorical status of language. No mode of discourse, not even the language of science, can be literally literal. All writing is, by its very nature ironic, simultaneously literal and figural."[38]

The very occurrence of the words "discourse" and "figure" in Kugler's above text prepares the appropriate context for introducing French postmodern philosopher J.F. Lyotard, who has something important to say regarding psychology vis-à-vis the emergent postmodern condition. In imaging the postmodern condition, Lyotard is operating with two differential (not oppositional) notions: discourse and figure. For Lyotard, modernist sensibility accords primacy to discourse; it gives central emphasis to words. But postmodernism gives primacy to figure, the figural, image and the visual. Lyotard's differential distinction between discourse and figure is parallel to American cultural critic Susan Sontag's distinction between the modernist "interpretation" and the postmodernist "sensation". For Lyotard, the figural sensitivity in the condition of postmodernity has, indeed, something to do with the creative manifestation of sensation where the "pleasure principle" is not slavishly subordinated to the "reality principle". Scott Lash tells us about the psychoanalytic implication of Lyotard's postmodern philosophy: "Lyotard's discourse is the Freudian secondary process, the ego operating in terms of the reality principle. The figural, by contrast, is the primary process of the unconscious which operates according to pleasure principle."[39] Furthermore, "Discourse discharges energy through the transformation of the external world, while figures are perceptual memories through which psychic energy is straightway discharged by investment in them."[40]

In this context, Lyotard is speaking about "libidinal politics" where desire becomes real. Here, "desire is not self-effacing. [...] desire does not need to be infused with reason in order for society to survive; creativity is a sufficient political motive."[41] This is politics of a new kind where the body politic is not only instituted anew in the human body but the body itself is participating in a politics of transformation. John Murphy sensitizes us to the politics of embodiment in the condition of postmodernity which may make desires real. Murphy writes in his insightful study, *Postmodern Social Analysis and Criticism*: "Postmodernism is consistent with what might be called radical democracy. With the periphery suddenly everywhere, a decentralized polity is not an anomaly. With the omnipotence of authority placed in question, decisions can finally be made that embrace public sentiments. The body politic is thus instituted."[42]

Thus, postmodernism does offer a set of challenges to psychology for rethinking its assumptions in the light of the contemporary transformation of self, society and culture. If psychology is to continue to act as an emancipatory perspective, then it has to help us articulate a new language about ourselves describing anew what we ought to be and redescribing what we take for granted about ourselves in our present-day world. It has also to help us understand both the work of culture and the work of the unconscious in our lives as both of these continue to be profoundly affected by the challenge of the postmodern condition – by the challenge of its structural and discursive transformation. For this, psychology has to renew itself by participating in a genuine "blurring of genres" and transform itself in a way that would enable us to live healthily, meaningfully and with dignity in a world increasingly marked by fragmentation and chaos.

Notes

1. Scott Lash, *Sociology of Postmodernism* (London and NT, Routledge, 1990).
2. Clifford Geertz, "The Uses of Diversity," *Michigan Quarterly Review* (Winter, 1986), p. 118.
3. David Harvey, *The Condition of Postmodernity* (Basil Blackwell, 1989); Lash, op. cit.; and Mark Poster, *The Mode of Information* (Polity Press, 1990).
4. A. Portes et al. (eds.), *Informal Economy* (Baltimore: The Johns Hopkins University Press, 1989) and Theierry Noyelle, *Beyond Industrial Dualism: Market and Job Segmentation in the New Economy* (Boulder, CO: Westview Press, 1987), XXIX.
5. Jurgen Habermas (ed.), *Observations on "The Spiritual Situation of the Age": Contemporary German Perspectives* (The MIT Press, 1984), XXIX.
6. Marlis Buchman, *The Script of Life in Modern Society: Entry into Adulthood in a Changing World* (Chicago, 1989), p. 48
7. Michael R. Wood and Louis R. Zurcher, Jr., *The Development of a Postmodern Self* (NY: Greenwood Press, 1988), p. 137. Also, David Menkin, *Towards a Post Industrial Psychology*. New York: John Wiley and Sons, 1978),
8. Fred Dellmayr, *The Twilight of Subjectivity: Contributions Towards a Post-Individualist Theory of Politics* (Amherst, 1981).
9. Alain Touraine, *Return of the Actor: Social Theory in the Post-industrial Society* (Minnesota, 1988).
10. Richard Rorty, *Irony, Contingency and Solidarity* (Cambridge: Cambridge University Press, 1989).
11. Mark Poster, op. cit., 1990, p. 11.
12. Ibid., p. 6.
13. Lash, op. cit., 1990, p. 23.
14. Jacques Derrida quoted in Michael Ryan, *Marxism and Deconstruction: A Critical Articulation* (Baltimore: The Johns Hopkins University Press, 1982), p. 12.
15. E.T. Barnett, *Structuralism and the Logic of Dissent* (London: MacMillan).
16. Lash, op. cit., 1990, p. 23.
17. Ronald Inglehart, *Culture Shift in Advanced Industrial Society* (Princeton University Press, 1990), p. 152.
18. Ibid.
19. Ashis Nandy, "The Idea of Development: The Experience of Modern Psychology as Cautionary Tale and as an Allergory." In Carlos A. Millnan and Oscar Nudler, (eds.), *Human Development in Its Social Context: A Collective Exploration* (London et al.: Hodder and Stoughton, 1986).
20. Nandy, op. cit., 1986, p. 250.
21. Ibid.
22. Ibid.
23. Ibid.
24. Abraham Maslow, *Towards A Psychology of Being* (New Jersey: Van Norstrand Co., 1962).
25. Anthony Giddens, *The Constitution of Society* (Cambridge: Cambridge Polity Press, 1984).
26. Agnes Heller, *Beyond Justice* (Cambridge, MA: Basil Blackwell, 1987), p. 273.

27. Ibid., p. 326.
28. Jurgen Habermas, *Moral Consciousness and Communicative Action* (Cambridge: Polity Press, 1990), p. 108.
29. For instance, in cultural anthropology, the postmodern turn has meant a fundamental questioning of "ethnographic authority". See James Clifford and George Marcus (eds.), *Writing Culture: The Politics and Poetics of Ethnography* (California, 1986).
30. Paul Kugler, "The Unconscious in a Postmodern Depth Psychology," in Karin Basrnaby and P.D.'acierno (eds.), *C.G. Jung and the Humanities: Towards a Hermeneutics of Culture* (Princeton University Press, 1990), p. 208.
31. Kugler, op. cit., 1990, p. 313.
32. Ibid.
33. Ibid., p. 313–14.
34. Ibid., p. 316.
35. Ibid., p. 312.
36. Mark Poster, *The Modes of Information: Post-Structuralism and the Social Context* (Polity Press, 1990), p. 12.
37. Ibid., p.13.
38. Kugler, op. cit.
39. Lash, op. cit., 1990, p. 177.
40. Ibid., p. 178.
41. John Murphy, *Postmodern Social Analysis and Criticism* (NY: Greenwood Press, 1989), p. 147.
42. Ibid.

24 Conquest of Self? Intimacy and Overcoming of Boundaries

> Sexuality and reproduction in the past structured one another. [...] when directly bound up with reproduction, sexuality was a medium of transcendence. Sexual activity forged a tie with the finitude of the individual, and at the same time carried the promise of its irrelevance; for seen in, relation to a cycle of generations the individual life was part of a more embracing symbolic order. Sexuality for us still carries an echo of the transcendent. Yet given that such is the case, it is bound to be surrounded with an aura of nostalgia and civilization. A sexually addicted civilisation is one where death has become stripped of meaning; life-politics at this point implies a renewal of spirituality.
>
> — Anthony Giddens (1992)
> *The Transformation of Intimacy: Sexuality, Love and Eroticism in Modern Societies*, p. 203

> Human society is a ceaseless growth, an enfoldment in terms of spirituality. If so, it must be based on ever increasing demand upon the restraint of the flesh. [...] Above all, a life of restraint presupposes an intense loving desire for reunion with god.
>
> — M.K. Gandhi (1946), *Conquest of Self*, p. 23, 21

> A closed government is bounded in a way that the self is supposed to be bounded and undisclosed in the individualist model of unethical freedom that permits us to victimize, appropriating and acquiring power of wealth behind our boundaries, without disclosing and assuming relational responsibility [...]
>
> — Michael Ryan (1989)
> *Politics and Culture: Working Hypotheses for a Post-Revolutionary Society*, p. 225

I

Commenting upon the sexual revolution taking place in American society, Pitirim Sorokin had written in 1956: "Since the 'marriage-family' school increasingly fails to graduate well-adjusted individuals and since there seems to be no other agency which can better discharge this task, the nation, and mankind at large, is bound to be made up more and more of individuals less and less capable of getting along with others. [...] Charity or love begins at home, at the cradle of the helpless baby. If there is no baby, no cradle, there can be no loving and caring parents" (1956: 11, 20). Anthony Giddens' *The Transformation of Intimacy: Sexuality, Love and Eroticism in Modern Societies (1992)*, which comments upon the same American condition but in its later phase of development, provides us not only a different – an affirmative – answer to the nagging doubts Sorokin had raised but also a different meaning of the elementary terms of conversation such as home, family and marriage. Giddens shows in this engaging book how changes taking place in the realm of intimate relations in American society in particular and western societies in general have broken asunder the supposed, teleological unity among sexuality, marriage and reproduction. Recent developments in sexual relations, for Giddens, show that it is possible to get along with each other in companionate marriage, while fighting with each other in heterosexual marriages, and nurture each other without having the need of the opposite sex and having a child as a medium.

Basing upon the ethnographic observation of men and women, and boys and girls, carried out by researchers such as Lilien Rubin and others, Giddens argues: "Heterosexual marriage superficially appears to retain its central position in the social order, making the prior discussion of lesbian relationships at best rather marginal In reality, it has been largely undermined by the rise of the pure relationship and plastic sexuality" (ibid.: 154). For Giddens, "Plastic sexuality is decentered sexuality, freed from the needs of reproduction [...] it frees sexuality from the rule of the phallus, from the overwhelming importance of male sexual experience" (ibid.: 2). This is manifested in gay, lesbian as well as in heterosexual relation where sexuality is an act of intimacy in itself, is not tied to reproduction and is not servant of an imposing long-term commitment. It goes hand in hand with the rise of "pure relationships" in the realm of sexual intimacy where one enters inside a relationship as an autonomous and free individual without any constraint. Pure relationship does not presuppose sexual purity – in fact it considers this as a liability – and is capable of accommodating multiple sexual relationships. Giddens calls it episodic sexuality as he tells us:

> A pure relationship has nothing to do with sexual purity, and is a limiting concept rather than only a descriptive one. It refers to a situation where a social relation is entered into for its own sake, for what can be derived by each person from a sustained association with another, and which is continued only insofar as it is thought by both parties to deliver enough satisfactions for each individual to stay within it. Love used to be tied to sexuality through marriage but now these are connected more and more via the pure relationship. [...] The pure relationship, to repeat. is part of a generic restructuring of intimacy. It emerges in other contexts of sexuality besides heterosexual marriage. it is in some casually related ways parallel to the development of plastic sexuality (ibid.: 58).

Episodic sexuality earlier was the preserve of the males. Giddens argues that recent developments in the sphere of intimate relations show that girls have also entered this exclusive male privilege. In fact, the significance of Giddens' present work lies in bringing to the core of the discussion the sexual experiments of the girls in the recent times. The bad/good girl distinction is not total any longer and girls feel that "they have an entitlement to engage in sexual activity, including sexual intercourse, at whatever age seems appropriate to them. [Girls now do not have to] fight to achieve sexual freedom: such freedom exists. And the problem is to make something of it in the face of male attitudes which still carry more than an echo of the past. The girls therefore emerge as the main social experimenters" (ibid.: 10).

But when girls pursue sexual experimentation, it is no longer a reiteration of the earlier male "romantic lover" but is a pursuit of what Giddens calls "confluent love". While "in romantic love attachments, the element of sublime love tends to predominate over sexual ardour'' (ibid.: 51), confluent love is contingent in which a person's sexuality "has to be negotiated as part of a relationship" (ibid.: 40).

For Giddens, in the transformation of intimacy underway in Europe and North America, both lesbian and gay relationships are examples of reflexive sexuality: "sexuality as a quality or property of the self" (ibid.: 63). But, in this transformation of intimacy there has been a transmutation of the biological categories of male and female, including the transmutation of phallus into "mere penis" (ibid.: 14). While this transmutation has made sexuality "torn between assertive sexual dependence, including the use of violence, on the one hand, and constant anxieties abut potency on the other" (ibid.: 118), in the case of women it has certainly led to liberation. According to Giddens, "Women can now see men, at least on a cognitive level, as just as much a functionless appendage as the male sexual organ itself" (ibid.).

II

Giddens describes both the limits and possibilities in the rise of such plastic sexuality. The limits are mainly the problems of compulsive sexuality and pathological co-dependency. With the public legitimation of lesbian relationships and sexual freedom, the sexual addiction of girls has come to the force. But Giddens offers a normative criticism of sexual addiction, whether it is in the male or in the female, by arguing that it is a "defensive reaction" and a "negative index of the degree to which the reflexive project of the self moves to centre-stage of late modernity" (ibid.: 153). Sexual addiction is a form of "compulsive behaviour" where the "integrity of the self as a whole is menaced" (ibid.: 76). The same problem of "reverse reflexivity" is also at work in the rise of co-dependency in the field of emergent plastic sexuality. A co-dependent is someone who is dependent upon another person for his or her definition and "cannot feel self-confident without being devoted to the needs of others" (ibid.). "Lack of self-esteem," because of abusive parentage, is a primary reason for co-dependency and therefore co-dependent persons are advised to "heal the child within" (ibid.: 89).

The promise in contemporary changes in intimate relations lies in the germs of a "non-repressive" society that it carries within itself. It is also harbinger of a companionate marriage where marriage is used as a home base by both partners who have "only a slight emotional investment" in each other (ibid.: 99). The rise of free and non-coercive engagement in sexuality is an index of "revolutionary processes, already underway in the infrastructure of personal life," which press for "psychic as well as social change" (ibid.: 155). Transformation of intimacy carries with it the promise of a "democratic personal order" not only in the area of sexuality but also in the realm of parent-child relations, and other forms of kinship and friendship (ibid.: 182). According to Giddens, "the prohibition of violence" and "avoidance of emotional abuse" are continuing challenges that current transformation of intimacy has to face.

Though Giddens locates the transformation of intimacy in social and cultural transformations taking place in the recent past, he does not agree with the Foucauldian account of the history of modern sexuality. For Giddens, *contra* Foucault, modern preoccupation with sex has not been set by the regime of power and its origins are not merely institutional; rather its origin lies in the reflexive project of the self – a project helped but not exhausted by changes in reproductive technologies. Giddens argues that to explain changes in sexuality "we have to move away from an overwhelming emphasis on discourse" (ibid.: 188). For him, "[...] sexuality has the importance for us today that it does, not because of the significance for the control systems of modernity, but because it is a point of connection between two other processes: the sequestration of experience and transformation of intimacy" (ibid.: 25).

III

Giddens traces the emergence of an "ethical framework for the fostering of non-destructive emotion" in individual and communal life in the non-coercive intimate sexual relations underway in our times (ibid.: 180). Such intimate relations provide for the "possibilities of a revitalizing of the erotic" through mutuality rather than through unequal power (ibid.: 202). Giddens has also brought the autonomy of individual action to the centre of intimacy but does not explore the question of negotiation between autonomy and mutuality. In his quick characterization of all co-dependent relations as pathological, Giddens argues that "defining personal boundaries is regarded as fundamental for a non-addictive relationship" (ibid.). For him, boundaries "counter the effect of projective identification" (ibid.: 94). But without overcoming boundaries is real love, any love for that matter, possible? Giddens privileges personal boundaries thus reiterating the vocabulary of possessive individualism which is in urgent need of transformation. Therefore, he can uncritically accept the current therapeutic labelling of co-dependency as pathological. If co-dependency also means being dependent on the other and giving love to a partner despite felt abuses, then why should it be viewed as pathological? If the task of sociological engagement is also to subject the dominant style of thinking to a critical scrutiny by bringing in different styles of non-institutional reflection, then is it not important for Giddens, who is interested in reflexive mobilization of self, to explore different alternatives possible within a labelled type? After all, what is the meaning of self-confidence when one is part of a relationship? This exploration would help us raise further questions to the contemporary discourse rather than just celebrate it, such as: is it not challenge for pure relationship to overcome the boundaries between self and non-self? With a view of intimacy based upon inviolable boundaries and self-confidence, how do we come to terms with the view that love makes us vulnerable rather than powerful?

In this account of transformation of intimacy, Giddens himself points out the contradictions in pure relationship. He shows us the tension existing in lesbian relationships because of promiscuity and the use of violence in such relationships. Therefore, on the part of women, lesbian sexuality can be looked upon as a step towards a more democratic sex but cannot be treated as an end in itself. Giddens himself talks about the "return of the phallus" in some of the sexual activities lesbians are engaged in such as hair pulling and beating. Here, along with the challenge of overcoming boundaries, there is also challenge of overcoming one's ego. Children, men, women – all have ego, and distortions ego can bring to the work of a "pure relationship" are enormous. Though modern feminist scholarship has looked at the problem of gender at the conjunction of race and class, it has by and large left the problem of ego untouched. However, whether we speak of intimacy or democracy or intimacy as democracy, the next battles are to be fought vis-à-vis the challenge of ego in individual and collective lives. Overcoming one's egoistic boundaries certainly constitutes an arena of "life politics," which is concerned with generativity rather than distributive power, in Giddens' sense.

Giddens looks at the transformation of intimacy as an instance of both institutional reflexivity and self-reflexivity. Though he shows us reflexivity of self vis-à-vis modern institutions, he does not provide the account of reflexivity of the self vis-à-vis itself. What is the nature of the self and what place intimacy and sexuality have got in its total scheme of things – its scheme of being and becoming? How does sexual engagement relate to seeking of meaning in other engagements? At what point does sexuality itself become an addiction to be distantiated from in the meditation of the self? The meditation of self, according to Charles Taylor, involves discovering and realizing a set of "qualitative distinctions" (Taylor 1989). Lately, even political scientists have started speaking of higher desire and lower desire – "the inner conflict between what the individuals themselves experience as their more desirable and less desirable desires" (Offe and Preuss 1991). I am not arguing that sexual engagement is an instance of lower desire but does a reflexive mobilization of the self come to term with such questions at all at any point? About sexual over-indulgence, Sorokin had written: "[...] over-indulgence of sex urge tends to undermine the physical and mental health and vitality of the individual, destroys his sense of morality, diminishes his creative energy?" (Sorokin 1956: 56). One can probably disagree with Sorokin's assertion but does a reflexive self at all confront such questions in its sojourn? Can a reflexive self totally discount what Sorokin hints at "the possibility of transmuting an unsatisfied sexual drive into a form of creative achievement?" (ibid.: 72). These questions inevitably bring us to the issue of the nature of the self – its sources and its manifold aspirations. Though Giddens (1984) had told us in his *Constitution of Society* that he is more interested in questions of ontology than epistemology he does not really probe into ontological questions such as the nature of self and culture (see Pande 1989). Without a deeper reflection on the nature of the self, it is no wonder that Giddens can only work with the visible boundaries of the self.

Of many contradictions in pure relationships that Giddens talks of what is conspicuous by its absence is the question of purity of action and intention in a relationship. Giddens says that a pure relationship can accommodate multiple sexual encounters. But he himself admits that such sexual encounters bring tensions to a relationship. A processual analysis of resolution of such tensions would have made Giddens grapple with the question of purity of action and intention of actors rather than dismiss it as a non-issue. Giddens says that confluent love can revive the "aesthetic qualities" of actors as participants of sexual activity (1992: 202). But does this aesthetic experience not have at least the potential to make actors reflexive about "eroticism as cultivation of feeling, expressed through bodily sensation" (ibid.) and use it as a basis for a transcendent spiritual realization. In other words, does not sexual pleasure beginning with the denudation of body, in its aesthetic turn end with its cultural and spiritual adornment? Do these moments of aesthetic realization not initiate a process of reflection within actors to purify their instruments of pleasure? If the kind of changes that Giddens is describing are a step to future, then, the issue of purification of intention and action cannot be dismissed totally.

The delinking of sexuality from reproduction is probably the most important feature of the transformation of intimacy that Giddens talks about. He makes a reference to contraception and other reproductive technologies in this regard. He looks at this delinking in the context of technological changes as well as of shifting mentalities. But he takes for granted the non-contentious articulation of this delinking as offered by the dominant discourse. In the American heartland itself, a serious ideological battle has been going on around the issue of abortion where the participants are not only those women who celebrate the freedom of sexuality from reproduction but also women in pro-life movements who have consistently questioned the delinking of sexuality from reproduction. In fact, they have offered a cultural critique of such delinking. Faye Ginsburg's (1989) engaged ethnography of the abortion debate presents the voices of some such critics of contemporary culture of sexuality. Ginsburg writes about the vision that animates pro-life women in the American community that she studied. Pro-life activists

> [...] accept differences but not necessarily hierarchy in the social and biological roles of men and women. Their reform efforts are directed toward creating and promoting a social and political context that they feel will protect and enhance essential condition that, in general, distinguishes men from women: pregnancy and motherhood and the central attribute assigned to it in this culture – the self-sacrificing nurturance of dependents (1989: 7).

Ginsburg also tells us how in their fight against abortion, pro-life activists are fighting against the forces of "materialism and narcissism" that are "displacing the nurturant ties of kin and community" and to "reform the more dehumanizing aspects of contemporary capitalist culture" (ibid.: 9). They strive to control destructive male sexuality and transform "raw masculinity" into a nurturant power. They associate abortion with the profit-making motive and liken abortion clinics to "7–11" convenience stores (ibid.: 5). In their attacks against abortion, they are not only concerned with women and womanliness, gender and sexuality but also with what Touraine might call "self-production of society" and the reproduction of American culture as a whole (see Giri 1989). In the right-to-life view, abortion comes to signify "not only a withdrawal of unconditional, self-sacrificing nurturace but the devaluation of culture itself" (Ginsburg 1989: 109).

The above account of Ginsburg shows that there are still many women in American society who value motherhood and would like to take responsibility for the foetus that is born of sexual relation.[2] In his earlier work on modernity and self-identity, Giddens had told us that reflexive mobilization of the self which is not an extension of the control systems of modernity takes place primarily, though not exclusively, in the field of contemporary social and cultural movements. If he had brought some related social movements such as the pro-life movement into the orbit of discussion he would have encountered a more differentiated ideological landscape where the point about delinking sexuality from reproduction is itself subjected to intense ideological criticism.

The genius of Giddens lies in elevating sociological analysis to a level of normative criticism which is evident from his critique of sexual addiction. With this Giddens would be open to the possibility of taking such normative criticism to still greater heights and explore the pathways that Bellah and his colleagues open up: "Attending means to concern ourselves with the larger meaning of things in the longer run, rather than with the short-term pay offs. The pursuit of immediate pleasure, or the promise of immediate pleasure, is the essence of distraction. A good society is one in which attention takes precedence over distraction" (Bellah et al. 1991: 273). In his own account, Giddens many times refers to manifold relationships between spirituality and emergent plastic spirituality. Therefore, to ask such questions as can sexuality be a source and field of spirituality would not be unfair to Giddens. But to come to terms with such questions Giddens would have to meditate on the frontiers of spirituality at the present juncture. From *The Class Structure in Advanced Societies* (Giddens 1973) to *The Transformation of Intimacy*, Giddens' career has been a quest of creativity and continuous transgression of boundaries. The next thing we can expect from this remarkable interpreter of our times is a work on spirituality which is in fact long overdue given his preoccupation with what he himself calls the "transformative capacity of actors" (Giddens 1984). But for this Giddens would have to be not only an ethnographer but a spiritual seeker questioning not only the "post-metaphysical thinking" of the time but also going beyond the exclusionary rationalistic foundation of European sociology and philosophy.

Notes

1. This chapter explores the way sociology can relate to contemporary issues and go beyond some of its canons by discussing Anthony Giddens' work *The Transformation of Intimacy: Sexuality, Love and Eroticism in Modern Societies* by (Cambridge: Polity Press, 1992).
2. Here we also cannot forget the practice of surrogate motherhood and its implication for the narrative of plastic sexuality that Giddens speaks of.

References

Bellah, Robert et al. 1991. *The Good Society*. NY: Alfred A. Knof.

Gandhi, M.K. 1946. *Conquest of Self.* Bombay: Thacker & Co.

Giddens, Anthony. 1973. *The Class Structure of Advanced Societies*. New York: Harper & Row.

——. 1984. *The Constitution of Society*. Cambridge: Polity Press.

——. 1991. *Modernity and Self Identity: Self and Society* in *the Late Modern Age*. Cambridge: Polity Press.

——. 1992. *The Transformation of Intimacy: Sexuality, Love and Eroticism* in *Modern Societies*. Cambridge: Polity Press.

Ginsburg, Faye D. 1989. *Contested Lives: Abortion Debate in an American Community*. Berkeley: University of California Press.

Giri, Ananta Kumar. 1989. "Narratives of Creative Transformations: Constituting Critical Movements in Contemporary American Culture." *Dialectical Anthropology* 14: 331–43.

Habermas, Jurgen. 1993. *Post-metaphysical Thinking*. Cambridge: Polity Press.

Offe, Claus and Ulrich K. Preuss. 1991. "Democratic Institutions and Moral Resources". In David Held (ed.), *Political Theory Today*, Oxford: Polity Press, pp. 143–71.

Pande, G.C. 1989. *The Meaning and Process of Culture as Philosophy of History*. Allahabad: Raka Prakashan.

Ryan, Michael. 1989. *Politics and Culture: Working Hypotheses for a Post-Revolutionary Society*. Baltimore, MD: The Johns Hopkins University Press.

Sorokin, Pitirim A. 1956. *The American Sex Revolution*. Boston: Porter Sargent Publishers.

Taylor, Charles. 1989. *The Sources of the Self*. Cambridge, MA: Harvard University Press.

25 Anthropological Imagination and Forgetting

A Glimpse into Milan Kundera's A Book of Laughter and Forgetting

An anthropological imagination is an imagination of a bird which flies into other spaces and brings "views from afar". This view is presented to others through a "thick description" of the human condition observed. The encounter of the anthropological imagination with the human condition is a unique one. The anthropological imagination encounters the human condition in a specific space and in a specific time under some general theory of man, culture and society. The anthropological imagination observes man, society and culture in a specific locale and many times puts these specific locales in the wider complex of a general theory and the world system. The problems of the general and the particular, data and theory, thick description and theoretical generalization and localization of the human condition and the universal implications of it are integral aspects of the anthropological imagination.

In so far as the proclivity of the anthropological imagination to discover human condition in a specific locale is concerned, it shares goal, method and spirit with the craft of an historian and the mind of a novelist. All the three observers and commentators on the human condition – the anthropologist, the historian and the novelist – share a basic commonality in their sensitivity to the particular. If, as Clifford Geertz tells us, every discipline is like a culture providing the interactive field for the ethos, world-view and imagination of the practitioners, then there are some close parallels among the three disciplines – the disciplines of anthropology, of history and of novel (Geertz 1983). The parallelism between history and anthropology has been widely discussed in the literature. On the other hand, the close neighbourliness between anthropology and novel requires further elaboration.

In recent years those who have spoken about *Writing Ethnography* have made us aware of the links between anthropological constructions and the construction of a novel. Hence, James Clifford speaks of anthropological allegory. Anthropological truth is certainly allegorical. But, the common foundation of the culture of the novelist and the anthropologist that I seek to stress here is something different. The anthropologists as members of a tribe train themselves how to observe the particularities of the human condition and describe it thickly. The same is also of the training of the novelist. A novelist like an anthropologist has to be an astute observer of detail. Both of them have to train themselves to observe clues and to make mountain from this molehill of the clue. Hence, in so far as professional training and acculturation is concerned, anthropological imagination not only requires an encounter with other ethnographies written by other anthropologists but also reading, understanding and analysing novels as observations on the human condition. This motivates the border-crossing conversation between anthropological imagination and the themes in Milan Kundera's *A Book of Laughter and Forgetting* (1981) in this chapter.

Kundera's novel has a number of themes which could be of interest to students of anthropology and sociology. The central theme, of course, is the significance of memory and the politics of forgetting. In this novel, most of Kundera's characters encounter the problems either of memory or of forgetting or of both. Kundera has two stories under the same title "Lost Letters". In the first story, the hero Mirek is struggling desperately to have his lost love letters from his previous woman of love Zdena. Mirek in this story had loved an ugly girl. He loved her because his inferior social condition could not have allowed him to anchor upon a better one. But somehow he left this ugly girl, got married, and had children. Now, he wants to remember the secret of his youth, hence wants to get hold of his letters lying with his old girl friend. For Kundera, "The reason Mirek wanted to go back to his origins was to have a better idea of where he had gone wrong". Mirek wants to get of hold of his lost letters because he wants to erase his past with Zdena by destroying these letters. In the second story, Tamina struggles to regain the lost love letters of her husband left in Prague, Czechoslovakia. Tamina and her husband had to leave Czechoslovakia because of their opposition to the totalitarian regime there. Tamina's husband dies shortly after his migration to some place in Western Europe. Tamina works as a waitress in a restaurant. She has to struggle hard to regain the memory of her husband and also to regain her lost letters. Her lost letters are the most desired object of her life. Unlike Mirek, she does not want to erase the past and rewrite it. Rather, by getting hold of these letters, "she wants to give the past back its lost body" (ibid.: 88). This object of her past is the source of her strength in the present. This is her most significant possession. She wants to recover the letters untouched by anybody else. Kundera here contrasts the spirit of Tamina with the spirit of a poet. For a poet, it is a crucial defeat not to have been read by a single reader. But for Tamina, if a single individual reads her lost letter, the worth of her letter loses its significance for her.

As Kundera argues, the intensity of the individual's will to retain memory in the novel has to be understood in the context of the constant struggle of the state to erase people's memory. Kundera writes: "The basic event of the book is the story of totalitarianism, which deprives people of memory and retools them into a nation of children" (ibid.: 233). So, after long years of struggle, Tamina ends up in the island of children. Metaphorically, childhood here represents forgetting and lack of memory. These children in the island are addressed by the president of forgetting. The president addresses the children as the future of mankind. This president, it seems, is no other than the president of Czechoslovakia. For Kundera, "The reason children are the future is not that they will one day be grown-ups. No, the reason is that mankind is moving more and more in the direction of infancy, and childhood is the image of the future" (ibid.: 186).

Kundera also tells us: "The first step in liquidating a people is to erase its memory" (ibid.: 169). To be able to remember one's past, one's tradition is to be able to live truly and independently. Forgetting, on the other hand, is a type of death. "Forgetting is a form of death ever present within life" (ibid.: 235). The story of conquest in history is in a way the story of the conquest of a people's memory. Conquest of a group is accompanied by efforts of organized forgetting. As Kundera writes, "The struggle of man against power is the struggle of memory against forgetting" (ibid.).

It might be argued that Kundera's use of terms like "people's memory" reflects the problematic nature of his conceptions. People are stratified along lines of class, status, ethnicity, religion, power and gender in a national community. Hence, to speak of the memory of a nation might be misleading from an anthropological point of view. But, the problem here is not one of absolute inappropriateness, rather one of level. Kundera is basically faced with the problem of a nation subjected to domination by another outside power. So, at this level, he speaks of the memory of a nation.

The theme of memory and the struggle over it delineated in this novel is interesting from the point of view of discussion on production of history in history and anthropology. In this discussion, the significance of the communicative and symbolic aspect of the past in social and political struggles is strongly emphasized. Struggle takes places not solely around material resources. If memory, as Margaret Mead argues, is the basis of the people's communal life, the control of this memory is also the clue to the control of a people. "Real community is based upon memory, on shared experience over time, continually revivified by comment, by reference, by telling the story over and over again" (Mead in Cassidy 1982: 169).

To understand the significance of memory in social life, both in structure and in its practice, we have to understand the true meaning of memory. "One might suppose that memory simply refers to the past. [...] If time is not a succession of 'present' but 'presenting', in the sense attributed to this by Heidegger, then memory is an aspect of presenting" (Giddens 1984: 450). Hence memory is not simply "remembrance of things past" rather an active element in "presenting" (ibid.: 46). Moreover, for Giddens, memory, perception and language are closely linked (ibid.: 45–46). As perception is a simultaneous mechanism of selection and elimination (ibid.: 46), human memory is also "a marvelous instrument of elimination and transformation – especially what we call the collective memory" (Bloch 1961: 114). On the other hand, if language is close to memory and if communication is at the centre of language, then forgetting represents the pathology of communication (Levi-Strauss 1985: 187). Having a view of memory as "presencing" and forgetting as "pathology of communication," it is easy to make sense of Tamina's intense desire to retain her memory in spite of the constant efforts of both the children in the island and her aspiring lover to make her oblivious of her past. In the novel, we see different agents involved in the struggle over the memory and the past. The individuals are constantly producing and recreating their own histories. This is evident in the characters of Mirek and Tamina.

In the first story in the book, Mirek wants to rewrite his own history. For Kundera, "Mirek is as much a rewriter of history as the Communist Party, all political parties, all nations, all men" (1981: 22). People are fighting for "access to the laboratories where photographs are retouched and biographies and histories are rewritten" (ibid.). If Mirek and others want to erase their memory, Tamina wants to preserve it despite all odds. Tamina had spent eleven years with her husband in Bohemia and eleven note books remained behind with her mother-in-law. She is aware, of course, that there might be many unpleasant things in the note books. But she is not intrigued by it because she wants to derive the inspiration for living from the realities of the past. In her search for the past, she is not "compelled by a desire for beauty". So, both the individuals and the state are constantly involved in the struggle over the past, some to preserve its memory, others to erase it. In this struggle, we can see parallels with the discussions on "Invention of Tradition" and "Production of History" (Hobsbawm and Ranger 1983; Cohen 1986). As Cohen tells us, "The control of voices on the past has been critical and remains critical in all sorts of settings" (Cohen 1986).

In the novel, linked with the theme of memory, are the themes of resistance and body as the final repository of resistance. Tamina with the memory of her husband constantly strives to resist the forces of domination and temptation. Even though Kundera is not explicit about the fact that her strength to resist resides in her memory, there are enough clues in the novel to make this inference. For example, when Tamina feels seemingly oblivious of her husband's memory, she wants to find it out by traveling all over the world. When she is no more in touch with her husband's memory, she goes out with another boy. Here Cohen's points are helpful: "History and memory are as much about resistance and suppression as they are about creation and recollection" (ibid.: 4). In anthropological discussion on the ability to resist the larger forces of domination and penetration, an individual's membership in a close familial and communal relationship has been considered a critical variable. Herbert Gutman's study demonstrates the creative power of kinship bonds and kinship symbols in organizing the defense and the survival of the slave population (see Medick and Sabean 1984: 22). The fact that an individual's memory of and participation in a close intimate bond, personal or social, enhances his or her power of resistance is also stressed by Levi-Strauss: "A certain restoration of partial societies offers a final chance of providing ailing freedoms with a little health and vigor" (Levi-Strauss 1985: 285).

If forgetting is a key concern in Kundera's novel, so is body. There is a close link between memory, forgetting, body and resistance. If we understand Tamina's memory as not simply remembering past events but rather as an active element in "presencing" this is also an embodied presence with potential of embodied memorization and resistance. Kundera himself writes about body: "The old duality of body and soul has become shrouded in scientific terminology, and we can laugh at it as merely an obsolete prejudice" (Kundera 1984: 40). In this novel, Kundera shows, in many places, how body is the irreducible locale of one's own identity. Tamina does not want to see her husband disgraced by the violations done to his corpse. Hence, she wants to burn her husband's corpse.

Body is also a source of resistance. In her discussion of women's body and its resistance, Emily Martin writes: "Women find in the concrete experience of their bodies a different notion of time that counters the way time is socially organized in our society" (Martin 1987: 197). In many varieties of structuralism, it is presumed that mind is the product of society and body is the domain of the individual. But we can reverse this: if body is the domain of the individual, it also contains the potential to resist the mind of society.

This potential is reflected in the character of Marketa. Marketa's husband Karel is a flirt. One fine morning when the phone rang for her husband, Marketa could be sure that it was from a girl. This ring did not count nearly so much as what it represented: "an eloquent condensation of her whole life situation" (Kundera 1981: 37). In her entire life, Marketa has played the role of the better partner and has suffered silently her husband's infidelities. But when Marketa is not able to tolerate anymore, she wants to be "all body" and to do away with all these "unwritten agreements" (ibid.: 50). When Marketa is in bed with her husband Karel and with her friend Eva, she is tempted to make love to Eva. But just looking at her husband brings her back to her usual role. Even though she is with Eva, the presence of the man she loves too much weighs heavy on her and dampens the pleasures of the senses. Kundera shows that the minute she severs Karel's head form her body, she feels the "new and intoxicating touch of freedom'. At the height of her passion, Marketa "tried to be all body, a body pressed against a dear friend and a headless man" (ibid.). The fact that Marketa's resistance is accompanied by her imaginative severance of Karel's head from his body suggests that one's resistance and search for freedom requires a break from mental conventions and a return to one's body.

In Kundera, not only is the body a source of resistance, but the shape resistance takes may be very unconventional and implicit, hence requiring more sensitivity to make sense. Let us reflect upon the way Tamina resists the violation of her body by Hugo, a violation which would constitute a violation of her husband's memory. Hugo promises her that he would get back her lost letters from Prague. This compels Tamina to a very complex situation, to go to bed with Hugo. But, the image of her husband comes constantly before her eyes. Even in his 25th attempt, Hugo is not successful in engaging her in sexual act. Tamina is not completely submitting herself even though she is in bed with Hugo. This shows the subtle line of demarcation between submission and resistance. The complexity of situations in which a novelist's characters live, give him or her more dialectical and relational view of resistance where it is not easy to know where resistance begins and passivity ends. Moreover, it is the mind of the novelist which can inform the anthropological imagination that passivity may be a type of resistance.

The relationship between the private and the public is another theme in this novel that can actively engage one's anthropological imagination. In his talk with Philip Roth, Kundera shows how forgetting is a problem both in the private and in the public domain. Kundera writes: "The metaphysics of man is the same in the private sphere as in the public one. [...] Politics unmasks the metaphysics of private life, private life unmasks the metaphysics of politics" (ibid.: 235). This has two implications: (a) the relationship between the private and the public has to be redefined, and (b) in understanding everyday life which may supposedly belong to the domain of private life we have to be sensitive to the outside structuring forces. Hence, as C.W. Mills told us long ago, biographies and histories should be studied in their mutual implication (Mills 1959). Alf Ludke also argues: "the interdependence of private and political should be systematically included in a historical reconstruction" (Ludke 1982). This means in understanding the private, we are obliged to take note of the public and the vice versa. This means in understanding the larger structures of society and history, we have to take note of the realities of "everyday life".

In the last decades, "common sense" (1983) and "everyday life" (Giddens 1984) have been central themes in human inquiry ranging from philosophy to anthropology. The discussion on "everyday life" and "practice" in sociology and anthropology has to be understood in the light of the fact that this is meant to empower the common sense of the actor. Hence, it is not just an accident that those who have spoken of the centrality of everyday life have also spoken of the significance of practical consciousness, as opposed to discursive consciousness (cf. Giddens 1984). In Kundera's novel, like any other novel, the discussion of everyday life gives us clues to understand the creativity and constraint of the agents in their relationship with the large structures. The point I seek to make here is that the recent fascination of anthropological imagination with practice can gain a lot from the close observation of everyday life in novels.

Moreover, the reality of everyday life is marked by uncertainty and ambiguity. Hence, it is the source of creativity and resistance. In Kundera, ambiguity and lack of boundary are persistent themes. These come out most clearly in his sections on "The Angels" and "The Border". He shows how the boundary between the angel and devil is not a clear and a fixed one. For him, this is also not desirable. As he writes, "If there is too much uncontested meaning on earth (the reign of the angels), man collapses under the burden; if the world loses all its meaning (the reign of the demons), life is every bit as impossible" (1981: 61). This, in a way, is linked to his arguments about border. In Jan's character in his novel, Kundera is eager to correct Jan's view of the border. While for Jan, border represents a kind of cataclysmic break, for Kundera border is perennially with us at every moment. For Kundera, "But I feel Jan is wrong in thinking that the border is a line dissecting man's life at a given point, that it marks a turning point in time, a definite second on the clock of human existence. No. In fact, I am certain that the border is constantly with us [...]" (ibid.: 217). We can gain a lot by applying Kundera's notion of the border to the reality of social life, especially to the relationship between structure and agency and between rules and practice. With such a notion of the border, we can understand that agents have the potentiality to cross the border between the omnipotence of rules and its negation and transformation. With this view, we can laugh at both the angels and devils in social theory and social life. The angels who laugh at the omnipotence of rules do not see that behind the border, there is the domain of ambiguity, 'liminality' and unpredictability. Hence, like Kundera's angels in the novel, they are infinitely laughable. The devil who sees no rule is also a laughing-stock. To an anthropological imagination, both the angel and devil miss the "border" as the intermediary ground between "rule" and its negation.

Apart from the significance for social theory, Kundera's novel has rich insights for substantive issues in anthropology, such as gender and the family. Kundera shows how women, even though considered as objects, know how to protest. Here, Kundera uses the analogy of the worker and the hammer. "The worker may be the hammer's master, but the hammer still prevails. A tool knows exactly how it is meant to be handled" (ibid.: 209). So, Kundera is according more power and creativity to those individuals and groups which are considered as objects by those who wield more power. He writes: "It would therefore seem that a woman undergoes cosmic transformation in two directions; up from object to being, down from being to object" (ibid.). Marcel Mauss' discussion on the inalienability between person and thing is relevant to all varieties of relations where beings are supposedly made into things. Kundera shows how we have to add the dimension of time to understand woman both as thing and as being. The introduction of time is not only revealing in the context of the supposedly master-slave, person-'thing' relationship; it is also crucial to understand roles in many different social contexts, especially in the context of the family. Kundera's discussion of the mother-in-law over a period of time is insightful for students of family and society. Marketa's mother-in-law in her old age is almost like a child. She can no more exercise power over Marketa. Rather, she is defenseless like a child. This has parallel to what two most distinguished students of family role write: "Roles within the family then are not to be analysed out of context in terms of a universal set of judgments. Rather, in fulfilling roles, individuals are carrying on a series of exchanges, which may involve inequality at one level, with a reversal of inequality at another" (Medick and Sabean 1984: 18).

The philosophy of history that emerges in novel is equally provocative. For Kundera, the struggle over the future and the present is, in fact, a struggle over the past. He further implies that the past contains the variations from which present and future have to choose. This view of history seems closer to works in historiography as reflected in the works of Marshall Sahlins. As against western historiography, Sahlins pleads for another historiography to capture another mode of history that he calls heroic history. In such historiography, "The life that the ancestors lived forth in history is the same as that active in the living" (Sahlins 1983: 528). Contingent events, in this historiography, are understood as the recurrent manifestation of the same cosmogonic experiences. But such a view of history has a potential conservatism embedded in it. If all the creative potentialities of human society are to be moulded by the variations contained in the past, then where is the room for innovation and cataclysmic transformation? Moreover, the issue of memory as an active element of historical consciousness and reconstruction leads us to understand the links between historical truth and narrative truth. Kundera's novel shows that the past is not simply the condition for the realization of the present, rather it is the crystallization of memory.

With this dialogue between anthropological imagination and Kundera's *A Book of Laughter and Forgetting*, we can conclude with Kundera's arguments about the role of the novel in arousing man's critical consciousness: "The novelist teaches the reader to comprehend the world as a Question. [...] In a world built on sacrosanct certainties the novel is dead" (ibid.: 237). This is also, in a way, the vocation of the historian. As Marc Bloch writes: "[...] a historical work should make its readers hungry – hungry to learn, that is, and above all to enquire" (Bloch 1961: xx). Anthropology with its "views from afar" also raises perplexing questions for the civilization (Diamond 1974). Anthropology tries to question the familiar assumptions in one's own society by bringing the perspective of the excluded and the marginalized (Martin 1987). Anthropological imagination inspires those who are involved to question the naturalization of history and culture in one's own society and thus helping in its transformation.

References

Adams, R.M. 1981. "The Cold Comedian". *New York Review of Books*, Vol. 28, February 5: 22–23.

Bloch, M. 1961. *Feudal Society*. Chicago: The University of Chicago Press.

Bold, A. 1981. "Half Love, Half Joke". *Times Literary Supplement*, February 5, 131.

Bourdieu, P. 1977. *Outline of a Theory of Practice*. Cambridge: Cambridge University Press.

Cassidy, R. 1982. *Margaret Mead: A Voice for the Century*. New York: Universe Books.

Cohen, D.W. 1986. "The Production of History", position paper for the Fifth Roundtable in Anthropology and History, Paris, July.

Diamond, S. 1974. *In Search of the Primitive: A Critique of Civilization*. New Jersey: Transaction Books.

Geertz, C. 1983. *Local Knowledge*. New York: Basic Books.

Giddens, A. 1984. *The Constitution of Society*. Cambridge: Polity Press.

Hobsbawm, E. and T. Ranger (eds.) 1983. *The Invention of Tradition:* Cambridge: Cambridge University Press.

Kundera, M. 1981. *The Book of Laughter and Forgetting*. New York: Penguin Books.

——. 1984. *The Unbearable Lightness of Being*. New York: Harper & Row.

Levi-Strauss, C. 1985. *The View from Afar*. New York: Basic Books.

Ludke, A. 1982. "The Historiography of Everyday Life: The Personal and Political", in Raphael Samuel and G.S. Jones (eds.), *Culture, Ideology, and Politics*. London: Routledge.

Martin, E. 1987. *The Woman in the Body: A Cultural Analysis of Reproduction*. Boston: Beacon Press.

Medick, H. and D. Sabean (eds.) 1984. *Interest and Emotion: Essays on the Study of Family and Kinship*. Cambridge: Cambridge University Press.

Miller, N. "Review of Kundera 1981". *The Antioch Review*, Vol. 39 (Spring): 260.

Mills, C.W. 1959. *The Sociological Imagination*. New York: Oxford University Press.

Sahlins, M. 1983. "Other Times Other Custom: The Anthropology of History". *American Anthropologist* 85 (13), 511–543.

26 Epistemological Crisis in Anthropology

The Case of the Quest for the Real Samoa

The publication of Derek Freeman's critique of Margaret Mead has generated widespread controversy in anthropology all over the world. Because of the wide popularity of Margaret Mead, this Mead-Freeman debate also attracted great media attention. In American anthropology, the response to this debate has been of two different styles. For the majority of American respondents to this debate, Freeman is equally wrong in his ethnography of Samoa, and his critique is less a scholarly exercise and more a personal vilification of the work of Margaret Mead (Holmes 1986; Shankman 2009; Schneider 1983; Weiner 1983). This style of response presupposes the same naturalistic, positivistic and realistic epistemological framework as that of Freeman. In this perspective, there is a real Samoa which for Freeman is missed, misconstrued and misrepresented by Mead, and which for Mead's enthusiastic American defenders, is totally misrepresented by Freeman.

But another style of response in American anthropology has tried to understand Mead-Freeman controversy from the point of view of epistemology and its crisis (Clifford 1986; Schwartz 1983). In this framework, the problem is not the correct depiction of Samoan reality; rather, it is the construction of many supposedly "accurate" descriptions of Samoan reality. The central issue here is the crisis of epistemology and "ethnographic authority" entailed by multiple constructions of Samoa. Schwartz writes: "Beyond Samoa what is at stake is the epistemology and status of anthropology" (Schwartz 1983: 923). Clifford's response best reflects this perspective:

> Two competing portrayals or Samoan life are cast as scientific projects; but both configure the other as a morally charged alter-ego. Mead's 'experiment' in controlled cultural variation now looks less like science than allegory – a too sharply focused story of Samoa suggesting a possible America. Derek Freeman's work ignores any possible literary dimensions in ethnographic work, however, and applies its own brand of scientism, inspired by recent developments in sociobiology But as Freeman heaps up instances of Samoan anxiety and violence, the allegorical frame for his own understanding begins to emerge (Clifford 1986: 102).

In this chapter, my objective is to try to understand Mead-Freeman controversy as an instance of epistemological crisis in anthropology. In the history of anthropology, critiques of earlier monographs by later ethnographers are not something new. But, only Mead-Freeman controversy has generated such intense debate. In order to understand this, we have to treat this debate from the point of view of the sociology of knowledge.

For the last many decades both scientists and laymen have been intensely aware of the simultaneous integration and the fragmentation of the contemporary world system (Bright and Geyer 1987). Critique of hegemony in the socio-economic domain of the world system has paralleled a fundamental critique of "representation," "ethnographic authority" and "cross-cultural" translation in the domain of social sciences. This has made all of us aware of the contested and "ideological" nature of the representation of other societies. Hence, the intensity of Mead-Freeman controversy is due not so much to the internal elements in this debate but to the general critical "anti-representational" discourse of our time.

In the treatment of Mead-Freeman controversy, I have been influenced by two recent anthropological restudies. The first is Robert Borofsky's restudy of Pukapukan social organization in his *Making History* (Borofsky 1987). The foreword to this book declares: "Whereas Freeman is intent on attacking the credibility of Mead as a field-worker [...] Borofsky is more concerned with understanding how the inevitable biases of ethnographers influence the results they achieve. Borofsky is engaged in the archaeology of ethnography" (Borofsky 1987: xiii). Another is the restudy of Tchambuli, a society studied by Margaret Mead, and by Errington and Gewertz (1987). In their restudy, they are interested to show how Mead misunderstood and misrepresented Tchambuli social categories of individualism. Errington and Gewertz's work is interesting in its own right, because it is another restudy of Mead. In order to understand Mead-Freeman controversy as an instance of epistemological crises in anthropology, it is essential to understand the nature of anthropological epistemology.

Anthropological Epistemology and Its Crisis

In Western society, anthropology emerged as an institutionalized field of study of the other societies in the second half of the 19th century. For Marshall Mcluhan et al. (1989), anthropology is the only field of human inquiry that has broken Western society's characteristic narcissistic preoccupation with itself and has opened up for a genuine understanding of other societies and cultures. However, from the very beginning, the others have not been understood on their own terms; rather they have been constructed in particular ways for the Western audience. What Edward Said (1978, 1989) proposes about the essential nature of Orientalism is helpful in understanding anthropology. For Said, Orientalism has less to do with Orient than it does with our world. The basic objective of Orientalism is to claim "a kind of intellectual authority over the Orient within Western culture" (Said 1978: 18).

Clifford's (1983b) arguments about "ethnographic authority" shows that the representation of reality, rather than the depiction of "truth", is the basis of "ethnographic authority". For Clifford, textuality is the basis of ethnographic authority. In the construction of anthropological texts, the native is almost always excluded, his or her voice never comes to the force. In Mead's work many elements of ethnographic epistemology are present. In all her ethnographic cases, she is interested in how the study of an ethnographic case can illuminate our understanding of problems in modern Western society, especially the American society. Mead also believes that the nature of primitive life is simple and one can understand its structure in a period of five or six months. Therefore, she assumes that she can grasp Samoan culture within four or five months. Her positivistic epistemology is fully revealed when she writes in the conclusion to her book on Samoa: "As far our materials permitted, an experiment has been conducted to discover what the process of development was like in a society very different from our own" (Mead 1928: 195). In her preface to *Male and Female,* Mead (1949) shows how anthropological representation of another society has an authoritative superiority over other types of descriptions of other cultures. She asserts that the study of other societies by the amateurs lack the authority of an ethnographer. However, she is not aware of the problems in convincing the readers the natural superiority of anthropological accounts over other types of descriptions of other societies. Mead's belief in the absolute authority of anthropological construction is revealed in her attitudes toward restudies. L.D. Holmes (1986), who made a methodological restudy of Samoa, shows Mead's systematic and well-argued antipathy to such restudies. For Mead, restudies should be based upon what an earlier study did rather than on what it did not accomplish. This suggests Mead's attachment to the facts she herself has collected and her own portrayal of a particular cultural reality. Even though she considers it a necessary task to show the process by which anthropological conclusion is arrived at, she never rises up to this challenge and ends up only asserting her own ethnographic authority.

Mead's Study of Samoa

Mead had gone to Samoa to investigate whether the stress and strain common to adolescents in Western culture was to be found in primitive cultures. In other words, are the adolescent troubles peculiar to Western culture an inherent aspect of adolescence as "biological process"? At the age of twenty-five, she arrived at Samoa in 1925. In November 1925, still far from being fluent in the language, Mead decided to study adolescent girls in Tau island of the Mauna group of islands. From November 1925 to June 1926, Mead lived in Tau village on the screened back porch of the village dispensary.

In her study, Mead starts with the young children and their socialization in Samoa. Here, each child is disciplined through responsibility for a still younger one. The girls learn to weave. Boys learn the skill of the ranked elders so that the cream of becoming a *matai* (the family head) would be realized one day. In the household, a disagreement with the father leads to leaving the household on the part of the children. Here, intergenerational sentiment is diffused and not fixed. When a girl comes of age, her *matai* will send an offering to the house of the chief. Mead argues that girls and women are not of central interest to the community. When a woman commits adultery, her punishment is light compared to similar cases committed by the males. Similarly, a *taupe* (a virgin) who is found not to be virgin is simply cast out.

Before adolescence, boys and girls do not have much communication among each other. Brothers and sisters have a relationship of strong avoidance. But, after adolescence, the situation changes from pre-puberty avoidance to post-puberty free love. Even without referring to any of Mead's critics, one can easily discover inconsistencies and contradictions in her field material. For instance, Mead does not discuss this process of transition. When adolescent love starts, it is always initiated by a boy through the mediation of another boy. But there is a problem here. If the lover chooses an inexperienced boy, there is every possibility that his initiative may be spoilt by the inexperience of his mediator. On the other hand, if he chooses a handsome and expert wooer, then the girl may prefer the second to the principal. The contradictory and the critical role of the mediator is similar to the situation in English love described by Alain Macfarlane (1986).

Among the adolescents, Mead discusses a type of sex activity which is called *moetotelo*. This refers to the sex activity of sleep crawling. "The motives are given for this unsavory activity – anger and failure in love" (Mead 1928: 94). Sexual assault in the form of rape is uncommon in Samoa. Elopements are much less frequent than clandestine love affairs because these involve more risk. By eloping, she renounces even her normal claims to virginity. Afterward, her family members beat her soundly and shave her head. "Her lover's only motive is vanity and display, for the boys say, 'This girl hates a *moetotelo* but they all love an *avaga* (eloping) man'" (ibid.: 104).

Mead also discusses Samoan attitudes towards virginity. As Holmes shows, Samoans have been Christians for the last one hundred and fifty years. Mead writes: "But virginity definitely adds to a girl's attractiveness; the wooing of a virgin is considered far more of a feat than conquest of a more experienced heart" (ibid.: 99). She discusses briefly the *taupe* system. But Mead is aware of the problem this "curious attitude" towards virginity poses in her general interpretation of adolescent behaviour in Samoa. But such contradictory awareness does not affect her conclusions about Samoan adolescence.

Mead devotes a chapter to the discussion of deviants among adolescents in Samoa. The upward deviants include those girls who are highly ambitious about their career and who take recourse to modern education as a means of social mobility. These girls stay in the pastor's house where chastity is much emphasized. On the other hand, the delinquents are deviants in a downward direction. These girls violate group standards and become unmanageable for the group.

Mead argues that the Samoan attitude towards adolescence reflects the general Samoan ethos and the preferred type of personality. In Samoa, "evaluations of personality are a curious mixture of caution and fatalism" (ibid.: 122.). She generalizes that there is not much rivalry and competition in social life. But she herself writes: "Comparisons are not habitual, although in the rigid structure of the community, relative rank is very keenly observed" (ibid.: 125).

In the conclusion to her book on Samoa, Mead asserts that adolescence is not accompanied by stress. But if we carefully go through her own portrayal of Samoan reality, inconsistencies in her own description strike us immediately. She concludes that "sex is natural pleasurable thing; the freedom with which it may be indulged in is limited by only one consideration, social status" (ibid.: 210). But, she still concludes that in Samoan ethos, competitiveness is not a determinant factor. So, there is a tension between her ethnography, which captures a complex picture of Samoa, and her conclusions, which tailor Samoan reality into crude simplicity. This again reflects the essential limitations built into ethnographic presentation of other societies.

Freeman's Critique of Mead

In his critique of Mead in *Margaret Mead and Samoa: The Making and Unmaking of an Anthropological Myth,* Freeman refutes Mead's conclusions about Samoa on the basis of his own fieldwork in Samoa for forty years and uses this refutation as a case against cultural determinism in American anthropology (Freeman 1983). In the end, the book pleads for a more scientific paradigm which integrates biology and culture in anthropological explanations.

Freeman rightly argues that Mead in no way allowed the deviations to interfere with her conclusions (ibid.: 93). Even independently of Freeman, any careful reader can discover this in Mead's book on Samoa. But Freeman also goes to refute systematically Mead's previous evidence. In this he involves the work of ethnographers such as R.L. Stevenson, G.B. Miller and George Brown.

Freeman argues that Mead never understood the *fono* or the political structure of Samoa. As a woman, Mead, of course, was not permitted to join the *fono*. Freeman argues that in *fono*, there is a sharp distinction between the talking and titular chiefs. Contrary to Mead's comments, the titular chiefs are not simply nominal heads. In the *fonos* of major concern, the titular chiefs voice their opinions in the most forthright terms. In *fonos* the judgment of a particular chief is also called *tonu*, meaning an exact decision. In Samoa, those who are of superordinate rank exercise authority over those who are below them. Mead argues that there are titles for everybody, eliminating competition. But, for Freeman, there is an intense competition for titles at all levels of the rank structure. Such struggle has occurred frequently in the course of Samoan history.

Freeman argues that individuals, families, and local politics of Samoa are indeed arranged in hierarchies according to rank and the relationship between them is a relationship of intense hostility and competitiveness. In the performance of oration, competition is especially marked among the talking chiefs. Sometimes this competitiveness becomes so intense that the talking chiefs even resort to physical violence. There is also intense competitiveness over valuables such as fine mats. Linked with this competitiveness is the fact of Samoan aggressiveness and warfare. Basing upon historical sources of the European observers, Freeman argues that wars were frequent in pre-Christian Samoa. Fights also commonly occur between rival extended families of the same village which may continue intermittently over several days until those involved are either apprehended and fined by the local *fono* or restrained by the police. Mead had no knowledge of the nature of Samoan history. Among warlike Samoans, it is not surprising to find numerous war gods. So, for Freeman, Mead's generalizations about Samoan adolescence and culture are completely decontextualized from the broader ethos of Samoan culture and history.

Freeman argues that in discussing sexual mores and behaviour, Mead had misunderstood Samoan puritanism manifested in its *taupo* system. A *taupo* is sexually mature virgin of rank. These virgins are different from Christian virgins in that their virginity is maintained and guarded by their family members and can result in a prestigious marriage with a titular chief. A *taupo*'s marriage with a titular chief is also accompanied by lots of prestations and gifts. Hence, in pre-Christian Samoa, virginity was a "social asset rather than a moral virtue" (ibid.: 220). The culminating point in the marriage of a *taupo* was her ceremonial defloration. In this the bride stood naked in front of the bridegroom and the groom ruptured hymen with two fingers into her upper lips. If a hemorrhage ensued the bridegroom drew his finger from her upper lips. But if the hemorrhage did not occur the bride was abused by her friends and sometimes clubbed by her father and brothers. In her stress on free love, Mead completely ignored the influence of Christian institutions such as Church. Freeman shows how the Church pastor is not simply an external agent but is involved with the social and political processes of the village. For instance, he has a place in the village *fono*. In Mead's ethnography, there are a lot of clues to understand this. Mead nowhere discusses the social relationships between the pastors and the villagers who leave their girls in the house of the village pastor.

Freeman also gives the result of his survey of prevalence of virginity in which 73 per cent girls were found to be virgin in the age group of 12–22. Adultery in the case of spouses is strongly punished by the juridical *fonos*. Moreover, for Freeman, rape in Samoa, both surreptitious and forceful, is among the highest to be found anywhere in the world. The rate of rape in Samoa is approximately 160 rapes per 1,000,000 females per annum. Moreover, the mauve behind sleep crawling is to force a girl to marry the person or elope with him.

Freeman has given a large number of tables and graphs to demonstrate that the adolescent transition in Samoa is accompanied by stress and strain. Moreover, these stressful situations are sexual in origin.

From this specific refutation, Freeman launches an attack on the supposedly absolute cultural determinism in the Boasian tradition in American anthropology. Mead's study of adolescence was meant to prove that adolescence is culturally, not biologically, determined. Towards the end, Freeman pleads for a more inclusive scientific paradigm which would give equal importance to the biological and cultural factors in human behaviour.

Foundational Assumptions in Mead and Freeman

For Mead, it is culture which is central to the human condition. Culture is the determining factor in the constitution of all significant human processes including the human biological development. Here, she works with the Boasian approach to the human condition in which culture plays the most crucial role.

While Mead operates with the foundational principles of cultural determinism and cultural relativism, Freeman operates with a naturalistic approach to human behaviour. As early as 1962, Freeman draws a clear line between his scientific-cum-naturalistic approach and the Boasian method of cultural determinism. Freeman challenges one of the central tenets of cultural determinism, i.e., the radical distinction between nature and culture. For him, "There is no disjunction between nature and culture as Levi-Strauss and some other anthropologists have been led to suppose" (Freeman 1966: 339). Moreover, unlike the abandonment of the notion of "truth value" in cultural relativism, Freeman argues that cultural behaviours can be evaluated in terms of their truth value which since these behaviours are "functionally related to man's phylogenetlcally given nature and the outcome of the evolutionary process" (Freeman 1967: 133) must also be seen in terms of their adaptive value.

Response to the Mead-Freeman Debate

Freeman's critique, as pointed out in the beginning, received responses of many different kinds. The controversies were carried out to the media. It supposedly shook the very foundations of American cultural anthropology. However, in most of the cases, the response was hysterical. Anthropologists, such as Goodenough, Robert Murphy, Eliott Skinner, L.D. Holmes, Bradd Shore, Annette Weiner, David Schneider and many others, replied back to Freeman. For example, Schneider wrote, "This is a bad book. To make matters worse, the book has been promoted in ways that seem to have precluded whatever useful serious discussion it might have provoked" (Schneider 1983).

Critics point out that Freeman is incorrect in his ethnography of Samoa. Holmes, who made the first methodological restudy of Mead's work, has argued in his recent book that Freeman has misrepresented Samoa to suit his own scientific paradigm of sociobiology (Holmes 1986). As Holmes writes: "Throughout the thirty two years I have been researching Samoan culture, I have observed that teenage and young adult males are given a great deal of personal freedom. By adolescence, Samoans have learnt to regulate their own personal conduct and there is practically no testing of the limits of sanctioned behavior" (ibid.: 164). For Holmes, Freeman shifts back and forth between Samoan ideal behaviour as projected in ceremonies and day-to-day social interactions, always to the advantage of his theories. "While young people in Samoa are not promiscuous, as Mead suggested, neither are they models of chastity, as Freeman would have us believe" (ibid.: 167). For him, Freeman should have written a book on the ethnography of Samoa instead of simply refuting Mead. He argues that Freeman's book speaks more about Freeman than about Samoa. Annette Weiner also finds problems in Freeman's data on Samoa. "The ideal of virginity has more to do with the intricacies of titles and rank than with a woman's physical condition. [...] Premarital intercourse and virginity both were publicly marked with fine mats, the most sacred Samoan objects" (Weiner 1983: 916). Shore, himself an ethnographer of Samoa, argues that Freeman's insistence on residential stability is in peculiar variance with the detailed information on fosterage (Shore 1983: 939). "Samoan children undergo a kind of double socialization, in which values asserted in one context are undercut systematically in a different set of contexts" (ibid.: 942).

The nature of relationship between biology and culture and the fact of absolute cultural determinism in the Boasian paradigm becomes the other concern for the respondents. Weiner argues that Freeman misunderstands Boas. Boas never rejected biology *per se*. Moreover, Freeman does not discuss the actual social and political implications of the controversy over eugenics and culture in which Boas was involved. Schwartz argues that Mead starts with the facts of adolescence as a universal biological fact. "Rather than rejecting the biological, Mead dealt with the question of how a given culture responds to the generic events of the life-cycle" (Schwartz 1983: 924).

Two Other Instances of Ethnographic Allegory

In looking at the Mead-Freeman controversy as an instance of the ethnographic allegory, two recent anthropological restudies, mentioned in the beginning of this chapter, provide an insightful vantage point.

Margaret Mead and the Tchambuli

Mead's ethnography of Tchambuli in her *Sex and Temperament in Three Primitive Societies* (1935) has been subjected to a restudy by Frederick Errington and Deborah Gewertz (1987). In case of the Tchambuli, Mead argues, women do the fishing and weaving while men's occupations are simply ceremonial. Over the top of men's houses there are wooden figures of women with an enormously exaggerated vulva, which symbolizes men's fear of women. "In Tchambuli society, men are theoretically dominant in which they play an emotionally subservient role" (Mead 1935: 263). But, for Gewertz, this is a complete misunderstanding of Tchambuli cultural view of personhood and individuality. "To be a person, among the Tchambuli is to be a member of the patriclan [...] Tchambuli describe a patriclan as the people with the same totems. All clan members together assume responsibility for payment of the bride price and the affine debts incurred by a co-member, and together they receive the affine presentations owed to the clan. Each individual also inherits several totemic names from his or her affines. Thus, Tchambuli becomes repositories of both their patriarchal and matrilineal relationships through their possession of certain names. To be a person among them is to embody these relations" (Gewertz 1984: 618).

For Gewertz, Mead misrepresents Tchambuli when she explains the relative strength and weakness of Tchambuli in individual terms. Gewertz argues that Tchambuli female dominance should be understood in contextual and historical terms. "When Mead and Fortune worked among them, 52 per cent of Tchambuli men between the ages 15 and 45 were away from their village, probably for the purpose of labour migration. Those women who remained were busy rebuilding their ceremonial houses which had been razed during a war with the Parambeiltamul. [...] With so many men away Tchambuli women had begun to assume control of the trading relationships previously dominated by their husbands and fathers. It seems possible therefore that Mead was wrong to attribute either the emotional insecurity-cum-artistic preoccupation of Tchambuli men or the cooperative, work-oriented solidarity of Tchambuli women to cultural performances. Both could simply be seen as reflecting socio-historical circumstances" (ibid.: 621).

Mead discusses young widows in Tchambuli who are thought of possessing a particular threat. She explains this fact in terms of a Western cultural preoccupation with the power of sexuality rather than in terms of the Tchambuli cultural preoccupation with the totemic power. "A widow is feared not because of her sexuality but because of her knowledge of the totemic name of the clan which when revealed would bring disaster to the group" (Errington and Gewertz 1987: 81). Mead fails to perceive the Tchambuli cultural construction of individuality thus misinterpreting it as relations of domination. Errington and Gewertz write: "In her effort to make cultures such as the Chambuli relevant to our own, she described non-Western personality configurations of men women as permutations of established western patterns" (ibid.: 8).

Borofksy's Restudy of Pukapukan

In his *Making History: Pukapukan and Anthropological Constructions of Knowledge*, Borofsky (1987) shows how Pukapukan social organization has been constructed differently within different intellectualist contexts by different ethnographers. He starts with Pearl and Ernest Beaglehole's ethnography of Pukapukan. The Bargeholes argue that Pukapukan social organization is predominantly matrilineal. In his study, Borofsky does not find evidence for this matrilineal assertion. But, unlike Freeman, Borofsky does not want to put the Beagleholes on trial.

Implications of Mead-Freeman Debate

In Mead-Freeman debate, the problem of "ethnographic authority" is quite central. In a way the "deep structure" of the debate is the invocation of different types of ethnographic authority. Freeman tries his best to show that his account of Samoa is more authoritative than Mead's. Mead did not know the Samoan language. Freeman complains that she stayed there only for nine months whereas he has spent forty years in his study of Samoa. In another context, Geertz (1969) has spoken about the phenomenon of "the intense struggle for the Real". In this debate, in the intense struggle for the Real, the contenders, in claiming their superior ethnographic authority, marshal all their virtues and linkages before the audience.

Freeman argues that many inhabitants of Samoa had looked forward to him in the hope that one day he would challenge the misrepresentation of their society. He claims that his version is close to the native point of view. His wife and children are also brought into the scene to add to his credibility. He also gives us the list of title he has been awarded in the village juridical structure, which is presented as a qualitative advantage over Mead. When Holmes in his critique of Freeman also invokes his "ethnographic authority" it is interesting to see the response of Freeman. Freeman refutes Homes' claim that he has been offered a title in the village. Freeman even goes to the extent of informing us that while Homes has not paid the regular dues to the village council he has never failed in his payment of dues.

Freeman's epistemology is a positivistic one. He believes that there is a real Samoa. He successfully shows the intellectual and the paradigmatic context within which Mead's construction of Samoa took place. But he considers this as only an exceptional instance. His own epistemology does not permit him to see that the problem with Mead is a problem basic to all ethnographic constructions. Hence, he discounts the possibility that his own construction of the supposedly "real Samoa" might have been influenced by his own scientific paradigm. To paraphrase James Clifford (1986), Freeman rightly points out that Mead's Samoa is an allegory while not realizing that his own construction too is allegorical.

The tension between the ethnographic chapters and the concluding chapters in Mead's book reveals the fact that the tension between theory and ethnography in anthropology is a real and a perennial one. Anthropological theory building is a unique combination of the "abstract" and the "concrete". Schwartz (1983) rightly points out that the Mead-Freeman debate has one positive effect of stressing again the obvious: in anthropology, data do not constrain interpretation as they are made out to be. This chapter, on the other hand, has sought to show that this is not really the case. In anthropology and other social sciences, we have to break from the epistemology of "speaking in the name of the real" and bring to the forefront our own self and our whole intellectual, theoretical and cultural contexts active in our construction of the ethnographic universes.

By the Way of Conclusion: Beyond the Mead-Freeman Debate and Imagining Alternatives to the Epistemological Crisis in Anthropology

But such an outline of anthropological epistemology has to take issue with anthropologists, such as Sidney Mintz, who have defended the realism of ethnographic authority and the anthropological representations. To make sense of the contemporary challenges to the prevalent anthropological epistemology, Mintz (1988) operates with two images or "rhetorics" of anthropology: "science" and "self". The recent postmodern critics of anthropological epistemology, for Mintz, operate with the rhetoric of self. "'Objectivity', in this image, is impossible. It requires the ethnographer to realize that there is no such thing as fact; there are only interpretations, because he or she, as well as the informant, is a human being. One must deobjectify the data collection process by remembering that one is part of the data [...]" (ibid.: 27). For Mintz, the contemporary postmodern challenge is not bound naturally to any political ideology. "Both the scientist and the self-person may be of the Right or Left. [...] It is merely that forty years ago there seem to have been more scientists now there appear to be more selves" (ibid).

The crisis of ethnographic authority that Mead-Freeman debate illustrates and the postmodern challenge has heightened requires an anthropological imagination of striking a balance between realism and representation, theory and data. The postmodern challenge to the naturalistic relationship between the observer and the observed has made the task of constructing ethnographic universes and asserting its supposed naturalized authority problematic. In subsuming this challenge, which is part of a wider crisis of representation in Western society and discourse (Giddens 1975; Goldthrope 1984; Touraine 1988) under the image of self, Mintz is partly making a caricature of this postmodern challenge. Postmodern challenge to anthropological epistemology cannot be simply reduced to reflexive anthropology, though it is an important part of the total scheme.[1]

Clifford Geertz's (1986) response to the contemporary epistemological crisis seems to be arguing that the authority of the ethnographer ultimately depends upon the ethnographer's ability to be "authors", rather than simply writers. But as Michalea de Leonardo (1989) has rightly pointed out, such a defense ultimately seeks to establish an avuncular relationship between the ethnographers who can elevate themselves to the status of the "authors" and the less elegant anthropologists who continue to remain as writers of anthropological texts. In this scheme, Malinowski, Levi-Strauss, Evans-Pritchard and finally Geertz come out as the pioneering "uncles" "and the less articulate writers become the "nephews" who look forward to the "authors" for avuncular secret codes (Leonardo 1989).

But Mintz's passionate plea for fieldwork and his stress on distinguishing between "better interpretations and less good interpretations" of reality deserves careful consideration. Such a view of the task of anthropology makes clear that the days of fieldwork are not over. Nevertheless, the ethnography of the real can enrich itself by the recent critique of the anthropological epistemology. To be able to respond to the epistemological crisis in anthropology heightened by the Mead-Freeman debate and the postmodern critiques, we need to strike a creative balance between Sidney Mintz and James Clifford by not simply calculating an Archimedian mean between them but by transcending both of them. The lesson from the Mead-Freeman debate seems to be suggesting that we need to refine an anthropological epistemology where the ethnographers specify relationships in reality but break away from the natural authoritativeness of "speaking in the name of the real" and bring to the fore his or her own self and *a priori* theoretical and political presuppositions.

Note

1. Here I have in mind the works of Clifford (1983b), Clifford and Marcus (1986) and Marcus and Fischer (1986). But these postmodern critiques of anthropology have to be situated in the broader discourse of postmodernism (Harvey 1989; Lyotard 1984; Madison 1988; Rorty 1989). The postmodern critics of ethnographic realism seem to be taking inspiration from Derrida and Rorty but do not exhaust the scene of postmodern imagination. There is a hermeneutic agenda in postmodernity which is just not deconstructive but also reconstructive. For example, Gadamer does not discard reality and representation rather the objective of his hermeneutic postmodernism is to understand truth through self-transformation. As Madison argues: "Gadamer's concentration on play as a metaphor for the understanding process is not meant as a Nietzschian rejection of rules or of the subject; its purpose is rather to enable us to conceive of subjectivity anew, in a postmodern, post-epistemological fashion" (Madison 1988: 117). Here, "Truth refers not to a static, mirroring relation between a subject and an object but to the transformation process which occurs in all instances of genuine understanding; truth refers to the self-enrichment and self-realization that occurs as a result of the play of meaning." In this context. anthropologists such as Mintz (1988), Trouillot (1988), Sangren (1988), and Gudeman and Rivera (l989) who strive to rescue the ethnographic reality from the supposedly postmodern nihilistic predators can strengthen their agenda by deconstructing the project that the postmodern critics of anthropology have constructed and build on alternative pathways, experiments and traditions in postmodernism such as Gadamerian hermeneutics of postmodernity (cf. Madison 1988).

References

Appel, G. and T.N. Madan. 1987. *Choice and Morality in Anthropological Perspective: Essays in Honour of Derek Freeman*. Albany: State University of New York Press.

Borofsky. M. 1987. *Making History*. Cambridge: Cambridge University Press.

Bright, C. and M. Geyer 1987. "For a Unified History in the 20th Century". MS.

Clifford. J. 1983a. "Power and Dialogue in Ethnography: Marcel Griaule's Initiation". In *Observers Observed,* edited by G. Stocking, Jr., Chicago: The University of Chicago Press, pp. 121–156.

——. 1983b. "On Ethnographic Authority." *Representations,* 1.

——. 1986. "On Ethnographic Allegory." In *Writing Cultures: The Politics and Poetics of Ethnography,* ed. by J. Clifford and G. Marcus, Berkeley and Los Angeles: University of California Press.

Clifford, J. and G. Marcus (eds.), 1986. *Writing Cultures: The Politics and Poetics of Ethnography.* Berkeley and Los Angeles: University of California Press.

Errington, F. and D. Gewertz. 1987. *Cultural Alternatives and* a *Feminist Anthropology.* Cambridge: Cambridge University Press.

Freeman, D. 1983. *Margaret Mead and Samoa: The Making and Unmaking of an Anthropological Myth.* Cambridge, MA: Cambridge University Press.

——. 1984. "Oh rose, thou art sick." *American Anthropologist* 86: 400–405.

——. 1962a. "Review of Trance in Bali by Jane Balo." *Journal of Polynesian Society* 71: 270–73.

——. 1965. "Anthropology, Psychiatry and the Doctrine of Cultural Relativism." *Man* 65: 65–67.

——. 1966. "Social Anthropology and the Scientific Study of Human Behaviour." *Man* (New Series) 1: 330–42.

——. 1967. "A Matter of Values." *Man* (New Series) 2: 132–33.

Geertz, C. 1969. *Islam Observed.* New Haven: Yale University Press.

——. 1988. *Works and Lives: Anthropologist as Authors.* Stanford: Stanford University Press.

Gewertz, D. 1984. "The Tchambuli View of Persons: A Critique of Individualism in the Works of Mead and Chodorow." *American Anthropologist* 86: 615–629.

Giddens, Anthony. 1975. *The Class Structure of the Advanced Societies.* London: Hutchinson.

Goldthrope, J.H. (ed.), 1984. *Order and Conflict in Contemporary Capitalism.* Oxford: Oxford University Press.

Gudeman, S. and A. Rivera. 1989. "Colombian Conservations: The Strength of the Earth." *Current Anthropology* 30: 267–283.

Harvey, David. 1989. *The Condition of Postmodernity.* Cambridge, MA: Basil Blackwell.

Holmes, L.D. 1986. *Quest for the Real Samoa: Mead/Freeman Controversy and Beyond.* South Hadley, MA: Bergin & Garvey.

Leonardo Michalea de. 1989. "Malinowski's nephews", *The Nation.* March 3. pp. 350–352.

Lyotard, J. 1984. *The Postmodern Condition.* Minneapolis: University of Minnesota Press.

Macfarlane, A. 1986. *The Hermeneutics of Postmodernity: Figures and Themes.* Bloomington: Indiana University Press. Ch. 7. "Beyond Seriousness and Frivolity: A Gadamerian Response to Deconstruction."

Madison, G.B. 1988. *Hermeneutics of Postmodernity.* Bloomington: Indiana University Press.

Marcus, G. and M. Fischer. 1986. (eds.) *Anthropology as Cultural Critique: An Experimental Moment in the Human Sciences.* Chicago: The University of Chicago Press.

McLuhan, M. et al. 1989. *The Global Village.* New York: Oxford University Press.

Mead, M. 1928. *The Coming of Age in Samoa.* New York: Blue and Ribbon.

——. 1935. *Sex and Temperament in Three Primitive Societies*. New York: William Morrow & Co.

——. 1949. *Male and Female: A Study of Sexes in a Changing World*. New York: W. Marrow.

Mintz, Sidney. 1988. "The Sensation of Moving While Standing Still". Paper presented to the Seminar in Atlantic Society. Culture and History, The Johns Hopkins University. This has later been published in *American Ethnologist* 16: 786–796 (1989).

Rorty, Richard. 1989. *Contingency, Irony and Solidarity*. Cambridge: Cambridge University Press.

Said, Edward. 1978. *Orientalism*. New York: Pantheon.

——. 1989. "Representing the Colonized: Anthropology's Interlocutors." *Critical Inquiry* 15: 205–225.

Sangren, Steven. 1988. "Rhetoric and the Authority of Ethnography: Postmodernism and the Social Reproduction of Texts." *Current Anthropology* 29: 391–405.

Schneider, D. 1983. "The Coming of a Sage to Samoa." *Natural History*.

Schwartz, Theodore. 1983. "Anthropology: A Quaint Science." *American Anthropologist* 85: 919–929.

Shankman, Paul. 2009. *The Trashing of Margaret Mead: Anatomy of an Anthropological Controversy*. Madison: University of Wisconsin Press.

Shore, Bradd. 1983. "Paradox Regained: Freeman's Margaret Mead and Samoa". *American Anthropologist* 85(4): 935–944.

Touraine, Alain. 1988. *Return of the Actor: Social Theory in Post Industrial Society*. Minneapolis: University of Minnesota Press.

Trouillot, M. 1988. *Peasant and Capital*. Baltimore: Johns Hopkins University Press.

——. 1991. "Anthropology and the Savage Slot: The Poetics and Politics of Otherness." In R.G. Fox (ed.), *Recapturing Anthropology: Working in the Present*. Santa Fe, New Maxico: School of American Research Press.

Weiner, Annete. 1983. "Ethnographic Determinism: Samoa and the Margaret Mead Controversy." *American Anthropologist* 85: 909–919.

27 The Power of Word, The Language of Religion

> It is impossible to do justice to the sacred scriptures of most religious traditions, or their public utterances, if we fail to notice just how much of language is used, not to make claims about supernatural realities, but to urge on believers in their chosen ways of life
>
> — Donovan (1976: 86)

> First a religious faith may be identified with its language, or to speak more appropriately, as a kind of discourse. Whatever ultimately may be the nature of so-called religious experience, it comes to language, it is articulated in a language and the most appropriate place to interpret it in its own terms is to inquire into its linguistic expression.
>
> — Ricouer quoted in King (1980: 192)

Language has been a key concern for students of human inquiry in the 20th century. The preoccupation with language has cut across many disciplinary boundaries from philosophy to anthropology. Philosophy of language has been an influential discourse for more than a century now. But in this domain of philosophy of language, religious language as a linguistic type has posed many challenges. It has been the source of many riddles to the philosophers of language who are otherwise concerned with the 'truth value' of linguistic statements. The empiricist philosophers such as A.J. Ayer (1936) have been compelled to respond to the challenges emanating from the operation of religious language.

In this context, the present chapter seeks to explore what a religious language is and its various features that make it such a contested terrain for the skeptical analytic philosophers and the defending theologians.

Language of Religion

Religious language does not mean specifically sacred languages of antiquity. Nor does it refer to an artificial or a special language constructed by the specialists. Religious language is not simply a language containing certain theological words like "God", "Universe", "Brahma" and "Cosmos". Religious language is "rather the way any words (often quite ordinary ones) play a role within some context of religious belief and observance" (Donovan 1976: 1).

In the study of religious language, as Peter Donovan argues, use of religious language is as much important as religious language itself. The emphasis is less on the words themselves, rather it is on in what circumstances these words are occurring. "Religious, then, rather than being taken as an adjective describing a certain kind of language, is better understood adverbially, indicating a mode or manner in which language is made to work" (Donovan, ibid.). In his book, *The Study of Religious Language*, Andes Jeffner also takes a similar stance. For Jeffner, religious language is a number of interrelated written or spoken religious sentences. Taking inspiration from Ramsey in whose approach to religious language religious situation plays a key role, Jeffner argues that religious sentences are those which are connected with religious situations which mean: "(a) that the uttering of the sentence is part of what constitutes the situation, or (b) the sentence says something which is taken for granted by a group of believers when they participate seriously in a religious situation [...]" (Jeffner 1971: 10).

Religious sentence, according to Jeffner, performs four-fold function of statement, expression, prescription and performance similar to the function of utterance of a sentence in natural language. For Jeffner, one important problem in the study of religious language is that most of the sentences are "problematic". Problematic sentences are those sentences whose reality are difficult to verify. These are the sentences which pose the problem of verification, more specifically the problems of "anchorage" and "localization". The anchorage of a statement is its "reference" and it is the state of affairs which makes the statement true. "Localization" refers to the locale to which reality and reference of the statement belong. To distinguish the problematic sentences from the ordinary sentences, Jeffner gives the following examples:

Ordinary sentence: Jesus was born in Bethelheim.

Problematic sentence: Jesus is the son of God.

While the truth-value of the first sentence cannot be contested, the truth-value of the second is difficult to verify.

Jeffner argues that problematic statements are, most of the times, indirect statements and they are metaphorical. It also points to the figurative dimension of religious language which makes it different from ordinary sentences and linguistic utterances. Donovan also argues that oblique statements are typical of religious language. Religious language is figurative, affective. Similar to Austin's distinction between "performative" and "constative" statements, Donovan makes a distinction between the evocative power of language and its informative function. Religious language for him is predominantly affective as contrasted with the ordinary informative sentences.

If, as Jeffner and Donovan argue, figurative language and problematic sentences are characteristic of religious language, they also make them an "empty talk" in the eyes of the skeptical analytic philosophers. The pioneering critique in this domain seems to spring from A.J. Ayer who has influenced subsequent critiques in this tradition. In 1936, Ayer published what was to become a widely influential book, *Language, Truth and Logic*, in a bold attempt to show how philosophy can get rid of empty talk. For Ayer, "[...] a sentence which does not express either a formally true proposition (like a proposition in arithmetic or deductive logic) or an empirical hypothesis (a claim based on the observation of world around us) is devoid of literal significance" (1936: 54). Kai Neilson makes such an empiricistic stance clear: "God-talk does not lend itself open to experimental confirmation or disconfirmation as other linguistic statements, hence, it is, no matter how evocatively meaningful, is without factual significance and truth-claim" (quoted in Donovan 1976: 17).

However, in an attempt to respond to such empiricistic challenges, other philosophers of language such as Ramsey, Braithwaite and Hare have put forward an alternative formulation of verification. Hare argues that while religious statements might be factually empty as statements, they still have meaning because it offers what he calls "bleaks" or principles to live by or to use in the interpretation of one's experience. Similarly, Braithwaite argues that religious statements have a meaning because they can be shown to have a use. This use can be discovered by suitable observations, and stated in straightforward propositions. This is how he believes that religious language can meet the challenge of the empiricist. Religious assertion, though non-factual, does more than just expressing emotion or evoking feelings. Braithwaite suggests that they be regarded as "[...] being primarily declarations of adherence to a policy of action, declarations of commitment to a way of life" (quoted in Donovon 1976: 25). King (1980), whose work on religious rhetoric will be discussed later, rightly places Braithwaite's declarative religious statements against the background of Searle's speech acts.

This reformulation of Braithwaite and Hare is widely known as the non-cognitive account of religious statements. One of its principal advocates is Ian Ramsey whose major work in this field is *An Empirical Placing of Theological Phrases*. For Ramsey, instead of asking the truth-function of religious utterances, our primary objective should be to show how certain religious sentences evoke a certain kind of situation. This is similar to Austin's arguments about performative statements which he contrasts with the constative. For Austin, these two types of statements function in two different planes: the performative statements are concerned with happiness or unhappiness of the statements while the constative statements are concerned with truth or falsehood. When Ramsey identifies religious situation as the central aspect in the study of religious language, the links with Austin has to be borne in mind.

Religious situations for Ramsey are the situations of discernment and commitment. As situations of discernment, they provide sudden revelation to the believers and participants. But these situations also demand a total supra-logical commitment from the believers. But, as J. Macquarrie argues, Ramsey's theory of religious language can account for more the situations of commitment than those of discernment. Macquarrie writes: "With the new stress on use, many analytic philosophers might be willing to place religious language in situations that might be called 'religious' but perhaps most of them would stress 'commitment' rather than 'discernment' that is to say, they would tend to see the meaning of religious assertions in ritual or social terms and would be reluctant to acknowledge the cognitive dimension of 'discernment', especially if this was supposed to do with disçernment or disclosure of some transhuman reality" (Macquarrie 1967: 118).

Braithwaite, Ramsey and Hare represent the non-cognitivist school of the meaning of religious statement. As King argues, the chief criticism of non-cognitivism has been that religious statements are not merely non-cognitively meaningful, they are also believed to be true. In the words of King, "Ultimately, even Braithwaite and Hare have to admit some relationship between religious language and truth. Then, there might be a factual assertion behind the adoption of a 'bleak' even though the 'bleak' may not be an assertion of fact" (King 1980: 195).

Main Genres of Religious Language

After meeting the empiricistic challenge to the reality of the religious language, we have to identify the main genres of religious language. However, a typology of religious language cannot ever be exhaustive. Hence, we can attempt to identify only some of the more familiar genres. Broadly, these are: hymns, rhetoric, sermons and chanted preaching. All of these have their influence on the feeling, cognition and thought of the listeners.

Donovan entitles his chapter on the typology of religious language as "Doing Things with Religious Language". This title seems apt as it points to the way different genres of religious language perform with words. As Donovon argues, all of these are not only affective but also effective. It is effective in the sense that it achieves things: "it enables believers to live out their beliefs, and to do various things, as parts of their religious life" (Donovan 1976: 78). Both Donovan and Jeffner treat these languages as a part of the broader genre of "performative utterances".

Donovan discusses the following main types of religious language:

Worshipping

Some important acts of worship take place with very few words; their power lies not in what is said so much as what is performed with it. We find a striking evidence of the performative role of word in the sacrament of baptism. The utterance "I baptize you in the name of the Father, the Son and the Holy Spirit", accompanied by other rituals, turns the happening into an effective Christian baptism. "The same is true of other sacraments and ceremonies, where prescribed words used at certain key points are intended to make the whole activity achieve what it sets out to achieve" (Donovan 1976: 80). In Hindu religious tradition, both in the text and in the ritual contexts of worships, there are designated *mantras* which are essential to be uttered for the effectiveness of the ceremony.

Reminiscing

Because words are able to bring to mind events of the past, they also help us in re-living the experience of the past by reminiscing. "A large proportion of the narrative and stories told in religious contexts are of the reminiscing kind" (Donovan, ibid.: 82). Religious language helps us in remembering forgotten or half-forgotten things in the religious tradition. Especially religious language plays a great reminiscing part in the Christian piety. This is seen in the systematic reading and re-reading of the Bible, attending church regularly and hearing to quite predictable sermons.

Committing

Religious language as a performative language helps us in committing ourselves to certain things. Creeds, statements of faith and words of consecration within worship are familiar instances of committing and self-involving language. In the religion of Israel, we are familiar with the covenant between God and the people of Israel. By formal words and utterances, the covenant was ratified and accepted.

Invoking, Praying and Blessing

Asking questions or making requests are further non-stating uses of words, as are wishful expressions like "if only if", "may it be so", or "we pray that [...]". As Donovan argues, "many psalms and hymns are in the form of prayers, either asking, or expressing a desire or a wish which is believed to be in accord with the will of God and so proper to express his hearing" (ibid.: 85). In blessing phrases like "God be with you", "The Lord bless you", and "Peace be unto you" involve a combination of request and performative utterances.

Solemnizing

Many uses of religious words have the effect of solemnizing some natural occasions or utterances by setting it in a religious light. Certain verbal formulae are especially common for solemnizing purpose. The Christian formula, "In the name of the Father, and of the Son, and of the Holy Ghost" performs soleminizing function in many occasions.

Exhorting

Exhorting is perhaps the archetype of performative religious utterance. In religion, more words are probably used for exhorting than for any other purpose. Exhorting commonly takes the form of urging or encouraging others to join in worshipful activities. It stirs up worshipful behaviour within the believers. It is almost like the utterance of a cheerleader. Well-known phrases of exhorting like 'Praise the Lord' and 'Sing to the Lord a new Song' appeal to the listeners to worship God in various ways. The power of exhorting becomes manifest when it appeals to the non-believers invoking a religious response.

Sermon and chanting are the more familiar types of exhorting. Later on we shall see how these two perform a crucial role in the shaping of belief in an ethnographic context.

Inspiring

Closely related to exhorting is the use of language in religion for worshipping, arousing feelings and stimulating actions. Like exhorting, inspiring is very much an effective function of words.

The Performative and the Power of Words

The above discussion shows us how the power of religious language in producing effect and affect lies in the fact that most of the religious utterances are performative utterances. As Jeffner argues, performative utterances are important aspects of religious language. In his contribution in the volume *Talk of God*, N.H.G. Robinson also writes: "When, for example, the religious believer declares 'I believe in God the Almighty' it is clear that he is not simply giving assent to proposition. His words have something of a performative character" (Robinson 1969). Hence, to understand the way religious utterances perform powerful functions we must discuss the performative power of utterances in general.

And here we can begin with J. Austin and J. Searle. Austin (1962) shows how we do things with words. He questions the assumption that to say something is always to state something. To be true or false is traditionally the characteristic of a statement. But performative utterances are not true or false in the conventional sense. Rather, they are happy or unhappy or imbued with some affective and effective load.

For Austin, the idea of the performative utterance is that it is to be the performance of an action. Actions can only be performed by persons and in this case, the utterer must be the performer. Hence, Austin treats the first person utterance as the archetype of performative utterances. He makes a performative analysis of the statement "I know". In his influential essay "Other Minds", Austin argues that the phrase "I know" has a performative function; what I do when I say "I know that S is.P is that I give others my words for saying that S is P".

To elucidate his arguments about performative utterances, Austin discusses three types of speech-acts: locutionary, illocutionary and perlocutionary. In locutionary act, a person simply utters a sentence which could be true or false, as in the statement, "The door is closed". In perlocutionary act, a person affects someone by uttering a sentence. An example of it is the statement: "Please open the door". The person to whom the statement is addressed is affected in some way: either he opens the door or becomes irrational, angry or apologetic. But, in an illocutionary act, one accomplishes something by uttering the sentence, without regard to whether or not any one or any thing else is affected. The truth-claim of the illocutionary act performed does not depend upon production of any particular set of effects. It can be true that "I request, I promise, I think of order" whether or not my requesting, promising etc. has any effect at all. For Austin, to determine what illocutionary act is, we must determine in what way we are using the locution: "asking or answering a question, giving some information or an assurance or a warning, announcing a verdict or an intension or an appeal or pronouncing sentence, making an appointment, or a criticism" (Austin 1962: 99). Illocutionary acts, however, might be strong or weak depending on the intensity of the involvement of the speaker's intent. The strong illocutionary acts such as 'requesting' are the acts in which the intention of the actor is strongly involved. In case of weak illocutionary acts like 'wishing', the effects are not necessarily intended at all (Martin 1979: 1)

Searle further adds to the study of illocutionary acts with his notion of a declarative. A declarative has two defining characteristics:

1. The successful performance of one of its members brings about the correspondence between the prepositional content and the reality. Declaratives bring about some alteration in the status or condition of the referred to object of objects solely in virtue of the fact that the declarative has been successfully performed.
2. The mastery of these rules which constitute linguistic competence by the speaker and the hearer is not in general sufficient for the performance of a declarative. In addition, there must exist an extra-linguistic institution and the speaker and the hearer must occupy special places within this institution (Searle 1969).

Austin, Searle and most of the students of religious language assert that performative utterances must be studied and understood in their speech context. For Austin, "We must consider the total situation in which the utterance is issued-the total speech act-if we are to see the parallel between statements and performative utterances and how each can go wrong" (Austin 1962: 52). Hence, in his theory, Austin gives utmost significance to the "circumstances of utterances".

Austin makes it quite clear that while at one level of analysis, performative may refer to a type of statement, at another level, it constitutes an essential aspect of all sorts of statements. The performative is not altogether so obviously distinct from the constative. As Austin argues, "Furthermore, in general, the locutionary act as much as the illocutionary act is an abstraction only: every genuine speech act is both" (Austin 1962). This means that every statement has a performative dimension as it has got a referential and locutionary dimension. This means that statements of all types have a power of their own.

In his widely-read essay, "Magical Power of Words", Tambiah shows how words have a magical power. As in case of Austin here it is helpful to go beyond the absolute distinction between the performative and the constative. Tambiah also argues against the Taylorian and Frazerian distinction between the revealed religion and natural religion to formulate a general statement about the widespread belief in the magical power of words.[1] Both the religions have rituals where words uttered have a magical power of spell. In usual anthropological treatment, spell is considered to act mechanically and is intrinsically associated with magic. Spell is also opposed to prayer which is thought to connote a different type of communication with the divine. But with the example of the spell of the *mantra* from the Singhalese exorcistic ritual, Tamibiah shows us that even though the *mantra* corresponds to a stereotype of spell, it has a sophisticated logic of its own. "[...] Far from being nonsensical and indiscriminately concocted, the spells show a sophisticated logic" (Tambiah 1985: 21). So Tambiah suggests that even though there is a distinction between prayer and spell at one level[2], at another level *mantra* like prayer does not fall outside the requirement of language as a system of communication, and their literal intelligibility to humans is not the critical factor in understanding their logic. Hence, it is not only the *mantra* (the secret language in Sinhalese ritual) that has the magical power, the prayer and other verbal utterances in the ritual such as Kannalava and Kaviya have their magical power as well.

Malinowski argued that magical utterances are completely different from ordinary speech. The difference is that magical utterances are believed by the natives to produce supernatural effects which they do not expect ordinary speech to produce. The very basis of verbal magic was the creative metaphor of magic – a suggestive phrase that he interpreted as "the belief that the repetitive statement of certain words is believed to produce the reality stated" (Malinowski 1965: 238).

That language in magic is different from other ordinary speech, utterance is also postulated by other theorists of language, most notably Ernest Cassirer. To propound a philosophical-cum-linguistic theory to account for the basis and origin of the word veneration reflected in religious thought, Cassirer argues that belief in magical power of words is a part of the mythic node of thought which is different from the rational/scientific mode.

For Tambiah, it is helpful to go beyond these dualistic approaches to understand the essentials of word veneration and its magical power. The power of word in magical utterances is not altogether different from the power of words in ordinary utterances: "Trobriand magical language is intelligible language, not mumbo-jumbo shot through with mystical ideas resistant to rational examination. It is not qualitatively different from ordinary language, it is a heightened use of it. The same laws of association that apply to ordinary language apply to magical language" (Tambiah 1985: 35).

In the Terrain of Ethnography

We can follow up the above discussion about power of words and language of religions in some ethnographic contacts and here we can start with the power of the rhetoric in the religious experience of some contemporary religious cults as has been documented by Susan Harding (1987), Betsy Taylor (1987) and Karen Mae King (1982).

Ethnographies of Religious Rhetoric

Rhetoric, as Peter Dixon tells us, is a speech in the public where the speaker addresses a public audience in order to make an impact upon it. Dixon starts with the root word 'rhetor' which refers to "a man skilled in speaking who addresses a public audience in order to make an impact upon it" (Dixon 1971: 2).

Rhetoric is a useful device not only in the study of literary criticism but also in the study of religion. For Kenneth Burke (1961), language and religion share a common ground in so far as what we speak in ordinary language has some implications for gods, deities and God in religion. Word is related to the "word", theology is related to logology. For this matter, the subject of religion falls under the head of the rhetoric.

To come to the arena of ethnography, we can begin here with Sushan Harding's study of Moral Majority in Virginia, USA where she shows us the power of the rhetoric in fundamentalist Baptist conversion. For Harding, "At the center of the language of fundamentalism is a bundle of strategies – symbolic, narrative, poetic, and rhetorical – for confronting individuals, singly and in groups, stripping them of their cultural assumptions, and investing them with a fundamentalist mode of organizing and interpreting experience" (Harding 1987: 167). Harding continues, "Witnessing, and conversion talk more generally, is rhetorical in the sense that it is an argument about the transformation of self that lost souls must undergo, and a method of bringing about that change in those who listen to it. Fundamental Baptist witnessing is not just a monologue that constitutes its speakers as a culturally specific person, it is also a dialogue that reconstitutes its listeners" (ibid.).

Harding discusses the power of the rhetoric in converting the "unsaved" in the situations of witnessing. Witnessing is different from preaching. Preaching is a formal religious address delivered to a body of believers in church services and revivals. But witnessing is more informal. It occurs as a conversation between the witness who is saved, and an unsaved listener. But, when the witness and the "unsaved listener" converse, they talk in different language in so far as they have different understanding of reality. In witnessing, the witness wants to strip the novice listener of his prior cultural assumptions and to impress the reality of Bible, God and the word upon the novice. "The reality or the truth constituted in witnessing is, in part, a linguistic one: the Supernatural is experienced as god's voice and his spirit is communicated and experienced through words" (ibid.: 168). While use of rhetoric characterizes all conversion situation, it is formalized to an unusual extent in the fundamentalist Baptist conversion.

Harding discusses her witnessing experience with one Reverend Cantrell of the Moral Majority and shows the power of Cantrell's rhetoric to induce a feeling of "liminality" in her. Harding had intended to interview with Cantrell but he reframed her appointment to witness to her for an hour and a half. There are five rhetorical moments in Cantrell's witnessing talk: equating his present listeners with listeners in his stories, defining the listener as lost, defining the speaker as saved, transforming his narrative listeners into speakers and exhorting his present listeners to speak.

Cantrell, as Harding presents his witnessing conversation, used numerous poetic and performative features in his speech. These are verse makers ('and' 'now'), special codes, figurative language, symbolic and metaphorical parallelism in his speech. These features mark the text as an oral performance. It also indicates a special relationship between the performer and the listener. This special relationship is indicated in the use of pronouns.

Harding writes, "Reverend Cantrell communicated my relationship to his speech more directly through his use of pronouns: 'I still had not heard the gospel story of Jesus Christ and how that he died for our sins'. 'Because, though we have never seen God, we are still aware of the fact that He is present, we know that He is there.' Cantrell continued to place me in his narrative during the rest of the time by using the royal 'we', ambiguously as a personal and impersonal pronoun. His listeners by this means became the subject of a whole range of presuppositions posited in such a way that they were difficult to resist."

Harding continues, "Reverend Cantrell at one point in this initial speech and at several points later on quite overtly identified me with his narrative listeners. The central, reiterated narrative structure in his witnessing was a dialogic encounter between person and God, or between a lost listener and a saved speaker" (ibid.: 172).

Cantrell reminded Harding of her position in this narrative several times. Cantrell told Harding, "I found that I could win others the same way I was won; by simply telling them that there's a heaven to gain and a hell to shun."

In this witnessing rhetoric, Cantrell placed Harding in his narratives. Cantrell also introduced and located God within another level of dialogic imagination, between God and Biblical figures. Harding must listen to Cantrell as Moses and Cantrell listened to God. From this Harding argues that witness's words and rhetoric, though they appear to be about the witness and about other characters in the narrative surface, are on a deeper level about the listener. The listener also becomes a character in this story.

Cantrell concluded his narrative by asking, "Now Susan, let me ask you a question. Do you know Christ as your personal saviour? [...] Do you believe in God? What if you died today? Have you ever sensed the presence of God?" Cantrell brought his exhortation to a rather striking conclusion:

> Now in this life, the Bible says, only we have hope then we of all men are most miserable. But you see my life, my hope is in the life to come, and I realize this life is a passing thing. Jeremiah says it is like a vapor. It appears but for a while, then vanishes.

His conclusion of the narrative with this apocalyptic picture is meant to create a sense of disruption and lack of rootedness within the listener so that the listener could be converted to the message of the preacher.

So, in this ethnographic account, Harding shows how the rhetoric used in the witnessing has the power to evoke an intended response from the listener. This rhetoric actualizes its power by making the unsaved listen to the narrative. "The single most important clue I gave Reverend Cantrell that was susceptible to conversion was that I was willing to listen to the gospel." His language was so intense and strong, yet deceptively plain and familiar, full of complex nuances and pushes and pulls, that I had no time, no spare inner speech to interpret him, to rework what he said into my own words, as he talked. I just willfully uncritical as well, in the sense that I wanted to understand, as best as I could, his words from his point of view. [...] It was not exactly what Reverend Cantrell said that brought me under conviction; it is that I took it up, namely by listening to him actively and uncritically" (Harding 1987: 982).

The power of the religious rhetoric in converting the unsaved listeners also comes out in the study of Betsy Taylor, once a student of Susan Harding at Michigan. Taylor did her fieldwork in a coal-mining community of southern West Virginia. Taylor argues that the rhetoric of the speaker performs two inversions on the normal intentionality of the self. "First, it collapses the hermeneutic cycle that provides most metaphors for self-reflexivity and knowledge. Secondly, it stretches out the normally collapsed zone of choice to create a conative pressure so intense that the choice for Jesus seems inevitable (Taylor 1987).

The Power of "Rhetoric" in the New Religious Cults: The Case of the Moonies

While Harding's account shows the power of the rhetoric in the situation of witnessing, King's brilliant study of the rhetoric of the Unification Church broadens the focus to arenas like preaching. The objective of King's study is to show how rhetorical vision plays a key role in the process of persuasion and is able to achieve a fully functioning theocracy.

In the Unification movement, the power of the spoken word is very much emphasized. The leader of the movement, Reverend Moon, advises his followers, "If you want to be a good leader, you must be a good speaker. You must be able to express yourself well" (quoted in King 1980: 183). Most of the evangelical activity in the church is done by means of the spoken word: be it in the form of a lecture or a story for enjoyment. Earlier, the American branch experimented with tape-recorded sermons but later on they were abandoned in favour of the spoken word. Moon himself prefers the spoken word compared to other methods of communication.

In the new religious cults and movements in contemporary America, as King shows, spoken word is the single most important channel of communication. While the power of the spoken word has been recognized and utilized in all religions, the new religious cults distinguish themselves in their emphasis on orality. Their performance with the words have been so successful in persuading others that it has led to the charges of brainwashing against them. Responding to the charges of brainwashing, Neil Solomon of the Unification Church argues, "We do not brainwash. We simply argue that a careful analysis of the new religious movement is required to gain an understanding of this washing process."

To understand the rhetorical strategy of the Unification Church, King employs the method of fantasy theme analysis, developed by the sociologist Bales in his study of the small group interaction. Fantasy theme refers to the statement made by one member of a small group that has the power to capitalize on the suppressed feelings of others. Speakers present themes that form the composite dramas which catch up large group of people in a symbolic reality to a rhetorical vision. Fantasy theme analysis requires that the critic search a variety of rhetorical artifacts from a given group in order to discover dominant themes, heroes, villains, and praiseworthy or blameworthy behaviour. From this the analyst is able to reconstruct the rhetorical vision of the group.

The basic drama of the Unificationist vision involves around the principle or purpose of creation, the fall of man, and providence of restoration. Unificationist theology holds that man was created to be one with God in a state of absolute perfection. However, before perfection was achieved, Adam and Eve fell to Satan. By engaging in an illicit love relationship with the serpent angel and then joining in a premature conjugal relationship centred on Satan, Adam and Eve created a sinful lineage and destined mankind to struggle to perfection. At various times throughout the history of mankind Satan has been able to prevent a resolution of the conflict.

The key dramatis personae of the Unificationist movement are the new Messiah, the followers of the movement, and the opponents of the movement.

Reverend Moon is at the centre of the movement. The principal enemy of the movement is selfish individualism. Specifically, the Unification Church finds the enemy manifest in the godless ideology of communism. It is this ideology that must be challenged and defeated if the movement is to succeed.

Five basic themes dominate the rhetorical vision of the Unification Church. First, every individual must have the freedom of choice to join the movement. Mankind must choose freely to believe and to follow. Second, God-centredness is seen as the ultimate goal. The hallmark of God-centredness is sacrifice. Third, discipline and hard work are encouraged. The story of Reverend Moon's life is repeated throughout Unification Church rhetoric. Like Moon who while starting the movement in Korea had undergone a lot of hardship, the Unification Church followers must courageously face the continuing persecution in the United States. This persecution will culminate in the final theme that dominates the rhetorical vision of the movement, namely, the final battle and victory. How the battle will be fought depends upon whether or not Unificationism has become an ideology strong enough to triumph over communism. If not, the battle may have to be fought with weapons.

Both the content and the form of Unification Church rhetoric contribute to the effectiveness of the vision. In terms of content, the essential elements of a civil religion appear consistently throughout the rhetoric. The United States is seen as the catalytic agent in the process of restoration. The United States must be the nation to choose God over Satan. The importance of nation is stressed throughout Unification Church rhetoric, for while the movement begins with individuals it must progress to families, tribes, and ultimately to nations.

The rhetorical vision of the movement is communicated to others in the jeremiad form. The jeremiad is a traditional European form that was brought to America and adapted to meet the particular needs of Americans. Essentially, the form leads to listeners to view themselves as a chosen people facing a crucial time. The people are directed to take action in order to fulfil God's wishes or face dire consequences. The strength of the jeremiad form lies in its ability to unify and sustain commitment and to explain evens that occur unexpectedly.

Thus, the rhetorical vision of the Unification Church employs a variety of acts, action and themes. Taken together, they create a kind of myth or fantasy type. Its rhetorical vision follows a mythic pattern. Moon's speeches fall within the province of the caring circle. By virtues of their content, they foster the attitude that the members of the Unificaiton Church are a special circle from which others are excluded. The fantasy type created has displayed considerable power in motivating action.

Finally, King argues that the success of the new religious cults is due to the fact that their language is performative and declarative. Declaratives aim to create a consistency between the content of the proposition and reality; that is to say, they attempt to get the world to match the words.

Power of Religious Utterance: The Case of New England Sermon and the Shaping of Belief

Teresa Toulouse, in her book *The Art of Prophesying: New England Sermons and the Shaping of Belief*, discusses the sermon forms of the New England preachers. She is interested in the structure of the sermon – the structure in which arguments were presented and how a definite sermon used was instrumental not only in expressing religious and social assumptions, but also in shaping them.

To understand the shaping of belief in New England in the 17th and 18th centuries, it is essential to understand the structure in which they were presented. For her, matters or belief cannot be separated from the question of their actual presentation and actual structuring within the sermon form. Toulouse wants to show how "[...] sermon structures do not merely frame the content of faith, but also can be used to reconstruct the preacher's sense of his role, his attitude towards his listeners, and wider cultural assumptions underlying these attitudes" (Toulouse 1987: 8). To substantiate her argument, she discusses sermon structure used in the preaching of four New England ministers: John Cotton (1584–1652), Benjamin Coleman (1673–1747), Channing (1978–1982) and Emerson (1803–1982).

William Perkins' *The Art of Prophesysing*, originally published in 1592, was a standard preaching manual for the ministers providing them the structure and the format within which to present their arguments. John Cotton, the influential New England preacher, started with Perkins' model, but he in course of time transformed the original sermon structure. Toulouse shows how alteration in the sermon structure was crucial in the shaping of belief at that time.

According to Toulouse, Perkins suggests a preaching form that consists of a logical development from the divine text to its practical applications in the daily lives of his congregation. He describes four steps:

1. To read the text distinctly out of the canonical scripture;
2. To give the sense and understanding of it being read by the scripture itself;
3. To collect a few and profitable points of doctrine out of the natural sense; and
4. To apply the doctrines rightly collected to the manners of men in a simple and plain speech (ibid.: 21).

The progression from a text to doctrines to reasons and to uses is the pattern Perkins assumes most clearly manifests God's intended meanings to a congregation. In the progression from description to explanation and application, Perkins also plays out his desire both to address the piety of the elected and to move his whole congregation to compliance with a moral law.

The Perkins sermon model, as Toulouse argues, "[...] involves a preacher and listener in a nascent narrative that unfolds in the logical movement from the sacred text to its application in the temporal human world" (ibid.: 22). John Cotton uses both Perkins' interpretive method and the semantic model of text-doctrine uses. Adhering to Perkins' model, Cotton also transformed his previous ornate style of preaching to the style of plain preaching recommended by Perkins. But Cotton transforms the Perkins' model by detracting from its progressive, logical and deductive movement. Cotton gives excessive attention to his text, doctrines and reasons which creates a fragmentation of the pattern and of its movement. This fragmentation of the original Perkins' sermon form is the crucial issue here. Toulouse's main objective is to show how this transformed fragmented sermon form was crucial in the shaping of belief in New England at that time.

In order to illustrate this transformed sermon form, Toulouse gives the following example of how John Cotton breaks the original text in the document. The text is from Rev. 3: 20: "Behold I stand at the and knocke, if any man heare my voice and open the door I will come into him, and will supp with him and he with me" (ibid.: 29). Cotton breaks this text into three larger sections, each including its corresponding reason and use:

> That the heart of a man is the doore of the soule.
>
> The patience and bounty of God is great towards sinners, even admirably great in calling them home to himself.
>
> Such as do heare the voice and knocks of Christ and doe open the door of their hearts to him, he will vouch safe fellowship with them, feasting of them, and be feasted by (quoted in ibid.: 30).

In the afore-mentioned sermon, instead of progressively moving forward, Cotton stops at the word "behold" at the beginning and he broadens the scope of the message conveyed in this word by referring to examples of this usage elsewhere in the Bible. In this process of broadening and collation, Cotton uses a lot of figurative images. Hence, unlike the Perkins' model, the movement of the sermon is not progressive and rational, rather it is fragmented and emotional. He uses a lot of evocative and organic images in his sermon. The gradual accumulation of images in this passage is directed at engaging an audience's emotional rather than its rational acquiescence.

In order to come to the central argument about the sermon structure and its instrumental role in the shaping of belief, Toulouse argues that Cotton's fragmented sermon form, compared with the earlier Perkins' progressive and rational model, helped him in shaping a distinct view of election among the audience. This refers to the view that the elect are graced by the scripture and the holy spirit to understand the complicated message transmitted in the scripture. The elect are specially different from the non-elect because they have been graced and saved by the holy spirit. Hence, they do not require the presentation of the essence of the message of the sermon in a simplified and logical form. In this view of election, "The preacher should not maladroitly translate Scripture, nor should he forbid the spoken and sung use of the psalms for his own edification and that of his congregation. Above all, he should not limit the possible meanings of his text in order to reduce God's will to a single moral truth easily graspable by those eager to find assurance of their blessedness" (ibid.: 41).

But Perkins' sermon form, with its obvious 'movement' towards the applications and with the objective to present the message of the sermon in a clear simplified logical statement, was particularly meant to the needs of the elect who apparently did not have any special grace to understand the message of the complex sermon in its original and non-simplified form.[3] As Toulouse writes, "Given Perkins's emphasis on the varying needs of his different listeners, however, it seems clear that, practically speaking, the model suggests his leanings towards a non-elect than an elect audience" (ibid.). But John Cotton's fragmented model helped him shaping a particular view of election both within himself and among the listeners.

In this essay, our concern has been how the way words are uttered, affects and shapes the beliefs of the listeners in a particular way. The above discussion shows how two different sermon structures (more exactly two different structures of sermon utterances) express and shape beliefs differently. It also shows how the fragmented sermon structure of John Cotton was instrumental in shaping a particular view of election.

The Power of Word: The Art of the American Folk Preacher

Here, in this section, we shall discuss the power of the religious utterances with specific reference to the chanted formulaic sermons used by the American folk preachers. The ethnographic material here is presented by B.A. Rosenberg (1970).

In case of Toulouse's study, we were concerned with the power of the (non-chanted) sermon structure. But Rosenberg is concerned with the chanted spiritual sermons. In the chanted sermon, the verses are predominantly formulaic, there are extended passages with parallel syntax, and the constructions are direct with almost no periodicity. This chanted form is used by a few of the spiritual preachers in America. These men are found largely in the South where they learned to preach, though some now live in every major city in America. Although most of these men are Black, there are Whites also in the eastern Kentucky hills and in parts of Ohio and Pensylvania who still preach this way.

In case of the chanted sermon, what is important is not language, but rhythm. These sermons are composed spontaneously by the preacher which contains formulae and themes. Spontaneous composition is the key issue, because it is not effective when read. The two key features of the chanted sermon are that it is formulaic and based around themes. Considering the spontaneous nature of the composition and performance of the chanted sermons, formulae and themes act as a sort of mnemonic device in the chanted sermon.

Formulaic systems as genres of oral performance were first reported by Parry and Lord during the thirties and fifties in their study of the Yugoslav epic singers. For Rosenberg, "It does not matter that the Parry-Lord singers composed narrative epics while the American preachers compose sermons: the modes of creation are similar" (1970: 47). Rosenberg argues that it is difficult to define what a formula is in case of the chanted sermon. He further argues that it is safe to conclude that repetitiveness is an essential feature of the formulaic quality of the chanted sermons.

Rosenberg analyses the chanted sermon of one spiritual preacher named D.J. McDowell. The sermon is entitled "The Christ of the Bible". In it one finds a striking repetition of the following phrases:

The Christ of the Bible	24 times
Am I right about it	15 times
I know that's right	11 times
Amen (used as metrical line)	11 times
Keep your hand in God's hand	5 times

Rosenberg states that it is natural to expect that the phrase "Christ of Bible" would occur in a sermon with that title. But twenty-four times is far more than accidental, and a bit more rhetorical. "Furthermore, McDowell uses the same phrase (though not as frequently) in other sermons, just as many of the phrases-and entire sections or themes-are used elsewhere and in different contexts" (ibid.: 48).

Most of the McDowell's work is heavily formulaic. In this, the highly repetitious quality of the passage is evident even at first glance. Analysing this sermon, Rosenberg writes, "Of the twenty-three lines, nine (including 2 and 23) are repetitions of others within the same sermon. Eight lines are nearly identical: the syntax is consistent, with the verb in the same relative position, though the nouns are varied (florist, geologist, physician, baker). Four lines are syntactically similar to phrases found outside the, either communally or personally. At least twenty-one of the lines, then, are in effect repetitions – or 91 per cent. The remaining lines (19 and 22) may also have been repeated elsewhere in sermons not recorded or heard" (ibid.: 50).

Formulae used in the chanted sermons may be of different types. Two types that are very important are the ones that help the preacher to refrain and to stimulate the discussion. The refrain formulae used by McDowell is "I know that's right". The formulae like "I do not believe you, know what I am talking about" stimulate the audience in a particular way.

The chanted sermons not only use formulae but also themes as mnemonic devices. "Themes give a great deal of coherence to the language in a sermon; the preacher depends upon them to hold his sermon together and he uses them as a departure point. Without themes and a coherent narrative plot line, most sermons would be structurally (and probably semantically) chaotic; with them the sermon does not become inflexible, but rather just strong enough to allow communication with the shifting moods of the congregation" (ibid.: 73).

Rosenberg argues that themes are not altogether different from the formulae. Particular use of formulae helps to bring forth a particular theme used in many different contexts by the same preacher. As Rosenberg writes, "The sermon theme is a sequence of formulae nearly memorized, used to describe recurrent scenes, ideas, or actions within the sermon."

Rosenberg analyses four sermons delivered by a preacher named Reverend Brown. The first sermon was recorded by Rosenberg in June 1967, the second in July 1967, the third in August 1967 and the fourth in May 1968. Rosenberg finds out that Brown uses the formula "The same man" when he is using the theme of Jesus' miracles. The formula "This same man (Jesus/One)" comes up again and again whenever Brown delivers sermons on the miracles. In a way, this formula calls forth the theme of the miracle of Jesus.

The chanted sermons, through the use of formulae and themes, become spontaneous powerful performances. They also build up the emotions of the congregation as no other means does. In case of the chanted sermons, what moves and excites is not the particular idea and the message, but a preacher's rhythm, his musical chanting and the great passion he expresses through gestures and repetition.

Rhythm and repetition play an important role in arousing heightened emotional intensity in the audience. In such performance, the listeners in the audience also play an active role. As Rosenberg shows, they determine the length of the sermon: if they are bored, the sermon is likely to be cut short, and if they are caught up in the passion of the moment they may induce the preacher to extend his moments of ecstasy. Further, the congregation can improve the quality of the preacher's performance by their active participation in the service: they urge him on, and infect him with their cries and their clapping.

In the chanted sermon, as has been shown with the help of Rosenberg's material, what arouses the attention of an audience is not a particular message but a particular structure of chanting and utterance. Most of time, the message conveyed in these performances is not audible. Hence, the meaning of the sermon is not the absolute determinant in the passionate response of the audience. What moves the mountains here is the rhythmic, formulaic and repetitive quality of the sermon. It is the chanting itself – its rhythm, repetitiveness and the formula – that has the magical power here. Hence, Rosenberg writes, "The first thing the incipient chanting preacher learns that will influence his style is not language but rhythm" (1970: 76).

Social Religion and the Power of the Hymns in 19th Century America

During the 19th century in America, there emerged a complex of religious practices which was different from the earlier Puritan religious practice. This was a new complex of religious practices which dissolved the earlier Puritan distinction between the private and public religious behaviour. In the Puritan tradition, conversion was a private experience,. shared directly only with one's intimates. Even when private religious life was linked to the Church by means of conversion narrative, it was distinguished from the public ones which centred on the Sabbath services. But in 19th century there grew a social religion with its different sets of religious practices. The earlier language of conversion was adapted to the social context of revivals. In this social religion prayer, testimony and exhortation were employed to create a community of intense feeling in which individuals underwent similar experience. In his book *Gospel Hymns and Social Religion: The Rhetoric of Nineteenth Century Revivalism*, S.S. Sizer (1978) tells us how gospel hymns and spiritual revival songs played a major role in the formation of this social religion.

For Sizer, gospel hymns simultaneously encourage the audience to participate in it by singing and provide a general description of the world. Gospel hymn is rhetorical in the sense that it wants to encompass a situation by persuasion. As rhetorics, gospel hymns should be viewed as offering by opponents. Similarly, they provide a collective identity which are defined in contrast to other identities.

To show the distinct features of the gospel hymns and their power, Sizer chooses three dimensions for analysing the rhetoric: metaphor, theme and form. With regard to the first, gospel hymns are largely constructed around series of metaphors. Such metaphors consistently appear as elements in a group of contrasting sets. This gospel hymn exhibits a set of polar metaphors. This polarity of the metaphors in the gospel hymn had the magical power to affect of the audience.

The themes of the gospel hymns are positive and affirmative. In this respect, these hymns are different from earlier hymns where the constant theme was the degrading passivity of the humans and their sinful nature. But, in gospel hymns, the image is that of a wonderer, not of a worm. The gospel hymns emphasize the transient nature of this worldly life by using verbs in their progressive forms: the contrast between the 'ing' forms and the measured, evenly accented "I shall be soon" serves to reinforce the contrast between the changing world below and the unchanging world above. Furthermore, the striking aspect of gospel hymn was that it was full of metaphors. This metaphorical nature of the hymns had the power to create a community of feeling and social religion.

By the Way of Conclusion

In all the genres of religious language discussed in this chapter, we have found the predominant occurrence of metaphors, more particularly organic metaphors. All the students of religious language who theorize about 'God-talk' at an abstract level also argue that 'indirect talks' and metaphors are the striking and the constitutive properties of the religious language. In this context, some comments on the power of metaphors in general is helpful.

In recent decades, the power of the metaphor in human perception, cognition and abstraction has been given special attention. It is through metaphors, not through abstract concepts, that we live by. Our thinking is not the sovereign operation of a disembodied mind; rather it is the operation of an embodied mind. As Johnson and Lakoff argue, we think through and live not by abstract categories but by metaphorical 'prototype' (Lakoff and Johnson 1979: 125). Our everyday consciousness and practice, as Anthony Giddens tells us, is not a discursive consciousness but a practical consciousness (Giddens 1984: 7). In this, body and metaphors play a crucial role.

What is striking about metaphor as a mode of cognition, perception and abstraction is that it involves our whole experience. Metaphors operate and are born in our "embodied practice". Because metaphors involve our whole being – body as well mind – it has the power to strike and affect us as a totality. Because of this holistic, experimental and embodied nature, metaphors have the power to affect our language, thought and reality in an unimaginable way. Martin (1987) shows the power of metaphors in current day medical practice.

To connect this to our central concern, power of metaphor in religious language is the basis of the power of the "word". It is through metaphorical language that religion becomes a language game. The participants, believers and those who are at the "threshold" of religion play interesting game with it. Metaphors in religious language provide the point of reference around which the faithful play game, it is through the evocation of these metaphors that the proselytizers try to exhort the unbelievers.

Levi-Strauss (1966), Tambiah (1985) and Martin (1980) try to apply the analogy of game to the study of ritual. Martin shows how peasant religion and rituals are like learning games which teach them about the basic elements of political order. Similarly, by participating in the linguistic game of religion, mostly set by its metaphors, the participants learn their basic elements of faith and the non-believers the force of it for a probable change of faith.

The basic postulate of this chapter is that religious utterances have a power to effect and affect, to convert and convict, to shake and to move, to disrupt and to bind. Through the works of the scholars of religion, we saw that this is due to the performative nature of religious language. But from the work of Austin, it became evident that the performative, contrasted with the constative, is not a qualitatively different type of statement. Rather, it is an aspect of all speech utterances. The power of religious utterances has a magical character and extending Tambiah we can similarly argue that as sacred language in religious rituals is not altogether different from magical language, the performative power of religious language is not qualitatively different from the performative power of ordinary speech utterances, rather it is a heightened and concentrated form of it. Spoken words of all sorts have a power. As Ricouer argues, word initiates a specific action upon others and this pertains to influence (1965: 205).

Notes

1. Martin (1979), who is also concerned with the problem of efficacy of utterances and speech acts argues from her Chinese study of rituals that an absolute Frazerian distinction between magic and ritual cannot be sustained.
2. Prayer is an audible invocation and a supplication while spells are muttered utterances using the language of command, and emphasizing a series of metaphorical images.
3. The argument presented above simplifies the contrast between the sermon structure of Perkins and John Cotton to a greater extent. As Larzer Ziff, who taught English at Johns Hopkins and who is one of the established authorities on the Puritan sermon structure, argues (personal communication), the actual situation was much more complex and it is a contested view that the changed sermon structure gave rise to the transformed view of election.

References

Austin, J. 1962. *How To Do Things With Words.* Cambridge, MA: Harvard University Press.

Ayer, A.J. 1936. *Language, Truth and Logic.* Gollancz.

Burke, K. 1961. *The Rhetoric of Religion.* Boston: Beacon Press.

Dixon, Peter. 1971. *Rhetoric.* London: Metheun & Co.

Donovan, P. 1976. *Religious Language.* London: Sheldon Press.

Giddens, A. 1984. *The Constitution of Society.* Cambridge: Polity Press.

Harding, S. 1987. "Convicted by the Holy Spirit: The Rhetoric of Fundamental Baptist Conversion". *American Ethnologist* (14) 1: 167–81.

Jeffner, Andes. 1971. *The Study of Religious Language.* London: SCM Press

King, Karen Mae. 1980. *The Rhetoric of the New Religious Movements.* Ph.D. Dissertation: University of Iowa.

Lakoff, G. and M. Johnson. 1980. *Metaphors We Live By.* Chicago: University of Chicago Press

Levi-Strauss, C. 1966. *The Savage Mind.* Chicago: University of Chicago Press.

Macquarrie, J. 1967. *God-Talk: An Examination of the Language and Logic of Theology.* New York: Harper & Row.

Malinowski, B. 1965. *Coral Gardens and their Magic.* Vols. 1&2 Bloomington: Indiana University Press

Martin, E. 1979. "The Problem of Efficacy: Strong and Weak Illocutionary Acts", *Man* 14: 1–17.

——.1980. *Chinese Rituals and Politics.* Cambridge: Cambridge University Press.

——.1987. *Woman in the Body: A Cultural Analysis of Reproduction.* Boston: Beacon Press.

Ramsey, I.T. 1957. *Religious Language: An Empirical Placing of Theological Phrases.* New York: Macmillan.

Ricouer, P. 1965 "Work and the Word". In idem, *History and Truth.* Evanston: Northwestern University Press.

Robinson, N.H.G. 1969. "The Logic of Religious Language". In *Talk of God.* London: Royal Institute of Philosophy.

Rosenberg, B.A. 1970. *The Art of the American Folk Preacher.* New York: Oxford University Press.

Searle, J. 1969. *Speech Acts: An Essay in the Philosophy of Language:* Cambridge: Cambridge University Press.

Sizer, S.S. 1978. *Gospel Hymns and Social Religion: The Rhetoric of Nineteenth Century Revivalism.* Philadelphia: Temple University Press.

Tambiah, S.J. 1985. *Culture, Thought and Action: An Anthropological Perspective.* Cambridge, MA: Harvard University Press.

Toulouse, Teresa. 1987. *The Art of Prophesysing: New England Sermons and the Shaping of Belief.* Athens: University of Georgia Press.

Taylor, Betsy. 1984. "On Fundamentalist Preaching". Manuscript.

28 Sociology, Theology and Spirituality

Nurturing Spaces of Emptiness and Striving from Fullness to a Different Fullness

The 'secret silence' and 'darkness' are not emptiness, but indicators of that fullness, not yet accessible to us and on the face of which everything else gets relativized.

— Felix Wilfred (2008), *Margins: Sites of Asian Theologies*, p. 348

Between the experience of something and the experience of nothing lies the experience of one's own passivity.

— Georgio Agamben (1999), *Potentialities: Collected Essays in Philosophy*, p. 217

The voices from the 'margins' come from people who have learned of Christ and the gospel in contexts that are vastly different from that in which European Christianity has existed for centuries. Their faith has not passed through the filter of the Enlightenment and their Christ is not associated with imperial or colonial power and privilege, with the result that they are able to recognize the truly radical nature of the gospel. What is more, from the so-called margins of a globalized world, they are able to discern the extent to which Western Christianity has been shaped, and often compromised, by its relationship with a culture that underpins and justifies the political and economic interests of powerful and dominant nations. Such discernment leads them to ask uncomfortable questions.

— David Smith (2007), *Moving Towards Emmaus: Hope in a Time of Uncertainty*, p. 49

I

In his creative *ouvre* spanning over the last three decades, Felix Wilfred has made insightful contributions to a deepening of our understanding of theology, sociology, philosophy, religion, spirituality and society. In one of his many heart-touching essays, Wilfred tells us that there are two poles in Christianity: the pole of emptiness and the pole of fullness. In his own words, "The Christian attempts to cross over to the other, to the different, has been made by and large from the pole of being or fullness. This naturally creates problems, which can be overcome by activating also to cross over from the pole of nothingness or emptiness. The central Christian mystery of Jesus Christ offers the revelation of both fullness and nothingness – the total self-emptying. Many frontiers which are found difficult to negotiate and cross over could be crossed by making use of the other pole represented in the Christian mystery of emptiness as self-abnegation, so as to reach a deeper perception of the mystery of God, the world and the self. Perhaps here lies something that could become an important program for Christianity and its theology at the turn of the millennium" (1999: viii). Walking with Wilfred and seeking souls from all around, Christianity has to now cultivate spaces of emptiness and this cultivation would also be a fertile ground for following the paths of Jesus, giving birth[1] to Him in our daily lives and social relationships, renewing Christianity in our contemporary world and also walking together with people of other faiths – religious and non-religious – for fuller realization of the potential of humanity, nature and the divine.

A space of emptiness is a creative space of encounter and emergence where we strive to live lives of truth, goodness and beauty and we live together with all our fellow seeking souls without *a priori* judgment, discrimination and exclusion. A space of emptiness is not just dark night of the soul but is an originary space and time of birth and bringing forth of life. It resonates with the notion of vacuum in quantum physics, *sunyata* in Buddha's paths of knowing and being and silence as the originary and continued mother of speech. The world is not only born out of vacuum or *sunyata*; vacuum and *sunyata* are a continued constituent part of our unfolding reality and possibility.[2] Emptiness is an ongoing part of our reality of fullness and striving from fullness to a different fullness. We are born both empty and full and are invited continuously to be on the road of fuller realization: a never-ending journey from emptiness to fullness and to a different fullness. This striving is touchingly presented in the following lines of *Isopanisad*: *Purnat Purnamodachyate* – from fullness to fullness.

But when fullness gets too certain about itself there emerges the problem of closure and violence where a particular conception of fullness is put in a prison of finality by the powers – be it religious, spiritual and political. Probably it is our original sin that we forget that we are simultaneously empty and full and we become a prisoner of one-sided self-denial or uncritical self-valorization. This is as much a predicament for individuals as for collective formations such as world religions which assert exclusionary fullness for their beliefs, rituals and dogmas. These world religions forget what Wilfred (2008) calls the universal destiny of religion that each religion is a member of the human family and furthermore part of our unavoidable existence in Nature, part of what can be called continued planetary realizations (Giri 2004). Collective groups – tribes, nations, religions, castes, communities – assert only one pole of the identity – fullness and fail to realize that all these identities are foundationally characterized by an integral emptiness. This assertion of fullness – exclusionary fullness – becomes a source of violence and the religious history of humanity as well as the history of nationalism and other group identities is a testimony to unimaginable brutality, violence and crime committed in the name of exclusionary fullness of one's group – be it social, religious or national. While these groups have claimed exclusionary and fully realized fullness for themselves they have portrayed individuals within these groups as only empty without any spark of fullness. Major world religions have presented an essentially demeaning view of ourselves and religious systems of relegates powers have abused the notion of original sin or *karma* to perpetuate the existing structure of the belittling of the individual and valorization of the fullness of the group. We see examples of this in both Christianity and Hinduism where the papacy and the caste system have made violent use of notions of original sin and *karma* to suppress individuals and to perpetuate the tyranny of the system. Even before the rise of nationalism which despite the notion of citizenship gave primacy to the nation-state over the aspiration of self, collective formations in the tribal world also many a time did not give enough spaces for the self-realization of individuals thus perpetuating a cult of fullness of groups and emptiness of individuals. Nurturing spaces of emptiness in this context is part of a great evolutionary journey moving beyond the cult of emptiness and fullness on the part of both self and society, individual and group, believer and a community of faith, inquirer and a community of learning and citizen and nation-state.

Emptiness is a space and process; it is not a point. Emptiness is a relational field animated by processes of self-emptying or *kenosis* as well as societal processes of mutual interaction and learning about our integral self-limitation and relativization. Emptiness is a mother of creative and emerging relational fields and in these relational fields we touch others by emptying ourselves while the touch of others also make us empty. When we love, the process of love – divine and human – makes us empty and, at the same time, make us realize that we are bathed with the stream of fullness. In the field of interaction between human and the divine, individuals and individuals, individuals and collectivities, collectives and collectives, religions and religions, and religion and science, each of the partners of interaction even while asserting its *a priori* fullness realizes its integral emptiness in terms of its self-limitation to claim the whole truth, nature, divine and humanity only for itself and only in its way. These interactions have often been violent in history, especially when these partners of interaction have lived with a machinery and illusion of absolutist power. But through violent painful interactions in the relational fields in societies and histories we have learnt our own limitation in a hard way. But there have also been non-violent and self-initiating and mutually initiating ways of acknowledging our essential limitation and embracing the other, learning with and from the other.

Emptiness as a relational field and process thus involves processes of self-emptying on the part of both individuals and groups and it is a multi-dimensional process in the lives of souls, societies, histories, gods, goddesses and the divine. Human life and cosmic life are perpetual journeys in which all of us in interaction are learning how best we can realize our potential of beauty, truth and goodness in our manifold relationships. In this the divine is in a co-journey with us as much the human. Images and perceptions of God in earlier times were ferocious and now the images of ferocious and angry God even in monotheistic religions are changing. God is not only a judge but a mother. May be in the cosmic evolutionary journey the divine is also co-learning with the human how to be a compassionate mother while humans, both male and female, are also learning how to give birth to this divine mother in our lives and societies.

Spaces of emptiness are generative spaces – these are spaces of self-generation, self-production and co-creation. Meister Eckhart, the great mystic, had once said that Jesus Christ was not born once in history, we have to give birth to him at each moment of our lives. It is in our spaces of emptiness that we become mothers of our higher self of simultaneous emptiness and fullness as well as give birth to more dignified, truthful and beautiful relationships in society.

Spaces of emptiness as relational fields of interaction, learning, mutual fecundation, co-bringing forth new modes of human, societal and divine realization involve both self and other, ontology and epistemology. But ontology here is a weak one what Giani Vattimo (1999) calls weak ontology and the epistemic practices of co-learning here involves self-transformation (Giri 2005). In this way spaces of emptiness become dynamic fields of ontological epistemology of participation where weak ontology gives rise to the ability and humility to co-learn and this accompanying emergent co-learning is not confined only to an alienated epistemic process but is accompanied by processes of participation and transformations.

Spaces of emptiness are not only spaces of utterances but also spaces of silence. It is the epiphany of encounter that makes spaces of emptiness spaces of silences. It is in these spaces of silence that we realize that truth is not only a point but a landscape of realization where there are not only many ways to truth but also many dimensions to truth. This is the originary ground of the rise of a multi-valued and multi-dimensional ontology and epistemology of truth. The many-sidedness of truth calls for journey of many kinds and realization of this also calls for realization of truth as a rainbow.

Spaces of emptiness are spaces of new fertilization and cross-fertilization. It is in spaces of emptiness that we can cross-fertilize different symbols of emptiness and fullness. During my recent visit to different churches in Europe I felt that crosses in different spiritual traditions are painted in different ways, while in some such as the Lutheran tradition we have much more a linear representation of the cross, in many others such as the Celtic we have a representation of cross as cross-section of blossoming circles. The space of cross is also a space of blossoming flowers and I started seeing a meditative Christ along with a crucified Christ on the cross. From Wilfred's recent sharing of realization it is possible to see a flute playing Christ along with a crucified Christ (see the next section). We can realize simultaneously Buddha, Christ, Krishna as well as Divine Mother on the cross where cross becomes an expanding symbol of many circles of cross-fertilization, co-realization and mutual transformations.[5]

II

Wilfred's life of *sadhana* as a teacher, co-learner and friend as well as his creative *oeuvre* from *Emergent Church in New India* to *Margins: Sites of Asian Theologies* provide us with many valuable insights and shared co-realization to cultivate spaces of emptiness and strive from fullness to a different fullness. With Wilfred we learn how spaces of emptiness are spaces of self-criticism. In Wilfred it is an inspiriting journey of self-criticism and courage to grow not only as an individual but as a member of an aspiring community of faith. Writes Wilfred in his *Margins: Site of Asian Theologies*:

> Reading the New Testament will reveal how it has all the things necessary for salvation. But I have been struck by the lack of one thing in the New Testament: the humour. Though the gospels are meant to convey joy and peace, yet humour does not seem to have a due place. A reading of the divine intervention in human history as through the avatar of Sri Krishna would bring in the element of play, both in God and also in human life. This play, in reality, is not expression of any privolity. Through the play (*lila*) of Krishna is expressed the *unbound freedom of God and God's creation*. In fact creation is viewed as the play of God What is happening at the microcosmic level with the play of Krishna is in fact the mirror of the macrocosmic reality of infinite freedom. [...] The magnetic pull of the milkmaids towards Krishna playing flute is nothing but the irresistible way the Divine power draws everything to itself. In Christian tradition we speak of the way the cross as the power of God's mystery draws us all [...] In short, a reading of the New Testament symbolism of the cross through the story of Krishna playing flute could be very enriching for both the traditions. A cross-scriptural reading of the New Testament message of the cross with the play and aesthetics (*rasa*) involved in the play of flute by Krishna could save us also from the possible danger of masochistic trends (2008: 182).

This foundational self-criticism in the direction of self-opening and cross-fertilization of symbols of self-realization finds a sociological resonance in Wilfred (2000) when he writes in *Asian Dreams and Christian Hopes* that Christian social institutions of service delivery are not always part of the wider civil society with accountability and consideration for fears and concerns of non-Christian neighbours. For Wilfred, "Many Christians may dispute how unfounded are the fears of our neighbors regarding conversion and how much it may be substantiated by hard facts. But, the fact is that there is such a wide-spread impression that Christians are concerned about increasing their numerical strength in addition to the power and influence they already wield in terms of their institutions and foreign flow of funds. Such impressions create a lot of difficulties in our mutual relationship" (ibid.: 236). In this context, Wilfred urges our Christian brothers and sisters to develop a "relational language" "ending the epoch of the language of isolation," participate in civil society, and make their service organizations accessible to the public and open to democratic community control. For him, "Christian services today exhibit a certain parallel to what is being done either by the State or other voluntary agencies. Though in principle co-operation with the larger society is recognised, in practice, however, there is the attitude of self-isolation and segregation. This is fostered at various levels by confidence in money, institutional power and servile and uncritical dependence on elsewhere. There is greater need to practice greater collaboration with the larger civil society" (ibid.: 194).

There are many inspiring paths of self-criticism in Wilfred, which should inspire other people of faith to be engaged in a similar process of self-criticism vis-à-vis their own initial spaces of religious formation. The 19th century Hinduism had more movements of self-criticism than now where leaders from within this space such as Swami Vivekananda and Iswara Chandra Vidyasagar were engaged in foundational acts of criticism of Hinduism such as the casteism and treatment of widows (cf. Beteille 2003; Das 2006). But in recent times on the wake of Hindu fundamentalist mobilization spaces of internal criticism of Hinduism have dried out and let us hope that self-assertive Hindus would learn to be, at least, as self-critical about their initial Hindu identity space as

Wilfred is of Christianity. Wilfred is critical of missionary zeal in Christianity as well as the propensity to convert on the part of some institutional leaders with the power of money and other resources. In his essay, "Christianity and Religious Cosmopolitanism: Towards a Reverse Universality," Wilfred writes:

> The idea of Christianity as mission spanning the whole of humanity as the recipient of its Good News, is a unilateral universality, whereas Christianity to be more completely universal requires multilateral universality which calls for the reading and interpretation of its message by diverse peoples through their conceptions of the destiny of the human family. If the outgoing universality is from God; so is incoming universality for which Christianity needs to make room. It is dogmatism and fostering of stratified Christian identity that makes it difficult to accept the incoming universality. The incoming universality is the movement by which Christianity receives the ways of the Spirit from other religions (2008: 160).

Wilfred is also a critic of anthropocentrism in Judeo-Christian tradition. For him, "The exaggerated anthropocentrism in Christian worldview and theology could be considerably tempered by the Asian approaches to harmony" (ibid.: 134).

Let us learn with Wilfred and nurture our spaces of belonging as spaces of incoming universality whoever we are – Hindus, Muslims or Christians. Giani Vattimo (2002), another self-critical contemporary Christian, speaks of "After Christianity" and explores pathways of a post-Christian world. Love and non-violence are the perennial flows of such a world. For Vattimo, love and non-violence are the perennial legacy of Jesus. In a similar way, could we all of us concerned explore pathways of "After Hinduism," "After Islam," "After Buddhism" from our mothering spaces of belonging?[3] Religions are our mothers but our mothers are not destined to die as mother's wombs and it is through cultivation of incoming universality that all of us concerned can realize the potential that our mothers love for all children and species of the earth and not only as human members of our group boundaries called Hindus, Christian, Muslims and Buddhists etc.

If spaces of emptiness are spaces of nurturing generativity in Wilfred's *ouvre* there are a profusion of symbols of mother and mothering which inspire us to realize that God is also a mother. Building upon new developments in feminist theology, Wilfred writes: "The approach to Jesus as the Sophia of God allows women to find themselves drawn in to the mystery of God. God's self itself is viewed in maternal terms as a corrective to a male dominated understanding of God as a Father. The image of God as Mother dovetails with the Divine nurturing of the whole universe" (Wilfred 2008: 222). In the introduction to *Margins: Sites of Asian Theologies* Wilfred writes: "Jesus' privileging of the small, the hidden and the insignificant in the eyes of the world has the double purpose. First it is to show how the mercy and compassion of God is with the lost and the least. Second, it is among them that God reveals her very self like a Mother who is particularly fond of a physically weak or handicapped child" (ibid.: xi). God is compassion and for Wilfred compassion means to suffer with – suffer together – and here again Wilfred tells us the *sadhana* of a mother:

> A widowed mother, for example, from a poor family undergoes great suffering when she has to work very hard the whole day to be able to feed her children, and to be able to educate them. Here suffering is transformed, and it acquires a different

> meaning. This is very different from pain, frustration and anxiety suffered all by oneself, without reference to the other. In this case one may be driven to desperation and helplessness (ibid.: 239).

Wilfred also writes how Jesus has no hesitation to "compare the compassion of God with a woman who sweeps the whole house to find the lost coin" (ibid.: 221).

Spaces of emptiness are creative spaces where we discover ourselves as mothers. This discovery transforms our relationship with space and time. We will not try to keep all the space occupied and marked but keep it empty for the emergent, the unborn and unknown Christ. Spaces of emptiness also call for a new relationship with time where we are not just slaves of time. In modernity God has been replaced by time and today we all have become its slaves. This slavery creates unprecedented misery, suffering, alienation where we do not have time neither with ourselves nor with each other. Cultivating spaces of emptiness is part of a cultivation of a new spirituality and society where we learn to live with time as our mother. Our non-anxiety, compassion and mutual care also enables us to give birth to a nurturing time as we give birth to a nurturing God. In this emergent spatio-temporal rainbow of emptiness and striving for a different fullness time waits with us as does the divine. We become mothers of time and divine as the divine and time become our mothers. This maternal constitution of time contributes to a maternal constitution of space liberating it from being just a factor of exploitation in the valorization of capital.

III

Nurturing spaces of emptiness as spaces of generativity, co-realization and creative relativization, Wilfred writes: "It may be surprising nevertheless true, that the cause of Christian faith has been most served in history and in present times by a committed and engaged relativism than by defending absolutism. It is like the bamboo tree which contrary to its weak appearance and its bending is in fact strong; it may be tossed around by winds and powerful storms, but it springs back and does not break" (ibid.: 346). Emptiness becomes a space of nurturance of a creative relativism. In the words of Wilfred, "[...] Christian relativism that enables us to live through the ambiguities of human life is not about ego-centeredness but has to do with detachment and the deeper kind of freedom it entails. [...] Christian relativism acquires its depth and seriousness from the fact that it results as a fruit of spiritual enlightenment and awakening. In this experience of faith the relative character of the entire reality appears as illumination" (ibid.: 347, 348). Nurturing relativism, which is creative and not a prisoner of the dualism between relativism and universalism, challenges us to understand the deeper meaning of Christian relativism. Wilfred writes:

> Absolutism is a kind of solipsism. Christian relativism, far from being solipsism, is an expression of solidarity and relationship with others, which call for the spirit of detachment. It is not leveling down matters of divine revelation to the democratic process and egalitarianism, as is often alleged, but a confirming to the nature of divine revelation which happens through self-emptying of God's self. Christian relativism is an existence of detachment and a refusal to hold on to anything less

> than God. Love and Wisdom beckon us to a life of relativism – love by inviting us to new bonds in such a way as to define ourselves relatively with reference to the other, and wisdom by integrating and relating everything. Finally, relativism opens the way for us to migrate to the margins and discern the presence of God among the poor (ibid.: 354).

Wilfred's relativism is not relativistic but moves with joy, love, compassion and wisdom from relativity to post-relative planes of relationship and co-realizations. This involves a fundamental re-conceptualization of each of us as invitees, witnesses and addressees for a greater task of fuller realization. Sin is forgetting of our identity as a journey man and woman and for being a prisoner and violent executioner of an *a priori* fullness for the whole humanity. For Wilfred, "the practical reduction of salvation to freedom from sin would appear as something too restrictive. The approach through harmony could help broaden the understanding of salvation as a state of communion with the entire creation" (ibid.: 134). Lack of realization of our potential is our sin.[4] We realize our potential by not forgetting that all of us belong to the human family and Nature. This Wilfred calls the 'Universal Destiny of Every Religion': "If we search deeply we would find an "overlapping consensus" on the truth that all religions belong to the entire human kind, and no religion is in possession of the immediate community of believers" (ibid.: 154). This finds a resonance in the work of the great sociologist of religion Robert Bellah. He says, "[...] genealogically the history of religion is singular, that all existing religions have developed out of common roots and have constantly intertwined ever since" (Bellah 2007: 9). For Bellah, this recognition that "we are ultimately related, part of a single history, might, just might, if we give it enough effort, move us closer to mutual intelligibility, even toward a recognition that we are ultimately members of one another [...]without abandoning our indelible particularity, the fact that we are our history, we can move to a new history in which we see that those of other faiths are not as other as the post-modernists like to claim, that we have much in common with them, that, in spite of all the differences, we are part of the same story, the human story" (ibid.: 9, 23).

This realization that we are all part of a connected story and journey of human, nature and the divine calls for border crossing where we learn to exchange our assertive boundaries of fullness and embrace the emergent emptiness of a different shared fullness.

Wilfred is a superb artist of negotiating borders which becomes an art of practical spirituality and mysticism. For Wilfred (2008: 188), "The art of negotiating the borders could be viewed, I suggest, as the contemporary form of mysticism in practice". Through the art of negotiating borders Wilfred cultivates in-between spaces of creativity, emergence and transcendence. Wilfred nurtures spaces of emptiness as multi-dimensional struggles and movements from fullness to a different fullness. Let us cultivate new spaces of nurturance in between emptiness and fullness drawing inspiration from the following lines of Wilfred:

> The experience of crossing and negotiating borders is the unitive mystcism of everyday, and indeed an act that can be practiced in everyday life by all those who

are in a journey towards those marvelous ultimate realities, namely: *Satyam, Sivam, Sundaram* or *Verum, Bonum & Pulchrum* – truth, goodness and beauty (ibid.: 188).

Notes

1. It was the great Christian mystic Meister Eckhart who had urged us to realize that each of us are invited to give birth to Jesus in our lives. See Mieth (2008).
2. To understand the continued presence of originary source such as emptiness in reality I find many resonant thoughts in Agamben's (1999: 226) essay, "Absolute Immanence": "Immanence flows forth; it always, so to speak, far from leaving itself, remains incessantly and vertiginously within itself."
3. From a Hindu space, Ramachandra Gandhi's (1993) *Sita's Kitchen* can be taken as an attempt towards outlining a path after Hinduism. For Gandhi, all of us always have the compassion of emptiness and Gandhi carries out dialogue between non-dual aspirations between Buddhism, Hinduism and all aspirations for blossoming. For Gandhi, "[…] Sita's kitchen is the entire field of her self-imaging Sakti, powerfully represented by the earth. It is on earth, in the embrace of the Divine Mother, that all are born, all creatures great and small; all forms manifest, noble or evil; and all are nourished" (1993: 16). Gandhi further says, "Indian spiritual self-knowledge cannot become self-realization without encounter with non-Indian spiritual traditions, and without sharing space and time with them. Held in topographical and historical embrace by the birth place and kitchen zone of Ayodhya, the Babri mosque is evidence not of Hindu humilitation but its venturesome sadhana of self-realization" (ibid.: 17). In the first part of the book Gandhi reflects upon his grandfather Mahatma Gandhi's murals in St. Mary's church in Oxford where he was a graduate student: "Perhaps his mural in St. Mary's drew attention to the neglected inclusivist dimension of Christ's teaching that man does not live by bread alone, but by every word that proceeds from the mouth of God, i.e., we are adequately nourished by nothing less than the full range of truth's manifestation" (ibid.: 9–10).
4. It is helpful here to take note of a foundational rethinking of sin and evil in many different religious, spiritual and philosophical movements of the world. For Swami Vivekananda, "Sins are very low degrees of Self-manifestation (Vivekananda 1991: 300). He further says "Vedanta recognizes no sin, it only recognizes error and the greatest error says the Vedanta is to say that you are weak, that you are a sinner" (ibid.). From a Christian perspective, Giani Vattimo (1999) redefines sin as failure in love. For Vattimo, we have all sinned not because we have fallen in love but have failed in love. Love is not a conditional exchange but unconditional and from this point of view we all can always be more unconditional in our loves overcoming our integral original sin of not being quite up to mark in our practices of love. God is unconditional love. From the point of view of unconditional love we fail in on our lives of love as realization of unconditional love is always a journey. Given our human limitation no matter what we do our love is always in need of much more intimate non-dual realization and this becomes our condition of original sin. Thus, our task is to overcome this through more love and grace and continue our strivings with gratitude and not simply for fear of punishment from a God conceived as a moral law commanding us not to do evil. Here creative theologian I.U. Dalferth also helps us with a new hermeneutics of evil:

The problem is rather to construe God's will as law, and God´s law in moral terms as a set of divine commandments as to what humans ought or ought not to do. The result is a misleading *moral sense* of evil: If evil is that which is contrary to God's will, God's will identified with God's law, God's law reduced to moral instructions of what humans ought or ought not to do, then doing evil is equated with trespassing God's commandments and evil is *everything that God prohibits us to do*. But this is a misleading way of stating the point of the Torah, the gospel, and arguably also the Koran. They are not a set of divine prescriptions, commandments and prohibitions which humans must obey in order not to do evil. At least in the case of the Torah and the gospel they are better understood in terms of God´s gift of a blueprint of a good and just human life in community with God and one another, the presentation of what God has done for his people and all humankind, and the unfolding or unpacking of its implications for human life at its best – as it could and should and ought to be. They outline a way of life that responds in gratitude to the goods received from God rather than to a set of arbitrary divine commandments and prohibitions that are to be obeyed on pain of punishment (Delferth 2006: 18–19).

Similarly, from the shores of contemporary critical philosophy, Georgio Agamben (1993) redefines evil as deficit of human existence and anything that blocks the realization of fuller potential including the potential of fuller God realization and world realization is evil. Here, Bhaskar (2002) also speaks about structural sin and ill-being referring to such fields as contemporary capitalism, which leads to exploitation and blocks universal self-realization.

5. Here I wish to offer the readers the following poem of mine on Cross:

Oh Cross!
Our Mother
Your Four Sides
The Crucified Middle
Are Not Only a Square
Of Torture, Suffering and Cruelty
You are a Circle of Compassion
Of One and Many—
Nature, Divine and Evolution
Oh Cross
You are a Field
In Your Field
We Learn our
Limitations and Possibilities
In your lap
Hands of compassion
Give us strength
Trust and Hope
We embrace you
Our pain and suffering
Become circles of awakening
From ashes arise the Gold
Flowers of Transformations

(Originally written in Odia by the author and then translated into English by him).

References

Agamben, Giorgio. 1993. *The Coming Community*. Minneapolis: University of Minnesota Press.

——.1999. *Potentialities: Collected Essays in Philosophy*. Stanford: Stanford University Press.

Bellah, Robert N. 2007. "All Religions are Cousins. Religions in Human Evolution." Text of a Lecture at Pacific School of Religion.

Beteille, Andre. 2003. "Hinduism in Danger?" *The Hindu*. January 3.

Bhaskar, Roy. 2002. *From Science to Emancipation*. Delhi: Sage.

Das, Chitta Ranjan. 2006. *Drustanta-Purusha Iswara Chandra* [Iswara Chandra: An Exemplary Person]. Bhubaneswar: Sikshasandhan.

Dalferth, I.U. 2006. "Problems of Evil: Theodicy, Theology, and Hermeneutics." Unpublished Paper.

Gandhi, Ramachandra. 1993. *Sita's Kitchen: A Testament of Faith and Inquiry*. Delhi: Penguin.

Giri, Ananta Kumar. 2004. "Self, Development, Inclusion of the Other and Planetary Realizations." In *Religion of Development, Development of Religion*. Delft, The Netherlands: Eburon.

——. 2006. "Creative Social Research: Rethinking Theories and Methods and the Calling of an Ontological Epistemology of Participation." *Dialectical Anthropology* 30: 227–271.

Mieth, Dietmar. 2009. "Meister Eckhart: The Power of Inner Liberation." In *The Modern Prince and the Modern Sage: Transforming Power and Freedom*. Delhi: Sage.

Smith, David. 2007. *Moving Towards Emmaus: Hope in a Time of Uncertainty*. London: SPCK.

Vattimo, Giani. 1999. *Belief*. Cambridge: Polity Press.

——. 2002. *After Christianity*. New York: Columbia University Press.

Vivekananda, Swami. 1991. *The Collected Works of Swami Vivekananda*. Calcutta: Advaita Ashram.

Wilfred, Felix. 1988. *The Emergent Church in New India*. Tiruchurapally.

——. 1999. "Introduction: The Art of Negotiating the Frontiers." The Special Issue of *Concilium* on "Frontier Violations: The Beginnings of New Identities." April.

——. 2000. *Asian Dreams and Christian Hopes*. Delhi: ISPCK.

——. 2005a. *The Sling of Utopia: Struggles for a Different Society*. Delhi: ISPCK.

——. 2005b. *On the Banks of Ganges: Doing Contextual Theology*. Delhi: ISPCK.

——. 2008. *Margins: Sites of Asian Theologies*. Delhi: ISPCK.

29 Literature, Society and the Calling of Creative Public Spheres

Towards a New Art of Cross-Fertilization

He who takes his stand in relation shares in a reality, that is, in a being that neither merely belongs to him nor merely lies outside him. All reality is an activity in which I share without being able to appropriate for myself. Where there is no sharing there is no reality. Where there is self-appropriation there is no reality.

— Martin Buber (1958), *I and Thou*, p. 63.

Who is my audience? It took me a long time to understand that the "public" I am waiting for is the same that I am living for: humanity at large.

— Raimon Panikkar (1995), *A Dwelling Place for Wisdom*, p. 85.

What would the world be if there were no needle and thread? Naturally, no stitched garments!

— Kapila Vatsayan (2010), *Sui Dargha: Crossing Boundaries Through Needle and Thread*, p. ix.

It is not the elements or the sets which define the multiplicity. What defines it is the AND, as something which has its place between the elements or between the sets. AND, AND, AND-stammering.

— Gilles Deleuze & Claire Parnet (2002), *Dialogues*.

Literature and Society

Exploring and realizing creative relationship between literature and society is an adventure in co-realizations and transformations going beyond the logic of the fields of both literature and society. It also calls for understanding their manifold conceptualizations and realizations. Our conventional understanding of literature is that it is created by men of literature. It is not always realized that literature is a part of life and society; when it is done so it is usually conceptualized and represented in a language of mirror and adaptation; literature is either a mirror of society or it adapts to the logic of society. But literature is not only a mirror of society but also a field of creative expressions and confrontations, which breaks existing mirrors of society and creates new languages of self and social realizations and new landscapes of imaginations. Both literature and society are not only fields of adaptation but also fields of transcendence and transformations in which individuals and groups strive to go beyond adaptation and create new conditions for self-realization, co-realizations social realizations. These are fields in which there is interrogation and confrontation of the existing logic of literature and society. Literature is thus not only a field of murmuring but of grumbling and a field of contestation and confrontations of the existing grammar of society based upon a higher grumbling of self and awakened social groups and movements.[1]

In exploring relationship between literature and society, the language of interdisciplinary transaction, as it happens in conventional academic corridors, is not enough. We need a new language and practice of transdisciplinary cultivation, beyond adaptation and meditative verbs of transformations. In this striving for a new language and relationship, realizing the distinction between noun and verb is crucial. In our conventional languages, literature, society as well as such important terms of personal, cultural and national identity as person, nation, writer, India, Shakespeare, etc., come to us as nouns which we also uncritically use, adopt and adapt to. These nouns already from the beginning are imprisoned in a logic of possessive pronouns – this is my self, this is our literature – and any foundational critique of such possessive pronouns are met with resistance and sometimes violent annihilation. But literature, society as well as such fundamental fields of life as self are not only nouns but also verbs. They embody verbs of unfoldment, emergence and realizations.[2] But as verbs they are not only activistic (which is the way verbs are constructed and realized in modernity) but also meditative (see chapter 3). But these meditative verbs of action, expression, communication and co-realizations are manifold – sitting, walking as well as dancing verbs of life. Literature and society are verbs of co-realization and meditative transformations involving walking, sitting and dancing verbs (see the next chapter). Public sphere is an important sphere in which such verbs of co-realization and transformations are at work.

And, in such transformative co-realizations, the nature of "and" plays an important role. If we conceptualize "and" in a logic of juxtaposition, as it mostly happens in the logic of interdisciplinarity, the terms and fields on both sides of "and" do not get mutually interpenetrated and transformed. "And" becomes a helpless presence repeating the logic of "end" (which simultaneously means end of meaning as well as ultimate end or purpose). But if our conception and realization of "and" is one of mutual interrogation, transmutation and mothering bridge then our inhabitation, meditation, dance, walk and work in the space of the "and," the space in between, becomes a work of transformation – transforming a one-sided conceptualization, realization and organization of fields such as literature and society. While our conventional understanding and work in the space of "and" reproduces a logic of "end" and "noun," in beyond adaptation and meditative, interrogating and mothering verbs, "and" is a space of transformations. "And" is a space of quest for infinity from the actors and fields on its two sides rather than a reiteration of the totalizing logic of totality of either of them.[3] "And" is a mothering ground and bridge of quest for and embodiment of responsibility. In his work, *Sahitya O* [Literature and...] Chitta Ranjan Das (1923–2011), a creative seeker, writer and experimenter from Odisha, who has written more than two hundred books on different aspects of literature, society, education, and social criticism suggests such a transformative, interrogative and mothering meaning and realization of "and" (see Das 1989a, Giri 2011). This also comes out in a joint work of co-creation in which the poetic critic and essayist Chitta Ranjan Das and poet Srinivas Udgata co-create poems and reflections on poetry together in the work *Ebam* which also means and (Das 2009b).[4]

Public sphere helps us in realizing such a meaning of "and" beyond the adaptive, already determined and ultimate logic of "end". Literature helps us to express ourselves to ourselves as well as to the others and the public. Expression in the field of literature is simultaneously self, mutual and public, and helps in the creation of public spheres in societies. In the creation of modern public spheres, as Jurgen Habermas (1989) himself tells us, literature has played an important role. He calls it literary public sphere. But it is one thing to talk about literary public sphere as a type of public sphere or even as a segment of public sphere and it is another thing to realize the integral literary dimension of public sphere itself. In later conceptualizations and realizations, literature becomes an integral part of public sphere through work of rhetoric, language, style of argumentation and mutual co-presence in such modes as co-walking and co-labouring.[5] In their vision and practices, writers such as Chitta Ranjan Das, U.R. Ananthamurthy and Mahesweta Devi from India embody this later realization of public sphere. They are tireless participants in public discourses and public spaces through speech, writing; and in case of Das through regular columns in newspapers. They not only help us realize the literary dimension of public sphere but also recreate public sphere through creative and critical literary interventions.

Unfortunately, our understanding of public sphere in social sciences do not fully appreciate its literary dimension and constitution. It has a very prosaic and intellectualist rendering of public sphere without realizing public drama and public poetry in it. The other limitation of contemporary social science understanding of public sphere is that it is part of an uncritical telos of modernity; originating in modernity, it can only become part of an "unfinished agenda of modernity." Such conceptualizations of public sphere do not help us realize the work of public sphere in pre-modern and non-modern societies (cf. Giri 2002; Giri 2008; Uberoi 1996). But literature in all societies have created public spaces and public spheres for mutual communication though depending upon the nature of social arrangement and mode of government, the nature of such social manifestation of creativity has varied. In societies where creators of literature seeking critical public dialogue with their literature of protest and alternative imagination are not tolerated, humiliated and killed, meditative verbs and streams also dry up and die. Such conditions existed in the past in many societies, especially those under authoritarian regimes, and it does continue to exist even in liberal modern democracies.

Literature and Society: Beyond Adaptation and Dynamics of Creative Expressions

In order to understand the relationship between society and literature, we need to understand the transformed understanding of both these fields. Society is a field which helps individuals to come together and express themselves. In sociological theorization of society, there is an acknowledgement of the fact that society is not just a field of *a priori* determination and embeddedness but also a field of self-realization, co-realizations and creative emergence (cf. Sunder Rajan 1998). G.H. Mead, one of the pioneers of modern sociological thinking and author of *Mind, Self and Society*, helps us realize the limits of the social, and urges us to realize that neither "I" nor "me" is a reiteration of the existing conventions of society. As Mead tells us:

> [...] me may be regarded as giving the form of the "I." The novelty comes in the action of the "I," but the structure, the form of the self is one which is conventional.
>
> *This conventional form may be reduced to a minimum.* In the artist's attitude, where there is artistic creation, the emphasis on the element of novelty is carried to the limit. This demand for the unconventional is especially noticeable in modern art. Here the artist is supposed to break away from convention; a part of his artistic expression is thought to be in the breakdown of convention (1934: 209).[6]

Among contemporary philosophers and sociologists we also get an intimation of a post-conventional and post-social conceptualization of society. Jurgen Habermas (1990) tells us that morality is not just reproducing the conventional logic of society rather it is to learn how to think and act in post-conventional ways taking into consideration the calling of universal and universalizable justice. Alain Touraine (2007) tells us about sociology beyond society which explores the way individuals become subjects. For Touraine, becoming a member of society is integrally linked to the process in which one becomes a subject but to be a subject is to have the ability to say "no" to the existing logic if this does not allow creative self-realization. But what Touraine and Habermas have not explored sufficiently is how by cultivating the literary field on the part of self and society one can realize the post-conventional dimension of society, have the capacity to say "no" in the face of an overwhelming compulsion for "yes," and go beyond the logic of an *a priori* social. What they have not explored is how practice of creative literature can contribute to co-creating society as a field of creative expression, co-realization and confrontation. This we find in the works of seekers and experimenters such as Chitta Ranjan Das.

From the field of literature, we also have a connected move to realize society as a field of self-expression and co-realizations. Das, for instance, urges us to realize that society has been built by those who do not confirm. Personality and self for him is not just a logic of adaptation and socialization; it is a field to realize an emergent wholeness building upon one's quest for self-realization, co-realization and world realization (Das 2010). Touraine's appeal for sociology beyond society finds a creative resonance in Das who urges us to realize how boundaries of sociology are now being transcended in creative experiments and adventures.

The Calling of Creative Public Spheres

We usually look at literary creativity in an individualized way but now we need to link both to the fields of creative public spaces and spheres. For our *tapasya* of creativity in literature and society, we need the spheres of the creative self, intimate groups of mutuality as well as public spheres. But in each of these spheres, we continue the modernist logic of linearity. Despite the language of sphere in public sphere, our conceptualization and organization of it is linear. It is hardly a sphere where the spherical nature of our being is at work or finds an expression.[7] In this context, we need to conceptualize and realize public spheres as manifold circles and *chakras*. Public spheres as *chakras* bring interested people together where people through creative sharing and contestation generate mutual energy. Literature can help realize public spheres as *chakras* where individuals and groups can express themselves and through processes of communicative dialogues and contestations can generate mutual energization. These *chakras* can inspire and enable the participants to bring together their vertical dimension such as quest for transcendence and horizontal dimension such as commitment to fellow beings and realizing solidary praxis with others.

The concept and organization of public sphere in modernity is also bound to a logic of double contingency and dualism. For example, we look at self, other and society through the logic of what Strydom (2009) calls "double contingency" of self and the other. This double contingency is also imprisoned within dualism. But now we need to bring the concept of "triple contingency" to each of these spheres. In triple contingency, along with self and other, there is also a public (Strydom 2009). But this public is not fixed, it is emergent, it is not only observing but also participating. Triple contingency does not lie only outside but also works inside. Triple contingency is also a bearer of transcendence as it transcends the dualistic logic of double contingency of self and the other.

In literature, spiritual traditions and creative imaginations, we are familiar with the concept and reality of third eye. This third eye exists not only in Shiva, the meditative *tapaswee* and dancer, but also in all of us.[8] Triple contingency can be linked to the work of third eye. Literature and creative public spheres can help us realize and cultivate not only the triple contingency of life thus going beyond the arrogance and exclusionary assertion of either self or other but also develop and realize our third eyes, a challenge missing in contemporary theorization of society and public sphere. Public sphere and creative meditation can help us realize both triple contingency and third eye and then move it further to the fourth, fifth and further dimensions of our contingencies, aspirations and struggles.[9]

Life Worlds and Living Words

But for this we would have to recreate the link between what is called life worlds and system worlds through the categories of lived worlds and living words. Our lived worlds everywhere are multiplex and plural but the language of life worlds and system worlds as it comes in sociology and in the works of critical theorists such as Habermas usually present a one-dimensional logic and rationality such as the primacy of rational in modernity and hierarchy in traditional societies. Life worlds everywhere are also subjected to dominant logic of the system worlds such as market, state, caste and gender which does not encourage creative wandering and critical reading.[10] In this context, to cultivate lived worlds with their creativity, courage, transcendence and multidimensionality is a challenge which calls for us to go beyond the existing logic of life worlds and system worlds. The challenge of creativity is simultaneous: simultaneously nurturing lived worlds of vibrancy, energy, soulful togetherness and meditative solitude, and living words which move us not to hatred and annihilation but to mutual blossoming and co-realization. Both lived worlds and living words do *tapasya* for and with beauty, dignity and dialogues in the face of and in the midst of ugliness, indignity and violence.[11]

Living words work as new *mantras* of life, to put in the words of Sri Aurobindo, and embody what Martin Heidegger (1994) calls "way making movement." They just do not mirror "forms of life" but create new ways of life. They just do not reproduce existing language but create new languages of self and social realizations.[12] They just do not reproduce the rationality of either tradition or modernity but possibly embody strivings towards what Latin American thinker Enrique Dussel (2010) calls "transmodernity" which builds on tradition and modernity in critical and creative ways. They are not just part of either the "logic of transcendental awe" in tradition or "the linguistification of the sacred" in modernity (see Das 2004).[13] While they seek to make the Divine and Nature part of the communicative field of humans and express it in ways understandable to modern rational mind, it nonetheless does not reduce either of them only to what is comprehensible in the language of modern rationality. It seeks to cultivate the ineffable and ever-present and dynamically moving Beyond in both lived worlds and living words while at the same time making them part of our everyday conversations. Both lived worlds and living words become sites of courage, creativity and transcendence working in between and in the margins of fear, drudgery and pull towards an imprisonment in closed walls which is often justified in the name of immanence.

Going beyond the "linguistification of sacred" (cf. Habermas 1990) in modernity and the consequent disenchantment and dualism between the religious and secular, both life worlds and living words embody new border crossing between rational and emotional, religion and reason, nature and human, mental and supramental. The life worlds and living words embody such a new border crossing among humans, nature and divine in continuously emergent ways.

Towards a New Art of Cross-Fertilization

Literature, society and public spheres are fields of living words and lived worlds. Living worlds and lived words can make us pregnant, pregnant with a new creativity. While our existing space and time are empty and continuously being emptied out with the logic of the system such as money, market and capital, life worlds and lived worlds help us cultivate pregnant spaces and pregnant times. Both lived worlds and living words work as seeds for a new pregnancy thus helping us realize the concept of immaculate conception in new ways. Our living words can impregnate us as our lived worlds of *tapasya* can make each other fertile which is an embodiment of a new spiritual eroticism.[14] Our compassion and confrontation can make us conceive new ideas and new relationships.

Our fields of literature, society and public sphere have become dry and deserted and we need to make them fertile. But for this available fertilizers from the market and external world are not adequate. We need to make them fertile through self, mutual and cross-fertilization in which our quality of life, relationships and living words play a crucial role.

It is earthworms which make the land fertile but today we need to be earthworms to each other as well as to ourselves. But once the land is fertile we would have to cultivate the land as a garden for which we need to be gardeners. But both earthworms and gardeners can remain bound only to the field thus uncritically reproducing the logic of embeddeness which also becomes hostile, opposed and violent not only to forces of emergence from the field itself but also to other fields. In this context, the calling of cross-fertilization and cross-pollination calls us to grow wings and be simultaneously birds and bards, fly and sing together, wonder and wander.[15] Literature, society and creative public spheres can help us simultaneously become earthworms, gardeners and birds.[16] It can also help us become Socratic gadflies, as Socrates, Antigone, Gandhi, Chitta Ranjan and many other seekers and fighters of humanity have exemplified, striking the powers which hinders our potential, aspiration and efforts for self-realization, mutual blossoming and world transformations.

Notes

1. In our seminar on "Literature and Society" at North Eastern Hill University, Shillong in March 2010 where some of the ideas were first present, Professor Mrinal Miri in his keynote address said that literature is an act of murmuring. In my presentation, I said that literature is also an act of grumbling, especially higher grumbling of self and awakened social groups. In offering this argument I am building upon the work of Chitta Ranjan Das (2010) who talks about the work of higher grumbling in personality and society based upon the work of Abraham Maslow.
2. We may note here that in different philosophical, cultural and spiritual traditions, body, mind and being are considered verbs. As T Wei-ming writes about body in Chinese culture and philosophy: "There's a beautiful term, *ti*, which means the body. But, that word, *ti*, can also be used as a verb. It means just my body, but also to embody. The embodiment is a process of understanding other human beings experientially as well as intellectually and spiritually" (Weiming 2000: 50). In his *Art and Experience*, John Dewey also writes about mind: "Mind is primarily a verb" (quoted in Elbridge 2000: 244–245). And theologian and philosopher Raimon Panikkar writes about Being: "Being is a verb, an action, and it has rhythm" (Panikkar 1995: 26).
3. This resonates with the thoughts of Emmanuel Levinas. Franson Manjali (2001) also explores such pathways in his *Literature and Infinity*.
4. So does poet and novelist Rabi Narayan Dash (2008) in his book of poems, *Ebam Kadha* (and buds).
5. While Habermasian public sphere is mainly one of sphere of argumentation, I make it plural by bringing such activities as love and labor into it. Cf. Giri 2008.
6. In this context, what Tabish Khair (in Khair & Doubinosky 2011: 236) has recently written from the field of literature also resonates with Mead's spirit:

   Thus the 'individual' who is indivisible from society but this is also [...] the 'individual' who cannot and should not be reduced to or conflated with 'society.' It is in this creative tension that we, as creative writers and 'individual' readers, have to trace out or locate a value for literature

7. Philosopher Peter Sloterdijk urges us to realize the distinction between a spherical approach and a linear approach.
8. In this context, what Troy Wilson Organ writes below deserves our careful consideration:

   > In India looking at something from a different point of view is called 'seeing with the third eye.' Augustine, in the midst of an analysis of the nature of memory, abruptly asked: 'What third view is this?' And Plotinus advised, 'You must close the eyes and call instead another vision which is to be walked within you, a vision, birth right of all which few turn to use (Organ 1987: 2).

9. This calls for cross-cultural dialogue and border-crossing dialogue between critical theory and religious and spiritual ways of thinking. It would be interesting to explore further dialogue between the concept of triple contingency in critical theory and trinity in Christian religious and spiritual tradition. For Panikkar, "Trinity is not a number but the depth and unfolding of the riches of reality, which is a living relationship" (Pikaza 2010: 119). "Panikkar thereby seeks to move beyond a form of dualism, following the best *advaita* experience (of non-dualism), opening a way to dialogue [...]" (ibid.). In the same way we can realize triple contingency not as a number but as the depth and creativity of relationship beyond the dualistic logic of self and other. But triple contingency also urges us to realize that Trinity whether it is in Christian tradition or Hindu tradition is also confronted with the challenges of public – an observant and meditative public.
10. In this context, what Sebastien Doubinosky writes deserves our consideration:

    > The system has understood that reading is a subversive act that goes beyond the mere 'food for imagination.' As Proust pointed out in his essay 'On Reading', one can be disappointed by books because they have no reality – and we want them to have one. And that desire, precisely that desire, is dangerous because it involves – hopes and frustrations – with reality (in Khair & Doubinosky 2011: 133).

11. In this context, what Margaret Chatterjee tells us about different lifeworlds that we inhabit is touching:

    > On this side of the wall children have milk to drink at least once a day. On the other side, one *pawa* of milk has to stretch for glasses of tea for five adults plus children. A six year old girl told me this. Near the milk stall there are three *mithai* [sweet] shops. This is where the bulk of the milk goes. Consciousness cries out for transformation, a consciousness imbued with conscience. Such a consciousness would grow laterally, horizontally, turning the search light of attention on the endless anomalies around us, the endless injustices, the lack of any sense of priorities (Chatterjee 2005: 16).

    In the above paragraph, Chatterjee talks about the growth of consciousness hortizontally and this resonates with Husserl's emphasis on horizontal ontology (see Mohanty 2002).

12. As expressed in the following poem:

    > Oh friend
    > You said
    > We need a new language
    > A new *sadhana* of words and *tapasya* of worlds
    > This is not a language of victory

Nor is one of self-advertisement and aggrandizement
Neither is it a language of doomsday
This is a language of walking our ways together
Walking our dreams, *sadhana* and struggle

II

In our co-habitations of affection
Of compassion and confrontation
Words become *mantras*
Of a new life, a new responsibility
Of wiping tears from our eyes and
Again taking each other into our laps
Renewing our strength from embrace
We create new paths by walking
We create new language
Our language is the language of walking
Stars of *mantras* leap from our lap

(originally written in Odia by the author and then translated)

13. Habermas (1990) talks about "linguistification of the sacred" where sacred becomes part of ordinary language and conversation. But in this there may be a danger of reduction of sacred to language that Habermas does not explore.
14. Note here what philosopher Luc Irigaray (2002: 115–117) writes:

    Carnal sharing becomes then a spiritual path, a poetic and also a mystical path. [...] Love takes place in the opening to self that is the place of welcoming the transcendence of the other. [...] The path of such an accomplishment of the flesh does not correspond to a solipsistic dream [...] nor to a fin-de-siecle utopia, but to a new stage to be realized by humanity. [...] Nature is then no longer subdued but it is adapted, in its rhythms and necessities, to the path of its becoming, of its growth. Caressing loses the sense of capturing, bewitching, appropriating. [...] The caress becomes a means of growing together toward a human maturity that is not confused with an intellectual competence, with the possession of property [...] nor with the domination of the world.

    For Irigaray, "sharing breath" is an important aspect of this aspired for spiritual eroticism, giving birth to life and each other and making of a spiritual community. For Irigaray, "This proto-ethical plane of shared breath is the eternal germ of a spiritual community, i.e., a community of embodied individuals, caring for each other" (quoted in Skof 2011: 136).
15. A poem written by my friend Francis Regis Bouquizabout "Le Trdoubador," the wandering musicians in medieval France can be of interest. The following line from the poem in French tells us how the troubader visit from place to place:

    Je suis le troubader du chemin qui me mene vers Lui
    Et le passager des temps visibles, invisibles [...]

    Also this poem "On Wings" by Rabi Narayan Dash (2007) can help us realize many meanings of growing wings:

    When I emerged
    Broken and aimless
    She came out on to her terrace
    To ask if I had seen a flying cat
    And a little sparrow crying in sorrow
    If I knew leaves are already yellow.

The world I came of, seeking
Care, if I am I love with
Money or work with a
Passion for becoming
Somebody and something
I have already read
'the child is the father to man'
Sharing her words and unending dream

I started to scream:
'God! Return me to her,
To child, the mother!"

About wings, Rumi tells us about its significance in the following ways: "Something open our wings, something makes boredom and hurt disappear."

16. When I present these three modes of being, I always ask what are the words in local mother languages. While presenting it in Hanoi, my Vietenese partiticpants told me that the word for earthworm is *Konchin*, for garderner is *Kechia* and for bird *Lantivuan*. During our conversation we created a symphony of *knoching*, *kechia* and *lantivuan*.

References

Buber, Martin. 1958. *I and Thou*. New York: Charles Scribner's Sons.

Chatterjee, Margaret. 2005. *Lifeworlds, Philosophy and India Today*. Shimla: Indian Institute of Advanced Study.

Das, Chitta Ranjan. 1989a *Sahitya O... [Literature and...]. Berhampur*: Pustaka Bhandar.

——. 1989b. "Ethara Udiba Neta." In (eds) Chitta Ranjan Das and Srinivas Udgata, *Ebam*. Cuttack: Books & Books.

——. 2004. *Mahimandalara Gita: Sri Arakhita Das, Eka Adhyana* [The Mahimandala Gita of Sri Arakhita Das, A Study]. Bhubaneswar: Odisha Sahitya Akademi.

——. 2009. "Afterword." In *The Modern Prince and the Modern Sage: Transforming Power and Freedom*. Delhi: Sage Publications.

——. 2010. *Byakti o Byaktitya* [Person and Personality]. Bhubaneswar: Pathika Prakashani.

Dash, Rabi Narayan. 2007. *On Wings and Other Poems*. Huddinge, Sweden: Prima Verba & Balasore, India: New Race.

——. 2008. [...] *Ebam Kadha* [...and buds]. Balasore, Odisha: Samara Graphics.

Deleuze, Gilles & Claire Parnet. 2002. *Dialogues*. New York: Columbia University Press.

Dussel, Enrique. 2010. "Transmodernity and Interculturality: An Interpretation from the Philosophy of Liberation." Paper presented at the International Symposium on "Learning Across Boundaries," University of Luxembourg, June.

Elbridge, Richard. 2000. "Dewey's Aesthetics." In *Cambridge Companion to John Dewey*, (ed.) M. Cochran. Cambridge: Cambridge University Press.

Giri, Ananta Kumar. 1990. *Moral Consciousness and Communicative Action*. Cambridge, MA: The MIT Press.

——. 2002. *Conversations and Transformations: Towards a New Ethics of Self and Society.* Lanham, MD: Lexington Books.

——. 2008. "Civil Society and the Calling of Self-Development." *Sociological Bulletin*

——. 2011. "Chitta Ranjan Das: A Creative Thinker." *Social Change* 41 (3): 359–380.

Habermas, Jurgen. 1989. *The Structural Transformation of the Public Sphere*. Cambridge, MA: The MIT Press.

Heidegger, Martin. 1994. "The Way to Language." In idem, *Basic Writings: Revised and Expanded Edition*, (ed.) Farrell Krell. London: Routledge, pp. 393-426.

Irigaray, Luc. 2002. *Between East and West*. New York: Columbia University Press.

Khair, Tabish & Sebastien Doubinosky. 2011. *Reading Literature Today: Two Complimentary Essays and a Conversation*. Delhi: Sage Publications.

Manjali, Franson. 2001. *Literature and Infinity*. Shimla: Indian Institute of Advanced Studies.

Mead, G.H. 1934. *Mind, Self and Society*. Chicago: University of Chicago Press.

Mohanty, J.N. 2002. *Explorations in Philosophy: Western Philosophy*. Delhi: Oxford University Press.

Organ, Troy Wilson. 1987. *Third Eye Philosophy: Essays in East-West Thoughts*. Athens: Ohio University, Press.

Panikkar, Raimon. 1995. *A Dwelling Place for Wisdom*. Delhi: Motilal Banarasidass.

Pikaza, Xavier. 2010. "Raimon Panikkar (1918–2010)." *Concilium* (5): 117–120.

Skof, Lenart. 2011. "Pragmatism and Deepened Democracy: Ambedkar between Dewey and Unger." In *Democratic Culture: Historical and Philosophical Essays*, (ed.) Akeel Bilgrami, Delhi: Routledge, pp. 122–142.

Strydom, Piet. 2009. *New Horizons of Critical Theory: Collective Learning and Triple Contingency*. Delhi: Shipra.

Sunder Rajan, R. 1998. *Beyond the Crises of European Sciences: New Beginnings*. Shimla: Indian Institute of Advanced Studies.

Touraine, Alain. 2007. "Sociology After Sociology." *European Journal of Social Theory*.

Uberoi, J.P.S. 1996. *Religion, Civil Society and State: A Study of Sikhism*. Delhi: Oxford University Press.

Vatsayan, Kapila. 2010. *Sui Dargha: Crossing Boundaries, Through Needle and Thread*. Delhi: India International Center and Wisdom Tree.

Weiming, Tu. 2000. "The Complex Bridges between China and the West." In *A Parliament of Minds: Philosophy for a New Millennium*, (eds.), Michael Tobias, J. Patrick Fitzerald & David Rothenburg, Albany: State University of New York Press, pp. 46–59.

Appendix

Crocodile and Sabari *Sukta*: Shankara, Buddha and Ambedkar

1

Oh Crocodile
Pull my leg
As you had pulled
The tiny legs of Shankara
If you pull my legs
Towards the other shore
Across deep waters
My *Sannyasi* soul
Would surrender
I would be a *Sannyasi*
With the ways, with light
With home and the world
With self and non-self
A new blossoming of relationship
And the world
A new *Sannyasa*
Transformation of Life!

2

New Encounters
With Soul, with the *Chandala*
But the *Chandala*
Does not turn into Shiva
Chandala Becomes Buddha and Ambedkar
A new Constitution in the hands of the Chandala
Meditating he asks:
Oh Shankara
You had said
We are neither body nor intellect
Chidanada Rupa
But where is here
The festival of soul
In the sacrificial pyre
Of Caste systems
So many souls get killed and burnt
Shnakara embraces Chandala
Holding hands together
Buddha, Shankara and Ambedkar
Walk together
A new Sannyasa of begging of life

3

Walking together
They feel hungry

Says Shankara:
I am supposed to have only my own cooked food
But I do not know how to cook

Would you know?
Buddha the Enlightened says no

Says Ambedkar:
I had coordinated the writing of the Constitution
But forgot to learn how to cook
In hungry stomachs
They meet Sabari
But Sabari does not give them fruits
Brings the three Greats to
The kitchen
By the fire
Blowing the rods of Sabari
Shankara, Buddha and Ambedkar
Learn to make rice and *dal*

4

Cooking and eating
Rice and dal
Around the kitchen
A new *Sannyasa*
Singing *Saundraya Lahari* and reading
Tripitaka Sutra and Constitution
We join them in
This path of *tapasya*
We learn the *sadhana* of cooking
We transform the tears of history
A new garden of creativity
Holding the hands of crocodile
And around the kitchen of Sabari
A new *sannyasa* of Life.

(A poem originally written in Odia and translated by the author)

30 With and Beyond Plurality of Standpoints

Sociology and the Sadhana *of Multi-Valued Logic and Living*

Ideologies by their very nature make use of concepts and symbols which are ambiguous and rich in implicit meaning. The process by which these implicit meanings are made explicit is both complex and uncertain in its course; it is a process in which both the proponents of an ideology and their adversaries take part. [...] An ideology addresses itself to the possibilities contained in the human condition and not merely to existing conflict of interests.

— Andre Beteille (1980), *Ideologies and Intellectuals*, pp. 22, 20.

There are no simple concepts. Every concept has components [...]. It is a multiplicity [...] Components are distinct, heterogeneous, and yet not separable. The point is that each partially overlaps, has a zone of neighborhood [...] something passes from one to the other, something that is undecidable between them. There is an area *ab* that belongs to both *a* and *b*, where a and b "become" indiscernible.

— Gilles Deleuze & Felix Guattari (1994), *What is Philosophy?*, pp. 17, 19–20

Observations are unavoidably position-based, but scientific reasoning need not, of course, be based on observational information from one specific position only. There is need for what may be called "trans-positional" assessment – drawing on but going beyond different positional observations. The constructed "view from no where" would then be based on synthesizing different views from distinct positions. The positional objectivity of the respective observations would still remain important but not in itself adequate. A trans-positional scrutiny would also demand some kind of coherence between different positional views.

— Amartya Sen (1994), "Positional Objectivity," p. 130.

But some of the greatest achievements in philosophy could only be compared with taking up some books which seemed to belong together, and putting them in different selves, nothing more being final about their positions than that they no longer lie side by side. The onlooker who doesn't know the difficulty of the task might well think in such a case that nothing at all had been achieved.

— Ludwig Wittgenstein (1958), *The Blue and Brown Books*, p. 44–45.

Introduction and Invitation

In his essay, "Sociology and Ideology" Andre Beteille (2009) discusses a range of issues on the relationship between sociology and ideology such as the need for sociology to maintain a focus on the empirical and make a distance from a zealous commitment to ideology. Towards the end of his essay, Beteille presents us the challenge of pluralism through a brief pointer to what he calls "plurality of standpoints." Beteille has been consistently a champion of a plural approach[1] in the study of society but his discussion of plural standpoints in his essay raises further questions which call for further collaborative search and reflections. For example, what is the nature of standpoint in these plurality of standpoints – is it partial or absolute? Do these different standpoints communicate among each other? Is it a responsibility for sociology to understand and contribute to communication among plural standpoints?[2] In this chapter, I wish to think together with Beteille on these questions and discuss further the challenge of pluralization emanating from Beteille's reference to plurality of standpoints in his essay. I do not make an exhaustive discussion of all the issues raised in Beteille's essay but mainly focus on the theme of pluralism and plurality of standpoints and discuss how ideology and theology also do embody plural streams. I then briefly touch upon the issue of empirical and normative aspects of social reality raised by Beteille and argue how sociology needs to go beyond the dualism of the empirical and normative and understand the normative strivings and struggles at work in the very heart of social reality itself.

Sociology and Plurality of Standpoints

For Beteille, an ideological approach to reality tends to present an absolutist picture while sociology and social anthropology present us plural standpoints:

> [...] there is no one unique or privileged standpoint in the study of society and culture. Even within the same society there generally is a plurality of standpoints, varying with religion, class, gender or moral and intellectual predilection, and besides different outsiders may view the same society from different standpoints. Sociology and social anthropology cannot move forward unless the plurality of standpoints is accepted as a fundamental condition for the systematic and comparative study of society and culture. But it is one thing to acknowledge the value of, say, studying marriage from the standpoint of a woman, or discrimination from that of a *dalit*, and quite another to have the standpoint itself defined by a particular agenda (2009: 210).

Sociology and anthropology present us plurality of standpoints of actors and institutions. But what is the nature of these standpoints? Are they partial or absolute? Building upon Beteille and also Mannheim,[3] the pioneer of sociology of knowledge, we can realize that each of these standpoints is partial though they may claim absolutism on their own behalf.[4] But realizing the partial nature of one's standpoint and realizing that ones' standpoints is interpenetrated or needs to be interpenetrated by others' standpoints calls for further work on self-transformation – transformation of one's one-dimensional epistemology and politics – mutual communication and institutional nurturance where institutions of society facilitate such realization of one's partiality and communication among partial standpoints through institutionally facilitated spaces and processes. This calls for understanding the way plurality of standpoints become part of multi-dimensional processes of pluralization. This is a further challenge for sociology. Here it is not enough only to confine sociology to the empirical study of society and not to accept the normative challenge of how sociological research can contribute to creating a field of knowledge, reflections, social relations and institutional space where plurality of standpoints go beyond their initial closures – self-justification and absolutist claim – and communicate with each other.

Beteille does not want one's standpoint in the study of society defined by a particular political agenda. Beteille also does not want study of religion to be confined only to the followers of a particular religion. As Beteille writes: "The sociologist's obligation to be even-handed and value neutral in the study of religion in a country like India where different religions with different world views and ideologies co-exist and are allowed and encouraged to grow and flourish. The comparative study of religion becomes difficult where study of religious beliefs and practices become divided among sociologists according to their religious identities so that Hinduism is studied only by Hindus, Islam only by Muslims, and Christianity only by Christians" (2009: 206). But the sad reality is that we find very few sociologists and anthropologists in India who study a religion other than the one to which they are born.[5] For overcoming such binding and bondage as well as the problem of one's standpoint in the study of society defined by a political agenda, as Beteille challenges us, we need to cultivate a process of pluralization where as students of society as well as living embodiment of it we learn of the partial nature of our standpoints, accept the responsibility of going beyond these and open ourselves to other standpoints and ways of seeing, being and living. This way a standpoint does not continue to remain only an "inheritance" but a project[6] and an achievement[7] – sometimes a joint project and joint achievement – in the life of self, culture and society. Pluralizing our plural standpoints and making them open to mutual interpenetration constitutes a challenge for a creative joint project.[8]

Such a challenge creatively confronts us in contemporary ways of knowing and articulation of epistemological standpoints such as feminist standpoint epistemology. Feminist standpoint epistemology challenges us to see and the understand the world through "the eyes and experiences of oppressed women" and "apply vision and knowledge of oppressed women to social activism and social change" (Brooks 2006: 55). But feminist standpoint epistemology is faced with all the questions of standpoints raised above including the need for going beyond one's standpoint. In this context, feminist standpoint epistemologists are themselves realizing that there is not one standpoint of women and there is the need for dialogue across standpoints of different women. As Brooks writes: "Many feminist scholars emphasize the need for open dialogue between women and different perspectives [...]" (ibid: 74). Sympathetic yet self-critical feminist epistemologists themselves are realizing: "The very term 'standpoint' evokes an image of a position where one stands and views the other from a particular 'perspective.' Even though this image has been fruitful in feminist epistemology, it is time to acknowledge that it creates more problems than it solves. One problem is that it imports a fundamentalist theory of epistemic justification into feminist epistemology" (Rolin 2006: 134). In place of a fundamentalist theory of epistemic justification and what Sandra Harding, the pioneer of feminist standpoint epistemology, calls "maximally objective standpoint," Kristen Rolin presents us a "contextualist theory of epistemic justification" where in a particular context, different standpoints including standpoints of different women interact with each other and through such mutual interaction and dialogue justify each other. This leads to socially grounded perspective which, it is important to note, "is not simply a view from a social position" (ibid: 135; also see Harding 2004). "It is a matter of doing research with certain moral and social values" (ibid). In line with our above discussions such values embody efforts to go beyond one's absolutist social positions, be open to each other and be part of multidimensional processes of pluralization.

From Plurality of Standpoints to Pluralization

Pluralism is a much talked about ideal today but we need to understand the distinction between pluralism and pluralization. A discourse of pluralism can often be imprisoned within a logic of status quo without transforming the very condition such as nation-state and modernist epistemology which is prone to propound and assert a singular view of self, culture, method, disciplinarity, citizenship and the world (cf. Connolly 1995; Dallmayr 2010).[9] Most of the time we approach pluralism though the language of the noun which is a language of statis. Such a condition of statis is amenable to looking at our mode of being in condition of plurality as one of standpoint as if we are standing still. In this context pluralization challenges us to realize plural modes of being, intersubjectivity, culture and society in dynamic ways as verbs.[10] But as verbs they are not only activistic but also meditative. We need to transform the existing discourse and practice of pluralism into meditative verbs of pluralization (see chapter three in this volume).

Beteille uses the language of standpoint to point to conditions of plurality. Apart from this being a language of noun, this is also primarily the language of an observer[11] which has its inherent limitation if not transformationally supplemented with the lived experiences of actors of society. Participants in condition of plurality live a life of plurality and do not have only standpoints about it. An observer's being in condition of plurality is not the same as that of a participant. For example, participants in life worlds of both society as well as ideological field learn as well as fail to learn how to exist and co-exist going beyond formal absolutist claims.

Standing is one mode of self-presentation and interaction with others but in our spectrum of self-presentation there are other modes as well such as sleeping, sitting and walking. Sleeping is a creative moment of reflection and regeneration which can give us an opportunity to think beyond our own positions and create new realities and possibilities.[12] When we sit together and communicate and walk together it may lead to different possibilities of pluralization. While people from plural backgrounds of both society, culture, gender, caste and ideology sit together it creates new realities and possibilities of going beyond their absolute claims and closures and creating spaces and processes of communication. Thus creative spaces for sitting together with and for people from different backgrounds has been one of the practices of human society – from tribal villages in the remote past as well as present to varieties of spaces of dialogues in the modern and postmodern world. [13] Similarly when people from diverse backgrounds walk together it creates new conditions of pluralization including co-walking meditation where they ruminate "when walking" (Thoreau 1975: 596).[14] Let us look at the significance of epochal marches such as Gandhi's Salt March in 1930 and walk across riot-hit Noakali in 1947 which contributed to calming down communal fire and bring about peace,[15] Martin Luther King Jr's famous Washington March for Freedom in 1963, and marches organized by the women's movements. In the March in Washington walkers realized that they are not only Blacks and Whites as Martin Luther King addressed these walkers of "creative suffering": "We cannot walk alone." In his epochal "I have a dream" speech King also hoped for a day when people "will not be judged by the color of their skin but by the content of their character." Similarly when a man takes part in the marches organized by the women's movements it creates a moving condition to realize that one is not just a man. In these marches participants get an opportunity to realize that they just do not have one standpoint, their standpoint is not an inheritance but a project, a joint project. For realizing pluralization we need to go beyond the existential fact of plurality of standpoints and explore how in the fabric of daily life and in struggles for co-realization such as varieties of struggles and mobilizations for dignity and dialogues participants go beyond existing logic of closure and pluralize their lives and modes of relationships.

Pluralization and the *Sadhana* of Multi-Valued Logic and Living

Sociology for Beteille presents plurality of standpoints. But our realization and living of plurality with a predominant focus on standpoint is different from a mode which emphasizes and practices sitting together and walking together. Furthermore, all these standpoints belong to a field and from the perspective of the field, each of these standpoints is partly true and also not partly true. Moreover, each of these standpoints is also interpenetrated by the standpoint of others. For example, a Dalit standpoint on society is interpenetrated by a Brahminical standpoint in the ontology of reality as a field which holds both the Dalits and Brahmins together even though both of them may deny that their standpoint is interpenetrated by the other. Similar is the situation vis-à-vis the standpoint of man and woman about society. While this is an aspect of reality which holds us, our epistemological construction of it is, many a time, one-dimensional which is fuelled by an uncritical bondage to a single political ideology. In this context, how do we go beyond a one-dimensional epistemological construction of reality where the ontology of reality is inherently plural? How do we pluralize our plural standpoints which at the level of self, ideology and even sociological method, present themselves in a singular, absolutist and exclusionary way? Pluralizing plural standpoints calls for generosity and expansion of points of view into circles of views[16] on the part of both participants and observers which is not necessarily articulated and embodied in the sociological method as it is prevalent today. This calls for *sadhana*[17] (striving) of multi-valued logic and living as well as spiritual transformation of our consciousness, method, self and society which are prone to cling to the absolutism of a singular standpoint. *Sadhana* or striving makes our knowledge, including locational knowledge of standpoint, not just received and taken for granted but evolving, interpenetrative and emergent.

Multi-valued logic, as recently presented to us by J.N. Mohanty building upon multiple traditions of humanity such as the Jaina tradition of *Anekantavada* (many paths to truth), Husserlian phenomenology of overlapping contents and Gandhian pathways of non-violence, emphasizes that "every point of view is partly true, partly false and partly undecidable" (Mohanty 2000: 24).[18] This is different from a dualistic logic where each point of view claims absolutism for itself or its absolutist claim is accepted at face value by the observer as well as the participant. One might claim absolutism for oneself but the fields of life, history and society compel us to realize the partial nature of our absolutist claims. This is also the calling of life. In life there is an inescapable pluralization which calls for cultivation of a multi-valued logic and living where we move beyond our initial standpoints and interact with each other sometimes going inside each other. Such a multi-valued logic and living embodies an art of autonomy and interpenetration where our autonomy is not fixed but transforms itself in the process of mutual interaction and communication.

One important aspect of multi-valued logic is overcoming what Sri Aurobindo calls "egoistic standpoint" of subject positions or position of actors (Sri Aurobindo 1962: 258).[19] In sociology we mainly conceptualize, perceive and relate to actors as holders of social roles and social identities. But an actor as an occupant of social role and positional-cum-social identity such as a wife or a Dalit can enact one's positional standpoint as an ego or a self. While one's egoistic standpoint can be more closed, one's standpoint as a self can be much more open. Transformational streams in psychology, sociology, philosophy and spiritual traditions urge us to realize the distinction between ego and self. Thus overcoming our standpoint as that of an ego and cultivating the standpoint of self in our enactment of positions and embodiment of transpositionality helps us to move beyond our own initial standpoints and be open to and embrace the standpoints of others. This contributes to pluralization of our subject positions, first of all realize the subject position of self in place of the subject position of ego, overcoming positional fixation and realizing transpositionality and a multi-valued logic and living.

Multi-valued logic and living is an aspect of reality which needs to be understood and explored and not asserted. Here I am not making an *a priori* assertion about it and just pointing to the need for investigating multi-valued aspects of reality as an indispensable empirical task for sociology. At the same time, by investigating it empirically sociology can contribute to a public enlightenment as to the nature of its existence or lack of it and in the process contributing to the normative task of contributing to building a self and society of pluralization. But this challenges sociology to understand some of its own limitations, for example, its uncritical bondage to a logic of dualism. In a dualistic sociology plurality of standpoints are likely to be understood dualistically and even left at that by the empirically minded sociologist. But despite ideological construction and valorization of our absolutist standpoints communications do take place or fail but in order to understand lack of or failure of communication we also need a multi-valued sociology pursuing a multi-valued logic. Thus multi-valued logic and living challenges both sociology and ideology to pluralize; it challenges sociology to understand its own limitations such as bondage to dualism and cultivate non-dual modes of investigation and cultivation of knowledge, self and society.

The *sadhana* of multi-valued logic and living challenges us to pluralize both sociology and ideology. For Beteille (2002), sociology is a modernistic project as different from a project of tradition or postmodernism. This way, sociology becomes a part of post-traditional telos of modernity.[20] But modernity is not only a condition of life; as the difficult journey of the modern world reveals and different critiques of it such as those offered by Foucault and the postmodernists have shown, modernity itself has an element of ideology. Following Beteille's own plea for maintaining a distance between ideology and sociology, should not sociology maintain and self-consciously cultivate a distance from the ideology of modernity? If sociology is a study of our world, this world consists of plural modes and organizations of life – traditional, modern and post-modern. If sociology only follows the post-traditional teleology of modernity how can it study varieties of forms of life – traditional, modern as well as postmodern? These varieties of forms of life exist not only in the so-called traditional societies such as India or Lapland but in all contemporary societies – be it India, Indonesia, Sweden, France, England, Germany, Singapore, China or the USA. If sociology is only bound to an ideology of post-traditional telos of modernity, is it capable of even empirically understanding the plural worlds it claims to understand?

Plural Streams in Ideology and Theology and Challenges for Sociology

Pluralization is also a challenge for ideology. As already suggested, in the condition of ideological plurality there is a dimension of plulralization at work. During the cold war, protagonists of communism and capitalism learnt how to live with each other in the world system. This was in the midst of violence, war and propensity for mutual annihilation. This was not an easy co-existence but for both sides there was no alternative. Both sides also influenced each other – socialism influencing welfare policies in capitalistic societies and market principles influencing socialitstic organization of the economy leading to the principle and practices of market socialism. So there was communication across the ideological divide and, despite and in the midst of difficulties, both sides learnt how to live together. This is also an aspect in all ideological situations. For example, the way followers of different political parties with their different ideologies such as Congress, Communist and BJP live in a social space – be it that of a village or a nation, point to an indispensable aspect of co-survival which is difficult and fragile. But to understand the ideological field as a practical field of life we need to move beyond a representational and typifying view of ideology and adopt a communicational view, especially a perspective of pragmatics of communication. If we look at the work of ideologies from the point of view of pragmatics of communication we realize that ideologies are much more plural in their lived realities and histories. Beteille himself has shown us this in his discussion of plural streams within Marxism. This work of plural streams from the point of view of intellectual history which is true of not only Marxism but many other ideologies can be linked to a pragmatics of communication which challenges us to realize plural streams in existing ideological practices and communication among them.

Plural streams in the discourse and practice of ideology also challenges us to understand plural streams in the theological and the theologian. Beteille writes: "The distinction between the normative and the empirical approaches is seen most clearly in the contrast between the theological and sociological approaches to the study of religion. The theologian is concerned primarily with questions of truth and efficacy of religious beliefs and practices. Such questions do not concern the sociologist in the same way. His primary aim is to observe, describe, interpret and explain the ways in which religious beliefs and practices actually operate" (2009: 204). But in the actual work of many theologians today there is a greater embodiment of empirical approach to study of religion deploying social science methods such as participant observation, historical study and survey work. The work done by faculty and students at Department of Christianity, University of Madras, led by the pre-eminent social theorist, philosopher and theologian Felix Wilfred uses social science methods in the study of religions. The Department is not confined only to the study of Christian religions. Here students and faculty who are Christians also study religious practices of other religions employing the methods of social sciences. As Felix Wilfred writes in his essay, "Christian Studies: The Contours of a Discipline and Its Future Prospects" in the Silver Jubilee Volume of the Department *Transforming Religion: Prospects for a New Society*: "In the Department of Christian Studies of the University of Madras, there have been several dissertations written through empirical investigations applying qualitative and quantitative methods of study" (2009: 244; also Maliekal 2002). As Beteille draws the distinction between sociology and theology, Wilfred draws the distinction between theology and Christian Studies:

> A good theology serves an important purpose of motivating and inspiring the believing Christian community by elucidating the meanings of the truths of faith and drawing its practical implications. But the discipline of theology has its serious limitations when done from within its religious precincts. [...] Christian Studies does not necessarily call for confessional approach, nor does it exclude it. Therefore, those who believe explicitly in Christianity and those who are not Christians but are interested in knowing what Christianity is all about, could find that knowledge and continue their search. *This open-endedness is necessary to allow people of other faiths to find a point of intellectual intersection with Christianity. This could be different from what traditional theology projects* (ibid: 245; emphases added).

For Wilfred, Christianity Studies (ibid: 244) does not continue the project of an absolutist claim about one's religion:

> [...] all religions fall into the temptation of claiming the particular belief system it represents as something universally valid. Christian Studies does not aim at such universalizing of the particular, which is a centripetal movement. Christian Studies needs to understand itself as part of a centrifugal movement. It tries to find the universal lying outside its boundaries and relates the particularity it embodies with this universality in a process of dialogue and inquiry.

Methods of social sciences including methods of sociology and anthropology become a partner in this process of moving outside ones' boundary. At the same time, Christian Studies does not just give an objective picture of its subject of study because it does not presuppose that one can study religion or, for that matter, any aspect of reality without the involvement of the subject. But this involvement is not an extension of one's faith but working out one's role as a student of faith, religion and society. In the words of Wilfred:

> *Comparative religion, like its kindred discipline of phenomenology of religion, is non-judgmental about religion, and therefore it claims to give an "objective" picture of religion. Christian studies, on the other hand, presuppose that in the process of knowledge the subject is deeply involved. Many studies in sociology of religion have underlined that one does not understand a religion and its expressions unless one enters a certain way into the world of its believers.* Christian Studies does not pretend to give a neutral picture of Christianity, but goes into the world of faith of Christians as they would like to be understood. *This epistemological approach to Christianity – for that matter in the study of religion – does not necessarily presuppose faith in the student and researcher of this discipline* (ibid: 246; emphasis added).

Some of the themes in the above narration of Wilfred do speak with themes in Beteille's discussion. For example, while presenting Srinivas's work as an epitome of sociological approach to Hindu religion as different from a theological approach, Beteille nonetheless tells us how Srinivas did not like representation of his religion which he perceived to be misrepresentation: "He once returned from a seminar, infuriated by a participant who had described Hindu beliefs and practices as 'mumbo-jumbo." (Beteille 2009: 205). Beteille reads Srinivas' reaction in this way: "It is no easy matter to remain detached, objective and value-neutral in the study of religion, and particularly of one's religion" (ibid). But in showing his reaction was Srinivas becoming less value neutral or was he expressing his genuine need that the religion that he was born with and that sustains his faith should be understood properly and, least of all, not misrepresented? This possible wish of Srinivas is a universal wish as all of us, whatever locations we come from, want to be understood properly and with care and respect in terms of representation of our locational identities. This way Wilfred's charting of pathway of Christian Studies as an effort to "go into the faith of Christians as they would like to be understood"[21] resonates with Srinivas' possible wish that his religion should be properly understood which does not mean an uncritical glorification of it or "wholesale condemnation" (Beteille 2009: 205). But to understand the religion of one's own or other's is not to impose one's *a priori faith* or belief on one's study. This is the approach of sociology as well as that of Christian Studies which does not necessarily presuppose "faith in the student and researcher of this discipline" (Wilfred 2009: 246).

In the University of Madras the Department of Christian Studies is part of the School of Philosophy and Religious Thought which has also other departments such as Islamic Studies, Vaishnavism, Buddhist Studies, Jaina Studies and Saiva Siddhanta. At Oxford there are both the Oxford Centers of Hindu Studies and the Oxford Center for Islamic Studies which are, however, not part of the University of Oxford. But I do not know if proponents of other religious studies departments within University of Madras as well as Oxford Centers of Hinduism and Islamic Studies have the same open-ended approach of Wilfred and make it clear not to impose one's *a priori* religious belief in the study of one's religion on that of the other.

Though like Beteille's distinction of sociology and theology, Wilfred makes the distinction between Christian Studies and theology (Wilfred's Christian Studies comes closer to Beteille's sociological approach), he, at the same time, as in the above cited paragraph, challenges us to realize that in order to understand the religious life of a people we would have to go inside it and it is not enough to stand outside as an observer. This challenges Beteille's approach to the sociology of religion which may like to stand outside and not enter into religious belief of the believers.[22] Without entering inside the religious life of the believer which is different from acting out one's faith or uncritically borrowing other's faith how can sociology of religion fulfill its task? This, in turn, calls for a simultaneous cultivation of the subjective and objective in one's study of religion and society.

Wilfred makes a distance from the theological approach to religion starting with his own journey, at least formally, as a student and teacher of theology (see Gnanapragasam & Schussler Fiorenza 2009). This journey itself points to critical and self-transforming plural streams in the theological which is much more than what is typified in the noun theology in both Beteille and Wilfred. What we find in Wilfred is a continuation of a rich legacy within theological engagement with religion, society and the world. Let us consider here the seminal work of Paul Tillich. Tillich was a theologian but as a theologian he talked about the need for skeptical belief in matters of not only study of religion but in one's faith.[23] Such an articulation of faith – faith with skepticism and vulnerability – now finds a creative resonance from the other side of intellectual spectrum, for example, from the shores of critical theory and postmetaphysical thought, where sociologists and philosophers such as Jurgen Habermas (2003, 2008) are challenging us to understand the limits of rational knowledge and rework our relationship between faith and knowledge. Habermas (2006: 5) pleads for a "complementary learning process" in which both people of faith and reason take part. In this learning process "true belief is not only a doctrine, believed content, but a source of energy that the person who has a faith taps performatively and thus nurtures his or her entire life" (ibid: 9). Habermas also urges us to realize that what is needed at this contemporary juncture is a "correlation of reason and faith, of reason and religion, both being summoned to mutual cleansing and healing."[24]

In the theological legacy we also find the inspiring work of Raimundo Panikkar (1977) who embodied deep and meditative pluralization. He studied the Vedas starting with his initial journey as a Catholic priest and his *The Vedic Experience Mantramanjari: An Anthopology of the Vedas for Modern Man and Contemporary Celebration* is a testament to the deep quest for the other from within theology. In our representation of theology in sociology we are invited to acknowledge these plural streams and cultivate it further (cf. Giri 2011b; Wilfred 2008; Vinayraj 2010).[25] In these plural streams of theology there is a great deal of appreciation for sociological strivings as David Smith, an insightful contemporary theologian, writes: "Indeed, there are times when the work of contemporary sociologists is characterized by such depth and seriousness that one is inclined to think that they are the true inheritors of the ancient prophetic traditions working in the world today" (2007: 83). Similarly from the sociological side there is also an openness to the theological. As Robert Bellah, the great sociologist of religion of our times, tells us: "Some of the systems theorists such as Parsons and Karl Deutsch have conceived of human action as multi-layered and open. Deutch, for example, has spoken of the propensity for all highly complex systems to break down, and has borrowed the theological term 'grace' to designate the indispensable but unpredictable situational conditions that seem to be necessary in order for any complex system to function at all" (1970: 241; also see Bellah 2011).[26] And John Clammer, himself a sociologist and anthropologist, urges us to understand the significance of theology in giving us a sense of whole and the need to pursue it in our complex world.[27]

Beyond the Dualism of the Empirical and Normative

This brings us finally to the difficult issue of the normative and the empirical. For Beteille, sociology has to study the empirical but the empirical itself has many layers of reality and realizations. To study the empirical, sociology has to be much more than empirical and also go beyond empiricism as a singular method.[28] Moreover, the normative has also multiple meanings and modes of realizations. Normative does not just mean what is coded as norms and expected and uttered by the formulaic interpreters and defenders of social norms. Normative also refers to aspirations, strivings and struggles to make life and society more beautiful, dignified and dialogical. Such a quest for the normative is not just an extension of existing norms in society as most of these norms in traditional, modern and postmodern worlds are islands of problematic justice, dialogue and beauty. Normative refers to a dimension of *sadhana*, striving and struggle in our very existent world and it is that way a part of reality itself. It is a fragile, ambiguous and uncertain quest as the very project of life, reality and society which nonetheless challenges us to understand and cultivate this normative quest for beauty, dignity, dialogue and pluralization in the midst of ugliness, violence and monological absolutism of various kinds. Should not sociology try to understand this quest of the normative and cultivate it further in self, culture, knowledge and society?

Notes

1. As, for example, in his M.N. Roy memorial lecture on "Marxism, Pluralism and Orthodoxy" presented near three decades ago Beteille (1982) had argued how Marxism is not a singular and monolithic ideological system and consists of plural streams of reflections and practices.
2. It must be noted here that cultivating plurality of standpoints and facilitating communication among them is also part of the dialogue philosophies and works of our times. There is a long genealogy of multiplicity of standpoints in philosophy and other fields as exemplified, for example, in the works of Martin Buber (1958). There is also attention to plurality of standpoints beyond absolutism in the work of Karl Mannheim (1936), the pioneer of sociology of knowledge. John Clammer also here draws our attention to the work of John Paul

Lederach in peace studies and Marjorie Green in philosophy (personal communication).

3. In his *Ideology and Utopia* Mannheim (1936: 75–76) writes:

   > It may be true that every form of expression, in which we clothe our thoughts, tends to impose upon them an absolute tone. In our epoch, however, it is precisely the function of historical investigation [...] to analyse the elements that make up our self-assurance, so indispensable for action in immediate, concrete situations, and to counteract the bias which might arise from what we, as individuals, take for granted. This is possible only through incessant care and determination to reduce to a minimum the tendency to self-apotheosis. Through this effort the one-sidedness of our point of view is counteracted, and conflicting intellectual positions may actually come to supplement one another (ibid: 75–76).

4. Here Marcus Bussey insightfully comments: "Phenomenologically they are experienced as absolute until some event shatters the illusion – transformation requires such a disjuncture so that identity can shift to incorporate multiplicity" (personal communication).
5. This is also true of M.N. Srinivas whose sociological approach to religion Beteille celebrates. Srinivas did not study any other religion except Hinduism. Even his essay, "The Social Significance of Religion in India," does not discuss much the work and dynamics of non-Hindu religions in India (cf. Srinivas 2009; Giri 2010).
6. I draw this distinction from Nitasha Kaul's (2008) very illuminating discussion on the need for new kind of knowledge creation which seeks to put different parts, especially forgotten and excluded parts, together. For Kaul, "[...] modernist knowledge needs to be haunted by a post-colonial memory, a re-membering, which can be instigated by placing the question of difference at the heart of the story. When one re-members, one does not simply recall – to re-member is to put it altogether again" (Kaul 2009: 116). Such as standpoint of knowledge participation and generation is a project, "not an inheritance" (Kaul 2008: 141).
7. In her reflections on standpoint theory in epistemology, for example, feminist standpoint epistemology, Ahlstrom Kristoffer (2005: 88) tell us: "As standpoint theorists often emphasize (Harding included), a standpoint is an achievement. Women do not automatically accept a feminist standpoint just by virtue of being women, a standpoint has to be achieved, and the way to achieve it is to raise one's consciousness."
8. In this context, Shiv Visvanathan's description of the main character Jagannatha in the novel Bharatipura by U.R. Ananthamurthy shows us how one can embrace and grow into plural standpoints. What Visvanathan (2011: 70) writes deserves our careful consideration:

   > I think the genius of the book lies in the flat land called Jagannatha. He is a middling character [...] Yet Jagannatha is a seed that grows in power because of the humus of characters around him. In every chapter, he almost absorbs another point of view. His self grows as he discovers the richness of the other he wants to change.

9. As Connolly writes: "A conventional pluralist celebrates diversity within settled contexts of conflict and collective action [...] But what about the larger contexts within which the pattern of diversity is set? How plural or monistic are they? To what extent does a cultural presumption of normal individual or the preexisting subject precede and confine conventional pluralism? (Connolly 1995: xiii).

10. As Mannheim (1936: 20) writes: "The world of external objects and psychic experience appears to be in a continuous flux. Verbs are more adequate symbols for this situation than nouns." What Connolly (1995: xxi) writes below provides us pathways of pluralism as multi-dimensional verbs:

    A pluralizing culture embodies a *micropolitics* of action by the self on itself and the small-scale assemblage upon itself, a *politics of disturbance* through which sedimented identities and moralities are rendered more alert to the deleterious effects of their naturalization upon difference, *a politics of enactment* through which new possibilities of being are propelled into established constellations, *a politics of representational assemblages* through which general policies are processed through the state, a *politics of interstate relations*, and a *politics of nonstatist, corss-national movements* through which external/internal pressure is placed on corporate and state-centered priorities.

11. We can note here the title of one of Beteille's (1998) essay, "Comparative Method and the Standpoint of the Investigator." Beteille is a proponent of comparative method but this also raises the question if comparative method from the standpoint of an observer would be same as one from the experiential perspective of participants.

    In a related note, Amartya Sen also seems to look at the human condition from the point of view of observer which is different from that of a participant. Sen whose ideas have been presented in the third epigraph of this essay talks about positional objectivity but this objectivity is that of an observer: "[...] positionally dependent observations, beliefs, and actions are central to our knowledge and practical reason. The nature of objectivity in epistemology, decision theory and ethics has to take note of the parametric dependence of observation and observation on the position of the observer" (1994: 126). But here again there is the need of pluralization of the model and working of agents not only as observers but also as participants. Sen talks about the need for positional objectivity but once the agents are not only observers but also participants the objectivity that emerges is not only objective but also intersubjective and transsubjective. So we need to explore *transpositional subject-objectvity* – one which emerges out of pluralization of the subjects, border-crossing transmutations among positions and transformative cultivation of the objective and the subjective including intersubjective and transsubjective.

12. Here we can realize the significance of such symbols as Lord Vishnu in his eternal sleeping as well as the image of sleeping Buddha. These moments of sleep are moments of meditation, reflection and new creation. Social theorist and sociologist of religion Robert Bellah urges us to realize the significance of sleep in life which many a time has to do with "learning, with consolidating memories, sorting out importat memories, and removing evanescent ones; or with creativity" (Bellah 2011: xxi). On another plane, economist Kaushik Basu shares with us his experience of creativity arising out of sleep which can help us realize the significance going beyond a monolithic view of standpoint:

    Sleeps, as poets have written about and Dali has depicted so disturbingly, is a precarious indulgence [..] It comes easily and naturally if one has a puzzle in one's head which is engrossing and at the same time not personally intense. Some of my best slumbers have occurred when I have gone to bed with a research puzzle in economics and I remain convinced that some of my best papers have been written in my sleep (Basu 2010: 90).

13. We can look at the significance of public sphere in both in modern as well as premodern world in terms of varieties of spaces of meeting as well as walking together it sought to create and provide bringing people from different backgrounds amidst continued challenges of exclusions. In terms of possibility that sitting together offers, my student Rajakishore Mahana in his work on tribal movements in Orissa shares an insightful lesson from his fieldwork. In his fieldwork, Harabati, one woman tribal leader from Raigarh, Odisha tells him that when there was intractable conflict between the visiting police and tribals of the village she asked all of them, police and the tribals to sit down and it helped to calm the situation.
14. We have many moving meditations on the significance of walking in human life and for our expanding self and world-realizations. For anthropologist Tim Inglod, "[...] walking is not the behavioral output of a mind encased within a pedestrian body. It is rather, in itself, a way of thinking and knowing – 'an activity that takes place through the heart and mind as much as through the feet'" (Ingold 2011: S135). In his study of political processions in Tamil Nadu which is modeled on religious processions, Bernard Bates (2011) uses the term "walking utopia" which while creating condition of fellowship among participants does not necessarily enable them to go beyond their initial religious and political standpoints. But we see this in other modes of walking such as walking done in the Warkari movement in Maharastra which has a cross-caste dimension. As Dallmyr writes: "[...] periodic pilgrimages to Pandarpur are central to the Warkaris' life, but not in the same way as pilgrimage to other holy places such as Banaras or Dwarka. In the general Hindu tradition, the focus is typically on the destination of the pilgrimage, the sacred center of worship. But in case of the Warkaris, the accent is not so much on the destination as on the journey itself" (Dallmayr 2007: 56). What Dallmayr suggests is that in the journey there is an openness to others which is different from one's location at home. This openness emerges in other occasions of journey and encounters as well. In the same book where Dallmayr writes about the Warkari movement, he also presents us the following experience of a woman that he talked to from a train journey and the encounter that happened:

> [...] I talked to another Indian woman, the wife of a senior professor of English at the University of Baroda. She told me the story of a strange happening – an event that startled her and left her wonderng and amazed: She was traveling with her son by train from Delhi to Shillong, a journey of some twenty hours. In her compartment was a young man, a soldier in the Indian army. Given the long train ride, a conversation developed between them, starting at first haltingly and almost absentmindedly and then turning more serious. The woman had been raised in the Vaishnava tradition and had never devoted much thought to Muslim beliefs and practices. During the conversation, it emerged that the young man was a Muslim – deeply religious and knowledgeable Muslim. Prodded by her questions, the young man began to talk about the Islamic faith, the long history of Islam, and the deeper meaning of Quranic passages. It was as if he illuminated from within a building that had always seemed to her dark and uninviting. As she confessed to me, she was profoundly moved by this sincere (and nonproselytizing) disclosure of faith, and something happned to her on that train ride that she had not planned or anticipated. Somehow – and she was not quite sure how – the encounter had transformed her, ahd opened her heart to new possibilities ad a new dimension of human relations (Dallmayr 2007: 257–258).

In his recently published autobiography, *A Living Faith: My Quest for Peace, Harmony and Social Change*, Ashgar Ali Engineer also narrates a similar insight emerging during meeting in walking:

> Here, I would like to narrate an interesting encounter with a postman when I was in the 8th standard. In hindsight, I feel the postman was a very humble person but with a good understanding of religion. I was, on the contrary, very orthodox with the conviction that Islam was the only true religion. One day, the postman met me on the road and began to talk to me. He said in a very philosophical way that all paths, though they differ from each other, lead to God and that all paths are true. I protested and said that that could never be. For example, idol worship can never be a true path and it can never lead one to God. Islam believes only in one God and everything contrary to it is false. I remember the postman smiling at me and saying that if one has *shraddha* (faith) in idols that can also lead to God. I, however, stuck to my point and the postman left it at that. But whenever he met me, he smiled in a charming way.

I also used to read Sufi poetry, especially of the noted Sufi poet Mir Dard. His beliefs were of the kind that affirmed the truth of what the postman used to tell me. I could not quite fathom the stand he took [...] This would leave me quite perplexed (Engineer 2011: 11–12).

The above two narrations show how in complex ways, walking does add an element of pluralization to our ontology and epistemology of stand point. But to this condition of pluralization of walking and sitting on a train, we can also invite the experience of "sitting on a boat." It reminds us the symbol of Noah's boat described in the Bible and also the way Jesus and his followers sat on the boat and crossed over to the other side of the sea to meet with people there who were considered an other. Since our present discussion involves the border-crossing dialogue between sociology and theology what theologian Vinayraj writes about the significance of sitting on a boat deservers our careful attention:

> Sea, for Jews is a symbol of chaos. The land across this sea is pictured as a terrific land as we used to tell in the fairy tales. It is the abode of evils [...] It is a place of violence and terror. In our society we use these imageries to talk about Dalit/Tribal colonies! By exhorting the disciples to "go across to the other side," Jesus asks them to deconstruct their subjectivity conceptions and move beyond to an existence of fraternity. Jesus shows his interest to talk to them by "sitting in the boat." The "boat" symbolizes the reconciliation between "shores." [...] Here "crossing" means "bridging" and that is why it was a stormy journey for them. It was a symbolic journey from "hostility" to "hospitality" (Vinayaraj 2010: 50).

To the above experience we can also invite the recent effort of Freedom Fortilla where activists protesting Israel's blockade of Gaza were on the ship to cross over to Gaza. But their ship was brutally attacked by Israel in which many activists from Turkey were killed.

15. During his walk in Noakhali to bring about peace among Hindus and Muslims, Gandhi had once said, the greatness of a person lies not only what one or two spectacular thing one does in ones' life but how much "dust" one collects on one's feet.
16. Management thinker and poet Subhash Sharma calls it omega circle and is doing work on creating dialogues across omega circle. See Sharma 2008.

17. For Marcus Bussey, " *Sadhana* as a quest, striving, struggle involves *tapasya* – a sacrificing of one's veil of certainty – and opening to dialogue via vulnerability and inner reflection" (personal communication)."
18. What Mohanty (2000: 24; emphases added) writes below helps us understand the proposed multi-valued logic of autonomy and interpenetration:

    > The ethic of non-injury applied to philosophical thinking requires that one does not reject outright the other point of view without first recognizing the element of truth in it; it is based on the belief that every point of view is partly true, partly false, and partly undecidable. A simple two-valued logic requiring that a proposition must either be true or false is thereby rejected, and what the Jaina philosopher proposes is a multi-valued logic. To this multi-valued logic, I add the Husserlian idea of overlapping contents. The different perspectives on a thing are not mutually exclusive, but share some contents with each other. The different 'worlds' have shared contents, contrary to the total relativism. *If you represent them by circles, they are intersecting circles, not incommensurable, [and it is this model of] intersecting circles which can get us out of relativism on the one hand and absolutism on the other.*

    This multi-valued logic also resonates with what J.P.S. Uberoi (2002) building on Goethe, Gandhi and the Hermetic tradition of Europe calls "the four-fold logic of truth and method." In the above paragraph, Mohanty refers to the Jaina tradition of *Anekantavada* about which what B.P. Singh writes deserves our careful attention:

    > *Anekantavada* wad directly related to Mahavira's philosophy of non-violence. We have to recognize that ordinarily violence is rooted in dogmatic and mistaken knowledge claim that fail to recognize other legitimate perspectives. *Anekantavada* provides us with an alternative epistemology to support dialogue among people of diverse viewpoints. It does not mean conceding that all views are valid. It does, suggest, however, that logic and evidence determine the validity of a given view. *Anekantavada* allows us to accept a pluralistic approach to reality (Singh 2008: 96–97).

    K.S. Singh, the heart-touching anthropologist and seeker of pluralism, also writes the following about *Anekantavada* which is insightful:

    > It should be noted that while diversity of perceptions, approaches, and practices are recognized by some schools including those of the idealist philosophy, it is Anekantavada described by S. Radhakrishnan as a doctrine of realistic pluralism that tries to explore diversity logically and in depth.
    >
    > [...] there are three tenets of Anekantavada. One, that there is a possibility of many perceptions of an object; two that everything is relative and multi-dimensional; and three, that there is an in-built co-existence of opposites, that one dimension is possible as another and it is only in relation to other factors like time, place, and context that one dimension gains predominance over another. All this is subsumed under the doctrine of *syadavada* or *saptabhangi*. From the acceptance of the multi-dimensional nature of objects and their probability is derived the moral imperative of *ahimsa* or non-violence (2011:).

19. In this context, what philosopher Ashok Gangadean tells us deserves our careful attention: "Spirituality is a philosophical point of view concerning the rational awakening that enables you to break free of your ego perspective, your closed view, the egocentric point of view, and become, instead dialogical, open to multiple views. And it helps you to negotiate them. You become a more mature, awakened rational being" (Gangadean et al. 2000: 287). Mrinal Miri also talks about the need to overcome "egocentricity" which "distorts, to a greater or less

extent, most of our perceptions of reality, and this is especially true of our perception of human reality" (2003: 42). Egocetricity also distorts our efforts to know another person thus the need to overcome it. But for Miri,

> [...] the overcoming of ego in attending to another person is never an isolated phenomenon; to be able to transcend one's ego is also to be able to achieve true humility; and with humility comes the realization of the infinite difficulty of being just to another person, the realization, in other words, of the ever-present possibility that one has blotted out, from one's attention, vital, if subtle aspects of the other person's behaviour. A natural accompaniment of such a realization on the way to achieving the true emotion of love, or what Gandhi might have meant by *ahimsa*. And it is the possibility of ahimsa in this sense that makes knowledge of the other as a person possible (ibid: 43).

Thus overcoming ego centricity helps one realize humility and *ahimsa* in ones's knowledge of and relationship with the other which also contributes to overcoming one's one-sided standpoint. In a related move, philosopher Peter Singer who has also urged us to go beyond anthropocentric standpoint and realize the suffering and pain of non-human beings challenges us to cultivate "the point of view of the universe" and "thereby transcending not only our individual point of view but the point of view of our society and species. Of course, Singer doesn't believe that the universe has a point of view, but he thinks that this is an apt metaphor for the human capacity to take up a standpoint of impartial and equal concern for the welfare of all sentient beings" (Nagel 2010: 26).

20. This is also the approach of Giddens and Beck (Beck et al. 1994).
21. In this context, what the Dalai Lama (2011: 19) writes below is an inspiring example of how to understand religion of people other than one's own:

> For some people, then, the concept of a Creator, God, is very helpful. I once asked an old Christian monk why Christianity does not believe in previous lives. He said, 'Because this very life is created by God. Thinking that gives a feeling of intimacy with God. This body comes from our mother's womb and so we have a feeling of closeness and comfort with our mother. So. the same is the case with God. The closer one feels, the stronger the intention to follow God's advice, which is love, compassion'. Therefore, the theistic approach is very powerful and much more helpful for many people than a non-theistic approach.

It must be noted here that many streams in Buddhism do not have a theistic approach and the Dalai Lama is able to understand and appreciate the need for theistic approach in Christianity. He also does not want any body to convert from one religion from another, for example from Christianity to Buddhism. What he writes below is also an example of how one can go beyond oneself in understanding the religion of another person:

> It is better to keep one's own religious tradition [...] The best is to have information. This helps to develop respect. Therefore, keep your Christian tradition, if you are a Christian, but gain understanding and knowledge of other traditions. As for methods, all teach the same practice-love, compassion, tolerance. Since the practice is shared in common, it is alright to adopt some methods from Buddhism. But as for the Buddhist concept of no absolute – this is strictly Buddhist business. It is not helpful for others to learn. One Christian father asked me about emptiness, voidness, and I told him that this is not good for him. If I teach complete interdependence, this might harm his strong faith in God. So it is better for such people not to listen to talk about voidness (ibid).

While the above passage shows remarkable generosity of the Dalai Lama, it still leaves us with some further questions. Are concepts from a religious tradition such as emptiness from Buddhism meant to be limited to the believers and practitioners of these traditions? Are they not universal? Even if they unsettle believers in other traditions, is there a responsibility to share and learn on the part of people in interaction. In inter-religious interaction is there not a necessity to go beyond one's tradition and explore paths of seeking in emergent ways? Is it not possible to realize God even in Christian tradition not only as fullness but emptiness? The Dalai Lama and proponents of such view may note what Felix Wilfred and Griffths write below. For Wilfred (1999: xiii),

> The Christian attempts to cross over to the other, to the different, has been made by and large from the pole of being or fullness. This naturally creates problems, which can be overcome by activating also to cross over from the pole of nothingness or emptiness. The central Christian mystery of Jesus Christ offers the revelation of both fullness and nothingness – the total self-emptying. Many frontiers which are found difficult to negotiate and cross over could be crossed by making use of the other pole represented in the Christian mystery of emptiness as self-abnegation, so as to reach a deeper perception of the mystery of God, the world and the self. Perhaps here lies something that could become an important program for Christianity and its theology at the turn of the millennium.

For Griffiths, "[...] We often find that the Christian concept of God becomes personal that it needs to be corrected by the impersonalism of Buddhism" (Griffiths 1976: 86).

22. Borrowing the language of Weber, Beteille (2002) presets his approach to religion as that of the "religiously unmusical".
23. Tillich (1957: 20) writes in his *Dynamics of Faith*:

> The doubt which is implicit in every act of faith is neither the methodological and skeptical doubt. It is the doubt which accompanies every risk. It is not the permanent doubt of the scientist, and it is not transitory doubt of the skeptic, but it is the doubt of him who is ultimately concerned about a concrete context. One would call it the existential doubt, in contrast to the methodological and skeptical doubt. It does not question whether a special proposition is true or false. It does not reject every concrete truth, but it is aware of the element of insecurity in every existential truth. At the same time, the doubt which is implied in faith accepts this insecurity and takes into itself in an act of courage. Faith includes courage

Tillich speaks about doubt in act of faith which finds a resonance in Iqbal's approach to Islam. According to Ayesha Jalal, "[...] Iqbal asserted that the principle of doubt was the beginning of all knowledge. And the opening word in the Muslim creed, *la*-literally 'there is no God' – was a statement of that doubt. Without the power of negation in the *la*, the affirmation of God in *illaha ilallah* loses its true in meaning" (Jalal 2009: 461).

Tillich is a source of inspiration to critical practitioners of faith in Islam such as Amina Wadud who has fought against patriarchal structures of Islam. In her words:

> I have fought the gender *jihad* to remove the blinkers that see only the illusion of fragmentation and then build structures and formulate systems to sustain the perception that it is real, and then to give divine sanction to the illusion of human independence from transcendent peace and unity [...] The significance of Tillich's work was simply that it expressed itself in response to the moral-spiritual

> dilemma of modern consciousness. I ran up against a scarcity of information in response to such dilemmas from modern Muslim thinkers. They were obsessed with *realitic politique* (everything was power, authority, and control) through the medium of legal operation (Wadud 2006: 258–259).

The above also shows how critical theological work transcends religious boundaries as a woman in Islam who is struggling for gender justice is drawing inspiration from a Christian theologian.

24. Habermas had shared this in his now famous dialogue with Cardinal Joseph Ratzinger (now Pope Benedict XVI) held on January 19, 2004 at the Catholic Academy in Munich in which both agreed that: "Religions and secular rationalities need to engage in a mutual process of dialogue in order to learn from each other and to protect the planet from the destructive potential of the uncoupling of faith and reason" (Heythrop Institute 2005: 2; also see Bellah 2008; Ratzinger & Habermas; Eder 2007).

    Apart from this celebrated dialogue with the present Pope, Habermas had had a long dialogue with the great theologian Johannes B. Metz from Germany that is relevant here. Metz has a critical-practical approach to theology as he writes: "It is surely true that the frontiers of modern theology runs across confessional boundaries. In this case, how could theology itself determine the distinctive unity of what it is concerned with? The quest, its dwelling place is not pure theology but [...] faith in practice" (1970: 82). In his dialogue with Habermas Metz had argued that reason cannot just continue the tradition of critical thought from Athens, that is from Greek tradition, it also must be open to the other tradition of reason what Metz calls "anamenestic reason," a reason which remembers the memory of struggle for self and spiritual transformation. For Metz, this is the tradition of Israel. For Metz, for a fuller realization of reason, there should be interpenetration of both the tradition of Athens and the tradition of Israel. But Habermas in this dialogue a decade ago was reluctant to open the tradition of argumentative reason to the tradition of "anamenestic reason" of Israel. But with his contemporary rethinking of faith and reason in which Habermas argues that both sides should go beyond their absolutist claims Habermas may be more open to such a foundational border-crossing which has also deep implications for border crossing between traditions of critical sociology and liberation theology.

25. For Vinayaraj, doing theology involves a "new journey of re-understanding of our faith, theology and ontology. [...] doing theology means reconstituting our ontology. Faith is a total commitment to the ongoing journey of finding ourselves dialogically" (2010: 32).

26. Another example of possible border crossing between sociology and theology is the simultaneous moves such as public sociology from sociology and public theology from theology which challenges both these disciplines to be much more communicative with and responsible to the public (see Clawson et al. 2007; Wilfred 2010). In Indian context, Dalit theology is an aspect of emergent public theology but Dalit theology is not asserting Dalit identity in an exclusionary way. Rather it is a "political theology that re-locates the 'missionized' as the social agents of a democratic civil society and envisage a dialogical community where everyone celebrates together their differentiated identities" (Vinayaraj 2010: 73). It would be insightful to explore further Dalit theology and Dalit sociology together.

27. Clammer is not shy of arguing that when sociologists have lost a sense of the whole it is the theological approach which constantly challenges us to not to forget that we are part of a bigger whole. In the words of Clammer:

    While in a secularized and globalised world in which many faiths contend for attention, as do the insidious demands of the consumerist culture of neo-liberal capitalism, theology (understood in its specifically Christian context) may well appear to have lost its status as 'Queen of the Sciences.' But perhaps not, since not only is (Christian) theology in a globalised world necessarily forced to confront the reality of other faith traditions and to enter into dialogue with them, but it also remains, even today, *the most integral of the disciplines, containing as it does history, linguistics, archaeology, anthropology, textual criticism, sociology, psychology and the applied dimensions of these fields in pastoral care, counseling, development and social work*, as well as its specifically 'religious' dimensions and their expressions in such areas as liturgy. With the rising perception that the roots of our current crisis are essentially spiritual, theology takes on a new salience, as witnessed by the number of students world-wide who enter the discipline with no intention of ever taking up a pastoral career. *In a world in which new models of education are urgently needed, theology, when informed and permeated by an Earth-spirituality (the definition of which in a Christian context is itself a challenge and an adventure), stands poised to renew itself and as such to provide a renewing force in the wider world, far outside the boundaries of the narrowly defined faith community* (Clammer 2010: 226; emphasis added).

    As sociologists we need to pursue the meaning and working of a bigger whole in our lives and society though this whole is not necessarily the theistic whole of the theologian nor the systematic whole of the believer. The whole that invites both the sociologist and theologian is what philosopher Vattimo (1999) calls a contingent whole and Simogy Varga (2009) calls a "limited whole."
28. We may note here that T.N. Madan in his insightful essay on M.N. Srinivas talks about the possibility of 'transempirical' understanding (see Madan 2011).

References

Ahlstrom, Kristoffer. 2005. "Incorporating Feminist Standpoint Theory." *Nordic Journal of Philosophy* 6 (2): 79–92.

Basu, Kaushik. 2010. *The Retreat of Democracy*. London: Anthem Press.

Bates, Bernard. 2011. *Tamil Oratory and the Dravidian Aesthetic: Political Practice in South India*. Delhi: Oxford University Press.

Beck, Ulrich, Anthony Giddens and Scott Lash. 1994. *Reflexive Modernization*. Cambridge: Polity Press.

Bellah, Robert N. 1970. *Beyond Belief: Essays on Religion in a Post-Traditional World*. NY: Harper Row.

——. 2008 "Challenge of Secularism: Is God Absent?" Text of a lecture at University of Detroit Mercy, April 22.

——. 2011. *Religion in Human Evolution: From the Palaeolithic to the Axial Age*. Cambridge, MA: Harvard University Press.

Beteille, Andre. 2009. "Sociology and Ideology." *Sociological Bulletin* 58 (2): 196–211.

——. 2002. *Sociology: Essays on Approach and Method*. Delhi: Oxford U. Press.

——. 1998 "Comparative Method and the Standpoint of the Investigator." *Sociological Bulletin* 47 (2): 137–154.

——. 1982. *Marxism, Pluralism and Orthodoxy*. Delhi: India Renaissance Institute.

——. 1980. *Ideologies and Intellectuals*. Delhi: Oxford University Press.

Buber, Martin. 1958. *I and Thou*. New York: Charles Scribner's Sons.

Brooks, Abigail. 2006. "Feminist Standpoint Epistemology: Building Knowledge and Empowerment Through Women's Lived Experience." In *Feminist Research Practice: A Primer* (eds.), P.Levy & S. Hesse-Biber, pp. 53–82. Newbury Parks, CA: Sage

Clammer, John. 2010. "Learning from the Earth: Reflections on Theological Education and the Ecological Crisis." In *Socially Engaged Religions*, ed., John Calmmer, pp. 221–229.

Clawson, Dan et al. 2007. (eds.), *Public Sociology: Fifteen Eminent Sociologists Debate Politics and the Profession in the Twenty-First Century*. Berkeley & Los Angeles: University of California Press.

Connolly, William E. 1995. *The Ethos of Pluralization*. Minneapolis: University of Minnesota Press.

Dallmayr, Fred. 2010. *Integral Pluralism*. Lexington: University of Kentucky Press.

——. 2007. *In Search of The Good Life: A Pedagogy for Troubled Times*. Lexington, Kentucky: University of Kentucky Press.

Deleuze, Gilles & Felix Guattari. 1994. *What is Philosophy*? New York: Columbia.

Eder, Klaus. 2007. "Secularization, Desecularization and the Emergence of a Postsecular Modernity: Making Sense of the Religious Field in Europe." Humboldt University, Berlin: Paper

Engineer, Ashgar Ali. 2011. *A Living Faith: My Quest for Peace, Harmony and Social Change*. Hyderabad: Orient Blackswan.

Gangadean, Ashok, Ewert Cousins, Robert Muller, Karan Singh. 2000. "A Dialogue on Global Thought and Spirituality." In *A Parliament of Minds: Philosophy for a New Millennium*, (eds.) Michael Tobias, J. Patrick Fitzgerald & David Rothenburg, pp. 281–300. Albany: State University of New York Press.

Gnanapragasam, Patrick & Elisabeth Schussler Fiorenza (eds.). 2008. *Negotiating Borders: Theological Explorations in the Global Era: Essays in Honour of Prof. Felix Wilfred*. Delhi: ISPCK.

Giri, Ananta Kumar. 2010. "The Challenge of Understanding Indian Society: Critique, Generosity and Transformations." *Sociological Bulletin* 59(2): 256–277, May–August 2010.

Griffiths, Bede. 1976. *Return to the Center*. London: Fount Paperbacks.

Habermas, Jurgen. 2008. *Between Naturalism and Religion*. Cambridge: Polity Press.

——. 2006 "Religion and the Public Sphere." *European Journal of Philosophy*.

——. 2003. "Faith and Knowledge." In idem, *Future of Human Nature*. Cambridge: Polity Press.

——. 1997. "Israel or Athens, Or To Whom Does Anamnestic Reason Belong? On Unity in Multicultural Diversity." In *Liberation Theologies, Postmodernity and the Americas*. (eds.) David Batsone et al. London: Routledge.

Habermas, Jurgen and Joseph Ratzinger. 2007. *The Dialectic of Secularization*. The Ignatius Press.

Harding, Sandra. 2004. (ed.) *The Feminist Standpoint Theory Reader: Intellectual and Political Controversies*. New York: Routledge.

Ingold, Tim. 2011. "Footprints through the Weather-World: Walking, Breathing, Knowing." *Journal of Royal Anthropological Institute* (N.S.), S121–S139.

Jalal, Ayesha. 2009. "Freedom and Equality: From Iqbal's Philosophy to Sen's Ethical Concerns." In *Arguing for a Better World: Essays in Honour of Amartya Sen*, (eds.), Kaushik Basu & Ravi Kanbur, pp. 452–469. Delhi: Oxford U. Press.

Kaul, Nitasha. 2008. *Imagining Economics Otherwise*. London: Routledge.

Madan, T.N. 2011. "M.N. Srinivas: The Man and His Work." In idem, *Sociological Traditions: Methods and Perspectives in the Sociology of India*, pp. 174–194. Delhi: Sage.

Mannheim, Karl. 1936. *Ideology and Utopia*. London: Routledge and Kegan Paul.

Miri, Mrinal. 2003. "On Knowing Another Person." In idem, *Identity and Moral Life*, pp. 35–45. Delhi: Oxford University Press.

Metz, Johannes B. 1970. "Does Our Church Need a New Reformation? A Catholic Reply." *Concilium* 4 (6): 8162. -91.

Mohanty, J.N. 2000. *Self and Other: Philosophical Essays*. Delhi: Oxford U. Press.

Nagel, Thomas. 2010. "What Peter Singer Wants of You." *New York Review of Books* LV11 (5): 24–26, March 25-April 27.

Panikkar, Raimundo. 1977. *The Vedic Experience Mantramanjari: An Anthopology of the Vedas for Modern Man and Contemporary Celebration*. Delhi: Motilal Banarasidas.

Rolin, Kristen. 2006. "The Bias Paradox in Feminist Standpoint Epistemology." *Episteme: A Journal of Social Epistemology* 3 (1): 125–136.

Sen, Amartya. 1994. "Positional Objectivity." *Philosophy & Public Affairs* 22 (2): 126–145.

Sharma, Subhash. 2008. *New Mantras in the Corporate Corridors*. Bangalore: New Age International.

Singh, B.P. 2008. *Bahudha and the Post 9/11 World*. Delhi: Oxford U. Press.

Singh, K.S. 2011. *Diversity, Identity, and Linkages: Explorations in Historical Ethnography*. Delhi: Oxford University Press.

Smith, David. 2007. *Moving Towards Emmaus: Hope in a Time of Uncertainty*. London: SPCK.

Sri Aurobindo. 1962. *The Human Cycles*. Pondicherry: Sri Aurobindo Asrham.

Srinivas, M.N. 2009. *The Oxford India Srinivas*. Delhi: Oxford U. Press.

Thoreau, David. 1975. "Walking." In *The Portable Thoreau*. Edited by Carl Bode. Penguin.

The Dalai Lama. 2011. "The Relevance of Religion in Modern Times." *Integral Liberation* (Journal of Bangalore Social Action Trust) 15 (1): 15–23.

Tillich, Paul. 1957. *Dynamics of Faith*. New York: Harper & Row.

Uberoi, J.P.S. 2002. *European Modernity: Truth, Science and Method*. Delhi: Oxford U. Press.

Wadud, Amina. 2006. *Inside the Gender Jihad: Women's Reform in Islam*. Delhi: Viva.

Vatttimo, Giani. 1999. *Belief*. Cambridge: Polity Press.

Wilfred, Felix. 2008. "Christological Pluralism: Some Reflections." *Concilium* 3: 84–94.

——. 2009. "Christian Studies: The Contours of a Discipline and Its Future Prospects." In *Transforming Religion: Prospects for a New Society*, edited by Felix Wilfred, pp. 241–259. Delhi: ISPCK.

——. 2010 *Asian Public Theology: Critical Concerns in Challenging Times*. Delhi: ISPCK.

Wittgenstein, Ludwig. 1958. *The Blue and Brown Books*. Oxford: Basil Blackwell.

Vinayaraj, Y.T. 2010. *Re-Visiting the Other: Discourses on Postmodern Theology*. Tiruvalla, Kerala: Christian Sahitya Samiti.

Visvanathan, Shiv. 2011. Review of U.R. Ananthamurthy's *Bharatipura*. *Seminar* 619. March: 68–70.

Varga, Somogy. 2009. "Sub Specie Aeternitatis: An Actualization of Wittgenstein on Ethics and Aesthetics." *Nordic Journal of Aesthetics* No.39: 35–50.

Index

Abbott, Andrew, 1, 4
advanced industrial societies, 186, 187
legitimation crisis of, 198
aestheticization of production, 280
in contemporary capitalism, 279–80, critique of, 283–86
aesthicization of empowerment, 284
aesthicization of politics, 284
aesthtic ethics, 310
aestheticized consumption, 280, 281
critique of, 281
aetheticized commodity of postmodernity, 273
Agarwala, Binod Kumar, 15, 16
Albanese, Catherine, 221
Alvares, Claude, 261, 283
Ankersmit, F.R., 22, 166
anthropological allegory, 345
anthropological epistemology, 354
and its crisis, 354–55
anthropological imagination, 345
anthropology, 354
epistemological crisis in, 353–55
Ananthamurthy, U.R., 399, 421
Antonio, Robert J., 78, 83
Appadurai, Arjun and Carol A., Breckenridge, 286
Appadurai, Arjun, 196, 311
Apter, David, 198, 209
Arif, Yasmeen, 152, 155–56
Austin, J., 371, 372
Avadhuta, Acharya Tadbhavananda, 199
Ayer, A.J., 366, 367–68
Bahuguna, Sunderlal, 190, 232
Bailey, Joe, 190
Bajaj, J.K. and M.D. Srinivas, 301
Baldwin, John, 49
Banerjee, Mukulika, 137
Basu, Kaushik, 422
Bates, Bernard, 423
Baudrillard, Jean, 208, 268, 277, 280, 282
Bauman, Zygmunt, 14, 37–38, 188, 257, 319
Baviskar, Amita, 200
Beck, Ulrich and Elizabeth Beck-Gernsheim, 14, 57
Beck, Ulrich, 3, 14, 18, 34, 57, 157, 248
Beidelman, T.O., 228
Bell, Daniel, 190
Bellah, Robert et al., 76, 81, 88, 106, 200, 209, 221, 222, 282, 343
Bellah, Robert N., 96, 97, 99–102, 103–4, 105–8, 109, 112, 222, 406, 422
sociological quest of a good society of, 99–104
sociology of, 98–99
Benjamin, Roger, 255
Berman, Russell, 187
Berreman, G.D., 227, 228, 230
Beteille, Andre, 6, 98, 104, 140, 152, 154, 155, 166, 167, 240, 256, 323, 410–414, 416, 418–420
beyond sociology, 14
Bhaba, Homi K., 33
Bist, A., 229
Bloch, M., 347, 351
Blue Planet, x
Bluestone, Barry and Bennett Harrison, 253, 272

Bocchi, G. and M. Ceruti, 44, 72
Borofsky. M., 354, 360
Bourdieu, Pierre and Loic J.D. Wacquant, 22
Bourdieu, Pierre, 21–22, 23, 122, 151, 153, 273
Bouquizabout, Francis Regis, 405
Brandt, Willy, 197
Brecht, Bertalt, 307
Bright, C. and M. Geyer, 196, 218, 354
Brooks, Abigail, 412
Buber, Martin, 47, 397
Buchman, Marlis, 253, 329
Burawoy, Michael, 3–4
Burdick, John, 190
Burke, K., 373
Burns, T. and R. Uberhst, 187, 255
Bussey, Marcus, 421, 424

Calhoun, Craig, 187
Capra, F. and C. Spretnak, 187
Carrette, Jeremy R., 17
Cassen, Bernard, 300
Cassidy, R., 347
Castells, Manuel, 188, 189, 190
Chakraborty, Dipesh, 141
Charsley, Simon, 167–68, 170
Chatterjee, Margaret, 404
Chatterjee, Partha, 142
Chekki, Dan, 198
Chipko movement, 225
  ecological shift in, 232
  objective of, 226
  origin of, 229–30, main demands of, 230
  people's understanding of, 232–33
citizen diplomacy, 197
civil labour, 34
civil society
  concept of, 98
Clammer, John, 47, 54, 58, 67, 68, 301, 420, 428
Clammer, John, Sylvie Piorie and Eric Schwimmer, 21
Clifford. J., 353, 354, 361
Cohen, Anthony, 19
Cohen, D.W., 348
Cohen, Gerry, 297
Collins, Randall, 151, 309
communal self-management, 37
companion species, 57
confluent love, 339
Connolly, William E., 48–49, 90, 196, 421–422
consumerism, 88
consumption
  process of, 280, aestheticization of, 280–81
contemporary American society, 268
  the great U-turn in, 253, 268
contemporary global reality, 196, 197
contemporary globalizing economy, 291
  call/need for rethinking, 291–97
contemporary homelessness
  causes of, 272
Corlett William, 220
Cortese, Anthony, 76
Cousins, E.H., 89
Cox, Harvey, 189, 263
creative transdisciplinarity, 317
  need for, 319–25
critical traditionalism, 190
Croker, David A., 287
cross-species dignity, 57, 67
cultural mass, 191

Dae Jong, Kim, 301, 303
Dahl, Robert, 257
Dalai Lama, 110, 307, 427
Dallmayr, Fred, 21, 23, 24, 32, 35, 56, 66, 71, 75, 84, 97, 121, 141, 323, 324, 329, 423
Das, Chitta Ranjan, 1, 60, 110, 286, 323, 390, 398–400, 403
Das, Veena, 57–58, 120, 151, 319
Dasgupta, Partha and Ismail Serageldin, 35
Dash, Rabi Narayan, 403, 405

Davidson, Miriam, 195
de Barry, Wm. Theodore, 71
de-alienation, 31
deindustrialization, 253
Deleuze, Gilles and Felix Guattari, 410
Deleuze, Gilles and Claire Parnet, 397
Derber, Charles, 187
Derrida, Jacques, 108, 139, 151, 330
Deshpande, Satish, 177
destructuration, 253
development, 252
  in developing societies, 260, impact of science and technology on, 200–61
Devi, Mahesweta, 399
Dewey, John, 77, 403
Diamond, S., 351
Dirlik, Arif, 36, 37
discourse ethics
  of Habermas, 79, 87, 332, criticism of, 80–81; and moral consciousness, 81–83
Dixon, P., 373
Dogra, B., 229
Donovan, P., 366, 367, 368, 369, 370
Doubinosky, Sebastien, 404
Downey, Garry L., 190
Dussel, Enrique, 37, 402

economic development, 252
economics, 291–92
  as forms of life and quest for a good society, 292–94
economy, 291
  and economics, 291–92, distinction between, 292
Edelman, John T., 87
Eide, Asbjorn, 196
Eliade, M., 228
Elias, Norbert, 14
emerging transnational spaces, 196
Engineer, Ali, 423
entrenched institutionalism, 97
episodic sexuality, 338
Errington, F. and D. Gewertz, 354, 360
Esteva, Gustavo, 196
ethical formalism, 80
ethics of reconciliation, 307, 308
  emergence of, 308
ethics of social affiliation, 33
ethnographic allegory, 359
ethnographies of religious rhetoric, 373–75
Ezzat, Hebba, 57, 67

Falk, Richard, 35, 190, 196
Farid, Baba, xv
Faubion, James D., 18–19, 55
Fischer, Michael M.J., 185
Foucault, Michel, 71, 267
Fourth World colonialism, 228
Frank, Andre G. and Marta Fuentes, 189
Fraser, Nancy, 188, 189, 258
freedom
  perspective of, 256
Freeman, D., 357–58
Frietag, Michel, 14–15
Fromm, Eric, 21
Fuchs, Martin, 15
Fuller, Millard and Linda Fuller, 212, 220
Fuller, Millard, 198, 211, 213, 214, 214–15, 221

Gadamer, Hans-George, xv, 307
Galbraith, John Kenneth, 277
Gale, D., 188
Galtung, Johan, 197, 255
Galtung, Johan and Daisaku Ikeda, 311–12
Galtung, Johan and Graeme MacQueen, 291, 301
Gandhi, M.K., 337, 414, 424
Gandhi, Ramachandra, 49
Gangadean, Ashok, 425
Gans, Herbert, 188
Gasper, Des et al., 53–54, 56, 165
Geertz, Clifford, 76, 186, 317, 318, 328, 345, 350, 361, 362

Georgescou-Roegen, N., 282
Gewertz, D., 360
Giddens, Anthony, 89, 121, 195–96, 100, 200, 209–10, 219, 331, 337–41, 343, 347, 350, 362, 383
Ginsburg, Faye D., 193, 342
Giri, Ananta K. and Quarles van Ufford, 34
Giri, Ananta Kumar, 3, 19, 24, 34, 35, 44, 45, 47, 49, 55, 56, 59, 60, 69, 70, 71, 83, 84, 89, 98, 100, 108, 109, 126, 139, 141, 152, 155, 164, 166, 169, 194, 196, 198, 199, 201, 210, 221, 254, 255, 258, 283, 284, 286, 294, 296, 297, 298, 309, 310, 312, 320, 342, 387, 389, 419
global justice, 296
  and calling of peace, 301–2
  concept of, 297–98
  realization of, 298–300
globalization, 76
globalizing economy, 291
Gnanapragasam, Patrick and Elisabeth Schussler Fiorenza, 419
Goldthorpe, J.H., 362
good society, 252
  concept of, criticism of, 98
  quest for realizing a, in sociological traditions, 97, 256; in Bellah's study of Japan, 99–100
Gorz, Andre, 14, 30, 34
grass roots social movements, 186, 188, 255
Greco, John, 21
Griffiths, Bede, 427
Guha, Ramachandra, 136, 139, 140, 143, 151, 154, 228
Gundelach, Peter, 185
Gunter, Gotthard, 3

Habermas, Jurgen, 14, 55, 68, 70, 72, 75, 76, 77, 78, 79–80, 80–81, 82, 87, 88–89, 98, 126, 136, 139, 186, 198, 214, 219, 246, 248, 256, 258, 296, 297, 307, 319, 331–32, 400, 405, 419
Habitat for Humanity movement (US), 208, 211, 293, 298
  activities/programmes of, 212–13
  significance of, 218–20
Hall, Stuart, 191, 195, 253, 259
Han, Sang-Jin, 109
Haraway, Donna, 57, 126
Harding, Sandra, 412
Harding, Susan, 373–75
Hardt, Michael and Antonio Negri, 303
Harrington, Michael, 253, 272
Harrison, Bennet and Barry Bluestone, 253, 268
Harvey, David W., 39, 141, 189, 191–92, 209, 222, 259, 260, 267, 272, 273, 274, 275, 284
Haug, W.R., 280, 281
Hegedus, Zsuzsa, 185, 187
Heidegger, Martin, 402
Heller, Agnes, 84, 331
Hellman, Stephen, 187
Henderson, M.G., 317
Hertz, S., 194
herzenbildung, 285
heterosexual marriage
  origins of, 338
Hettne, Bjorn, 197, 198, 199
high technology, 255
  and human freedom, 255–56
Hirsch, Joachim, 187
Hirschmann, A., 193
Hirschorn, Larry, 188
Hobsbawm, E. and T. Ranger, 348
Holmes, L.D., 353, 355, 359
home ownership
  crisis in, 268
  in American culture, 267
homelessness, 268
  as a postmodern simulacrum, 268
  in contemporary times, 272, factors behind, 272
Hometh, Axel, xv
Hopper Kim, 271
Hopper, Kim and Jill Hamberg, 270

Hopper, Kim, E. Baxter, S. Cox and L. Kloin, 272
Hornborg, Alf, 282, 285
human security, 53
human unity
ideals of, 302–4
humanism, 56, 66
limits of, 56–57
humanity
concept of, 66, in Asian traditions, 66; in modernity, 67

ideal communication community
Habermas' idea of, 79
ideal society
of Sri Aurobindo, 86
Indian society, 163, 328
challenge of understanding, 163
informal economy, 329
Inglehart, Ronald, 190, 191, 218, 259, 330
Ingold, Tim, 165
inner planet, 71
Iqbal, Muhammed, 427
Islands of problematic justice, 139, 296

Jalal, Ayesha, 427
Jasper, James, 33
Jasper, Karl, 109
Jeffner, A., 367, 371
Jonas, Hans, 86
Jordan, Clarence, 213
Joshi, G., 286
justice, 296
theories of, 297

Kabeer, Naila, 300
Kagarlitsky, Boris, 36
Kant, Immanuel, 75
Katz, Stanley N., 318, 321
Khair, Tabish, 403
Khare, Ravinder, 139
King, Karen Mae, 366, 368, 369, 373, 376
King, Martin Luther, 414
Knor-Cetina, Karin, 16–17
Knox, Paul, 273, 274, 275
Kothari, Rajni, 188, 190, 196, 198, 319
Kovack, Ilona, 198
Kozol, Janathan, 268–69
Kriesi, Hans, 258
Krishna, Daya, 55, 120, 123, 125–26, 126–27
Kristoff, A., 421
Kropotkin, Peter, 44
Kugler, Paul, 332–33
Kundera, M., 346–47, 348, 349, 350–51
Kurien, C.T., 291

Laclau, Ernesto, 84, 210, 211
Lakoff, G. and M. Johnson, 383
Lasch, Christopher, 278
Lash, Scott and John Urry, 279–80, 283, 284
Lash, Scott, 273, 274, 275, 328, 330, 334
Laughlin, Kim, 199
Lee, Dallas, 213
Lee, Martyn J., 280, 281
Levi-Strauss, C., 347, 348, 383
Lieberson, Stanley, 221
life world, 187, 189
and system world, fight between 254
Lippmann, Walter, 97
Lowe, Stuart, 189
Ludke, A., 349–50
Lyotard, J., 333–34

Macfarlane, A., 356
MacIntyre, Alasdair, 157, 325
Macquarrie, J., 368–69
Madan, T.N., 429
Madison, G.B., 209
Maheshvarananda, Dada, 294, 301
Malinowski, B., 373
Mandel, Ernest, 272
Manjali, Franson, 403
Mannheim, Karl, 42, 44, 411, 421, 422

Mansbach, Richard et al., 197, 198
Marcuse, Peter, 272, 273
Margalit, Avishai, 31, 97
Marglin, F., 263
Martin, E., 189, 190, 348, 351, 371, 383
Mathur, Shubh, 157
McAdam, Doug et al., 193, 218
McCarthy, Thomas, 78, 79, 81, 83
McDonald, Malarie, 212
McDonaldization of the World, 286
McLuhan, M., et al., 359
Mead, George Herbert, 42, 45–47, 48, 400
Mead, M., 347, 355, 360
Medick, H. and D. Sabean, 348, 351
meditative action, 49
Melucci, Alberto, 32–33, 58, 71–72
Miri, Mrinal, 403, 425
method of modern science, 240, 246
  critique of, 261–62
methodological Hinduism, 163, 166–70
methodological individualism, 166
methodological pluralism, 163
Metz, Johannes B., 89
Meyerson, Ann, 273
middling grass-roots, 109
Millennium Development Goals, 296
Mills, C.W., 349
Mintz, Sideny W., 164, 362
Mishra, A. and S. Tripathy, 230
Mishra, Godavarish, 168
modernistic humanism, 67–68
modernization trap, 283
Mohanty, J.N., 142, 143, 415, 424
Mohanty, Manoranjan, 30, 36, 97, 137, 256
moral consciousness
  and communicative action, Habermas' agenda of, 78–80, 256–57
  spiritual foundations of, 85, Sri Aurobindo's agenda of, 85–86
Morris, Charles W., 44
Mouffe, Chantal, 36
movement towards a better society, 30–31
Mukherjee, Ramakrishna, 240–41, 252
Murphy John, 334
Murphy, Robert F., 164
Murphy, Y. and R. Murphy, 227

Nadkarni, M.V., 163, 173, 175
Naidu, Ratna, 137
Nagel, Thomas, 426
Nandy, Ashis, 185, 190, 198, 261, 330–31
Nederveen Pieterse, Jan and Bhikhu Parekh, 37
negative freedom, 255
negative peace, 311
Neilson, Kai, 368
Neville, Robert C., 80, 241
new class/bourgoisie, 273, 275
new global humanity, 67, 69, 72
  planetary realizations of, 71–72
  the inclusion of the 'other' in, 70
new homelessness
  causes of, 272
  in the US, 267, 268–72
new social movements, 193, 264
  emergence of, 189–92, 258
  idea of, criticism of, 192–96
new technologies
  challenge of, 254–55, 256, 257
new built-environment, 272–75
Newman, Katherino, 253, 268
North-South divide, 78
Nussbaum, Martha, 67, 68, 294, 299

Offe, Claus and Rolph G. Heinze, 283
Offe, Claus and Ulirch K. Preuss, 211, 287, 341
Offe, Claus, 253, 287
Ogata, Sadako and Amartya Sen, 54, 60
Olson, Mancur, 193
ontological epistemology of participation, 157, 164, 298

field of, 13, rethinking sociology research as a, 21–22
ontological sociality, 14
role of, in reconceptualizing society, 14–18; in rethinking subjectivity, 18–21
Oommen, T.K., 157, 163, 164, 165, 166, 170, 174–75, 176, 193
Ortner, Sherry, 122, 186
Osborne, David, 253
Osborne, Thomas, 277, 278

Pande, Govind Chandra, 82, 120, 210, 258, 285, 341–42
Pandian, M.S.S., 174
Panikkar, Raimundo, 397, 404, 419
Parajuli, Pramod, 195, 199, 260
Pathak, S., 233
performative utterances, 371
Perin, Constance, 267
Pillai, P.V., 23
planetary society, 71
plastic sexuality, 338
pluralism
and pluralization, 400
distinction between, 400–1
ideal of, 400
plurality of standpoints, 398
sociology and, 398–400
Pollock, Sheldon et al., 18
Poole, Dorris, 219
positive freedom, 255
positive peace, 311
post-citizenship movements, 33
post-colonial cosmopolis, 71
post-conventional morality
theory of, 76–76
post-empiricism, x
Poster, Mark, 330, 333
post-industrial opportunities, 187
post-industrial societies, 187
post-industrial transition/transformation, 187, 253
challenge of, 187–88
postmodern architecture, 274, 275
postmodern new built-environment, 274
postmodern self, 329
postmodernism, 328
as a movement, 329
post-positivism, x
Poulose, Thomas, 267
power-free existence, 71
practical spirituality, 310
Preteceille, Edmond and Jean-Pierre Terrail, 188
production
aesthetic turn in the, 278–81
process of, in contemporary advanced societies, 278
programmed societies, 190
psychology
postmodern challenge to, 332–34
Puligandla, Ramakrishna, 169, 323, 324
purusastha
concept of, 126–27
new vision of, 58–60
Putnam, Robert D., 35

quality of life, 239, 240
critical understanding of, 240–46
and the method of science, 246–49
Quarles van Ufford, Philip and Ananta Kumar Giri, 310

Radhakrishnan, R., 18
Raina, Vinod, 199, 263
Rapp, Rayna, 188, 254
rational society
Habermas' idea of, 79
Sri Aurobindo's views on, 85–86
Rawls, John, 297, 298
reflexive production, 279
religious evolution, 101
stages of, 101–2
religious language, 366

major genres of, 369; worshipping, 369; reminiscing, 369–70; committing, 370; invoking, praying and blessing, 370; solemnizing, 370; exhorting, 370; inspiring, 370
study of, 367, problems in the, 367–68
religious sentence, 367
functions of, 367
religious situations, 368
religious utterances, 371
power of, 377–80, in American folk preachers, 380
revolving fund for humanity, 211, 219
rhetoric, 373
power of, 374, in the new religious cults, 376–77
Ricouer, P., 366, 384
Ritzer, George, 286
Robinson, N.H.G., 371
Rochon, Thomas, 194
Rolin, Kristen, 412–413, 422
Roof, Wade Clark, 221–22
Rorty, Richard, 196, 319
Rose, Dan, 275
Rosenberg, B.A., 380, 381, 382
Ross, Fiona, 309
Rosseau, Jean-Jacques, xv
Rousseau, Jerome, 44
Roy, Bhaskar, 17, 18, 19–20, 30, 31, 69, 72, 104, 110, 154, 296
Ruiz, Lester Edwin J., 196
Rumi, 406
Ryan, Michael, 337

Saberwal, Satish, 137
sadhana (spiritual practice), 83, 122, 401
Sahashrabudhey, Sunil, 262, 283
Sahlins, M., 351
Said, Edward, 354
Sanskritic Hinduism, 172
Sanskritization
understanding of the, 170–75
Santos, Boaventura de Sousa, 38
Sapir, Edward, 285
Saxenian, A., 188
Scarpaci, Joseph L., 189
Schester, Susan, 194
Schiller, Friedrich, 153
Schneider, D., 353, 359
Schwartz, Theodore, 353, 359, 361
Scott, David, 37
Searle, J., 371, 372
self
concept of, 69
self-development
concept of, 69–70
Sen, Amartya, 3, 59, 66, 70, 97, 210, 240, 241–43, 244–45, 252, 255, 256, 292, 297, 299, 319, 322–23, 410
Seshadri, C.V., 261, 262, 263, 283
sexual addiction, 339
sexual revolution
in American society, 337
shacks, 267
Shah, A.M., 152, 153, 163, 170, 171, 172, 175, 176
Shaiken, Harry, 188
Shanks, Andrew, 24
Shankman, Paul, 353
shelter
challenge of, 267
Shore, Bradd, 359
Simon, Herbert, 321–22
Singh, B.P., 425
Singh, H.K., 230, 231
Singh, K.S., 425
Singer, Peter, 425
sister-city movement, 196–97
Sitas, Ari et al., 308–9, 310
Sitas, Ari, 308
Sivakumar, S.S., 319
Sivaraksha, Sulak, 291
Sizer, S.S., 382
Sloterdijk, Peter, 404
Smith, Adam, 22
Smith, David, 96, 386, 419
Snow, David et al., 194

'social'
  concept of, in Indian traditions, 120–27
social development, 252
  challenge of, 263–64
social movements, 186, 218
  in contemporary advanced societies, 187, emergence of, 186; objectives of, 187; types of, 187
social quality, 53
social science research
  in India, 136–43
socio-centrism
  limits of, 57–58
sociology, 13, 401
  and plurality of standpoints, 398–400
  and the limits of loyalty, 151
  as a quest for good society, 98–100
  challenges to, 17
  discipline of, 2, origin of, 2
  Habermas post-conventional practical discourse on, 77–84
  need for transforming, into ontological and epistemological engagement, 13
  new paths of criticism and creativity in contemporary discourses and practice of, 30
Soja, Edward, 208
Sorokin, Pitirim A., 195, 337, 341
speech acts, 371
  types of, 371: locutionary, 371; illocutionary, 371–72; perlouctionary, 372; declarative, 372
spiritual society, 86
spiritual transformation, 83
Sri Aurobindo, 53, 59, 67, 85–86, 87, 89–90, 102, 210, 303–4, 402
Srinivas, M.N. and M.N. Panini, 153
Srinivas, M.N., 138, 153, 154, 155, 166, 167, 170–71, 171–73, 175–76, 421
Srinivasan, Amrit, 23
standard of living, 252–53
Staveren, Irene Van, 15, 292, 294
Steiner, Rudolf, 52
Stolcke, Verena, 284
Strydom, Piet, 2, 2–3, 44, 48, 104, 401
Sunder Rajan, R., 20, 38, 67, 298, 317, 318–19, 319, 325
Swaraj (self-governance), 37, 70
symbolic realism
  Bellah's concept of, 104
system world, 187, 189

Tagore, Rabindranath, 24
Tambiah, Stanley, 252, 372, 373, 383
Tarrow, Sidney, 193
Taylor, Betsy, 373, 375
Taylor, Charles, 32, 71, 82, 83, 121, 341
Terchek, Ronald J., 37
Thapar, Romila, 30
(the) human and (the) social
  concept of, 53; rethinking the, 53–56; approaches to, 53–54
(the) new American poverty, 253
(the) third system politics, 197–98
Therborn, Goran, 35
thermodynamics of imperialism, 282
Third World, 267
Thompson, E.P., 228
Thoreau, Henry David, 414
Tillich, Paul, 427
Tilly, Charles, 193
Tocqueville, Alexis de, 195
Tomlinson, Alan, 280
Tomsho, Robert, 195
Toulmin, Stephen, 18
Toulouse, Teresa, 377, 378
Touraine, Alain, 1, 14, 33–34, 43, 187, 187, 189, 190, 190–91, 195, 198, 258, 329, 362, 400
Towsey, Michael Vaktavirya, 199
Toynbee, Arnold J., 71
Trachtenberg, Alan, 275
transcendental identification, 19
transcendental immanence, 48
transcendental institutionalism, 70
transcendentally really self, 69
transformative non-duality, 49
  fellowship of, 49

transformative reconciliation
  and striving for peace, 311–12
  process of, 308, need for, 308–11
transnational movements, 196
  as the third system of power, 197–200
tribal religions, 100
triple contingency, 401
Trouillot, M., 318
Trouillot, Michel-Rolph,
Tucker, R., 229
Turner, V., 186
Tutu, Desmond, 293, 301
twinned towns, 197

Uberoi, J.P.S., 17, 83, 98, 104, 136, 137, 199, 318
Udgata, Srinivas, 399
Unger, Robert M., 32, 84, 213, 218, 219, 286
universal self-realization, 296
urban social movements, 189
Urry, John, 16
Uttarakhand (an Indian state located in Central Himalayas), 226
  history of, 228–29
  society and culture in, 226–28

Vasudheiva Kutumbakam
  concept of, 71
Vatsayan, Kapila, 397
Vattimo, Giani, 21, 71, 111, 389
Verma, Roop Rekha, 211
Vinayaraj, Y.T., 424
Vincent, Joan, 186
Visvanathan, Shiv, 421
Vivekananda, Swami, 89, 125
voluntary poverty, 245, 246
vulgar functionalism
  of modernist mass consumption, 273

Wagner, G.R. and H. Zipprian, 88
Wagner, Peter, 318
Walker, R.B.J., 189, 190
Wallerstein, Immanuel et al., 18, 186, 318
Wallerstein, Immanuel, 17, 36
Walzer, Michael, 38, 39, 83, 209, 215
Weiming, Tu, 403
Wein Berger, Jerry, 246
Weiner, Annete, 359
Weiner, Robert P., 38–39
Welz, Frank, 170
Wignaraja, P., 186
Wilfred, Felix, 35, 39, 56, 167, 169, 302, 324, 386, 387, 389–90, 391–94, 417–419, 421
Williams, Bernard, 82, 243–44
Williams, Brett, 274–75
Wittgenstein, Ludwig, 52, 410
Witz, Klaus, 324
Wolf, Eric, 320
Wood, Michael R. and Louis R. Zurcher, Jr., 329
Wordsworth, William, 52
world power, 380
Wuthnow, Robert, 31–32, 208

yoga, 87
yuppie radicalism, 260

Zald, M.N. and J.D. McCarthy, 192, 193
Zelinsky, Wilbur, 197
Zohar, Donah and Ian Marshall, 126, 321, 323, 324
Zuboff, Soshana, 188, 254